FRENCH WOMEN PHILOSOPHERS: A CONTEMPORARY READER

'*French Women Philosophers* seems to me to be remarkably timely . . . and will find a ready audience which has been primed by all the work done in feminist philosophy throughout the last two decades.'

Margaret Whitford, *Queen Mary and Westfield College, London*

This reader is the first of its kind to present the work of leading French women philosophers to an English-speaking audience. Many of the articles appear for the first time in English and have been specially translated for the collection.

Christina Howells draws on major areas of philosophical and theoretical debate including Ethics, Psychoanalysis, Law, Politics, History, Science and Rationality. Each section and article is clearly introduced and situated in its intellectual context. The book is necessarily feminist in inspiration but draws on an unusually wide range of thinkers, chosen to represent the philosophy of women rather than feminist philosophy. It will be ideal for anyone coming to this area for the first time as well as those seeking to extend their understanding of French thought and Continental Philosophy.

Articles by the following writers are included: Françoise Collin, Sylviane Agacinski, Catherine Chalier, Luce Irigaray, Françoise Proust, Françoise Dastur, Barbara Cassin, Natalie Depraz, Elisabeth de Fontenay, Elisabeth Badinter, Françoise Héritier, Hélène Cixous, Monique Schneider, Julia Kristeva, Sarah Kofman, Monique David-Ménard, Françoise d'Eaubonne, Geneviève Fraisse, Michèle Le Doeuff, Natalie Charraud, Françoise Balibar, Anne Fagot-Largeault, Colette Guillaumin, Dominique Schnapper, Myriam Revault-D'Allonnes, Nicole Loraux, Mireille Delmas-Marty, Blandine Kriegel.

Christina Howells is Professor of French at the University of Oxford and Fellow of Wadham College. She is author of *Sartre's Theory of Literature* (1979), *Sartre: The Necessity of Freedom* (1988), *Derrida: from Phenomenology to Ethics* (1998), and editor of *The Cambridge Companion to Sartre* (1992).

FRENCH WOMEN PHILOSOPHERS: A CONTEMPORARY READER

Subjectivity, Identity, Alterity

Edited by Christina Howells

Routledge
Taylor & Francis Group

LONDON AND NEW YORK

First published 2004
by Routledge
11 New Fetter Lane, London EC4P 4EE

Simultaneously published in the USA and Canada
by Routledge
29 West 35th Street, New York, NY 10001

Routledge is an imprint of the Taylor & Francis Group

Editorial matter © 2004 Christina Howells.
All articles copyright of the contributors.

Typeset in Times and Bell Gothic by
Keystroke, Jacaranda Lodge, Wolverhampton
Printed and bound in Great Britain by
MPG Books Ltd, Bodmin

British Library Cataloguing in Publication Data
A catalogue record for this book is available from the British Library

Library of Congress Cataloging in Publication Data
A catalog record for this title has been requested

ISBN 0–415–26139–2 (hbk)
ISBN 0–415–26140–6 (pbk)

CONTENTS

CONTENTS

CONTENTS

ACKNOWLEDGEMENTS

I should like to thank the *Division de l'écrit et des médiathèques* of the French *Ministère des Affaires Etrangères* for their generous help with the translation rights of these texts; the Faculty of Modern Languages at the University of Oxford for assistance with funding for the translations themselves; and Tony Bruce and Siobhan Pattinson of Routledge for their friendly support. I am deeply grateful to my three translators – Oliver Davis, Stephen Forcer and Tom Baldwin – for their wonderful work and commitment, which has been accurate, stylish and scholarly. I am indebted also to the philosophers represented in this reader for their cooperation and enthusiasm, and especially to Françoise Collin who has given me unstinting advice and assistance throughout. I should like to thank Alain Viala, Elizabeth Fallaize, Colin Davis and Toril Moi for their encouragement, intellectual stimulus and affection; and John Flemming, who died too soon to see this book, for being a source of inspiration and renewal over the past year. As always, far more than gratitude is due to Bernie, Marie-Elise and Dominic for their love and tolerance.

The publishers would like to thank the following authors and publishers for permission to reprint their material in this book.

Part 1 The Ethical Subject
1 **Françoise Collin**, 'Praxis de la différence: notes sur le tragique du sujet', *Les Cahiers du Grif*, 1992, pp.125–141. Reprinted with permission of the author.
2 **Monique Canto-Sperber**, 'L'éthique et les défis de la philosophie morale' from *L'inquiétude morale et la vie humaine*, Presses Universitaires de France, 2001 © PUF. Reprinted with permission of the publisher.
3 **Sylviane Agacinski**, 'La question de l'autre' from *Critique de l'égocentrisme*, Galilée, 1996 © Editions Galilée. Reprinted with permission of the publisher.
4 **Catherine Chalier**, 'Introduction' and 'Don et obligation' from *De l'intranquillité de l'âme*, Payot, 1999 © Editions Payot & Rivages. Reprinted with permission of the publisher.
5 **Françoise Proust**, 'La doublure du temps', *Les Conférences du Perroquet* 38, May 1993. Reprinted with permission of the publisher.
6 **Luce Irigaray**, 'The Question of the Other' from *Democracy Begins Between Two*, Athlone Press, 2000 (UK); Routledge, 2001 (US). Reprinted with permission of both publishers.

Part 2 Borders of the Human Subject

7 **Barbara Cassin**, 'Aristote avec et contre Kant: sur l'idée de la nature humaine' from *Aristote et le logos: contes de la phénoménologie ordinaire*, Presses Universitaire de France, 1997 © PUF. Reprinted with the permission of the publisher.

8 **Natalie Depraz**, 'Imagination and passivity: Husserl and Kant, a cross-relationship' from Depraz and Zahavi (eds.), *Alterity and Facticity: new perspectives on Husserl,* Kluwer Academic Press, 1998. Reprinted with permission of the publisher.

9 **Françoise Dastur**, 'Mortality and Finitude' and 'Death, Speech and Laughter' from *Death: an essay on finitude*, Athlone Press, 1996. Reprinted with permission of the publisher. (Originally published in French as *La Mort: essais sur la finitude*, Hatier, 1994.)

10 **Elisabeth de Fontenay**, 'Comme des pommes de terre (Kant)' from *Le Silence des bêtes: la philosophie à l'épreuve de l'animalité*, Fayard, 1998 © Librairie Arthème Fayard. Reprinted with permission of the publisher.

11 **Françoise Héritier**, 'D'Aristote aux Inuit: la construction raisonnée du genre' from *Masculin/féminin: la pensée de la différence*, Odile Jacob, 1996 © Editions Odile Jacob. Reprinted with permission of the publisher.

Part 3 The Psychoanalytic Subject

12 **Hélène Cixous**, 'Alterity: being human' from Cixous and Calle-Gruber, *Rootprints: memory and life writing*, Routledge, 1997. Reprinted with permission of the publisher. (Originally published in French as *Photos de Racines*, Editions des Femmes, 1994.)

13 **Monique Schneider**, 'Repudier le feminin' from *Généalogie du masculin*, Aubier, 2000 © Aubier. Reprinted with the permission of the publisher.

14 **Julia Kristeva**, 'Might not universality be . . . our own foreignness?' from *Strangers to Ourselves*, Columbia University Press, 1991. Reprinted with permission of the publisher. (Originally published in French as *Etrangers à nous-mêmes*, Fayard, 1988.)

15 **Sarah Kofman**, 'Miroir et mirages oniriques: Platon, précurseur de Freud' from *Séductions: de Sartre à Heraclite*, Galilée, 1990 © Editions Galilée. Reprinted with permission of the publisher.

16 **Monique David-Ménard**, 'Introduction', 'Les structures de désir et le concept d'universel' and 'La pensée est-elle sexuée?' from *Les constructions de l'universel*, Presses Universitaires de France, 1997 © PUF. Reprinted with the permission of the publisher.

Part 4 The Rational and Scientific Subject

17 **Françoise d'Eaubonne**, 'Introduction' from *Féminin et philosophie (une allergie historique)*, L'Harmattan, 1997. Reprinted with permission of the publisher.

18 **Geneviève Fraisse**, 'Individu, actrice, sujet féministe' from *Les femmes et leur histoire*, Folio Gallimard, 1998 © Editions Gallimard. Reprinted with permission of the publisher.

19 **Michèle Le Doeuff**, 'How Intuition Came to Women' from *The Sex of Knowing*,

Routledge, 2003. Reprinted with permission of the publisher. (Originally published in French as 'Déshérences: comment l'intuition vint aux femmes' in *Le Sexe du savoir,* Aubier, 1998.)

20 **Nathalie Charraud**, 'Sujet apparent, sujet réel' from Françoise Collin (ed.), *Le Sexe des sciences: les femmes en plus*, Autrement, 1992. Reprinted with permission of the author.

21 **Françoise Balibar**, 'Y a-t-il une science feminine?' from Françoise Collin (ed.), *Le Sexe des sciences: les femmes en plus,* Autrement, 1992. Reprinted with permission of the author.

22 **Anne Fagot-Largeault**, 'Problèmes de fondement' from *L'homme bio-éthique: pour une déontologie de la recherche sur le vivant*, Maloine, 1985. Reprinted with permission of the publisher.

Part 5 The Juridical and Political Subject

23 **Colette Guillaumin**, 'The specific characteristics of racist ideology' from *Racism, Sexism, Power and Ideology*, Routledge, 1995. Reprinted with permission of the publisher and the author. First published 1972 in *Cahiers Internationaux de Sociologie.*

24 **Dominique Schnapper,** 'Racisme et condamnation radicale de la modernité' from *La relation à l'autre: au coeur de la pensée sociologique*, Gallimard, 1998 © Editions Gallimard. Reprinted with permission of the publisher.

25 **Myriam Revault-D'Allonnes**, 'Kant et l'idée du mal radical' from *Ce que l'homme fait à l'homme: essai sur le mal politique*, Seuil, 1995 © Editions du Seuil. Reprinted with permission of the publisher.

26 **Nicole Loraux**, 'The Athenian name: imaginary structures of lineage in Athens' from *The Children of Athena,* Princeton University Press, 1993 © Princeton University Press. Reprinted with permission of the publisher. (Originally published in French as *Les enfants d'Athéna: idées athéniennes sur la citoyenneté et la division des sexes*, Maspéro, 1981.)

27 **Mireille Delmas-Marty**, 'Démocratie et humanité' from *Trois défis pour un droit mondial*, Seuil, 1998 © Editions du Seuil. Reprinted with permission of the publisher.

28 **Blandine Kriegel**, 'Les déclarations des droits du XVIII siècle et leur destin' and 'La philosophie du sujet n'est pas la source des droits de l'homme' from *Les droits de l'homme et le droit naturel*, Presses Universitaires de France, 1989 © PUF. Reprinted with the permission of the publisher.

INTRODUCTION

Philosophy has not traditionally been considered the natural domain of women. Along with rationality and scientific thought, philosophy has been deemed predominantly masculine. Geneviève Lloyd's *Man of Reason* (1984), Michèle Le Doeuff's *Le Sexe du savoir* (1998), and Françoise d'Eaubonne's *Féminin et philosophie: une allergie historique* (1997) are among the many studies to examine this alleged incompatibility. Women philosophers can of course be cited in an attempt to refute this preconception, along with socio-historical evidence which demonstrates that the apparent paucity of women philosophers must be, at least in part, produced by social, financial and educational circumstances. All this is may well persuade us that there is no 'natural' disjunction between women and rationality. But more compelling, perhaps, is the paradoxical 'effect' produced in the last fifty years by the traditional exclusion of women from philosophy. In the West at least, women have been led precisely to reflect on their own irrational exclusion from the realm of supposedly universal reason, and thereby to produce an extraordinary vital array of philosophical texts. Many of these have an explicitly self-reflexive nature, that is to say that they explore the meaning and implications of the identification of philosophical reason with the masculine, despite its claims to objectivity. This collection is dedicated to contemporary French women philosophers, and shows them exploring their own status and identity as philosophers, as human subjects and as rational women. It shows them examining questions of the relation between self and other, individual and collective, subject and object, in domains as diverse as ethics, psychoanalysis, politics and law. It shows how consideration of the nature of gender and of the degree to which it should be viewed as natural or as socially constructed has repercussions in other areas such as race and nationality. The very concepts of universality, objectivity and nature are subject to analyses which refuse to accept them on their own terms as self-explanatory and transparent, but rather submit them to the close and sometimes hostile scrutiny afforded by other domains such as psychoanalysis, history, and anthropology. In the process, the history of philosophy itself is frequently revisited through perspectives which offer some rigorous and at times contestatory new interpretations.

The sub-title, *Subjectivity, Identity, Alterity*, captures some, but of course not all, of the diversity of production of contemporary French women philosophers. It also names the primary focus of attention of the texts themselves, which, however varied their methodology, share, at least in part, the aim of self-understanding and self-knowledge, mediated not so much through introspection as through reflection on relations with others and otherness. It is this focus which also explains in part some of the omissions from this Reader; the rest of the explanation lies in factors such as constraints of space, my own knowledge and judgement – or lack thereof – and the always pervasive aleatory element which has inevitably meant that I discovered certain writers and certain texts at 'the right moment' and others just a little too late. To list the many other philosophers whom I would have wanted to include would be equally open to error, so I will simply apologise to those whose omission has weakened this anthology, and to those readers who have suffered from such omissions.

Part 1

THE ETHICAL SUBJECT

INTRODUCTION

The six essays presented in this section take us to the heart of the preoccupation with subjectivity that is manifest in the work of so many French philosophers in recent years, and especially in the work of women. The questioning and deconstruction of the subject in its classical sense arguably started at the very inception of the classical conception itself (that is to say with Descartes), and increased in strength and visibility in Hume, Kant, Nietzsche, Heidegger, Sartre, Levinas and Derrida, to name but a few. The self-sufficiency and autonomy of the subject were put into question, as well as its centredness and self-identity. Levinas in particular attempted to free the philosophy of the Other from the epistemological problematic in which he believed it had been embedded and to resituate it in the domain of ethics. Once the Other is not seen primarily as an object of consciousness the subject/object divide ceases to have any absolute pertinence for human relations. It is no longer possible, since Levinas, to consider subjectivity without a simultaneous awareness of alterity and of its constitutive role in the self-understanding and even in the generation of the subject. Women philosophers in France have been quick to develop and extend the implications of this new view of subjectivity in a wide variety of domains. The essays of this section, all written since 1990, demonstrate clearly that ethics and subjectivity are inseparably entwined for contemporary women philosophers: the question of the constitution of the subject leads inevitably to the question of relations with others, precisely because the subject is no longer envisaged as radically autonomous.

Françoise Collin's essay on 'le tragique du sujet' gives a thought-provoking account of this ethical turn in the history of conceptions of subjectivity. Her essay on 'The Praxis of Difference' sets the scene for the section as a whole as she explores the aporias in which feminist critiques of the subject seem to be trapped. 'On the one hand, the advent of the feminine spells the death of the subject – the opposition between subject and object being a phallic position. On the other hand, after centuries of subjugation, women want to become "subjects in their own right" '. If the deconstruction and death of the subject has dismantled the 'self', how can women assert their rights, political and other? What is more, deconstruction would seem to have already led philosophy towards a 'feminine future' in its concern with *différance*, dissemination, passivity, receptivity, vulnerability, alterity and so on. However, Collin argues, this link between the post-metaphysical 'end of the subject' and the feminine is in fact deeply problematic. In the first place it is highly selective, retaining only certain aspects of the so-called 'feminine'; and second, the apparent reversal of values is not in reality relevant to the positions of actual men and women. What is worse is that the values themselves (such as passivity and welcome) are apparently incompatible with the political 'voluntarism' that is endemic in any attempt to change the world, thereby associating the political will-to-change with the phallic position that has been rejected. From this point of view, feminism may seem to be a paradoxical betrayal of the feminine.

> Poor seconds as ever, women aspire to be subjects when the subject no longer exists. Waving the flag of autonomy, they fail to grasp that truth is now on the side of heteronomy, that this is the new law . . . They have adopted a language of futurity and becoming without realising that these out-dated categories have been replaced by the prudent disillusionment of the 'post'. In a world without history, they cling to historical temporality.

In Collin's view, the feminisation of truth, despite and also because of its attractiveness, represents a real danger for women in the political arena. Male philosophers take over the 'feminine' by erasing the boundaries between male and female and embracing the abolition of sexual difference; women philosophers continue to preserve sexual difference, still considering the 'feminine' to be their birthright, and failing to recognise that it has been annexed. In short, Collin believes that 'the feminine' risks taking the place of actual women, but that the problem with contesting such a substitution and reaffirming the link between women and the feminine is that such a strategy involves another risk: that of imprisoning women in an ontological definition. Her practical solution seems to involve a separation of domains: the metaphysical 'death of the subject' must not kill off women's political right to be treated, at long last, as subjects. But such a separation does not provide any real solution. This is the tragedy referred to in Collin's sub-title: how is the claim that the subject is fundamentally heteronomous – inhabited by the Other or others – to be reconciled with its autonomy? The problem is felt more acutely by women, since those (men) who have held the subject-position for so long need not fear that their relinquishing it will be identified with their alienation. How then, asks Collin, can we actually conceive of a non-metaphysical politics? How can we fight against alienation while remaining open to the 'alter-ation' of otherness? Collin turns to Emanuel Levinas and Hannah Arendt for contributions to the debate on alterity in the ethical and the political spheres respectively. The death of the subject does not, and should not, entail the end of agency. Indeed, even if the subject has been stripped of its pretensions to autonomy and mastery, this is not to say that there is nothing of the subject left. On the contrary, 'there is no "I" altered by the Other which does not resist this very alter-ation, no deconstruction from which the beginnings of reconstruction are entirely absent, no self-effacement without self-assertion . . . there can be no separating self-presence, or identity, from alterity, and even no separating identification from alteration'. The two incompatible but inseparable faces of being in the world are both part of our undecidable and aporetic finitude. Despite the 'tragedy' in her title, Collin's essay seems to relish the struggle in a way which, in her terms, would seem better described as feminist than feminine.

INTRODUCTION

Monique Canto-Sperber is one of the philosophers represented here whose preoccupations may seem closest to those of Anglo-American philosophy. In *L'Inquiétude morale et la vie humaine*, she takes the side of so-called moral philosophy with its concepts, rational arguments and discipline against what she sees as the current preoccupation with the supposedly looser, more practical domain of ethics. She contests from the outset the equation of moral philosophy with the law, and ethics with the art of living: in her account ethics and moral philosophy are synonymous. In this extract from her work, Canto-Sperber sets out the reasons behind her disquiet with the French obsession with modernity as progress, through an analysis of the current understanding of the 'modern individual', a critique of the domination of Kantian ethics, and an appeal for a less superficial understanding of Greek moral philosophy. Canto-Sperber's conclusion is that the impossibility of deriving a universal ethics from abstract rationality does not entail any scepticism with respect to the existence of universal moral obligations. In her view, what matters is not so much to ground such obligations but rather to discover and define them.

The title of Sylviane Agacinski's book, *Critique de l'égocentrisme*, gives a clear expression of the significance of her reflections, in which she maintains that a false view of the subject lies at the root of ethical and political irresponsibility and injustice. Although coming from a very different philosophical position, closer to Derridean deconstruction than to Anglo-American philosophy, Agacinski shares Canto-Sperber's wariness of Kantian ethics. In this extract, 'La question de l'autre', Agacinski argues against all types of ethics that are not based on the relation to the other. She maintains that the metaphysical emphasis on the self-sufficiency and self-reflexivity of the subject is precisely egocentric in ethical terms. The Kantian subject, for example, is deaf to the other in so far as it sets itself up as sole arbiter of what is right through the faculty of reason, just as Cartesian doubt casts aside all authority except its own. For Agacinski, subjectivity is immediately shared with the other, solicited by the other, and cannot and must not bracket off the experience of the other in an attempt to ground its own self-sufficiency. Her approach, which is carried out through reflection on Kiekegaard, involves a radical questioning of notions of identity, communication, community, ethics and love.

Catherine Chalier's essay on interiority explores the link between this philosophical development and Judaic philosophy. In her discussion of 'l'intranquillité de l'âme', it is precisely the *lack* of tranquillity that enables ethics. Chalier analyses attempts to justify war in the cause of peace, which she calls the 'messianic' perspective, but she does not conclude in favour of a simple pacifism. On the contrary, she uses Kant's essay on perpetual peace to argue that his hope that a good legal constitution could lead us towards morality has been outpaced by the two world wars, and that a new perspective is now necessary. Levinas provides this perspective with his conception of a form of peace that is not a matter of individual serenity of soul but rather one that recognises and embraces alterity. Chalier's view is that the Jewish notion of peace as *chelemut* may provide a key: *chelemut* is not a private and personal inner peace but rather involves the recognition of the vulnerability of peace and the necessity to protect and nurture it. Chalier argues that peace is, in the last analysis, more important than truth, and is a part of what she calls the 'irreducible fraternity' of human co-existence, in which it is alterity rather than interiority that allows the psyche to thrive.

INTRODUCTION

The penultimate essay of this section take an ethical approach to one of the major topics of philosophical reflection, time, which is once more explored in conjunction with the question of relations between self and other. Françoise Proust shows how the imbrication of self with other means that temporality loses its pure, linear quality, which is exchanged for a more complex interweaving. Like several of the essays in this section, Kant is again one of the most significant reference points, whether for development or attempted rebuttal. Here Proust explores Walter Benjamin's deconstruction of Kant's analytic of temporality, which she envisages as a response to Heidegger's own critique of Kant. Time, she argues, is neither successive nor projective: it is rather self-entwined, 'imbricated', forming loops and arabesques. This unusual view implies a notion of temporal doubling, according to which all events produce a double self-overlapping moment, described by Proust as a 'doublure', a term with multiple connotations involving the idea both of doubling and of an inner lining. Proust attempts here to explore the implications of this notion, which she refers to as a 'law of temporal survival' or 'ghosting', for ways of thinking about history.

In *Democracy Begins Between Two*, Luce Irigaray calls for a radical reconsideration of the so-called democratic bases of Western culture. In this essay, 'The Question of the Other', which was originally given as part of a seminar at the University of Verona and which offers a clear account of the major lines of her position, she argues for the urgent need for our society to recognise both genders fully, rather than considering woman as other than, and second to, man. For Irigaray this should not entail a Beauvoirian attempt at equality and identity between the sexes, but rather a recognition of difference in the form of specific civil rights guaranteeing women a separate civil identity of their own. Her main focus in this essay is on the philosophical aspect of the question, that is, on gendered subjectivity and identity. Her argument is that while empirical differences are recognised and respected by philosophical discourse, the model of the human, at least in Western philosophy, has remained unchanged and invariable: 'singular, solitary and historically masculine'. From this perspective, differences, be they of age, race, culture or sex, are necessarily regarded as deficiencies. Irigaray's argument is that female otherness is more radical than this model can cope with: the female subject is radically irreducible to the male. This leads her to a conception of what she calls 'The Two', that is an attempt to overthrow the authority of the One as dominant, be it expressed in terms of man, the father, the one God, the unique truth. The subject, for Irigaray, is neither one nor singular, but two. Recognition of this 'scandal' is, she maintains, vital not only to women's liberation but also to ethics and indeed to democracy.

1

FRANÇOISE COLLIN

Françoise Collin is a feminist philosopher, critic and writer, born in Belgium, with a doctorate from the University of Louvain. After teaching for a while in Brussels, she was until 2002 Professor at the Critical Studies Centre of the American University in Paris. In 1973 she founded *Les Cahiers du Grif*, a major journal of feminist philosophy, which she continues to edit. She is a member of the Collège International de Philosophie. Her interests lie on the one hand in Maurice Blanchot and the philosophy of literature and art, and on the other in political philosophy and in particular Hannah Arendt. She has also published widely on Borges, Burroughs and Levinas, and has written numerous works of fiction. These apparently unrelated domains are linked in her reflections through the question of what she calls 'the praxis of the unrepresentable', which is the working title of her next book, and which underlines the impor-tance of the act (without representation of its end) as constitutive of human existence. Her most recent work is a vast critical anthology of texts concerning women by sixty philosophers from Plato to the present day.

Her academic publications include the following:

Maurice Blanchot et la question de l'écriture, Paris: Gallimard, 1971 and 1986.

Le Sexe des sciences: les femmes en plus (ed.), Paris: Autrement, 1992.

Politique et pensée (ed.), Paris: Payot, 1997.

Le Différend des sexes: de Platon à la parité, Nantes: Pleins Feux, 1999.

L'Homme est-il devenu superflu? Hannah Arendt, Paris: Odile Jacob, 1999.

Les femmes, de Platon à Derrida, critical anthology (co-edited with E. Pisier and E. Varikas), Paris: Plon, 2000.

Her novels and recits include the following:

Le Jour fabuleux, Paris: Seuil, 1960.

Rose qui peut, Paris: Seuil, 1962.

Le Rendez-vous, Paris: Tierce, 1988.

Le Jardin de Louise, Montreal: NBJ, 1989.

THE PRAXIS OF DIFFERENCE
Notes on the tragedy of the subject

> . . . to be the free speaking subject and to vanish as the patient does, as
> the passive one does who will not show their face and through whom
> death is passing . . .
>
> (Maurice Blanchot)

Post-metaphysical critiques of the subject would appear to have coincided with the collapse of the political and of the attempt to think the political. And yet two seemingly contradictory assertions are to be heard today. On one hand, the advent of the feminine spells the death of the subject – the opposition between subject and object being a phallic position. On the other hand, after centuries of subjugation, women want to become 'subjects in their own right'. These notes are intended to offer a survey of this aporia. How can that which 'is' not be a self? In the following discussion, this question will be approached from the perspective of sexual difference, one of several areas upon which it has a bearing.

The death of the subject

The death of the subject has been variously interpreted by different branches and registers of a key trend in contemporary philosophy: that described as 'post-metaphysical', or indeed 'post-modern'. The claim is that the subject was an invention of the modern era, or even, to heed Heidegger, of the entire history of philosophy since Plato. The subject's death knell [*le glas*] has been ringing for some time now. But who tolls the bell? And 'for whom does the bell toll?'

  The thinking man has resigned himself to the loss of the firm foundation which grounded his attempts to apprehend the world before him as a totality, or at least as a field which might potentially be grasped as a totality. Gone is that 'view from nowhere', from which all that is appears as it is, devoid of either perspective or shadow. Suspicions have even been raised about the status of vision as a leading metaphor for knowledge. The thinking man has given up his attachment to the first of all privileged objects, the ego itself. The paths of knowledge and truth have diverged, knowledge being bound up with those ends immanent in the technical means of its production and truth being dependent upon the repudiation of mastery. From now on, 'the eye listens'. Speech has become the contemplation of being, or of the Other. Writing deconstructs the book. The person speaking is no longer at the origin of either speech in general or their utterance in particular. The era of representation and self-representation has given way to the unfolding of presence-absence. Man is 'the one who does not accompany himself'.[1] He is the one who comes afterwards. To the self-assured sound of 'I think, therefore I am' comes the echo, three centuries later, of 'I think, therefore I am not'.[2]

So when women, when feminists, denounce the dominant philosophical tradition as a means of exerting mastery by imposing the duality of subject and object and accordingly recognize in it the masculine position, they are advancing along established lines of attack. The master-subject they are disputing committed hara-kiri some while ago, at least in the philosophical arena. Has not Derrida himself made the connection between the logocentric and the phallic positions by coining the term 'phallogocentrism' to refer to the metaphysical/scientific tradition which Heidegger called into question? (And certain elements of psychoanalysis allow the masculine tendency to favour the visible and the manipulable to be explained in terms of sexual morphology, on the basis of the detachable object.) Thus there would no longer seem to be grounds for complaint. Philosophy has embarked, of its own accord, on a 'feminine future', in its concern with issues such as the not-one, difference and *différance*, dissemination, passivity, welcome, receptivity, vulnerability, the 'not all', the indefinite, radical alterity . . .

Room nevertheless remains for a question: does not the attempt by certain philosophers (aided and abetted by one particular form of feminism, jubilant that women are finally 'on the right side') to forge a link between the post-metaphysical – the end of the subject – and the feminine actually give rise to confusion? Is it appropriate to use sexed metaphors to designate logical and ontological categories? Do these metaphors not carry a weight of historical and ideological meaning which resists this attempted reduction? Moreover, although the deployment of these metaphors in philosophical discourse is necessarily selective, this selection is never itself either justified or explained. They retain only the 'payload', or better part, of the feminine: receptiveness and even a form of captivity refined from the servitude, or from the reputation for being unsuited to the symbolic, which have been traditionally associated with this term.

Crucially, the sense of novelty is derived here from the reversal of the values traditionally attributed to sexual difference. Truth is henceforth on the side of the not-one. But this reversal of values remains speculative. It does not affect, nor is it even relevant to, the positions of actual men and women, these effectively being placed within brackets. No sooner have these metaphors of femininity been extracted from one group of empirical human beings – women, that is – than they are detached from them. Thus one immediate effect of this glorification of the feminine is to reduce the political to the ontological. One pernicious consequence of this confusion, if taken to extremes, although this is clearly not what the philosophers in question intended, is to restrict women to their positions of today, on the grounds that these are supposedly identifiable with that of the any truly human being in the world. If to persist in truth is to welcome that which gives itself then any form of 'voluntarism' – the (political) determination to change how things are – accordingly appears to be a throwback to the phallic position, a bid for mastery now that mastery has been stigmatized – delusions of grandeur. From such a perspective, feminism (as a movement for change) may appear to represent not

9

the work, but rather the betrayal, of the feminine: women's male future. This clever reversal leaves the male philosopher the bearer of the feminine and the feminist woman a proud occupier of the recently abandoned phallic position, a charge which some have been only too keen to throw back at her. Yet this conversion to the feminine does nothing to deprive him who would undergo it of the authority he enjoys, the authority of speech which his position in society affords him. The mere act of attributing to being in the world qualities thereafter determined as feminine does not of itself entail that the lot of women will be shared, or even accorded a moment's consideration, by each and every human being. The *mea culpa* of the Western phallogocentric subject does not jeopardize the position of the one who intones it.

Such interpretative games which deal in the masculine and the feminine do not, then, have all that much to do with the real situations of men and women, situations which these games are even prone to obscure. For in the post-metaphysical critique of the subject, it is men – poets and writers – who step in to illustrate the feminine position: Hölderlin, Artaud and Joyce. Has not a semantic slippage occurred here? Can writing and the feminine really be used interchangeably as figures for dissemination and the undecidable?

Feminism, when it revives the discursive dimension within writing and re-emphasizes the project within the errant, appears accordingly to be a reincarnation of the metaphysico-dialectical position. Poor seconds, as ever, women aspire to be subjects when the subject no longer exists. Waving the flag of autonomy, they fail to grasp that truth is now on the side of heteronomy, that this is the new law. They would keep their heads while all around are losing theirs. They are claiming the right to speak, having failed to understand that in the place where 'I' speaks, nobody speaks. Such is the triviality of their demands. Latter-day converts to the Marxist Hegelianism of yesteryear, they remain locked into that infamous struggle between master and slave, a logic which values dialectic over and above difference. They intone a chant in a world of disenchantment. They have adopted a language of futurity and becoming, without realizing that these outdated categories have been replaced by the prudent disillusionment of the 'post'. In a world without history they cling to historical temporality.

Conscious of this apparent anachronism, it is understandable that one branch of feminist thought, particularly well-developed in the American world, should have endeavoured, sometimes in a rather confused fashion, to find sustenance if not salvation in an intellectual approach which brings into dialogue work as different as that of Derrida, Lyotard, Heidegger and even Lacan. The feminine, after having been stigmatized for such a long time, finally becomes an emblem for the truth of the human. What was negative becomes positive. And feminism in turn rallies around the banner of the post, becoming post-feminism.

Yet does this indirect act of homage to the feminine – which may understandably seem gratifying for women – really constitute a recognition of women as such? Is the 'feminization' of truth not simply the latest ruse, a tactic of non-violent seduction designed to supplant women?

When they decamp entirely to the side of the critique of the subject, do women risk finding that they are just as subjugated there as they were under the aegis of the subject? What if the appeal of a certain mode of thought, one described with questionable justification as feminine, threatened to spawn misunderstanding about what is really at stake for women in the world? To overvalue one category of thought is to let that particular minority from which it has been extracted be devalued. In the same way, the incorporation of so called 'negro art' into Picasso's work and the fascination with 'raw art' in that of Dubuffet evinced a concern that was principally for art, rather than for either people of colour or the inhabitants of the asylum. To what extent can theatrical, or mimetic, actions have a bearing on the real? A prince in disguise is still a prince. Perhaps every oppressed group is bound to be incorporated superficially into the folklore of the oppressor. "We are all black", "we are all mad", "we are all women", "we are all Jews" – the meaning of all such claims is highly questionable.

The feminine within/without women

Philosophers (men) and women (philosophers) each have their own way of entering the centreless space of the 'post' and do so under different guises. For the former it is a question of putting the negative to work – not negativity but rather the neuter of ne-uter, neither one nor the other – of undoing, deconstructing and decentring (that which is). Images of this work border on the side of castration and circumcision. For women (philosophers) it is a matter of pro-phanation (of making things appear, transgressively), or the joyful affirmation of what is not (yet). The Trojan Horse smuggled into the bastion of metaphysics is clad in different garb: for men, it betokens retiring self-effacement. For women, it is thought, not without a hint of triumphalism, to mark the advent of their time. It is as though this entry into the post were at once a funeral rite and a celebration of birth, the discovery of nativity in negativity. For these women do, in a sense, embody that which they mime, provided that the truth is henceforth a woman. 'The eternal irony of the community' – they have always known, since time immemorial, that the One is not, or that the One is the oppressor's trap. To dismantle the statue of the Commandeur is thus an act of celebration – their act. They are dancing on his remains. The rite of Reason's collapse seems to prove them right or to restore a birth-right.

Except that there is no horse. When philosophers (men) talk about the feminine, it is as though this were a category severed from its ties to a particular sex. When women (philosophers) voice the feminine, they hesitate to cut the umbilical cord which attaches it to women as such. The strategy of the former consists in the attempt to erase, or erode, the boundary between the sexes, to use the feminine as a way of short-circuiting this boundary, or even as a way of short-circuiting the sexes themseleves: the end of the One is the end of the two. The strategy of women (philosophers), by contrast, consists in priding themselves on the feminine as though it were an inalienable right. Now that it has acquired positive connotations, they choose to retain their rights to the infamous 'not all', which had for centuries been thrown back at them as evidence of inferiority, even if they are prepared for these rights to be non-exclusive. Whereas the former approach asymptotically the point where sexual difference vanishes, the latter preserve the mark of this difference, because they sense that, were they to strive to obliterate it, they would, so to speak, be shooting themselves in the foot. It is here that psychoanalysis comes to their rescue: if both sexes have their share of the feminine, this accordingly means that women and men are not indistinguishable positions. One throw of the dice will never

FRANÇOISE COLLIN

destroy chance.³ Difference can never imply indifference. For the former, the non-subject describes the underlying ontological character of being-in-the-world, *dasein*, to which writing testifies. For the latter, it essentially characterizes women's being-in-the-world, or indeed women's way of writing [*l'écriture féminine*], even though this may not necessarily rule out the possibility of its being manifested in the writing of a number of men.

The substitution of the post, the time after, for the clash of opposites, the end of the subject and the assertion of the not-One – when these figures nonetheless characterize one of the two sexes and can be termed 'feminine' on this basis, they do not in fact put an end to the binary logic which they were supposed to have destroyed. The *régime* of the indeterminate 'feminine' still sounds like an antonym for the masculine or the phallic. The attempt to think the not-one, when it engages with sexual difference, by opposing the not-one (the feminine) and the one (the masculine), remains a prisoner of that order of the one plus one which it ostensibly rejects, even if one of these two ones is the not-one. The dualistic referent of sexual difference – which, if not biological, is at least morphological – that Freud put in place in what was still the era of positivism (to have it or to lack it) is alive and well at the heart of one particular branch of feminist thought, even as it aspires to repolarize those values attributed to each sex, as when the non-objectifiable not-one of 'touching lips' or the 'insurpassable volume'⁴ is given credit over and above the one of the phallic part-object.

Yet even a mode of thought that manages to free itself of the ascription of sexual difference to biological or morphological terms, thereby allowing it to conceive of the feminine and the masculine purely as categories and independently of the sites of their empirical inscription (i.e. men and women), remains contaminated by this dualism, a dualism which we must struggle to overcome. There is a sense in which the indefinite remains definite by being linked to the definite. The end of metaphysics, the end of the subject, are 'deconstructive' movements that must be initiated again and again, rather than definitive acts of destruction. There is no end to ending. Worklessness [*désœuvrement*] unworks the work. The not-One becomes detached from the one. There can be no let up for the feminine in the battle against the phallic, not even when the phallic has been overcome.

So this way of approaching the question of the positions of men and women by way of the masculine and the feminine is not without its own very particular consequences. While for feminists the masculine and the feminine may be superimposed onto men and women (the feminine being that which belongs to women), for the philosophers these categories may be substituted for the individuals concerned, such that the feminine takes the place of empirical women and in a certain sense allows them to be 'done away with'. By confining their discussions to the feminine, the philosophers side-step the questions of empirical women, while nonetheless appearing to take them into consideration. When feminists (who are also philosophers) make out that there is an inexorable connection between women and the feminine, they imprison women in an ontological definition, whereby women are defined by a feminine that is ostensibly an essential quality yet which nevertheless serves implicitly as a standard for discriminating between "real" women – who live up to the feminine – and bogus ones, who have fallen prey to the lure of the phallic.

12

The foregoing considerations do not represent a denial of either the importance or the interest of post-metaphysical branches of philosophical inquiry. They do, however, question the intelligibility and the pertinence of using the category of the feminine to designate the end of the master-subject and they cast doubt on whether it is appropriate to use this category as an organizing principle for discussion of the situation of women, whether this be a feminine which crosses the boundary between groups of different sexes or a feminine attached to one of these groups in particular, women. The former avoids recourse to a metaphysics of the sexes but only at the price of ignoring real women, while the latter reinstalls metaphysics by reasserting a logic of sexual difference that is both dualist and essentialist. In the former, men and women no longer mean anything. In the latter, men and women mean everything. Perhaps we should conclude that they mean less than everything but more than nothing.

Both these ways of appealing to the feminine (to the feminine as human being in the world or to the feminine as women's being in the world) would appear, perhaps unwittingly, to be driven by hopes of reconciliation. The first, which emphasizes the porous or undecideable character of the frontier between the sexes and which tends to make the difference between the sexes into a matter of indifference, evades not only the figure of oppression, that is the political dimension which permeates it, but also all hint of any tragic dimension to the relation between the sexes. It makes immediate the 'end of history' by jumping free of the intervening phases in the dialectic to a climate of felicitous indeterminacy in which there would no longer be either men or women (and neither Jews nor Greeks, neither masters nor slaves . . .) – an atopia that differs by a mere letter from utopia. The second, by planting women firmly in their essence – that of the indefinite, the not-one – obliterates for its part all trace of the dialectical and tragic aspects of women's relations with one another: it unites women in a greater 'we', the plurality of which – affirmed as it most certainly is, albeit within the margins of a certain sameness – is supposed to be heaven-sent.

Women without the feminine

In view of the obstacles encountered by those philosophical approaches in which the category of the feminine plays a leading role, would it not perhaps be preferable to reorientate the discussion around the real situations of men and women *qua* groups in society? No branch of feminist thought either can or does ignore this aspect of the question, for the prime concern of feminist thinking will always be to properly recognize, and to ensure that women recognize, women's rights and being.

Even if women promote, or help to promote, a way of thinking and a way of relating to the world that can do without the position of the calculating subject, one which tells tales instead of keeping books, they must do so not by proxy but in their own right. It is vital that they first be not only in the world but of the world, for to be condemned to acosmia (as Hannah Arendt said of the Jews and Beauvoir of women) is always to be held back. There is indeed something scandalous here – not the kind of scandal proper to one philosophical approach in particular, but rather the scandal engendered when any branch of philosophy would turn away from, or shirk, the political. The fact that a handful of women are busy dancing in the big boys' playground to the strains of the feminine is no

FRANÇOISE COLLIN

reason to forget those multitudes of silenced women for whom the feminine is still bound up with the hardships of a position which they have not chosen, those women who, from birth and even before, are destined to know of the subject's lack only in their experience of subjection. The ways in which men and women are actually treated cannot be reduced to the categories of masculine and feminine, regardless of how exactly these are combined or conjugated. Difference is a lesson taught by oppression, one inscribed in the real in a multiplicity of guises and which can no more be pinned down to a single cause than it can be ascribed to one originating moment in history. This move towards a theory of the (good) feminine, however subtly contrived, involves a certain denial of the real.

Yet the attempt to think sexual difference in terms of oppression alone has certain unexpected consequences. For those who confine themselves to such an approach (encouraged in this, perhaps, by the work of Simone de Beauvoir, or at least by *The Second Sex*)[5] the claim that sexual difference may be identified entirely with its status as a historico-cultural construct implies that the end of oppression will entail the end of sexual difference, or at least that there will come a time when it ceases to be of any consequence. Understood literally, 'One is not born a woman, one becomes a woman', leads us to believe that once the age-old burden of an unhappy lot has been shaken off, woman (man) will no longer make sense and Man (that is, the human) will attain wholeness in a humanity that is fully in control of its own fate, one that is pure freedom. According to this hypothesis, women and men mean nothing other than what centuries of subjection of one by the other have made them mean. Once subjection has been overcome, only the subject will remain, just as the humanist had always affirmed: Man, finally restored to transcendence, will no longer be alienated, no longer 'altered'.

This position confuses equality and identity: to be equal means to be identical, whereas to be different necessarily implies inequality. We may discern here, in its application to women and men, a trace of that Enlightenment assumption that the only way to achieve equality is through identity – the belief that there is only one kind of Man. And assimilation is always construed in terms of identification with the dominant party. Under the guise of universalism, the foreigner is only entitled to equal treatment if he goes native (or pretends to) and a woman only becomes fully human by becoming a man (or pretending to). The defeat of alienation is also that of difference.

Thus the desire, which feminists share, to overcome the structural oppression informing sexual difference, gives rise to two opposing positions which nevertheless both aspire to restore the metaphysical claims of the subject. On one side there is 'women's subject', qualified as feminine – the position described today as essentialist – and on the other, there is the rationalist 'human subject'. Each position assumes that the meaning of 'women' can be taken as read: all or nothing. Each approach presupposes a certain representation of sexual difference, either as determinable or as null and void. Either there is women's logic, or human reason. Women are reconciled to themselves, or else Man (the human) is reconciled to himself. Either oppression conceals a recognizable difference, or else it projects a semblance of difference that is nothing but illusion. Two interpretations of a characteristic property and its sphere of appropriate usage: the distinctively feminine as against the distinctively human. Implicit in political projects of either kind is a certain vision of the desired end: the feminine identity of women (as distinct from that of men) or, alternatively, the one identity of the human being.

The question of the subject must, therefore, be rephrased in political terms, in such a way as to leave open the issue of its metaphysical foundation. Women, at any rate, including those who insist on the 'death of the subject' because of its links to the phallic, still demand the right to be treated, at long last, as subjects. And to be a subject here means this: to be able 'to figure in speech and action', in public and private spheres alike; to become agents within this shared world, where being an 'agent' is not to be confused with being an 'author', in line with the crucial distinction proposed by Hannah Arendt,[6] who was subsequently most careful not to speak of the subject, preferring more often than not the Latin *quis*, the 'who', the 'someone'.

The tragic conflict

How to act, then, without renewing the bond of mastery? How to hold fast to the passivity which lets be, while working to change that which is? Is there indeed a mode of action which allows room for quietude? The impossibility of this dual allegiance cannot but be experienced as tragic. In this tearing apart, poetics, politics and ethics begin to come into relation with one another.

How indeed is the claim that the subject is fundamentally heteronomous – inhabited by the Other or by others – to be reconciled with its autonomy? How can the non-subject (whether this be thought of in general terms, as being-in- the-world, or more specifically as women's being-in-the-world) demand to be recognized as a subject? The burden of this struggle, or internal contradiction, is borne far less by the oppressors than by the oppressed and it falls to them to think it through. Indeed, it is all very well for someone who occupies the subject-position, at least politically – whose voice can be heard – to bear witness to their having been altered by the other, for there is no risk of this being identified with their alienation.[7] There is a sense in which such an individual unwittingly has a foot in both camps. He has the authority to denounce the authority of the subject. It is with a loud voice, strong in the assurance that he will be heard, that he calls to mind the weak. It is in the work he produces that he is able to gesture towards the absence of work. By contrast, someone who has yet to be in authority, who has still to be recognized as a speaking subject and who has still to be admitted to that space of 'self-assertion by word and deed', must needs first demand their right of entry. And so it is that women have conceived the desire to be subjects, or to occupy the subject-position, if only to gain a hearing when they testify to the dispossession of the subject.

For the struggle to give voice to silence and inaction must be waged in words and deeds. For the sound of the neuter can only issue forth in assertion and self-assertion. For only those who comply with the norms of the discourse of mastery may cross into the country of the murmur. For those who aspire to the place of the non-subject must stand firm as subjects. For the right to speak alone can only be won by speaking with one, collective, voice. For the way to open a passage through the self towards the abyss of the 'I' lies in assuming the figure of woman, or women, in all its substantiality. For those who would be silent must cry out. Such is the terrible necessity of the inevitable ordeal that is the political. To be condemned to the political is the harshest sentence that oppression of any kind can pass on the oppressed party.

The way out of this theoretical impasse is, no doubt, to be found by distinguishing between the position of the subject of a right – that is, the position of the individual *qua* political subject – and the position of the ontological subject. Being a citizen who belongs to a community by no means offers the subject infallible protection from the experience of ontological lack. Someone who speaks and acts in the public arena may yet feel, and indeed be, radically altered by otherness. Yet it is nevertheless within one and the same person that these two principles coexist: one does while the other undoes, one masters while the other lets go, and one comes forward while the other steps back. However, the ability to distinguish in theory between these two registers does not of itself resolve the real conflict that exists between them: the background to such distinctions is one of underlying tension. This ambivalence cannot be resolved into an 'either/or', but must rather be expressed as 'one and the other', or, at the very most, in the alternation of 'first one, then the other', which is indeed the knot that lies at the heart of tragic experience and the expression of an impossible ordeal.

It is only by passing through the dialectic of mastery and servitude, at the risk of getting drawn in, that members of any minority can hope to escape it. This throws some light on the unfortunate and unlikely common trajectory of almost all liberation movements: in the course of confronting mastery in order to overcome it, they become contaminated by the very position which they set out to challenge. To be obliged to fight for one's fundamental rights can end up reducing a human being to this role of combatant. And by the time they finally come out the other side, the oppressed have become like their masters, that is, like the members of that very group against whom they rose up in revolt. (So it is that every revolution sows the seeds of dictatorship.) And yet there can be no killing the master without killing the master within.

The 'dislocuted subject': alienation and the alteration that is otherness

How then is it possible to emerge from that bitter struggle which is the only way to become a subject of rights, without falling prey to the imaginary of the master-subject in which essences are restored once more and the self is reconciled to itself, as if 'I', or worse still, 'we', could be a self? Or, in other words, how are we to conceive of a non-metaphysical politics? How are we to envisage a political movement that avoids reducing those men or women who devote themselves to its cause to their status of political subjects, one which does not confine them to the collective identity which they must needs embody in order to assert themselves?

The attempt within the political to escape from the reductionism of the political can only succeed by constantly reopening the political to rupture by the non-political, by striving to welcome within the political that which transgresses and eludes it, by allowing the infinite heterogeneity of language to resonate within the homogenous field of discourse and by preserving in what is done the memory of the undoing. There can be no end to this labour of criticism and self-criticism, within and upon the political, one which perhaps bears some resemblance to the critical work which writing performs both in and against the book. For to guarantee its survival, the political asks only to be forgotten. This critical project can only be realized by attending to the weakness of the 'I' in every 'me' and every 'we' of which there are instances (me, a woman; we women).

For if I am a woman, 'I' is not a woman. And women's admission to the position of the subject of rights would expose them, in perpetuity, to the risk of abandonment to the drifting stream affecting every 'I', substituting plurality for collectivity, as they make their way through the dangerous waters of Manichaean dualism, on a journey that every liberation movement must undertake.

So it is a matter of fighting against alienation in order to respond and remain responsive to the alteration that is otherness. As long as vulnerability to the other means being appropriated by the other, finitude or alter-ation risks being confused with alienation. Thus the oppressed are often the last remaining champions of the humanism of identity, the last believers in the reconcilation of the self with the self (woman's self or the human self). They easily fall prey to the totalitarian temptation which promises that they will be, that they are, divine. Women's liberation is also liberation from the belief in liberation. The struggle against subjection must be waged without bolstering the myth of the subject. The fight against injustice, if obliged to hold up the ideal of justice, must not itself fall for this myth.

The difficulty faced by every movement striving for political freedom – to resist confusing the struggle against subjection with the myth of the subject, that is, to resist reducing the unknown to the known – will be made manifest in its relationship to works of art. There can be no denying that such movements (Marxism and feminism, to give but two examples) rarely sponsor the emergence of new artistic forms and tend to reduce (in their interpretations) those which do arise to mere expressions, illustrations or proofs of an abstract truth already established.[8]

It turns out that even in the social arena, political reductionism values, paradoxically, only those actively involved in campaigning, or only that part of their lives which is given over to this. The collectivity will inevitably fix its own limits, for it can only operate under such conditions. It jealously guards all entrances and exits to the space in which 'we' can be used legitimately.

A political reading of the world excludes that which is not useful to it and, more generally, that which is not useful. With this in view, it comes as no surprise to discover that a way of thinking which took root in the rich soil of a political movement is unable to confront loss when this is conceived in terms of waste. For a postulate of the political is immortality: the weak 'I' is replaced by the strong 'we' and all pain is put down to injustice. Thus theorizing will often arise from the political, but seldom thinking.

To fight against alienation while remaining open to alter-ation – such is the path ahead of what may still, today, be called the subject, which has only persisted by keeping these two movements apart, either by submitting to alienation or eluding alteration. For any struggle against alienation which has no time to be attentive to the alteration that is otherness is in danger of seriously losing its way.

The unconditional experience of dialogue is capable of warding off the subject's metaphysical temptation to self-sufficiency or the reconciliation of self with self: dialogue is a space in which the 'I' is freed simultaneously from its delusions of identity and the wretchedness of objectification. Levinas' contribution, here in the ethical sphere, is decisive, no less than Arendt's in the political. The subject is vulnerable to the other, is altered by the other and thus will never be self-sufficient. The ruse of oppression is to elude this alteration by placing the other in the object-position and by substituting discourse *about* the other for dialogue *with* the other. This has characterized those dominant modes of thought and action alike in which men, instead of being ready to listen to what a woman says and does, have for centuries tried to say what a woman is, what women are, ascribing to them at once a definition and a place, as though men were destined for all eternity to speak but never to be spoken to, or at least never by a woman who would take the initiative in conversation, a woman who would be more than (an) echo. (Yet, paradoxically, this inability or refusal to hear anything that has not been said already can also afflict those men or women who would speak for a minoritized group: all 'representatives' have their own limiting conceptions of what it is they represent.)

The shuttle of alterity passes back and forth through the weft of dialogue, which, as Jean-Luc Marion[9] suggests beautifully, leaves the subject 'dislocuted', 'dislocuted' because subjected to interlocution and 'dislocuted' because left out of joint, deprived of self-assurance, taken by surprise, reduced to stupefaction. The other person, that other person that is the other of the other sex, deprives me of all certainty, both about what I am and what the other is. Such is the shock of encounter: the subject is rendered speechless, a ban is placed on the subject's position without there being any compulsion to adopt that of the object (nor to become embroiled in the variant of this figure that is the subject/object dialectic – the confrontation, which Sartre evokes, of the 'looker' and the 'one looked at'). The other, as other person, will no more allow me to say "I" than to say "we". Identities are not prejudiced in the encounter, but nor is the reality of their effects avoided: they are respected just as they present themselves and no attempt is made to subject them to definition. For it is up to each party to come forward in the encounter without being obliged in so doing to name themselves.

This is what Levinas suggests in his discussion of radical alterity, the otherness which can only be spoken *to*, but never spoken about in the third person. But this 'speaking to' must constantly be detached and distilled from the temptation to 'speak about'. The encounter is not a given but must be worked upon, for there is always the risk that the adversary may resurface in the other. The *differend*[10] expresses both difference and what it is about that difference which forestalls conflict. The alteration which takes place in the encounter is perceived as a threat to the subject, whose defences lie alternatively in mastery or trickery.

A non-metaphysical politics can have no preconceived ideas about either its mode of operation or the identities of its agents. It lends agency to new centres of resistance, ones which had previously been excluded, thereby releasing their unmasterable potential for change. In the encounter, only action, in all its unforseeability, may be foreseen, for better or for worse.

Sexual difference as *praxis*

"What does a woman want?" Or, in other words, what is a woman? This is not a question that can be answered within the theoretical arena, or not without turning it into the bogus question of one who already knows both the questions and the answers. This question only acquires substance in the trial of dialogue. (And the same can probably be said too of that rather more deeply hidden question, 'What is a man?', or 'What does a man want?')

This is to say that the question of the difference, or differend, between the sexes proves resistant to all forms of theoretical investigation. Rather, it partakes of the order of *praxis*. Man and woman do not come within the substantial and definable realm of the utterance.

There can be no disputing the fact that there is a difference between the sexes. Yet the idea that this difference 'must' disappear, or else that it will become fixated on itself once oppression has been overcome – these are mere postulates. Difference there is, even though what differs cannot be essentialized. Both claims – woman does not exist and woman is such and such – are similarly speculative and similarly inquisitorial.

Sexual difference is elaborated in real relations between women and men and cannot be discussed in the third person. There is only one way in which it can be articulated: in the trial of dialogue, with its conflictual dimension, in which a man and a woman, or men and women, confront each other, whether in private or in public. Sexual difference and the knot of the differend which lies at its centre is, then, a question of address. No one can understand the meaning of woman (or man) – what 'woman' means and what she means to say – other than by listening to what it is that a woman actually says. She who speaks does not know who she is (nor who the other is) and yet she speaks, she is the one who is speaking and who wants to be understood on the basis of what she says. This difference, which in theory is undecidable, is decided over and over again in every relation.

So feminism, no less than psychoanalysis and philosophy, needlessly exhausts itself in the attempt, which is doomed to fail, to say what a woman is or what women are, or to define what a man is and what men are. The exponential growth of discourse on the matter only heightens its obscurity. Yet at least it teaches us not to know, to uproot the question of sexual difference and that of the definition of the differing parties from the sphere of knowledge, in order to make of it an act, an ethical and political *praxis*. From now on, sexual difference will be work in progress, undertaken independently of any particular representation of what one or the other is, or should be. Sexual difference, which for centuries has in both theory and practice been construed in terms of substance, is now brought into play, not in accordance with the shifting forces of history but rather in action. And even if this is still largely the action of women – who are often compelled to act unilaterally – it is potentially and already, here and there, actually a shared undertaking, a joint action in which the agents are no longer certain of their roles and lapses of memory serve as spurs to invention, whether in private or on the public stage. There could never, in all this, arise grounds to assert either that there is no difference between the sexes, or that the difference is insurmountable, for all the evidence would suggest, indistinctly and simultaneously, both that there is no difference and that there is a difference. Herein lies the way out of any metaphysic of the sexes: not by substituting the assertion that there is no difference for the old belief in two localizable sets of differences, nor by fixing their new positions – their 'rightful places' – but in the action of the differing parties, just as they are in the here and now. For the rejection of servitude does not in itself provide the model for an egalitarian future.

It is purely speculative to attempt to foreclose discussion about what difference will be like once the deforming yoke of oppression has been lifted. The desire to overcome inequality by engaging plurally in speech and action, by adopting plurally the positions of women and men who are agents in a shared world, this desire is not a licence to determine the nature of human identity by reducing sexual difference almost to nothing, nor to establish the status and significance of the difference that would, hypothetically, survive the obliteration of this unequal world. Neither the fight against inequality, nor the bid for women to assert themselves as the initiators of words and deeds, need imply any attempt whatsoever to define them as they are (their nature) or as they should be.

So there can be no representing the difference between the sexes. It is neither a fact nor an idea but rather an ongoing activity which can operate either by perniciously repeating the oppressive pattern imposed and represented over the course of centuries, or by embarking on a difficult process of reinvention in which no one (woman or man) can be sure at the outset where their place will lie. Sexual difference is a way of acting out a differend, a mode of understanding in which misunderstandings may nevertheless be heard and accommodated. "I'm not sure I understand what you mean" at least suggests an attentive ear and is preferable to the "You're not saying anything", or the "What you're saying isn't worth anything" of the master conveniently deaf to all but the echo of his own voice.

If this enactment of sexual difference can only take place within the weakness of the subject, of speaking subjects and of the subject who lords it over speech, it cannot do without its women agents. To bring about the death of the subject is to give free reign to those men and women who are the actors (but not the authors) of their speech. The undecidable is constantly elaborated and re-elaborated in a praxis of two which eludes dualization and not in that discourse which is always the discourse of the one. Women's struggle is basically not to devise yet another theory of sexual difference, but to seek the end of all theories and in the midst of the proliferating discourse on the subject, to discern the hope of that silence which is alone able to listen and understand.

The ever unquiet dead

The foregoing discussion took as its point of departure the aporia which arises when post-metaphysical critiques of the subject, often expressed metaphorically in feminine terms, are confronted with the claim to subjecthood presupposed by any form of political thought. To proceed thus was to situate from the outset the re-emergence of the subject on the side of the political. Only then did an enquiry into the conditions of the possibility of a non-metaphysical politics commence, or indeed an enquiry into a non-metaphysical assertion of subjecthood in the very work of the political.

The assumptions implicit in such an approach have yet to be established, as does the extent to which it remains attached to the subject, even while denouncing oppression and mastery. Such a line of enquiry, which we cannot pursue here, would require a thorough re-examination of the very notion of the subject. Should we consent to a definition of being in the world which entirely purges this of any ego component, which makes it out to be pure contemplation, nothing but dissemination and the alteration that is otherness? Or to one which sees this ego component only as something to be erased? In other words, is being in the world 'pure' alter-ation, to the exclusion of that 'care of the self' which women cannot afford to forget?

The critique of the subject, the placing of the subject in question, has inspired much contemporary thinking and, on occasions, has played a part in apologies for the feminine.

Yet in its attempt to invert 'modern' thinking by stressing otherness and difference, has it not itself become mere ideology? For even if there is no such thing as a pure subject, there is still something of the subject in every human 'being there', or to use one of those sexed metaphors, there is always something of the phallic, the virile, in every instance of the feminine. There is no 'I' altered by the Other which does not resist this very alteration, no deconstruction from which the beginnings of reconstruction are entirely absent, no self-effacement without self-assertion. And these are not just the remnants of what was destined to disappear: they are co-constituents of that which is. The undoing of writing writes – it writes a book, or in the space of the book. Ruin and reconstruction are closely, indeed inextricably, linked. The fact that the subject is not the master (of the other or the world) does not deprive it of its status as subject. There can be no separating self-presence, or identity, from alterity, and even no separating identification from alteration. When they are given over to celebrating the death of the subject, attempts to think the feminine (whether by philosophers (men) or women philosophers) end up simply hiding the reality of its being. Negation resembles denial. For in death, even by execution, the king is restored to life. There is no 'feminine' that can be definitively detached from the phallic, even if the phallic is placed under erasure by what we call the feminine. The end of oppression is not the end of the subject: the ego lives on in a society of equals and egoism is just one mode, one manifestation, of an ego component which cannot be dispensed with, an inextinguishable 'care for the self'. The 'you' and the 'we' are connected to the 'I' that neither can do without. The attempt in ethical, as in political, thinking to arraign its delusions of grandeur by recalling it to its place within a plurality does not entail the abolition of this 'I'. Equality presupposes recognition of multiple, different, egos; if every ego is, in the first instance, related to itself and, in a certain sense, prefers itself, then it is not alone in having such a preference. To set about listening to the other is to understand that he is to himself what every 'I' is to its self (an alter ego, one unlike the ego but similar to an other ego), for all are called to 'persist in their being', to reveal themselves, and yet also to disappear. There is neither an ethics nor a politics that can get round the recognition of the subject, yet the thing to remember is that this subject is plural. Being in the world consists in being torn apart in an 'altercation' between self and other, for alteration is attendant upon this confrontation with other selves. For I can (sometimes) die for the other, but never in the other's place. And it is up to everyone to value their own place while also leaving room for others, to be a 'friend to themself' in order to 'become a friend to another'.[11] The undecidable, which is suspended in every repeated judgement, lies at the limit both separating and uniting persistence in one's being and the call on the other to come into being, respect for the other's being. And this is how speaking together works: both parties speak (without knowing either who they are or even what they are saying) and both listen to speech of the other.

For, as psychoanalysis will insist, every 'I' is an other, is inhabited by an other which it cannot assimilate; every I is unnameable. What it says, what it does, even in the political arena, is informed by that which lies beyond both mastery and representation. This other which inhabits the 'I', dividing me from myself, can also be embodied in the radical alterity of an other person, thereby providing a vivid reminder, in plurality, of the internal difference at the heart of every self. However, this alteration by the other cannot quite efface the enduringly stubborn 'I', which, at least in Western cultures, remains transfixed by its own impossible self-coincidence. For if its name is never its own, it is nonetheless played upon by the desire for ownership, even if this is only made manifest in a concern over signature. (Remember those early days of the feminist movement when signature was forbidden, not just in a bid to break with the 'Name of the Father' but also every name? The moment was short-lived.) Even after abandoning the hope of self-knowledge, the subject continues to assert itself. Anyone serious about the 'death of the subject' would have to fall silent, or at least into a form of silence, the time of the instant, the instance without insistence . . . or would lean towards suicide. Yet from the moment of birth, the newborn's first cry is the sign of a stubborn will to live. It could seem surprising that each one expends so much energy on surviving when nobody calls upon it to do so (for he or she is never called on in particular, not even by its parents) or indeed that it should take up abode in a place which has not been marked out for it. This subject that is supposed to be dead proves to be remarkably obstinate. It is this obstinacy which moves the adult in the cry of the infant, that cry which contains condensed everything that it will have to negotiate later, verbally and actively, for years to come, in order to assert his or her semblance of self. And this cry of "I am", with all its pain and anger, will be regurgitated in the throes of death. The subject's demand for 'a place', which can be translated into political terms, is not, on this understanding, a betrayal but rather an enactment of the ontological condition of being in the world – neither pure otherness nor pure self. The beginning is multiple. Finitude is not the great myth of the subject's disappearance but rather the testing experience of its limits. And the fact that action (as *praxis*) cannot be reduced to the execution of projects (to a *technê*) does not, for all that, render it null and void.

The post-metaphysical does not betoken the death of the subject but rather its inscription between the frontiers of life and death. Awareness of the alteration involved in exposure to the other, awareness that the subject is not master and is not a transparently self-reflecting relation, only spells death to those who confuse the subject with the One, but not to those for whom "the one won't go without the other",[12] death for those in search of a 'mother tongue' but not for those who know that to dwell in language is always 'to live in several languages', in a 'monumental *quid pro quo* . . .'.[13]

To welcome that which is and to intervene with the determination to change that which is – these are the two incompatible but inseparable faces of being in the world, of living in the midst of that confusion of 'things which depend, and do not depend, on us'. If 'to think is to thank', then to think is also, always, to act. And to act is one way of giving thanks.

This text, in an earlier version, was first read at the inaugural ceremony marking Rosi Braidotti's accession to the Chair of Feminist Studies at The University of Utrecht. It is dedicated to her, in friendship.

Translated by Oliver Davis

Notes

1 Paraphrase of the title of a book by Maurice Blanchot, *Celui qui ne m'accompagnait pas* (Paris: Gallimard, 1953).
2 Maurice Blanchot, *Thomas l'obscur* (Paris: Gallimard, 1950); Hannah Arendt, *The Life of the Mind* (Orlando: Harcourt Brace & Co., 1978), vol. 1, p. 210: 'Only insofar as he thinks, and that is insofar as he is *not*, according to Valéry'.
3 A paraphrase of the title of Mallarmé's *Un Coup de dés jamais n'abolira le hasard* [*Translator's note*].
4 Well-known expressions of Luce Irigaray's which attempt to describe the feminine.
5 Beauvoir's position elsewhere is not always so clear-cut.
6 Hannah Arendt, *The Human Condition* (Chicago: The University of Chicago Press, 1958), pp. 176–7.
7 There is some risk of confusion in the use of the term 'alienation', on account of its Hegelian connotations. Here, 'alienation' [*aliénation*] is contrasted with 'alter-ation' [*altération*], the alteration that otherness occasions in the subject. Alienation denotes a specific kind of alter-ation in which oppression features, without this implying any prior commitment to the possibility of pure self-coincidence.
8 See Collin, F., 'Le sujet et l'autre', *Cahiers du Cedref* (Paris: Université de Paris VII, 1988), no. 2 and Marini, M., 'D'une création minoritaire à une création universelle', *Les Cahiers du Grif*, no. 45, 1991.
9 Jean-Luc Marion, 'L'interloqué', *Cahiers Confrontation*, no. 20, 1989, 'Après le sujet, qui vient?' [Marion's elegant expression exploits the dual meaning of the French 'interloqué', which can mean either to be engaged in a spoken exchange, an interlocution, or to be stupefied, struck dumb. The English neologism 'dislocution' suggests something of both the interlocutory and dislocatory aspects of Marion's 'interloqué'. – *Translator's note*].
10 Jean-François Lyotard writes: 'A case of differend between two parties takes place when the "regulation" of the conflict that opposes them is done in the idiom of one of the parties while the wrong suffered by the other is not signified in that idiom', *The Differend*, tr. Georges Van Den Abbeele (Manchester: Manchester University Press, 1988), p. 9. See also Collin, F., *Le différend des sexes* (Paris: Pleins feux, 1999).
11 Aristotle, *Nicomachean Ethics*, IX, 5, 25.
12 A paraphrase (which changes the sense) of the title of a book by Luce Irigaray: *Et l'une ne bouge pas sans l'autre*.
13 Rosi Braidotti, 'L'usure des langues', *Les Cahiers du Grif*, no. 39, 1988.

2

MONIQUE CANTO-SPERBER

Monique Canto-Sperber is currently Director of Research at the CNRS (Centre National de la Recherche Scientifique), Paris, and Professor at the EHESS (École des Hautes Études en Sciences Sociales). She was previously Professor of Philosophy at Amiens. She is a specialist in Greek philosophy, in particular Plato, and in moral and political philosophy. She is the mainstay of the recent revival of interest in moral philosophy in France, and has made a huge contribution to the introduction of Anglo-American moral philosophy into France. She edits a collection of works of moral philosophy for PUF (Presses Universitaires de France), and is editor of a 1840-page dictionary of ethics (1996) as well as of a book on British moral philosophy. In 1998 she edited a special edition of the *Magazine Littéraire*, devoted to 'les nouvelles morales', which focused attention on the wealth of moral philosophy being developed outside France, in Britain, Germany and the USA in particular. In Canto-Sperber's view, French moral philosophy, having been dormant for many years, has impeded its own reflourishing by its obsession with Kantian ethics.

Monique Canto-Sperber's major works include the following:

Platon, Ménon, Flammarion, 1991.

Les Paradoxes de la connaissance, Paris: Odile Jacob, 1991.

La Philosophie morale britannique, Paris: PUF, 1994.

Dictionnaire d'éthique et de philosophie morale (ed.), Paris: PUF, 1996.

La Philosophie grecque, Paris: PUF, 1997.

Les Ethiques grecques, Paris: PUF, 2001.

L'Inquiétude morale et la vie humaine, Paris: PUF, 2001.

MORAL ANXIETY AND
HUMAN LIFE

The myth of Modernity

[Synopsis of pp. 59–64: French moral philosophers, by contrast to their Anglo-American counterparts, have insisted in recent years on the importance of our being 'Modern'. Their references to 'Modernity' are not merely descriptive but suggest that it consitutes the inevitable goal of human moral development. Yet such deterministic talk of the laws of historical development glosses over the persistence of numerous Judaeo-Christian and Classical elements which are, in fact, central to our 'Modern' world-view. Their reliance upon the notion of historical stages involves a degree of caricature; instead of philosophy, what most contemporary thinkers offer are sociological analyses, necessarily both superficial and ephemeral. The advocates of Modernity – Gilles Lipovetsky and Luc Ferry in particular – simultaneously overdramatize the phenomenon and yet seem to dismiss it as, in essence, nothing new. The philosophical discourse of Modernity is as open to argument as that which proclaimed the Death of Man.]

* * *

I would like here to advocate a rather different way of approaching the study of Modernity. The world in which we live is not the end result of a chain of historical necessities, nor is it a product of the perfect enactment of a transcendent process; nor has it arisen from the complete emancipation of the human being; nor indeed from the secularization of society. It occurs to me that we are depriving ourselves of the means to understand the nature of our Modernity when we think of it as a unified whole that could not have been other than it is. I do not believe either that we have simply found our freedom nor that we have entirely left behind any of the supposed forms of alienation that are religion, nature and tradition. I aim here merely to offer my own sketch of our current moral situation.

The world we live in is complex, differentiated and, in certain respects, contradictory. There are many sources of moral value. These include the existence of universal, impersonal, duties, the weighing up of consequences, ties imposed by the specific obligations we have towards other beings, not to mention the ideals and values of self-realization. The very forms in which morality is present in our world are many and varied: we may be forced to encounter it in the form of obligations or prohibitions, but also in the shared truth of righteous indignation, or praise, or indeed in the certainty that

25

every act must be governed by its very own set of norms. It would be reductive and inaccurate to attempt to establish a fixed hierarchy of these sources of value, these various different meanings of the normative.[1] Accordingly, the specificity of our present moral situation lies, to some extent, in the diversity of its constituent parts. Among these elements are those concerned with the various ways in which we may be held to be responsible for our actions and their consequences. They also include others which relate to a single overriding value, respect for the human person and his or her rights; others still refer to the idea of human perfection or the intrinsic value of effort and merit. This list is not intended to be exhaustive. For the main point is this: far from following successively one from the other, these elements exist alongside one another; they coexist in a fragmented or conflictual state.

It may be that the contingencies of human history have allowed these moral beliefs of various origins to remain in existence even after the particular world-view in which each prevailed has itself fallen into eclipse.[2] It may also be that our experience of the normative can only take shape amid this differentiation of the various sources and aspects of morality. It is even possible that we may only be able to gain access to one or more aspects of the reality of the normative, in a fairly irregular way and depending upon historical, cultural and political factors. And it may indeed be that the terms and categories with which we think about our moral life have emerged from two defining experiences (even if their historical moment has passed): the moral purpose of the City in the Ancient World and that of the painful, stormy and intermittent recognition of the link between a people and their God, or indeed between humanity in its entirety and its God. The particular characteristics of today's moral situation are rooted in attitudes from what is sometimes the distant past, attitudes which we have no reason to believe were necessarily the best or indeed the only ones available. Our moral situation cannot escape this condition of contingency and diversity. In this sense, it is necessary in its singularity: although there are powerful reasons why we should have arrived where we have, this does not imply that it was necessary for us to have arrived here, nor that our Modernity should be viewed as that which it was always, necessarily, destined to be. This analysis is no barrier to our acknowledging the unique specificity of our era, one marked, not least, by the emergence of a worldwide sense of human belonging. But a singular occurrence of this sort ought to be subject to an ongoing process of anxious questioning rather than being taken for granted as an unassailable point of departure.

If we opt for any of these interpretations of how we arrived at Modernity – the determinist, the progressivist or the 'instantaneous' interpretations (it had to happen, it happened little by little; it happened all at once), then we deny ourselves the necessary intellectual resources with which to reflect upon this process. First, because what we have to think about – the end result – tends to dissolve into the process which gave rise to it. What is Modernity? We are told that it is the end result of the processes of emancipation and secularization. Yet there is no guarantee of the legitimacy of such a view of our history. The underlying thought is that humanity, having reached Modernity, has simply become what it was destined to be from the very beginning: democratic, rational and emancipated. A simplistic interpretation of this kind (which is historicist, self-satisfied and vaguely Hegelian) has no more to be said for it, intrinsically, than those interpretations which purport to identify in Modernity a form of barbarity and madness (as in the case of Kierkegaard and Nietzsche) or a close – if paradoxical – association between reason and superstition, between free diversity and constraining uniformity. Indeed it is no more justifiable than those ways of thinking which deny or remain unaware of the significance of the phenomenon that is Modernity.[3] Moreover, the reality of Modernity may be considered to be, in part, the creation of philosophy. Our world has been shaped, to some extent, by a number of powerful philosophical concerns . . .[4] The 'criterion' of Modernity has indeed been generated by the power of philosophical thought, reflective and speculative. It is a 'criterion' which endeavours to distinguish between and oppose, on one hand, the bygone world of prejudice, madness, nature, religion and authority and, on the other, the Modern world of reason, autonomy and self-possession. A 'philosophical history' of this sort, which informs both the consciousness of being Modern and the desire to be Modern, does itself have an origin, one which lies at the end of the sixteenth century.[5] Yet we cannot be sure that it alone will allow us to gain the kind of access we need to the phenomenon we seek to explain – one which it has helped, in part, to constitute. For, once more, we must be careful to recognize fully the role played by contingency in the world in which we live. Few of the characteristics of this reality, not to mention its ambiguities, are susceptible to explanation in terms of a single philosophical and historical interpretation.

The reality of the Modern is a mix of democratic enthusiasm and the glorification of abilities or personalities which happen to have risen, by chance, to positions of exception; a blend of pedantic rationality and superstition, of emancipation and dependency. The claim that 'secularization', or 'emancipation', from authority, are in themselves the criteria which allow us to gauge the divide between thought and truth, is wishful thinking and could only be found credible in the context of a very restricted view of reality. Above all, this way of viewing our present leads us astray because it convinces us that we have arrived at Modernity when the process, if process there is, is far from complete. Things may remain as they are without developing further, the process may prove to be self-cancelling, or to take shapes which are either outmoded or as yet unheard of, for its meaning has yet to become accessible to us.

The ill-treatment of individualism

A textbook case, but one that I can only discuss very briefly here, is the way in which Modern individualism has been understood. The 'Modern individual' has been dressed in some of the most splendid, as well as some of the most miserable, of the costumes our world has to offer. At one moment the individual is he who 'finally comes to be what he is, in a society of human rights and autonomy',[6] who is able to get free of nature in all its guises, of every tradition and all forms of authority. But generally – and to paraphrase Descartes, this cud has been well-chewed – the Modern individual is characterized overall in terms of 'the instant gratification of desire, the passion for ego, happiness of an intimate and a material kind, well-being and the dynamics of subjective rights', as the source of neither norms nor values, as a 'floating space, lacking both points of reference and fixity, a pure openness'.[7] The most pronounced tendency today is to take the denigration of the individual as a mark of lucid awareness of the pathologies of the Modern.

These characterizations of the subject of Modernity – grandiose and miserabilist alike – strike me as open to argument.[8] It is difficult to see which historical or philosophical arguments could be adduced to justify them. In fact, these characterizations are so extreme that their first and only effect is to stop thought in its tracks. They prevent us from understanding the intrinsic difficulties bound up in what it means to be a human being today. Why is it that the positive definition of Modern individuality always, without fail, leads to this idea that a wrenching-away from nature, tradition, or the group, is a necessary condition of autonomy? Do the painful contorsions by which we detach ourselves from everything that is not the self really allow us to find that self? Why is it necessary to preempt the reality of the Modern human being by conceiving of it in terms of the demand for radical self-determination? What reason is being invoked to make a freedom as empty and abstract as this into the source of all meaning and value, by dismissing everything that does not comply with such a demand as an archaism or a hangover from the past? Is not the self in fact defined in a continuous process of interaction with that which is not itself? Indeed, is it not rather the case that the self's autonomy takes shape in a process of critical evaluation, elaboration and revision of its own psychological material? In fact, this conception of the individual of today – as a butterfly, flitting high above values, gathering up the norms which please it, concerned always with its own pleasure – is simply a decorative and reactionary portrait which corresponds to almost nothing, real or psychological, in our surrounding field of human reality. To attempt to defend such an extreme conception of the Modern individual is surely to consign oneself to the realms of incoherent fantasy. What real understanding of individuality can we hope to gain from the artificial opposition between 'subjectivity as the awareness of principles made out to be universal and as one pole in intersubjectivity' and 'the May '68 notion of Modern individuality'?[9]

The individual may be thought of as the autonomous source of a particular conduct, but the representations, goals and values which direct this action cannot be 'self-determined'. The atomistic conception of the individual is both ontologically and psychologically untenable.[10] Modern identity, together with the relation to the self and the possibilities for action which accompany it, has come into being at the end of a long historical process, the earliest developmental stages of which (the Greek and Judaeo-Christian) remain with us today. Insofar as it is a product of humanity's incessant reflective and interpretative activity, Modern identity is by no means bound fast to the historical causes which gave it shape. But nor does it exist independently of a society in which human practices come into being, a culture and the many ties which are formed with, and around, the individual. The principal features of Modern identity – freedom, autonomy, self-restraint and the search for well-being – can neither originate in a subject's choice of its own position nor in an act of rational self-determination. Rational autonomy is a basic good – both as a real orientation towards morality and as the source of a practical reason that is not exclusively formal and procedural – because the condition of its value lies in an anthropology of human sociality.

Today's glorification of the rational will must be accompanied by an acknowledgement of the fundamentally non-determined character of human will. If there were a single characteristic of Modern man, it would be that of being almost unable to know what he wants. This explains why the will can both do freedom's work and why it may prove to be the locus of dependency. An infinity of reflections in the mirrors that are others' desires incessantly incites the individual's will to determine itself but without always lending this will either a direction or an object. To the extent that the individual is a discordant being in which a disparate mix of aspirations, some of them opposites, are bound together, to the extent that this being must always constitute itself on the basis of that which is external to it (social reality, practices, ties of cultural belonging and loyalties), the life of a 'Modern' individual is more of a challenge than it is the result of a necessary process of emancipation. It is the product of much hard work, work both indeterminate and ongoing, undertaken without hope of fulfilment – work which is necessitated by the universal struggle in which all are striving to be recognized as singular beings.[11] From Benjamin Constant on, many thinkers have explored this ambivalence of the Modern individual. A more worthwhile task for today's thinkers than the glorification of autonomy or the condemnation of the triviality of their contemporaries' desires, would be to uncover the multiple, sometimes contradictory, faces of today's individual, a reality both very stable and very fragile, bound up as it is with the democratic conditions in which it came into being.[12]

Those whose contribution is limited to identifying a 'structural conflict' between 'two incompatible logics of individualism' – on one side, 'individualism tied to moral laws, to equality and the future' (responsible individualism) and, on the other, 'the individualism of each man for himself and *après moi le déluge*' (irresponsible individualism) – simply repeat what amounts to little more than a truism, namely that it is better to prefer responsibility to irresponsibility.[13] The key question is, rather, why one form of individualism is, without fail, tied to the other. How are we to find the necessary critical tools to analyse the Modern individual if we deprive ourselves from the outset of the intellectual resources with which to understand its ambivalence, one far more complicated than a simple opposition between rule and licence?

One way of trying to understand Modernity would be to carry out a reflexive and normative study of the intellectual conditions of our epoch, of its representations and justificatory procedures. Such an undertaking would require concepts that are better suited, more rational, more specific and less questionable than those I have just criticized. It would involve an unprejudiced description of the forms of contemporary humanity, with the aim of demonstrating both the divisions and the connections between autonomy and dependency, elitism and the sense of democracy, rationality and the particular ways of renouncing rationality that are peculiar to our age.[14] This kind of understanding has to be based on analysis and reflection which must, first and foremost, be realistic and compelling, humanly and psychologically suited to what we are and what is going on around us.

One of the aims of the present essay is to demonstrate that moral philosophy has a real role to play in this bid for understanding and that critical thinking can only advance when all the glorification and all the denigration have subsided. To deny that moral reality is varied and ambivalent and to attempt to unify it arbitrarily under the categories of autonomy and emancipation plunges us into the depths of self-delusion. This might almost be described as a moral failure, a failure in our attempt to understand our own situation as completely and accurately as we can. The consequence of such a failure will be an inability to think about and analyse anything that might happen in the future which had not already been mapped out deterministically in the Spirit's destiny of secularization and emancipation. For there can be no predicting the future of such processes, which are by definition ongoing.

Every moral situation is contingent, because it could have been different and also because, in spite of the fact that moral beliefs can aspire to objectivity and validity, it is impossible to find non-moral reasons which would guarantee their truth, whether these supposed reasons are rooted in the metaphysical nature of rationality, in universal forms of argument, or the necessary advance of Modernity. The fact that we are entirely unable to engage in moral reasoning without first starting out from a moral standpoint is one sign of this moral contingency. In the *Nicomachean Ethics*, Aristotle emphasizes that moral teachings can only be understood by those who have been brought up to behave decently. Kant reminds us at the beginning of the *Groundwork to the Metaphysic of Morals* that he is merely elaborating on the common conception of morality as duty. At the end of the nineteenth century, the English philosopher Henry Sidgwick set himself what he considered was the only task in moral philosophy: to analyse and expound the 'methods of ethics', which are simply the rationalization and justification of those moral elements that are already present in the common consciousness of all humanity.[15] Moral thinking can only be fostered within a pre-existing moral context which lends it meaning. It is because we are part of an age-old process of moralizing the human being – a process both irregular and decidedly imperfect – that moral thinking is possible. In the absence of this real process, none of the supposed foundations of ethics – whether in rationality, practices or linguistic norms – would be conceivable.

'All books lie open before me'

By way of conclusion, I would like to say something about how the critique of too unified or compact an understanding of Modernity and the Modern individual can have an impact on moral philosophy. Paul Ricoeur recently remarked that his moral thinking has been nourished by contributions from a wide variety of different philosophers. He observed that 'I see myself as a consummate reader, master of all I survey'.[16] Such a reminder is only necessary because it has almost become gospel truth that a 'Modern' moral philosophy can only ever be developed in the space of a rupture with the 'Ancients' and from a Kantian philosophical perspective. This is the argument I would like to criticize here, one which presumes to make unreserved adherence to Kantian philosophy the condition of the relevance of all moral thinking.

I have already commented on how the return to Kant, in which Luc Ferry and Alain Renaut have played pioneering roles, has sparked new interest in moral philosophy among the wider public. Yet it would be regrettable if such a return to Kant were to be all there is to the renewal of moral philosophy. First, because it is not clear that Kantian philosophy really includes a requirement for an independent moral philosophy. Second, because there are certain difficulties involved in the interpretation of Kant's position with respect to the role of practical reason and the determination of categorical or universal imperatives. And finally, because Kantian philosophy remains silent on many of the questions which are vitally important in moral philosophy – issues relating, for example, to the understanding of human motivation, the role of moral feelings, the existence of moral conflicts or the justification of moral beliefs. Yet Classical philosophy (and indeed other philosophical traditions such as intuitionism, Humean moral thinking and non-Kantian forms of contractualism) has considerable conceptual and critical resources which may be brought to bear on precisely these issues.

There would be no need to argue this case further were it not that the question of 'Philosophical Modernity' tends to be framed today in such inexact and question-begging terms, with one philosophical point of reference being assumed to naturally exclude every other. Yet because morality is a complex and disparate phenomenon, it should not come as any surprise in intellectual terms that several moral perspectives may be required to analyse it. The misunderstandings I alluded to at the beginning of this work – that every form of morality is law-based, that ethics is only concerned with happiness, that the moral philosophy of the Ancient World depends upon a particular notion of the cosmos – are all premised upon arbitrary, prior, decisions of meaning. Moreover, the bid to exclude philosophers from the Ancient World rests on a distorted sense of the historical character of moral philosophy.

The are some aspects of our moral image of the world – the universality of obligations, the idea of humanity – which probably are rooted in our Modern condition. It is unlikely that the philosophers of Antiquity would have had much of a sense of history and improbable that the idea of universal moral obligation would have played a central role in their conception of the ethical. Moral categories are not, then, independent of history but it would be incorrect to suggest that their only meaning is an historical one. I argued above that it would be wrong to imply that the entirety of our moral experience is circumscribed by the characteristics of 'Modernity'. Some key themes of Classical moral philosophy lie at the heart of our moral thinking. What is more, the philosophers and tragedists of Antiquity displayed an awareness of the wide variety of the sources of their morality and the conflict which this could engender. When they describe the difficulty of making moral decisions or address the irreducible character of moral dilemmas or discuss what form of life is implied by a particular conception of morality, we cannot neglect the richness of their moral thinking and their capacity to frame pointed quest-ions – which are sometimes so very close to our Modern investigations in so far as they betray an acute awareness of the heterogeneous character of our morality. In this sense, there is much to be learned from Greek thought, yet its role as an exemplar has nothing to do with the psychology of reassurance and wisdom to which it is all too often reduced today.

The thinkers of Classical Antiquity defined morality as a profound theoretical and practical understanding of action. The analysis of the practical side to rationality (that which applies to action) was a particular strong point, above all in Aristotle. And a great many of the ontological and epistemological problems posed by the definition of moral objectivity are set out in Plato's work. The field of practical reason encompasses every-thing pertaining to the normative character of acts, above and beyond morality in the strict sense. If the first challenge facing any morality is to define the principle which governs the way in which the intellectual grasp of reality is to be co-ordinated with the definition of the rule and the rectitude of desire, then such a challenge has rarely been met with greater lucidity than in Greek moral thought. Regardless of the other ways in which Greek thought may be inadequate or errant, no branch of moral philosophy today can afford to neglect this definition of the practical sphere, whether we choose to readopt it or merely to position ourselves in relation to it.

Most of the objections to Greek moral philosophy are merely taking issue with an artefact that Modern philosophy has constructed, one which goes by the name of 'Greek philosophy' yet usually in the absence of any precise historical reference. What masquerades as the thought of 'The Greeks' tends to be little more than a diluted and naturalistic version of Aristotelianism. Whole swathes of Greek thought are generally left out of this ad hoc composite, particularly the intellectualist and rationalist strains embodied in the Socratic tradition. Moreover, the history of Greek philosophy, which spans ten centuries, from the Presocratics to the last of the Stoics, one rich in discussions, controversies, schisms and polemics is represented here as a unified whole in which anti-rationalism, anti-formalism, and anti-universalism all have their proper place. This probably makes it rather easier to take issue with 'The Greeks'. The problem, however, is that the target of such criticism is no more than an artificial creation, a composite – the artefact I just referred to – and not a real, historically-instantiated, mode of thought.

The most pronounced differences between Modern moral theories and the ethics of the Ancient World lie in their respective understandings of the scope of moral philosophy. For Aristotle, in particular, the incisiveness and suitability of moral thinking is not to be measured by the presence in it of formal and procedural components nor by its ability to deal with every unusual or difficult case. Yet both these requirements – the capacity of a particular moral theory to supply a maxim or decision-making criterion which holds good in every difficult case and the capacity to abstract from the particular, concrete, features of an individual or a situation – are characteristic of the moral theories of today. Here, then, the difference between Classical moral thought and contemporary theory is very pronounced. However, moral thinking in the Ancient World varied in the degree to which it aspired to be systematic: Plato and the Stoics were great system-builders, Aristotle less so. Most importantly of all, inspiration can be found in the dominant themes of Greek moral thinking[17] for a far-reaching programme of rational inquiry, even if the aim of this undertaking is not to arrive at a unified theory capable of guiding our decisions. If there is no reason to reduce Modern moral philosophy to the two leading theories of today – Kantianism and Utilitarianism – we should certainly not attempt to reduce the entire history of morality to the sum of these two theories.[18] The very common assumption that 'Greek' thinking, because it cannot be reduced either to a form of Kantianism or a form of Utilitarianism, can have no impact on Modern thought, rests upon an erroneous conception of the nature of morality.

Another oft-repeated criticism of Greek thought – that it has nothing more to offer than a philosophy of how to live well, of happiness, or an art of living – is not only question-begging but rests upon a lack of historical awareness. It is alleged that Greek thought fails to provide a philosophy of law, rule and obligation and that, in this sense, Greek moral thinking cannot really be considered to be moral philosophy; put bluntly, the 'moral' in Greek moral thinking is something of a euphemism. This objection begs the question of whether morality must, by definition, be based on rules. I think I have already refuted this claim.[19] The historical misconception lies in the assumption that Greek thought in its entirety may be reduced to the search for happiness (happiness here being understood in the most pedestrian of ways, as the satisfaction of material needs independently of any notion of rational autonomy). According to those who kneel at the altar of Modern philosophy, Greek thought has no place for the human.[20] Yet this involves a confusion between, on one hand, a particular, substantive, claim which is indeed to be found in the work of a number of Greek philosophers – namely that moral goodness is the same as happiness and the search for happiness is the only way of becoming moral – and, on the other, a generalized interpretation imposed upon the entirety of Greek thought, namely that the Greeks could not conceive of a source of the morally normative in terms other than the search for happiness, or that Greek thought is constitutionally unable to conceive of morality other than in terms of self-fulfilment. It is this obsession with happiness that, according to the critics, makes Greek thinking structurally unable to have the merest inkling of the specificity of moral reasons, the nature of obligation and the integration of others' points of view. Yet this general claim is false. Happiness is fundamental to the moral thought of the Ancient World, yet it is clear that happiness alone cannot form the basis of the normative aspirations which thinkers of Antiquity recognized were part of moral thinking. For the majority of Greek philosophers, the source of morality could not be framed in terms of happiness and the principle underlying the prescriptive and impersonal character of moral norms is not the search for *eudaimonia*. For Plato, in particular, there exists a moral principle which determines both the value of virtue and that of happiness. This is the Form of the Good, understood as a wholly intelligible, real, presence and a principle of order. The case of Plato alone suffices to show that the customary accusation that all Greeks confused morality with the search for happiness is grossly unfair.[21]

Another equally unjustified objection has also become part of the stock-in-trade of contemporary thought. The notion that Greek morality in its entirety is dependent upon a certain idea of the cosmos is the result of a misunderstanding of references to natural ends. In Plato, the cosmos serves as a model of order. For Aristotle, nature is used as a conceptual paradigm for an immanent form of the normative. For the Stoics, the existence of the cosmos testifies to the presence of an ordering principle. It goes without saying that there is no trace whatsoever in these three philosophies of the idea that human ends or moral concepts are given by nature.[22] It is quite clear that Aristotle did not see human freedom and political action as modelled upon falling bodies. Rather, when he endeavours to understand the normative aspect to human action, he merely refers to the teleology which appears to be at work in nature and in technical decision-making, using these as instructive, productive, models. This is in no sense a dogmatic insistence on the intrinsic value of the natural, in no sense a claim that human actions should conform to natural processes.

It is sometimes said, moreover, that we can safely do away with Greek thought in view of the morally repellent realities of the world in which it originated (slavery, infanticide). The Greeks, it is claimed, had no understanding of the idea of humanity and had yet to grasp that history can shape social and political ideas. A necessary precondition of being able to think in terms of humanity or history, it is claimed, is to live in a situation in which these really exist. There can be no denying that both concepts lack concrete, historical, referents in the Ancient World. But how can we be quite so sure that they would also have been inconceivable to Greek philosophers? As for the objection based on the morally repellent features of the society in question, this is a *non sequitur*. First, because the history of the twentieth century should be sufficient safeguard against such ethical self-righteousness. Moreover, the fact that certain practices are repellent does not mean that attempts to analyse, understand and criticize them by philosophers are also, by the same token, repellent. Philosophy does not necessarily offer a mirror-image of the world in which it exists. In the case of Plato, in fact, philosophy is radically detached from this surrounding world. The right-thinking critics of today who complain indignantly of Aristotle's failure to take a stand against slavery, are probably unaware that Aristotle is reflecting upon a social reality in order to understand the basis of its legitimacy. It is quite possible to find philosophical interest in Aristotle's reasoning without being obliged to judge it according to the moral value of his conclusions. It is a misunderstanding of the role of examples in philosophy to make the intellectual worth of a particular argument depend upon its proposing a morally correct solution. The condition of philosophical legitimacy cannot just be moral legitimacy.

Another way in which a critical understanding of Modernity can impact upon the aspirations of moral philosophy is in terms of the relation between formal rationality and moral content. It has become a commonplace to assert that democracies allow *de facto* a high degree of moral pluralism. Individuals today do seem to entertain radically different conceptions of good and of human perfection. Some contemporary philosophy is driven by the hope that a kind of universality and objectivity can be attained by exposing people's opinions to mutual criticism that is both rational and public.[23] There has been much discussion of this enterprise and I shall only mention two objections here. First, the notion that a consensus may arise freely as the conclusion to a limitless process of inquiry or discussion is somewhat utopian, especially if it is also left to the citizens to come up collectively with a definition of the conditions of truth itself.[24] But above all, to suggest that the foundations of the normative ought to emerge from such rational processes of discussion is surely to start out from a position in which we are unable to think through all that is it is most pressing to understand about the Modern world: the conflicts, the inequalities, the persistence of tradition, the strength of the archaic. To describe all this as heteronomous and argue that, by contrast, the only source of autonomy lies in argument, is to dispose of what should have been the very object of inquiry.[25]

Can moral philosophy confine itself to being no more than an explanatory tool, adding a layer of reflection to various moral concepts and enabling, by force of reason alone, a formal core of universal obligations to be derived, which may be considered moral precisely in the sense that they are detached from beliefs and traditions? According to the advocates of this kind of moral universalism, the way to arrive at an ethics that is both rational and universal is to wrench oneself away from one's particularity, history and community and find in public argument the basis for all moral rationalism. This path, which presupposes, in principle, a radical distinction between reason and historical context, has led in France to a critique of all philosophical movements which stand opposed to a philosophy of the subject, be they deconstructionist or relativist.[26]

I think it would be desirable, however, to build a body of critical thinking around so clear-cut a distinction as that between reasons and convictions. This distinction, which is a precondition of the elaboration of a rational, universal, ethics, demands close scrutiny in its own right. I shall limit myself here to three reservations. The hope of deriving a universal ethics from reason alone (universal in the full sense: not just a criterion for identifying moral actions but a body of obligations capable of determining the will and which can inspire adherence) has never even begun to be realized, nor has it ever been established exactly how such an ethics would look. I would also emphasize that it is no easier to work out what exactly is meant by such a project than to reach agreement about the nature of the rational. Those who back so extreme a position today are relying on a quasi-metaphysical conception of human reason which logicians, mathematicians and cognitive psychologists appear to have more or less abandoned, in favour of a definition of rational ways of behaving which takes into account the coherence of the means, the context and how they developed. In other words, it is not clear why exactly moral philosophers should alone be permitted to entertain so absolutist a view of rationality. The first duty of a moral philosophy is to be realistic, by which I do not mean prosaic or materialistic, but close to the real. Finally, those who live in Modern democracies are so very aware of the extent to which subjects rely on pre-existing ways of being; they are also somewhat sceptical about the possibility of deriving norms from human reason. They are accordingly unlikely to be convinced that the only form of moral thinking to which they may aspire is this very limited and abstract rational exercise. It is even less likely that to demand of them a brutal emancipation from their beliefs will prove the most effective way of guarding against the return of these beliefs.

For my part, I am sceptical about the possibility of deriving a universal ethics from so absolutist and abstract a conception of rationality. But I must insist that this scepticism about the ability of reason to form the foundation of an ethics in no way entails my being sceptical about the existence of universal moral obligations. The most important questions about such obligations seem to me to be those of how they are discovered, defined and 'stabilized' and not those concerning their foundations. Moreover, the pressing need for moral thinking which we see today, and which I have evoked elsewhere, is by no means limited to the scrutiny of the formal conditions of life in a community. The question is whether moral philosophy has something more to offer, without abandoning, in the process, its critical and universalizing mission. Certain aspects of moral thinking are derived from the particular moral beliefs which it evaluates, puts together and criticizes in order to extract their ways of understanding the world. These beliefs, which are rooted in the commitments of individuals, are not however confined to their particularity: they may also be representative of shared obligations or imperatives imposed on all and which, in spite of being violated on occasions, are norms that may be applied to human conduct in general. Whilst there is nothing imperative about this understanding, it seems difficult to demand that it be deprived of its capacity to influence the way in which individuals view the norms governing their actions.

As well as declarations of principle and genealogies of Modernity, the renewal of moral philosophy must be based upon precise studies of the role of pre-existing convictions, universal obligations and practical norms, whatever the underlying ontological and epistemological commitments, be they founded in moral realities or not and regardless of whether they require moral understanding. The philosophical task here is considerable and will represent a decisive contribution to the development of moral philosophy in France. For it will involve work on the normative aspect of various ways of behaving, critical discussions which confront inherited moral concepts with principles and norms of action, as well as global reflection on the nature of practical rationality, on autonomy (that is, rational agents' capacity to act) and on the forms of deliberation and ethical decision-making. This is a brief outline of the kinds of questions which, it is my contention here, have specially preoccupied moral philosophers over at least the last two thousand years. In conjunction with the analysis of moral thinking, these themes go some way to showing that moral philosophy, once shorn of the dogmatism and bombast which has sometimes adorned it, is now, more than ever, capable of becoming a very powerful tool for understanding and critically evaluating the realities of today's world.

Translated by Oliver Davis

Notes

1 Thomas Nagel, 'The Fragmentation of Values, *Mortal Questions* (1979) and Charles Larmore, 'Reasonable Disagreement and Moral Pluralism', *The Morals of Modernity* (Cambridge: Cambridge University Press, 1996) and, in the same volume, 'The Ambitions of Moral Thinking', pp. 120–3.

2 See, for example, Charles Taylor, *Sources of the Self. The Making of Modern Identity* (Cambridge: Cambridge University Press, 1998), Isaiah Berlin, *The Crooked Timber of Humanity. Chapters in the History of Ideas* (London: Fontana, 1991) and Alasdair MacIntyre, *After Virtue* (London: Duckworth, Second Edition 1985).

3 Wittgenstein viewed with disdain 'the idea of moral progress in history and the notion that the world is a better place to live than it ever used to be. He is skeptical of the future of mankind. He attends to the detail of specific human beings' lives and does not meddle in mankind or in popular movements. He is attracted to Kierkegaard and Dostoyevsky, both of whom share and develop these thoughts.' – J. L. Craft & R. E. Hustwit, editors' Introduction to O. K. Bouwsma, *Wittgenstein, Conversations 1949–1951* (Indianapolis: Hacket, 1986), xxiv. See also Jacques Bouveresse, *Essais I. Wittgenstein, la modernité, le progrès et le déclin* (Marseilles: Agone, 2000), pp. 89–124.

4 On interpreting the relation between concepts and events, intellectual history and political history, or philosophy as a 'phenomenology' of the political and moral life of the last three centuries, see Leo Strauss & Joseph Cropsey, *The History of Political Philosophy* (Chicago: Rand McNally, 1972) and Leo Strauss, *The City and the Man* (Chicago: Rand McNally, 1964).

5 On Machiavelli's work as the 'point of departure' for Modernity, and also for an exemplary demonstration of 'against the grain historicism', see Pierre Manent, *La Cité de l'homme* (Paris: Fayard, 1993).

6 Luc Ferry, *L'Homme-Dieu ou Le sens de la vie* (Paris: Grasset, 1996), pp. 14, 34–7, 31 and 46.

7 Gilles Lipovetsky, *Le Crépuscule du devoir*, pp. 15, 18. This recalls somewhat the terms in which the subject was denounced in *Anti-Oedipus*: 'a floating space, with neither fixation nor reference, a pure openness', ch. 1. The congruence is highlighted by Luc Ferry and Alain Renaut in *La Pensée 68, essai sur l'anti-humanisme contemporain* (Paris: Gallimard, 1985), p. 284.

8 On the distinction between a subject and an individual, see Alain Renaut, *L'Ère de l'individu* (Paris: Gallimard, 1989). The question asked by Renaut is whether we should 'give up trying to analyze the history of Modernity in terms of subjectivity and instead see it, as a totality, in terms of the progressive unfolding of individuality' (p.22). In Descartes, there is no clear-cut distinction between a subject and an individual. Leibniz, by contrast, allows himself a strictly individualistic (monadic) ontology which forms part of a theodicy. Contemporary individualism is born in the aftermath of the exhaustive critique of theodicy (in particular, by

Nietzsche). It is born of the obligation to divorce an individualistic ontology from the belief in an underlying rational order governing the relations between individuals. In the opposite direction, Kantian philosophy emphasises the importance of the subject's thinking of itself as autonomous; for on this condition alone depends its ability to be able to institute values for itself as 'norms which humanity has set itself, as constitutive of the intersubjective realm' (p. 258). This is not the place to discuss an argument which is incisive yet open to a number of objections which I shall merely list here: 1) the sharp contrast between an individual and a subject is not a matter of fact but rather of philosophical interpretation and accordingly the legitimacy of the opposition between an individual and a subject is grounded entirely in this interpretation; 2) this interpretation serves here as an ad hoc hypothesis, used to derive the desired conclusion; 3) criticism of the link between ontological individualism and theodicy does not in itself destroy every possibility of regulation in a world of individuals (we might think in terms of the combined effect of the establishment of norms for co-operation, their internalization, specularity and self-sacrifice); 4) Kantian self-determination is not the only way of understanding autonomy; 5) the Kantian definition of the subject is not needed in order to provide rational grounds for the objectivity of values. In the works I am discussing here, the distinction between individual and subject is not present and I shall therefore refer only to 'the Modern subject'.

9 Luc Ferry and Alain Renaut, *La Pensée 68*, p. 163.
10 Charles Taylor, 'Atomism', *Malaise of Modernity. The Ethics of Authenticity*. (London: Harvard University Press, 1991).
11 Cf. Pascal Bruckner, *La Tentation de l'innocence* (Paris: Grasset, 1995), pp. 14–15. The Modern individual wants both to be autonomous and, at the same time, innocent.
12 Ibid., p. 271.
13 Gilles Lipovetsky, *Le Crépuscule du devoir*, pp. 20, 241–2, 245, 265.
14 However individualistic our societies may appear in their self-representation, a constant struggle remains between the image which they have of themselves and a social reality made up of ties of solidarity, dependency and subordination. Durkheim suggested that the principal intellectual challenge for Modernity lay in the attempt to understand just such a mix of autonomy and dependency. Cf. *The Division of Labour in Society*, tr. by W. D. Halls (Basingstoke: Macmillan, 1984). See also Louis Dumont, *Homo aequalis* (Paris: Gallimard, 1977) and *Essays on Individualism. Modern Ideology in Anthropological Perspective* (Chicago: University of Chicago Press, 1986).
15 By contrast, Plato and the first utilitarians attempted a complete reconstruction of morality and in so doing were guilty of psychological implausibility.
16 *Magazine littéraire*, no. 361: January 1998, p. 39.
17 Namely the drive to find a way of understanding the normative which also takes into account the particular characteristics of the subject and the ontological reality of the actions concerned, coupled with the effort to embrace every facet of moral life and to defend a conception of the rational as more than merely instrumental. Aristotle is adamantly opposed to Plato on both the question of the ends of morality (morality is neither an inquiry into essences nor a disinterested *theoria*) and that of its means.
18 There is, moreover, a very pronounced anti-theoretical trend within contemporary moral philosophy. Cf. Stanley G. Clarke & Evan Simpson, *Anti Theory and Moral Conservatism* (State University of New York Press, 1989).
19 See *L'Inquiétude morale et la vie humaine*, pp. 34–6.
20 This is probably the inspiration behind the relentless ongoing critique of Michel Foucault's late philosophy. It is assumed that the Greeks were unable to conceive of the notion of autonomy. Thus Michel Foucault's return to the Greek conception of the human is dismissed from the outset as an insidious form of anti-humanism because it was inspired by the Greeks. In other words, to invoke 'The Greeks' today is supposedly to pursue the fruitless avant-garde project of undermining the subject. For detailed coverage of this argument, which seems to depend upon turning a blind eye to the place of rational autonomy in Greek thought, see Luc

Ferry & Alain Renaut, *La Pensée 68*, pp. 162–3: 'From the beginning to the end of his career, Foucault sang from the same hymn-sheet [. . .] The anti-humanism of the thinking of 68 opens out onto a form of "barbarity".'

21 Cf. Monique Canto-Sperber, 'La moralité du bien chez Platon', *Les Éthiques grecques* (Paris: Presses Universitaires de France, 2001).

22 'In Plato and Aristotle, the idea of right was derived [. . .] from the observation of nature, understood as a cosmic order or hierarchy [. . .]', Alain Renaut, *Histoire de la philosophie politique* (Paris: Calmann-Lévy, 1999), I, p. 18. What could be the meaning of such a claim? Could it be empirical? That would be absurd. Conceptual? In which case, the term 'nature' would not have the same meaning as it does in Modernity and recourse to this term alone would be insufficient to serve as a refutation.

23 Such is the blueprint of Jürgen Habermas's project: a Modern, constructivist, progressive and universalist project which stands opposed to the retrograde and obscurantist, antimodern, tendencies in contemporary philosophy.

24 Vincent Descombes, 'La rationalité politique', *La Pensée politique* (1994), p.148.

25 'If the advance of individualism logically entails the critique of traditional values [. . .] this critique and, moreover, any new declaration of values can henceforth only claim to be legimate on the basis of argument. Legitimacy must cease to be "traditional" and become "legal".' Luc Ferry & Alain Renaut, *68–86, Itinéraires de l'individu*, pp. 42 & 71.

26 Luc Ferry, *Philosophie politique* (Paris: Presses Universitaires de France, 1984), III, 74; Alain Renaut, *L'Ère de l'individu. Contribution à une histoire de la subjectivité* (Paris: Gallimard, 1989); Alain Renaut & Lucas Sosoe, *Philosophie du droit* (Paris: PUF, 1991), p. 414.

3

SYLVIANE AGACINSKI

Sylviane Agacinski is a French philosopher, living in Paris and married to Lionel Jospin. She was a pupil of Gilles Deleuze in the 1960s in Lyon, and a member of Greph in the 1970s. Her work is associated with philosophers of deconstruction such as Jacques Derrida, Jean-Luc Nancy and Philippe Lacoue-Labarthe. She teaches at the École des Hautes Études en Sciences Sociales. She is author of works on a variety of subjects from Kierkegaard to architecture and the politics of sexual difference. Her approach is one of ethical reflection on the destiny of the 'other', of the stranger (foreigner), and of woman. She was one of the prime movers in the Parity movement which aimed for a more equitable role for women in political life in France via an equal number of female and male candidates in every election, on the grounds that sexual difference is a universal human trait that should be fully reflected in a representative politics. In this sense she opposes the Beauvoirian feminist position that female liberation depends on a denial of sexual identity.

Agacinski's works include the following:

Aparté: Conceptions et morts de Soren Kierkegaard, Paris: Aubier-Flammarion, 1977.

Volume: Philosophies et politiques de l'architecture, Paris: Galilée, 1992.

Critique de l'égocentrisme: L'événement de l'autre, Paris: Galilée, 1996.

Politique des sexes, Paris: Seuil, 1998.

Le Passeur de temps: modernité et nostalgie, Paris: Seuil, 2000.

THE QUESTION OF THE OTHER
(*Critique of Egocentrism*)

Can the metaphysical subject hear the question of the other? Or can it only hear its own question?

Philosophies of the subject – of which there are several – always ascribe to the subject the capacity to self-question, to ask something of itself, to undertake its own self-interrogation. Thus the subject lays hold of whatever had been troubling it, on the inside or the outside, and makes this the object of its question.

It would appear that there can be no separating the philosophical issue of the subject from that of the question and its origin. We might claim, for example, that the subject is, in the first instance, the one who asks, or asks itself, the question. Subjective consciousness presents itself as that which, essentially, is capable of asking itself its own questions and answering them.

But there is *another way of experiencing the question*. This experience is no longer one of a question which thought asks itself but, more radically, one of a question which arises from an arrival, a call or a gesture that I had not anticipated.

Yet philosophical questions, at least since Descartes, do not come to me from an other, do not come from elsewhere. Thus they can neither take me entirely by surprise, nor uproot me from myself, contrary to what might be said of the call of an other, such as God, or even of an event which comes about.

The necessity with which the philosophical question is endowed arises from my freedom. The question does, of course, appear to ask itself and to impose upon my thinking, yet it originates in the kind of questioning thought which aspires both to provide the answer *to* its own question and to answer *for* that question. Questioning thought is free with respect to the question which it poses itself. Such thought does not, therefore, involve my responsibility for an other, as it would if the question were to come to me from the other. It is in this sense that the subject of philosophy – as a subject which asks itself the question, even when this is the question of the other – is a subject with diminished responsibility, as it were. This is a subject which asks a lot of itself, forcing itself to answer its own question and, in so doing, to answer for itself. (Descartes' aspiration in his *Meditations*.) But the thinker of questioning thought can, nonetheless, remain deaf to the call which may come from the other, substituting its own 'question of the other', its inquiry into the condition of the other, for the question which comes from the other (or from others, as we should say here, for they are always several).

Thus self-questioning thought always runs the risk of reducing the *experience* of responsibility – an experience of having to respond to a question which has arisen – to a *question about responsibility*, one which becomes its own question and which is only obliged to itself. The subject which questions itself about its responsibility at first hears only the sound of its own voice and has no need to hear another's. Yet, in fact, the sound of this other voice has always already reached it.

Can philosophical thought get around the experience of the other? Is this not precisely what the philosophical subject is trying to do by claiming that it is itself the foundation not only of its relationship to being, but also to others, in an ethical, juridical and even a political sense?

The voice of the other cannot be heard from, for example, the position of Kantian ethics because, at the outset, every last trace of the empirical has been expelled from the moral domain. Yet that which comes from the other, for example the other's question, will always be empirical.

For Kant, the other is the other rational being: there is no need for me to listen to the other in order to discover how I should behave towards them, for my reason will tell me. The metaphysical question of duty, here, that which the subject asks itself concerning its obligations in general, can neither be based upon nor tailored to any particular encounter with, or empirical request from, the other. From the Kantian perspective, I should already have foreseen the ethical validity of such a request, *a priori*, by the light of my own inner faculty of reason.

The question of duty, put in this way, concerns only the subject's relation to itself and the form which its will takes. The requirement of practical reason that the subject's will be good – universalizable without this entailing a contradiction – is demonstrated by the infamous example of the categorical ban on lying and making false promises, on the grounds that these acts would, if universalized, involve contradictions. The lie could not be made into a univeral law of the will because the lier wants to be believed, that is, simultaneously wants trust to be the rule. One cannot want, at same time, to raise to the level of universal law the imperative to truth and that to falsehood.

Everything there is to say has probably been said about the consequences – whether cruel or absurd – of this absolute ban on lying. Yet no such argument can shake this Kantian rigour, for the consequences of an act, the work of my will, its effects on myself or on others, have been ruled out a priori and cannot feature in the process of determining my duty. Kant's position is invulnerable once it is accepted that ethics, insofar as they must be grounded in metaphysics, do not have to take the other's experience into consideration. It has rightly been emphasized, for example, that it is not the risk of inspiring others' mistrust that should be thought of as the foundation of the ban on lying and making false promises. If that were the case, we would be dealing with an extrinsic contradiction – one between consequences of the will – when, in fact, it is because lying is self-contradictory that it must be forbidden.

Kantian ethics, by entirely excluding empirical considerations from its basic principles, thereby excludes the relation to the other and the other's voice, relegating both to the sphere of Anthropology. That which is merely empirical belongs in the domain of Anthropology. In these terms, moreover, Kant is indeed keen to condemn the various forms of egoism (logical, aesthetic and moral) which imprison the subject in a presumptuous indifference to the judgment of others, as though it had no need of this 'touchstone'.[1] However, this condemnation of egoism from a pragmatic point of view does not weaken in the slightest what I would call the absolute egoism (or egotism) inherent in a metaphysical point of view which is reaffirmed here: 'in philosophy, we are not required to call upon the judgement of others to confirm our own'. This moral and metaphysical egoism is clearly not that of a subject concerned only with the search for its own happiness but rather that of a subject which sets itself up as the sole judge of what is right, when right has been entirely reduced to *good will*.

In this scenario, it is not to the other that I owe something – the truth, for example – but to myself, in accordance with an imperative which is, in the final analysis, more logical than ethical (my will must not contradict itself). And herein lies the folly of this ethics: it remains deaf to the other, or at least to any other that cannot be exclusively determined as a rational being or who, for example, might ask of me – implicity or explicitly – for something other than the truth, or an other who might *not always* want the truth from me. An other who could rely on me, place their trust in me, in a different way.

For instance, can you trust a doctor who, sure of himself, his knowledge and his duty, informs a patient that he has but a few weeks to live? (I have a real case in mind, where the patient was twenty years old.) Kantian ethics has no interest in the empirical qualities of the rational other to whom the subject is indebted, for these have been ruled out from the very start: the other has neither age nor sex, is neither young nor old, in good health or bad. And yet it is by way of these very qualities that the other's existence is *other* and in virtue of them that it is singular. Yet that is exactly what the metaphysical subject just does not want to know.

A remarkable thing about the classical mode of philosophical questioning – self-questioning – is that it remains closed to the question of the other, except where this other has already been conceived, in advance, as being the same: another ego, another subject, another man, even another *Dasein*.

The question takes place in the relation of consciousness to itself, as it performs an experiment on itself, moving 'ever more behind its self', to quote Heidegger's characterization of this experience of consciousness in Hegel.

Consciousness, as a questioning agency, strives to rid itself of all that is either 'behind' or 'in front' of it. In philosophies of the subject, if we understand by this ways of thinking in which consciousness is the foundation of all that is, the question can only come from consciousness itself. Consciousness is its very own need. Indeed, we can hardly even speak here of an experience of the question, if experience is understood, minimally, to imply an openness to alterity and to presuppose the acceptance of something *given*.

We might wonder, in particular, whether the question (which I ask myself) can be conceived of as that which takes the place of the gift, or of a certain experience of the gift. This strikes me in reading, for example, Descartes' 'Address to the Doctors of the Faculty of Theology',[2] in which the undertaking of the human mind 'reflecting on itself' is presented as a compensation for the lack of that faith which is 'a gift from God'. Those who have not received the gift of faith can be shown, by means of thought, that 'what may be known of God can be made manifest in reasons which we need only look inside ourselves to discover and that our mind alone is able to deliver unto us'. Descartes declares here that the subject of his *Meditations* will be the question of God and that of the soul: it is, then, no longer God who calls forth or asks the question. 'God' has become the object of the question, a question which the mind poses itself and to which it may give its own reply.

The extent of the difference is clear here between a question that comes from the other, which presupposes the experience of a gift, and a question that I ask myself concerning the other. By giving itself its own question, thought affirms its absolute autonomy and constitutes itself as subject.

This does not mean that the other need be God. Critiques of the subject can manage without harking back nostalgically to kinds of religious thinking in which alterity is not the alterity of other people but that of the Great Other which a searching finite existence approaches, in love or in obedience, as it strives to overcome its finitude.

As for the philosophical subject, it bows only before itself, its own faculty of reason, its own law.

Just as Descartes replaces God with 'the question of God', so Kant completes the conversion of the religious into the moral, bringing religion entirely *within the limits of reason alone* by developing the concept of purely rational faith. At the opposite extreme, the man of faith – Job or Abraham – bows piously before the sacrifice of the intellect and abandons any attempt to understand the commandment which comes to him from God. Neither divine law nor moral law involve me in an experience of others in the sense of other existences, different but finite, which are neither the big, absolute, Other nor an other rational being assumed to be similar to myself.

Something that has always interested me, however, in a religious thinker such as Kierkegaard . . . is the way that he takes into account the encounter with the other, who is not only God, an encounter to which the existing being is immediately subjected for the simple reason that he starts out as a child – that is to say, a son – and that it is thereby impossible for consciousness to have an absolutely independent beginning. Subjectivity is not, here, the kind of free autonomous consciousness that imagines it can ask itself its own questions but an existence which is originally aware of its own descent and derivation and thus of its finitude. The other is already there, in the shape of a father from whom the son differs and who from the very beginning impinges upon the identity of the son.

What counts is whether the question of the other is being asked on the basis of an inaugural experience of the other – in which case, subjectivity is immediately shared, immersed in its co-existence with the other, solicited by the other before being able to isolate itself in a relationship to itself – or whether it is legitimate to begin from this self-relating consciousness which brackets off the encounter with the other in order to seek to ground its relation to the other.

The metaphysical subject can only assert its autonomy by first detaching itself from existence and maintaining a distance from the experience of the other. And what could be more striking than this movement in which thought withdraws into itself and becomes disengaged from that with which it co-exists. This withdrawal is what constitutes the transcendental subject and it has a decisive influence on the way in which moral and juridical relationships are established.

For this subject, the other can only ever be another subject, just as abstract and just as autonomous as itself. The duty of respect owed to this other is based upon the power of free self-governance attributed to the faculty of practical reason imputed to each and every subject. My relationship to the other is determined *a priori* by my subjective freedom as a rational being. My relationship to the other is something I settle upon *with myself* and not with the other. This involves the idea of a community that is not already given but which must be built along rational lines.

Thus it is also of decisive importance for political philosophy to know whether it is starting out from questions which consciousness asks itself (and therefore with the autonomous subject) or whether, following Aristotle, 'the point of departure for, as well as the purpose of, argument in political science, including ethics, is experience of the things of this life'.[3] Vague though this dictum may seem, it suggests, as is always the case for Aristotle, that political philosophy can neither fall short of nor lie beyond the experience of community. Aristotelian empiricism begins with the common life, with the irreducible plurality of those voices which would make themselves heard; it begins, let us say, with the reality of a kind of co-existence which forbids the initial separation of thought from this being-together, in an attempt to better grasp or organize it. The ideas of community and, as I shall argue later, of justice, do not transcend the encounter with the other; rather, this is an encounter which they cannot afford to do without.

All talk of an empirical approach always implies, ultimately, the need to constantly take into consideration those experiences which deprive thought of its desire for self-sufficiency and thus of its *self-satisfaction*, in a moral sense. Thought is exposed to that which prevents it from coinciding with itself and which bears witness to its original belatedness, its forever being destined to come after whatever has been given it to think – those things which, along with existence as such, it can neither entirely avoid nor appropriate: the body, matter, other people, the community, language . . .

The metaphysical position, by contrast, shields subjective consciousness from the trial of these experiences and allows it the possibility of a pure self-relation.

Accordingly, the philosophy of communication remains metaphysical in character whenever it presupposes the independence of the subject's thinking, even if this is sub-sequently confronted by the other. This is the case, for example, in Habermas because, even though he asserts that communication is irreducible, he fails in so doing to break with the philosophy of the subject. The author of *The Theory of Communicative Action* writes, for example, that argument as a mode of discourse allows interlocutors to *go beyond* 'their initial subjective preconceptions' and to meet in the common ground of 'a community of rationally-motivated convictions'. This view of community, as *beginning* with communication, presupposes the prior existence of separate, or separable, subjects which each have their own *initial* preconceptions. These subjective preconceptions, which are assumed to be 'initial' and which must be overcome, are therefore imputed to isolated subjects which have not yet communicated, individuals in whom neither community nor language as yet have a share. The community established by the dis-course of argument seems to be a community of thinking subjects, in which each is initially self-coincident and only then encounters the other and becomes able to co-operate with that other. This community first provides itself with its subjects, each of which represents to itself the reasons for its action, and only then elaborates a community of subjects. Yet a set of behaviours, a fabric of practical relations (whether harmonious or conflictual), *already* constitutes the community and does so 'prior to' any declaration of convictions, whether shared or different. Is it the case that all forms of shared action necessarily presuppose the existence of representations, or thoughts, of common 'convictions', or reasons? There is surely room for discussion here. (A Wittgensteinian question.)

Furthermore, the community of consent could be simply another manifestation of insular subjectivity: by way of a community *of convictions* which are 'rationally motivated', the community could seek to overcome its divisions. But how far is the existence of a community of convictions a guarantee that the political community it establishes will be both more rational and less restrictive than other comparable communities, ones which also strive for unity through shared convictions and indeed achieve it by less rational means (even if argument always figures among these)? Can the assenting "Yes" of however many real interlocutors – 'illocutionary success' – really be taken as decisive proof that a particular line of argument is 'rational'? The fascist "Yes", uttered with one voice (the leader's), also constitutes, in its own way, the assent of the interlocutors; it too builds a consensus. It is no straightforward matter to calmly distinguish the 'force without violence of the discourse of argument' from 'manipulation', as long as agreement with a consensus of common convictions remains both the criterion of rationality and the ideal of society.

My purpose in drawing attention to this difficulty is clearly not to dispute the legitimacy of argumentative discourse – for it always has *some* legitimacy – but rather to point to its limitations and, above all, to ask whether the community of consent, as a collective manifestation of self-satisfied, insular, subjectivity is necessarily the kind of community that always leaves room for the other, that is, for others, for a plurality of voices and therefore also for conflict.

It is from quite the opposite position that Aristotle embarks on his attempt to think about justice: from an initial experience of plurality rather than an ideal of unity, from an initial experience of the conflicts and relationships between others who *are already compromised*. For Aristotle it is, at best, a matter of arbitrating these disputes and relations with prudence rather than trying either to create or ground them. The role of reflection is to think through the way in which the world has been shared and divided, but this has already occurred and it must serve as the point of departure. Social and political relations are not *established* by philosophy: they are already there, like bonds, exchanges, or the complex mix of rights and obligations. Because others are already there, others who already have a stake in the things of the world and in the world as such.

The metaphysical subject, by contrast, questions itself about the conditions of its freedom and about the compatibility of this freedom with that of other subjects no less abstract than itself. It strives to define *a priori* the conditions in which free subjects can coexist. Herein lies the root of the legalistic bent that has afflicted the metaphysics of morals, preventing it from engaging with real cases in their singularity, and also the cause of the resistance to any conception of jurisprudence in terms other than simply the application of the law. Singularity is foreign to law-giving reason, which has only to know the law in its universality and not the other. It has already decided *who* the other is: another rational subject, another autonomous subject, whose expectations it can determine in advance. Prior to the existence of any bond to the other, any questions from, communication with or experience of that other, the law has already told me what I owe the other and formed the foundation of my relationship with that other.

The particular way in which thought *asks itself* the question of the other, or by contrast allows itself to be questioned in the experience of the other, is a direct result of the metaphysical or empirical position adopted at the outset. A question of beginnings: *either* thought serves as its own beginning and refuses to be impinged upon by that other whose status and the conditions of whose appearing it fixes after its own image – in which case it is difficult to see how the subject could encounter in experience anything apart from its own creation, for there could be no way for the other to surprise the subject. *Or* thought is originally exposed to the other and the other comes to me, in an event that can never be entirely anticipated, never determined *a priori*. And it is by virtue of this very singularity that the other is *other* and not the same. The other is only possible as a singular event. In this sense, the possibility of an encounter with the other, if such a possibility exists, stands in contradiction to the self-satisfaction of the metaphysical subject and its own peculiar way of asking itself the question of the other.

If the other is the one that I cannot disclose to myself, the one that can only be given to me *a posteriori*, I cannot – by the same token – disclose to myself the question that is the *other's* question. I can only ever be attentive, or not, to the other's question; all I can do is respond, or not. But if this is a question that I cannot anticipate and if I am prepared to allow myself to be surprised by it, then there is no law that can direct my response *a priori*. Responsibility, in its fullest sense, resides in this obligation to invent an answer to a question that may be unprecedented, strange or obscure.

So it is possible to frame questions of duty and justice, in the sense of what the other is owed, less in terms of law than on the basis of experiences of need and complaint. The question would then become one of establishing where these complaints come from, who is complaining, and of what.

If room is to be allowed for questions from others, then there can be no fixing in advance who has the right to voice a complaint. It must be possible to depart from the law (which has already stipulated who is and is not owed what) in order to take a complaint into account. If the possibility of voicing, or hearing, a complaint is circumscribed by law, then this would also determine once and for all who is and who is not entitled to voice their grievances.

Yet the law has a history precisely to the extent that there has remained in the idea of justice the possibility of responding to the question of the other.

We must choose between the metaphysical conception of a law capable of being rationally and absolutely grounded and the thought of a law (even, at first, of a custom), of which our experience would entirely coincide with that of our being-together.

The metaphysical question of foundations, resting as it does on the autonomy of reason, on the liberty of the subject, works by suspending experience and placing in brackets those ties, relations and relationships which already determine in concrete terms the nature of being-together and in which existence is always already implicated.

Thus it is always the case that *whenever experience is placed in brackets*, as it typically is in the demand for foundations, *so too is the other*.

The foundations are laid in this mode of thinking for a relation to the other that is not the product of any relationship involving real others, but which is, rather, an *a priori* construct. Foundations are always required in this process of construction, a process of which rational thought is the one and only judge.

Kant's legal philosophy is a direct descendant of that Cartesian rationalism which likened the work of the legislator to that of the architect: law and architecture alike are always better for being the work of one man, provided he be prudent, that is, guided by reason. For Descartes, laws conceived by one man alone are always preferable to those which nations have built up gradually, in response to the demands of particular crimes and conflicts.

This ideal of a form of rational construction which establishes its own working principles always allows the thinker to dispense with division (one rather than several) and the passage of time (all at once rather than little by little). By contrast, legislators and judges are engaged in the empirical business of defining and correcting relations between people, of arbitrating disputes as and when they arise. They proceed on the basis of particular cases as much as principles – the latter being no more than provisional hypotheses.

The call for a return to first principles, to the unconditional, to the universality of the law, is heard only where there is neither history nor future; principles must explain, or apply to, that which happens repeatedly. The event, by contrast, if there is such a thing, must, at least to some extent, evade the law.

A birth is an event not just because *one* child is born, for this happens repeatedly, but because this child is unique and will look upon the world with new eyes.

To say that I cannot disclose the other to myself is the same as to say that the other cannot be conceived of on the basis of a law. Only by evading the law can the other arrive. There is no such thing as the other *in general*. The experience of the other is, on every occasion, a singular event.

Moreover, we should not be led astray by the fact that others (my father, mother and so many more) are already there: this *already* is not a licence for me to appropriate them by incorporating them into a past that would be entirely my own. I shall never be able to move back in time in order to precede them, to anticipate and reappropriate them for myself. I can no more appropriate the *already* of the other or their past than I can the *not yet* of what is still to come. Paradoxically, what is already there, such as the past, can only ever happen to me, never stops happening to me.

Everything that can still reach us, in one way or another – even from out of the past – all that can still happen to us manifests itself as an event. The 'already there' of the other, like the other's past, is no less new to me than what is to come, in the future: this 'already there' also comes to me.

So in the attempt to think the other such that they truly remain other, one possible motto, or motif, could be the 'to come', the not yet.

The other will necessarily have been awaited and will necessarily be unexpected.

(Anyone who was once a child will probably never stop *waiting* for his father and mother, just as they once awaited him.)

Love, especially, is an encounter with the other.

What we call love consists in an experience of the other that whoever undergoes it cannot grasp entirely in their own terms, as subject. For love will not come to a free, autonomous, self-sufficient subject. It is not a bond between two subjects but rather the experience of an essential dependency.

As a free consciousness – one originally and essentially free – the subject cannot conceive of involvement except in terms of its own action, its decision, or the act by which it forges a bond, or enters into a contract or an association, etc. Subjective consciousness both wishes and assumes itself able to rest permanently on its own foundations and to return to its self. Such a subject is capable of desiring the other – and even the desire of the other – but it cannot *fall* in love without foregoing the security of its autonomy. English and French both put it the same way: they refer to a fall, they speak of an experience of weakness. The existence of one who loves is revealed or rediscovered to be, in spite of itself, resting in the hands of the other, involved with the other, offered as a pledge, and as though entrusted to the other for safe-keeping. Were it not for this strange experience of expropriation, nobody would ever have wanted to die for unrequited love.

This experience would neither be one of dependency nor of self-giving if the self in question remained free to decide whether to give itself or not. She or he who loves, at the same time as becoming aware of their inadequacy also acquires a sense of elective responsibility for the other, of care: it is as though this responsibility were older still than the question of the other.

By contrast, the Kantian conception of a loving relationship – in marriage – reduces this to desire and the subject's opportunity to enjoy the other as they would an object. Such enjoyment consists in 'the natural use made by one sex of the sexual organs of the other'. Yet this enjoyment, which transforms both parties into objects, is incompatible with the freedom of each of these subjects. They are accordingly obliged . . . to get married in order to 're-establish their personalities'. At the same time as one partner is being acquired by the other, '*like an object* [emphasis added], they in turn acquire the other, reciprocally; in effect, this is how the first partner re-establishes both their self-control and their personality'.

It is less than clear how reciprocal ownership, as guaranteed by contract, is supposed to allow each party to re-establish their personality when such ownership looks a lot like mutual, albeit legally enshrined, disrespect. That aside, this mercantile description of marriage – as an *exchange of goods* – stems directly from the individualist and subjectivist foundations of the 'sexual community' (*commercium sexuale*). In this transaction, the other first appears to the subject as no more than an object to be used, entirely given over to their partner's enjoyment, who is 'compensated', so to speak, for this act of self-devotion, by the reciprocal nature of the arrangement. The freedom of the subject, as subject, lies in the enjoyment of the other. Both parties must, on this basis, demand and consent to reciprocity. We can recognize in this the legal principle which states that there is no such thing as rape within marriage. In what for him is a familiar move, Kant lends metaphysical legitimacy to tradition. In fact, he would have us assent to two rather questionable presuppositions: that all trace of dissymmetry may be removed from sexual difference and that the other, in 'sexual commerce', may be reduced to the status of an object (to their sexual organs).

To imagine that husband and wife 'regain control over their personalities' on the grounds that their rights of ownership over one another are 'reciprocal' is either naive or cynical. For the property right to the 'sexual organs' of the other could not be exercised equally and symmetrically by women and men. The equality which the reciprocal nature of this right would bring about is entirely bogus. In concrete terms, a man has the physical and the sexual means to abuse the woman he has 'acquired' by contract, which is not the case in reverse. Thus the purported reciprocity of the acquisition of the other in marriage *in actual fact* licenses the legal purchase of the woman, 'as an object', by her husband. The positions of subject and object, which seemed to be interchangeable, are in reality those of the male subject and the female object. There is no need to emphasize, then, that this example of juridical egocentrism is also one of androcentrism.

The second of the two presuppositions which Kant relies upon – and the more clearly visible in his account – is the identification of the other, in 'sexual commerce', with their sex organs, thereby effectively transforming them into an object. This objectification of the other is one of the pernicious effects of egocentrism. The subject which starts out from its own desire, from its own freedom, in trying to conceive of a relation to the other, necessarily makes this other into the passive object of its own enjoyment. We have just witnessed the consequences of such an approach for the attempt to think about marriage and we underlined the fact that the pretence of reciprocity in this scenario by no means diminished its intrinsic violence.

We now know, of course, that the question of love is certainly not identical to that of marriage. Let us frame these questions differently. It would be interesting if, instead of trying to position the subject in terms of the principle of sexual commerce, we were to ask what becomes of the 'subject' in the encounter that is love. Could the autonomy of the subject ever provide the basis for an understanding of this encounter, of what what Georges Bataille called 'the community of lovers'?

The very special inclination that is usually called love, the combination of giving and abandon which it involves, is a decentring experience for the so-called subject. But above all, aside from either contractual reciprocity or sexual pleasure, there is, in the event that is love, an absolute trust – absolute and also, therefore, secret and obscure. Each lover trusts the other and entrusts themselves to the other, frantically and passionately. An event of this kind, if and when it happens, owes nothing to either freedom or autonomy. It lies outside ethics and law and outside ties of violence or respect. No contract can manufacture trust; no contract can insure against risk. By undermining the ego's self-sufficiency – a process which no doubt began in the relation to the mother – and by preventing the 'subject' from simply resting on its own foundations, this kind of event also exposes it to the constant possibility of unhappiness, betrayal, mourning, loneliness and even death. In Othello, Faust and Don Juan, what terrifies us is not the invocation of God or the Devil but rather the fact that love brings death. The metaphysics of the subject can only put all this down to passion and madness. But the poets, who have thought more deeply about this than the philosophers, know that it arises from an experience and a weakness that are both essential.

In short, alongside limit experiences (those in which joy always rubs shoulders with the very worst there is), the decentring of the subject can also be experienced in every kind of friendship and, indeed, of social existence. We are 'attached' to one another, even in hatred.

'To be *attached* to the other' is the lot of finite mortal beings who cannot, as gods can, rest securely on their own foundations.

It might seem paradoxical that beings prone to weakness should be able to become *attached* to one another. However, it is precisely because none are sufficient unto themselves, precisely in virtue of their shared finitude, that they are brought to support one another. And it is this which bestows on each existence its semblance of necessity. In the depths of distress and destitution, the young Gwynplaine, hero of Hugo's *The Laughing Man*,[4] takes it upon himself to care for an orphaned child and thereby discovers, in this unexpected responsibility, the strength to go on.

Existence, its lack of self-sufficiency, is shared and exposed from the outset to the other by the similar *insufficiency of bodies*.

They are less readily separated, less individualized than might appear to be the case – except in death, which separates them once and for all. The boundaries of my physical existence have already been crossed by the other.

Not to begin as a lone self, in the first instance, is to be born – to be what grows out of other bodies. The processes of reproduction and rearing, so to speak, pose along the way the question of the boundaries of organic existence – the limits it sets on ownership, its confines and its inner and outer dimensions. And organic existence is that aspect of existence which consciousness finds most repugnant of all and which it resists ('repugnance' originally meant 'resistance').

In all species of mammal, the newborn clings onto or plugs into the mother's body while it suckles, in such a way that each is, for a moment, the organ of the other (each fulfils a need of the other). This disturbing connection – disturbing because, like sexual relationships, it disturbs the boundary between what is mine and what is foreign to me – cannot be described as a relationship between subject and object, any more than it admits of a distinction between active and the passive participants.

If the other body is, at the same time, the body of the other, another body and an organ of mine, then these bodies are all encroaching upon one another, spilling over one into the other. Subjective consciousness finds this idea repugnant, but is beginning to become accustomed to it in the medical context of transplant surgery.

Not only is the subject suspicious of the other's body, from which it wants to be unequivocally distinguished, but it is also determined not to allow itself to be submerged by its 'own' body. For it knows that the body can exceed its limits. So the subject must seize the initiative and get ahead of the body by representing to itself, where possible, this body's functions, anticipating and learning how to trigger or suppress them. This is the struggle of consciousness, and still more so that of the philosopher as he strives, in his own life, to push his campaign for reappropriation to the utmost extremes. There is something moving, comic and full of pathos about the effort Kant expends in trying to ensure that he will be neither disturbed nor surprised by his body (but we all, more or less, resemble Kant in this): a regime of constant self-surveillance, strict rules of daily life which aim to prevent sweating, sneezing and coughing – 'Breathe through the nose!' – to ensure good digestion and vestimentary comfort (hence the invention of a specially-designed suspender belt), etc. These are just a few examples of techniques of control aimed at making this philosophical machine function without upset. An unmarried machine, of course, or almost, for the faithful servant Lampe is the attentive and indispensable supplement to this passionately autonomous existence.

It is worth considering seriously why Kant could not bear sneezing and coughing (nor indeed, in all probability, spasms of any other kind). It seems clear enough, indeed, that the autonomy of a subject who coughs is compromised – if not seriously then at least perceptibly. One really ought to be sufficiently free to prevent oneself from coughing . . .

This would be the moment to embark on a discussion of the status of organs and techniques and how they relate to consciousness, an area that I shall merely touch on here.

Philosophies of the subject conceive of techniques in terms of the conscious implementation of certain means with a view to a particular end, an end which the subject has in mind. The representation of the end and the mastery of the means are thought to be the criteria of a free action, that is, a human action.

The metaphysical humanist understanding of techniques presupposes the control of a conscious subject over those processes which it sets going in order to reach the goal it has in mind. Thus the use of various techniques forms the dividing line between the animal and the human. And since I have already mentioned mothers and children, I shall refer here to Spengler's view of parenting in his essay entitled *Man and Technics*.[5] According to Spengler, it would be wrong to say that the female animal 'is concerned for' her offspring. The feeling of concern presupposes the projection of a mental image into the future, a preoccupation with how things *will* be. 'Animals know neither bitterness nor disappointment. And their behaviour as parents [. . .] is an obscure, unconscious, response to the same kind of prompting that undergirds many other forms of life.' The particular kinds of techniques proper to individual species are thus not considered here to be techniques at all.

The distinction between the human and the animal is based on an opposition between the ability to *project a mental image*, on one hand, and *obscure, unconscious, response* on the other – that is, between the freedom of the subject and the constraints of the species.

These oft-repeated clichés can leave you perplexed. Until, that is, you suddenly ask what exactly it is that a mother thinks about. What is the 'mental image' that this real mother, this human mother, projects when she takes care of her children? Does she really look ahead to how things will be? It is not clear that she does. She keeps watch, she stands guard, remaining alert for signs of the vague but infinite danger of a constant threat. Her concern precedes and encompasses all possible risks. Which is why her concern will always seem excessive and exaggerated – to be frank, irrational. And this to the point that it is not at all sure whether she is quite as free as Spengler would like to believe of that 'species pressure' to which animals are supposedly, for their part, entirely enslaved. The poets have sometimes used less humanist language: Hugo, for example, in his *Ninety-three*, opined that 'There's no way out of motherhood; it brooks no discussion. What makes a mother sublime is that she's a kind of animal.' There are few experiences to rival motherhood for revealing this primary, pre-rational, responsibility which pulls consciousness out of its egotism and forces it to experience its being-alongside the other, its being inhabited by the other.

I do not seek, however, simply to return mothers to their instincts, or even to their bestiality, but rather to question the degree of autonomy which consciousness experiences with respect to techniques in general. I do seek recognition for the role of the other in acts governed by techniques, a role which arises as much from particular circumstances as from socio-cultural conditioning. And thus to deconstruct the metaphysical opposition between natural necessity – entirely devoid of consciousness and species-determined – and the supposed freedom of subjective consciousness with respect to the technique which it implements and, in particular, the bodily habits which accompany it.

This is what Marcel Mauss did in his innovative approach to the question of bodily techniques. Such techniques – in sport, dance and even the erotic sphere – are traditional and acquired. Consciousness does intervene, to a certain extent, in the repetition of particular composites of actions which these techniques encourage, but less as a free, decision-making, power and more as one element in the chain. Bodily techniques are described here as 'syntaxes of traditionally efficacious actions', or put differently, 'physio-psychosocial composites' in which mental components function merely as 'cogs in the machine'. This characterization of the place of psychological factors in the overall composite, which is itself technical – the 'cog in the machine' – demonstrates that conscious thought neither grounds nor transcends the technical process. Rather, it is in some sense only one component in that process. It is not in control of every action at every moment, as though it were their external cause. And this is why, for example, once Mauss the swimmer had learned the swimming technique that was taught in his day, he could no longer do things differently: he continued to swallow water and spit it out again while he swam, as he had become accustomed to doing early on. 'It's silly', Mauss observed, 'but I just keep doing it. I can't rid myself of my technique.'

Once the technique has been learned, that is, once the habit of a particular combination of actions has been acquired, the source or cause of the mechanism ceases to lie in reflexive thought. And there is more: not only does reflexive thought not control the technical mechanism but, on the contrary, it is possibly this which creates the opportunity for thought as such. The sang-froid, or *presence of mind*, that is typically put down to the controlling influence of subjective consciousness, may depend upon those bodily habits or techniques that are procedures for delaying and inhibiting unruly movements. The set of techniques that together constitute a (physical) discipline are just so many habitual means of resisting 'emotional disturbance' – they liberate consciousness, to some degree, more than they rely upon it. Thus bodily techniques stand at a crossroads between the physical, the mental and the social. They allow subjective consciousness a measure of freedom that is not to be confused with sovereign authority. In so far as my technique is a traditional pattern of behaviour, it always belongs, in the first instance, to others. Marcel Mauss makes us become aware of the belatedness of reflective thinking, of the extent to which subjective consciousness lags behind its own bodily techniques. Before the subject thought to ask itself the question of the other, the others were already there, inhabiting its body and actions alike.

Let us return now, however, to our opening question about the self-questioning subject and also to the question which Jean-Luc Nancy once asked me: 'Who comes after the subject?'[6]

In framing this question, it is impossible not to turn to Heidegger, who, of the thinkers who have called into question philosophies of the subject, is one who has thought long and hard about a different experience of the question or, if you will, the experience of summons and response, naming *Dasein* that which will come after, and must be thought in the aftermath of, the subject.

Dasein is indeed the name for a new power of questioning, one which is neither a subject nor this 'fiction' of a consciousness without a world or other people. *Dasein* is not the consciousness that represents to itself the world and others but it does relate to the world and to others, in the modes of concern (*Besorge*), assistance and solicitude (*Fürsorge*). It is with-others and in view of others, even if this coexistence can in concrete instances become mere indifference. The way in which we care for one another is a property of our existential and ontological condition. This takes us very far indeed from the thought of an ego detached from existence, from the world and from the experience of the other. 'The world in which I am is always one I share with others, for being-in-the-world is a being-in-the-world-with . . . The world of being-there is a shared world (*Mitwelt*). Being-there . . . is a *being-with* others. The intramundane being-in-itself of others is coexistence.'[7]

Yet at the same time, it is not from being-with-others that the question comes, but from being, and it is towards being that the question is orientated. And there is no authentic, original, relation to the other. The possibility of a *we*, of a community, is dependent upon an experience of the fundamental question, the question of being – it is dependent upon *Dasein*'s acceding to its responsibility.[8]

In the first instance, *Dasein* in its initial and everyday mode of existence is not yet anyone: 'not this one, not that one, but the the neuter 'they', the 'they' which presents every judgement and decision as their own, thereby depriving the particular *Dasein* of its responsibility. In *Dasein*'s everydayness, the agency through which most things come about is one of which we must say that "it was no one" '.[9]

Dasein only accedes to itself on the basis of a new experience which is an experience of the question. For Heidegger, the attempt to conceptualize this new experience gives rise to a new kind of freedom: the question is the decision that most befits the mind, it is its freedom.[10]

This being the case, the question is always in some way or other directed towards that which it is asking after. While expanding on the idea that the question of the meaning of being must be *asked*, Heidegger turns to the general structure of every question and asserts that is is in the nature of the 'formal structure' of the question to be a search for that which it asks after and toward which the question is directed.[11] 'To ask is always, in one way or another, to address a question *to* something.' It does not follow from the structure of the question that it will be addressed *to someone*, about something, but simply to what is being asked after. Yet questioning thought asks after the meaning of being; to answer this question – indeed, to ask it in the first place – is the responsibility of thought. This does not, necessarily, involve any responsibility towards another person: it is not addressed to the other, nor is it mediated by the question which comes from the other.

We might hazard the suggestion that the community, this being-with, the original sharing of existence, the 'we' is not the condition of the possibility of the question of being, but rather, conversely perhaps, the possibility of a 'we' depends upon the sharing of a single experience, the experience of that fundamental question which is the question of the meaning of being.

But perhaps these two things have never really allowed themselves to be wholly separated?

Perhaps the crux of the question of being and the question of the other is already to be found in Plato. Not just because the question of being can only be asked in a dialectic. The art of thinking cannot, of course, do without the other's voice: it needs the other to agree with its thoughts, as a way of guaranteeing its own self-agreement (in contrast to Kantian philosophy, which has no need, in principle, of the confirmation of the other's judgement). However, over and above the dialectical search for agreement about whatever it is that they are discussing, the interlocutors – before any questions can be either asked or answered – must first 'agree' on this one point: that they will speak to one another, *with* the other and not against the other (as in a debating match). As Socrates says to Meno: the prior condition of the dialectical method is friendship.[12]

What friendship denotes here, at the very least, is the obligation to attend to the voice of the other and listen to what is being said – before any question of whether we agree with the other on this or that particular issue. This method, which starts out with what the other says and thinks, would not be possible without such initial, 'friendly', attentiveness (which need not imply any particular affection). So if dialectic is the condition of thought, and friendship is the condition of dialectic, the possibility of asking the question of being is already bound up with the question of the other.

If the philosophical question is a shared one, *philosophy* must already be home to a certain *philia*.

This *philia* inhabits the philosopher from the moment when, in speech or in writing, he addresses his question to someone (or indeed receives it from someone).

For even when philosophers are not engaged in spoken discussion with one another, like Socrates and Meno, they are writing – that is, writing to one another – even if to express their disagreement. Each exposes themself to the other, who is always to come, and to the thought which is to come, just as each responds to thinking that has already come – even when in the most idiosyncratic of ways, even when articulating the most particular of experiences, experiences such as that of 'Descartes the doubter'.

Nothing could be more 'egotistical', as Valéry would later remark,[13] than these Cartesian *Meditations*: the story of a singular experience of error and doubt by 'someone' who rashly decides to 'suddenly abandon all the privileges of authority'. As ever, to abolish authority is to set oneself up as the sole authority.

But at the same time, this authorial authority, the writer's, is *not yet* that of the subject. It is the authority of someone who doubts, of a bare ego, of a voice with a unique ring articulating an experience of pre-subjective singularity.

Subjectivity was only decreed to be 'the centre of thought', thereby inaugurating the era of modern subjectivism, in the aftermath of this singular experience: imperial dominion was made to emerge from a revolutionary event . . . Heidegger would later write that, 'Descartes the doubter compelled men to doubt, he led them to think about themselves, their "I".' And to think of the other as a subject.

This 'story', which Descartes told in his *Meditations*, only went down in the history of thought as the foundation of a philosophical era because its author wrote 'to us', sent it to us, dispatched it to us – and because, by answering him, we have identified ourselves as those to whom the story was addressed.

The correspondence continues. And it is in this exchange of letters that the philosophical question is always inscribed. It is a question we ask *between ourselves*, before and after the coming of the subject.

The question of the other is at once that which I allow others to utter and that which, as soon as it discloses itself, chooses its (cor)respondents, those who will take a share in it. But delivery cannot be guaranteed.

Translated by Oliver Davis

Notes

1 *Anthropology*, 'On Egoism', Book 1, § 2.
2 Descartes, 'A Messieurs les Doyen et Docteurs de la Sacrée Faculté de Théologie de Paris', *Œuvres et lettres*, ed. André Bridoux (Paris: Gallimard 'Pléiade', 1978), pp. 257–8.
3 *Nicomachean Ethics*, I, 2.
4 Victor Hugo, *The Laughing Man*, translated by Paul Hardy (London: Collins, 1920).
5 Oswald Spengler, *Man and Technics. A Contribution to a Philosophy of Life*, translated by Charles Francis Atkinson (London: Allen & Unwin, 1932).
6 Jean-Luc Nancy, *Who Comes After the Subject*? (New York & London: Routledge, 1991). The answer I gave him then formed the basis for the present discussion.
7 *Being and Time*, tr. Macquarrie & Robinson (Oxford: Blackwell, 1962), § 26.
8 [The standard French translation from which Agacinski quotes (by De Waelhens) rightly gives the noun 'la responsabilité' for Heidegger's adjective *verantwortlich*; I have followed this here, with the English 'responsibility'. Note however that the established English translation (by Macquarrie and Robinson) gives the somewhat abstruse 'answerability' for *verantwortlich*. – Translator's note]
9 *Being and Time*, § 27.
10 Jacques Derrida writes: 'Nothing precedes the question in its freedom. What comes *before* and *in front*, that which anticipates and questions ahead of everything (*vor*), is the mind, is the freedom of the mind.' *De l'esprit* (Paris: Galilée, 1987), pp. 69–70.
11 See § 2 of *Being and Time*, 'The formal structure of the question of Being'.
12 *Phaedo*, 75 d.
13 Cf. Valéry's 'Une vue de Descartes', 'Fragment d'un Descartes', 'Descartes' and 'Seconde vue de Descartes', *Oeuvres* (Paris: Gallimard Pléiade, 1968), vol. 1, p.787 ff.

4

CATHERINE CHALIER

Catherine Chalier teaches Philosophy at the University of Paris X (Nanterre). She studied for many years under Levinas. She specialises in moral philosophy and the philosophy of Judaism. Many of her works explore the relationship between philosophy and its Hebrew sources, as she aims both to convey the richness of the Hebrew tradition in terms that are accessible to philosophers and to show how that tradition can help to renew the concepts of philosophy. She has also translated several works from Hebrew into French.

Her major works include the following:

Figures du féminin: lecture d'Emmanuel Levinas, Paris: La Nuit surveillée, 1982.

Judaïsme et Altérité, Paris: Verdier, 1982.

Les Matriarches, Paris: Cerf, 1985.

La Persévérance du mal, Paris: Cerf, 1987.

L'Alliance avec la nature, Paris: Cerf, 1989.

L'Histoire promise, Paris: Cerf, 1992.

Levinas, l'utopie de l'humain, Paris: Albin Michel, 1993.

Pensées de l'éternité: Spinoza, Rosenzweg, Paris: Cerf, 1993.

Sagesse des sens: Le regard et l'écoute dans la tradition hébraïque, Paris: Albin Michel, 1995.

L'Inspiration du philosophe, l'amour de la sagesse et sa source prophétique, Paris: Albin Michel, 1996.

De l'intranquillité de l'âme, Paris: Payot et Rivages, 1998.

Pour une morale au-delà du savoir: Kant et Levinas, Paris: Albin Michel, 1998.

Judaïsme et Christianisme, l'écoute en partage (with M. Faessler), Paris: Cerf, 2001.

La Trace de l'Infini, Emmanuel Levinas et la source hébraïque, Paris: Cerf, 2001.

PEACE AS GIFT AND OBLIGATION

The end of the twentieth century was a happy hunting ground for intolerant and sinister ideologies, what with the insidious and brutal agony that continued to reign over the millions of people exposed to military madness, the outrage of famine and the unpredictable threat of ordinary violence. By reciting sovereign and incontestable words that herald persecution and death for others, people suspend their fear of living through an exaltation of the great right to be, to dominate and to enslave. These words are sometimes spoken in the name of a God who is supposed to justify both the mortal excesses of hearts and minds, and the horrors of war between different peoples. These words of ideology are also constantly rooted in the fear of living and dying. It is the Book of Genesis that gives the first account of a man being murdered by his brother,[1] and here our right to kill one another is celebrated, even though 'such blood spills pollution which endures and fouls beyond cleansing'.[2] Hatred has been making its way to the fore ever since, and we now find ourselves in a situation where the world is being destroyed so as to avoid its having to be shared. Hatred feeds on the incomprehensible certainty of the lonely demise of us all, and on the anxiety of coming face to face with the Other, here and now, without any sort of reason or justification. The refusal to share life – which is signified by hatred – dramatically defies this certainty and anxiety. It creates the illusion of the great right to *be*, whether or not this involves humiliating, terrorising or destroying other people. The refusal to share life transforms the idea of an individual's own mortality by making it more desirable than life itself, however tragically.

There are certainly multiple economic, social, religious and political causes behind current and former wars. However, most of the time it is claimed that war is justified by noble and unshakeable principles which are greater than the life of an individual person, and which demand sacrifice. Sometimes a war is fought in the name of future peace, as if the right to peace derived from an infinite capacity to put up with violence and death. Philosophy – especially in its dialectical form – defends this idea and consequently holds that, despite wars and because of them, the historical progress of reason promotes peace. That is to say that, regardless of their own moral codes, States and individuals will move in stages towards the ideal prescribed by the idea of rights. Thanks to the communal, rich life that will follow the resolution of oppositions, the internal logic of the armed conflicts that have so persistently plagued history should ultimately allow everyone to find his or her place in the world. Thanks, that is, to the integration of differences – in terms of both subjective thoughts and lives – within a higher unity or political totality. The peace of an individual State would depend on its ability to assimilate each of its citizens within this unity without constraining or subjugating them. Foreigners, widows and orphans should also be able to find a place for themselves in such a State. Over the course of history, dialectical philosophy says that this political peace will come to tame the terrible cycle of violence, and bring humanity together in the acceptance of common values. In this context, political peace would therefore take on a universal aspect.

European culture has been much marked by this 'messianic' perspective, and in particular by the great secular frescos of human destiny that belong to philosophies of history. These philosophies comfort men about their lost lives: they teach that human suffering and sacrifice will one day make sense in that, despite all appearances, wars depend on a higher rationality which will, in the end, reconcile us with reality. These philosophies encourage us to think about peace in legal and political terms, and instrumentalise feelings and passions which, according to Hegel, serve this rationale without our realising it. However, despite the weight of philosophical thought that supports this process, confidence in it seems to have been betrayed by a century of anguish and crime. The weak are left to die slowly of destitution and hunger, and we resignedly accept the violent death of the victims and participants in endless ongoing conflicts. All this flies in the face of the idea of humanity's advance towards universal reconciliation. Even today the immorality of a philosophy or politics that accepts the death of innocent people as an indispensable step towards fulfilling an idea is to be found in multiple religious and ideological expressions, whether or not that idea is connected with the divine absolute. However, should such philosophy and politics expect that we simply come to terms with the nameless, faceless and irreplaceable people who are killed by war, famine and attacks, as if we were dealing with necessity or fate? Should cruelty be formalised as the price to pay for the uncertain and obscure tomorrows that philosophy predicts for humanity?

In this discussion I certainly do not want to imply any sort of approval of the established order and its profound injustices; but nor do I intend to fight the cause of some second-rate form of pacifism. For the planet has been damaged by the evil that men do to each other and horrifically torn by the hate that people hold for their enemies: in this kind of world we will not banish the shadows if we allow ourselves to advocate reconciliation and peace at any price. This attitude will not quell a people's anger or obsession with an outrage they have suffered; it will not stop their inconsolable grief or day-to-day fear. Moreover, pacifism almost always ends up supporting violent acts of injustice suffered by the weak. Rather than safeguarding weaker people and taking on their adversaries, pacifism abandons the weak without defending them. History has shown any number of times that concessions to violence in no way satisfy its claims; on the contrary, such concessions encourage violence, and pacifism does not save peace. For example, when in 1938 Czechoslovakia was obliged to cede the Sudeten mountains to Hitler, what was satisfied was the defeat of courage and not the expansionist desires of the aggressor. Above all, pacifism seems devoted to sparing the worry and anxiety of those who support it. In a troubled world, pacifism seeks a harbour where people can enjoy their limited days on earth without conquering anyone else, but also without fighting against things that threaten them. In their calls for peace and their efforts to calm anger, pacifists believe – and would lead us to believe – that love is simple and immediate. Does this mean that pacifists are generous and unselfish? Or are they committed to ensuring inner peace and serenity at precisely the time when pacifists' concern for others is sharpening their perception of the world and troubling them despite themselves? For, at a time when others suffer increasingly from drought, can our human conscience content itself with wishing to continue undisturbed enjoyment of the shade of our own garden, even if this ideal of happiness is very modest?

In 'The Doctrine of Right' (1797) Kant contends that moral reason instils in each of us 'its irresistible veto: *there is to be no war*, neither war between you and me in the state of nature nor war between us as States . . . ; for war is not the way in which everyone should seek his rights'.[3] Kant goes on to say that the maxim about working tirelessly to put an end to the disastrous state of war applies to any moral conscience, however pious or fanciful this may seem. On pain of discarding reason and plunging into animalism, for Kant it is an indisputable moral duty to seek to institute peace and to use the law to guarantee 'the state of "mine" and "yours"' among a mass of neighbouring men. However, Kant says that peace – which he describes as 'the sovereign political good' – can only be maintained between men and States by a 'legal bond'. It is from this perspective that, in *Perpetual Peace* (1796), Kant attempts to think through the conditions that allow institutions, treaties and alliances to put a provisional then definitive end to barbarous freedom. For Kant the state of peace does not in fact pre-exist, but must be instituted. He says that in the state of nature – a non-legal realm where the rule of the strongest (that is, the rule of war) prevails – 'the man or nation that live[s] in a state of nature . . . attacks me without being an aggressor, by the mere circumstance of living contiguous to me'.[4] This proximity therefore immediately arouses anger and the desire for vengeance, as well as fear and the frantic quest for protection. How, then, are we to sustain an inevitable state of proximity with other individuals or States without immediately feeling threatened, harmed or victimised? Kant argues that because the intrinsic principles of morality remain dormant in most individuals, the response to this question must be left to the legal brilliance of treaties and constitutions alone. He also believes that the principle of rights to which States pay homage (if only by lip-service, by claiming their right to go to war with one another) proves the presence of an originary moral disposition. Despite the almost constant lethargy of this disposition and its terrible subordination to melancholy and aggression, it slowly manages to open up new pathways and overcome the propensity for evil that characterises natural selfishness. How else, says Kant, are we to understand the way States use the word 'rights', however hypocritically, to begin or end armed conflict? However, somewhat paradoxically the philosopher also holds that the outward behaviour of States henceforth comes quite close to what is demanded by the idea of rights, 'though the intrinsic principles of morality do certainly not contribute towards it'.[5] This in any case seems normal to Kant, and he writes that 'it is not for morality to lead to a good constitution, but for this latter to produce the moral reform in man'.[6]

Two centuries on, it is obvious to everyone that man's murderous rage persists, and that the scale and crimes of World Wars I and II exceed anything that Kant could have envisaged. In 'The Idea of a Universal History from a Cosmopolitical Point of View' (1784), Kant expresses the hope that – thanks indeed to conflict and to what he calls 'an intention of nature' that is inseparable from the personal intentions of those who shape history – the human race is progressing towards peace and that it will one day achieve harmony between morality and politics. World Wars I and II shattered this hope: as Jürgen Habermas has said, 'the idea of a world war simply never occurred to Kant'.[7] Today, however, this terrible fact cannot be forgotten, and it obliges us to think out a peace that is able to confront the excess and terror of war on a global scale. Although many of the crimes against humanity committed in World War II were carried out with the support of various State institutions, Habermas joins with Kant in supporting the idea that the key to the problem lies in law. Thus, 'If the alliance of peoples has to be a legal rather than moral organisation, then that alliance absolutely needs the qualities provided by a good constitution.' In this way, Habermas opposes the idea of a peace that is dependent on moral norms by one based on a legal alliance, and which is free from any evaluation that talks in terms of 'good' and 'bad'. For Habermas, this latter form of peace is the only one that could guide modernity in its quest for consensus on the rights of man. He says that we should free 'the subjects of rights from moral imperatives' and 'accord to active participants the legal margins of action based on the preferences of each individual.'[8] Habermas argues that this legal alliance would avoid any sort of moral or religious fundamentalism, and that it would lead to the foundation of a universal legal State. With all peoples henceforth united, this State could hope to eradicate war altogether.

However, the question remains as to whether peace is essentially a legal and political concept. For example, is it appropriate to see in peace Kant's 'sovereign political good' and to entrust the power for its care to a law that has been purified of any moral interference? And does the ultimate meaning of peace reside in the ability to use laws to guarantee, as Kant has said, 'the state of "mine" and "yours"'? On the other hand, ours is a world full of despair and anger, a world where, in the face of injustice and humiliation, 'there is no pain of heart nor any grief when a man is fighting for his possessions'.[9] Does Levinas's suggestion that 'peace is a concept that goes beyond purely political thought' open up another pathway?[10] While certainly not an alternative to political and legal research on peace, would this pathway never the less open up discussion as to what this same research neglects?

In the Bible, Abram is the first person to speak to others in the terms of peace. The shepherds of Abram's flock are arguing with those of Lot, for the area of land they are on is too small for them to remain together.[11] 'Then Abram said to Lot, "We are relatives, and your men and my men should not be quarrelling."' Abram asks Lot to do him the honour of leaving him: 'So let's separate,' he says. 'Choose any part of the land you want. You go one way, and I'll go the other.' However, this desire for peace, which is inseparable from the idea of sharing things out, only provides the premise of how to think through the proper maintenance of 'mine' and 'yours' without a legal guarantee. For this desire for peace is a frequent characteristic of Biblical lessons about hate and fratricide, and the episode with Abram and Lot is significant in that it is the first of the Bible's responses to such questions, slowly gaining momentum as the Bible progresses, and subjected to numerous assaults and blasphemies along the way. In this instance, at least, the Bible's response to hate and fratricide implies approval of the idea that man be freed from the bewitching notion that an individual could ever own land exclusively and definitively. Despite the sometimes extreme pain occasioned by lost dreams, the Bible says that sharing and separation are worth infinitely more than the savage shame of conflict. Through this renunciation and the grace of sharing comes the hope of saving fraternity, or of rescuing it when it falls into the clutches of hate. Further on in the Book of Genesis, Joseph tells this to his brothers. Having endured their terrible misdeeds, he looks at them and says, 'Peace be with you (*chalom lakhem*), you have nothing to fear (*al tiraou*).'[12] Peace (*chalom*) therefore goes beyond the idea of an equal sharing between 'what is mine' and 'what is yours', delivering us from hate and fear. Fragile and at the mercy of the very worst human acts, peace emerges in the words of a man who, having had his soul ravaged by jealousy, hate and violence, realises that all these things come from fear. Fear, that is, of living and dying, of being one among many others and lost in the vast succession of generations, bereft of reason and rights in the absurdity of a destiny that will soon be annihilated.

Peace does not bring the bitter taste that is always left by the conquering of others, however passionate or philosophical the conquerors. Moreover, while it is of course true that the peace treaties and judicial guarantees that legally protect people are preferable to injustices, wars and massacres, these obligations only give a very rough idea of the perfection (*chalem*) that is characteristic of true peace. However, this perfection would seem to be indistinguishable from an internal function whereby man faces his fear of dying not to withdraw into solitude and seek some kind of individual salvation, but precisely in order to confront in a different way the cruel and tormented world that continues to prevail. This is the kind of peace meant by the Bible when it paradoxically describes peace as both a gift and an obligation: as a gift from Heaven that we have to accept.

The desire for peace has been ceaselessly beaten and suppressed. In order for it to recover, surely political realism must also be alert to the significance of peace as both a gift and an obligation?

'Peace as gift and obligation'

To talk of 'irreducible fraternity' as a corollary of peace is not to describe an empirical fact: rather, this reminds us that the perfection (*chalem*) of peace (*chalom*) goes against any attempt to think of it as the realisation of an essence. If fraternity actually turns out to be irreducible, this is not because of a concern, be it selfish or not, to live in peace with those who temporarily share our existence, but because fraternity inhabits the psyche itself. The realisation of an individual essence or identity cannot therefore be assimilated with peace. This is because individual essences or identities have always had fraternity within them, and always will. Through the rupture that fraternity creates within the self, the assimilation of peace with essential fullness is indefinitely deferred. However, in attempts for peace that are also motivated by the desire to give everyone the possibility of realising his or her own identity, it remains impossible to attend to the demands of fraternity. Thus, even when people manage to live side-by-side without attacking each other, they still refuse fraternity. Peace therefore implies that everyone – despite the primacy of self-concern that is inherent to the concept – accepts the authority of abstract and universal principles or of a truth that transcends individualities and brings them together.

So what do we mean by the 'rupturing of the psyche by fraternity'? At first glance, the expression seems to be incompatible with any idea of peace when thought of as serenity, tranquillity or a state beyond conflict achieved through common truth. In fact, the expression implies a different way of thinking about peace that operates outside of a relationship with these states. This is because fraternity posits an irreducible anxiety – namely, the absence of peace and quiet – within the most secret part of the psyche. Moreover, since this fraternity does not derive from any freely accepted principle, it does not claim or announce itself. Neither is fraternity a generous metaphor that serves to evoke the mortal condition in which we are all supposed to share and believe. Rather, in spite of the anxiety that it arouses and, indeed, because of this anxiety, fraternity lies deep within the psyche as a promise of deliverance. But what kind of promise and deliverance do we mean here? Can the peace that is heralded by the anxiety that lies embedded within the psyche have significant effects on political peace?

Jewish commentaries on the Bible often say that peace is of superior value to truth. Contrary to the idea that peace comes from knowledge, in this perspective truth finds itself subservient to the protection of peace. According to the rabbis of the Talmud, this is why the book's stories may be modified in the interests of peace. Of course, this moral possibility does not give one free licence to transform the truth in order to avoid arousing anxiety or challenging other people's feelings by announcing painful or difficult realities; nor does it allow one to lie in the name of 'a bit of peace and quiet'. Rather, this moral choice presupposes that, in each and every case, the protection of peace involves the subordination of knowledge to the cause of individuals. For instance: 'In the school of Rabbi Ismaël it was taught that peace is an important thing, for even a blessed Saint modified in its honour the tale of Sarah.'[13] Another example is given by the Bible: when the birth of Isaac is announced, Abraham's wife ironically talks about her husband's old age;[14] however, when the everlasting Lord comes to tell Abraham of this, He omits to mention this mocking. When it comes to the transmission of knowledge in relation to the words that are actually said, the concern for peace shown in the house of Abraham and Sarah (*chalom bait*) is superior to precision. Thus: 'the ultimate criterion for the appreciation of a particular truth is peace'.[15] Peace, that is, between people, and not in the sense of an individual's own tranquillity or serenity (*chalva*). In morality, the criterion for judging a question of truth should therefore not be drawn from irrefutable proof – much less any sort of dogma that has to be defended at all costs – but instead from an ability to keep alive the bond with the Other, a fragile bond which is continually under threat. On the other hand, it is easy to see the extent to which man is inclined to destroy peace in the name of truth: for example, by using the idea of 'charitable' warning as an excuse for telling someone of a insult that has been made against them; or by demanding that someone who has signaled their desire for reconciliation further explain him or herself to the point of shame, since this person is so obviously in the wrong about the disagreement that has brought the two parties into conflict. Indeed, in this sort of instance, truth serves first and foremost to generate animosity, jealousy and hate.

However, once adorned with the grand name of 'truth', the desire for the rupture of the human bond becomes even more dangerous and effective because it escapes clear thinking. When men claim to fight for ideals of private or collective truth they are in fact colluding with their own desire for destruction. They approach the question of the human bond as if it were an object of knowledge. However, to argue that peace must prevail is not to scorn truth and side with lies: rather, the case for peace assumes that the meaning of the human bond exceeds any argument about the truth of how things are. By holding onto the norms of this conception in order to safeguard peace, we therefore inevitably subordinate the human to an order to which it does not belong. Contrary to the ideals of the Enlightenment, it also remains very uncertain that the hope for peace lies within the intellectual development of humanity according to the diffusion of knowledge and the mastering of 'truth' by science and technology.

In saying all this I do not wish to imply a scornful opinion of progress, knowledge and truth. Nor am I taking peace as a pretext for preaching for anti-Enlightenment philosophy, for prejudice and ignorance continue to torture the earth, and the acts of murder and destruction they provoke are all too visible even today. Even those who argue that we should in each case approach truth as subordinate to the unrivalled nobility of peace are themselves always in search of knowledge and truth. That is to say that they, too, hope that the terrifying power of hate may be curbed by shedding light on the soul. This is the angle from which Maimonides, a twelfth-century Jewish sage, says that if one day we come to have true knowledge of God, then all rivalry, war and tyranny will disappear.[16] However, while we wait for this uncertain and improbable moment, we must not let up in our thoughts, reasoning and examinations of texts, nor in the transmission of our interpretations.

At a time when there is the threat of war between peoples (in other words, all the time), talking about the superiority of peace over truth does not mean that truth has been abandoned. On the contrary, such a choice makes for a constant exchange (*makhloquet*) about truth. It is simply the case that this exchange sometimes comes in the form of war, which takes place against the background of a text that is open to interpretation. In a conflict between two individuals the grim will to assert oneself over one's foe is disguised as the defence of one's point of view; in war fought over a text, however, once the book is closed the war ends immediately. This kind of war does not seek to satisfy personal interests (such as prestige, power or fascination) to the detriment of others, and it does not therefore contradict the priority for peace. Rather, such a war is based on the certain belief that, like life, truth is always shared, and that it is achieved through exchange with the Other. As Rabbi Haïm de Volozin has stressed, this involves humility, and a mistrust of anything that colludes with the arrogant desire to control both other people and truth itself.[17] From this angle, a moral disposition towards other people is therefore an essential condition of the quest for truth. This can be seen in the word *makhloquet* (constant exchange), which is derived from the linguistic root of 'kh.l.q' meaning the noun 'share' in Hebrew. That is to say that *makhloquet* cannot become the will to impose our 'share' as the sole location of truth without running into mortal peril. In French, the recurrence of the letters 'm', 'o' and 't' suggest that death ('la mort') lies within words ('les mots'): men can only challenge death by exchanging living words, and never by the imagined certainty of being right. However, as Levinas has said, living peace between peoples 'is produced as this aptitude to speak'.[18] Thus, living peace resists all forms of submission to anonymous truth (be it that of fate or history), as well as the bewitching powers of truth promoted by a single individual.

The quest for truth led by Jewish scholars in their study of the Torah therefore means that the primary concern is *either* peace or the idea of speaking and sharing. The Torah will only remain a text for life (*Torat haïm*) if its readers attend to the idea of mutual sharing. Rabbi Haïm de Volozin says that through modesty, hesitation and an absence of arrogance or fanaticism, a person who speaks in this spirit will renew the meaning (*hidouch*) of exchange and that his or her words will come to join with those of the living God (*divrei Elohim haïm*). However, the importance of *hidouch* does not take peace as a pretext for making concessions to the relativism of different opinions. Rather, it makes the more challenging assumption of a truth that can be shared with others.

To forget this way of thinking is to perpetuate war and exile. For example, under-standing hate as the rejection of the Other for the simple reason that he or she is different from oneself, Jewish scholars charge gratuitous hatred with responsibility for the ills of human history. Man has a furious desire to declare that, despite his efforts, he has been unable to assert himself in his own right and truth (as if it were a question of universal rights and truth): in so doing, man is in fact always at risk from the all-consuming power of hate. This, say Jewish scholars, is why exile and war persist, with exchanges made in order to attack and dominate other people, and with any question of sharing stubbornly denied through the incitement of hatred. 'There is no greater idolatry than this,' conclude the scholars.[19]

This way of thinking suggests a form of peace that cannot be reduced to what Levinas has called 'the ideal of unity of Oneness that is disrupted by any sort of alterity'.[20] The idea of a living peace does not mean a pure serenity of the soul that is enjoyed in spite of the cruel days endured by so many people. However, neither does the language of sharing life and truth mean that men and their words are fragments of a complete whole, the philosophical and historical reconstruction of which would equate to peace. This kind of peace would destroy alterity, or would at least reduce it to a way of making logical distinctions within a single category of person. Levinas writes: 'It is in fact obvious that peace with another person is transformed into hate by thinking of that person as a simple individual from a particular class, gender or race.'[21] Thus, gratuitous hatred and its attendant destructiveness are passed down through the generations by what Levinas calls 'an approach to other people that thinks of them in terms of "a this or a that"'.[22] This approach considers that the circumstances surrounding the birth of an individual inscribe him or her as a copy of a particular identity; the individual therefore belongs to the history of a people which has come into conflict with other peoples. It is this way of thinking that generates hate and the feeling that one is within one's rights to kill or wage war on other people. Sinister and daily reminders of this are provided by the fate and misery of deported children who, as little more than babes-in-arms, come to know the hate of other children who have inherited a different history and who have been told that it is legitimate to attack and kill them, especially in cases when their respective histories conflict with each other.

The sharing of life and truth remains impervious to dialectical transcendence. For all the murderous frenzy of the twentieth century, the call for peace will not be answered by social totality and a definitive synthesis of opinion. This is because totality and synthesis, despite their appearances, can only ever alienate lives: more often than not, they reduce people to silence and obedience, fascinating or terrorising the individual with fear. Peace, on the other hand, is achieved by agreeing to share and by an incontrovertible access to humanity. The idea of a person's share means that each human being is thought of not as a single, barely distinguishable example of the innumerable members of the human race, but as a unique individual among many other unique individuals. Thus, peace is kept alive by accepting and welcoming irreducible uniqueness. On the level of the quest for truth, this means that no one may be so proud as to assume that superior intelligence or power allows his or her share to be imposed on everyone else without discussion. For example, it is not an ideal of peace that different interpretations of biblical texts be unified. On the contrary, Jewish scholars tell us that such contradictory interpretations will survive until the end of time, provided that they are selfless (*lismah*). No single person contains the ultimate meaning of holy verses, and the words of men can only cause this meaning to grow if they allow it to be engaged with by a multiplicity of other individuals. Thus, every one of us can illuminate the holy verses with our own most personal questions and our own irreducible uniqueness: our joys and sorrows, our calm and passion, our gentle honesty or our acumen. In this way, we can take part in a truth that needs us in order to live.

The decision to make truth subordinate to peace therefore cannot be reductively described as a wisdom that, when it comes to interpreting the complexities of a text or situation, shows a modest attentiveness to the views of other people. More radically, the subordination of truth presupposes that peace is never a simple state or settled situation, even if it has been achieved as the result of a noble struggle. Rabbi Tsadok haCohen reminds us that, no matter what the location, self and Other are always caused harm by the act of settling,[23] and that those who are just cannot ask to settle peacefully (*chalva*) within the world. Thus, an individual in fact becomes shielded from the demands of peace if he is allowed to believe that he may settle with a clear and carefree conscience, that he has at last found a place of serenity and certitude that is protected from any sort of dispute, and that this place may be enjoyed with perfect entitlement. This shielding from the demands of peace is especially true if the individual comes to settle at the end of years of toil or after troubles that have been overcome. Peace does not consist in resting or in settling somewhere tranquil; nor does it occupy a particular place, be it physical, or abstract, as in the location of knowledge. Rather, peace is the obligation to protect the unique and fragile life that is given to everyone. The meaning of peace cannot therefore be thought of in terms of a psyche that is in harmony with itself or with God, either in the sense of the pure serenity of the soul or of deliverance from one's normal suffering. Peace is directed towards a type of perfection known in Hebrew as *chelemut*. Because *chelemut* is not the same thing as the realisation of a personal essence, it requires the individual to take the obligation of peace into the heart of his or her daily life, and to think it through and take responsibility for it not with meanness or pure chance, but with the care that is due to a goodness that is irreplaceable but vulnerable. How should we understand this idea? Previously I evoked the notion of 'irreducible fraternity' (which, as we have seen, does not mean shelter from remorseless, terrible hostilities) as something that counterbalances the temptation for war – does *chelemut* allow us to shed further light onto this idea?

Certain thinkers from the Jewish tradition say that, of all the names of God that man may utter, the most high is that of 'Peace' (*Chalom*), which surpasses even that of 'Truth' (*Emet*).[24] In this perspective, God is not so much the source for all things as He who, above all, makes and gives peace. The Jewish liturgy recalls all this at various points, most notably in the words of the priest's benediction (*Cohanim*):[25] 'May the Lord look on you with favour and give you peace.'

However, are all these edifying words not also heavy with a piety that is alien to most individuals, and therefore of little interest to a discussion about a type of peace that cannot be reduced to the beliefs of a particular people? Are these simple words of consolation that are spoken in order to make us accept our troubles and woes, and to give the illusory hope that there is a God who is watching over each of us and concerning Himself with our own individual peace? It is obvious enough that, when reading holy texts, everyone often gives in to the temptation to hear words of comfort that are meant for him or herself alone. Despite this, however, we should also remain attentive to what these words inspire when they are *not* read for oneself. This kind of reading, which should be done without self-satisfaction, brings to mind the idea that the meaning of peace resides in the face-to-face: that is, in the welcoming of an unknown guest who comes during the fleeting and invigorating break of day, when comfort resembles an obligation to be hospitable. While it seems strange next to the popular conception of peace as a state of serenity or safety, it can therefore be said that the gift of peace is assured by defeating the desire to receive something for oneself and for one's own pleasure or comfort. For peace is not a state of satisfaction that is achieved by deserving or anguished souls; nor is it a reward or response that is bestowed when one's troubles disappear or when one's desires are fulfilled. Peace is an infinite obligation. However, in liberating the self from its immobility and imprisonment within its demands for itself, peace reveals a path that leads the self away from the tragedy and death with which it colludes in the belief of securing self-preservation and self-love. By rising up in the name of other people, and by going to them having been freed of an imperious state of mind that may have gone unnoticed, the self is released from a great and disabling burden. In honour of the unknown guest mentioned earlier, the self forgets the fiction of its own sheltering identity, which it is ready to defend and to impose on others. However, this does not cause the self to become lost. On the contrary, it finds new direction and becomes aware of the life that was being obscured by the fiction of selfhood. All that remains is the face-to-face encounter, the moment when the Unique One turns to look at the self and in so doing gives birth to the self's own uniqueness.

It remains the case that this moment of the face-to-face – this awakening of uniqueness by uniqueness – is not described by any body of learning. Theology, for example, despite its speculative aims, lacks the conceptual means to discuss the gift of peace when thought of as the birth of uniqueness within every individual. However, is this gift an imperfection in that it does not shed any light onto the essence of God? In fact, nothing is less certain. This is because perfection – the work of accomplishment, or *chalom* – consists here not in revealing a God whose name is Peace, but in the fact that the individual whom He turns to face becomes sensitive to the precious and fragile uniqueness of each human being. The gift of peace 'strikes in separate beings the exact same note that lies deep within every individual'.[26] In so doing, it is as if peace awakens to the meaning of 'irreducible fraternity', which is for the moment subjugated within disaster, hatred and war, as well as the drive for wrongful seizure of other people's space, violence and the killing of those whose existence is felt to be too much to bear.

Fraternity does not banish hate, and can even exacerbate it. However, in that fraternity presupposes the idea of a common origin, it implies the thought that peace between people depends upon the welcome that is reserved for this origin. According to the various religions that have grown out of the Bible, fraternity is a fundamental part of the divine Name, no matter how each religion actually speaks this Name. The implication, therefore, is that one of the qualities of fraternity is an orientation towards God. But just what kind of quality is this, given how clearly, even today, human faith in God continues to justify the spilling of blood? Rather, does not the successful establishment of peace between peoples suppose that, as a prerequisite, they stop claiming the Name of God and accept that they are alone?

* * *

The desire for peace – *chalom, salam* – directs us towards other people. However, when these words are spoken from a pre-history that has been divested of the stories individuals tell themselves in order to justify their hatred, they do not simply announce to a person or a people the undertaking to abstain from harming them. Rather, the words bless their days and say that their existence is to be rejoiced in. However, this conquest of jealousy will only be possible by finding within oneself – in an internal space that has been freed from the burden of an identity that is self-satisfied or on the defensive – the direction that brings life. If undefeated, this jealousy continues to haunt the psyche, to the point where the temptation arises to destroy other people in order to appropriate what it is that makes them live. However, although this may seem strange to those who believe that the internal is the opposite of the external, each time that the self weaves a seductive attempt to reassert itself the orientation towards other people patiently unpicks its stitches, without allowing itself to become caught up in the thread. For the interiority from which peace derives will not let itself become ensnared within a play of alternatives, such as the internal and the external, the personal and the foreign, or sameness and difference. On the contrary, this interiority means that the secret of alterity is what allows the psyche to live. It is this that directs the psyche towards others who live within this secret, without really being aware of it, and who even sometimes become angry about it. When the day comes to welcome this secret into one's self – a day which has always yet to happen – the eradication of the divine Name will become an obligation of peace towards other beings.

Translated by Stephen Forcer

Notes

1 Genesis, Ch. 4, v. 8.
2 Aeschylus, *Seven Against Thebes* (trans. Anthony Hecht and Helen H. Bacon; London: Oxford University Press, 1974), p. 50 (lines 689–90).
3 Immanuel Kant, 'The Doctrine of Right' in *The Metaphysics of Morals* (trans. and ed. Mary Gregor; Cambridge: Cambridge University Press, 1996), 7–138 (p. 123).
4 Immanuel Kant, 'Containing the Definitive Articles for a Perpetual Peace among States' in *Perpetual Peace* (intro. Nicholas Murray Butler; New York: Columbia University Press, 1939), 10–11 (p. 11n).
5 Immanuel Kant, 'Supplement – Of the Guarantee for a Perpetual Peace' in *Perpetual Peace*, 27–37 (p. 34).

6 Immanuel Kant, *Perpetual Peace*, p. 34.
7 Jürgen Habermas, *La Paix perpetuelle, le bicentenaire d'une idée kantienne* (trans. R. Rochlitz; Paris: Cerf, 1996), p. 13.
8 Jürgen Habermas, *La Paix perpetuelle*, pp. 23 and 90.
9 Homer, *The Odyssey* (trans. A. T. Murray; London: Heinemann, 1946), p. 187 (lines 469–71).
10 Emmanuel Levinas, *L'Au-delà du verset* (Paris: Minuit, 1982), p. 228.
11 Genesis Ch. 13, v. 8–9.
12 Genesis Ch. 43, v. 23.
13 See the Talmud Babli, Yebamot 65b.
14 See Genesis, Ch. 18, v. 12–13.
15 Marcus Wald, *Jewish Teaching on Peace* (New York: Bloch, 1944), p. 97.
16 See Maimonides, *Le Livre de la connaissance* (Paris: PUF, 1990), p. 418. This book is available in English as *The Book of Knowledge*, 2 vols., newly revised and edited by Moses Hyamson (Jerusalem and New York: Feldheim, 1981).
17 See Abraham Sagi's Hebrew study on the status of halakhic exchange, *Elu va Elu* (Tel-Aviv: HaKibbutz hameuchad, 1996). For example: 'halakhic exchange (about the Law) is a battle between master and pupil . . . that takes place at the heart of a respectful relationship' (p. 152). See also p. 153 on humility.
18 Emmanuel Levinas, 'Preface' in *Totality and Infinity* (trans. Alphonso Lingis; Pittsburgh: Duquesne University Press, 1979), 21–30 (p. 23).
19 Rabbi I. D. Epstein (ed.), *Mitsvot haChalom* (New York, 1970), p. 64. This collection of texts from within the Jewish tradition is written in Hebrew.
20 [Translator's note] NB. Although the author attributes this and subsequent quotations from *Totality and Infinity* to a section entitled 'Paix et proximité' ('Peace and Proximity'), no section of that name, either exact or approximate, appears in the English translation consulted here. The reference given by the author for these quotations is: Emmanuel Levinas, 'Paix et proximité' in *Totalité et Infini: essai sur l'extériorité* (La Haye: M. Nijhoff, 1961); this first quotation is from p. 143.
21 Emmanuel Levinas, 'Paix et proximité' in *Totalité et Infini*, p. 145.
22 Emmanuel Levinas, 'Paix et proximité' in *Totalité et Infini*, p. 145.
23 See Rabbi Tsadok haCohen, *Otzar haMarchava* (Jerusalem, 1991), p. 76. The text is in Hebrew.
24 See, for example, Maharal de Prague, *Netiv haChalom* in *Ntivot Olam* (London: L. Honig, 1961), p. 203. This text is in Hebrew.
25 See the Book of Numbers, Ch. 6 v. 22–27.
26 Franz Rosenzweig, *L'Étoile de la Rédemption* (trans. A. Derczanski and J. L. Schlegel; Paris: Seuil, 1982), p. 100. This text is also available in English as *The Star of Redemption* (trans. William H. Hallo; Notre Dame, IN: Notre Dame Press, 1985).

5

FRANÇOISE PROUST

Françoise Proust (1947–98) was Professor of Philosophy at the University of Paris I and programme Director at the Collège International de Philosophie. Her work centred on the question of how to conceive the political, and she translated several of Kant's works of political philosophy. Her most recent work on resistance enters into a debate with Foucault and Deleuze and argues for a conception of resistance as an active experience of subjectivation, on the side of life, freedom and the passions. Together with Françoise Collin, she also co-edited a special issue of *Les Cahiers du Grif*, devoted to the work of Sarah Kofman.

Her works include the following:

Kant: le ton de l'histoire, Paris: Payot, 1991.

La Doublure du temps, Paris: Le Perroquet, 1993.

L'Histoire à contretemps: le temps historique chez Walter Benjamin, Paris: Cerf, 1994; reprinted by Librairie générale française, 1999.

Point de Passage, Paris: Kimé, 1994.

De la Résistance, Paris: Cerf, 1997.

TIME'S DOUBLE

A lecture given by Françoise Proust on 18 May 1993

The deconstruction of Kant's Analytic of temporality mounted by Walter Benjamin may be viewed as a response to that of his contemporary, Heidegger. Time is not, in essence, successive but nor is it projective; it is imbricated and forms loops or arabesques. These temporal loops are time's doubles, its inner lining. Whenever something happens, this moment doubles itself immediately, forming two lines, or spaces, which overlap. We shall endeavour to explore the implications of this law of temporal survival, or ghosting, for ways of thinking about history.

At the beginning of his article from 1936, 'The Storyteller' (*Der Erzähler*), Walter Benjamin writes:

> Experience has fallen in value. And it looks as if it is continuing to fall into bottomlessness. Every glance at a newspaper demonstrates that it has reached a new low, that our picture, not only of the external world but of the moral world as well, overnight has undergone changes which were never thought possible. With the [First] World War, a process began to become apparent which has not halted since then. Was it not noticeable at the end of the war that men returned from the battlefield grown silent – not richer but poorer in communicable experience? What ten years later was poured out in the flood of war books was anything but experience that goes from mouth to mouth. And there was nothing remarkable about that. For never has experience been contradicted more thoroughly than strategic experience by tactical warfare, economic experience by inflation, bodily experience by mechanical warfare, moral experience by those in power. A generation that had gone to school on a horse-drawn streetcar now stood under the open sky in a countryside in which nothing remained unchanged but the clouds, and beneath these clouds, in a field of force of destructive torrents and explosions, was the tiny, fragile human body.[1]

Often only partially quoted, this is a passage which, in consequence, is often only partially understood. The 'lost experience' described by Benjamin is not the loss of experience. It is, rather, the experience of a 'lost generation' and a 'lost time', which

70

points to the new form that experience takes under modernity. Modernity has no knowledge of the destruction (or explosion) of experience but rather undergoes an experience of destruction (or explosion), which is something altogether different. Therein lies the significance of the First World War: those involved in it, or who lived through it, knew from the outset that their experience was decisive, in both its novelty (which came at breakneck speed) and its radicality. It pushed every experience *to the extreme* and, if indeed it has always been death that has lent experience its truth and dignity, one of the essential characteristics of this modernity is that death too is extreme. Extreme in intensity (radical) and in extent (global). Construction and destruction come to be equivalent, not because one follows the other in some infernal cycle (although this has proved to be the case empirically) but because, more fundamentally, both are governed by the same logic: war and peace (the technologies, situations and so on, of war and peace) become interchangeable because both are subject to the same law of battle. It is this law of the extreme (the law of destruction), which those who lived through the First World War were the first to experience, that constitutes the *primal scene* of modernity.

Like every primal scene, this one was cloaked in denial. And in fact, from that moment on, the process by which living beings are destroyed becomes so radical that it also occasions the destruction of its truth, that is, of the truth of the very existence and forms of existence of that destruction. It is of this that Benjamin reminds us: when the State spoke of patriotism, human beings were experiencing the barbarity of the trenches; when capital spoke of growth, they experienced the poverty brought on by inflation; when governments spoke of morality, they experienced deceit and corruption, etc. And let us be clear that it was because these decisive experiences were cloaked in deception that those involved preferred to remain silent, at the risk of others believing that they had not experienced anything at all and *a fortiori* nothing new.

Yet it is quite clearly the same law – that of *destruction* – which governed both the murder and the deception. And it would appear that this law was the opposite of that which had governed experience – as it had been lived and conceptualized – at the dawn of modernity, namely in its Hegelian form. Since Hegel, experience had been understood as the process by which consciousness is formed, that is the establishing of subjectivity in truth. But what are the characteristics of modernity? Shattered existences, traumatized consciousnesses, lost generations and experiences that have been stripped of the possibility of articulation and narration (of transmission). And indeed, if these experiences were deprived of meaning and appeared empty, if they were lived as though they were 'natural phenomena', this is because they could no longer be placed within the frame of a coherent picture, because they could no longer be situated on any horizon. After 1914, to die at war is to die for nothing and perhaps after 1917, the fight for justice is all for nothing. Better still, by the same logic, things come full circle when these experiences that have been emptied of significance are overwritten by a spiritualizing language that may be just as dangerous as the inability to speak. The massive 'oversignification' of this present *fin de siècle* may prove no less deadly to the experiences concerned than forgetting. We know it by the name of pious remembrance.

It will be clear from this last remark that experience under modernity is, despite appearances to the contrary, the completion or *radical implementation* of Hegelian experience. Hegel had hoped to stop the *destructive* process by naming it negativity, that is by replacing it within a whole that would give it meaning, that would show that its truth lay in its becoming rather than its being. But once its becoming has been fully realized, when it no longer has any exteriority to devour and internalize, its absolute positivity (the absolute positivity of the absolute) changes into absolute negativity. It is condemned to destroy itself unceasingly in order to produce and reproduce itself. The *paradise of meaning* reaches its apotheosis when it reveals itself to be a *hell of meaning* in which self-production demands self-destruction. This is indeed modernity: every novelty has always already been recycled, all alterity has always already been re-appropriated and all exteriority always already internalized. An excess of meaning is condemned, infernally, to secrete non-meaning in order to make more meaning, indefinitely, so as to extract from it a surplus value of meaning.

Thus the attempt to do justice to the decisive experiences of modernity demands, first of all, that they be made to speak their naked truth. It demands we recognize the regime of truth proper to experience under modernity: the regime of destruction, of naked destruction (and not of destruction converted or raised into negativity). Destruction is terrible: it places experience in mortal danger, for by dint of the structural necessity we have already described, destruction is not simply the destruction of being but also that of the being of destruction. There is a risk that both destruction and the experience of destruction will vanish without leaving a single trace. For the trace is already a space and a time and the deception consists precisely in claiming that nothing took place, that there was absolutely no experience of a new space and a new time.

Yet paradoxically, destruction (and particularly destruction by explosion) also offers an opportunity, perhaps the final opportunity. For the experience of destruction also marks the destruction of traditions of deceit, of false accounts and, at the same time, this dismemberment, this shattering of experience and its tradition, leaves behind it small shards, tiny stones, sometimes just a scattering of ashes, which may permit the restoration of meaning and truth to the experience of destruction.

To talk of experience after Kant is to talk of *synthesis*. Experience is synthesis, 'the synthetic unity of the manifold'. Let us briefly remind ourselves of what is involved in this threefold synthesis: the synthesis of *apprehension in intuition*, the synthesis of *reproduction in the imagination* and the synthesis of *recognition in the concept*. In the first of these, consciousness must be able to connect or bring into relation two or more 'absolute units' in time, to refer one to the other as taking place in the same time and forming a temporal series. We call this series a moment in time or a *unit* of time. The first synthesis is, then, one of apprehension or comprehension (*Zusammennehmung*). In the second, consciousness must reproduce in its 'inner sense' those representations which preceded the new representations and hold the manifold of these representations together in a single gaze, for 'if I were always to drop out of thought the preceding representations (the first parts of the line, the antecedent parts of the time period, or the units in the order represented), and did not reproduce them while advancing to those that follow, a complete representation would never be obtained; none of the above-mentioned thoughts . . . could arise'.[2] Thus a second synthesis is required, a synthesis of reproduction. And finally, consciousness must be conscious of its act, must apprehend itself as the subject or author of its synthesis; it must grasp the two preceding syntheses as acts of a single consciousness, itself; for were they not to have a single author, these syntheses could merely follow one another as distinct syntheses and the manifold would remain manifold. So a third synthesis is required, the synthesis of recognition.

Each of these three syntheses testifies to the necessity for consciousness to grasp the manifold, the chaos of data, in one minimal unit of sense. Experience always involves the unification of an amorphous multiplicity of raw data into a meaningful form, the gathering of 'theses' in a 'synthesis'. For there to be experience requires that consciousness can apprehend (in the first synthesis), recollect (in the second) and recognize (in the third) two impressions, two distinct data, and assemble them into an identifiable and meaningful unit. The condition of the possibility of experience is thus the synthesis of data by consciousness, 'the synthetic unity of experience'.

In other words, synthesis is the synthesis of time (and space). More precisely, synthesis *is* time (and space): time (space) *is* the synthesis of the manifold. This is why, as Kant states repeatedly in the 'Transcendental Aesthetic', there is only one space and one time, because all possibile relations to space and time already presuppose, as the condition of their possibility, time and space, or if you prefer, transcendental temporality and spatiality. It follows that there is no form of experience other than *synthetic* experience. Every experience occupies a given time and space. If that were not so, then, purely and simply, nothing would happen. In the absence of a temporal datum allowing identification and recognition and in the absence of a spatial datum designating location, strictly speaking nothing has happened.

So how are we to synthesize that which manifests itself as the destruction of all syntheses? How are we to posit, without contradiction, both the dissolution of every synthesis of space and time and the necessity of there being a synthesis? In sum, what are the conditions of the possibility of an *experience of the loss of experience*?

Under modernity, every event comes in the form of an *impact* [*coup*] (or 'shock', to use Benjamin's term): the *coup d'État* (if by State we understand every kind of institution – political, economic, military, cultural, etc.), the *coup* plotted or thwarted, the advertising *coup*.[3] It is not that modern times are newer or more unpredictable than those which came before: every age has its share of innovations and transformations. Every age is struck by surprising events which rear up as if from nowhere and lead to the decline and dissolution of the times which gave them birth. Yet under modernity, since the end of the eighteenth century, the pace at which events have followed one another has prohibited their forming the basis or foundation of enduring institutions. These are beginnings, but ones which do not, in Kantian terms, mark the beginning of any series and which do not constitute the principle (the beginning and inspiration) of an epoch or situation. They are pure beginnings, ends in themselves, and their simple but terrible power is to strike and mark. Similarly, there can be no pretending that the modern age is more violent than those which preceded it. Earlier centuries were ravaged by wars (of religion), riots and oppression (exploitation, persecution and colonization). Modern violence, however, is such that it abolishes the distinction between violence and non-violence, between war and peace. The language of war is now in common usage in times of peace: 'salvo' of information, sex 'bomb', terrorist 'commando', 'army' of journalists, party 'HQ', etc. Modern events take place at breakneck speed and strike with disproportionate force. This is why their violence is aggressive, shocking and dazzling, why they leave consciousness violated and traumatized.

Yet the fact that events as experienced under modernity are *impacts* means that we cannot, as Kant thought, grasp the 'conditions of the possibility of experience' in the 'synthesis of the manifold'. To clarify:

1. An impact is a blow, a mark, an *impression*. An impact is measured only by what it leaves behind – a scratch, groove, notch, incision, etc. – and not by its content, which dissipates at precisely the moment when it hits home. The only evidence, or rather the only testimony, which the impact leaves is its trace. What is more, this trace does not point to anything in particular and is entirely lacking in meaning, intention and significance. A trace is simply the trace of a *having-happened*. It is a pure inscription, an 'archi-écriture', in Derridean terms, which bears witness to the fact that 'something' has happened in this place at a given moment. It does not tell us whether the event in question was historical (the product of human freedom and action) or natural (a natural phenomenon). Nor does it tell us whether someone *wanted* to leave a trace or whether this just happened by itself. It bears neither the signature of its author nor the date of the event which left its trace here. It is only in the act of reading and interpreting ('remarking' upon the trace, if you will), that the mark is grasped retrospectively as being the mark of *this* or that. It is only in the aftermath of its having struck that the impact will be understood as meaningful and expressive. It is only in the act of reproduction – that is, with the addition of a second blow, in apposition – that the first, which in itself is insignificant, has the opportunity to become a meaningful event, the bearer of a proper name, of a *date*.

In the meantime, there is an inscription, but the signs inscribed do not yet constitute writing: there is only the pure trace of a having-happened. On this point, Kant is unquestionably right: the condition of the possibility of any phenomenon is its being *given in space and time*, that is, both the presence of matter (space which lies open, *a priori*, to impact and inscription) and form (a process, an intervention, a temporality) are required. Whenever a phenomenon is given, in keeping with the originary character of this act, a space is laid open and a time is born. But in order for there to be such an opening and such a birth, we must conceive of a space and time that are more original than those proposed by Kant in his first synthesis. Prior to the 'synthesis of apprehension in intuition', an impression is made which makes both possible and impossible the 'running through and grasping of the manifold'.

Every manifold, indeed, is already a form of unification of what Kant himself calls 'absolute unities'.[4] For it to be possible for the manifold to be apprehended as a manifold and its constituent parts united, these 'unities' must already have been bound into 'indivisible' units. Yet this is precisely what is no longer available in modern experience: a given is never unified, it is a many-layered and infinitely divisible multiplicity of impressions which are merely differential and inherently meaningless. A series of points can give rise to a shape, a line or a figure. But this presupposes an intervention, a decision as to its meaning, a 're-marking' upon the mark. The synthesis is thus both possible and impossible; or, better, it is only possible under the force of a second *impact*, regardless of whether this be desired or accepted. The synthesis is the bringing of unity by force to a sequence of impressions which do not allow themselves to be unified without resisting and persisting 'in the wild'.

To summarize: the impression is the condition of the impossibility and the possibility of the 'unity of intuition', that is, of space and time (in the first synthesis).

2. If the impression can be reproduced, this is because it is, in essence, reproducible. If the mark can be 'remarked upon', this is because it can be reiterated. The impression can be reproduced because it is itself a reproduction. The impression is always the fragile and provisional unity of a play of forces which necessarily strike on several occasions, in succession, or in other words, which reproduce one another. Reproduction is an effect of both necessity and chance. There is necessity in the time that passes and the necessary scansion of the indefinite number of impacts which strike. There is chance in the precarious way in which these impacts are assembled into a figure of the moment that is destined soon to disappear.

One aspect of reproduction is erasure. An impression reproduced is thereby obliterated: another impression is installed where the first once was, is superimposed upon it as its substitute. Thus between 'the old' and 'the new', between same and other, there is no longer any difference; repetition, in this case, is reappropriation. The previous impact, which presumed to be unique, is reappropriated, or recycled, in the 'present' of the impact which follows, just as the impact which is to come is anticipated and internalized in advance. This is characteristic, moreover, of conceptions of time since Augustine: the past and future are modes of the present, for the past is that which I remember *at present*, just as the future is that which I await (in hope or fear) *at present*. In other words, memory and anticipation are modes of a temporal structure which is itself necessarily repetitive, a structure which modernity has made its own by systematically archiving and simulating. Every new event, whether it has already taken place or has yet to occur, is susceptible to return as the same, to return *as though* it were the same. Nietzsche, with prescience, had already identified this loop in modern time, a loop in which every novelty is caught, brushed aside and finally recycled: 'eternal recurrence'.[5]

But if reproduction is the inevitable risk attendant upon the production of every spatio-temporal given (every impact), it is also its opportunity. It is, indeed, the only opportunity for meaning. As we have already noted, the mark only attains sense when remarked upon. If recapture can always also be reappropriation, it is, by the same token, an opening (which can neither be predicted nor anticipated) onto another blow, which will itself be entirely new and original. This novelty and originality which cannot, at least for a moment, be reappropriated, are given in spite of and on account of reappropriation. They result from the interlacing of those scraps of that form of memory known, since Proust, as 'involuntary' (which are manifested 'intermittently', despite but also because of the form of memory described as 'voluntary') and the expectation of what remains unexpected, in spite and because of these anticipations. All originality comes both too late and too early. Too late, because every event can always be reappropriated – if indeed this has not already happened – and too early, for as we have seen, an event only acquires a date (becomes historical) as a result of a second event which gives it meaning retrospectively. The first impact, the 'originary' impression, is never knowingly so; it calls for a second impact which will be the only true 'first impact', even though it presupposes its antecedent. Thus we are obliged, with Benjamin, to hold to the following paradox: 'A work of significance either founds a genre or dissolves one and, when perfect, does both at the same time.'[6]

To summarize: reproduction both threatens and enables, ineluctably in both cases, the unity of the impression. The fact that events may be *reproduced* is the condition of both the possibility *and* the impossibility of that 'reproduction in the imagination', or in memory and anticipation, which is necessary in order to achieve the synthetic constitution of the given (in the second synthesis).

3. Thus, in a sense, every event recalls one which came before and one which, although there be no memory bearing its trace, nonetheless, as the common expression would have it, 'looks familiar'. This relationship, or 'family resemblance', to use Wittgenstein's term, between a 'now' and a past which was never a present (since the 'first' impact was not knowingly this) is manifested in the (far from pathological) feeling of 'déjà vu'. In another respect, this same event promises (or threatens) to repeat itself and to return. Every event appears to point forward to another and herein lies the meaning of that characteristic feature of modernity, usually referred to as the 'race against time': it seems as though every event is 'running after time', trying to catch up with time, to pass or overtake it. So every event has a border and a lining – on one side, spectres and revenants and on the other, omens and portents – as though time were always lagging behind itself (coming, as it does, after the second impact which should have been it) and as though, in equal measure, it were always ahead of itself (coming before the first real impact which it simply supports and prefigures).

Thus Kant, in a way, is right: there can be no experience without the 'recognition', that is the 're-cognizing', of a phenomenon. This 're-' prefix in recognition makes explicit the transcendental condition of every event which we have just mentioned: every event *reproduces* a preceding one, in relation to which it is, however, prior and 'unprecedented', just as it points forward to an event which is to come, which it anticipates as a decisive revelation and with respect to which it will have been a mere forerunner. In other words, an event (a 'phenomenon'), in order to qualify as such, must be *recognized* by consciousness. Consciousness must be able to locate it within a series and give it a place: the 'present', which lies between an 'already happened' and a 'still to come'. However, and this is where the third of Kant's syntheses breaks down, the 'already happened' and the 'still to come' do not follow one another but, rather, intertwine inextricably to form a loop or arabesque. For the present has 'always already' happened, since it has always already been reappropriated by another imminent present, in the same way (at the same time) as it is 'always already' still to come, for it calls for yet another event, the one which would finally be decisive. It follows that no event takes place in the present, *now*. The event has never entirely vanished into the past, into the preserve of memory's archives, just as (at the same time as) it is never still to come, because every future is articulated in the present.

The present, therefore, does not come; it *comes back*. It returns from afar, from the most distant past and the most far-flung future. As such, it is both unrecognizable and recognizable, unidentifiable and identifiable. It is unrecognizable because it does not constitute a single unit of time capable of being separated from, or detached within, a flow of time and, once again, the act of separating off an 'already' and a 'still to come' can only ever occur by force or intervention. Yet it is, at the same time, recognizable: it certainly takes place and has its date in history, for an indelible act of inscription must have occurred (even if the inscription had in fact always and necessarily remained under erasure) in order for there to be remembrance ('still') and recurrence ('already').

To summarize: *return* is the condition of both the impossibility and the possibility of 'recognition in the concept', that is of the unity of the manifold as outlined in the third of Kant's syntheses.

Modern experience is ghostly. Experience certainly implies synthesis. Yet this synthesis must be aborted when it comes up against the resistance of the non-synthesizable. The temporal unity of the manifold is always *haunted* by revenants, by the return of an 'again'. This 'again' belongs neither to the past nor the future: it is the past which returns ever and again, as though it were the future coming back from the past.

If Benjamin provides the guiding insight which enables us to conceive, in a faithful infidelity to Kant, a new or second Analytic of temporality, this is because his analysis is rooted in the ordeal of modernity. Modernity is marked by the loss of magic; it is disenchanted and this disenchantment is essential to it. All the distinguishing characteristics of 'Modern Times' flow from this disenchantment: radicality, extremity and reproducibility. Modernity has been denied the opportunity to conceive of a *beyond* (and whether this be considered cause for rejoicing or lamentation, the fact is undeniable): a *beyond* time (eternity) and a world beyond this one ('the other world'). Modernity cannot provide its experience with a *horizon* of sense, whether this be construed dialectically (a gradual process of totalization, with the possibility at any moment of subsuming under a whole, even a partial one, all the experiences which occurred in preceding moments) or 'transcendentally' (another world which gathers up, takes hold of and elevates this world into its 'transfigured' counterpart). Any attempt to look forward to, or hope for, a 'hereafter' which lies 'ahead', has come to look like 'running away into the future', a 'race' against time. Meaning can no longer be located *ahead* or *in front*. Or better, the horizon of a bygone era is made coextensive with the world, or time, and functions as a mirror, reflecting and magnifying. It reflects time back at itself and thereby reveals its true nature: time repeats itself, it returns, it turns on its axis and forms loops or arabesques.

To put this differently, the process of disenchantment which has been taking place before our very eyes for the last two centuries, provides us with a valuable clue: the dyad of linearity and eternity is no longer in force. Eternity was a compact version of the successive nature of time and, conversely, this successive character was the unfurling or 'unfolding' of timelessness. There can be no question of overturning or inverting this dyad; it is rather a matter of *diverting* it, giving it a gentle push, a flick or tap, in order to restore its balance or turn it the right way round and thereby, from the depths of disenchantment, to elaborate a new way of finding time enchanting.

Time in its place (time the right way round) is the place of time's taking place. And this 'taking place' is, in a sense, *eternal*: whenever something happens, there is an impact, whenever something happens there is yet another impact which makes its mark. This eternity is not paradisaical but *infernal*, diabolical, satanic. Time is mechanical and, as such, it reproduces itself identically, as a machine churns out mass-produced manufactured goods. Thus, paradoxically, it is time which saves us from eternity. It is the promise that time will run on, will continue to give itself, which *saves* us from this *infernal* eternity. Herein lies the *irony* of modernity: it is not eternity which saves time, it is time (the time of the lucky break, 'Messianic' time) which preserves us from the threat of eternity.

Time is double, which means three things: it repeats itself, it doubles back on itself and it 'restores' itself.

1. Time is *repetitive*: it is only by returning that it comes at all. As we described above, time is a series of impacts, each of which presupposes, by definition, a preceding one, yet this impact (this 'foreshock') can only be perceived as such, as *temporal*, after a second impact has hit home; that is, in the aftermath. Time is repetitive because temporality is *scansion* and scansion ('before/after') is a secondary phenomenon derived from the originary scansion that it the repetition or return of the same. Time becomes tangible, in the first instance, in the return to sameness of a sonic or visual impact and this is why two originary, archaic, impressions of time are boredom (time as empty and pointless) and inebriation (time coiling back on itself). This is also clearly demonstrated by music, that 'art of time'. Music is born of the return of sonic impacts. It is the repro-duction at varied intervals (or different tempi) of the same sound which gives rise to a sequence of sounds and thereby changes noise into sound. The differentiated play of repetition is what allows us to recognize a sound, to articulate it in a meaningful way and it is this recognition which produces an emotion, a certain enchantment. Music is chant and this chant is none other than the round of sonic impacts.[7] Enchantment tends towards intoxication, indeed hypnotic trance, when the reproduction occurs without differen-tiation, when the return of the sounds is a return to the same, when the same is no longer inflected or troubled by the other (by an altered sound), when there is no longer a *play* of sounds and the sound sequence is devoid of 'jumps of key'.[8]

Reproduction is the *guardian* of time.[9] In one respect, to stand guard is to keep watch on, to keep away from prying eyes and exposure to possible attack; it is to preserve something in its initial state. Yet to guard is also to remain watchful for, to exercise care, to hold back, in reserve, and to keep 'for'. To guard is thus to guard *against* and to watch *for*. It is at once to preserve and to promise. Time can make no promise to come (can neither come nor continue to give itself) without being preserved; conversely, it can only be preserved by being returned to the present and if the present kindles its 'messianic flame'. In Benjamin's terms, *memory* requires *remembrance* in the present. The past dies when stacked for preservation in archives and, conversely, a present which does not take hold again of a past is empty. Remembrance is the arc or loop between past and present.

2. Time is *double*. Whenever something happens or takes place, it inscribes itself and this writing (or inscription) is the remains of an event. There is never an event without an inscription of one form or another, nor by the same token without remains of some sort. These remains will not *subsist*; with time, the inscription becomes illegible, anonymous and silent. It is gradually erased and only after a new impact (a new act of inscription) – after the fact – does the inscription speak, awaken and reveal itself as writing. Yet this necessitates a first incription which, as such, *insists* and *resists*. 'Like ultraviolet rays, memory shows to each man in the book of life a script that invisibly and prophetically glosses the text.'[10] Every event is *doubled* by the inscription which outlives it. *Survival* (the remains, the trace, the memory) is not what follows an event but is instead its double and accompaniment. Living and outliving coexist as contemporaries: life is always edged with phantoms, spectres and revenants. An event always has, or is, a *deposit*. For one thing, what always remains of an event – particularly those events which come at breakneck speed to hurl themselves at consciousness – is a deposit, a precipitate, a heap, be this of ashes. Such violent and extreme events are events of fire: they consume and incinerate, they are both destructive and self-destructive. And yet after

action of such suicidal violence, ashes always remain, for even if they are dispersed, this itself is an act which leaves a trace. Every event, intentionally or otherwise, entrusts itself *as a deposit* for safe-keeping into the hands of another event which, when it follows, will restore to life (again, intentionally or otherwise) the spectre or ghost in waiting, deposited in the preceding event, and will be haunted by it. And, to be sure, such a deposit requires someone to keep it safe, someone who feels that it has been consigned to them. *Deliverance* for imprisoned promises can only be achieved if there has first been an act of delivery, one which has been experienced as such. Yet even before this can take place, something must first have left a deposit or precipitate and this is a still more originary act. A new event will awaken the secret or spectre sealed within this deposit and be haunted and possessed by it. It is one and the same movement which reawakens the past, recalling to mind its 'spirit' in the present, giving the present life, and which renders the present still-born, haunted by the past, alive in death, surviving.

So there are two lines, or lineages, two spaces of a time which double one another, continually follow one another: the line of traces ('phenomenal', as Kant would have qualified it) and the line of phantoms ('noumenal', in Kantian terms). An event occurs when the two lines intersect and one intercepts the other, when instead of lying on top of one another, two spaces cover each other and merge into one. When a ghost from the past comes (back) to haunt the present, this ghost is dissolved and consumed and in doing so gives life to a new present. Yet precisely because it does so, the present explodes in turn, it shatters, and from the fire of the event, smoke rises – which, when it dissipates, will reveal a heap of rubble and cooling ashes in which some captive 'spirit' lies awaiting rebirth in another form, at another moment.

3. Time *restores* itself: time is a series of impacts, which is to say a series of *jumps*. By definition, a jump jumps over, but never out of, the temporal flow or continuum. There is, plainly, a time-line which is causal or successive. This is what we are rightly accustomed to call the passage of time and is quite simply the repetition of the same which we discussed earlier. But there is another time-line – a dotted line – which jumps from point to point. An event, in fact, extracts itself from time – it is a *leap* in and of time. It interrupts time and even interrupts itself, though stopping short of self-contradiction. Every event is destined to be abortive, to remain still-born, to disappear as soon as it has appeared, to be fleeting, precarious and transient. For the same reason, however, it is destined to return, as though it hoped, on this occasion, finally, to fulfil and complete itself, to offer up its secrets and accomplish what it promised. Yet once more and for the same reason, the historical event abandons – until the next time – the task at hand and the fulfilment of its neglected promises. 'There is a secret agreement between past generations and the present one. Our coming was expected on earth. Like every generation that preceded us, we have been endowed with a *weak* Messianic power, a power to which the past has a claim.'[11]

All these jumps form a series which is both broken and continuous. A broken series, because there is nothing to stop one thinking that the most recent event will be the last there is; because there is nothing to stop one imagining that time will stop and cease to be given; because there is no guarantee that another event will assume the legacy of the promises made in a preceding one; a broken series, at an even deeper level, because an event is, by definition, broken, suspended, in suspense. A continuous sequence, however, because where there is an event, all events refer retrospectively to one another along a broken line and form a *tradition*. This tradition is, to be sure, suppressed, underground, clandestine. It can remain dead for an age, only to be reborn unexpectedly and in a new guise. It can remain secret or unknown and, come what may, it always remains 'hidden', to echo Hannah Arendt, because it is always covered over in the passage of time, either by forgetting or by commemoration. Yet this tradition is still the only way to save time in the kingdom of disenchantment.

A tradition *resumes* and *restores*. To restore is, in one respect, to defer, to put off the completion of a task or the fulfilment of a promise. It is an attempt to insure the present against the demands for payment which would encumber it, allowing it to remain free and sovereign both in relation to the legacy of the past and the promise for the future. Thus, in one respect, restoration increases both the risks and the opportunities. The present gains free space but at the same time runs the risk of arriving late, too late, when payment is due, that is, when the *present* moment arrives. But from a different angle, to restore is to deliver, to confide, and this implies the involvement of something or someone to whom restoration is made. Restoration connects – invisibly but definitively – the next moment to the one before, attaching the past to the present with gentle cunning. Restoration obliges the future to account for the deposit with which it has been entrusted and to assume it with fidelity. Restoration brings the future to pass, summoning it as of now, sooner than it would have wished, to the point where it becomes one with the present. Here too there is both opportunity and danger: opportunity, because this is probably the only way not of holding time in one's grasp but rather of summoning it and being sure that it will come. There is danger because this hidden undertaking can insulate from other obligations and impede recognition in other legacies.

This is why restoration must assert itself as renewal and remembrance as making-present. History presupposes neither the preservation nor the destruction of tradition, nor indeed the reproduction or abolition of time, but rather the *restoration of presents*. Every present (every situation) is in peril, either of returning to the same, or of disappearing without trace. Every present (every situation) is virtually lost to both itself and the future. Deferring to the next present can place it in mortal danger, for it can never be sure that another present will come. Yet this is its only chance of salvation. Should such a present 'brush history against the grain'[12] and by turning its back on time's arrow become entangled with the preceding moment, then do we have a chance to make it yield its secrets and release its ghosts which await salvation; it, in return, has the opportunity to be saved from the empty and intert temporality which threatens it. What we see here is neither succession nor linearity, but rather a loop, just as there is no eternity, but only a series of jumps or leaps from one instant to another. They form a 'broken sequence', in the shape of a circle.[13] Every present which encircles its precursor brings with it both enchantment and salvation. This is not lost time regained, nor is it a fragment of 'time in its unadulterated purity',[14] but rather, it is the capacity of every present to be an *act of salvation*: remembrance 'stripped the future of its magic [. . .] For every second of time [is] the strait gate through which the Messiah might enter.'[15]

Translated by Oliver Davis

Notes

1 Benjamin, 'Der Erzähler', *Gesammelte Schriften* (hereafter *GS*), vol. II, p. 456. Tr. by Harry Zohn, *Illuminations*, ed. by Hannah Arendt (London: Fontana, 1973).

2 Kant, *Critique of Pure Reason*, A 102. Tr. by Norman Kemp Smith (London: Macmillan, 1950).

3 On the concept of the *coup*, cf. Benjamin, 'Paris under the Second Empire in Baudelaire' (Frankfurt am Main: Suhrkamp, 1972), p. 14.

4 *Critique of Pure Reason*, 'Transcendental Deduction', A 99.

5 Here and elsewhere, Benjamin is close to Nietzsche. Cf. my 'Melancolia illa heroïca', in *Furor*, nos. 19–20 (Geneva: 1990), pp. 85–109.

6 'The Origins of the German Baroque Drama', *GS*, vol. I, p. 225.

7 It is music and not the narrative dear to Ricoeur which seems to me to produce time. Music is the hidden schema lying in the depths of narrative.

8 On the subject of music, see my *Kant, le ton de l'histoire* (Paris: Payot, 1990), ch. 9, 'L'art des sons'.

9 Cf. my 'Walter Benjamin, la littérature à temps', *Les Temps modernes*, nos. 529–30, 1990, pp. 28–47.

10 Benjamin, *GS*, vol. IV, p.142. English translation: 'Madame Ariane: Second Courtyard on the Left', from 'One-Way Street', in *Selected Writings*, vol. I, ed. by Marcus Bullock & Michael W. Jennings (Cambridge MA: Harvard University Press, 1996), p. 483.

11 Benjamin, 'Theses on the Philosophy of History', Thesis II, in *Illuminations*, op. cit., pp. 245–6.

12 Ibid., Thesis VII, p. 248.

13 This implies a certain way of writing history: if you want to employ the theatrical mode, then comedy; if you want to write a story, this will be a series of anecdotes or *tableaux*; if you want to write a philosophical treatise, then a series of theses.

14 This quotation (in the original, 'un peu de temps à l'état pur') is from Marcel Proust's *A la recherche du temps perdu*.

15 'Theses on the Philosophy of History', Thesis XVIII, op. cit., p. 255.

6

LUCE IRIGARAY

Luce Irigaray is a feminist philosopher and psychoanalyst, born in Belgium and attached to the CNRS, who has specialised in questions of sexual difference, language, alterity and the feminine. She published much of her early work in linguistics and this approach still underpins her most recent production, though psychoanalytic questions have also informed her work since the 1970s, and she taught a course in psychoanalysis at the University of Vincennes until 1974. Her work is influenced by German philosophy – Kant, Hegel, Heidegger, Nietzsche – as well as by Lacan and Derrida, whose work she also contests. She is associated with the 'écriture féminine' movement – which maintains the essential difference of women and their writing and refuses the patriarchal straitjacket of supposedly masculine rationality and logic – and is one of the most philosophical writers of that movement. Recurrent themes in her work include subjectivity, identity, death and desire.

Her major works include the following:

Le Langage des déments, The Hague: Mouton, 1973.

Speculum. De l'autre femme, Paris: Minuit, 1974.

Ce Sexe qui n'en est pas un, Paris: Minuit, 1977.

Et l'une ne bouge pas sans l'autre, Paris: Minuit, 1979.

Amante marine. De Friedrich Nietzsche, Paris: Minuit, 1980.

Le Corps-à-corps avec la mère, Montreal: La Pleine Lune, 1981.

Passions élémentaires, Paris: Minuit, 1982.

L'oubli de l'air chez Martin Heidegger, Paris: Minuit, 1983.

Éthique de la différence sexuelle, Paris: Minuit, 1984.

Parler n'est jamais neutre, Paris: Minuit, 1985.

Sexes et parentés, Paris: Minuit, 1987.

Le Temps de la différence: pour une révolution pacifique, Paris: Hachette, 1989.

Je, tu, nous, Paris: Grasset, 1990.

J'aime à toi, Paris: Grasset, 1992.

Le Souffle des femmes, Paris: ACGF, 1996.

Être deux, Paris: Grasset, 1997.

Entre Orient et occident, Paris: Grasset, 1999.

A Deux, nous avons combien d'yeux?, Russelheim: Christel Gottert Verlag, 2000.

THE QUESTION OF THE OTHER[†]

(*Democracy Begins Between Two*)

[*]Two uses of the term 'the other' should be distinguished throughout this chapter. The Italian 'l'altro' (masculine) appears without an asterisk; the more complex 'l'altro(a)', combining masculine and feminine, appears asterisked.

Western philosophy, perhaps all philosophies, have started from a singular subject. For centuries, no-one imagined that different subjects might exist and, more particularly, that man and woman might be different subjects.

Of course, from the late nineteenth century onwards, attention turned increasingly to the question of the other. The philosophical subject, by now more sociological in nature, became a little less imperialistic. The existence of identities different from his own was admitted: children, for example, or mad people, savages and workers.

Certain empirical differences were, then, to be respected; not everyone was the same and it was therefore important to be a little more attentive to others and to what made them different. Yet the fundamental model of the human being remained unchanged: one, singular, solitary and historically masculine; that of the adult Western male, rational, competent. Diversity was therefore still conceived of and lived hierarchically, with the many always subordinate to the one. Others were nothing but copies of the idea of man, a potentially perfect idea which all the more or less imperfect copies had to try to equal. These copies, moreover, were not defined in their own terms, in other words, according to a different subjectivity, but in those of an ideal subjectivity and as a function of their deficiencies with respect to it: age, race, culture, sex, etc. The model of the subject thus remained singular, and the 'others' represented more or less good examples within the hierarchy established in relation to the singular subject.

This philosophical model corresponds, in fact, to the political model of a single leader, judged the best, and the only one capable of governing more or less civil citizens possessed of a more or less human identity.

Such a conception of the other perhaps explains Simone de Beauvoir's refusal to be treated as an other[*]. Since she does not, as a woman, accept coming 'second' to the male subject, she claims subjective status as man's equal, as the same or similar to him.

[†]Seminar held at the University of Verona at the invitation of 'Ariadne's Thread' and of the Department of Philosophy (30 April 1994).

On a philosophical level, this demand implies a return to the singular subject, historically masculine, and the cancellation of the possibility of any subjectivity other than man's. Although Simone de Beauvoir's critical work on the devalorization of woman as culturally 'secondary' is often accurate, her refusal to consider the question of woman as 'other'* represents philosophically, and even politically, a significant regression. Her position is, in fact, retrograde as regards those of certain [male] philosophers who enquire into the possibility of relations between two or different subjects: existentialists, personalists or more political philosophers; and it is also less driven by that of women who are struggling for the recognition of an identity of their own.

Simone de Beauvoir's positive proposals contain, in my opinion, a theoretical and practical error inasmuch as they imply the negation of an other* of an equivalent value to that of the masculine subject.

The other: woman

My work on female subjectivity develops in the opposite direction to that of Simone de Beauvoir's work as regards the question of the other*.

Instead of saying as she does: I do not wish to be the other* of the masculine subject and, in order to escape this secondary position, I claim to be equal to him, I argue: the question of who the other is has not been well formulated in the Western tradition, in which the other is always the other of a singular subject and not another subject, irreducible to the masculine subject and of equal dignity.

This means that in our tradition there has not yet really existed an other for the philosophical subject and more generally, for the cultural and political subject.

> In the subtitle of *Speculum of the Other Woman*, – the other is to be understood above all as a noun. In French, but also in other languages such as Italian and English, this noun is usually read as designating both man and woman. In this subtitle, I wanted to indicate that, in reality, the other is not neutral, neither grammatically nor semantically, and that it is not, no longer, possible to use the same term, in an undifferentiated way, to refer to the masculine and the feminine. Now this is, in fact, what happens in philosophy, religion and politics. The existence of the other, love of the other, concern for the other, etc. are evoked, without the question of who or what this other represents being asked. The lack of definition of the alterity of the other has paralysed thought, the dialectical method included, in an idealistic dream appropriate to a single (masculine) subject, in the illusion of a singular absolute, leaving religion and politics to an empiricism fundamentally lacking in ethics insofar as respect between individuals is concerned. In fact, if the other is not defined in his actual reality, he remains another me, and not a real other. In this case, he can be *more* or *less* than I, he can have more or less than I have. The Other can thus represent absolute greatness and perfection: God, Master, Logos; he can designate the smallest or the most vulnerable: children, sick people, poor people, strangers; he can name the one whom I believe equal to me. In all of this, there is not really any other, but rather only the same: smaller, greater, equal to me.
>
> (*I Love To You*, p. 61)

Rather than refusing, as Simone de Beauvoir does, to be the other gender, the other sex, I am asking to be recognized as really an other*, irreducible to the masculine subject. I can now see just how much the subtitle of *Speculum* may have irritated Simone de Beauvoir: *Of the other as woman*. At that time I sent her my book in good faith, hoping for her support with the difficulties that I was facing at that point. I never received an answer and it was only recently that I understood the reason for her silence. Probably I offended her without wishing to. I had read the Introduction to *The Second Sex* long before I wrote *Speculum*, and I didn't remember what the problematic of the other in her work was. Perhaps she didn't understand that, for me, it wasn't a question of admitting that my sex and gender should remain 'second', but of wanting the sexes and the genders to become two, without there being a first or a second.

I was pursuing, in my way, and unaware of their work, a goal which was closer to that of militant American neo-feminism, a feminism that promotes difference, one more closely related to the cultural revolution of 1968 than the egalitarian feminism of Simone de Beauvoir. Let us recall, briefly, what is at stake here: the exploitation and the alienation of women are located in the difference between the sexes and the genders, and have to be resolved in that difference, without trying to abolish it, which would amount to yet another reduction to the singular subject. In *Speculum* what I am interpreting and criticizing is precisely the fact that the philosophical subject, historically masculine, has reduced every other to a relation with himself – his nature, his universe, his complement, his projection, his inverse, his instrument . . . – within his own world, his own horizon.

Whether it is a question of Freud's work or of the most important philosophical systems of our tradition, I try to reveal how the other always remains the other of the subject himself, and not a real other.

So the criticisms which I level at Freud all come back to the same interpretation: he views the sexuality and, more generally the identity, of the little girl, the adolescent girl and the woman solely in terms of the sexuality and identity of the little boy, the adolescent boy and the man.

According to Freud, for example, the auto-eroticism of the little girl lasts for as long as she confuses her own clitoris with a little penis, for as long as she imagines she has the same sex organ as the little boy. When she discovers through the mother, that the woman does not have the male sex organ, the little girl renounces her own feminine identity and turns to the father, to the man, to obtain the penis through them. All her energy is from now on, according to Freud, engaged in acquiring the male sex organ. Even conceiving and giving birth to a child correspond, in his view, to a desire to appropriate the penis or the phallus and, for this reason, the birth of a male child is preferable to that of a baby girl. For Freud, no marriage can be happy, and no woman a good wife, without the birth of a male child.

Nowadays such a description would make some of the women here, and even some of the men, laugh. Yet a few years ago, not even twenty, any woman who pointed out the frightening machismo of our culture was laughed at, and excluded from teaching in the university. But things are not yet as clear as it may seem. Agreed, we are no longer completely in the Dark Ages but, if Freudian theory is macho, this is because it reproduces our sociocultural order. In a sense Freud did not invent machismo, he simply described it. His mistake – as, too, Simone de Beauvoir's – concerns how to overcome it. Neither she nor he recognize the other as other and, in different ways, both propose retaining the man as the subjective model whom woman should, so to speak, try to 'equal'. For Freud and Simone de Beauvoir, man and woman, by different strategies, should become alike. This ideal remains obedient to that of traditional philosophy which imposes a singular model of subjectivity, historically masculine.

This singular model can, at best, allow for an oscillation between the *one* and the *many*, but the one remains more or less obviously in charge of the hierarchy of the many: the singular is unique and/but ideal, Man. Concrete singularity is only a copy, an image.

Plato's vision of the world, his conception of truth, is in a way an inversion of the empirical reality of everyday. You believe that you are real, a singular truth but, in fact, you are only a more or less accurate copy of a perfect idea situated outside you.

Here again, before laughing too soon, we have to consider the continuing relevance of such a conception of the world. We are children of the flesh but also of the word, we are nature but also culture. Now, if we are children of culture, we are children of the idea, that is, more or less appropriate incarnations of an ideal model. Often, in order to draw closer to it, we mime, imitate, like children, what we perceive as an ideal. All these ways of saying and doing derive from a Platonic matrix, are the inheritance of a masculine idea of the truth. Even in the reversal which the privilege of the many over the one represents, a contemporary reversal in the name, amongst other things, of democracy, even in the privileging of the other over the subject, that of the *thou* with respect to the *I* (I am thinking, for example, of some of Buber's writings and of a part of Levinas' work, where such privileging is more moral and theological, perhaps, than philosophical), we remain subjected to a blind model of the one and the many, of the one and the same, a model on which a singular subject imposes one sense rather than an other. Similarly, granting precedence to concrete singularity over ideal singularity is inadequate in challenging the authority of a universal valid for all men and all women. In reality, no concrete singularity can designate an ideal valid for all men and all women, and to ensure the coexistence of subjects, particularly on the civil level, a minimum of universality is necessary.

If we are to get away from the omnipotent model of the one and the many, we have to move on to the *two*, a two which is not two times one itself, not even a bigger or a smaller one, but which would be made up of *two* which are really different. The paradigm of this two is to be found in sexual difference. Why here? Because it implies two subjects who should not be situated in either a hierarchical or a genealogical relationship, and that these two subjects have the duty of preserving the human species and of developing its culture, while respecting their differences.

My first theoretical gesture was thus *to free the two from the one*, the two from the many, the other from the same, and to do this in a horizontal way by suspending the authority of the One: of man, of the father, of the leader, of the one god, of the unique truth, etc. It was a question of releasing the other from the same, of refusing to be reduced to the other* of the same, to an other (male) or an other (female) of the one, not becoming him, or like him, but constituting myself as an autonomous and different subject.

Obviously this gesture challenges our entire theoretical and practical tradition, and particularly Platonism, but without such a gesture we cannot speak of women's liberation, nor of ethical behaviour with regard to the other, nor of democracy. Without such a gesture philosophy itself risks suffocating, defeated by, amongst other things, the use of techniques which, since the origin and in the construction of the logos itself, threaten and undermine man's subjectivity, a victory which will be that much easier and more rapid in that woman no longer ensures the pole of nature which resists masculine *techné*.

Only the existence of two subjects can lead the masculine subject back to his own being, and this would be possible if woman had access to hers.

For this reason, it was necessary to free the feminine subject from the world of man, and to acknowledge this scandal for philosophy: the subject is neither one nor singular, but is two.

The mediations needed by the feminine subject

It was essential to ensure that this barely defined feminine subject, lacking contours and edges, with neither norms nor mediations, have some points of reference, some guarantees, in order to nourish her and to protect her own becoming. After the critical phase of my work – a critique addressed to a monosubjective, monosexual, patriarchal and phallocratic philosophy and culture, – I tried to define the characteristics of the feminine subject, characteristics which are indispensable to her affirmation as such, to avoid falling back into a lack of differentiation or into subjection to a singular subject.

One of the crucial means of assisting the becoming of the feminine subject, and thus my own becoming, was to escape from a single genealogical power, to affirm: I am born of man *and* of woman, and genealogical authority belongs to man *and* to woman.

Female genealogies had to be disinterred from oblivion, not simply to eliminate the existence of the father, in a kind of reversal dear to the most recent philosophers, but to return to the reality of the *two*. But it is true that it takes time to rediscover and re-establish this two and it cannot be the work of one woman only.

Besides rediscovering and being reconciled with female genealogies, it was necessary to give woman, women, a language, images and representations which were appropriate to them: on a cultural, and also on a religious, level, since 'God' has always been an important accomplice of the philosophical subject. I began to carry out this work in *Speculum, This Sex Which Is Not One, Sexes and Genealogies, Thinking the Difference* and in *Je, Tu, Nous*. In these works, I discuss the characteristics of a world in the feminine, a world different from that of man as regards relationships with language, with the body (age, health, beauty and, obviously, maternity), and relationships with work, nature, culture. Two examples: I try to show how life unfolds differently for woman than for man, in that her physical becoming is marked by more crucial stages – puberty, loss of virginity, maternity, menopause, – stages requiring a more complex becoming than that of man. A further example: in the context of work, I maintain, with the support of evidence, that socio-economic justice cannot be limited to the application of the rule: equal work for equal pay. This rule is not, in fact, applied though it also implies respect for, and valorization of, women as regards the choice of means and ends in production, as of professional qualifications, relationships in the workplace, etc.

In these books I also initiated a discourse on the necessity of specific rights for women. As I have written, women's liberation cannot develop unless it goes beyond this stage, which is indispensable both for social recognition and individual growth, and for community relationships, between women and between women and men. My juridical proposals aroused interest and mistrust: interest on the part of women who are not specialists in jurisprudence who recognize the importance of rights for themselves, interest also on the part of feminists in certain countries who, for a long time, have been concerned with juridical mediation as a step towards the liberation of humanity, and particularly of women.

Two currents of women's thought oppose this perspective. Women in favour of equality generally fail to appreciate why positive rights for women are necessary.

They fight to obtain rights equal to those of men, they struggle against discrimination but they neglect the fact that some of the choices which women have to make are different from men's, and that such choices cannot remain individual or private but have to be protected by law. I'm thinking, for example, of the freedom of choice in work patterns, but also in matters of sexuality, or reproduction, concerning custody of the children in the case of divorce or separation and, more generally, in the framework of intercultural marriages where the diversity of customs often makes matters problematic.

In my opinion, the lack of positive rights appropriate to women prevents them moving from a state of nature to civil status. Most of them still remain nature-bodies, subjected to State, Church, father and husband, lacking the statute of civil persons responsible for themselves and for the community.

Even women more in tune with the culture and politics of difference deny the need for civil rights specific to women because they fear the law as an instrument ensuring submission to the State. On the contrary, civil rights for individuals represent a guarantee for male and female citizens, because they allow them to oppose the authority of the State. They maintain a tension between individuals and the State, and can ensure the passage from a society of a state-dominated kind to a civil society, whose democratic character would be preserved by individual rights for its members.

I hope that women will understand and pursue the goal of individual rights, both because such rights are necessary to them to protect and affirm their own identity, and because they are better prepared, as feminine subjects, to be interested in rights relating to individuals and to relationships between them, rather than simply in those which make up the bulk of masculine civil codes: rights of possession, of property ownership, of having as regards goods. What needs to be done is to complete already existing civil codes, constitutions and the Universal Declaration of Human Rights by adding rights for women and rights devised by women's spirit [genio femminile], that is, beyond sexed specificity, rights for male and female citizens as individuals.

The other: man

The uniqueness of this feminine spirit brings me back, in the final part of this talk, to the question of the other. Now that she has become an autonomous subject, woman, too, is obliged to situate herself in relation to the other, and the specificity of her identity leads her to privilege far more than man does the dimension of alterity in the process of subjective becoming. According to tradition, woman is the custodian of love, and is obliged to love, and in spite of all the misfortunes of love, without being given any reason for such a task.

I will certainly not become an accomplice to this kind of obligation with regard to love, nor to that duty with regard to hate which, it seems to me, is its complementary principle.

I prefer to pass on to you results obtained from research into how women speak, and to put forward an interpretation of the characteristics of a language in female mode (cf. *I Love To You*).

The language which pays most attention to the other is that of the little girl. She addresses the other – in my sample, the mother – asking for an agreement to do something together: 'Mamma, can I play with you?', 'Mamma, can I comb your hair?' In such statements, the little girl always respects the existence of two subjects, both of whom have the right to speak. In addition, what she proposes is an activity involving two subjects. The young girl could be a model for both, including the mother, who addresses her daughter with words like these: 'Tidy up before you watch TV', 'Bring me some milk on your way back from school'.

The mother gives her daughter instructions with no thought of a right to speech for both subjects, nor does she invite any shared activity, involving two subjects. Strangely, the mother speaks to her little boy in a different fashion, showing more respect for his identity: 'Do you want me to come and kiss you goodnight before you go to sleep?' As for the little boy, he already speaks like a little leader: 'I want to play ball, I want a little car'. Somehow the mother communicates to the little boy the *thou* that her daughter has given her.

Why such a taste for dialogue on the part of the little girl? Perhaps because as a woman, born of woman, with the properties and qualities of a woman, including those associated with giving birth, the little girl finds herself, from birth, better placed to enter into a relationship involving two subjects. This would explain her games with dolls, to whom she addresses a nostalgia for dialogue often left unsatisfied by the mother.

But the little girl will lose this, her first, feminine, partner in dialogue, as a result of her entry into a culture in which the subject is always masculine – he, He, they – whether it is a question of linguistic gender in the narrow sense or of various metaphors which supposedly represent human identity and its becoming.

Despite this, neither the little girl nor the adolescent girl renounces the relationship with the other, which they almost always prefer to the relationship with the object. Thus, when they are asked to form a sentence containing the preposition *with*, or the adverb *together*, female adolescents and students, and most adult women, will answer with statements like the following: 'I'll go out with him tonight', 'We'll always live together'; male subjects, for their part, tend to say: 'I came by [Ital. *con*] motor bike', 'I wrote this sentence with my pen', 'We get on well together, my guitar and I'.

A difference of this sort between the statements of subjects of the female gender and those of the male gender is expressed in one way or another in most of the replies given to questions whose aim was to define the sexed characteristics of language (this research is being carried out in various languages and cultures, in particular, the Romance and Anglo-Saxon ones).

Besides the alternation between the male choice of the subject–object relation and the female choice of the subject–subject relation, other characteristics can be noted. Women privilege the present or the future tenses, contiguity, the concrete context, relationships based in difference, being together, being-two; men, on the other hand, privilege the past tense, a metaphorical use of language, abstract transposition, relations between like and like by way of the object, relationships between the one and the many.

Women and men rely, then, on different subjective configurations and ways of speaking. These cannot be attributed solely to socio-historical determinations, nor to an alienation of the feminine which is to be overcome by making it equal to the masculine. Women's language does, of course, give signs of a degree of alienation and inertia, but it also demonstrates a richness of its own which has nothing to envy in men's language; and, particularly a taste for intersubjectivity which is definitely not to be abandoned in favour of the subject–object relation dear to men.

How could the feminine subject – and, first and foremost, myself – cultivate sharing with the other without becoming alienated? The gesture to be made here corresponds to the one already made at the time of *Speculum*: practising respect for the other as other. I live, we live, as women, a nostalgia for dialogue and relationship. But have we yet reached the point of recognizing the other as other, and of addressing him or her as such? Not really, not yet. The words of adolescent girls and of women do, indeed, reveal a tendency to favour the relationship with the other, but the desire for the *I–thou* relationship does not always care who *thou* is, nor what *thou* might desire.

Thus the female subject privileges the relation with the other gender, which the masculine subject does not do. This prioritizing of the masculine as partner in dialogue is proof, on the one hand, of cultural alienation and demonstrates, on the other, various characteristics of the feminine subject. Woman knows the other gender better: she engenders it within herself, she mothers it from birth, she nourishes it from her own body, she lives it inside herself in love. Her relationship to the transcendence of the other therefore constitutes itself differently with regard to man, for whom the other always remains outside the subject; and for whom transcendence of the other is marked by a mystery and an ambivalence associated with the problem of the origin, whether maternal or paternal. Woman's relation to man is linked to a carnal sharing, to an experience of the sensibility, to an immanence that is lived, even in the producing of children. The alterity of the other imposes itself on her because of the extraneity of his behaviour, and because of the resistance which he opposes to her own dreams and intentions. But she must constitute the transcendence of the other in a horizontal way, through a sharing of life which respects absolutely the other as other, beyond any intuition, any sense perception, any experiencing and knowledge. Women's inclination to dialogue runs the risk of reducing the other to a modality of herself unless she constructs the transcendence of the other as such, his irreducibility to herself through fusion, contiguity, empathy, mimetism, etc.

In *To Be Two* and *I Love To You* I've tried to open a path towards such a construction of the transcendence of the other. I have shown how the operation of the negative, which typically intervenes with a dialectic movement between self and self in order to reach a more spiritually evolved and cultivated becoming, ought to operate between two subjects, to prevent the reduction of the *two* to the *one*, of the other to the same.

Of course, the negative still intervenes in the development of my own subjectivity, but to delineate the irreducibility of the other to myself, and not to reduce its exteriority to myself. The subject, by a gesture of this kind, renounces being one and singular; instead, it respects the two in the intersubjective relation.

A gesture of this sort must intervene above all in the relation between the genders because alterity there is real and enables a new articulation of the relationship between nature and culture, in a more truthful and ethical way. It would thus be possible to overcome the guilt on which our culture is founded, which Hegel uncovered in speaking of the rejection and death of Antigone (*Phenomenology of Spirit*, Chap. VI).

The historical accomplishment of this passage from the subject as one and singular to the existence of two subjects of equivalent value and dignity seems to me an appropriate task for women as regards both philosophy and politics. Women, as I have already mentioned, are better able to commit themselves to a relationship between two, to the relationship with the other. Their subjectivity allows them to open up again the horizon of the one, the similar, and even of the many, in order to present themselves as an other subject, and to impose a two which is not a 'second'. Accomplishing one's own liberation implies, moreover, the recognition of the other as other to avoid the closing of the circle around the singular subject.

Recognizing man as an other thus represents not only an ethical task appropriate to women, but also an indispensable step towards the acquisition of their autonomy. The necessary deployment of the negative to respect the alterity of the other allows them to leave a solely natural identity behind and to accede to a civil identity without denying their own nature, thanks to their faithfulness to a gender identity.

All relationships with the other now involve a negative: in language, of course – for example; 'I love to you' and not 'I love you' – but also in perceiving, in listening, in touching. In *To Be Two* I try to define a new way of approaching the other, emphasizing how we can caress each other without losing either the *I* or the *thou*.

Carrying out this revolution, which goes from affirming the self as other to recognizing man as other, is a gesture which will then permit all the various forms of alterity to be respected without authority or hierarchy, whether one is dealing with race, age, culture, religion, etc.

Substituting the *two* for the *one* in sexual difference corresponds, then, to a decisive philosophical and political gesture, one which renounces being *one or many* in favour of *being-two* as the necessary foundation of a new ontology, a new ethics and a new politics in which the other is recognized as other and not as the same: greater, smaller, at best equal to me.

Part 2

BORDERS OF THE HUMAN SUBJECT

INTRODUCTION

The five essays in this section, published between 1986 and 1998, consider the ontological question of the nature of the subject from perspectives offered at its margins. It is in relation to its Other, be that the deficient humanity of women described by Aristotle and Kant, or the non-humanity of animals explored by philosophers from the Greek pre-Socratics through to the late twentieth century, that the question of the subject can best be approached. In other words, it is alterity that paradoxically but necessarily provides the most pertinent understanding of identity, just as it is death that provides the essential tools for an understanding of life.

Barbara Cassin takes us to the heart of the matter in her account of the contrasting analyses of human nature offered by Aristotle and Kant. Her essay, taken from *Aristote et le logos: Contes de la phénoménologie ordinaire*, explores the question as it is understood by Aristotle, Kant and Plato, amongst others. Cassin problematises the traditional opposition between an Aristotle who understands excellence as the perfection of our human nature and a Kant who understands merit as a fight against the natural. Through an analysis of Aristotle's claims concerning the 'natures' of masters and slaves, men and women, children and adults, and an exploration of Kant's conception of radical evil (and the extent to which that is, or is not, 'natural'), Cassin argues for a reappraisal of the opposition, and a serious reconsideration of the extent to which human nature can be seen as 'natural'. In her account, Aristotle is already critical of the concept of nature in an arguably stronger sense than Kant. For him, as for the Sophists, ethics and politics are not natural. Cassin's deconstruction of the opposition between Aristotle and Kant, excellence and merit, human nature and freedom, has led to a privileging of the political over the ethical, and a new understanding of the roots of democracy. Women, children and slaves are no longer excluded 'by nature' from the logos, nor, by extension, from the realm of the political.

Natalie Depraz also turns to Kant in her reading of Husserl's phenomenological perspective on imagination; her essay is drawn from the book in English on Husserl which she co-edited with Dan Zahavi. In it she proposes an interpretation of a certain form of imaginative passivity and self-alterity which allows us to avoid an exclusively ontic understanding of the world and to recognise the further possibilities of reality. Depraz argues against both the understanding of the passivity of imagination in terms of pure receptivity *and* against the view that, unlike perception, imagination is necessarily active and spontaneous. She also argues against Sartre's conception of imagination as a form of captive consciousness and against what she sees as

Merleau-Ponty's muddying of the waters and loss of conceptual rigour in his view of the inter-dependance of passivity and activity. Depraz describes three phenomenological meanings of passivity, all of which contain an element of alterity and reveal the self-alterity of individual consciousness. Indeed, in her sense, passivity implies not only an affective alterity within the self but also the 'experience of communitarian lived experience as sedimented deposits'. It is far from the suffered receptivity which the term might at first evoke, and involves rather an openness to the other which contributes to the overcoming of the individual I. In Depraz's terms: 'Being passive means being able to be completely open towards the other, to welcome him in full awareness: thus, you keep up with yourself at the very moment when you seem to be totally lost in the other and precisely *because* you are fully lost in the other.' Such a mode of being is 'deeply determined by self-alterity' 'which permeates the self at both the individual and at the communitarian level'. Depraz's final move is to link this imaginative passivity to freedom and to describe it as what enables us 'to resist the tendency to ontify our world'. The fixed borders between the faculties, between passivity and activity, and between the individual self and the other are thus put in question by Depraz through her meditation on imagination as it has been analysed by Kant and Husserl in a highly fruitful form of cross-relationship.

The next essay constitutes the final chapter of Dastur's work *Death: an essay on finitude*, in which she elaborates a Heideggerian phenomenology of mortality in opposition to a Sartrean approach. Dastur rejects Sartre's claim that death is not so much 'my possibility' as that which nihilates my possibilities, a claim which she sees as wrongly interpreting the human in terms of the brute facticity of nature. Dastur contrasts the biological notion of fulfilment, which applies to animals who reproduce themselves in their necessary perfection, with human fulfil-ment, which is never complete. Death can never come to a human being at the right time, when he or she has fulfilled all his or her possibilities: there could always have been more to achieve. Similarly, *Dasein* is always necessarily finite, constituted essentially rather than contingently by its birth and death. 'For it is not *despite* finitude and mortality that there is transcendence', argues Dastur. Death is not, as Sartre would have it, an accidental interruption and imperfec-tion of human life, but rather its foundational finitude. Dastur concludes with a brief discussion of language and laughter. Language enables us both to take a stand against death at the same time as radically revealing our finitude, in so far as it both separates us from being and binds us to it by enshrining absence and alterity. Anxiety itself, she argues, is equally double-edged, linked not only to death but also to laughter which explodes precisely 'when nothing fixed remains' and we find ourselves 'released into that more than human lightness by which existence as burden is transformed into grace'.

Elisabeth de Fontenay's essay on Kant is drawn from her extensive exploration of the ways in which philosophers have understood animality since Antiquity, and provides an unusual perspective on the history of philosophy, which complements that of Cassin and Depraz. Fontenay's essay on Kant's understanding of animals is drawn from her huge tome, *Le Silence des bêtes*, which comprises seventy-five chapters and covers over one hundred philosophers, ranging historically from the pre-Socratics, Plato and Aristotle to Derrida, Levinas and Françoise Dastur. Fontenay's own position, as outlined in her Introduction, involves a refusal of a radical break between animal and human, and an espousal of the notion of a gradation or continuity, which she traces back from Diderot to Leibniz via Buffon. In this chapter, Fontenay explores Kant's writings on animals and finds a discrepancy between his explicit refusal of any human duty towards animals, which, 'like potatoes', may be cultivated and 'which exist only as means', and the more enlightened vitalism and teleology that can be found elsewhere in his works. But Fontenay is not, of course, concerned with animals only for their own sake. Kant's attitude to animals has profound implications for his attitude to human beings also, and Fontenay asks whether an insistence on the specificity of the human and human rationality does not exclude the mentally deficient 'Cretins of Wales' (as Kant calls them) from the domain of the human because of their 'absence of soul'. It is painfully clear here that the sharp barrier between humans and animals risks breaking down, or indeed putting some people on the wrong side of the dividing line. Fontenay suggests that duty and respect, and even friendship, which Kant restricts to other human beings, should be extended to animals who are not, in Kant's view, subjects any more than they are the 'end' of nature, but who are part of a natural continuity with the human.

Françoise Héritier offers one of several essays in this volume specifically concerned with gender, from a descriptive, anthropological perspective. She examines the construction of gender as it has been manifest in thinking as diverse as that of Aristotle and the Inuit people, and argues that the idea of sexual difference structures human thought at its most basic level, in so far as it inaugurates the two primordial concepts of identity and difference. Consequently, she maintains, any change in the relationship between masculine and feminine will have profound repercussions, not only for human society and identity, but also for human thought. Héritier is interested in particular in the primacy of the symbolic in kinship relations, and this is the focus of one of her best known works on *Les deux soeurs et leur mère: anthropologie de l'inceste* (1994). The present extract comes however from *Masculin/féminin: la pensée de la différence* (1996), where Héritier explores similarities and differences in the way in which gender is constructed in ancient philosophical theories such as that of Aristotle, and more recent models such as those of the Sambians in New Guinea or of the Inuits (or Eskimos). Whereas Aristotle envisages the female infant as a deviant and 'monstrous' derivative of the male, the Sambians consider femininity to be complete and natural and masculinity to be acquired. For the Sambians, biological sex is not enough to ensure masculine gender, which depends on practices of insemination through fellatio from the age of seven onwards. The case of the Inuits is more complicated: for them, apparent biological sex may be misleading since the child is viewed as a reincarnation of an ancestor who may be of either sex and is raised accordingly till puberty, after which biological sex progressively comes to dominate. Such studies show that the determination of gender is not merely a matter of biology, but rather a function of the symbolic order. In Aristotle, for example, everything results from the prior oppositions between hot and cold, dry and moist, active and passive, potentiality and matter. And Héritier concludes by demonstrating that, contrary perhaps to what we might expect, such a mode of thought is far from alien to the discourse of contemporary science, which still speaks (in 1984) of the 'inert' and 'incapable' female cell that has to be 'activated' by the male cell with its 'vitalising potentiality'.

Despite their relative diversity of ostensible theme, the essays in this section once again reveal a preoccupation with the way in which human identity cannot be understood in isolation, and show the other, be it animality, femininity or death, as a key to the understanding of what may traditionally have been viewed as self-sufficient and self-identical.

7

BARBARA CASSIN

Barbara Cassin is a philosopher, philologist and specialist of Ancient Greece, working in particular on Parmenides, the Sophists and Aristotle. She worked with Martin Heidegger and René Char in 1969, and later with Pierre Aubenque at the Sorbonne. She is also actively interested in psychoanalysis and worked with Jacques Lacan in the 1970s. She is Director of Research at the CNRS and Associate at the Collège International de Philosophie. She has translated works by Hannah Arendt and Peter Szondi and is currently running an international research group that is working on a dictionary of untranslatable terms from European philosophy. Her most recent publication is a beautifully illustrated book that discusses a vast range of appearances of the figure of Helen in literature, philosophy, psychoanalysis and art throughout the ages.

Her major works include the following:

Le Plaisir de parler (ed.), Paris: Minuit, 1986.

Positions de la sophistique (ed.), Paris: Vrin, 1986.

Nos Grecs et leurs modernes (ed.), Paris: Seuil, 1991.

L'Effet sophistique, Paris: Gallimard, 1995.

Aristote et le logos: Contes de la phénoménologie ordinaire, Paris: PUF, 1997.

Parménide d'Elée etc, Paris: Seuil, 1998.

Voir Hélène en toute femme: d'Homère à Lacan, Paris: Institut d'édition Sanofi-Synthélabo, 2000. (Illustrated by Maurice Matieu.)

ARISTOTLE WITH AND AGAINST
KANT ON THE IDEA OF
HUMAN NATURE

What is there of Aristotle in the questions which preoccupy us today?

Aristotle is a model of the Phenomenologically Correct. *'Correct' not only in the ontological ease with which he describes the world as it is, offering a phenomeno-logy in which things, movements of the soul and the sounds of the voice coincide naturally. But 'correct', too, in a practical sense: for the men he describes live together in a shared world which is both poetically and politically 'presentable', that is, proper, respectable.*

This book probes this neat characterization, focussing on the inconsistences and hiatuses which the too-honest Aristotle never tries to hide. To describe the world? But there seems to be a gap between what we feel and what we describe, between the logic of feeling and that of the sentence. To speak as a man? But there are some men, the Sophists, slaves, women, for whom this does not go without saying.

By following the red thread of the logos *through Aristotle's work, we find that he works both with and against the leaps and transitions which the Greek language allows – a language which tends to be described, a little too hastily, as always already phenomenological.*

The Aristotle who emerges encourages us to be less easily taken in by the tales of ordinary phenomenology.[1]

* * *

Aristotle: 'Reason and thought is the ultimate end of our nature' (*ho de logos hêmin kai ho nous tês phuseôs telos*).[2] Kant: 'rational nature exists as an end in itself'.[3] Nature, end, reason, *nous*, rational nature – it seems that Aristotle and Kant are making use of the same ingredients and, what is more, the same kind of argumentative move, whereby what is given is also what we must strive to attain. I would like, with the assistance of Kant and in the light of certain of the uses to which Aristotle is put today, to return to this idea of 'human nature' (uncertain, as I am, whether it is anachronistic or timeless), an idea which lies at the the very heart of Aristotelian thinking about politics and education ('lead to the *logos* by way of the *logos*'), in the hope of gaining a clearer understanding of its meaning.

Never before has greater use been made of Aristotle's practical philosophy. Aristotelians are abundant, at least in this particular domain; Neo-Aristotelianism has become a political isssue, at times even a burning issue in its contemporary relevance, whether one is for or against, whether one finds in it the necessary conditions of real democracy or sees it as the symptom of an arid conservatism.[4] The debate began in Germany and has since spread to the Anglo-American world. The Italians, more so than the French, currently occupy the impartial observer's position and are able to assess, wisely and in full knowledge of the facts, the lineage and authenticity of the Aristotelianism in the various positions.[5]

What I find striking about this 'Neo-Aristotelianism' is the philosophically contradictory use which it makes of the term 'practical philosophy'. This contradiction does not correspond – as is broadly the case with other tensions in this movement – to the difference between the analytic and hermeneutic traditions. Rather, this contradiction, which crosses the boundaries between traditions, is more as follows: on some occasions, Aristotle is presented as a way out, a happy alternative to the unlivable rigidity of Kantian formalism and one which deserves to be championed once again. Yet on other occasions, Aristotelian prudence and free choice have been considered evidence of an intuition approaching Kant's, of the will and its freedom, but one which is capable of tempering and perfecting the life of practical reason. Thus two quite different ends and means are bound up in today's insistence on the importance of Aristotelian ethics. This either forms part of a reappraisal of the past, a reaction against Kantian modernity in its various incarnations, an attempt to rediscover ourselves as differently (or other than) Modern – and attempt in which Aristotle is definitively pre- (that is, non-) Kantian: Aristotle against Kant. Or, on the other hand, in a syncretic blueprint for the future, whereby Aristotle can help us become what we, in any event, are striving to be: Kantians, only a little more comfortable; here, Aristotle is a post-Kantian, Aristotle is with Kant.

It is worth adding that what these two alternatives clearly have in common (irrespective of their particular decisions and methods) is a concern with what we might call, along the lines of the rediscovery of 'everyday language', the recapture of everyday practical experience: an ethics in and of the quotidian. We could, accordingly, ask whether this is not in fact something approaching a sign of the times, a sign which is perhaps alone sufficient to allow these times to be characterized, if not as Aristotelian, then at least as 'Aristotelizing'.

Aristotle and Kant: two incommensurables?

To think Aristotle-and-Kant must surely be the common project shared both by those whose use of Aristotle is designed to perfect Kant and by those who would work Aristotle to Kant's undoing. Yet not even this initial assumption goes without saying. 'Any discussion of the notion of *proairesis* which proceeds in terms of the problem of the "freedom of the will" is doomed to look for things in Aristotle's work that are not there and to miss what is there.'[6] Implicit in this remark by Pierre Aubenque is an entire thesis on (or of) the history of philosophy, one which is attuned to to the incommensurability of what, after Heidegger, may be called different 'epochs'. There is a danger of our completely misunderstanding both thinkers if we attempt to measure Aristotle and Kant by the same yardstick, to place them side by side, even to recompose or perfect one with the aid of the other, as though they were contemporaries, or colleagues, both speaking to us of the same things. Or such is the tenor of the complaints, *mutatis mutandis*, addressed by philosophers from what is known as the hermeneutic tradition to those from the so-called analytic tradition, when the latter, convinced of both the unity of reason and the inevitability of its advancement, endeavour to correct, for example, the formulations and proofs of the principle of non-contradiction with the help of advances in propositional logic made by Frege, Peano and Russell.[7] Yet on this occasion, it is Arendt and Gadamer,[8] no less than MacIntyre and Nussbaum,[9] who emphasize, each in their own way, by turns the conflict between and the complementarity of 'Aristotle-and-Kant'. Before we get swept along on this particular tide, let us attempt to specify those considerations which can (or should) hold it in check.

'Excellence', 'merit' and 'authenticity': these are the characteristics which define the sequence of the 'three ages of ethical thought'.[10] Luc Ferry has done well to state simply something that we all knew but which, nonetheless, there is a tendency, or a desire, to forget in discussions of 'practical philosophy' entangled between Aristotle and Kant. According to Ferry, to speak of excellence (*arêtê*) is to say that Classical morality only makes sense in the context of a certain world-view, a 'nature which determines the ends of man and in so doing orientates his ethics' (p. 334). But we no longer all live in the same, shared, world. When the Moderns made the transition from the 'closed world to the infinity of the universe', they were forced 'to look within the subject' for reasons to justify a 'limitation which had thenceforward to be thought of as self-imposed, as autonomous'. 'Whereas the ethics of the Ancient World took as their point of departure a certain conception of the natural *end* of man, those of the Moderns start out from a theory of the "good will", of the free and autonomous will' (p. 336). Virtue could no longer consist in excelling in our nature, but lay rather in the fight against that which is natural within us: this, then, is the meaning of 'merit'. Kant spoke of 'Two things: the starry sky above and the moral law within'; 'two things' embraced by a disjunctive 'and', radically separate. Aristotle or Kant: the choice is yours – or, rather, since we are all prisoners of our time, the choice has already been made.

Unless, that is, we are living in a third epoch, one no longer characterized by the Modern subject but rather, by the contemporary individual. In which case, the appropriate ethical characteristic would be that of 'authenticity', which Luc Ferry defines (in what is, admittedly, a rather unconventional manner), as the conjunction of two demands, both of which seek to deny the legitimacy of the very notion of limitation: self-fulfilment and the right to difference. (p. 342) In fact, we cannot be characterized by authenticity alone, for authenticity is never alone: 'What is unprecedented in our epoch is the fact that the three ethical ages, which once indeed appeared to be antithetical, no longer cancel one another out: the demand for authenticity is not premised on the complete and final retreat of the principles of excellence and merit.' (p. 345) Authenticity, if it is to be valorized, must bear witness to something other than itself: 'the courage of virtue', 'the power of seduction'. Today's world is, according to Ferry, in essence syncretistic and eclectic.

So perhaps today we have finally gained the right to negotiate (albeit in aesthetic terms) the incommensurable and may accordingly speak legitimately of Aristotle-and-

Kant. Luc Ferry places a cautionary emphasis on the importance of the idea of human nature in understanding the ethics of the Ancient World and, in particular, on the amalgam of skill and practice which is as necessary a part of becoming a good flautist as it is in learning to become morally 'excellent'. Yet this warning of Ferry's nevertheless echoes the following comment by Pierre Aubenque: 'Even though it does not necessarily exclude a certain exercise of the will, only a *natural* gift can point out the path to follow and clear it of the obstacles with which it is strewn.' (And this, Aubenque argues, is the way to read Aristotle's remarks on 'deliberation' – not as prefiguring a Modern theory of the 'freedom of the will', p. 334). If we are to affirm the validity of both a distinction between epochs and the essentially syncretistic character of our own, the conclusion to be drawn is simply that contemporary philosophy – which is in the process of becoming – has rights which the history of philosophy would do better to desist from claiming.

The idea of nature in Aristotle: the slave by nature and the nature of man

Yet before concluding that the present discussion will be concerned more with philosophy than the history of philosophy, I would like first, as a historian of philosophy, to revisit what appears to be the key notion of 'nature' or 'human nature' in Aristotle. My aim in so doing is to make rather clearer why the practical use of this concept is so difficult and perhaps also, to cast a few doubts on this notion of clear-cut divisions between epochs.

Aristotle is, in essence, not Kant and only a fool would claim otherwise. Aristotle makes no distinction between the phenomenal and the noumenal, has no sense of a subject involved in the construction of reality, nor of the freedom of the will. Accordingly, in Aristotle, there is a continuity between the starry sky and that which could not at the time have been the moral law, etc. Yet even in the light of these considerations, is it true to say that, in the Ancient World represented by Aristotle, 'there is no way of raising oneself above one's nature and [that] one's self-definition constitutes, so to speak, the prison from which one cannot escape' (p. 333). This claim of Luc Ferry's concludes his discussion of what is, to a Modern, or contemporary, audience, one of the least acceptable aspects of Aristotle's practical philosophy: the idea of the 'slave by nature', expounded in Book I of the *Politics*. We must concur, initially, with Ferry that this aspect of Aristotelian doctrine is in no sense either marginal or accidental: the house, with its structure of different levels (free men on the one hand, slaves and beasts on the other) even functions as a metaphor for the universe.[11] Jacques Brunschwig has shown how Aristotle, far from trying to justify the institution of slavery as it was in the society in which he lived, chose to skirt around the realities of the day – the 'slave-producer' and the 'slave-commodity' (p. 30) – and instead to propose a new definition of slavery 'as it should be'. (By contrast, there may be cause to criticize today's Neo-Aristotelians for attempting to legitimize the established order in their own societies.) There are slaves by nature, but nature has failed to give us the ability to recognize them. ('There are some slaves who have the bodies of freemen, as there are others who have a freeman's soul . . . though it is not as easy to see the beauty of the soul as it is to see that of the body', *Politics*, I, 5, 1254 *b* – 1255 *a* 1.) Brunschwig continues as follows: 'What good is it to know that nature has ordained some to be slaves and others to be free, if we are unable to tell one class from the other and if we have no right to assume that the actual status of a person corresponds to the one allotted him by nature?' (Brunschwig, p. 26, cited in Ferry, p. 332). Yet Brunschwig's is a particularly shrewd variant on a classic line of defence against Aristotelian 'slavism': he insists on the difference between theory and practice, between law and fact. For Jacques Brunschwig, Aristotle intends to cast the shadow of a doubt on the institution of property-owning. For Martha Nussbaum, the definition of the slave by nature (he who cannot 'exercise forethought', which she renders as being unable to 'plan a life for oneself', *Politics*, I, 2, 1252 *a* 32) establishes a condition so restrictive that this class of person proves to be almost entirely empty. Most radical of all readings, finally, is that of W. W. Fortenbaugh: 'clearly, there is no such thing as slaves by nature in the world. Aristotle's, accordingly, remains a theoretical proposition'.[12]

Yet we cannot let Aristotle off the hook quite this easily. These various lines of defence suggest merely that Aristotle's thought has failed to move with the times, that he is simply stuck in the 'Ancient World'. For the key point, as Luc Ferry has shown, is precisely that there are slaves and free men by *nature* and that the ideal situation (even if it remains unrealized) is one in which the former obey and the latter govern. The 'abyss' separating the hierarchies of the Ancients from those of the Moderns consists in the fact that those of the former are 'in principle full' (even if they happen to have been 'badly filled'), whereas those of the latter are '*empty* a priori'. Thus 'law and fact occupy opposite positions in the two universes' (Ferry, p. 333). So we are confronted over and over again by this ubiquitous concept of 'nature' in the philosophy of the Ancient World, whether in the context of 'excellence' (as a natural goal prescribed in the order of things), or in terms of social hierarchy (where inequalities may be '*inscribed in the natures of individuals* and are, as such, *insurmountable*' – Ferry, p. 333).

This concept of an 'aristocracy' based on 'individual natures' also demands further investigation (Ferry opposes 'aristocratic excellence' to 'democratic merit'). In Aristotle's work, the word 'nature' applies at once to the physical world, to man (the human species), to every man in his particularity (in so far as he belongs to a 'class' such as that of slaves by nature) and even to what sets him apart as an individual (his variety of *êthos*, rhetoric, ethics, even psychology). Man, and every man (every 'individual', then), is 'by nature' such and such and, therefore, if you will, has such and such a nature to the extent that he is in the world, that is, in nature. There is, however, a nature which all men share by virtue of their being men, in accordance with the familiar, differential, definition of man as being 'alone of the animals' in possessing the *logos* (*Politics*, I, 2, 1253 *a* 9 s; VII, 13, 1332 *b* 4 s). Such is the nature which nature has prescribed for man.

So the question I ask myself is as follows: In what sense is 'a person's definition' purely a 'prison from which there is no escape'? (Ferry, p. 333). Phrased differently, are we entitled to affirm, without further ado, *by treating as equivalent all the meanings of 'nature'* (cosmic nature, human nature and individual nature), that the slave by nature stands beneath the free man in the same way that a stone falls to the ground and in the same sense that the human being stands forever above the plants and the animals and beneath the gods? Or does Aristotle's work suggest a certain conception of the nature of the human being as specifically different, a conception which, for example, would allow the human being to escape, to some extent (and to be precise, to the extent of its difference from other kinds of animal), from the fixed hierarchy of differences that is the order of things? (I think, however, that it would be wrong to speak of Aristotle's having 'anticipated' such a conception without also adding that such a conception preceded and 'influenced' his work, namely by way of tragedy, the Sophists and indeed Stoicism.) Is not human nature that property of every individual which is *exceptional as a matter of course* and does it not constitute, whatever the definition of each individual, the path of the transformation, or evolution, of this definition? We return here to the passing remark of a moment ago, which may be banal but on this occasion is by no means anachronistic: it is laid down in the order of things that human nature will be culture.

Before we can develop this particular line of argument, there is one critical objection that must first be addressed. Can we be sure that a slave by nature is a human being and thus that the definition of a human being applies in his case? We know that, in one sense, the slave constitutes a part of the 'house' (*oikos*), the 'eco-nomic' domain, and that he never rises to the rank of citizen. This objection is all the more serious in view of the fact that the opening of the *Politics* makes the ability to live in the city dependent upon possession of the *logos*. Moreover, slaves are merely cattle by analogy (2, 1252 *b* 12); indeed a slave is even described as an 'animate article of property' (*ktêma ti empsukhon*, 4, 1253 *b* 32). Here, then, are two reasons for doubting that the slave is truly a human being. 'The element which is able, by virtue of its intelligence (*têi dianoiai*), to exercise forethought, is naturally a ruling and master element; the element which is able, by virtue of its bodily power, to do the physical work, is a ruled element, which is naturally in a state of slavery' (2, 1252, *a* 32–34). According to this view, the slave by nature is not a human being but simply a body, the body of the master.[13]

I would suggest that, in spite of this division into two separate classes, and against the grain of the definition of the slave by nature – shocking, as it is, to our ears – we are nonetheless able to find the resources which will allow us, so to speak, to climb back up the ladder of humanity and to question again all such fixed hierarchies. The slave by nature is a body, granted. Yet a body, a *sôma*, is certainly not just the handle of a rudder – it is not made of 'ebony' – for the simple reason that such a handle is never 'animate', whereas a body (that is, an animal or human body) is always animate. Moreover, Aristotle states explicitly that the slave exists, for the master, as 'a living but separate part of his body' (6, 1255 *b* 11 s). In the same way that there is always, whatever happens, some amount of soul in a body, there is also, always, in one way or another, something of the *logos* in every soul, even the soul of a slave.

This emerges clearly when Aristotle, at the end of Book I, comes to divide up ethical virtues among members of the household: 'Here a preliminary question may be raised in regard to the slave. Has he any "excellence" beyond that of discharging his function as an instrument and performing his menial service – any "excellence" of a higher value, such as temperance, fortitude, justice, and the rest of such moral qualities? Or has he no "excellence" outside the area of the bodily services he renders? Either alternative presents difficulties. If slaves have an "excellence" of the higher sort, in what respect will they differ from freemen? If they have not it would be surprising since they are human beings, with a share in the *logos*'[14] (13, 1259 *b* 21–8 ; cf. 5, 1254 *b* 16). The resolution of this aporia is straightforward enough: there must be different kinds of excellence which correspond to differences between natures. The virtues of one who governs are not the same as those of one who obeys, no more than those of the male or the father can be confused with those of the woman or the child. However, there is more at stake in the resolution of this difficulty: it is striking, first, that the most fitting model to illustrate the relationship between the master by nature and the slave by nature is less that of the relation of the soul to the body which it animates, and more that relation which exists between different parts of the soul. It is not enough to assert merely that the master may be likened to the ruling part, 'that which has the *logos*' and the slave to the ruled part, 'that which does not have it' (*tou alogou*, 1260 *a* 7), for Aristotle adds immediately thereafter that 'all these people (i.e. slaves, women and children) possess in common (*enuparkhei*) the different parts of the soul; but they possess them in different ways' (10–12). The way to loosen the conceptual snare of the slave by nature is not to object that there is no way of knowing whether so-and-so is really a slave of this sort, but rather to acknowledge that, by rights, every slave by nature has, to however limited a degree, some share in the *logos*;[15] or, to recognize, as Aristotle puts it, that the slave is, nevertheless, a man.

If this point be conceded, it seems to me that the slave by nature cannot, in fact, any longer be considered a 'prisoner' of his nature. The *logos* alone allows him to transcend (or, more precisely, to transform) this slavish nature. The slave has just enough *logos* to be susceptible to the *logos*, that is, to be open to *paideia*, or education. This, moreover, is the last word on slaves in the first book of the *Politics*. As Aristotle puts it: 'those who withhold reason from slaves, and argue that only command should be employed, are making a mistake: admonition ought to be applied to slaves even more than it is to children' (1260 *b* 5–7). This relationship between the slave and the child, and particularly the status of the child, is a point of fundamental importance (and, perhaps, as we shall see, a touchstone) with respect to the radical character of the divide between epochs. If the slave may be compared to the child (as indeed the *Meno*, a dialogue which puts *paideia* into practice, already invites us to do by a turn of phrase that is surely far from incidental: 'tell me, little one . . .'), this is because both, in their different ways, are imperfect human beings: their *telos* lies beyond them, in a father or master (13, 1260 *a* 31–3), who represents for them the *logos* and the *nous* in complete possession of themselves, in action. The slave has just enough *logos*, as does the child, to be susceptible to cultivation, to reproach, to exhortation. This treatment, despotic though it is, bears a resemblance to the more kingly, paternal, task of bringing the child to the *logos* by way of the *logos*.[16] The effect is to make the slave, as Fortenbaugh notes, 'the judge of his own actions' (*Rh.*, 1391 *b* 10 s). Accordingly, whether or not this was the intention, the slave becomes more and more human. Yet none possess the *logos* from the beginning, nor indeed is it sufficient to have grasped it once to hold it forever. The definition of man reiterated in Book VII of the *Politics*, which addresses this very question of education, may be better understood by recalling that 'Reason and thought is the ultimate end of our nature' (VII, 13, 1334 *b* 15). This suggests the following line of argument: the slave by nature is a man, a man is an animal in possession of the *logos*, the *logos* is what allows man to come closer to the *logos*; so how could the slave by nature, in so far as he is a man, be denied this possibility of self-betterment?

Lastly, a clear indication of the importance of this 'in so far as he is a man' is to be found in the discussion of *philia*, in Book VIII of the *Nicomachean Ethics*, where

Aristotle specifies that I cannot feel *philia* for a horse, an ox, or indeed for 'a slave *qua* slave. For there is nothing common to the two parties'. However, he goes on to add that '*Qua* slave, then (*hêi men oun doulos*), one cannot be friends with him. But *qua* man (*hêi d'anthrôpos*) one can; for there seems to be some justice between any man and any other who can share in a system of law or be a party to an agreement; therefore there can also be friendship with him in so far as he is a man' (12, 1161 *b* 5–8).[17] 'One can never rise above one's nature' (Ferry, p. 331) – except, that is, by way of *paideia*, which is an aspiration by way of the *telos*. It may be objected that this argument is contradicted by the reality of life in Ancient Greece, for slaves, when freed, were not usually then educated and, even if they were, they never became citizens. Yet it would then be our turn to reply that we are talking here about principles rather than facts and that the theoretical question of the slaves' humanity remains in spite of this objection.

We must at least acknowledge that there are two opposing forces in play here. The first insists on the difference between the natures of slave and master whereas the second stresses that all human beings have a nature which is identical. The former appears to be entirely committed to positional fixity, whereas the latter allows room for development. Yet even the former is not quite so positionally fixed as it first appears: its function is to describe the structure of the household (master by nature/slave by nature, but also male/female and father/child). While the structure as such is set in stone, he who is by nature a child, who is born a child, will become, by nature, a man. It will already be clear where the crux of our discussion lies: is the slave by nature more like a woman or more like a child? Indeed the idea that a slavish nature is inscribed in the body has only been evoked (*banausoi*) in order to finally be rejected. There is no such thing as a biology of the *Untermensch* in Aristotle. Furthermore, the emphasis on exhortation, the insistence on the logos, the fact that the treatment of slaves and children often goes hand in hand, suggests that slaves are closer to children than to women. For no amount of education will ever free women from the world of silence.[18] If the slave is closer to a human being than an animal and closer to a child than to a woman, then the expression 'slave by nature' must primarily denote a place within a structure – that is, within a hierarchy which, in the final analysis, is empty *a priori*, just like that of Modernity.

I trust it will be clear that the point of honour at stake in this last stand is not Aristotle's 'slavism'; for Aristotle is, *in addition*, 'slavist'. Rather, this discussion aims to focus attention on the concept of nature in all its cosmo-anthopo-logical ambiguity. This ambiguity, inherited and handed down by Aristotle, combines a fixed order with the transformative potential that is a specifically human characteristic. This is why his understanding of the child's place is of such importance. During the era of excellence, the child [*l'enfant*] was required to be nothing more than a small animal whose sole right was the etymological one to remain silent [*infans*]. In the age of merit, the child was supposed to be a man in miniature and was expected to already be a morally responsible subject. There really ought to be an unbreachable divide between these two conceptions. And there is, but only if you ignore *paideia* on one side and *Bildung* on the other, both of which would be entirely (if inversely) deprived of their respective *raisons d'être*. This, to my mind, is the thought underlying Martha Nussbaum's objection to Terence Irwin's description (which Nussbaum calls 'Kantian') of Aristotelian education. Irwin makes out that education for Aristotle is a sort of behaviourist manipulation, necessary in order to provoke the metamorphosis of the child into an adult capable of making moral choices. Yet Irwin's account fails to lend due weight to the way in which the *aisthêsis* and the *logos* are conjoined and fails to do justice to the complexity of the concept of the *logos* itself, a concept which grounds the continuity between the child's animal nature and the pursuit of the *telos* of adulthood.[19]

A different way of phrasing the same reservations would be to suggest that the concept of nature as a teleological prison, which Luc Ferry ascribes to Aristotle, is the direct consequence of a Kantian reading of Aristotle. This is a reading which privileges the formal identity of concepts (nature, end) over and above differences of content (it is only for man that the end of nature is the *logos*). Thus what we have rediscovered here – in what is, essentially, simply a rather more 'Aristotelizing' reading of Aristotle – are the appropriate methodological principles of *Neo*-Aristotelianism.

From Aristotle to Kant: the slave by nature and radical evil

The concept of nature probably represents, in all honesty, one of the most considerable of the difficulties which each and every practical philosophy is called upon to face. It is a problem which is prone to cross the boundaries between epochs and which, I would suggest, contorts the thought of two figures as different as Aristotle and Kant in ways which are analogous.

I would like to prepare the ground with some cursory, even programmatic, comments, which aim to highlight the extent of the difficulty facing any comparative endeavour of this kind and to summarize the entire field of discussion by setting forth the issues which will demand further scrutiny. I shall then indicate how, latent in the concept of nature, is what I propose to call an *analogy of contortion* between the Aristotelian aporia of the slave by nature and the difficult Kantian doctrine of radical evil.

1. Aristotle comes so very close to 'inventing the will'.

For: Hannah Arendt,[20] among others: 'No other Greek philosopher came so close to recognizing the strange lacuna [. . .] in Greek language and thought';[21] Aristotle introduces 'a new faculty into the old dichotomy and thus settle[s] the old quarrel between reason and desire'.[22] The choice in favour of reason or desire is a matter for the faculty of choice (*proairesis*): 'It opens up a first, small restricted space for the human mind.'[23] Let it be noted here that in order to justify what has in fact become a rather common feeling about Aristotle (shared, indeed, by both Irwin and Nussbaum), what is required is a thorough re-examination of the three concepts of *boulêsis, proairesis* and *phronêsis*.

Against: the general line of argument pursued, in particular, by Pierre Aubenque, according to which Aristotle was bringing two different debates into contact with one another. The first was the traditional view that *proairesis* was the basis of imputability and the second, Aristotle's own, that *proairesis* has no bearing on the end but only on the choice of means. Thus what had formerly been known as *proairesis* (the determination of the end) became *boulêsis*, a process entirely rooted in nature and therefore never 'responsible', whether it strives for good (as a result of its definition and therefore without merit) or evil (against nature and therefore implying a pathology or teratology, yet still not implying responsibility). Thus, according to Aubenque, 'Aristotle's ethics is the only coherent ethics in Ancient Greece, because it locates good and evil not in the absolute of the will (as was later to be the case with the Stoics, who nonetheless also managed without a concept of sin), but in the choice of the means' (Aubenque, p. 138).

The problem with such an interpretation, which Pierre Aubenque makes no attempt to disguise, is that it splits the concept of *proairesis* into two different and incompatible meanings such that, in the final analysis, *proairesis* proves to be inarticulable. On one hand, in Book VI, for example, virtue is defined as 'a state of character concerned with choice' (*hexis proairetikê*) and is linked to *proairesis* understood as a 'deliberative desire (*horexis bouleutikê*) of things in our own power' (VI, 2, 1139 *a* 22 s). Yet on the other hand, in Book III, *proairesis* is thought of simply as the free choice of means, subject to a prior act of will (in other words, it is the 'predeliberated' of III, 4, 1112 *a* 15). In contrast to the first interpretation, which retained throughout a place for a practical will analysable in terms of its end or means, what we appear to have here is the mere juxtaposition of two concepts that are alien to one another, only the second of which is truly Aristotelian (op. cit. pp. 119–24).

The strength of the 'Kantianizing' reading of Aristotle is also derived from a second observation:

2. Aristotle comes so very close to inventing the difference between heteronomy and autonomy, the distinction between acting in conformity with duty but not from duty. Tricot, in his commentary on the *Nicomachean Ethics*, gives voice to a common view when he notes that 'we are getting close, here, to the rigorism of Kantian ethics' (n. 2, p. 309). Here are the two most salient passages:

– Aristotle levels the accusation of vicious circularity against his own argument that we become virtuous by doing virtuous things: for if we do virtuous things, he objects, does that not mean we are already virtuous? His answer: no more so than in the case of the *tekhnai*. For it is indeed by doing grammatical things that one becomes a grammarian, provided that one does them grammatically, which is to say neither by chance nor at another's behest. There is, nonetheless, one remaining difference: the property of being grammatical resides in the result, the product, whereas the property of being ethical resides in the subject. Thus 'if the acts that are in accordance with the virtues have themselves a certain character it does not follow that they are done justly or temperately. The agent must also be in a certain condition when he does them: in the first place he must have knowledge, second he must choose the acts, and choose them for their own sakes (*proairoumenos di'hauta*) and third his action must proceed from a firm and unchangeable character' (*NE*, II, 3, 1105 *a* 28–33). Equally, 'it is not the man who does these that is just and temperate, but the man who also does them *as* just and temperate men do them' (1105 *b* 7–9). The weak reading of these passages would have it that their aim is simply to rule out chance and obedience and to specify the importance of an understanding of the means adopted in the practical syllogism (and thus a declension of the act in accordance with the *kairos* of the categories). The strong reading – which is the more plausible – rules out, in addition, action which is merely in conformity with virtue.

– The second passage: 'As we say that some people who do just acts are not necessarily just, i.e. those who do the acts ordained by the laws either unwillingly or owing to ignorance or for some other reason and not for the sake of the acts themselves (though, to be sure, they do what they should and all the things that the good man ought), so is it, it seems, that in order to be good one must be in a certain state when one does the several acts, i.e. one must do them as a result of choice and for the sake of the acts themselves (*dia proairesin kai autôn heneka tôn prattomenôn*)' (*NE*, VI, 13, 1144 *a* 13–20). Then comes the distinction between skill (which is independent of the end) and prudence (which cannot exist without skill but which should not be confused with it) and Aristotle's analogy with what is sometimes called 'practical mutation', which is to say the difference between 'natural virtue' (*arêtê phusikê*) and ethical virtue (*arêtê êthikê*). Whence Tricot's note and his translation of *ariston* as 'Highest Good', one which is all the more suspect for having been presented as self-evident from the very beginning!

3. Yet Kant had himself blocked in advance the possibility of such a conflation of these two positions. The reason for his opposition is as follows: any other practical philosophy aside from his own, and in particular that of Aristotle, is in reality a philosophy of nature and will characteristically be dominated by the notion of the end. For a practical philosophy to be qualified as Kantian, it is not enough for there to be causation by the free will, or choice (which is very probably implied in *boulêsis-proairesis-phronêsis*); rather, by contrast with causality as it operates in the natural world, the will must be subject *only* to the concept of freedom, to a principle of law entirely divorced from reference to either ends or intentions.

Yet this is quite simply unthinkable from Aristotle's perspective. The notion of an act which proceeds from virtue rather than merely being in conformity with virtue cannot be expressed, nor can such an act be performed, in the Aristotelian universe without also willing the good or willing happiness; nor can it be performed without also taking into consideration the calculus of ends and means. There are Kantianizing and Aristotelianizing readings and both Luc Ferry and Pierre Aubenque are right to emphasize the difference. In Aristotle, there is always – at least to some extent – a natural dimension to the end (the will for good) and a natural dimension to the organ best able to discern this end (the 'eye' for the good). Accordingly, the alternative which Aristotle himself brings to the fore – is man given his end by nature or does he provide himself with an end of his own? – is always balanced in favour of the first option. This is particularly apparent in Chapter 7 of Book III of the *Nicomachean Ethics*: 'Whether, then, it is not by nature that the end appears to each man such as it does appear (*mê phusei ... phainetai*), but something also depends on him (*ti par'auton estin*), or the end is natural but because the good man adopts the means voluntarily (*hekousiôs*) virtue is voluntary, vice also will be none the less voluntary: for in the case of the bad man there is equally present that which depends on himself (*to di' hauton*) in his actions even if not in his end' (1114 *b* 16–21). The cautious way in which this is phrased ('something also depends on him') indicates that we are never more than 'joint causes' (*sunaitioi*) of the dispositions which lead us to posit any particular end. This suffices for responsibility, but not for freedom.

In Kantian terms, the will to an end (which refers either wholly or partially to the concept of nature) is not a will to act in accordance with the law (which refers exclusively to the concept of freedom and no other). This is especially clear in the First Introduction to the *Critique of the Power of Judgment*:

> The critique of pure *theoretical* reason, which was dedicated to the sources of all cognition *a priori* (hence also to that in it which belongs to intuition), yielded the laws of nature, the critique of practical reason the law of freedom, and so the *a priori* principles for the whole of philosophy already seem to have been completely treated. But now if the understanding yields *a priori* laws of nature, reason, on the contrary, laws of freedom, then by analogy one would still expect that the power of judgment, which mediates the connection between the two faculties, would, just like those, add its own special principles *a priori* and perhaps ground a special part of philosophy.[24]

Hence the recurrent distinction (which is also apparent in the *Groundwork to the Metaphysic of Morals*), not just between a 'skill' (a 'technical imperative' indifferent to its end, whether good or evil) and 'prudence' (a 'pragmatic imperative' which establishes a non-arbitrary end for itself, namely happiness), but also between a skill and this new arrival, the categorical imperative. Thus the concept of the 'pragmatic' (a free act but one not determined solely by the concept of freedom) allows for the rejection of all 'moral' doctrines of prudence and accordingly fends off the baleful misunderstanding that would end up making prudence and thus ethics into a technical branch of the human sciences.

All of the above is made quite explicit in the work of Pierre Aubenque and Luc Ferry alike.

4. Can this really be the last word on the matter? It seems to me that the Aristotelian reader's counter-offensive can only really be targeted at the internal difficulties generated by Kant's own use of the concept of 'human nature', with all the limitations it imposes.

'Nature', in the Kantian sense of *kuriôs*, is quite clearly the other face of freedom. This is manifestly the case when, for example, Kant asks: 'is man by nature morally good or bad? He is neither, for he is not by nature a moral being. He only becomes a moral being when his reason has developed ideas of duty and law.'[25] So what does it mean to say, as Kant himself does in *Religion Within the Boundaries of Mere Reason*, that '*The human being is (by nature) either morally good or morally evil*'?[26] Answer: 'This only means that he holds within himself a first ground (to us inscrutable) for the adoption of good or evil (unlawful) maxims, *and that he holds this ground qua human, universally* – in such a way, therefore, that by his maxims he expresses at the same time *the character of his species.*'[27] This is an '*innate* characteristic', yet one for which Nature is nonetheless not 'responsible'. For to avoid witnessing the collapse of his entire ethical system, Kant is obliged to hold to the principle that 'this subjective ground must, in turn, itself always be a deed of freedom';[28] it is 'thus represented as present in the human being at the moment of birth – not that birth itself is its cause.'[29] In other words, human 'morality' has nothing to do with nature but is nonetheless a characteristic expression of the species.

In this Kantian scheme of things, there are three 'original dispositions' which together constitute 'human nature' (cf. *Religion*, pp. 50–2 / 6:26 – 6:29): the disposition to animality (the human being as living entity – *The Critique of Pure Reason*), the disposition to humanity (the human being as both living and rational – *The Critique of the*

Power of Judgment) and the disposition to personality (the rational human being capable of responsibility – *The Critique of Practical Reason*). The position of the concept of 'radical evil' in Kant's scheme is pinpointed with the utmost precision and should be perfectly clear: radical evil is the remainder left once all 'systematically impossible' meanings have been eliminated. Yet it is hardly surprising if this concept has, as Alexis Philonenko remarks, been 'constantly misunderstood'.[30] Here, for example, is one of the definitions which typifies Kant's use of this residual compatibility approach: 'The statement, "The human being is *evil*", cannot mean anything else than that he is conscious of the moral law and yet has incorporated into his maxim the (occasional) deviation from it. "He is evil *by nature*" simply means that being evil applies to him *considered in his species*; not that this quality may be *inferred from the concept of his species* (i.e. from the concept of a human being in general), for then the quality would be necessary.'[31] This paragraph deserves to be quoted in its entirety. For in order to safeguard both freedom (and thus 'contingency') and universality (and thus the connection to the species), Kant ends up positing the existence of this '*radical* innate *evil* in human nature (not any the less brought upon us by ourselves)'. The term 'nature', then, is a way of referring to a characteristic of the species which is universal without being necessary.

It might be thought that, for our purposes, it would be possible to overlook the contorsions to which original sin gives rise in Kant's practical philosophy. However, the definition of radical evil, in all its subtlety, determines not only the concept of nature but also that of education, to which it is clearly connected. Radical evil – fragility, impurity, malice – is only 'perverse' because it 'inverts' the ethical order by prioritizing the motive of self-love over that of obedience to the law. It is this reversal which education is charged with correcting in the child; furthermore, we know that because the child is a moral subject, he or she is aware from the outset of the presence of the moral law within. Thus the 'Methodology of Pure Practical Reason'[32] should allow him or her to become better aware of the fact that the motive of obedience to the moral law ('virtue only has so high a value here because it comes with such a heavy price') is of greater worth than that of self-love in however altruistic a guise ('not because it brings any profit'). Moreover, there is perhaps the prospect of the human race putting right this same inversion in its own species. Moral education is both a progressive 'reform' of the way we feel (virtue, for Kant as for Aristotle, is acquired little by little, through the performance of virtuous acts from the still inappropriate motive of self-love) and a 'revolution' in our way of thinking, whereby the maxim of self-love is cast aside for that of saintliness (cf. *Religion*). Moreover, Kant accepts the paradoxical notion that this revolution – just like the child's awareness of the law – must be always already present in order for reform to take place. 'With education is involved the great secret of the perfection of human nature. It is only now that something may be done in this direction . . .'.[33] The human being will become 'disciplined' (tamed), 'cultivated' (skillful), 'civilized' (prudent), and 'moral' (capable of choosing good ends, namely ones which may be universalized). To this list of stages, Aristotle would probably have added that the human being will, finally, become 'political'. Either way, for both thinkers, 'All the natural endowments of humankind must be developed little by little out of man himself, through his own effort':[34] it is a question of man (or, for Kant, explicitly 'humankind'), or in other words that these potentialities be transformed into realities.

For 'Aristotle-and-Kant', then, 'a man can only become a man through education'. There is no doubt that the tone changes markedly when Kant assigns determinism and freedom respectively to the phenomenal and noumenal realms, as indeed it does with the conception of progress as generic. Yet the method remains the same: it is education which perfects nature's work. Between 'rational nature exists as an end in itself' (*Groundwork*, p. 37) and 'Reason and thought is the ultimate end of our nature' (*Politics*, VII, 15, 1334 *b* 15), there is certainly more than just a passing resemblance.

The slave by nature is also by nature a man. Man is evil by nature but is naturally neither evil nor good. Are not both these paradoxes – which are formally analogous – symptoms arising from the use of this concept of human nature? Practically impossible though the use of this concept proves, it still seems to be required from time to time, in order to convey with a minimum of confusion, if too with a strong dose of ideology, that a 'reality' (slavery, sin) is being worked on by philosophy.

On the uses of a practical philosophy

Radical though the differences may be between practical reason in Aristotle, a composite concept, and Kant's view of the moral subject as constituted by the freedom of the will, what we have been calling, for the sake of convenience, Neo-Aristotelianism, puts forward a series of reconciliatory solutions, the accuracy of which as history of philosophy is quite openly inflected by the strategic needs of a philosophy in the process of becoming. In order to scrutinize the contradictions between these various responses, I would suggest that it is worth taking into account the 'third man' in each case – not he who benefits from the interpretation but he in whose shadow it takes place. Thus on the chessboard which the history of philosophy quickly becomes (for better and for worse), the respective positions of Aristotle and Kant are determined by that of an other, of the other – by the choice of a third term. Once again in other words, I am suggesting that the typology of the Aristotle–Kant relationship is comprised of the two pure cases we have briefly discussed[35] – Aristotle/Kant, through a Kantian lens (Ferry), and Aristotle/Kant through an Aristotelian one (Aubenque) – and a virtually indeterminate variety of somewhat finer blends, of which I wish to question neither the interest nor the legitimacy. To make matters clearer, I shall choose two of these, drawn from the recent work of Anglo-American philosophers, both of which have had a decisive influence in terms of the large body of critical discussion they have generated, discussion which helps make them susceptible to comparison.

Plato, Kant, Aristotle

One of the interests of Martha Nussbaum's work lies in the way she attempts – with the assistance of Aristotle – to 'deplatonize' Kantianism. This is certainly not her main objective – this being, rather, the 'fragility of happiness' – but it is nonetheless a necessary phase in order to 'justify and give point to the ethical practices in which we actually engage' (*Fragility*, p. 286) and to address 'the daily conduct of our lives' (p. 287).

In order to demonstrate more fully the complexity of the bond between Aristotle and Kant, united against Plato, I shall begin by drawing on an article of Nussbaum's which

I have already quoted, one which is devoted to an Aristotelian critique of Plato: 'Shame, Separateness and Political Unity: Aristotle's Criticism of Plato'. The Greece of the *aidôs*, which is that of Plato no less than that of Aristotle, is a civilization of 'shame', or if you prefer, of 'self-respect'; the question is whether, as Aristotle suggests but as Plato denies, 'separateness and autonomy of choice are . . . necessary for self-respect' (p. 397).

The question which preoccupies Martha Nussbaum's Aristotle is accordingly: 'What is the relationship between self-respect and autonomy of choice?' (p. 404). Aristotle privileges, as he constantly states in the *Politics*, the distributive over the collective (1261 *b* 16 s, quoted in Nussbaum, p. 417 *s*), the properly political interrelation of separate free beings over and above organic unity (which is simply 'economic', in the sense of familial) and prefers to look for an ethical foundation in 'the considered consensus of the greatest number and of the wise' rather than in 'the vision of a single expert'. By contrast, to return to the topic of slavery, almost all of Plato's human beings are no more than slaves by nature in relation to the philosopher-king; what is more, they are probably ineducable in the Aristotelian sense. In short, Aristotle tolerates 'a certain amount of disorder for the sake of autonomy' (p. 422). Martha Nussbaum is careful to emphasize the fact that this is a 'deliberative autonomy' (p. 423), the very form of freedom which the slave *qua* slave lacks, and without which no life could really be a 'good life'. For a life to be 'good' in the Aristotelian sense, it must be chosen 'from within' by the power of practical reason which is common to all. This limited form of freedom, which is compatible with – and may even demand – the distinction between slaves and masters, is by no means identical to the kind of absolute freedom which resides in the realm of the Kantian noumenon, upon which any restriction whatsoever would be a contradiction in terms. This notwithstanding, it is clear that Aristotle and Kant are on the same side: against Plato.

Yet the relationship between these philosophers changes in *The Fragility of Goodness*. For here, Nussbaum is concerned in the first instance to guard against any Kantian, or indeed Kantianized reading of the Greek texts, on the grounds that the immediate effect of such a reading would be to force an inappropriate distinction to be made between moral and non-moral values, for example 'luck' (the 'hap' in 'happiness'). Nussbaum equips the reader with a handy table of reference in the form of a purposely sketchy list in two columns, intended to allow the reader to identify two (and perhaps the only two) of the 'normative conceptions of human practical rationality' (p. 20). On one side there is the entirely active agent who cuts himself off from all external influence and leads a good life in isolation. On the other, the combination of positive elements with elements rejected from the first column produces an agent who is both active and receptive, who strikes a balance between control and risk, between internal and external influences and who aims to lead a good life alongside friends and loved-ones – in a community. The first is a Platonic vision; the second, an Aristotelian one which reaches back, past Plato, in a return to the origins of tragedy. Yet at this point in Nussbaum's account it is already assumed – as it will be throughout the work – that the Platonizing tendency is also a Kantian tendency, as the following remark, typical of many, suggests: 'The middle-period Platonist (and the modern Kantian) might reply . . .' (p. 361). On this occasion, Kant is on Plato's side: against Aristotle.

Yet I do not believe for one moment that these two approaches are incompatible. When Aristotle and Kant are aligned together, against Plato, Aristotle is with Kant in seeking to recognize the existence of something like freedom – the capacity and the duty to choose freely in practice, shared by all men in so far as they are men. But Aristotle is also opposed to Kant, who here is on Plato's side, when Aristotle argues against the right of the moral agent to live in exclusion, one which would allow all relation between his inner being and outer reality to be severed. As we have already suggested, it is this continuity of the inside with the outside and similarly of the animal and child with the adult man, that provides the most compelling reason to reject Irwin's indissolubly Platonic-Kantian perspective on the appearance of *proairesis* and the supposed mutation into a moral subject. After all, we do not bring up our children as either Plato or Kant would have done.

According to the interpretation outlined by Nussbaum, which becomes more intelligible once the presence of Plato is acknowledged, if Kant may at times have got in the way of our reading Aristotle, it is now Aristotle's turn to let us live Kant.[36]

Kant, Nietzsche, Aristotle

Alasdair MacIntyre, at least in *After Virtue*,[37] orchestrates the confrontation between Aristotle and Kant to the accompaniment not of Plato but Nietzsche, a philosopher who, in that he hardly risks being confused with either of the other two, perhaps makes one of the fiercest of third-parties.

The key to MacIntyre's argument – which is dramatized at the beginning of his book in the 'disquieting suggestion' of a catastophe affecting the discourse of the natural sciences – lies in becoming aware of the fact that 'modern moral utterance and practice can only be understood as a series of fragmented survivals from an older past' (pp. 110–11). This is why the project of the Enlightenment must itself fail, for as Kant acknowledged magnanimously, it remains within a theological frame, a frame presupposed explicity in the concept of pure practical reason, the disappearance of which renders the entire project quite simply incomprehensible. It is at this point that Nietzsche steps in, 'as the Kamahameha II of the European tradition', one competent to inform us Polynesians that 'good', 'right' and 'obligatory' are linguistic vestiges that have become severed from their historical roots and today have no more meaning than 'taboo'. Thus in *The Gay Science*, ethics takes a kind of *linguistic turn*.

It is in this context that MacIntyre seeks to promote Aristotle. For if the defeat of Kant goes without saying, Nietzsche's triumph still depends upon a hypothesis: 'the only alternatives to Nietzsche's moral philosophy turn out to be those formulated by the philosophers of the Enlightenment and their successors' (p. 114), or in other words, those of 'liberal individualism in some version or other' (p. 259). But this is not the case; indeed quite the opposite is true. The failure of the Enlightenment and subsequently the failure of Nietzsche's demonstration of its failure, are in fact 'nothing other than an historical sequel to the rejection of the Aristotelian tradition' (pp. 117–18). Thus MacIntyre calls upon Aristotle on two occasions: first, because his theology and his teleology provide the interpretative matrix without which any form of Kantianism is little more than a tattered garment. Second, because Aristotle's is the only other available conception of morality and even the only form of moral reasoning that is truly consistent.[38] Which means that the underlying question is and always has been: 'Was it right in the first place to reject Aristotle?' (p. 117).

MacIntyre's Aristotle stands, of course, in the great tradition of Greek anthropologico-philosophical thinking (*aidôs, agôn, polis*), in which virtue denotes the excellence required on each occasion by the role or function of a mortal being. Furthermore, from the Sophists to Cicero, it is a question not of virtue in the singular but of *virtues*.[39] By anchoring the domain of the practical in the nature and specific end of man, Aristotle forges the moral thinking that undergirds the 'classical conception of man' and lends such weight to the allegation of naturalistic fallacy, effectively overloading it such that it ceases to hold. This is the happy chance of an ethics of happiness: the individual is, by nature, in continuity with both the world and his fellow beings.

Education adds the finishing touches to this harmonization of feeling and action: 'To act virtuously is not, as Kant was later to think, to act against inclination; it is to act from inclination formed by the cultivation of the virtues. Moral education is an "éducation sentimentale"' (p. 149). Education also adds the finishing touches to the perfect harmony of goods distributed in accordance with *philia* within a human community. It is only when 'men came to be thought of as in some dangerous measure egoistic by nature; it is only once we think of mankind as by nature dangerously egoistic that altruism becomes at once socially necessary and yet apparently impossible and, if and when it occurs, inexplicable. On the traditional Aristotelian view such problems do not arise' (p. 229).

Nietzsche's critique loses all foothold once it ceases to be the case that rules determine virtues (or, worse still, that the formalism of the moral law determines virtues) and instead it is virtues that govern rules. However, the requirement for intelligibility is entirely satisfied: Aristotle's insistence on the practical syllogism amounts to an attempt to elaborate the necessary conditions for giving account of any human action, such that a life may indeed have the appearance of a 'narrative unity'. It will come as no surprise, then, to find that the Aristotelian tradition can be 'restated in a way that restores intelligibility and rationality to our moral and social attitudes and commitments' (p. 259).

These analyses of MacIntyre's hold few surprises in themselves. However, the conclusion is unexpected, and strives to surprise by its brutal naivety: Nietzsche *or* Aristotle, Trotsky *and* St Benedict. Exactly what kind of worlds, or communities, does that particular partnership promise? It is quite likely that liberal discourse is made up entirely of bits and pieces. But could one imagine a fragment more *kitsch* than this Aristotle who only allows us to read Aristotle yet who is immersed in a form of society that is so very opposed to the Aristotelian vision? Unless perhaps MacIntyre is asking us to imagine the virtues of Aristotle's practical philosophy in a non-Aristotelian world – in the world of merit and authenticity, of Kant and *Heidegger*. In which case, the first of these virtues will surely be to restore the intelligibility of the everyday, along with a degree of good conscience, to 'us', to every 'I', in daily life. For we do not think of ourselves as phenomena at one moment and noumena the next, as physically determined then morally free, bridging the gap with an ever-resourceful philosophy of judgement. Rather, we perceive ourselves, and accordingly conceive of ourselves, as individuals who – body and soul – have but one single history. 'The history of nature begins with Good, for it is the work of God. The history of freedom begins with Evil, for it is the work of Man' (Kant, *Conjectures on the Beginning of Human History*). If instead of this dichotomy and this noumenal anguish we were now to begin to look instead to something along the lines of Aristotle's dictum that 'Every art and every inquiry, and similarly every action and pursuit, is thought to aim at some good' (*NE*, I, 1, 1094 *a* 1 s.), we would show ourselves to be more Aristotelian than we are Kantian in our elaboration of an inalienable right to *wellbeing*.

The Sophists, Aristotelianism, Kantianism

I would now like to draw together the various strands of the preceding discussion, one prompted by the constant juxtaposition of Aristotle and Kant in contemporary thinking: the distinction between epochs, the difficulties of the concept of nature and the presence of philosophical third-parties who serve to suggest that Aristotle and Kant are, by turns, staunch allies and bitter enemies.

Nature – as we have seen both in the case of the slave by nature and in that of radical evil – is the cross which every form of practical philosophy is obliged to bear. The use of this concept of nature as a means of distinguishing one epoch from another can only lead to further difficulties. We might use the concept more profitably to mark out a transhistorical difference between, let us say, one *style* of philosophizing and another.

Were I, from this perspective, to propose a new grouping, it would be the following: the Sophists, Aristotle and Kant. It would then be immediately clear that the idea of nature is by no means a characteristic of Antiquity in its entirety, even after we had distinguished between the various different meanings of the concept. This is a commonplace in the work of the Sophists, at any rate, which gets repeated on every possible occasion and in every every possible domain: there is no such thing as nature and, in particular, there is nothing natural about so-called 'human nature'. Gorgias wrote a treatise entitled *On Nature or the Non-existent*, in which it is convention par excellence, the *logos*, which finally provides the antiphysical model of this nature which is not, or is not one. Protagoras maintained that all is relative to a standard which differs on every occasion, to a convention which it may prove expedient to extend and make stable or preferable to attempt to improve. Nor indeed are ethics and politics ever matters of nature, even in the case of the famous myth of the *Protagoras* (of *aidôs* and *dikê*, this additional gift from Zeus, which is the source of all 'political virtue'), which is reinterpreted by Protagoras himself, in the course of the very narration which gives meaning to the myth, in terms of a sharing of the *logos* by way of pedagogy throughout the entire city, from the wet-nurse to the magistrate. Antiphon is renowned for being (unlike Aristotle) on the right side with respect to the question of slavery, in that 'by nature we are all just as much barbarians as we are Greeks' and because we all breathe the air 'through our nose and mouth'; yet even he makes of nature a mere horizon which is always secondary and forever being pushed into second place, beyond the initial sphere of the *nomos* which governs the arrangement of the public sphere in which we are immediately immersed. (And this complicates quite considerably the task of those of his interpreters who seek to present him as a precursor of 'natural law'.)

BARBARA CASSIN

I would assert with confidence that some of the tensions which permeate Aristotle's work, in particular in the area of politics and rhetoric, of which the problem of the slave by nature is a clear example, can only be explained in terms of a hesitation on the philosopher's part between the Sophists and Plato. Aristotle's final decision to stand with the Sophists represented an attempt to guard against a danger inherent in Platonism that was felt to pose the more serious threat. That aside, the idea that Antiquity could be distinguished by the undisputed preeminence of the concept of nature can probably be rejected: in Aristotle's time there existed, moreover, a critical awareness with respect to this concept which was often lacking in Kant's era, indeed even in Kant's work itself.

All this has repercussions when it comes to deciding on the nature of democracy. 'If excellence is essentially aristocratic, the idea of merit derives, by contrast, from democratic sources because it is not situated on the same level as innate abilities and therefore nobody is deprived of it *a priori*' (Ferry, p. 340). A claim of this sort can, it seems to me, be dismantled in the following manner. First, because we re-encounter here the same ambiguities with respect to the concept of nature and the idea of ascribing constitutive sense to the concept of human nature. For nor is anyone (any man) deprived of humanity *a priori*. There is no formal difference between having the *logos* and having a good will. The concept of nature can only ever fix in place the *a priori*.

Let us for a moment examine the matter not from an ethical standpoint but rather from the socio-political perspective called for by these very terms, aristocracy and democracy. When we say that a democratic society functions, or should function, 'on the basis of merit', we mean that instead of valuing so-called natural inequalities (race, strength, beauty), it should endeavour instead to encourage work and effort – but also, most probably, skills and results. It is accordingly no coincidence that, in republican schemes of value, excellence and merit are closely intertwined (the children get the prizes for excellence and those who reared them are honoured for their 'agricultural' merit). The Sophists, in this sense, were true republicans. They held that one skill alone – the *logos* – was the equal of every other and perhaps also their one source. This skill is both shared by all (hence Zeus's demand that everyone be given their portion of political virtue) and is capable of achieving excellence (hence the idea that Protagoras both speaks and teaches others to speak better than anyone else).

Once again, merit and excellence are not to be found in the ethical domain but, from the very beginning, in the political. This distinction, at least in theory, is perhaps among the most important of those elements of democracy handed down by the Sophists – through the intermediary of Aristotle, who chose to write both an *Ethics* and a *Politics* rather than a single *Republic*, and through Kant – to the world of today.

Translated by Oliver Davis

Notes

1 The back cover of *Aristote et le logos. Contes de la phénoménologie ordinaire* (Paris: Collège International de Philosophie/Presses Universitaires de France, 1997), from which the chapter which follows (Ch. III) is taken.
2 Aristotle, *Politics*, tr. by Ernest Baker (Oxford: Oxford University Press, 1995), VII, 15, 1334 *b* 15.
3 Kant, *Groundwork to the Metaphysic of Morals*, tr. by Mary Gregor (Cambridge: Cambridge University Press, 1998), II, p. 37 / 4:429.

118

4 This is very much the case with the following collections: M. Riedel, *Rehabilitierung der praktischen Philosophie* (Freiburg, 1972–4, 2 vols.) and W. Kuhlmann, *Moralität und Sittlichkeit. Das Problem Hegels und die Diskursethik* (Frankfurt, 1986).

5 Here are some of the most useful of these appraisals: E. Berti, *Aristotele nel Novocento* (Rome-Bari: Laterza, 1992); 'Les stratégies contemporaines d'interprétation d'Aristote', *Rue Descartes*, 1–2 (1991), pp. 33–55; 'Strategie di interpretazione dei filosofi antichi: Platone e Aristotele', *Elenchos*, X (1989), fasc. 2, pp. 289–315; C. Natali, 'Recenti interpretazioni dalla etiche aristoteliche', *Elenchos*, VIII (1987), fasc. 1, pp. 129–39; F. Volpi, 'Réhabilitation de la philosophie pratique et néo-aristotélisme', in P. Aubenque (ed.), *Aristote politique. Études sur la Politique d'Aristote* (Paris: Presses Universitaires de France, 1993), pp. 461–84.

6 P. Aubenque, *La Prudence chez Aristote* (3rd edition, revised: Paris, 1986), p. 125. The subject of Kantian readings of Aristotle and the fate of prudence in the face of practical reason are treated in the Third Appendix, 'La prudence chez Kant', pp. 186–212, from which I have drawn extensively in the course of the present discussion.

7 I am thinking of the trend-setting article by Jan Lukasiewicz, 'O zasadzie sprzecznosci u Arystotelesa' (*Über den Satz des Widerspruchs bei Aristoteles*), *Bulletin international de l'Académie des sciences de Cracovie* (Classe d'histoire et de philosophie, 1910), pp. 15–38, French translation by B. Cassin and M. Narcy, in *Rue Descartes*, 1–2 (1991), pp. 9–32. And also of C. Kirwan, *Aristotle's Metaphysics, Books Gamma, Delta and Epsilon, translated with notes* (Oxford: Oxford University Press, 1971).

8 As Berti and Volpi (op. cit.) have clearly demonstrated, the return to Aristotle's practical philosophy was initiated by both *The Human Condition* (Chicago, 1958, translated into German in 1960) and *Wahreit und Methode. Grunzüge einer philosophischen Hermeneutik* (Tübingen, 1960).

9 Alasdair MacIntyre, *After Virtue. A Study in Moral Theory* (London: Duckworth, 2nd edition 1985); Martha Nussbaum, *The Fragility of Goodness. Luck and Ethics in Greek Tragedy and Philosophy* (Cambridge: Cambridge University Press, 1986). I have chosen to discuss these two, more recent, works in order to illustrate my argument here. Similar issues are addressed in Giovanni Giorgini, 'Esiste un neoaristotelismo anglosassone?', in Berti & Napolitano Valditara (eds.), *Etica, Politica, Retorica. Studi su Aristotele e la sua presenza nell'eta moderna* (Rome, 1989), pp. 271–97, which appraises the work of Bernard Crick, Stuart Hampshire and Alasdair MacIntyre.

10 I am borrowing Ferry's terminology here and summarizing his argument in *Homo Aestheticus* (Paris: 1990), 'La question de l'éthique à l'âge de l'esthétique'.

11 See *Metaphysics*, A, 1075 *a* 17–23. This passage is quoted by Ferry (p. 331), who discusses Brunschwig's article, 'L'esclavage chez Aristote', *Cahiers philosophiques*, 1 (September 1979), pp. 20–31. According to the commentators, the stars correspond to free men, the sublunary beings to slaves and domesticated animals; the actions of the free men are 'orderly' (*tetaktai*) and they are not allowed – unlike the others – to act randomly. This passage, which occurs within a very specific context (is the good immanent in the structure of the whole, or transcendent, or both at once, as in an army?), is perhaps rather more difficult to interpret than it first appears. For this passage is not, in fact, concerned with action (*prattein*) but rather with manufacture, with the work (*poiein*); nor are these domestic animals (*hêmera*) but rather, wild, untamed, beasts (*thêria*; cf. *Politics*, I, 3, 1254 *a* 10–26).

12 Nussbaum, 'Shame, Separateness and Political Unity: Aristotle's Criticism of Plato', in A. O. Rorty (ed.), *Essays on Aristotle's Ethics* (Berkeley, 1980), pp. 395–435, especially p. 420. W. W. Fortenbaugh, 'Aristotle on Slaves and Women', in Barnes, Schofield and Sorabji (eds.), *Articles on Aristotle*, 2. *Ethics and Politics* (London, 1977), pp. 135–9, p. 137.

13 Fortenbaugh's bibliography of work on this question is recommended. See Fortenbaugh, p. 136, n.3

14 I have modified Baker's translation slightly, replacing 'goodness' with 'excellence' and restoring the *logos*, for the sake of continuity with Cassin's article and the work of the other French philosophers whom she cites. [Translator's note]

BARBARA CASSIN

15 The slave does not possess the finished form of the logical part of the soul – the faculty of deliberation (*to bouleutikon*) – which characterizes the male, the father, but he does possess the *logos* in the minimal sense in which the appetitive or desiring part possesses it, which is deprived of the *logos* but nonetheless, in a sense, shares in it. Cf. *The Nicomachean Ethics*, tr. by David Ross (Oxford: Oxford University Press, 1998), 1, 13, 1102 *b* 13 s. See also Fortenbaugh's article, cited above, which is particularly strong on this question of the bipartite division of the soul in Aristotle, how it differs from Plato's tripartite division and the relationship between the bipartite soul and the soul of the slave, the child and the woman.

16 On the admonition of the child by the father and more generally of the citizen by the law-maker, cf. the entirety of the closing section of *The Nicomachean Ethics*, IX (in particular, 1180 *a* s.) and ch. 13 of Book VII of the *Politics*. Some of the terms used are the same as those applied to the slave at the end of Book I of the *Politics*.

17 The difficulty involved in establishing precisely what this part of the slave consists in has occasioned a rather hasty reading of this same passage from Martha Nussbaum: 'This is probably a reference to the conventional slave, for he is assumed to have capacities that Aristotle denies to the natural slave' ('Shame, Separateness, and Political Unity', p. 434, n.54). This is clearly not the case, as the following passage from the *Politics* will, if need be, demonstrate: 'There is thus a community of interest, and a relation of friendship, between master and slave, when both of them naturally merit the position in which they stand. But the reverse is true, when matters are otherwise and slavery rests merely on legal sanction and superior power' (I, 6, 1255 *b* 12–15).

18 It is worth noting that Aristotle inserts here a line from Sophocles: '"Women should be seen and not heard" – the old, old story!' (*Ajax*, l.293), tr. by E. F. Watling, in *Electra and Other Plays* (London: Penguin, 1953).

19 Nussbaum, op. cit., pp. 283–7, discussing T. H. Irwin, 'Reason and responsibility in Aristotle', *Essays on Aristotle's Ethics*, op. cit., pp. 117–55. The relevant passages concerning the comparative 'morality' of animals and children are, in *The Nicomachean Ethics*, essentially 1, 10, 1099 *b* 32–1100 *a* 4 – the child, who takes no part in politics, is no 'happier' than an ox; III, 3, 1111 *a* 25 s. and 4, 1111 *b* 8–10 – the child resembles an animal in that he acts voluntarily (*hekousiôs*) but not through a deliberate choice (*proairesis*); VI, 13, 1144 *b* 8–17 – the child resembles an animal in that he possess 'natural virtue' (*phusikê*) but not 'virtue in the proper sense' (*kuriôs*), which presupposes *nous* and is to the natural disposition what prudence is to skill. Yet all these passages also show that if the child, like the slave, resembles an animal, unlike an animal (but like the slave?), he can come to acquire *nous*.

20 See, in particular, *The Life of The Mind* (New York, 1971), Part II, ch. 2, s. 7.

21 Ibid., p. 57.

22 Ibid., p. 61.

23 Ibid., p. 62.

24 Kant, 'First Introduction to the *Critique of the Power of Judgement*', in *The Cambridge Edition of the Works of Immanuel Kant, Critique of the Power of Judgment*, tr. by Paul Guyer & Eric Matthews, ed. by Paul Guyer (Cambridge: Cambridge University Press, 2000).

25 Kant, *Education*, tr. by Annette Churchton (Ann Arbor: University of Michigan Press, 1960), p. 108.

26 Kant, *Religion Within The Boundaries of Mere Reason*, tr. by Allen Wood & Geroge di Giovanni (Cambridge: Cambridge University Press, 1998).

27 *Religion*, p. 47 / 6:21. The italics are Kant's, the underlining is mine.

28 *Religion*, p. 46 / 6:21.

29 *Religion*, p. 46 / 6:21.

30 Alexis Philonenko (ed.), *L'Œuvre de Kant* (Paris: Vrin, 1969–72), II, p. 1131.

31 *Religion*, pp. 55–6 / 6:32.

32 *Critique of Practical Reason*, Part II. See *Kant's Critique of Practical Reason and Other Works on the Theory of Ethics*, tr. T. K. Abbott (London: Longmans, 1883), pp. 249–62. See also *Groundwork*, II; *Religion*, III; 'On the common saying: That may be correct in theory,

120

but it is of no use in practice', *The Cambridge Edition of the Works of Immanuel Kant, Practical Philosophy*, tr. & ed. by Mary J. Gregor (Cambridge: Cambridge University Press, 1996). On the relationship between education and nature, cf. Paul Moreau, *L'Education morale chez Kant* (Paris: Editions du Cerf, 1988).

33 Kant, *Education*, p. 7.

34 Ibid., pp. 2–3. [I have modified Churchton's translation slightly, restoring Kant's 'humankind' for her 'mankind' – *Tr.*]

35 Compare Pierre Aubenque's conclusion concerning the ban on a *moral* doctrine of prudence – 'What is in question here is not the coherence of the Kantian system, but its truth' (Aubenque, p. 211) – with Luc Ferry's remark: 'The extraordinarily compelling power of Kantian ethics derives from the fact that none of us are entirely able to think in other terms. I have yet to meet any Modern from among those who call themselves anti-Kantians who is wholly capable of living without the concept of merit, except of course in theory alone, and even then . . .' (Ferry, p. 338).

36 On this point, is seems to me that Nussbaum is in agreement with Irwin, who writes that, against the background of an agreement between Aristotle and Kant on 'the conditions of human responsibility', Aristotle offers an alternative response to Kant's question, one which avoids the metaphysics of Kantian freedom (p. 143).

37 *After Virtue. A Study in Moral Theory* (London: Duckworth, 2nd edition, 1985). I shall only be discussing this work here and not the broader sweep of MacIntyre's intellectual trajectory, of which this book is both typical and atypical, in more ways than one.

38 This is particularly clear at the beginning of the last chapter: 'After Virtue: Nietzsche *or* Aristotle, Trotsky *and* St Benedict'.

39 See, in particular, Chapter 16: 'From the Virtues to Virtue and after Virtue'. It is here that the difficulty inherent in the attempt to integrate Plato into a Greek tradition conceived along these lines becomes apparent.

8

NATALIE DEPRAZ

Natalie Depraz is a specialist in phenomenological philosophy with further interests in both theology and the cognitive sciences. She has published numerous books and articles on Husserl, whom she has also translated. She lectures in Philosophy at the University of Paris IV, and taught previously at the University of Poitiers. She is attached to the ENS (École Normale Supérieure), the CNRS and to the Collège International de Philosophie where she co-directs a seminar on 'Pratiques de l'exploration phénoménologique'. She is a founding editor of the phenomenological journal *Alter* and is a member of the editorial committee of *Husserl Studies* and *Orbis Phænomenologicus*.

Her major works include the following:

Transcendance et Incarnation: le statut de l'intersubjectivité comme altérité à soi chez Husserl, Paris: Vrin, 1995.

Alterity and Facticity: new perspectives on Husserl (ed. with D. Zahavi), Dordrecht: Kluwer, 1998.

Ecrire en Phénoménologue. 'Une autre époque de l'écriture', Paris: Encre Marine, 1999.

Husserl, Paris: A. Collin, 1999.

La Gnose, une question philosophique (ed. with J-F Marquet), Paris: Cerf, 2000.

La Conscience: approches croisés, des classiques aux sciences cognitives, Paris: A. Collin, 2001.

Lucidité du corps: de l'empirisme transcendental en phénoménologie, Dordrecht: Kluwer, 2002.

IMAGINATION AND PASSIVITY

Husserl and Kant: a cross-relationship[1]

Heidegger's interpretation of the Kantian imagination is well-known: it has often been commented on.[2] By underlining the central character of the schematism in the *Critique of Pure Reason* and choosing to emphasize the first Transcendental Deduction which highlights imagination rather than understanding, Heidegger gave the critical imagination a leading-role within the fundamental ontology he had just begun to build at that time. In short, he endowed imagination with the meaning of an ungrounded ground (*Abgrund*).

By contrast, Husserl's interpretation is in no way as consistent as the one that was developed in the Kant-Buch or even before:[3] first, it is not to be found in any one book. Second, the Husserlian theory of imagination is not as strongly unified as is the case in the Kantian philosophy.[4] Third, the Husserlian analysis of imagination may be understood almost without reference to Kant's thought, whereas Heidegger's hermeneutics intrinsically needs to be viewed with regard to the Kantian critical philosophy, since his ontological novelty is precisely founded upon it.

Needless to say, as far as imagination is concerned, Husserl and Kant are not related by anything like a father-son link. More exactly, the link between them turns out to be a cross-relationship. For the phenomenologist, imagination is nothing like a faculty, a power of the mind, as it is for a classical and even a Kantian interpretation. Like perception and remembrance, imagination is an act of consciousness, but one which does not entail that the intended object would have to be posited as existent or as real. On the contrary, the act of imagining consists in neutralizing the existence-character of the object, so as to change it into an object whose mode of givenness is reducible to a quasi-givenness.[5]

The only context in which the phenomenologist might encounter a kind of Kantian imagination, one which would accord with his own reductive prerequisites, would be that of aesthetic judgement in the *Critique of Judgement*. This is the only case where imagination depends upon a general suspension of the world-thesis: for aesthetic judgement is determined by a kind of open finality which does not include any specific purpose: it involves an interest which ends up being a kind of non-participant attitude which can be operative in any activity. Nonetheless, Husserl never refers to the *Critique of Judgement*, even though he quite regularly makes use of the "as if" (*als ob*) conditional syntagma to qualify the neutralizing act of imagining. Besides, I. Kern[6] has made it clear that the founder of phenomenology hardly ever lectured on this particular Kantian work, whereas he frequently lectured on the first two *Critiques*, as well as on the *Prolegomena* and the *Grundlegung der Metaphysik der Sitten*.

But Husserl was interested in the key role which imagination plays in the first *Critique*. In the course of carrying out his analysis of passivity understood as an associative synthesis,[7] the phenomenologist did indeed come to terms with the central role of the imagination in the first edition, the very edition Heidegger emphasized a bit later on, in 1929. For all that, Husserl never fully elucidated his own theory of imagination in the course of his analysis of passivity.

As a provisional conclusion, it may be held that, on the one hand, passivity meets the requirements of the imagination only in its narrow, critical meaning, that is, not in its strict, phenomenological meaning; in short, not as a presentifying (*vergegen-wärtigend*) act, but only by virtue of the philosophical theory of a cognitive and/or affective synthesis. On the other hand, when imagination becomes the theme of a properly phenomenological description, it is viewed as a pure presentifying act deprived of any kind of passive element.

Does this mean that a relationship between imagination and passivity is always wanting, at least at a properly phenomenological level? In other words, how can it make sense for a phenomenologist to speak of a "passive imagination"? In order to answer this question, we will identify and display the kind of equivalence which prevails between the Kantian productive synthesis of imagination and the Husserlian passive synthesis.

Let us consider first how the fruitful possibility of a "passive imagination", developed along Husserlian lines, drastically changes the classical conception of the imagination as a bodily faculty subject to the illusion of the senses.[8] Furthermore, we shall also need to consider how such a conception succeeds in escaping the Sartrean theory of imagining and dreaming consciousnesses as captive consciousnesses.[9] Both these questions furnish the critical background for this paper.

We will proceed in the following way: as a first step, we will endeavour to understand how a passive synthesis can be a synthesis of the imagination. In order to do this we shall clarify first, the several meanings of passivity in the Husserlian phenomenology; second, the way Husserl has incorporated the Kantian imagination into his philosophical project. We will then go on to take into account the very possibility of a passive imagination in a strong phenomenological sense. This account will be prepared by a critical study of the naïvely posited duality passive perception/active imagination. The centre of our investigation will turn around the need to provide evidence for the narrow relationship between fiction and fact; consequently, we will have to show how imagination is not lacking individuation.

Passive synthesis as a synthesis of imagination

Three phenomenological meanings of passivity

At first glance, it may seem odd to analyze the experience of passivity while stressing its connection with imagination, all the more so since passivity is often understood as something purely receptive, even as a re-action on the part of consciousness. For example, it is commonly held that we are passive when we simply accept an event that occurs suddenly and, even more, when we are subjected to it: I am called to the phone and I hear that a very close friend of mine has just been killed in a mountain accident. All I can do is take in the bare facts or react to them by crying or by rejecting them. But through this example, we see immediately that passivity immediately implies a number of different forms of activity: crying, etc. We will come back to this later on.

All the same, activity and passivity are traditionally presented as being as opposed to each other as spontaneity and receptivity. The contrast is all the more striking since the concept of imagination that is pertinent here is the Kantian one: the Kantian "power of formation" (*Einbildungskraft*) is a pure spontaneous imagination which, as such, is radically opposed to receptive passivity.

Such an understanding of passivity as receptivity, however, is stricken with a naïveté which makes it incapable of accommodating a phenomenological analysis of passivity.[10] In this respect, both Sartre[11] and Merleau-Ponty[12] fell into the trap: the latter went beyond what was required and the former fell short of it. The author of *L'être et le néant* does indeed stick to the Cartesian-inspired opposition between action and passion, whereas the author of *Phénoménologie de la perception* relies upon a mixed experience which leads to a dissolution of both notions: we no longer know whether to talk of an active passivity or a passive activity. The Merleau-Pontian way of thinking tries to avoid meta-physical distinctions by creating more and more intertwinings and interweavings. But the price to be paid might well be confusion.

Passivity is not opposed to activity. Still, this does not mean that it can apply to much the same experience, as if passivity was only a proto-activity, a feeble activity which has not yet reached its goal. This would mean that passivity would be no more than a lower order of activity – as if activity was in fact all that really mattered. Conversely, activity is not just a passivity that has reached a higher degree of intensity – as if passivity was that to which all activity secretly tended. Sticking to dualist distinctions or opting for an irreducible contamination of meaning through pseudo-inversions of one kind or another come down to the same thing. In both cases, we still have to do with a naïve metaphysics, grounded either upon conceptual dualisms or upon a monism achieved by the blurring of differences. Phenomenology, on the contrary, has to reduce both ways of thinking mentioned above. To reduce them means to get rid of them without being either opposed to, or identified with, one or other of them. In short, we have to prevent the contrasted powers of distinction and fusion – which on the whole amount to the same thing – from gaining the upper hand. The only way to do so is to practice a kind of detachment from both these attitudes, so as to open the way to a more properly phenomenological attitude, which involves a mindful absence of goal (or interest) directedness.

Let us add that passivity is neither a negative concept, the main meaning of which would be privation, nor a woolly and blurred concept capable of surreptitiously penetrating any reality. More radically, passivity is not at all a concept in the traditional (etymologically Latin-inspired) meaning of seizing (*capere*). Passivity is originally opposed to any active movement of catching or capturing, as intimated by the very word "concept". In this sense, passive experience has to do with heterogeneity and otherness. It is well known that the more identity and inner unity you acquire, the more closed-up, self-satisfied and homo- and endo-genous you may become. This attitude often goes hand in hand with a kind of activism that is voluntaristic (rather than authoritarian) in character. On the contrary, passivity gives way to a non-unified experience of plurality. But when we argue against the classical meaning of the concept, we do not intend to reject conceptuality as such. Quite to the contrary. Conceptuality is obviously the only healthy protection against the dissolution of meaning. What we are suggesting is that we become aware of both risks, conceptualization and confusion. Passivity is the key-word adopted to surpass both of these extreme tendencies.

Passivity has therefore to be defined in such a way as to allow for further differentiation, more specifically, by enriching the concept of plurality with more precise determinations and by providing a more satisfactory model for unity with reference to variation. By differentiating passivity with reference to its modes of appearance we will, mostly along Husserlian lines, be able to distinguish a primary, secondary and tertiary mode of passivity. The kind of settled plasticity that comes to light through a plural conceptuality provides the best account of what is at stake in the experience of passivity. In other words, passivity gives rise to a kind of experience that can hardly be grasped with the resources of conceptuality alone, even if the latter is also required in order to ensure correct expression. Conceptuality reveals its own limits when it comes to higher stages of experiential complexity. Indeed, some forms of cohesion exceed the grasp of conceptual thinking.[13] Of course, passivity is not the only kind of experience involving levels of analysis which include both conceptual and non-conceptual elements. Indeed, it might well provide an interpretative clue for other experiences of a similar kind in so far as it calls in question the success of any analysis which relies exclusively upon unity and identity.[14]

Central to any attempt to understand the method we propose to employ will be the notion of plasticity. As a primal structure of all living beings, it describes at best, in scientific biology, their way of constantly adapting to new circumstances and conditions. The notion of plasticity shows both how limited conceptualization is and, at the same time, how unlimited its own possibilities of inner transformation can be.[15] To conclude, the importance of a concept is never more evident than when it is exceeded. Now, plasticity depicts the very movement of this transformation. Even if thought, that is, rational and analytical thinking, always takes place by way of distinctions, the dynamics of a given thought lies in its ability to retain something of the original mobility of the idea in *statu nascendi*. Passivity is that very experience of the birth of thought before it has been crystallized in a word. Passivity could therefore rightly be regarded as another name for the very potentiality of thinking.

The primal modality of passivity is also the most radical of its dimensions. It is therefore appropriate to speak of an originary or original passivity. And yet, primal passivity is always inserted into an experiential context made up of many different kinds of activities and of secondary or tertiary modes of passivity. When I receive the call which announces the death of that close friend, I experience just such a radical passivity: I am deeply shocked to the point of being unable to react. But this inability, this silence, this immobility is already a certain form of activity. Later, I will cry, talk to others, etc. As such, primal passivity cannot be thought in complete isolation from our current flow of experience. Otherwise it would become an abstract stratum bearing no relation to our daily stream of pre-conscious and conscious experience. Now, what I want to do is show how that primal experience of passivity is all the more concrete in that it is both radical and originary. Its specific concreteness has to do with our on-going experience of self-opacity: I am observing a scene on the street and suddenly, something happens that makes me feel uneasy because it surpasses my understanding of the situation; or I am discussing something with a friend and find that my efforts at clarification are obstructed by ineliminable fragments of obscurity. Primal passivity livingly emerges into consciousness when these factors of vertigo or instability prevail. It makes itself known as a special affective peak in our self-opacity (the shock due to the sudden call), which does not imply that we are not intensively self-aware of it. If (and only if) we get acquainted with this experience of selfopacity, self-opacity and lucidity go hand in hand, by making it possible for us to create the right conditions for it to come up again. It is then fully incorporated into our experience as an experience of self-alteration. Every fragment of opacity in ourselves functions as a kind of inner alterity that we cannot control as such (as if we were inhabited by someone else) even if we are able to control the conditions under which it reemerges. We are therefore able to control this very lack of control itself. Consequently, primal passivity as a form of self-alterity, is its most concrete mode of givenness, precisely because it implies in itself a kind of originary and organic synthesis, what Husserl will call himself "passive synthesis".

In both of our last two examples the prevailing feeling is one of alien-ness: Now, this sense of otherness (in the self) is temporally and spatially determined. The self-alteration of our self occurs in relationship with the on-going temporal and spatial transformation of ourselves. At every moment and in every place, we discover that we are not exactly the same as we were the moment before. However, although the ego is constituted as an opaque consciousness by this originally temporal and spatial self-alterity, awareness of this same opacity is not precluded thereby. Not only are we directly affected by the alterity we find in ourselves: this same alterity also represents our highest form of freedom in so far as we may be lucid about inner affection and about the right means to use in order to make it become ever more stable. But since it can only be located in the depths of consciousness, it is never easy to bring it to light as such. Such a primal passivity is well-known to Husserlian phenomenologists as an *Urhyle*, another word for *Urimpression* (in the Time-Lectures from 1905–1912) or as *Uraffektion* (in the late manuscripts from 1929–1935). In fragments from manuscripts written in the thirties, Husserl accordingly describes the *Urhyle* as a synonym for what is foreign to the I inside the I (*das Ichfremde*).[16]

This primal passivity has to be separated from another passive mode of appearing or givenness, known as "secondary passivity". This should not be taken to mean that the latter is less important or even superfluous. Not at all. Its own radicality lies in its communal background and not in any proto-temporal and proto-spatial selfopacity, that is, in the self-alterity of an individual consciousness. In this respect, primal or originary passivity is shown to be limited: as an individually-located passivity, primal passivity runs the risk of producing an egology that, although genetic, would set individuality against community. Though innerly altered, a substantial (no longer merely methodological) subjectivity would then give rise to a correspondingly philosophical thesis with regard to the nature of consciousness. Hence, secondary passivity can be seen as the necessary phenomenological complement of the first and more primal mode of passivity.

So far as secondary passivity is concerned, we can say first, that we are affected in a communal way and not just as individuals. Indeed, the very power of the community makes this mode of affection much more profound: it gets enriched by each individual experience as it is sedimented through historical time and through a succession of generations. We inherit a secondary passivity in so far as we belong to a community, that is, in so far as we share a common history and a common life-environment. Experiences become sedimented through a common experiential history and common social references, be they intra- or supra-communal. This experiential stock is continuously shared and exchanged through daily interactions with the other members of our actual community. Previous generations, be they near to us or remote, as well as future generations, help to build up a common chain of generativity, the main rhythm of which is the succession of births and deaths.[17] Even if history is fractured, and even if species encounter and undergo mutations, the main values and cultural goods continue to be perpetuated and transmitted. This allows us both to presume and to anticipate the general form of a continuity transmitted from the present across to the future.[18] Unlike primary passivity, such a communal mode of appearing of passivity has no absolute character: communally sedimented lived experiences are (to be) re-activated or re-actualized at every moment and by every member of the community.[19] Passivity then is synonymous with a non-actuality that may be actualized at any moment.[20]

Affective alterity within my self and communitarian lived experience as a sedimented deposit that may always be actualized: these first phenomenological determinations lead us far away from the classical conception of passivity as a suffered receptivity. If being passive only meant undergoing or suffering, passivity would be restricted to a narrow etymological meaning, close to the Greek *pathein*. But passivity reveals a double dynamics of affective alteration, the alteration of individual identity and that of an actualization of communal sediments. What is at stake here is the need to distinguish the various modes of passive experience from any so-called "mystical" experience, which has much more to do with self-fusion or self-coincidence. With this latter kind of limit-experience, we would experience an absolute identification of the individual with the whole, be it divine, natural or social.[21] The ego would be immersed and captured by a transcendence which can also quite easily become a universal immanence. Nevertheless, mystical experience does not necessarily amount to fusion. It might therefore be better to insist upon a mystical passivity that would allow watchfulness to emerge; better still, that would train us to achieve lucidity; in other words, that would foster a special kind of self-alterity, both temporalizing (primary passivity) and pluralizing (secondary passivity),[22] without generating the well-known apathic "ataraxy" commonly vouched for by enlightened Stoics.

Thus differentiated, the modes of givenness of passivity provide us with a kind of plasticity, deeply anchored in the self-alterity primarily characteristic of the primal mode and which remains opposed to any fusional coincidence. In fact, this inner alterity can be expressed in three different ways, based upon the three passive modes: as a primary alterity, it has an affective character; as secondary, its dominant feature is communal; as tertiary, (which we now have to examine), it generates a specific kind of attitude which surpasses both activity and passivity. This third mode of passivity includes both previous modes of passivity within itself, the individual affective alien-ness as well as the communal de-sedimentation. As a communal self, the individual I is overcome – though it does not vanish. Passivity of this tertiary kind may also be understood as an absolute power, a power whose force excludes domination and gives rise to gift.[23] If it is correctly understood, the mystical experience of, for example, San Juan de la Cruz's provides an excellent illustration; and the same could be said of the experience of Christ during the Passion. In yet other respects, Buddha's "compassion" may also help us to understand the tertiary mode of passivity. Here the self is neither substantial nor formal. For all that, tertiary passivity does not reduce the self either to a mere structureless flow or to a sheer emptiness. Devotion to the other, freed from any sentimental feeling or care, calls for a total bareness of the self, which is very near to the Eckhartian *Abgeschieden-heit*. But it is not to be confused with any natural kind of "compassion" implying uncontrolled affection and vulnerability towards the other.[24] Being passive means being able to be completely open towards the other, to welcome him in full awareness: thus, you keep up with yourself at the very moment when you seem to be totally lost in the other and precisely *because* you are fully lost in the other.[25] All this attests to the pre-eminent power of a non-activity which is, as a matter of fact, a real activity engaged in observing itself at the very moment the act is being performed.[26]

Such a subtle and plastic passivity can be further differentiated from within: it includes different modes of temporalization which contribute intrinsically to that plasticity. The primary temporalizing begins with the hyletic affective *Anstoß*, which is constitutive for (if not constitutive *of*) time. My contention is that this hyletic affection has a constitutive role to play in the fulfilment of temporality: it has a part too in the process of constitution as a motivating impulse. Of course, this does not mean that affection would be alone in playing this part, nor that its role would be symmetrical with, or similar to, that of the ego. The latter is the constituting agency: as a functional pole of the lived acts and as a source of their sense, it bestows upon the intended object an a priori sense-giving structure. Static constitution has this powerfully deep but quite narrow meaning. Hyletic affection fulfils its constitutive function in a very different way because it acts as a passive motivation for the process of egoic constitution itself, that is, before any sense-giving. It plays the part of a facticial (non-formal) condition of the possibility of constitution: this is the true meaning of a genetic constitution. As far as secondary temporalizing is concerned, this has to be understood as an event that appears on the scene too late. It arises as an ever belatedly occuring moment which reflexion tries to catch up with afterwards. As a time of reflection, it is therefore a time of objectiva-tion. And as for tertiary passivity, this then gives way to a kind of temporality of self-anticipation where generally structured anticipation (previousness) and open future contingency of a singular event (unexpectedness) are organically linked.[27]

All the same, it goes without saying that we still need to know what kind of connection prevails between such a differentiated passivity (above all, its third mode of givenness, in which the first two culminate)[28] and imagination. In the next section, I will start by examining the way Husserl deals with the Kantian theory of imagination.

How Husserl deals with Kantian imagination[29]

No doubt, Husserl read the Critical Philosophy quite carefully, in particular the first two *Critiques* and the *Prolegomena* . . . It is well-known that the transcendental turning-point in his phenomenological development was fostered by his critical study of Kantian transcendentality.[30]

Nevertheless, unlike Heidegger, the founder of phenomenology never really appreciated the key role of the schematism for the theory of knowledge. Focussing upon the transcendental conditions of the possibility of knowing objects fully and accurately within the framework of phenomenal experience militates against any investigation at the level of an ontology of facticity, where imagination refers to the very power of nothingness. In other words, the mode of givenness of the imagination is that of absence as such. For Heidegger, on the other hand, coping with facticity means coming to terms with the radical possibility of nothingness, a possibility to which imagination grants us access. At first glance, even when analyzing the Transcendental Deduction, Husserl seems to concentrate upon the different levels of constitution of objectivity. Imagination, as we will discover in a moment, refers to one of these levels, but does not seem, at least within a static constitutional framework, to be endowed with any special and pre-eminent role. In other words, Husserl gives priority to the methodological mode of access to experience against any ontological mode of access.

Prior to Heidegger, however, he already highlights the Deduction in the first edition of the *Critique of Pure Reason* (1781), and he also insists on the productive synthesis of imagination as a specific stage within the constitution of objectivity. Although both notice how important imagination is in that first or "subjective" Deduction, they obviously do not draw the same conclusions from their investigation. At several places,[31] although sometimes still vaguely, Husserl carries out his analysis of constitution through a comparative investigation of both editions of the *Critique of Pure Reason*, with regard to the Deduction. Calling the first a "subjective Deduction" and the second an "objective Deduction", he emphasizes the key role devoted to imagination in the subjective one, as opposed to its subjection to understanding in the second one. Accordingly, he makes quite clear how the intermediate synthesis of the productive imagination in the so-called subjective deduction paves the way for a "genetic" constitution of the object, whereas the objective deduction will obscure this possibility by conferring the leading role upon the categorial synthesis of understanding.[32]

Let us be more precise: the Kantian imaginative synthesis in the subjective deduction plays a constitutive role in what Husserl calls a "phantomatic synthesis" in the context of his phenomenologically renewed transcendental aesthetics: it schematizes the sensible spatial datum.[33] Nonetheless, whereas the Kantian schematism is operative at the level of a transcendental analysis, Husserl refers the constitutive *Phantom*-stratum to the topic of a transcendental aesthetics. If imagination is part of the aesthetics and not of the analytics, it follows first, that this intuitive act has a leading-role to play in constituting objectivity; second, that it is not one-sidedly submitted to a pure categorial synthesis.[34] Since imagination is able to constitute eidetic categories, the phenomenological aesthetics in question ends up by covering higher levels of constitution, and especially since the disclosure of truth is granted to intuition. In this respect, the Phantom-stratum is the second step within the originary constitution (*Urkonstitution*) of space. The first and more primary step is kinetically oriented. As such, it refers to the Kantian transcendental aesthetics *stricto sensu*, except that (last, but not least!) for Kant, sensations are not primarily moved and moving, but are, above all, described as a "Gewühl der Empfindungen" (chaos of sensations). Now, it is worth emphasizing that a number of phenomenologists (among others, Husserl, Merleau-Ponty, Straus and Maldiney) have adopted an analysis of sensation as being primarily moved and moving.[35] The aesthetics in the *Critique of Pure Reason* does nothing but repeat the naïve duality of the forming activity of intuition and the receptive passivity of the many chaotic sensations: pure intuitions of space and time are able to in-form a diversity of unregulated sensations. As for the imaginative stratum, it is an in-between stratum. The categorial stratum is only able to constitute an objective and homogeneous space: in Kantian terms, it has to do with the faculty of understanding alone. According to the constitutional level adopted, either imagination or understanding prevail. Obviously enough, Husserl re-thinks the Kantian faculties of sensibility, imagination, understanding and reason[36] and changes them into genetic modes of constitution of objects of spatial perception.

Both strata, the kinetic as well as the phantomatic, are related to each other within the general constitutional framework. Both refer to specific processes of constitution of the body. Elsewhere, I have called the first sensible process "encharnement" (incarnation) and the imaginative one "incorporation" (incorporation).[37] As processes (and not as sheer strata), they give rise to a particular logic of previousness, whereby imagination can be anticipated within the primal synthesis of sensibility. It should therefore have become clear by now that the active/passive synthesis is an accurate synonym for static (in terms of strata) and genetic (in terms of processes) constitution. The relationship between both primary and secondary processes paves the way for an analysis of genetic constitution in terms of a logic of previousness.

Let us be more accurate with regard to this intertwining which has been understood here as an originary anticipation: the primary synthesis of sensibility is a passive associative synthesis which links sense-data related to every sense; the secondary phantomatic synthesis is also a passive synthesis in which the sensible is originally idealized through an originary imaginative figuration. Furthermore, sense-data (or hyletic data) are originally extended as presentative (*darstellend*): both contribute towards kinetic sensations. Imagination plays a central role in the constitution of objects: "as soon as" (that is, from the "beginning"!) a sensation becomes a figuration, imagination is already at work. In other words, within the very originary passivity of consciousness (the first mode of givenness we mentioned), imagination is operating under the immanent lived experience of originary figurative sensations. Here, Husserl takes into account Kant's notion of "associative Affinität", which is only to be found in the first Deduction.[39] Unlike Kant however, he founds it on the originary synthesis of time. True, only a temporal logic of previousness provides the genetic background needed to account for the way in which imagination is able to proceed back to such an elementary level of constitution: sensations are originary imagining movements of consciousness and they refer to a first associative linking for which previousness provides the processional dimension.

As far as Kantian passivity is concerned, it is useful to make a distinction between two different meanings. A first use of the notion operates above all in the Transcendental

Aesthetics: our bodily sensations are passive in the sense that our sensible faculty of knowing receives them as something coming to it from the outside; on the other hand, the intellectual faculty of knowing reveals the mind as primarily spontaneous.[40] A second (this time, phenomenological, or at least, pre-phenomenological) use of the notion of passivity makes itself known through the operations of the law of associative affinity in the synthesis of productive imagination. This second use also prevails in the Kantian *Opus Postumum*.[41] Passivity refers here to a prereceptive affection, that is, to a pre-categorial or pre-predicative synthesis. In the thirties, Husserl will call it a passive genesis of the categories of understanding.[42] Now, this synthesis, which is operative within the sphere of a pure passive affinity, appeals to imagination rather than to understanding.

The limitations of Kant's Transcendental Aesthetics are due to his failure to recognize the contribution made by the faculty of intuition to knowledge. Once this limitation has been overcome, the investigation of the productive imagination opens the way to a valuable elucidation of passivity as an originary synthetic figurative linking. It has often been claimed that Kant's conceptual framework can not be integrated within a phenomenological analysis precisely because of the limitations of his notion of intuition.[43] It is our hope that we have succeeded in showing, at least in part, that another view of Kant (a less well-known one) can contribute to a better understanding of the deeply rooted phenomenological relationship between passivity and imagination. Furthermore, interpreting the primary mode of givenness of passivity as an originary figurative synthesis makes it possible for us to side-step the aporetic debate on Husserlian phenomenology as a tension between realism and idealism.

Building upon what has been accomplished so far, we will offer an account of the very possibility of a truly phenomenological "passive imagination" by proceeding in the following way: First, we need to be reminded of the precise meaning of imagination as a specific act of consciousness. Thus far indeed, only the Kantian imagination has been taken into account. So we still need to determine which dimension of a more properly phenomenological imagination is to be related to the experience of passivity. Second, we will attempt to show that it is not just the first mode of givenness of passivity which is relevant for imagination. If the Kantian-inspired originary synthesis of imagination does indeed make possible a true and renewed access to the primary mode of passivity, we would like to suggest that other components of imagination might well be related to the third mode of givenness of passivity referred to in the first Part of this paper – provided, of course, that the imagination is interpreted in a properly phenomenological sense.

Passive imagination as a genuine phenomenological possibility[44]

Before we set about our task, it will be necessary to address a distinction which, however, naïve, still sometimes guides phenomenological analysis: the passivity of perception as opposed to a purely active imagination. Such a polarization still operates even within Husserl's analyses. Moreover, amongst phenomenologists it is Sartre who makes the most of this distinction. In the light of this distinction, the very possibility of a passive imagination seems to be excluded. Before we can even attempt to demonstrate the phenomenological possibility of a passive imagination, we first need to clear the ground by showing how un-phenomenological this distinction really is.

Passivity of perception/Activity of imagination

Seen from the standpoint of the static phenomenology of presentifications (*Vergegenwärtigungen*), perception, as a primary act supported by an originally intuitive mode of givenness, founds (*fundiert*) imagination. For, as an act of consciousness, imagination intends its object as non-given or, in other words, as quasi-being. Because it is a founded act, it remains, like remembrance, a secondarily structured act. Unlike the act of remembering, however, the positing of the object as existent does not belong to its mode of givenness: imagination neutralizes the mode of givenness of the object as existing. It therefore has still to be founded, either directly upon perception, or mediately, through remembrance. On the one hand, it looks as though it is founded in a secondary way; on the other hand, it is submitted to a double mediation and may be thought of as founded in a tertiary way.

Though it is a primary act, perception proves itself to be inadequate from the standpoint of its teleological structure. Even if, when perceiving, I always intend the *eidos* of a perceptual object as an identical whole, I can only perceive one of its sides at any given time. The act of perceiving can not achieve a saturated sense-givenness. It remains caught in a finite framework which is the very framework of our perceptual experience. In this sense, a certain kind of passivity can be identified within the very teleological ideality of perception. This only proves our powerlessness with regard to any experience of the world as a totality. The most we can do is intend the identity of an object through its different and changing profiles. Now, in so far as perception is *eidetically* structured, imagination is originarily required to account for the very structure of perception. At first glance, imaginary variation provides us with a pure and free activity, the goal of which is to give rise to the eidos. Moreover, if imagination is understood as the power of neutralizing its object as being, it may also be used to refer to a pure activity deprived of any ontic weight. From a strictly methodological standpoint, both these modes of appearance of imagination (variation, neutralization) emphasize its purely active role.

No phenomenologist has pushed the contrast between perception and imagination as far as Sartre. Indeed, he deliberately exaggerated the distinction in order to carry through his critique of static phenomenology. What the author of *L'imaginaire* is up to is obvious. His aim is to open the way for an alternative interpretation of imagination: imaging consciousness as well as dream consciousness are both captive consciousnesses,[45] whereas pure reflexion alone remains totally spontaneous. Although Sartre changes the emphasis he places upon imagination, he remains stricken in a naïve duality between activity and passivity. We are therefore right to wonder whether Sartre's interpretation (of the imagination as a captive consciousness) is the true phenomenological counterpart to his otherwise relevant critique of Husserl's one-sided opposition between passive perception and active imagination. In other words, this captive mode of givenness is not the only way imagination can be said to be passive, and moreover, the truly phenomenological possibility of a passive imagination requires that it be precisely not captive but free. We will have to consider to what an extent the free passivity of imagination tallies with the third mode of givenness of passivity we sketched out above.

The Sartrean critique of imagination as a mode of presentification squares well enough with the critical overview of the metaphysics of presence advanced by Heidegger. Like Heidegger, the author of *L'être et le néant* emphasizes the negative force which inhabits our imaginary world. On the other hand, imaginative presentification remains vitiated by its secondary role with regard to the more foundational structure of perceptual presentation and suffers from the inadequacy of the link established between them. As a matter of fact, the neutrality of imagination is but a pale reflection of the original power of negativity proper to the Sartrean imagination, and one which is, moreover, tarnished by the weight of presence. It is a criticism commonly directed against Husserl by phenomenologists that he invariably operated with just such a naïve metaphysics of presence: in addition to Heidegger, Merleau-Ponty, Levinas and Derrida also share this view. They all argue against a conception of imagination as an act whose basic intention is that of (mere) neutralization. Like many before and after him, Sartre sees in Husserl a late defender of a metaphysical activism which is ultimately referred to the pure act of being proper to God. He therefore persists in interpreting the Husserlian notion of imagination out of just such a conceptual framework. Even if it remains relevant, it does not provide us with a fruitful understanding of Husserl's most original intuition.

From this standpoint, Sartre is led to a critical description of any imaging consciousness as a captive consciousness: Passivity is here simply treated as an obscure heaviness, in contrast to any purely reflective consciousness, which is said to be translucid and therefore endowed with a pure spontaneity. A few years later, in *L'être et le néant*, this kind of self-transparency will become that pure kind of emergence from being called "Pour-soi". Even so, it is still nothing like a divine actus in so far as it is determined as the very opposite of an absolute fullness, that is, as a self-nothingness.[46] He is unable even to conceive of a kind of passivity that would not be straightforwardly assimilated to a full and hopeless opacity – which later he entitles an "en-soi". Only the Pour-soi can enjoy such a pure and lucid dynamics. Only by going beyond any naïve analogical duality in accordance with which opacity/lucidity matches passivity/activity will we be able to bring to light the specific quality and positivity of a passive conception of imagination.

Fiction and facticity

It should have become obvious by now that a phenomenologically passive imagination is neither merely associative, that is, receptive, nor yet one-sidedly captive, that is, alienated.[47] This would amount to mixing affection with passion. But we took care to separate them above: passion is a blind, and purely re-active passivity, the very kind of passivity we called non-phenomenological because naïvely opposed to activity. As for affection, it refers to the primary mode of givenness we mentioned.[48] Passion gives way to a contorted alienation, affection, on the contrary, opens the way for a temporality where the material fact is straightforwardly interpreted as a genetic self-differentiation. The dynamics of affective motivation change the immanently given fact (*Tatsache*) into a processional facticity which originally contains within itself its own temporalizing dynamics. If, as Nietzsche contended early on, there are no facts but only interpretations of them, facticity is inhabited by an originary plasticity. Since the fact conceals within itself a multiplicity of still unrealized possibilities, it harbours an inner differentiation.

Such a plastic facticity results from both the modes of givenness of passivity we thematized at the beginning of this paper. From the first mode of givenness, it inherits the affective and temporalized genetic dynamics. But the latter, as we already saw, remains the activity of an individual self. Only the secondary passivity supplies this factical plasticity with the plurality it requires as a self-differentiation. Last but not least, plastic facticity is achieved through the third mode of passivity, which incorporates both of the first modes. As we said, this third, pre-eminent mode of passivity presupposes previous modes of passivity, individual affective alienness as well as communal de-sedimentation. As such, it is deeply determined by self-alterity.

Now, it is well-known that the variety of possibilities contained within a single matter of fact (*Sachverhalt*) makes possible the very method by which the essence emerges as such, a method which requires a specific appeal to imagination. Thanks to our imagining faculty, we are able to vary individual facts. Those features which are regarded as being essential to the identity in question become the very features of the *eidos*; the others are set aside as merely contingent. Among the many possibilities contained within the matter of fact, the method of variation separates what is necessary from what remains contingent. Since the intuited essence is directly unfolded through the method of variation practiced with respect to matters of fact that are individually intuited, the former appears as a concrete entity As such, it is something factical rather than something factual, which latter would imply a naïve and purely abstract opposition between fact and essence. The concreteness of the essence lies in its ability to contain within itself a number of unactualized possibilities. In other words, the eidos is not a mere formal and identical necessity. Access to the eidos, which is also the essence itself as seen in the light of this very process, lies in imaginary variation, Now, dynamics and nonactualisation are features of both the first two modes of givenness of passivity, which in turn culminate in the third, a self-altering reception.[49]

It is imaginary variation which is responsible for changing factuality into facticity. Indeed, we know well that imagination is the key to the eidetic method in phenomenology. It paves the way for access to de-substantialized realities. In other words, *eide* are concrete and dynamical entities. Through variation, facticity emerges as an emergent core, the identity of which is dynamically constituted. Factical is therefore by no means synonymous for what is artificial, fabricated, built, as opposed to what is experienced in a bodily way. Quite to the contrary. Facticity is indicative of the dynamical plasticity of experience. In short, facticity is another name for what I we have called above a tertiary passivity.

Now, if, as is clear from Husserl's own statements, fiction is the essential element in phenomenological analysis, this is primarily due to the part eidetic variation plays in the constitution of phenomenological reality. Besides, the process of changing empirical facts into a factical essence is often presented in later texts by means of the verbal expression *sich umfingieren*. In short, essential facticity and fictionality are phenomenological equivalents, all the more so as both result from an identical process, the process of varying. Furthermore, and despite a dubiously common etymology, *Faktum* and

Fiktum refer to a kind of reality which is determined through its essential dynamical plasticity.[50] Clearly enough, just as "factical" does not mean artificial, "fiction" has nothing to do with a mere illusion that would be deprived of any vivid reality or that would be the pure creation of our fancy.

Hence the rather paradoxical result is that it is fiction which gives rise to a deeply embodied sense of reality. Just as the eidos is the most concretely intuited element in phenomenology and precisely because it is originally linked to individual facts used as effective clues enabling the essence to appear within a specific act, so fiction originates first and foremost in a true act of perceiving. A *Fiktum* is but a "*perzeptives Fiktum*". So it is most important to insist upon the intertwining of perception and imagination, rather than allowing them to lapse into an irreducible opposition. Accordingly, we have to disassociate ourselves from any conception of perception as a purely primary act giving objects in flesh and blood, and from any understanding of imagination as involving the neutralization of the existence of the object. We will have to show how perception is originally permeated by activities which obviously appeal to imagination, and how imagination wins for itself an element of radical freedom by appropriating the plastic and dynamical facticity we alluded to. In this respect, it is necessary to make a distinction between two meanings of perception and, correlatively, between two different senses of imagination. These two different meanings of perception coincide, in the German language, with two distinct words: *Wahrnehmung* and *Perzeption*.[51] German is fortunate enough to be able to make use of both Germanic and Latin roots, whereas French is lacking such a possibility. *Wahrnehmung* refers to so-called primary acts of consciousness which give objects in flesh and blood – although it is subjected to the teleological law of the inadequacy of what is perceived. Imagination then is a founded, neutralized act deprived of any intrinsic force. In a quite different way, *Perzeption* includes in its mode of givenness the different modalities of perceiving, that is, doubt, probability, possibility. Now, all these modalities are clearly potential germs of imagining contained within perception. In that sense, imagination is so deeply rooted in perception as to draw its very force from it.[52] In conclusion, we can say that both imaginary variation and perceptive fiction help in determining a new kind of passive imagination, the passivity of which is nothing but facticity.

In order to determine such a passive imagination more exhaustively, it is convenient to take a last step forward. Not only is facticity essential to passive imagination, it has to be supplemented by self-alterity, a self-alterity which permeates the self both at the individual and at the communitarian level. Is phenomenological imagination able to include self-alterity within itself? What follows from this as regards the unity of imagination in Husserlian phenomenology? To what extent does a self-altering imagination meet the requirements of the tertiary mode of givenness of passivity?[53]

Phantasie and individuation

As we saw at the beginning of this paper, passivity is far from being deprived of potentiality and even of power. Nevertheless, it has nothing to do, with either the traditional divine attribute of *potentia*, or with the Aristotelian *dynamis* as a still un-actualized act. The first suggests an understanding of the power of passivity as an (arbitrary) domination, that is. as a pure act. On the other hand, the second deals with a potential state which is teleologically oriented towards actuality. But over and beyond the obvious opposition of the two, both are linked through their secret interest in activity. So, the seemingly paradoxical power of the tertiary passivity lies in its open reception and in its capacity for self-observation.

In the same way, one might easily be led to concede that a phenomenological imagination would necessarily be deprived of any power. Since it provides many possibilities without having to effectuate or actualize any one of them, one might contend that it is a merely formal act, the force of which is quasi-reducible to nothing. In other words, imagination and embodiment would be quite incapable of fitting together.[54] Such a view would amount to a regression to the commonplace conception of imagining as the realm of phantasms and utopias. What we hope to show is the very opposite: imagination is able to accomplish a specific kind of individuation, that is, a particular form of embodied spatio-temporality. The question we then have to address is the following: what lies at the root of the individuation imagination might be able to provide us with? In other words, what is the nature of this particular passive power inhabiting imagination which makes it possible for it to give way to true individuation without being confused with sheer perception?

Our first two types of imagination (imaginary variation and perceptive fiction) were both determined by a constitutive link with the realm of fact and by their correlative change into a plastic facticity. As for *Phantasie*, it might appear at first that it is not so interesting for our purpose, since it shares with *Bildbewußtsein* the feature of being a presentifying, reproductive act. Nonetheless, its interest for us lies in its contrasted modalities of appearing: First, it is said to be a free imagination (*freie Phantasie*); second, it is called a perceptive imagination (*perzeptive Phantasie*).[55] In the first case, it looks like eidetic variation in that it functions as a method that is constitutively indifferent to the facts of the matter even though it takes the latter as its constitutive clue; in the second case, it is close to fiction, as it is permeated by perception through its constitutive modalities. As such, *Phantasie* proves to be an achieved synthesis of both the two earlier types.

Neutralization therefore results in a wholly one-sided view of imagination. For imagination is in fact constitutively related to spatiotemporality. By opening up possibilities of being which exceed our own limited belonging to space and to time, imagination makes possible an enlargement of our very notion of what is real. In particular, imagination makes it possible for us to accede to levels of experience which would previously have been thought unattainable. But to get these levels, which may be compared with Leibniz' "petites perceptions" or "perceptions insensibles" as presented in the *Monadology*, it is necessary to surrender our willfulness and to submit to what we have called "awaiting". In other words, if we are to individuate such very subtle and slight movements of consciousness, we have to let them come up by themselves rather than try to induce them for ourselves. What is specific to our imagination is that it does not have to lay hold of every possibility in order to actualize it immediately, but that it can let certain possibilities remain merely possible. Such a floating openness of our consciousness may enable us to reach a state of imaginative passivity.

This kind of individuation, through imagination, no longer refers to the well-known traditional principles, space and time, principles which prevailed from the Middle Ages right up to Schopenhauer, and passing via Leibniz. Such principles are here made dependent upon the new "principle" of imagination, which compels us to trace them back to their own possibility (*Vermöglichkeit*). As a matter of fact, such a principle is highly phenomenological: it brings to the fore the *possibilities* of reality and not reality itself, which may at any time lapse back into a naïve ontification. What we would like to suggest finally is that the tertiary passivity is the very attitude that makes possible such a plasticity of reality through its possibilities. All the more so since its core, that is, self-alterity, brings about a primary interplay between originary affective reality and its temporalization, the same kind of interplay as prevails between reality and its various possibilities. Only with reference to the structure of self-alterity does it become possible to resist the tendency to ontify our world and to assume, as the unique index of reality, just such an "ontified" world.

In the *Critique of Judgement*, which Husserl does not seem to have taken into account, Kant had already brought to light such a notion of *Spiel* as a "play" between faculties: Imagination was thus accorded a double power of free production and of reproduction, though subject, of course, to perceptual spatio-temporality. Now, although this game has its rules, these rules do not pre-determine the game. In this sense, the game is not subject to objective finality. Its freedom therefore approximates that of our imaginative passivity: the freedom to be a plastic power, the force of which is due to its own inner differentiation and self-alterity.[56]

Notes

1 This article is based upon "Comment l'imagination 'réduit' l'espace" (*Alter* No 4, Paris. Editions Alter, 1996b) and is also linked with "Puissance individuante de l'imagination et métamorphose du logique" (*Phänomenologische Forschungen*, 1996a). It constitutes a foundational programme for other later studies on the imagination as passively anchored and paves the way for the possibility of a "transcendental empirism" in phenomenology. For more on this subject, see my *Lucidité du corps. Pour un empirisme transcendantal en phénoménologie* (forthcoming). I wish here to thank Christopher Macann for revising the English version of this text.

2 See Schultz, 1965; Lichtigfeld, 1967; Makkreel, 1990: Courtine, 1990; Benoist, 1996; Dastur, 1996.

3 See Dastur, 1996. On the relationship between Husserl and Kant, see Dussort, 1959; Kern, 1964; Kockelmans, 1977.

4 See Saraiva, 1970, § 8 and 9, footnote 63, p. 172. and Depraz, 1996a and b.

5 See *Hua* 3, § 99–100 and § 110–111; *Hua* 23, n°20.

6 See Kern, 1964, p. 425–427. The only mention of Kant's Aesthetics is one which refers to the first *Critique*: In 1917 Husserl wrote "Philosophische Übungen im Anschluß an Kants transzendentale Ästhetik" (Kern, 1964, p. 426): through Kern we know that Husserl possessed two different editions of the third *Critique*, one edited by Hartenstein and one by Vorländer.

7 See *Hua* 11.

8 See *Les passions de l'âme* by Descartes, 1970, art. XX–XXI.

9 See Sartre, 1940, especially the fourth part.

10 See Holenstein, 1972.

11 See Sartre, 1943.

12 See Merleau-Ponty, 1945.

13 See Merleau-Ponty, 1964, where the author suggests the possibility of "non-conceptual

cohesions": "Remplacer les notions de concept, idée, esprit, représentations par les notions de dimension, articulation, niveau, charnière, pivots, configuration" (p. 277) In this regard the creative work of G. Deleuze is also an excellent reference.

14 See Levinas, 1966.

15 See Varela and Hayward, 1995, p. 93: "[. . .] à peu près tous les animaux, y compris les mouches et les vers, sont capables de changer de comportement en vertu d'une faculté que nous appelons 'plasticité'." See also Varela, 1989, p. 63–4: "Plasticité de l'ontogenèse", Varela, Thompson, Rosch, 1989, and van der Linden, Hupet, 1994, which deals with the possibility of a "functional plasticity" in the process of altering.

16 About time, alterity and affection, see Held, 1966; Derrida, 1964; *Alter*, revue de phénoménologie, n°2, "Temporalité et affection", 1994, Liminaire et N. Depraz, "Temporalité et affection dans les manuscrits tardifs (1929–1935)"; N. Depraz, 1995b, chapitre V.

17 See Held, 1981, *Alter* n°1, "Naître et mourir", 1993, and Steinbock, 1995.

18 See Husserl's *Origin of Geometry* (*Hua* 6) and Schütz, 1964.

19 Of course, that distinction between primary and secundary passivities is to be found in Husserl's texts, although not in a systematic form. See *Hua* 9, § 21, *Hua* 17, § 4 and *Beilage* II, *Hua* 1, § 38 and § 51, *Hua* 6, *Beilage* III, *Erfahrung und Urteil*, § 23 a. See also Ms. A VII 13 (1921) and the *Studien zur Struktur des Bewußtseins* worked out by Landgrebe. Besides, see Landgrebe's *Faktizität und Individuation*, where the distinction is more systematically brought about (in particular in "Das Problem der passiven Konstitution"). About the latter, see *Alter* n°3, 1995, p. 409–503.

20 See Holenstein, 1972, § 9: "Die Passivität als Inaktualität".

21 Among others, see Ruysbroeck's and Suso's suffering-oriented mystics.

22 See here the critical power of both Bouddha and Christ, as well as their ability to radically renew or recreate themselves and consequently the others. (See Thich Nhat Hanh, 1995; As for Husserl, he puts both of them together as being representative of a common eminent critical wisdom (Manuscript B I 2/88 and seq.)).

23 See Meister Eckhart's *Predigte*, in particular the one called: "Von der Abgeschiedenheit" which describes impassivity as a lack of every passion, as a preeminent power of self-observation.

24 See "Von der Abgeschiedenheit". On the contrary, E. Levinas emphasizes an ungrounded ethics where I am primarily exposed to the other within an infinite face-to-face relationship. It is an ethics which is deeply deprived of the measure, the very measure which is the token of Aristotle's ethics.

25 See Varela, Thompson, Rosch, 1989 and Vermersch, 1994.

26 See Depraz, 1995a.

27 For previous attempts, see Held, 1966; Brand, 1955; Henry, 1996. We made a first clarification of this notion of *self-anticipation* in "Can I anticipate myself? Temporality and Self-affection" in *Self-awareness, Temporality and Alterity. Central Topics in Phenomenology* (D. Zahavi ed.), Kluwer, Dordrecht 1998.

28 As far as I know, there are two kinds of experience which are quite near to that tertiary passivity, with a specific stress for each one: I mean "mindfulness" (Varela, Thompson, Rosch, 1989) and "transpassibilité" (H. Maldiney, 1992). Both provide a narrow link between intersubjectivity and temporal dynamics. Heidegger's *Gelassenheit* could he added here, although he does not emphasize the intersubjective background.

29 Holenstein, 1972. § 9, who accounts for the historical link there has been between Husserl and Kant with regard to the synthesis of associative affinity, and besides, their mediated structural relationships through H. Lipps and W. Wundt.

30 See Kern, 1962, § 17–19 and, for example, *Hua* 7/280–281.

31 See *Hua* 11/275; *Hua* 7. § 27 seq., and the Lecture "Kant und die Idee der transzendentalen Philosophie", *Hua* 7/282.

32 See Kern, 1962, § 22 and § 23.

33 See Kern, 1962, § 21 and Lohmar, 1993.

34 See Depraz, 1996a.

35 See in particular *Hua* 16, fourth Section and *Hua* 4, second Section, chapter III, Straus, 1935, Maldiney, 1991. More recently, see Barbaras, 1992.

36 See *LU* III, Sixth Investigation, Second Section, chapter VI; *EU*, Second Section, chapter II; Hua 3, Fourth Section.

37 See Depraz, 1995b, chapter III.

38 See Ms. B IV 12, p. 3 (around 1920), quoted by Kern, 1962, p. 259.

39 See Barsotti, 1994.

40 *Critique of pure reason*, A19/B33.

41 See Hübner, 1953, Marty, 1980 and 1991.

42 See *Hua* 1, § 36 seq. and *EU*, § 64 seq.

43 See Holenstein, 1972, § 9, and Husserl himself, Ms. B IV 1, p. 159 (1908), quoted by the latter.

44 As a matter of fact, such a possibility has yet to be demonstrated, even if it has to be *against* certain of Husserl's own statements. See for example *Hua* 9/77 (§ 9 c), where "passive Phantasie" refers to a goalless associative invention of images. This empirically inspired phantasy is rejected by Husserl and opposed to the eidetic process of *Umfingieren*. Passive means here purely receptive and even causal. We will therefore have to show that a passive imagination can still be a real phenomenological possibility.

45 See Sartre, 1940.

46 Although Sartre is here very far from any onto-theo-logical (at best Thomist) model of theology, the question arises whether he would not be quite close to a specific version of negative theology.

47 For these non- or pre-phenomenological conceptions of passive imagination, see the Cartesian bodily dependent imagination or the Biranian passive phantasy.

48 Such a difference between passion and affection (alias emotion) can be traced back to Kant's *Anthropology* (third Part, B).

49 See *Hua* 9/72ff., § 9, *EU*, fourth Section, Hua 3/311ff., § 149, and *Hua* 5/331, § 7.

50 See *Hua* 23, especially the texts n° 18, 19 and 20. These texts date from the early twenties.

51 See *Hua* 16, n°14 and n°21.

52 See Bernet, 1996 and Depraz, 1996a.

53 See *Hua* 23/574ff., n°20, where imaginary life is said to be a passive life.

54 See *Hua* 23/504, n°18 a.

55 See *Hua* 23, n°18 a and b. and n°20.

56 At the end of this paper, I would like to thank Sylvio Senn and Violeta Miskievitz, whose rich and valuable insights helped me in my investigation of a truly phenomenological passive imagination. Furthermore, I would also like to thank the students of the University of Poitiers, whose attention and patience encouraged me to carry on with my project. The quite demanding course of lectures which they attended was given in 1994–95 and entitled: Husserl and Kant: From One Transcendental Philosopher to Another. Last but not least, I wish to thank Dan Zahavi for some fruitful remarks.

9

FRANÇOISE DASTUR

Françoise Dastur studied in the Sorbonne in the sixties with Derrida and Ricoeur, and later in Freiburg with Eugen Fink and Werner Marx. She holds a doctorate from the University of Louvain in Belgium, which she prepared under the direction of Jacques Taminiaux in 1993. She is a phenomenologist who has taught in Paris I (1969–95) and Paris XII (1995–9) and is now Professor of Philosophy at the University of Nice where she is attached to the Phenomenological Seminar (a research group of the CNRS). She is President of the École française of Daseinanalyse, and gives a monthly seminar at the Sorbonne with the collaboration of psychiatrists. She has worked in particular on Heidegger, Husserl, Holderlin, Merleau-Ponty, Ricoeur and Derrida, and on the questions of time, language, death and tragedy. She has translated into French texts by Nietzsche, Husserl, Fink and Heidegger.

Her publications include the following:

Heidegger et la question du temps, Paris: PUF, 1990. (Translated into English as *Heidegger and the Question of Time*, Atlantic Highlands, N.J.: Humanities Press, 1998.)

Hölderlin. Tragédie et modernité, Fougères: Encre Marine, 1992.

Dire le temps. Esquisse d'une chrono-logie phénoménologique, Fougères: Encre Marine, 1994. (Translated into English as *Telling Time: sketch of a phenomenological chronology*, London: Athlone Press, 2000.)

La Mort. Essai sur la finitude, Paris: Hatier, 1994. (Translated into English as *Death: an essay on finitude*, London: Athlone Press, 1996.)

Husserl. Des mathématiques à l'histoire, Paris: PUF, 1995.

Hölderlin. Le retournement natal, Fougères: Encre Marine, 1997.

Comment vivre avec la mort?, Paris, Pleins Feux, 1998.

Chair et langage. Essais sur Merleau-Ponty, Fougères: Encre Marine, 2001.

Heidegger et la question anthropologique, forthcoming.

MORTALITY AND FINITUDE

The Heideggerian phenomenology of being mortal claims to concede to death whatever is radically unthinkable and impracticable about it, while showing how there can be a thinking and practice of what is here unthinkable and impracticable. But is that not ultimately the most subtle strategem by which we continue to convert the negative into a positive, and to give a meaning to what has none? This is the suspicion roused by Sartre who, taking Rilke, Malraux and Heidegger together as associates in the same idealist attempt to *recuperate* death', does not hesitate to speak of the 'sleight of hand' by which Heidegger, with 'an evident bad faith in the reasoning', individualizes death by means of *Dasein* and *Dasein* by means of death. Although this 'humanization of death' by Heidegger suits his own purposes, Sartre still proposes to 're-examine the question from the beginning'.[1] This 're-examination' is in fact based upon a radical failure to appreciate what makes of *Dasein* – which, following Henri Corbin, the first French translator of Heidegger, Sartre translates as 'human reality' – an ability-to-be-thrown, and of facticity an assumption of contingency. So it is not surprising to find Sartre asserting that 'death is not my possibility of no longer realizing a presence in the world, but rather *an always possible nihilation of my possibles which is outside my possibilities*', and concluding in opposition to Heidegger that 'far from being my own possibility, my death is *a contingent fact* which as such in principle escapes me and belongs originally to my facticity'.

It is not really the shortcomings of Sartre's reading of Heidegger that interest us here, but much more his wish not to grant any meaning to death, and to abandon it to its character of total absurdity: 'Thus death is never that which gives life its meaning; it is, on the contrary, that which as a matter of principle removes all meaning from life.'[2] This position in no way compels him to give up freedom for, according to him, death must be separated altogether from finitude, whereas the Heideggerian theory of being towards death seems, on the other hand, to be based entirely upon the strict identification of these two ideas. Because for Sartre death is a contingent fact, it does not in any way involve the structure of the existent in so far as it is *for-itself*; while finitude, by contrast, is a structure that determines intrinsically the being of the for-itself.

It is indeed not death that constitutes our finitude, but solely the choice by which the for-itself projects itself towards one possible to the exclusion of all the others. According to Sartre, there is a 'creation' of finitude by the very act of freedom: 'In other words human reality would remain finite even if it were immortal, because it *makes* itself finite by choosing itself as human.'[3] For the irreversibility of temporality would prohibit even an immortal being from being able to 'have a second chance', and would also give to a temporally indefinite existence a character of uniqueness: 'From this point of view the immortal like the mortal is born several and makes itself one'.[4] Finitude is here equated with singularity and at the same time separated from death which, for Sartre, retains the generality of a pure fact:

> Death is a pure fact as is birth; it comes to us from outside and it transforms us into the outside. At bottom it is in no way distinguished from birth, and it is the identity of birth and death that we call facticity.[5]

Singular subjectivity does not, therefore, assert itself in opposition to it, but independently of it, and there is no room for a distinction between a possible authentic attitude and a possible inauthentic attitude with regard to it, for 'precisely, we die always *into the bargain*'.[6]

Finitude is thus the work of freedom which, if it is to be effective, must set itself limits, but these have nothing to do with that external limit of death, for this is never *encountered* by the for-itself, and if it indeed 'haunts' all its projects, it does not, however, penetrate it: 'Since death escapes my projects because it is unrealizable, I myself escape death in my very project'.[7] By making of death a merely external limit Sartre provides the for-itself with an infinite freedom, and this seems hardly less 'idealist' than the 'humanization of death' that he wrongly attributes to Heidegger, since in this way, by his own admission, he succeeds in 'escaping' death in making of it, like Epicurus before him, a merely 'factual limit' which does not 'concern' us. But the whole question at issue is that of whether, in seeing death as an 'end' towards which we do not relate ourselves, we do not interpret our existence in terms of an inadequate model, that of the brute facticity of nature.

* * *

Finitude and totality

Is it really legitimate to regard human existence as the *series* of events that occur between birth and death? And if, like Sartre,[8] we compare existence with a melody, should we not first of all ask ourselves whether this is comprised only of a *succession* of notes? Out of the serial and the successive we shall never manage to make *one* existence. At the very most we shall manage to give an account of the thing's mode of being. This is why the representation of death as the mere 'final term' of a series utterly fails to give an account of the finitude of an existence. If Sartre dissociates the traditionally united ideas of finitude and death, it is because, in the case of death, he applies to *Dasein* – which is not a 'reality' but, rather, an existence – an inappropriate concept of end.

Can we suppose human existence to be made up of parts successively added on externally to one another from a first one to a last? Should we not recognize, rather, that the 'self' of the 'for-itself' constantly maintains a relationship with its beginning and its end, so that it constitutes a 'whole' in which no parts are to be distinguished? If it is capable of bringing itself into play 'as a whole', and projecting itself 'wholly' in each of its singular projects, this is just because its mode of being is fundamentally different from that of a *res*, a thing, whether this be simply present at hand, like a natural thing, or whether it be an artefact, a cultural object. It is possible to speak of the relation of 'parts' to a whole only in the case of a totality obtained by composition and addition, and it is impossible to regard the development of a living whole in that way, since its becoming is that of a self containing in itself all the 'moments' of its extension in time. In pointing out that there is therefore a *formal* identity between the being of *Dasein* and the living being, Heidegger not only reminds us that the difference between the two kinds of totality was already known to the Greeks, who distinguished *holon*, whole in sense of entire, from *pan*, whole in sense of sum; he also refers us to the development of concepts to be found in the third of Husserl's *Logical Investigations*.[9]

It is in the framework of a phenomenological logic that one can focus on the distinction, recognized by Hegel, between an independent part and a dependent moment. For such a logic, far from contenting itself with 'mere words' – here the words 'end' and 'whole' – prescribes for itself the precise task of returning to 'the things themselves' and to the intuitive data that underlie all signification.[10] According to Husserl, a distinction must be made between a fragment or independent part of a whole which may actually be separated from it, and a moment or dependent part of a whole which is separable from it only abstractly. What characterizes a moment is the relation of *belonging* to other moments and to the whole itself. What such a whole *is not yet* belongs to it nevertheless, whereas in the case of the whole composed of parts this is lacking from the assemblage of parts that are already present. The concept of lack, in the sense of incompleteness, is strictly applicable only to a whole composed of parts, and can have no application whatsoever to a totality in a state of becoming, like a living being. For this could never *become* what it is not yet unless in a certain fashion it was that *always-already*. Heidegger cites here the example of the fruit which can ripen only by bringing *itself* to ripeness, and this implies that ripeness is not simply added, like something else, to unripeness, but already belongs to the unripe fruit *as a constituent* of it.

'Become what you are. Such in fact is the law of the living, propounded already by Pindar,[11] from whom Nietzsche borrows this formula. It is not in fact possible for a living being to become radically other than what it is. This is why Aristotle understood the result of becoming, *energeia*, in terms of a power of becoming other, *dynamis*, meaning by this not an abstract possibility to be converted into a concrete realization, but a certain being disposed to . . . or being apt to . . . which is *already* orientated towards this result. So that the 'negativity' of the *dynamis* with regard to the perfecting of what Aristotle calls not only *energeia* (that which belongs to itself in its *ergon*, in its work, and is thus accomplished) but also *entelecheia* (that which has in itself its *telos*, its end) is never merely a determinate negativity, an *unfulfilment*. Although this is structurally different from mere incompleteness, no more than the latter can it serve to define the finitude of human existence. For, as Heidegger remarks, even 'unfulfilled' *Dasein* comes to an end and, conversely, it may have achieved fulfilment long before its end. So that for *Dasein*, coming to an end can never mean purely and simply fulfilling itself.[12]

The biological model of fulfilment none the less remains one of the ways in which the human being understands itself. Nietzsche, for example, remains locked into this schema when he defines man as 'the not yet determined animal'[13] – that is to say, the animal that has not yet succeeded in determining what might constitute the plenitude of its own being, its specific accomplishment. It is therefore prone to deem its existence, however long, always too short, and its death seems to it always premature. Seneca echoes this universal complaint, although he criticizes it, at the beginning of his famous treatise 'On the Shortness of Life', where he reminds us that the ordinary man and the sage agree in thinking that 'everyone is abandoned by life at the moment when they are preparing to live', and that Aristotle himself considers that nature has shown itself to be less benevolent towards humans than towards animals in assigning the former a much shorter life despite their being born for great achievements.[14] It seems clear that if the animal can perish after realizing everything of which it was capable, if it can have attained that fulfilment that the Greeks called *aretē*, the merit or specific quality in which it excels, so that the prolongation of its life would no longer make any sense, it is quite different for the human being. The human being always dies before it has exhausted all the possibilities of its being, as if it were violently prevented by death from accomplishing something it has not yet done.

Furthermore, what makes history and culture possible is the fact that human death is always felt to be 'not natural'. What the dead person has not had the time to complete can be taken up and completed by someone else.[15] For Aristotle, the human being, like other living beings, survives itself only through its descendants, since:

> for any living thing that has reached its normal development and which is unmutilated, and whose mode of generation is not spontaneous, the most natural act is the production of another like itself, an animal producing an animal, a plant a plant, in order that, as far as its nature allows, it may partake in the eternal and divine.[16]

One must distinguish, however, between the offspring of the animal – which reproduces only its own existence, since this has already reached its perfection – and the offspring of man, which is able to go further than its parent in accomplishing what the latter left unfinished. In this sense it can be said that with man paternity is always a 'spiritual' paternity, because it supposes not just the transmission of genetic 'capital' but also the legacy of a number of possibilities capable of being taken up or rejected. One can hardly seek to 'conquer death' by paternity unless one acknowledges the 'spiritual' dimension of the relation of 'exteriority' which unites the son to his father and at the same time 'ontologizes' this 'biological' category.[17]

However, although the biological schema of fulfilment may continue to form the structure of the idea man has of himself as a cultural being, it cannot provide a concept of 'ending' that could adequately represent the mode of being of *Dasein*. As we have already seen, *Dasein* cannot passively *undergo* any kind of 'end', whether this be the fulfilment of its maturity or the simple cessation of its existence, unless it is first related to its existence in, as it were, preceding it. In this way it *is* always-already its end, which can come to it from 'outside' only because it is already open to it from the beginning. This is why, instead of remonstrating against the brevity of life, as Protagoras already did – seeing in this, moreover, a reason for atheism and a motive for devoting himself to the purely human sphere[18] – and instead of thinking that death always comes too soon, one should on the contrary, as Heidegger maintains, consider that the human being is always old enough to die, because birth is in itself already an overture to death, and the fact of birth in itself invests us with the ability to die.

Hence it is in terms of such a *being-towards-the-end* that the finitude of existence may be understood. However, this does not at all mean, as Sartre would have it, that finitude can be chosen by an infinite freedom. For only the in-finite can *make itself* finite, whereas to exist means precisely *to be born* – that is, not to be at the origin of one's own being. Neither passively undergone nor freely created, the finitude of existence can only be *assumed*. The human being exists in a finite manner, and this means that, as being 'thrown into death',[19] it possesses less the capacity to give it freely to itself than that of *taking it upon itself*. One must be immortal if one is going to be able *oneself* to give oneself death, and it is upon this truth of Christianity that Hegel conferred a philosophical status in conceiving of the 'death' of the absolute, which, losing its transcendence, descends into history only to rise there again as spirit. A becoming finite of the infinite such as this can certainly not be likened to the radical *finitude* of a being who does not put himself in the presence of death by his own free decision, and who can therefore never be free with regard to death, but only free 'for' it. This is why Heidegger says, in 'What is Metaphysics?': 'So deeply is *Dasein* penetrated by finitization that our ownmost and most profound finitude refuses to give in to our freedom.'[20]

* * *

Finitude and natality

This mortal being *Dasein* is by no means free to *make itself finite*. Because it is thrown into the midst of being, and is not itself at the origin of its own being, it is *always-already finite*. For *Dasein* is not solely a being for that end which is death, but is equally a being for that end which is birth.[21] From the existential point of view birth is no more a past event than death is the future event of decease. *Dasein* exists 'natally', just as it exists 'mortally', throughout the entire length of its life.[22] But what does 'existing natally' signify for *Dasein*? At the point where Heidegger reaches the most original interpretation of *Dasein*'s being as temporality, he raises the question of what constitutes the 'totality' of *Dasein*, and himself acknowledges that the existential analysis has remained unilaterally directed towards being for death, and has not taken into account the phenomenon of birth. But there is in *Being and Time* an analysis of being-thrown which sheds some light on what being-born means for *Dasein*. For to say that *Dasein* is thrown into the world is, as we have already seen, to say that it is up to *Dasein* to take its own facticity upon itself, and from this it follows that it is, as it were, 'in debt' or 'at fault' with regard to itself. If Heidegger sees 'conscience' and 'being at fault' as existentials of *Dasein*, it is less because he is repeating at an ontological level a theme of Christianity[23] than because what has been 'thematized' by Christianity has an existential phenomenon at its foundation. It is because *Dasein* has not placed itself in existence and is not at the origin of its own being that it has to become responsible for what it is already, which means that it has to assume its own *de facto* being. It is therefore originally 'indebted' or 'guilty', because it exists only in terms of this debt which it has not itself contracted, or of this 'fault' that it has not itself committed. The Judaeo-Christian idea of 'original fault' itself could not have been formed except for the fact that the human being, in being born, sees stretching behind it an absolute past that it will never be able to appropriate completely, and for which, even so, it is 'originally' guilty. It is the same experience of an evil inherent in existence itself that is at the origin of the tragic sense of life in Greece, and it is this that leads the sage Silenus to say, when King Midas asks him what the best thing of all in the world is, 'The best of all things is entirely outside your grasp: not to have been born, not to *be*, to be *nothing*. The second-best thing for you – is to die soon.'[24]

So human existence contains something negative. This cannot be reduced to 'duty' in the moral sense of the word, since, on the contrary, it is presupposed by the latter. Nor can it be properly understood as 'lack', since this is a concept that cannot be applied to that temporal being which *Dasein* is. For although it has not laid the foundation of its own being, and can never become master of its own existence, nevertheless *Dasein* has, as an existing being, to take upon itself the being of founding itself.[25] So this 'negativity' peculiar to existence prevents it from being absolutely contemporary with itself, and it is this impossibility of ever being master of its ownmost being – in that it derives, as Sartre saw clearly, from the irreversibility of temporality, which constitutes its radical finitude.

It is thus on the basis of a 'negativity' and a fundamental lateness with regard to itself that *Dasein* is constituted as ipseity. This is why its position is necessarily one of an *heir* that on coming into the world finds already traced out possibilities which it can either assume as its own or not, but which it has not itself projected.[26] However, it is because it is capable of *opening itself* to these possibilities that it can truly become the heir that it is, and so assume its own facticity. The assumption of its being assigned to something already given, which refers to the existential phenomenon of birth, demands, then, the freedom of an authentic ability-to-be supposing the assumption of mortality. It is only in terms of this future which will never become present, this absolute future which is death, that *Dasein* can assume the absolute past of its birth, and thus be *one* existence. This is, as it were, the reply with which Heidegger anticipates Sartre's criticism. The choice of possibilities of existence can take place solely in the light of death, and only a *finite* freedom can therefore confront the irreversibility of temporality.

If the condition of birth is shown in this way to be death, the fact remains that philosophy has traditionally understood the essence of finitude in terms of what, by analogy with its mortality, may be referred to as the human being's 'natality'. In fact, it is not chiefly because it is destined to die, but because it is a created being, an *ens creatum* absent from its own origin, that the human being has only an *intuitus derivatus*, a 'derived intuition' – in other words, the kind of vision that is capable of grasping only something given, something already there, whereas the Creator's *intuitus originarius* is a kind of vision that is at the very origin of things. What is traditionally understood as *intuitus derivatus* is the necessity that the kind of intuition possible for a man as *ens creatum* be derived from a being that exists before he does. Here once more the Christian doctrine of creation discovers a foundation in 'the things themselves', since it amounts to a determinate interpretation of being-thrown, and of that original 'lateness' which prevents existence from being contemporary with its own emergence.

Kant, who takes over from the tradition the distinction between *intuitus derivatus* and *intuitus originarius*,[27] is led by this to develop a conception of finitude that makes this depend upon the necessarily sensible character of human intuition. For what is quite new in Kantianism as compared with Cartesianism, and its doctrine of sensibility as only confused intelligibility, is its recognition of sensibility as an altogether independent faculty of knowledge. Kant asserts that there are *two* distinct sources of knowledge: sensibility, by which objects are given; and understanding, by which they are thought.[28] Henceforth the problem is entirely that of how to define human knowledge. Is it intuitive thinking or thinking intuition? Is there complete reciprocity between an intuition which needs the concept in order not to remain blind and a concept which, without intuition, remains empty?[29] Where is the centre of gravity of human knowledge? In the interpretation of the *Critique of Pure Reason* expounded in *Kant and the Problem of Metaphysics*, Heidegger puts the accent on the first sentence of the Transcendental Aesthetic, which defines thought as a means to intuition, and sees in this a definition of human knowledge as finite in contrast to divine knowledge as infinite. The latter is wholly intuition, but intuition which is at the origin of what is seen, and totally transparent to it; whereas human sight, just because it is subservient to the given presence of an entity and secondary in relation to this, needs thought in order to know what it sees. However, the essential difference between human knowledge and divine knowledge is not that the one is pure intuition while the other is thinking intuition. The difference lies, rather, in the mode of intuition.

What distinguishes finite intuition? It is not creative. On the contrary, it is subservient to the object, secondary by comparison with it, *derived* in the sense of something whose origin is exterior to itself. Such intuition must allow itself to be provided with its object, since it is not capable of providing it for itself. Its distinguishing characteristic, therefore, is *receptivity*. But in order to receive, it must be capable of being touched by what will be received by it – as Kant in fact points out in the second sentence of the Transcendental Aesthetic, which explains that this intuition is possible 'only on condition that the object affects our mind in a certain way'. The reception of something given thus presupposes an affection, and this in turn presupposes organs capable of being affected: namely, *sense*-organs, for in the third sentence of the Aesthetic Kant defines receptivity as sensibility. Heidegger notes that these three sentences on their own lead to a reversal of the usual point of view. Human intuition is sensible not because affection is mediated by the senses, which would be no more than a factual limitation, but because it is finite, receptive – that is, subservient to the presence of an entity, because it must offer the entity the possibility of making itself known through the senses. The sense-organs that are in this way at the service of affectivity are not the 'causes' of our finitude but are, much more, its consequences; and far from sensibility explaining our finitude it is, on the contrary, in this that it has its raison d'être. From this Heidegger concludes: 'Kant for the first time attains a concept of sensibility which is ontological rather than sensualistic'.[30] It is this which enables him to develop the (from an empiricist standpoint) astonishing theory of pure sensibility. For sensibility is the *capacity* to receive impressions produced by objects and, as such, must lay out the conditions of this receptivity. It is not, therefore, to be confused with empirical intuition. Rather, it is it that which makes this possible.

Human knowledge, then, is in the first place intuition – that is to say, the immediate representation of an object. But to be fully knowledge, this representation must be made accessible always and to everyone. An intuited object is necessarily particular. It can become communicable only if it is determined *as* the same for everyone who intuits it. Such a determination consists, therefore, in a representation (a concept) of a representation (an intuition) which makes the individual object intended appear under the aspect of generality so that what is represented in intuition may be better represented – that is, made present for more than one person. Because finite intuition calls for determination, it is dependent upon the understanding. Not only does the latter participate in the finitude of the intuition in the service of which it remains, but it is itself still more finite than intuition, since it lacks intuition's character of immediacy. Heidegger concludes from this that it is the discursivity of the understanding that comprises the most significant mark of its finitude.[31]

Thus the Kantian conception of finitude interprets this as the tying of human knowledge to the prior givenness of an entity which can never be for it more than an object, a pre-existing entity with which it sees itself confronted, whereas infinite knowledge renders the entity manifest to itself by bringing about its original emergence. For, as Kant himself says, it is the *same* entity which, related to finite knowledge, is a phenomenon, but related to infinite knowledge is a thing in itself.[32] But in thus conceiving finitude unilaterally in terms of being-created, and so in terms of natality, Kant is led, like tradition as a whole, to locate in *another* being, in God, the power of creative intuition capable of bringing about a thing's emergence. It is therefore still in an *external* manner that finitude is determined according to him, since this is made to depend upon a divine infinitude which alone gives it all its meaning.[33] In bringing out the fact that dying is the condition of being born and death the condition of life, is it possible to gain access to an idea of finitude which is more radical in that it would no longer presuppose a transcendence of time as its correlate, an idea of original finitude which would no longer be based on infinity?

* * *

Original finitude

Of course, it is possible to produce a formal argument to the effect that all discourse about the finite and finitude presupposes a basis in the idea of infinity. It could be said that because finitude can appear only in the form of lack, imperfection and incompleteness, it implies the primacy of a relation to the infinite, the completed and the perfected, and that the finite being's understanding of itself derives, therefore, from its relation to an infinite Other. This is the argument developed in the third of Descartes's *Meditations* when, finding in himself the idea of infinity, he conceives the finitude of the *cogito* in terms of divine existence and not in terms of the mortality of the subject. Thus 'the Cartesian subject is given a point of view exterior to itself from which it can apprehend itself', as noted by Levinas, who sees the ethical relation itself in this relation to an infinity capable of being accommodated neither in intuition nor in reason.[34] And there is no doubt that the 'traumatic' way in which the infinite breaks into the finite ego corresponds to the authentic experience of that *independence* of what is thought with respect to the thinker which makes of *every* genuine act of thought an overwhelming event, since the parallelism between the *cogito* and its *cogitatum*, between the thought and its object, is here constantly affirmed and denied *at one and the same time*. In fact the whole problem depends on our interpretation of this experience. We can either *separate* the origin of the finite from the finite, in which case the exteriority of the infinite is the 'reason' for the finite, or we can *relate* the origin of the finite to the finite, in which case the interiority of the finite is the 'reason' for the infinite. In both cases finitude and infinity are intrinsically linked, the one necessarily requiring the other.

There is thus no finitude that is not at the same time an experience of infinity. This is substantially the objection Heidegger made to Cassirer when they met at the colloquium at Davos in 1929. Cassirer maintained that in Kant morality effects a break with the phenomenal world which is also a transcendence of the knower's finitude. Heidegger – underlining the fact that this exit towards the noumenal remains *relative* to the finite being precisely because the concept of the imperative as such is valid only for such a being – aims to show that the 'quite central problem' here is precisely the fact that infinity comes to light in the content of what is presented as the sphere where finitude is constituted.[35] The one thing a phenomenology focuses on and confines itself to is the *connection* between finitude and infinity which prohibits it from *positing* the one *outside* the other – as, by contrast, theology does. It is within the context of a *phenomenological* interpretation of the *Critique of Pure Reason* that Heidegger proposes to show that this connection has certainly been perceived by Kant, even though the traditional context in which his thought is developed continues to be decisively marked by theology.

Finitude, the receptivity of intuition, implies a directedness to what must be received in order that it may be encountered. In order that something may present itself as something over against us, as an ob-ject, a horizon of ob-jective appearance must be spread out in sensibility. For the very reason that it does not create what it intuits, the finite being must have the capacity to lay out the conditions that allow it to welcome it; that is to say, it must be able to 'form' spontaneously the view of what is presented. This is the role of the imagination, in so far as it furnishes forms or sensible schemata in terms of which objects of intuition may be thought. In calling the schematizing imagination *exhibitio originaria* – 'productive' imagination, imagination which is able to present the object originally – Kant is led to acknowledge an originality of the finite being itself, that is to say, a free creative power. But this creation is one not of the entity itself, for that pre-exists it, but of the horizon with reference to which it will be able to present itself as ob-ject. This free *donation* of an ontological horizon is therefore wholly relative to *ontic reception*, to the simple perception of the entities which present themselves to us. This is why Heidegger sees in it the strongest argument in favour of finitude.

No ontological horizon can be projected unless it is determined by *dependence* with respect to the preexistence of the entity. Ontology is possible, therefore, because existence is in itself finitude, not because this would find itself 'transcended'. For only a finite being, not God, *needs* ontology.[36] The 'transcendence' of the simply given that is carried out in every act of thinking is by no means the entry of the light of infinity from outside, but the manifestation of a need to understand on the part of a being allocated a dwelling in the world and forced to ignite by himself the fires that will illumine the walls of his prison. It is this transcendental need which is the very source of *Da-sein*, of that creative irruption of an opening which makes all presence possible and is at the origin of the very being of man. 'More original than man is the finitude of the *Dasein* within him.'[37]

Such a conception of finitude, one not dependent upon the *actual* infinity of a deathless and timeless divine being, is no longer in itself meta-physical or trans-cendental but is, rather, the very root of transcendentalism exposed to view, and the foundation of metaphysics exhibited at last. For it is not *despite* finitude and mortality that there is transcendence. There is, rather, a finitude *of* transcendence which stems precisely from the fact that as being towards death *Dasein throws itself beforehand* into the possibility of an absolute closedness to being, and of the abyssal obscurity from which it has emerged. It can be *open* to itself, to others and to the world only as long as it is constantly threatened by the possibility of becoming shut off from everything that is. This is how it is constantly held in the nothing by which it has a revelation of anxiety, that fundamental disposition through which – in being in relation to its own end, and in what Hegel so aptly described as 'the absolute fluidification of all subsistence' – *Dasein* experiences 'the constant, though veiled, precariousness that pervades all existence'.[38]

If the relation to mortality is a relation the human being has to its own end, the latter can no longer appear as pure accidental interruption, incompleteness and imperfection but, rather, as the 'foundation' which does not appear and the 'nocturnal' source of all appearing. Such a conception of finitude returns human being to its constitutive facticity, to its properly terrestrial, temporal and corporeal character. This conception of mortality as finitude constitutive of the opening to the world – as what, closely following Heidegger, Merleau-Ponty so fittingly calls *operant* finitude[39] – is at the same time a conception of birth as the finite capacity of having a world. For, as Hölderlin's Diotima says at the moment of her death: 'We part only to be more intimately united, more divinely at peace with all things and ourselves. We die in order to live.'[40]

Conclusion

Death, Speech and Laughter

> For we are nothing but the husk and the leaf.
> Great death, that each within him bears,
> is the fruit around which all revolves.
>
> Rilke[1]

We are open to the world only because we have a relatedness to that nothing which is death. And the sole foundation our existence ever has is the depths of a limitless occultation and oblivion from which we emerge only to bear witness to it.[2] It is *in existing* that we are witnesses of death – even and especially when we take up a stand against it, and 'work' to conquer it, employing all the means at our disposal to overcome it. Language, the primary and most powerful of these means, is also the one that most radically reveals our finitude. If, as Hegel recognized, language itself is a power of death, because to impose names on things is to annihilate them in their real existence, it follows

151

– as Blanchot makes clear in commenting on Hegel – that 'when I speak, death speaks in me', and that it is what both separates me from being and binds me to it.[3] The condition of the emergence of meaning and the prerequisite of the utterance of any words is thus 'a kind of huge hecatomb' by which the inaccessible singularity of the ineffable 'this' is put to death in order to make possible its resurrection in the form of the ideal generality of the *entity*. 'I say: a flower! and, outside the *forgetting* where no contour is banished by my voice, as something *other* than the calyxes known, arises musically, idea same and sweet, the *absence* from all bouquets.'[4] Speech, then, in the musicality of its intonation, is what rescues from deep oblivion and limitless occultation the very *being* of things, which is neither their mere sensible singularity nor their pure abstract concept, but the *alterity* of their absence which presents itself to us 'sweetly' – that is, sensibly – in the sonority of the words that name them. Being is therefore nothing other than the *gift* we are given by death in its omnipotence. This omnipotence is not in the least diminished by our 'work' of subjugating nature, which is aimed today, however, thanks to the progress of biology, at nothing less than the indefinite prolongation of human life.[5] What this omnipotence *grants* does not reveal itself in work directed at fixing up a place in which human beings may live, but in taking part in the *gratuitousness* of the *play* of the world to which only those have access who, in leaving behind themselves every ambition for the unconditioned and the absolute, have *become* mortals and henceforth live wittingly in the proximity of death.[6]

If in *Being and Time* authenticity is defined in a still quite Hegelian way as *Dasein*'s capacity to stand and face the gaze of death,[7] in later writings, when 'mortal' becomes the proper name of man,[8] it is a question of man's gaining access to and entering death.[9] It is thus death alone which, in its immeasurability, can give man the measure that Hölderlin had already found only in the emptiness of the heavens.[10] For, more than in the clearing itself, it is in the *heart* of this, in the *lēthē* of *alētheia*, that man truly belongs.[11] Because it is only from a bottomless darkness that the clearing of the world can spread out – just as, as Heraclitus suggests, at is from the 'crypt' favoured by it that *physis* may emerge, since 'self-revealing not only never dispenses with concealing, but actually *needs* it, in order to obtain essentially in the way it obtains as disclosing'.[12] Death as shelter of being and nocturnal source of all light is thus acknowledged to have an immeasurable power which remains unthought in all the stratagems we imagine in order to overcome it.

If this clearing that the world is cannot unfold itself otherwise than through the word, it follows that what speaks in this is actually death itself. What is called for, therefore, is not so much recognition that language can itself be the vehicle of death as seeing in it the phenomenal attestation of the hold death has over us. For we are, as it were, its mouth and it is, so to speak, upon its very lips that, as Hölderlin says, 'words, like flowers, are born',[13] words whose audible opening out gives rise to, rather than breaking, the immense silence from which it is born. And yet, far from grimacing and exhaling horror, this is instead a laughing, just as anxiety is cheerful and mourning itself full of joy.

For because anxiety is the revelation of the ecstatic character of *Dasein*, of its profound strangeness and its not belonging to the familiarity of being at home,[14] and because its being-thrown towards death is primordially disclosed in this anxiety,[15] this is secretly allied not only to joy and cheerfulness, as Heidegger himself maintains,[16] but also to laughter, in which Bataille – not without reason – saw 'nature's violent self-suspension'[17] and 'the point of rupture, of abandonment, the anticipation of death'.[18] In fact we *explode* into laughter only when, as in anxiety, there is no ground to stand on, when nothing fixed remains, and when in this state of suspense we find ourselves liberated from the burdens and attachments of daily life, and released into that more than human lightness by which existence as burden is transformed into grace.

Uncontrolled, uncontrollable, laughter bursts forth, shakes us, rends us more profoundly and opens us more infinitely than do affliction and tears, which bring us, instead, together with ourselves. Madly, it bears us to the edge of the abyss which we have in ourselves, towards the bottomless depths of an existence which in its radical mortality, far from being able to recoup its stake, is, on the contrary, carried away in the irresistible movement of an unjustified expenditure and innocent becoming whose emblematic figure is still that of the 'king of finitude'[19] – the playing child in Heraclitus, Fragment 52: 'The *aiōn* [that is to say, the span of life that each of us is granted, existence limited by death] is a child playing a game of draughts: the kingship of a child.'[20]

This kingship of finitude, and this irresponsibility and amorality of the play of the cosmos for which no expiation is desirable or possible, go wholly without recognition wherever, as in industrialized societies – hence today over an increasingly large part of planet Earth – there is forgetfulness of death.

Notes

1 Jean-Paul Sartre, *Being and Nothingness*, trans. Hazel E. Barnes (London, Methuen, 1969), pp. 531 ff.
2 Ibid., p. 539.
3 Ibid., p. 546.
4 Ibid.
5 Ibid., p. 545.
6 Ibid., p. 548.
7 Ibid.
8 Ibid., p. 531.
9 Martin Heidegger, *Being and Time*, trans. John Macquarrie and Edward Robinson (Oxford, Blackwell, 1962), p. 244, note.
10 Edmund Husserl, *Logical Investigations*, trans. J.N. Findlay (London, Routledge, 1970), vol. II, p. 435.
11 What Pindar actually says is: 'May'st thou become what thou art in learning' (Second Pythic Ode, line 72). It is true that, understood strictly, this applies to the human being, but to the extent only that *mathēsis*, spiritual growth through learning, is its own mode of becoming.
12 The very term *energeia*, which testifies that the source of the distinction between act and power is to be sought first in the model of production in the crafts, demonstrates the persistence of schemata borrowed from fabrication in Aristotle's explanations of natural phenomena.
13 See Heidegger's comments in Heidegger, *What is Called Thinking?*, trans. Fred D. Wieck and J. Glenn Gray (New York, Harper & Row, 1968), pp. 57 ff.
14 Seneca, 'On the Shortness of Life', in *The Stoic Philosophy of Seneca*, ed. Moses Hadas (New York, Doubleday, 1958), 15, pp. 47–8.
15 Alexandre Kojève, *Introduction to the Reading of Hegel*, trans. James H. Nichols, ed. Allan Bloom (New York, Basic Books, 1969), pp. 257–8.

16 Aristotle, *De Anima*, trans. J.A. Smith, 415a 26, in *The Basic Works of Aristotle*, ed. Richard McKeon (New York, Random House, 1941).

17 In order to see a 'pluralist existing' in paternity, as Levinas does, it is necessary, as he himself insists, to appreciate the 'ontological value' of the 'ego's fecundity'. For the ego becomes another self in the son, and the son is neither his work nor his property, but the very transcendence of existence. See Emmanuel Levinas, *Time and the Other*, trans. Richard A. Cohen (Pittsburgh, PA, Duquesne University Press, 1987), p. 92.

18 See the following fragment from the introduction to his work 'On the Gods': 'About the gods I am not able to know whether they exist or do not exist, nor what they are like in form. For the obstacles to knowledge are many: their invisibility and the brevity of human life.'

19 Heidegger, *Being and Time*, p. 329.

20 Heidegger, 'What is Metaphysics?', trans. David Farrell Krell, in Heidegger, *Basic Writings*, ed. David Farrell Krell (New York, Harper & Row, 1977), p. 108.

21 Heidegger, *Being and Time*, pp. 372–3.

22 Ibid., p. 374.

23 Jacques Derrida, 'Donner la mort', in *L'Ethique du don: Jacques Derrida et la pensée du don* (Paris, Métailié-Transition, 1992), p. 29; *The Gift of Death*, trans. David Wills (Chicago, University of Chicago Press, 1995), pp. 22–3.

24 Friedrich Nietzsche, *The Birth of Tragedy from the Spirit of Music*, trans. Shaun Whiteside (Harmondsworth, Penguin, 1993), para. 3, p. 22.

25 Heidegger, *Being and Time*, pp. 285.

26 Ibid., p. 384.

27 Immanuel Kant, *Critique of Pure Reason*, Transcendental Aesthetic, B 72.

28 Ibid., Introduction, B 29–30.

29 Ibid., Transcendental Logic, B75.

30 Heidegger, *Kant and the Problem of Metaphysics*, trans. Richard Taft (Bloomington, Indiana University Press, 1990), p. 18.

31 Ibid., p. 20.

32 Ibid., p. 21–2.

33 Heidegger, *Phänomenologische Interpretation von Kants Kritik der reinen Vernunft*, *Gesamtausgabe* 25, ed. Ingtraud Görland (Frankfurt am Main, Klostermann, 1977), p. 410.

34 Levinas, *Totality and Infinity: An Essay on Exteriority*, trans. Alphonso Lingis (The Hague, Nijhoff, 1969), p. 210.

35 'Davos Disputation Between Ernst Cassirer and Martin Heidegger', Appendix to Heidegger, *Kant and the Problem of Metaphysics*, pp. 174–5.

36 Ibid., p. 175. [However, in the English translation referred to in Note 35 Heidegger's ambiguous 'Denn Ontologie braucht nur em endliches Wesen' becomes 'for ontology requires only a finite creature', which reverses the point that the context seems to demand. – Trans.]

37 Heidegger, *Kant and the Problem of Metaphysics*, p. 156.

38 Ibid., p. 162.

39 Maurice Merleau-Ponty, *The Visible and the Invisible*, trans. Alphonso Lingis, ed. Claude Lefort (Evanston, IL, Northwestern University Press, 1968), p. 251.

40 Friedrich Hölderlin, *Hyperion*, in *Sämtliche Werke*, Dritter Band, ed. Friedrich Beissner (Stuttgart, Kohlhammer, 1957), p. 148.

Conclusion: Death, Speech and Laughter

1   Denn wir sind nur die Schale und das Blatt.
Der grosse Tod, den jeder in sich hat,
das ist die Frucht, um die sich alles dreht.

> Rainer Maria Rilke, *Das Buch von der Armut und vom Tode* (1903),
> in *Das Stunden-Buch, Gesammelte Werke*,
> Band II (Leipzig, Insel Verlag, 1927), p. 273.

2 Eclipse and forgetting, which in Greek are expressed in a single word, *lēthē*, since this noun, which is also the name of the Plain or River of Forgetting in the Underworld, comes from the verb *lanthanō*, meaning 'to be hidden', 'to remain concealed', like the Latin *lateo*, which derives from the same root.

3 Maurice Blanchot, 'La littérature et le droit à la mort', in *La Part du feu* (Paris, Gallimard, 1949), p. 326.

4 'Je dis: une fleur! et, hors de l'*oubli* où ma voix relègue aucun contour, en tant que quelque chose d'*autre* que les calices sus, musicalement se lève, idée même et suave, l'*absente* de tous bouquets.' Stéphane Mallarmé, 'Crise de vers', *Œuvres complètes*, Bibliothèque de la Pléiade (Paris, Gallimard, 1974). p. 368. (Emphasis added.)

5 On this point, see Hans Jonas, *The Imperative of Responsibility: In Search of an Ethics for the Technological Age*, trans. Hans Jonas and David Herr (Chicago, University of Chicago Press, 1984), pp. 18–19.

6 Martin Heidegger, 'The Thing', in *Poetry, Language, Thought*, trans. Albert Hofstadter (New York, Harper & Row, 1975) pp. 179–80, 182; Heidegger, *Der Satz vom Grund* (Pfullingen, Neske, 1957), pp. 186–7; *The Principle of Reason*, trans. Reginald Lilly (Bloomington, Indiana University Press, 1991). p. 112.

7 Heidegger, *Being and Time*, trans. John Macquarrie and Edward Robinson (Oxford, Blackwell, 1962), p. 382.

8 Heidegger, 'The Thing', in *Poetry, Language, Thought*, pp. 178–9.

9 Heidegger, 'Moira (Parmenides VIII, 34–41)', trans. Frank Capuzzi, in *Early Greek Thinking*, ed. David Farrell Krell (New York, Harper & Row, 1975), p. 101.

10 See the poem of Hölderlin's so-called 'mad' period, 'In lovely blueness . . .', in Friedrich Hölderlin, *Sämtliche Werke*, Zweiter Band, Erste Hälfte, *Gedichte nach 1800*, ed. Friedrich Beissner (Stuttgart, Kohlhammer – Cottasche Buchhandlung Nachfolger, 1951), pp. 372–4; *Poems and Fragments*, trans. Michael Hamburger (Cambridge, Cambridge University Press, 1980), pp. 600–5.

11 See Heidegger 'The End of Philosophy and the Task of Thinking', trans. Joan Stambaugh, in Heidegger, *Basic Writings*, ed. David Farrell Krell (New York, Harper & Row, 1977), p. 390.

12 Heidegger, 'Alētheia (Heraclitus, Fragment B 16)', trans. Frank Capuzzi, in *Early Greek Thinking*, ed. David Farrell Krell, p. 114, where Heidegger is commenting on Heraclitus, Fragment 123, *physis kryptesthai philei*, 'nature likes to hide itself'. (Emphasis added.)

13 Hölderlin, the fifth strophe of 'Bread and Wine', in Friedrich Hölderlin, *Sämtliche Werke*, Zweiter Band, Erste Hälfte, *Gedichte nach 1800*, ed. Friedrich Beissner, pp. 90–5; *Poems and Fragments*, trans. Michael Hamburger, pp. 248–9.

14 Heidegger, *Being and Time*, p. 188.

15 Ibid., p. 251.

16 Heidegger, 'What is Metaphysics?', trans. David Farrell Krell, in Heidegger, *Basic Writings*, ed. David Farrell Krell, p. 108.

17 Georges Bataille, 'Le coupable', in *Œuvres complètes*, vol. 5 (Paris, Gallimard, 1973), p. 349; *Guilty*, trans. Bruce Boon (Venice, San Francisco, Lapis Press, 1988), p. 103.

18 Ibid., p. 355.

19 This expression is to be found in Hölderlin's 'Hymn to Freedom', published in 1793. Hölderlin, *Sämtliche Werke*, Erste Band, Erste Hälfte, *Gedichte bis 1800*, ed. Friedrich Beissner (Stuttgart, Cottasche–Buchhandlung Nachfolger, 1946), p. 159.

20 See the translation and commentary in Heraclitus, *Fragments*, ed. M. Conche (Paris, Presses Universitaires de France, 1986), p. 446.

10

ELISABETH DE FONTENAY

Elisabeth de Fontenay teaches Philosophy at the University of Paris I (Sorbonne-Panthéon). She claims as major influences the three very different figures of Jankelevitch, Foucault and Derrida. She has worked on a wide variety of areas, from Diderot and Marx to her most recent explorations of the status of the animal – and, through the animal, the human – in philosophical discourse. De Fontenay is not easy to categorise: professing an anti-humanism which she sees as a true humanism, a feeling for tradition, which is a form of revolt, and a nostalgia for the past, which in her view lies at the heart of modernity. Her work on animals is similarly complex: she refutes what she sees as the excesses of both animal rights movements and those who construct a radical separation between humans and animals. And her professed enjoyment of hunting may surprise those who have either dismissed or championed her for over-simple positions that she does not hold.

Her major publications include the following:

Les Figures juives de Marx, Paris: Galilée, 1973.

Diderot ou le matérialisme enchanté, Grasset, 1979; Paris: UGE, 1986.

Interpréter Diderot aujourd'hui, (co-edited with J. Proust), Paris: Colloque de Cerisy, 1983; Paris: le Sycomore, 1984.

'La Raison du plus fort', in Plutarque, *Trois traités pour les animaux*, Paris: POL, 1992.

Le Silence des bêtes: la philosophie à l'épreuve de l'animalité, Paris: Fayard, 1998.

Des hommes et des bêtes, (co-authored with A. Finkielraut), Geneva: S. Kaplun, Tricorne, 2000.

LIKE POTATOES

The silence of animals

Introduction

It seems that we must proceed along a double line of enquiry if we are to determine the thought and passion of the animal. These are two somewhat divergent directions that tend, however, to coincide, not in the service of private or secret interests or to satisfy a taste in doublings, but for objective reasons and inasmuch as the aim of this study is to allow the animal to make its mark in the fields of history and philosophy. First, there is a Lucretian, pagan orientation that consists in subduing, indeed in abandoning, subjectivity – the subjectivity of metaphysics and reflexive practices – to a force that moves from distortions to identifications. These displacements are, of course, organised according to a system of philosophical deconstruction, but, above all, they depend for their organisation on an innocent wandering, the secret of which the Greeks and the Romans sealed mystically within the names of Dionysus and Bacchus, and philo-sophically under the concept of a 'plurality of worlds'. This deflection of individuality and subjectivity is played out within a tragedy that mixes pleasure, pity and cruelty, a cruelty that has nothing in common with that of modern times. Here, one can be drunk nostalgically on the multiplicity of living forms that are habitable and with which one can associate. The other orientation – Jewish, Christian, or, to put it bluntly, Republican, concerned with justice and compassion, perpetually full of pathos and always in danger of adopting an apocalyptic tone – asks where and when it was decided that animals must suffer unimaginably (through our deeds, for eternity and today more than ever), for the good of the techno-scientific, food-processing omnipotence of calculated self-interest.

This navigation of an almost phantom vessel on the isolated sea of metaphysics is conducted under the double flag of a *Miserere* and a deconstruction. We can criticise the lack of resolution in such an intention: must we not choose between pity and the overelaborate thought (which is unthinking) of philosophers? I admit that I have not been able to choose between the two approaches, because it seems to me that in this case pity has great powers of deconstruction. In fact, the aphasic *Kyrie eleison* addressed to the masters of *logos* and of the earth, this complaint that remains audible to some but which has been muffled twice by nature and by men, authorises a return to considering the distinct features of man and compels us to dismantle the mechanism of that which is given as an intangible and cardinal premise.

Philosophers who are attentive to the enigma of the animal are constantly taunted by the bogeyman of naturalism. There has been such permanent adherence to the

157

rudimentary disjunctions of matter/spirit, living/conscious, animal/man, subjection to nature/escape from nature that we might believe that history ended with Kant or Fichte. What is more, we would kick ourselves if we did not draw attention, if only in passing, to the power of naturalism, and above all of empiricism, to deflate the extravagances of the transcendental and the speculative. But what exactly are the crusaders of *humanitas* talking about? For them, 'naturalism' signifies anything from theology, to Thomism, vulgar materialism, ethology, and, for good measure, racism. To credit animals with any kind of capacity (even the capacity to suffer) or to be concerned with their fate at the hands of men would be automatically to deny the majesty of human suffering, to offend man by not affording sufficient status to the gap created by his escape from nature, his interiority, liberty and powers of self-constitution. These anthropolaters see only the excesses of the opposing camp. Konrad Lorenz reduces war to aggression[1] and Peter Singer values the life of a domestic animal over that of a disabled child:[2] these excesses and outrages are not philosopher's deeds, at least in the continental sense of the term 'philosopher'.

We must not become trapped in a situation that enjoins us to choose between two equally dogmatic discourses. Does Lévi Strauss's work not offer an example of a movement beyond these formal oppositions, in so far as his rigorous articulation of the nature/culture opposition breathes new life into the question of anthropological difference? The very same work enlightens us to the logic of the most distant of our fellow men and reflects on 'our' treatment of animals.

These quarrels with a so-called naturalism that would, inevitably, threaten any attempt to think philosophically about beasts, make no sense as soon as we are dealing with the animal, that is to say, with a sensitive being. Moreover, the animal has a world that tears it away from a simple naturalness, at least from the perspective of the phenomenological thesis that consists in a challenge to naturalisms and which eventually, it seemed to me, had to be sustained. To use other terms, the meanings of which will become clearer in the penultimate section of this study, we can provide a deconstructive critique of 'subjectivity' and trust to a certain extent in the concept or in the experience of 'consciousness'. This means that the animal, like man, is not a being of nature, it is simply more natural than man, but, like man, is capable, in accordance with the complexity of its organism, of a spontaneity and of a symbolisation that attest to what Hans Jonas refers to as 'the phenomenon of Life'.[3] In addition, as I wished occasionally to move beyond or beside a deconstruction of the metaphysical tradition that treats the animal as nothing but a trope, one particular statement that has caught my attention crops up in this study on several occasions: 'They sleep and we are awake'. In fact, metaphysics better withstood the test of beasts when it gave thought to the question of continuity. This generous distinction between those who are more or less awake and those who are more or less asleep comes from Diderot, who inherited it from Buffon, who, in a way, took it from Leibniz. Diderot said that vegetables, not animals, are asleep,[4] and used this basic gradation to differentiate between them and men. Nevertheless, I do not think that it would be to manhandle such a proposition if we were to allow those who it suits best to take it on: animals. Although Heidegger and Levinas have shown that the wakefulness of the subject is sometimes more forgetful of what is truly important than passivity and carefree being, there are, it seems to me, within the alertness and lucidity of wakefulness, flashes of responsibility and an invitation to offer guardianship to those who are other, but who remain infinitely close as inhabitants of the same earth.

'Animality, if this expression is permitted . . .'[5] In spite of Diderot's use of what was, at the time, an audacious neologism, and in so far as this term is employed more and more frequently in debates on the theme of 'man's animality', which is too vast for my purposes, I shall use it only rarely, preferring, systematically, 'animal' (with or without quotation marks) and also 'beasts'.[6] I wish to put philosophy, and more particularly, humanist metaphysics, to the test of animality, and not human reality. But this does not mean that we can forget for a single moment that 'animal' and 'beast' are first of all only signifiers that function in the history of our representations and practices like a structure that is susceptible to invariance, evolution and ruptures, the work of which we often misjudge – the ways in which this signifier operates in philosophical discourse is the very object of this study. But what will remain of the referent? Where are the beasts to take their flesh and bone, claws and fur, smells and cries? If they are to remain absent due to a methodological prejudice, wouldn't it have been better to keep our mouths shut about them? But how can we hope to consign the referent to memory, with its unruly multiplicity and mysterious singularity, at precisely the moment when the slightest mention of it causes problems for the analysis?

Remembering the truth of what is placed between parentheses and quotation marks can take place through the intervention of the sciences and the arts. It is through the arts that I have attempted, whenever the necessary level of abstraction suffocated me and led me to make the animal a question like any other, to rediscover and to keep a hold on what men can experience with regard to animals and what animals themselves can experience. 'I have drawn it in such a way that it will be able to find its body on the day of the Last Judgement.'[7] Lichtenberg's aphorism made me understand that, as captivating as the most recent data provided by ethology and artificial intelligence might be,[8] they cannot compete with the stunning facts of painting, music and literature. I have included long quotations because they reconstitute what is hidden from us by the exposition of doctrines, and because their concrete textuality engenders both worry and consolation. Perhaps I was reflecting timidly on Walter Benjamin's project of constructing a book entirely out of quotations . . .[9]

Like potatoes

Around 1760, as was customary at the university, Kant taught moral philosophy from successive editions of a manual by Alexandre Gottlieb Baumgarten, a distant disciple, through Wolff, of Leibniz. He discussed the official philosopher's *Ethica Philosophica* and the *Lectures in Ethics* were compiled from student notes. In paragraph 391 of Baumgarten's work, he speaks of 'duties to beings that are inferior and superior to us'. This invokes an entirely Leibnizian symmetry of what is above and below man, who is situated at the centre of the hierarchy of beings. As for spiritual beings, Swedenborg's future adversary[10] states that we are obliged to have no dealings with them. And what about animals? During his pre-critical period, he writes: 'Since all animals exist only as means, and not for their own sakes, in that they have no self-consciousness, whereas man is the end . . ., it follows that we have no duties to animals.'[11] There is no more striking formulation in Kant's work of the other side of the coin that is the categorical imperative, which demands that we treat man always also as an end. Kant adds that, while we may need to ask ourselves why animals exist, such a question – concerning the principle of reason – makes no sense where man is the issue. This means that between men and animals there is a difference in ontological status that renders them incommensurable, and this is why man has no obligations towards anything that is lacking in judgement, even if he has 'indirect duties to humanity'.[12]

Kant allows that if we take some animal actions to be the *analogon* of human actions, it is possible that we have 'mediate' duties to them. This decent treatment can have a formative function in that it provides us with exercises in the 'goodness of heart'. Kant's example is entirely Plutarchian ('The Greeks were high-minded in such matters'):[13] it is not 'indirectly just', 'human' or benevolent to kill dogs, the ancient servants of men, when they are no longer of use. This mediate obligation is illustrated in an engraving by Hogarth, *The Four Stages of Cruelty*, in which the artist exposes cruelty, 'where already the children are practising it upon animals, e.g., by pulling the tail of a dog or a cat; in another scene we see the progress of cruelty, where the man runs over a child; and finally the culmination of cruelty in a murder . . . This provides a good lesson to children'.[14] An edifying anecdote serves to reinforce this thesis: 'Leibnitz put the grub he had been observing back on the tree with its leaf, lest he should be guilty of doing any harm to it. It upsets a man to destroy such a creature for no reason'.[15] But it must be recognised that the Kant who wonders at this kindness is the author not only of the *Groundwork of the Metaphysics of Morals*, but also of the second part of *The Critique of the Power of Judgement*, in which he provides a critique of the power to judge teleologically. Does the reminder of the English law – to which Mandeville attached such great importance[16] – that prevented butchers and surgeons from sitting on juries on account of their being so accustomed to death come from Kant or Baumgarten? In the end, if it is indirectly immoral to make animals suffer for the sake of a simple game, it nonetheless remains that we cannot reproach anatomists for their experiments on living beings, in so far as those beings are instrumental in the furtherance of the end that is man: the anatomists have good grounds for their actions. In short, these lectures reveal a Kant who is fairly close to Leibniz and still marked by scholasticism, but who will scarcely evolve when it comes to ethical content, since, for him, morality remains a question of pure form.

A question arises here, and we must not hesitate in trying to answer it, even though it contravenes the chronology of Kant's work. Inspired by one of his later works, the *Anthropology*, this question emerges quite brutally and haunts, if it does not entirely crack – at least for those who read the history of metaphysics in the footsteps of Michel Foucault, who, incidentally, translated this text into French – the gleaming edifices of the *Groundwork of the Metaphysics of Morals* and the *Critique of Pure Reason*. The reader might well wonder where the dignity of those to whom Kant refers as the 'Cretins of Wales' resides. Are we to respect them as reasonable beings? 'Total mental deficiency is called *idiocy*. Here the mind may not even be up to animal use of the vital force (this is the case with the Cretins of Wales), or it may be limited to the sort of merely mechanical imitation of external notions that even animals can do (sawing, digging and so on). It cannot really be called a sickness of the soul: it is rather an absence of soul.'[17] Once again, a champion of the distinct features of man, who is self-assured in his expulsion of animals from the domain of duty, comes up against imbecility or madness and is not aware that if those who do not fit the criterion of rationality are excluded from humanity, then the definition of man lacks the universality which is its *sine qua non*. We know that Kant scorned the 'soul' of the metaphysician and that he replaced it with a subject that, far from being substantial, has only a functional reality – that which ensures the original synthetic unity of apperception, the 'I' that is precisely what the idiot from Wales and other 'cretins from the Alps' lack.[18] In fact, the question is clear: *either* the soul is nothing more here than a vital principle, as is the case in the vitalistic Aristotelian tradition that persisted even in Kant's time, in which case it is not clear why he should speak of a man who is simply disabled so scornfully; *or* it is the subject of all possible relations between perceptions and apperception, without which there would be nothing but a rhapsody of sensations,[19] in which case the deficiency of the 'I', of self-consciousness, introduces, on a practical level, a deficiency in liberty or in character. This renders the 'Cretin from Wales' and others like him more or less unworthy – but this 'more or less' is an ocean of troubles – of inclusion within a humanity that is only defined as rationality and the autonomy of will. In seeking to define man by separating him from animals we always end up stumbling into the same aporias, and we allow the self-proclamation, in which this upraising of the distinct features of man consists, to drift along aimlessly and without consequence.

Everything has a price. Only man, by virtue of the dignity accorded to reason, is worthy of respect, which means that there is something within him that cannot be evaluated or appreciated qualitatively. Respecting an animal is therefore senseless in Kant's practical philosophy. Would it be to commit an anthropomorphic or misologistic sin, or to abuse humanity, if we interrupted Kant's account of animals in order to give free rein to the shame we experience at the sight of the abuse of animals? We should have the right to speak of the secret dignity of animals, even though many of them do not mind doing their business or mating in public, even if they do not reason or speak, even if their operations are more subject to necessity than our own, or even though they do not know as much about death as we do. It is no doubt difficult to maintain animals in a position that does not transform their being and their functions radically (and which school of zoologists would determine what this status should be?), difficult not to denature them in treating them like inert things or like pathetic replicas of human beings,[20] not to speak to them only to laugh at their silence, or not to train them to perform silly contortions or petit-bourgeois tricks.[21]

René Char writes: 'Those who watch the lion suffering in its cage rot in the lion's memory.'[22] And those who are tempted by Kant's disjunctions would do well to remember that the displaying of men alongside animals in zoos and in the universal exhibitions of the techno-Christian Occident was for a long time a source of amusement. And they should reread Max Horkheimer's commentary on a painting by Longhi, a painting which dates from the eighteenth century and represents a captive rhinoceros being stared at by visitors to a town in Europe:

> Almost nowhere else is the stupidity of humans more evident than in this image. It is the only race that imprisons examples of other races and torments them, in various ways, for the sole purpose of self-aggrandisement. How wise [I would

say dignified] the stupid animal in the painting looks in comparison with these demented men who, at precisely this period, were torturing and burning their fellow creatures, supposedly for heresy, but, in reality, for reasons they themselves did not understand. This race of nature is indescribably mad and cruel.[23]

Do we need to drag up the Kantian vulgate, this 'critical' and formalist conception of morality that posits the unconditional character of the categorical imperative, an absolute requirement that reason prescribes, the maxim of which must conform to a universal legislation without consideration of extrinsic ends ever entering into the equation? '*So act that you use humanity, whether in your own person or in the person of any other, always at the same time as an end, never merely as a means.*'[24] This refers to man as rational being, or to any other rational being in general. True morality can only be based on principles that are not 'speculative rules, but the consciousness of a feeling that lives in every human breast and extends itself much further than over the particular grounds of compassion and complaisance. I believe that I sum it up when I say that it is the *feeling of the beauty and the dignity of human nature.*'[25] Here, in the domain of pure morality, we are situated poles apart from Leibniz and from an ontological gradation that accompanies degrees of consciousness or memory. We are dealing with – as is the case with Descartes, albeit in a different register – the principle of all or nothing. There can only be duties to people who are objects of obligation by virtue of their being free subjects capable of obligation. But, I should make clear, this does not mean that Kant thinks that we can behave towards animals in any way we please. Thus in the *Groundwork of the Metaphysics of Morals*, in the section entitled 'Doctrine of Virtue', Kant returns to the idea of indirect duties vis-à-vis inferior beings. He clarifies his position by distinguishing simple material nature, which is devoid of sensation, from that part of nature (minerals, plants and animals) that is endowed with 'sensation and choice'.[26]

He asks again: can there be relations of duty between men and animals? Strangely, the first element in the response belongs to the domain of what he refers to as 'inanimate beauty': the examples he provides are crystals and vegetables, even though he – in the manner of a true *Natur Philosoph* (which he is not, since he does not allow that life is a property of matter) – has just ascribed sensation and choice to minerals. The upshot of this is that we have difficulty in understanding his criterion for classification. He insists repeatedly that the destruction of 'inanimate beauty' amounts to a weakening of the sentiment that consists in loving something irrespective of its utility (a sentiment that is certainly not moral, but which favours morality), which is to neglect a sentiment towards oneself. As for the 'animate but nonrational part of creation', cruelty towards this appears to imply an even greater neglect of one's duty to oneself, in so far as a man, in performing such an action, dulls the shared feeling inspired in him by suffering, and this can only result in the annihilation of the disposition to morality that places men in relations of obligation to one another. The old horse and dog encountered by Plutarch in the life of Cato serve once again to illustrate this introduction to morality. As for the others, Kant makes a trenchant judgement: 'The human being is authorized to kill animals quickly (without pain) and to put them to work that does not strain them beyond their capacities (such work as he himself must submit to). But agonizing physical experiments for the sake of mere speculation, when the end could also be achieved without these, are to be abhorred.'[27] This remark demonstrates a level of prudence, a sense of moderation and reserve regarding experimentation that contrasts with the more permissive view of the *Lectures on Ethics* and which, during the same (or almost the same) period, the 'adventurers of the organisation' hardly bothered with. It should be noted that Kant's position here is highly moderate: it consists in allowing individuals to enjoy with complete impunity those rights granted to them by 'nature' and by the Christian tradition; it distinguishes use from abuse and does not separate – in this case at least – sensitivity from morality.

It is in the *Doctrine of Right* that we read the fateful words: man has the right to make use, in whichever way he sees fit, of that which, as regards its abundance, is a human product – potatoes and animals. 'Now just as we say that since vegetables (e.g., potatoes) and domestic animals are, as regards their abundance, a human *product*, which he can use, wear out, or destroy (kill), it seems that we can also say that since most of his subjects are his own product, the supreme authority in a state, the sovereign, has the right to lead them into war as he would take them on a hunt, and into battles as on a pleasure trip.'[28] But for Kant the analogy does not hold, since agriculture and breeding – both are capacities that exist on the same plane, to create and to nurture natural beings – confer a right to destroy that political power does not authorise. The difference is that while animals can be the property of men, men are subjects that are also citizens, the authors of the legislation they are subject to, and should not therefore be treated as means.

This haughty authorisation of use and abuse, which introduces a touch of contradiction into Kant's thought concerning animals, is also exhibited, this time from a genetic perspective, in the *Conjectures on the Beginning of Human History*:

> The fourth and last step which reason took, thereby raising man completely above animal society, was his (albeit obscure) realisation that he is the true *end of nature*, and that nothing which lives on earth can compete with him in his respect. When he first said to the sheep '*the fleece which you wear was given to you by nature not for your own use, but for mine*' and took it from the sheep to wear it himself, he became aware of a prerogative which, by his nature, he enjoyed over all animals; and he no longer regarded them as fellow creatures, but as means and instruments to be used at will for the attainment of whatever ends he pleased. This notion implies (if only obscurely) an awareness of the following distinction: man should not address other human beings in the same way as animals.[29]

This charter of near stoic anthropocentrism is not unlike the finalist foolishness commonly attributed to Bernardin de Saint-Pierre, and explicitly links rights over animals to duties to men. There are many further formulations of this teleology of nature in Kant's work. For example: 'As the sole being on earth who has reason, and thus a capacity to set voluntary ends for himself, he [man] is certainly the titular lord of nature, and, if nature is regarded as a teleological system, then it is his vocation to be the ultimate end of nature.'[30]

The brute force of the philosopheme 'animal' is demonstrated most strikingly if we play this Kantian argument off against some Spinozistic propositions. It should be noted that this *topos* is indifferent to the various lines of division that are in operation in the history of philosophy, and that its elevation with a view to reinforcing antinomically the thesis concerning the distinct features of man is to bring about an astonishing effacement of philosophical singularities. Schopenhauer was the first to establish a link between Spinoza and Kant – to engender an assimilation that everything should prohibit, given the apparent incompatibility of a-teleological monism and finalist dualism. If we avoid Schopenhauer's extrapolations and his shocking abhorrences, and pay attention to his obsessive and wandering readings in the history of philosophy, we discover that these irreconcilable philosophies, travelling along opposite lines, meet within the same discursive locus as soon as they reach the animal, a locus that Schopenhauer referred to abusively as 'Jewish' and which we should rather identify as constituting a metaphysical humanism.[31]

Basing his argument on a proposition that claims that desire – the effort to persevere in his own being – is identified as the nature of each individual (the desires of individuals must clash as a consequence),[32] Spinoza states that 'the emotions of what are called the "irrational" animals (for we can in no way doubt that the beasts feel, now that we have got to know the origin of the mind) differ from the emotions of men only in so far as their nature differs from human nature'.[33] Thus a horse's desire to procreate is different from a human's, and the same is true of the desire of insects, fish and birds: the 'contentments' that constitute the souls of these dissimilar beings are dissimilar. The difference in nature that persists between beings – but this does not mean that man can claim to constitute an empire within an empire – is the justification for man's natural right to make use of animals in any way that suits him. By saying that animals feel, Spinoza breaks with a Cartesian automatism that can be understood as the correlative of the twaddle that surrounds original sin: the theme of innocent suffering is as stupid as that of metempsychosis. It follows that

> the law against slaughtering animals is based more on empty superstition and effeminate pity than on sound reason. The principle of seeking what is useful to us teaches us the necessity of uniting with men, but not with the beasts, or with things whose nature is different from human nature; we have the same right over them that they have over us. Indeed, since the right of each thing is defined by the virtue, i.e. the power of each thing, we have much more right over the beasts than they have over men. I do not deny that the beasts have feelings, but I do deny that it is impermissible, on this account, for us to consult our own advantage, and to use them as we wish and to treat them in such a way is more convenient for us. This is because they do not agree with us in nature, and their emotions are different in nature from human emotions.[34]

These passages from the *Ethics* exhibit a stoic character that is all the more striking given that Spinoza, who follows Descartes on the question of mechanism, that is to say, in the critique of final causes, distinguishes himself from him by insisting in his principal texts that the beasts feel. Equally stoic are the ideal of virility, contempt for feminine sensitivity and the identification of the *conatus* with the proper interest that constitutes the soul of every being. Finally, the conception of association which holds that the nature of beasts does not 'agree' with ours, and that no union – and a union is as good as a contract, if we read chapter XVI of the *Theological-Political Treatise* – can exist between men and beasts, is also stoic. The *oikeiôsis* re-emerges in this *convenire*, along with the entirely Ciceronian consequence that the virtue of *humanitas* cannot be expanded to include beings that do not belong to the human race, and that benignity, the kindness of the Sceptics, Plutarch and Montaigne can only be addressed to rational beings. As for other kinds of animate things, since there is no association or 'agreement' between them and us, no kind of friendship is possible, and we are fully within our rights to use and abuse them. *Praeter homines* . . . 'Apart from men, we know of no particular thing in Nature in whose mind we can delight, and which we can join with us in friendship or in some kind of association. So a consideration of our advantage does not require us to conserve anything that exists in Nature apart from human beings: rather, it teaches us to preserve, destroy, or adapt it in any way to out advantage, in accordance with its various uses.'[35] The fatal and already Kantian *praeter homines*, which confers rights on men and reifies animals even though they are no longer machines!

This chronological digression, which is necessary for a presentation of a structure of thought that is trans-historical and trans-systematic, allows us to demonstrate that Spinoza is the philosopher whom we can view not only as the first reformer with regard to establishing the distinct features of man, but also as somebody who shelters his quasi deification of man – 'Man is a god to man'[36] – under the ancient idea of 'agreement', proposing a metaphysical humanism that we can identify, as it happens, as a return to the Ancients (another, more internal reading, would no doubt have to correct that reading which relates it to Kant).

However, what is new and singular in Kant is that the theme of the animality of man receives its full measure of explanation and exhortation. What Plato referred to as body and opposed to the soul, what Saint-Paul called flesh and opposed to the mind, becomes, through Augustinianism and no doubt Lutheranism, a decisive concept in anthropological analysis and moral prescription: animality. But, for Kant, animality is far from representing evil or sin, or even the 'warped wood' that man is made of.[37] It is, rather, an innate, natural and crude disposition that characterises the animate, to which we have duties and which, in man in his most basic form, requires uprightness, shaping, discipline, exertion, education, training, and culture in order that the individual and the human species can become civilised and moral, whereby the humanity that constitutes both their purpose and the ultimate goal of nature is realised. 'Man is the only being who needs education . . . Discipline changes animal nature into human nature.'[38]

That conceptuality which demands that we compare constantly the animality out of which man has emerged with the humanity he is or should be destined for can only have a negative effect on the status of the animal as such. The endless operations of continuity and fracture, this real obsession with the mending and correction of the animal by the human, of nature by society, history and morality, can only function with and according to a depreciation of the intelligence, sensitivity and sociability of animals, and are, of course, entirely at odds with the admiration of the virtues of the animal suggested by the traditions of the Renaissance and of antiquity. The cardinal disjunction between will or liberty and natural necessity, between reason and heteronomy, that emphasis on self-consciousness which is no less important to Kant than it is to Descartes (whatever imputations of paralogism can be aimed at the *cogito*),[39] provides the blueprint for modern humanism, in the form of Sartrian existentialism, for example. Any attempt to think about the animal in itself and for itself is doomed to failure as soon as we become rooted in this concept of animality. And anyone who would wish to take the escape route that runs closest to the enigma of the animal – even if they understand that no direct apprehension would be possible, but only a passage through mediations of and references to man – would still have to repudiate the ethical and culturist theme of the animality of man.[40] Only Husserl, in the chapter entitled 'Animalia' of *Ideas II* and elsewhere, succeeded in joining the motifs of the animal and of animality within a silent mediation, which is difficult because freed at last from ethical pathos.

So there we have it! Reading the *Critique of the Power of Judgement*, one realises that, as soon as there is mention of the animate, the epistemological maturity expressed in Kant's vitalistic cosmology is without equivalent in his century. It is the disproportion between, on the one hand, the fairly pitiful reduction of the animal to a thing that is entirely and naively referred to man on both a theoretical and practical level, and, on the other, the outpouring of an 'enlightened' vitalism and teleology that requires explanation. In a number of paragraphs in the third *Critique*, Kant writes, contrary to what has been quoted previously, that the judgement that posits finality – and the same goes for the finality that works in favour of man – is only subjective, a maxim of reason that is in no way objectively determinant, but functions only as a regulatory principle. Also, we cannot know if this principle of explanation is intentionally an end of nature, 'whether grass exists for cattle or sheep, and these and the other things in nature for human beings. It is even good for us to consider in this light things that are unpleasant and in certain relations contrapurposive for us.'[41] Could vermin be an incentive to cleanliness and therefore to health? The fact remains that there are some 'products' in nature that can only be thought of in terms of the final cause, and for which the mechanism – which is still required at the same time – could never be sufficient.[42] The beautiful description of the watch,[43] an instrument which Kant shows to be incapable of providing a paradigm for the 'organised being', demonstrates that like almost all of his contemporaries, albeit with the use of exceptional critical precautions, he was able to free himself from automatism. The 'organised being' is incomprehensible if we do not hold that the idea of the effect is already present in the cause. This anthropocentric teleology is bolstered in Kant by the assertion that it is only a matter of reflective judgement, whereby it escapes from all the dogmatism of finality. The critique of the work of Herder is similarly inscribed within the perspective that challenges teleological dogmatism: the latter does not grasp that explanation through finality can only ever provide a type of knowledge that replaces objective knowledge and intervenes where causalist, mechanistic and physicistic knowledge is lacking. However, as rich and as rigorous as this epistemological distinction may be, the fact remains that, in practical terms, the animal stays tethered to the status of instrument provided to man by nature and Revelation.

Translated by Tom Baldwin

Notes

1 Konrad Lorenz, *On Aggression*, trans. Marjorie K. Wilson (San Diego, New York, London: Harvest Books, 1974).
2 Peter Singer, *Animal Liberation* (New York: New York Review of Books, 1990).
3 Hans Jonas, *The Phenomenon of Life. Toward a Philosophical Biology* (New York: Harper & Row, 1966).
4 See the definition of 'Animal' in the *Encyclopédie*, 1751–1772.
5 Ibid.
6 There are three names for things that breathe in classical Latin. *Bellua* means 'beast', as opposed to 'man'. Sometimes, it is used to accentuate sheer size, ferocity and lack of intelligence, and can be used as an insult: to be stupid ['être bête'], an imbecile. Less familiarly, for grammarians and jurists, *bestia* is used to refer to ferocious animals. *Bestia* can also be used pejoratively, not in the sense of 'being stupid' ['être bête'], but in the sense of 'being a beast' ['être une bête'], a bestial being. Finally, *animal*, which signifies 'living being', comes from *animalis* ('that breathes') which comes from *animans* (that possesses breath), these terms being a translation of the Greek *empsuchon* and *psuchè*. *Animal* is often used in contrast to 'man'. In ecclesiastical language, *animalis* is opposed to *spiritualis*. In the Latin of the philosophers and the scientists, we find *bruta animalia* or simply *bruta*, the adjective *brutus* meaning morally and physically 'heavy'.
7 Georg Christoph Lichtenberg, *Aphorisms*, trans. R.J. Hollingdale (Harmondsworth: Penguin Books, 1990), p. 173.
8 Joëlle Proust, *Comment l'esprit vient aux bêtes* (Paris: Gallimard, 1997).
9 Walter Benjamin, *Paris, capitale du XIXe siècle. Le livre des passages* (Paris: Cerf, 1989).
10 Immanuel Kant, *Dreams of a Spirit-Seer and Other Writings*, ed. and trans. Gregory Johnson (Pennsylvania: Swedenborg Foundation, 2002).
11 Immanuel Kant, *Lectures on Ethics*, ed. and trans. Peter Heath (Cambridge, Cambridge University Press, 1997), p. 212.
12 Ibid.
13 Ibid., p. 213.
14 Ibid., p. 212.
15 Ibid., pp. 212–13.
16 Bernard Mandeville, *La Fable des abeilles ou les vices privés font le bien public* (1714), ed. L. et P. Carrive (Paris: Vrin, 1974), XIII, 3.
17 Immanuel Kant, *Anthropology from a Pragmatic Point of View*, trans. Mary J. Gregor (The Hague: Martinus Nijhoff, 1974), p. 82.
18 Cf. Hergé's *Tintin*, published in France by Casterman.
19 Immanuel Kant, 'The Deduction of the Pure Concepts of Understanding', in *Critique of Pure Reason*, trans. Norman Kemp Smith (London: Macmillan, 1929), § 17–19, pp. 155–60.
20 Françoise Dastur, 'L'Animalité', *Alter*, no.3, 1995, 303.
21 In *Les Voix de Marrakech*, Elias Canetti recalls the basic and surprising dignity exhibited by a donkey that has been mistreated and mocked.
22 René Char, *Les Matinaux* (Paris: Gallimard, 1950), p. 72.
23 Max Horkeimer, *Notes critiques (1949–1969)* (Paris: Payot, 1993), pp. 106–07.
24 Immanuel Kant, *Groundwork of the Metaphysics of Morals*, ed. and trans. Mary Gregor (Cambridge: Cambridge University Press, 1997), p. 38.
25 Immanuel Kant, *Observations on the Feeling of the Beautiful and Sublime*, trans. John T. Goldthwait (Berkeley, Los Angeles, London: University of California Press, 1960), p. 60.
26 Immanuel Kant, 'Doctrine of Virtue', in *The Metaphysics of Morals*, ed. and trans. Mary Gregor (Cambridge: Cambridge University Press, 1996), § 16, p. 192.
27 Ibid., p. 193.
28 Immanuel Kant, 'Doctrine of Right', in ibid., § 55, pp. 115–16.
29 Immanuel Kant, 'Conjectures on the Beginning of Human History', in *Kant: Political Writings*, ed. Hans Reiss (Cambridge: Cambridge University Press, 1991), p. 225.

30 Immanuel Kant, *Critique of the Power of Judgement*, ed. and trans. Paul Guyer (Cambridge: Cambridge University Press, 2000), § 83, p. 298.
31 Cf. *infra*, XVI, 1.
32 Baruch Spinoza, *Ethics*, ed. and trans. G.H.R. Parkinson (Oxford: Oxford University Press, 2000), Part Three, *Proposition 57, Demonstration*, pp. 209–10.
33 Ibid., *Scholium*, p. 210.
34 Ibid., Part Four, *Scholium* 1, p. 253.
35 Ibid., Appendix to Part Four, p. 285.
36 Ibid., Part Four, *Scholium*, p. 250.
37 Immanuel Kant, 'Idea for a Universal History with a Cosmopolitan Purpose', in *Kant: Political Writings*, p. 46.
38 Immanuel Kant, *On Education*, trans. Annette Churton (London: Kegan Paul, Trench, Trübner & Co. Ltd, 1899), p. 1.
39 Immanuel Kant, 'The Dialectical Inferences of Pure Reason', in *Critique of Pure Reason*, pp. 328–68.
40 See the fourth chapter of Florence Burgat's *Animal mon prochain* (Paris: O. Jacob, 1997), pp. 161–84.
41 Immanuel Kant, *Critique of the Power of Judgement*, § 67, p. 251.
42 Ibid.
43 Ibid., § 65, p. 246.

11

FRANÇOISE HÉRITIER

Françoise Héritier is a philosopher and anthropologist. In the 1960s she did several years of field-work in Africa, in particular with the Samo, Pana and Mossi populations. Amongst many academic posts and honours, she has been a member of the national committee of the CNRS, Directeur d'études at the École des Hautes Études en Sciences Sociales, Professor at the Collège de France, Chair of Comparative Studies of African Societies, and successor to Claude Lévi-Strauss as Director of the Laboratoire d'Anthropologie Sociale. She was also President of the governmental project ('mission') on National Museums for the Ministry of Education. Her teaching and research entail two main directions: the study of systems of marriage and kinship relations in Africa, and the study of structures of social practices and their symbolisation. She has also led research into the role of the anthropologist in a city environment, in areas such as the understanding of incest, violence, and questions of identity/alterity.

Her major works include the following:

L'Exercise de la parenté, Paris: Gallimard-Seuil, 1981.

De l'inceste, Paris: Odile Jacob, 1994.

Les deux soeurs et leur mère: anthropologie de l'inceste, Paris: Odile Jacob, 1994.

Masculin-féminin: la pensée de la différence, Paris: Odile Jacob, 1996.

De la violence, Paris: Odile Jacob, 1996.

Masculin-féminin II. Dissoudre la hiérarchie, Paris: Odile Jacob, 2002.

FROM ARISTOTLE TO THE INUITS

The reasoned construction of gender

On the theme of the generation and determination of the sexes, Aristotle composed one of the most elegant models. It is a well-argued and reasoned philosophical model that draws upon many of the arguments of the primordial genetics of so-called primitive peoples. I shall be referring to Book IV of *Generation of Animals*, a work written by Aristotle between 330 and 322 BC, at the end of his career.[1] He begins by reflecting on the works of some of the thinkers who preceded him.

For Anaxagoras, the sex of the child is determined by the father: boys come from the right testicle, the hotter one, girls from the left. For Empedocles, it is the temperature inside the womb, in accordance with menstrual flow, that determines the sex of the offspring. As we can see, in both cases it is a greater heat that causes males to be conceived.

Aristotle criticises his predecessors on certain points, and while he retains the opposition between heat and cold, he argues that it is no simple task to demonstrate that coldness is the decisive factor in the creation in the mother's womb of a foetus with a uterus.

But on a more fundamental note, he suggests that semen provides no material at all for the foetus; it is pure *pneuma*, breath and potentiality.[2]

By virtue of the intensity of his heat, it is the male who is able to concoct blood and to transform it into semen: 'he discharges semen possessing the "principle" of the "form"' (IV.1.765b), and 'principle' refers here to the proximate motor principle, whether it is able to act in itself or in something else. This is because the female – matter – is nothing but a receptacle. If all concoction works by means of heat, and if semen is concocted blood in its purest form, the male is attributed a greater heat than the female. Moreover, it is precisely because she is cold that the female is more abundant in blood and that she regularly loses it: if this were not the case, she would make it into semen.

This fundamental difference between heat and cold implies and justifies the anatomical differences between the sexes: the hot sex secretes, in small quantities, a pure residue that can be stored in the testicles; the other, which is cold and unable to effect concoction, requires a larger sex organ, the uterus. Each potentiality is assigned an appropriate organ.

But in that case, if the man who is hot dominates, how does he produce girls, and even girls who sometimes resemble their mothers?

A weakened male principle

'When the [male] principle is failing to gain the mastery and is unable to effect concoction owing to deficiency of heat, and does not succeed in reducing the material into its own proper form, but instead is worsted in the attempt, then of necessity the material must change over into its opposite condition' (IV.1.766a). Fathering girls is therefore the consequence of a partial weakness, because 'the opposite of the male is the female'.

This theory is, he argues, supported by the facts.

Both young and old parents tend to produce girls rather than boys. 'In the young their heat is not yet perfected, in the older, it is failing' (IV.2.766b). Such parents have more fluid and moist semen, and this is a sign of deficient body heat. Male offspring tend to be engendered when the wind is in the north, because when it is in the south it is richer in moisture, and under such conditions man has difficulty concocting. There are other accidental causes which play a part, as menstrual discharge takes place at colder and more fluid times of the month and when the moon is waning.

Climatic conditions and the type of food and water consumed are also influential: water, being hard and cold, causes the birth of females. It is a case of cold mixed with cold, and makes the concoction and transformation of blood into semen, which is the man's responsibility, an even more thankless task.

These remain purely accidental, additive causes. If male potentiality alone were in action, only males would be generated.

'The first beginning of this deviation', he writes, 'is when a female is formed instead of a male, though this indeed is a necessity required by Nature, since the race of creatures which are separated into male and female has got to be kept in being' (IV.3.767b).

Everything can change, and in changing, is transformed into its opposite. Hence, in terms of the generation of offspring, and in accordance with the lack of potentiality in the generative agent, that which does not dominate changes over into its opposite.

Aristotle identifies three elements in the male potentiality of semen. Each can change over into its opposite:

Generic masculine potentiality produces the male. If it does not dominate, the product will be feminine.

It is individual potentiality that makes any given male the particular individual he is. If this does not dominate, then the male offspring born of generic potentiality will resemble his mother instead of his father.

Generic potentiality, whether it dominates or not, determines sex; individual movement, whether it dominates or not, determines resemblance.

If both generic and individual male potentialities do not manage to dominate, to create the form of feminine matter, the offspring will be a girl who resembles her mother.

There is, however, no symmetry. There is no feminine potentiality that would determine the form should there be a weakness in the masculine, as there is for the Navaho Indians. All that matters to Aristotle is weakness in the masculine.

Resemblance in human form

There is more. Closely associated with the generic and individual potentialities is movement, as action and ability. The movements that fashion the embryo (they fashion it, yet provide no material for it) can either dominate or relapse.

It is the degree of the relapse of these movements, itself associated with weaknesses of potentiality, that explains why children resemble their more remote ancestors rather than their parents.

The perfect model: if male generic potentiality dominates, the offspring will be male; if individual potentiality dominates, he will resemble his father; if movement dominates, he will resemble his father exactly; the worst thing that can happen, if the movement relapses, is that he will resemble either his grandfather or paternal great-grandfather.

The most imperfect model: if generic potentiality is deficient, the offspring will be female; if individual potentiality is deficient, she will resemble her mother; if movement dominates, the hypothesis is that she will particularly resemble her mother; but if movement relapses, she will resemble her grandmother or her maternal great-grandmother.

There are two intermediary possibilities: if generic potentiality is weakened, but individual potentiality dominates, the offspring will be a girl who resembles her father. But if movement relapses, in accordance with the extent of this relapse, she will resemble her grandfather or paternal great-grandfather.

But if generic potentiality dominates and individual potentiality is weakened, the offspring will be a boy who resembles his mother. And if movement relapses, he may even resemble his grandmother or maternal great-grandmother.

And then, sometimes, 'the offspring is a human being yet bears no resemblance to any ancestor, sometimes it has reached such a point that in the end it no longer has the appearance of a human being at all, but that of an animal only – it belongs to the class of monstrosities, as they are called' (IV.3.769b).

So why do they exist?

The animal matter of femininity

I quote Aristotle: 'in the end, when the movements relapse and the material does not get mastered, what remains is that which is most general, and this is the animal' (IV.3.769b).

We must remember what we discovered earlier: movement comes from the man and characterises the generic and individual potentiality of man. Matter comes from femininity and, as we have seen, Aristotle states explicitly that the first stage of abnormality, of monstrosity, occurs when a female is conceived instead of a male. When the potentialities are deficient and movement has fully relapsed, all that remains is crude feminine matter, that is to say animal matter.

The hybrid monster is in a certain sense a clone of the feminine, a reproduction of that which is identical to matter and undominated by breath. It is a sign of the succumbing of masculine potentiality and of the irruption of the crude and animal forces of matter. There is no longer any harmony between the forces at hand. The resulting excess of the feminine, and therefore of matter, is a monster. But there can never be an excess of the masculine.

Not that Aristotle thinks that hybrids can be born. He states explicitly that they cannot: 'The occurrence of all these things is due to the causes that I have named; at the same time, in no case are they what they are alleged to be, but resemblances only' (IV.3.769b). Indeed, the birth of one animal within another is impossible, because (as he so matter-of-factly adds): 'the gestation-periods . . . are widely different' (IV.3.769b). But hybrids are not the only monsters: there are also those which qualify for the name by virtue of having additional body parts, or too few of them.

Monstrosity, an excess of the feminine

Contrary to Democritus, who explained the formation of monstrosities as the result of the conflict between two semens that have penetrated into the same uterus, Aristotle insists that the cause is to be referred not to the evanescent semen that comes from the male, but to the matter provided by the female. 'We ought preferably to hold that the seat of the cause is the material and in the fetations as they take shape' (IV.3.770a).

Indeed, he observes that when the uterus is extended lengthways, as is the case in snakes, or numerous eggs lie one after another in a row, or when the eggs are laid in separate cells, as is the case in bees, there are no monstrosities. This means, therefore, that we are bound to hold that the cause of such things is in matter itself, and above all in the arrangement of this feminine matter in certain species, especially in those which are multiparous, in which the offspring hamper each other's growth within the same organ.

'Because even in this species [human beings],' he writes, 'the occurrence is more common in those regions where the women are prolific, in Egypt for instance' (IV.3.770a). Indeed, as demonstrated by various texts of the period and by Aristotle himself in *History of Animals*, it was widely held that Egyptian women frequently gave birth to twins.

The problem that he addresses at this point of his argument, and quite logically it seems, is whether or not we should view the development of superfluous body parts in monstrosities and the mutiparous in the same way, that is to say, as having one and the same cause.

For us, as anthropologists, who are well aware that multiparity is never experienced as something ordinary, this is a pertinent question: is multiparity, as Aristotelian logic has it, another possible form of monstrosity, second only to femininity?

We know that conception is the result of one act of copulation, he says. 'The male's semen . . . acts by concentrating and fashioning the material in the female . . . just as fig-juice acts upon the fluid portion of the milk' (IV.4.771b). But when the fig-juice [présure] acts upon milk, it is condensed into a single mass.[3] Similarly, the concentration by semen of the animal and feminine matter can only produce a single embryo. 'If the male emits more semen [than is requisite] . . . the greatest possible amount will not make anything bigger . . . but on the contrary will dry the material up and destroy it' (IV.4.772a).

According to the logic of this argument, it seems that the desiccation is viewed as representing the opposite of monstrosity: if the excessive coldness of feminine matter produces monstrosity, an excess of heat due to excessive seminal production means that semen destroys itself as soon as it is expended wastefully. In elucidating this point, Aristotle employs a well-chosen metaphor: you may increase the amount of fire, but the heat of the water does not continue to increase; instead more and more of it evaporates, and finally it disappears and dries up.

Therefore, if there is multiparity, the seminal agent cannot be to blame: it is just acting upon a maternal matter that is disposed to multiparity.

Uniparous animals produce no more feminine matter than is conducive to the formation of a single embryo. 'If ever more of it is supplied, then twins are produced. And hence, also, such creatures seem rather to be monstrosities, because their formation is contrary to the general rule and what is usual' (IV.4.772b).

Thus multiparity and monstrosity are nothing but an excess of the feminine.

The birth of girls, multiparity and monstrosity represent, in ascending order, anomalies which stem from the dominance of Nature and of matter, which is feminine, and which man ordinarily fashions in his own image whenever he dominates it entirely.

The cause of the superfluity of parts, which occurs contrary to Nature, is also the cause of the production of twins: 'the cause occurs right back in the fetations, whenever more material gets "set" than the nature of the part requires' (IV.4.772b).

But monstrosity is only monstrous for man.

'A monstrosity, of course, belongs to the class of "things contrary to Nature", although it is contrary not to Nature in her entirety but only to Nature in the generality of cases, So far as concerns the Nature which is always and is by necessity, nothing occurs contrary to that' (IV.4.770b). This is a philosophical discourse which, in its own way, connects to a mythical discourse that is supplanted by those popular beliefs which refer to *teras* (monster) and *loimos* (curse).

The monster, the Sumerian's 'misshapen product', the Greek's *teras*, the Roman's androgyne or hermaphrodite and those ill-fated children thrown into the sea are all signs of the Scourge, of *loimos*, of *Pestilentia*.

Seeing it as punishment for a sacrilege committed against one of Apollo's shrines, Eschine describes the curse of God thus: 'may the Earth be barren, may women give birth to monsters instead of children who resemble their parents, and even among the herds, may newborns not conform to the nature of their gender'. As an evil sent by God, the *loimos* afflicts the collectivity of existence with sterility: sterile earth, women and animals.

Livy recalls the disasters of 200 BC: 'Each of these awful, hideous things appeared to be the result of a Nature that had confused and scrambled germs. People were particularly horrified by hermaphrodites. Some were thrown into the sea, as were foetuses with the same strange affliction.'

Only the gods can combine genders and generations. Hesiod believed that the human race would become extinct as soon as males were born with white hair – another form of monstrosity – in other words, as soon as the natural order of things and the apparent order of generations were inverted.

In the natural scheme of things, and if they obey social and divine laws, men and animals produce infants which resemble them and which have the features of their gender and their species.

For Aristotle, Nature, the Earth and – for popular belief – the gods produce monsters as natural objects, born of their will, and which are only unnatural at the level of man, his history and reproduction.

The gods are not bound to a contingent form; they can change form at will and nobody knows their face. For them, species are never fixed.

Thus Aristotle provides a complete, natural and philosophical model of generation, of the role of each sex in procreation, the determination of sex itself and of the existence of different kinds of monstrosity.

But, we might add, the process is always understood as beginning at birth. Offspring are always either masculine or feminine and usually conform to the definition of their sex, with the exception of hermaphrodites, who were, as we have just seen, the epitome of monstrosity in Rome.

The Sambia model: you are not born a man, you become one

Nevertheless, the determination of social gender is not always and everywhere modelled on the determination of biological sex. Sometimes it has to be constructed materially, and its apparent form is not enough to decide it. This is the case, for example, in a number of societies in New Guinea. I take as an example the Sambia, who have been described impressively by Gilbert Herdt.[4]

In this society, people do not think in terms of hot and cold: the identical and the similar are sought after rather than shunned; marrow does not go hand in hand with blood, and the concoction of blood does not intervene in the production of semen. Quite the contrary, in fact. Semen is not capable of self-production: it must be delivered.

Boys do not have an endogenous capacity to reach masculinity. They are said to possess the same organ as that which determines the feminine menstrual cycle, but it is dry and does not function. The masculine genital organ is empty at birth. Semen makes masculinity: solid bones, toned muscles, flat stomach. This empty reservoir must therefore be filled. We shall see how this occurs.

If it must be filled and if, unlike blood, semen cannot self-produce, a natural consequence is that this reservoir is perishable. Men therefore live in constant fear of losing their semen: sexual contact exhausts it and dries up life itself. Men are distinguished from one another by the extent to which they are afflicted by this specific anxiety.

Marriage to a niece or a sister of the clan is sought after, because semen is not thought to be wasted in the same way if it encounters a bodily substance that is at least partially identical. In pathological cases, certain men refuse all contact with women and the obligation to procreate that goes with it, which means that homosexual relations – which are also with the 'same' – are institutionalised, being infinitely less risky for the man. But what kind of homosexual relations are we talking about?

From the age of seven, the male infant is inseminated in the 'Men's House', through fellatio, firstly by his sisters' husbands and his fathers' parallel patrilateral cousins, and subsequently by unmarried young adolescents.

In all of this, one thing is imperative: the eldest inseminate the youngest. Psychological and affective investment between the partners of the operation is avoided as much as possible.

It is only when they marry that young men are considered to be exclusively heterosexual (except, of course, when they are required to fulfil their duty by inseminating their nephews by marriage, their wives' brothers' sons). Practically all of them cope with these changes without serious difficulty.

While femininity is viewed as complete and natural in an entirely innate way, masculinity must be constructed.

Semen is necessary for the activation of feminine blood and for procreation. Sexual contact is therefore highly regulated. However, men can replenish their stock of semen – but only in the context of heterosexual relations – by drinking the sap of a particular tree that grows in the forest. But however rare conjugal relations may be, they must be assiduous in their attention to the pregnant woman so as to fashion, at this stage also, the child that is to be born.

A distinction is made between being a male (for which having a penis and testicles is sufficient) and being a man. A male is only complete when his seminal reservoir is fully stocked. He must himself be filled so as to be able to fill others.

With paternity comes a fear of exhausting the seminal stock. Each man must accept the loss of the essence of masculinity for the sake of becoming a man, as his father did for him. As a life-choice, homosexuality is entirely refused.

The Inuits: gender and identity is disassociated from the sex organ

For the Inuits, otherwise known as Eskimos, it is a completely different story.

The child is certainly born with an apparent sex organ, but it is not necessarily viewed as its real one. Indeed, the real sex of the child is that which is brought by an identity disclosed by the soul-name, that is to say from the sex of the ancestor whose soul-name has penetrated the woman and installed itself within her womb so as to be born again, the identity of which is revealed by the Shamans when the child is born.

Thus Iqallijuq is the reincarnation of her mother's father (Saladin d'Anglure).[5] She remembers her intra-uterine life inside a tiny igloo. On either side of her were two benches, on which were placed the symbols of masculine and feminine labour. On leaving, as a reincarnated man, she voluntarily took hold of the masculine objects. A man by virtue of her soul-name, she was born with an apparently feminine sex organ.

Physiological differentiation is supplanted by the soul-name and the identity that goes with it.

Children are raised, therefore, as if they were of the opposite sex. They are dressed in the same way as individuals of the opposite sex and participate exclusively in the activities of that sex. Iqallijuq believed that she was a boy and excelled at hunting.

At puberty, everything changes brutally. Overnight, adolescents are expected to adapt their behaviour in accordance with their apparent sex organs.

This is not always a painless process. When, against her will, Iqallijuq had to wear feminine clothes for the first time, her mother cried at the sight of her father's reincarnation being subjected to menstruation.

In fact, individual personality is progressively readjusted to suit the apparent sex organ. Some methods of readjustment are quite subtle. Thus Iqallijuq's first partner was her cousin, who had experienced the inverse of her situation: he was born a boy, but raised as a girl. Their relationship did not last, and subsequently, both of them found partners whose identities had not been disassociated, but they had in the mean time adapted to the way of life and to the activities corresponding to their real sex organ.

However, the identity inherited from the soul-name remains with them for the rest of their lives.

Symbolic and natural orders

It is clear that, in the eyes of man, gender, sex, the determination of sex and the adaptation of the individual are not facts which are simply a function of the natural order.

Constructible and recreated, they are functions of a symbolic order, of ideology, even though the terms of this symbolic order seek to establish such things as facts of Nature which bear upon each and every member of society.

Thus, in the case of Aristotle, for example, everything results from the opposition, which he portrays as being natural, between hot and cold, dry and moist, active and passive, potentiality and matter, which connote the masculine and the feminine respectively. I should point out, in conclusion, that this Aristotelian mode of thought is not alien to modern discourse, including the scientific register.

We are still unaware of what exactly the fertilising power of semen consists in. In the 1984 edition of the *Encyclopedia Universalis*, in an article entitled 'Fertilisation' (Lavergne and Cohen), we can read the following:

> The particularity of female gametes is their specific metabolic regime. As soon as they are differentiated, these cells show an extraordinary inaptitude for development; they enter into a state of physiological *inertia* such that they are doomed to die if they are not activated. This demonstrates, then, the necessity of fertilisation: the male gamete takes on the *natural activating function* [our italics]. This seminal virtue has been recognised since the earliest antiquity. Nevertheless, the vitalising potentiality of male semen – or of pollen – has not been fully explained, even though it is accepted that it plays a key role in sexual reproduction.

It should be noted that the vocabulary used by these authors is the same as Aristotle's, and it is undeniable that it is used to express ill-defined concepts which rely upon a sense of the eternal in Nature and upon a set of popular beliefs: the 'inert' and 'incapable' feminine cell must be 'activated', if it is to escape death, by the male cell which is endowed with seminal 'virtue' and a 'vitalising potentiality', the nature of which remains a mystery.

We could no doubt call it *pneuma*.

Translated by Tom Baldwin

Notes

1 Aristotle, *Generation of Animals*, trans. A. L. Peck (Cambridge, Massachussetts and London: Harvard University Press, 1990).
2 Translator's note: I have translated 'puissance' as 'potentiality'. The latter is important in Aristotle's metaphysics: 'δύναμις [. . .] is the physical substance by means of which

impregnation is effected; and the distinctive physical characteristic with which we find this δύναμις closely associated by Aristotle is 'vital heat' or 'Soul-heat'. The most distinctive character, however, of this substance is that it is charged with a specific 'movement', capable of constituting and developing an embryo out of the matter supplied by the female; and hence we also find a close association of δύναμις with κίνησις. This is the most important extension of δύναμις in its ancient sense made by Aristotle, for it links up the old sense of the term with the typically and peculiarly Aristotelian sense of δύναμις = 'potentiality' (A. L. Peck in the preface to Aristotle, *Generation of Animals*, p. lii).

3 Translator's note: Aristotle uses the term 'ὀπός', which is translated by Peck as 'fig-juice' (see ibid., p. 432). Héritier translates the Greek term as 'présure', which is usually translated in English as 'rennet'. Rennet is defined as 'any means of curdling milk, especially a preparation of calf's stomach' (*The Chambers Dictionary* (Edinburgh: Chambers Harrap Publishers Ltd, 1993), p. 1458). Fig-juice is, then, a form of rennet.

4 Gilbert Herdt, 'Semen depletion and the sense of maleness', in *Ethnopsychiatrica* 3 (Paris: MSH, 1981), pp. 79–116.

5 Bernard Saladin Anglure, 'Iqallijuq ou les réminiscences d'une âme-nom inuit', in *Études inuit* 1 (1), pp. 33–63.

Part 3

THE PSYCHOANALYTIC SUBJECT

INTRODUCTION

This section, which constitutes one of the most fertile areas for reflections on subjectivity, contains essays by three of the philosophers in this collection best-known outside France: Kofman, Kristeva and Cixous. This is perhaps because French psychoanalysis has been both popular and deeply controversial for a long time, especially in the wake of Jacques Lacan. But none of the essays selected is truly Lacanian in method, though several use Lacanian concepts and categories.

In the extracts from *Rootprints*, interviews conducted by Mireille Calle-Gruber, Hélène Cixous explores the relations between self and other in particular through the question of love. For Cixous 'we are always prey to otherness' for it is the other who 'gives me I', 'it is the other who makes my portrait'. And Cixous sees the unknowable self of the other, his or her infinite foreignness, as part of love, and as exalting as knowing the other, which is also part of love. Love is described in terms of vulnerability and mortality. It is the other who holds my life in his or her hands, and who returns it to me. In love, I am second to the other whom I love, and in this loss of self-priority I am simultaneously augmented and exalted. These reflections are as much philosophical as they are psychoanalytic, and they pinpoint the thread of paradoxes that underly many of the meditations on identity and alterity in this volume. Cixous is known as a theorist of sexual difference and of creative bisexuality, but these interviews are not primarily concerned with gender.

Monique Schneider's book, *Généalogie du masculin*, represents another application of psychoanalytic theory to the question of identity. Schneider explores the patriarchal adage that 'anatomy is destiny' and puts in question the age-old identification of masculinity with verticality and power, and femininity with vulnerability and physicality. In Schneider's view, psychoanalysis may be in the thrall of this interpretation but is none the less able to question it through another interrogation of masculine eroticism based not so much on power as on the uncontrollable irruption of desire. In this extract, Schneider considers the origin of the identification of masculinity with verticality and elevation as described by Freud, and brings to the fore the nostalgia for sensuality and instinct that permeates his texts and undermines his ostensible celebration of male abstraction, purification and spirituality. She uses Merleau-Ponty and Freud to analyse the effect of what she calls the 'repudiation of the feminine' which dominates civilisation: in striving for transcendence of the corporal and tangible, human civilisation cuts itself off from some of the major regions of experience. Freud's espousal of

INTRODUCTION

the progress of intellect and monotheism is shown to be marked by ambivalence and doubt, and the passion for ascent is simultaneously a mark of exile.

In the following extract from *Strangers to Ourselves,* entitled 'Might not universality be our own foreignness?', Julia Kristeva brings together politics and psychoanalysis in a powerful account of the relationship between self and other, identity and alterity. Tracing a line from Kant through Herder to Freud, Kristeva explores the notion of cosmopolitanism with its attempt to account for both separation and union in a form of active, political hospitality towards foreigners. In Herder's hands, Kant's conception forms part of a meditation on the question of translation, and on the way in which national culture is rooted in the genius of a language. Kristeva considers that Herder was 'only indirectly responsible' for the appropriation of his ideas by nationalist politicians. But their appropriation by Freud has a quite different consequence, for Freud considered that the unconscious itself followed the logic of each natural language. In Freud, foreignness is not so much national or racial as internalised: 'foreignness is within us: we are our own foreigners, we are divided'. In Kristeva's terms, 'Psychoanalysis is then experienced as a journey into the strangeness of the other and of oneself, towards as ethics of respect for the irreconcilable'. And she concludes with a fascinating account of the implications of the uncanny, *heimlich* and *unheimlich,* for an understanding precisely of the strange uncanniness within my own psyche. If the foreigner is within me, there are, she argues, no foreigners: the ethics of psychoanalysis clearly implies a politics, and a new form of cosmopolitanism.

Sarah Kofman's essay also has an ethical and political dimension in its comparison of what Freud and Plato have to say about dreams and their role in the expression or repression of unacceptable desires. For Plato, dreams can and should be controlled; this is achieved through temperance, through positive bedtime rituals, and through the exercise of a similar control in waking life. A soul which falls asleep in complete self-mastery will, Plato believes, also be blessed with powers of divination and access to the truth. Freud's use of Plato, Kofman argues, to reinforce his own theories about the role of dreams, is based on either a careless or a wilfully blind reading. Whereas the Freudian subject may be split, and may relegate its evil desires to night-time, Plato is a philosopher who aims for self-integration and self-mastery, and posits the necessity for a total rejection of madness and tyranny. Dreams for Plato are not cathartic but rather serve to strengthen and feed evil and anti-social desires. Kofman concludes by proposing, perhaps not purely ironically, that we follow Plato rather than Freud and spare ourselves the need for a psychoanalytic cure.

Monique David-Ménard concludes the section with a rigorously argued critique of the concept of the universal which, she claims, organises our logic, political philosophy and ethics, as well as our understanding of sexual difference. David-Ménard argues that the confusions endemic in the concept of the universal arise from a failure to recognise the subjectivity of thought and its roots in desire; her analysis of the concept aims to produce a clearer understanding of the ineradicable relationship between fantasy and theory. Using a psycho-analytic approach, she attempts to reconnect concepts with the fantasy structures from which she claims they arise. In her view, our concept of the universal is acutely subject to blind-spots of understanding precisely because it has been severed from the context in which it was elaborated. And this context, as with conceptuality in general, is predominently masculine. David-Ménard does not claim that thoughts or concepts arising from feminine thinkers would present a higher truth, but rather that they would establish a necessarily different relation to truth because of the difference between the subjectivity and fantasies of men and women. This is an aspect of the nature of thinking which has been occluded in part precisely by the very notion of universality, the limited and situated nature of which has remained unrecognised. David-Ménard is not an essentialist: she does not consider sexual difference to be ontological, nor philosophical arguments or formulations to be more than provisionally linked to masculine or feminine preoccupations. But she does believe that the origin of concepts in fantasy structures needs to be acknowledged and their claims to universality consequently mitigated. Thought, she concludes, is only provisionally sexed, but it is not possible to eliminate such 'sexuation' which represents what she calls, in a memorably paradoxical phrase, the 'necessity of a contingency.

12

HÉLÈNE CIXOUS

Hélène Cixous is a major exponent and practitioner of *écriture féminine*. She was for many years Professor of English Literature at the University of Vincennes. Her early work is indebted to that of Jacques Derrida, especially her analysis of patriarchal binary thought, and her deconstruction of the hierarchical oppositions within its system of values. It is these ideas that lie at the heart of her conception of 'feminine writing', and the open-ended textuality which it embodies, in texts which undermine logic and promote rather difference, lyricism, and imagination. Cixous opposes philosophy and poetry, theory and life, and has produced a vast number of novels and plays which she appears to value above the theoretical texts with which she is most often identified in the UK and the USA. Even her 'theoretical' texts are, however, permeated with lyricism as the extract chosen from *Rootprints* (*Photos de racines*) illustrates.

Her major critical works include the following:

L'Exil de James Joyce ou l'art du remplacement, Paris: Grasset, 1968.

Un K. incompréhensible: Pierre Goldman, Paris: Christian Bourgeois, 1975.

La Jeune née, Paris: UGE, 10/18, 1975.

La Venue à l'écriture, Paris: UGE, 10/18, 1977.

Entre l'écriture, Paris: des femmes, 1986.

L'Heure de Clarice Lispector, précédé de Vivre l'Orange, Paris: des femmes, 1989.

Photos de racines, Paris: des femmes, 1994.

Voiles (with Jacques Derrida), Paris: Galilée, 1998.

Portrait de Jacques Derrida en jeune saint Juif, Paris: Galilée, 2001.

A selection of her fiction:

Dedans, Paris: Grasset, 1969.

Les Commencements, Paris: Grasset, 1970.

Neutre, Paris: Grasset, 1972.

Tombe, Paris: Seuil, 1973.

Prénoms de personne, Paris: Seuil, 1974.

Là, Paris: Christian Bourgeois, 1976.

Angst, Paris: des femmes, 1977.

Ananke, Paris: des femmes, 1979.

Le Livre de Promethea, Paris: Gallimard, 1983.

Manne, Paris: des femmes, 1988.

Déluge, Paris: des femmes, 1992.

La Fiancée juive, Paris: des femmes, 1995.

Messie, Paris: des femmes, 1996.

Or, les lettres de mon père, Paris: des femmes, 1997.

Theatre:

Portrait de Dora, Paris: des femmes, 1976.

La Pupille, Paris: Cahiers Renaud-Barrault, 1978.

Le Nom d'Oedipe, Paris: des femmes, 1978.

L'Histoire terrible mais inachevée de Norodom Sihanouk, roi du Cambodge, Paris: Théâtre du Soleil, 1985.

La Prise de l'École de Madhubai, Paris: des femmes, 1986.

L'Indiade, ou l'Inde de leurs rêves, Paris: Théâtre du Soleil, 1987.

On ne part pas, on ne revient pas, Paris: des femmes, 1992.

La Ville parjure ou le réveil des Erynyes, Paris: Théâtre du Soleil, 1994.

ALTERITY

Being human

Otherness (Altérité)

H.C.: *Otherness*, yes. But are we not *always* prey to otherness? The fever only lets up in appearance. At the exterior floor, 'up above', at the floor of the semblance – of myself – of order. Below, next door, we are always adrift. We respond straight ahead and think sideways. Always in the process of betraying (ourself), of leaving (ourself). We 'take decisions': in a stroke, we come down on one side – we cut out a part of ourself. We are tortuous, impenetrable. We do the thing we just decided not to do. We are the place of a structural unfaithfulness. To write we must be faithful to this unfaithfulness. To write in voltes. In volts.

The word '*entredeux*': it is a word I used recently in *Déluge* to designate a true in-between – between a life which is ending and a life which is beginning. For me, an *entredeux* is: nothing. It *is*, because there is *entredeux*. But it is – I will go through metaphors – a moment in a life where you are not entirely living, where you are almost dead. Where you are not dead. Where you are not yet in the process of reliving. These are the innumerable moments that touch us with bereavements of all sorts. Either there is bereavement between me, violently, from the loss of a being who is a part of me – as if a piece of my body, of my house, were ruined, collapsed. Or, for example, the bereavement that the appearance of a grave illness in oneself must be. Everything that makes the course of life be interrupted. In this case we find ourself in a situation for which we are absolutely not prepared. Human beings are equipped for daily life, with its rites, with its closure, its commodities, its furniture. When an event arrives which evicts us from ourselves, we do not know how to 'live'. But we must. Thus we are launched into a space-time whose coordinates are all different from those we have always been accustomed to. In addition, these violent situations are always new. Always. At no moment can a previous bereavement serve as a model. It is, frightfully, all new: this is one of the most important experiences of our human histories. At times we are thrown into strangeness. This being abroad at home is what I call an *entredeux*. Wars cause *entredeux* in the histories of countries. But the worst war is the war where the enemy is on the inside; where the enemy is the person I love the most in the world, is myself.

On the other hand, what I work on does not take place in the violent interruption – which opens up, and instead there is a sort of strange material which would be called '*entredeux*' – but always in the *passage*. In the passage *from the one to the other, de l'une à l'autre*.[4] Why do I say '*de l'une à l'autre*'? If I were to remain in the frame of the sober practice of the French language, I would say: '*de l'un à l'autre*'. This established expression has always irritated me. This is also a part of my work: to be irritated, as the skin is irritated, by the stubborn, outdated side of a number of idiomatic locutions which are not questioned and which impose their law on us. With '*de l'un à l'autre*', one expels the feminine – because neither of the two elements of the group carries the incontestable mark of the feminine. So I prefer to say: *de l'une à l'autre* (but I am playing at the same time). I think that when I write, it is because something goes from *l'une à l'autre*, there and back. But also, in play, I wrote: *de lune à l'autre*, from (the) *moon* to the other. It's a game, but a serious one. It is a way of dehierarchizing – everything. Being geocentric, because we are geocentric, we say: from the earth to. And the moon is the other. For a very long time I have felt myself to be in a poetic and fantasmatic relationship to the moon our other . . . to whom I always say – silently looking at her – excuse me for acting as if you were the other, whereas you are *lune*.

Let us change points of view. If I write '*de lune à l'autre*', in this case the other would be the earth. And it is a good thing. Each one should get her or his turn. In all ways. Not only because we must play musical chairs with hierarchies; it is also because, by dint of commanding without knowing, that is of being commanded in advance by language, we

> *No sooner I write . . . it is not true.*
> *And yet I write hanging on to Truth.*

deprive everyone of everything. We deprive ourselves of otherness – of the otherness of the earth.[5] We ourselves finish by no longer seeing it from another point of view, while it absolutely needs this. The earth seen from the point of view of the moon is revived: it is unknown; to be rediscovered.

This perhaps is one of my motives – I will not say one of the motifs because I prefer it to be more buried, an intention which is not voluntary but is spread throughout me – this tendency to rehabilitate what is forgotten, subordinated. Or else it is an unconscious leitmotiv: when I speak it comes forth exterior to myself and I recognize it. But basically, it is active in me, permanently, like one of the springs, like one of the sources of what I write. I write also with an incessant drive for re-establishing the truth, justice. I want to use this word: justice. We do not think with justice. The world is not just. The world-wide nonjustice that we all know politically has spread all the way to our imagination. It goes so far that we are not just with the earth, with the stars, with ground, with blood, with skin. In advance, and without our even being informed, everything is already ordered-classed according to a scale which gives primacy to one element over another. And power to one thing, or to one being over another. All the time. And in an unfounded manner.

So when I write, in the writingness [*écrivance*] itself, in the material, in the course of the writing, I am already in the process of shaking all this up. So that what is at the top stops being at the top by believing itself to be at the top; not so as to make the top fall towards the bottom, but so that the bottom has the same prestige, that it be restored to us with its treasures, with its beauties. And the top also. That the top not be only opposed to the bottom. That it be on an initial, augural level where we would discover, in a new way, all that it can bring us. I am saying the top and the bottom: I could obviously change the terms infinitely.

'Tearing of conventions, of '*received*' ideas, received feelings': you are right. It is what has been received for a long time, and never called into question, and dead for a long time, that I do not accept. It is even the sound of 'received' that alerts me. As if I had a sort of ear for cliché, in all the domains: and also for the cliché of *jouissance*,[6] the cliché in the body. There must be positions of the body and of the sensations that we have lost from the beginning, as our body is itself so much a cliché. More than ideas, it is feelings that are more important to me than anything in the world. My working material is what was once called the 'passions'; or, the 'humours' and what they engendered, that is to say the phenomena that appear first in our body, coming from the innumerable turbu-lences of the soul. In other words: what gives us suffering. Or what gives us joy. And the two touch, they are always in exchange. The most incredible is to notice to what extent we are all ignorant of ourselves. To what extent we are 'stupid' that is to say without imagination. To what extent we are sorts of corks without poetry, tossing about on oceans . . . Yet I am convinced that we all desire not to be corks tossing on an ocean; we desire to be poetic bodies, capable of having a point of view on our own destiny; on . . . humanity. On what makes humanity, its pains and its joys. Which is not the point of view of a cork. Of a cork without a bottle, of course! Which would also be great. I am sure that we are all thirsting after our virtuality of greatness. And it is without limits. It is as great as the universe. And we are deprived of it because we no longer even know how to let ourselves feel, how to allow ourselves to feel what we feel. Nor how to accompany this feeling with the song that echoes it and restores it to us.

> *a deluge*
> *We would have to annul Time, undo*
> *History. Un-recount. Un-know.*
> *Un-arrive*
> *Un a gree*
> *– Begin again at zero, all powerfully*

We receive what happens to us with 'received feelings'. We do not profit from it in any way. Neither in knowing how to suffer from it, nor in knowing how to enjoy it. We do not know how to suffer, this is perhaps the worst. It is our greatest loss. And we do not know how to enjoy. Suffering and joy have the same root. Knowing how to suffer is knowing how to have joy in suffering. Knowing how to enjoy is knowing how to have such intense joy that it almost becomes suffering. Good suffering.

That is my material. Where do I find it? In me and around me. What sets me writing is that lava, that flesh, that blood, those tears: they are in all of us. I am not the one who invented them. They are worked on in all the great tragic texts; it was their flesh, it was their body. I work on unknown events (because I find myself before them): what life brings me. The arrow that hits me in the face. The car that runs over the person next to me. Fire, prison; these are things which have a very high index of intensity. But in situations that are less acute one can also find material to work on and to rediscover what one has never had.

You are right, I work (on) relations all the time. We look at the garden together: the garden is a place of relations. We could express this place in a thousand ways. Relations of colours together; of different species together; between the vegetable and the human. In relation to all the phenomena of growing, to the question of preservation. Gardening is an act that is absolutely strange, in relation to life and death. And if I only listen to myself gardening, I have a very light sense of suffering in saying to myself: why garden when I know it will die? That, for me, is the other. Between us: death. Together we look at the garden.

M.C-G.: If I understand you correctly, alone, *I* does not exist. *I* is nothing. *I* is only with the other, and it is the other who gives me *I*. Is the other thus innumerable? Are *they* also of all sorts, my others?

H.C.: The other in all his or her forms gives me *I*. It is on the occasion of the other that *I* catch sight of *me*; or that *I* catch *me* at: reacting, choosing, refusing, accepting. It is the other who makes my portrait. Always. And luckily. The other of all sorts, is also of all diverse richness. The more the other is rich, the more I am rich. The other, rich, will make all his or her richness resonate in me and will enrich me. This is what people do not know, in general, and it's too bad. They are scared of those they consider to be stronger or richer or bigger, without realizing that the richer, the bigger, the stronger person enriches us, makes us bigger, stronger.

It's the other who makes my portrait

M.C-G.: That attitude is part of the hierarchizing spirit you spoke of.

H.C.: A spirit that rages between individuals, between people, between parties. All the time. The world is mistaken. It imagines that the other takes something from us whereas the other only, brings to us, all the time. The other is complex. He can be our enemy, and our friend.

M.C-G.: He is incalculable also. Which is not inevitably bad.

H.C.: Our enemy is not necessarily bad. Our enemy also teaches us something. He does not necessarily teach us hate. He makes a sort of mysterious map of all our points of vulnerability appear. He does not only teach us to defend ourselves. He teaches us to grow: because there are many possibilities to work with the enemy, when he is not death itself. When it is not the death drive or assassination.

And conversely, you said to be 'thwarted by the other': I think you must have been alluding to limitations?

M.C-G.: Or to displacements, to changes of position that awaken an ankylosis we had not suspected. Habits, mania, a routine. Because of this, the shock of the other is at once painful and salutary. At least it seems to me that we live through it at first in this way: painful because it involves a putting into question of the self-image that allows us to believe we know ourself, to believe we recognize ourself. That allows one to live with oneself. To rest . . . as long as some 'other' does not make this interior cliché vacillate.

So the other can be felt as a breaking, a point of rupture that is more or less painful according to whether one is more or less used to the self-image, whether a sort of defence has been established, an imagination that keeps us on the defensive.

H.C.: Here is difference between us, which is to say that we have been fabricated, moulded, written by millions of elements and authors ending in a different chapter. For you, if I take you literally, there is always breaking and for me, in a certain sense, not. What is it that makes a membrane, a defence, something I do not know, probably be situated in a different place for you than for me? . . .

H.C.: I did not follow you about the word *breaking*. Here is the end of language; it is a word that does not fit what I feel. Because in breaking I sense: irreparable. But there is *wounding*. The wound is what I sense. The wound is a strange thing: either I die, or a kind of work takes place, mysterious, that will reassemble the edges of the wound. A marvellous thing also: that will nonetheless leave a trace, even if it hurts us. It is here that I sense things taking place. The wound is also an alteration. Breaking, for me, remained in the domain of a less fleshy material. I see a stick being broken . . . of course, one can also break one's bones, but then the sticks of the body repair themselves, and there is no scar . . . I like the scar, the story.

Negative incomprehension
Positive incomprehension

To return to the eventual shock with the other, the violence of the other: there is one that happens daily, that is up to us to manage. We are always in a relation with *negative incomprehension*; not even an incomprehension, but very often a non-comprehension. Simply put: there is no openness. And this spreads out infinitely, in all our relations. But there is also a *positive incomprehension*. It is perhaps what we discover in love; or in friendship-love: the fact that the other is so very much other. Is so very much not-me. The fact that we can say to each other all the time: here, I am not like you. And this always takes place in the exchange, in the system of reflection where it is the other we look at – we never see ourselves; we are always blind; we see of ourselves what comes back to us through (the difference of) the other. And this is not much. We see much more of the other. Or rather, on the one hand, we see an enormous amount of

> *I love* dialogue *(this is why I love theatre)* – *work, dance, groping, rectification,* repentirs, *misunderstandings – (portrait of dialogues) – assault and battery – duet*

the other; and on the other hand, at a certain point we do not see. There is a point where the unknown begins. The secret other, the other secret, the other itself. The other that the other does not know. What is beautiful in the relation to the other, what moves us, what overwhelms us the most – that is love – is when we glimpse a part of what is secret to him or her, what is hidden, that the other does not see; as if there were a window by which we see a certain heart beating. And this secret that we take by surprise, we do not speak of it; we keep it. That is to say, we keep it: we do not touch it. We know, for example where the other's vulnerable heart is situated; and we do not touch it; we leave it intact. This is love.

But there is also a not seeing because we do not have the means to know any further. There are things that we do not understand because we could never reproduce them:

behaviours, decisions that seem foreign to us. This also is love. It is to find one has arrived at the point where the immense foreign territory of the other will begin. We sense the immensity, the reach, the richness of it, this attracts us. This does not mean that we ever discover it. I can imagine that this infinite foreignness could be menacing; disturbing. It also can be quite the opposite: exalting, wonderful, and in the end, of the same species as God: we do not know what it is. It is the biggest; it is far off. At the end of the path of attention, of reception, which is not interrupted but which continues into what little by little becomes the opposite of comprehension. Loving not knowing. Loving: not knowing.

> *to believe: to have faith in the other beyond*
> *all proof*
> *movement of faith*
>   *to believe the other even if he himself be-lies*
>   *to believe (in) God even if he does not exist*
> *There is no proof of the existence of God:*
>   *there is faith*
> *Faith:* my *movement. I exist God.*

You said: it is never psychology. Psychology is a bizarre invention, about which I understand nothing, a sort of verbal gadget. First of all we are sentient beings.

First of all we are sentient beings

The most impassioned, the most passionate in us is the quantity, the flood of extremely fine and subtle affects that take our body as a place for manifestation. It begins in this way, and it is only belatedly, and to go quickly, to sum up, that we give general and global names to a whole quantity of particular phenomena. In *My Pushkin*, Tsvetaeva says in passing: it begins with a burning in the chest, and *afterwards* it is called love. Now writing deploys itself before 'it is called'. Before . . . This is undoubtedly the cause of my problem with titles: I just finish writing a book, someone asks me what it is called . . . and there is never a title. Never. One must obey the law of the book which is to have a title. For me the book should not have a title. The book wrote itself before the title, without a title.

The dream is that someone who is my alter ego would take the magic decision to name, to give me the name.

M.C-G.: The title is a reduction – as if one could account for two hundred pages in a few words . . .

H.C.: Each (word or) sentence of a text has survived the shipwreck of two hundred pages. The process of writing is to circulate, to caress, to paint all the phenomena before they are precipitated, assembled, crystallized in a word. A practice which is not only my

191

> *So deep inside that there had* never been a name.
> *(No names in the stairwell, no names in the kitchen)*
> *It was voices that were seen, seeing.*

own. So it is not 'psychology', because it begins with this experimental annotation which, what is more, is always taken from life. That is to say always mobile. Which is dated; carries the dates of a certain moment that will not return. Or at times, what writing does well is this meticulous work that one does not have the time to do, one does not take the time to do when one is not writing. Such that in the end we will not have lived these innumerable intimate events that constitute us because we will not have recognized them. In a book, sometimes, all of a sudden, we see the portrait of a palpitation pass, the portrait of an instant of which we ourselves have been the lead character, without being able to detain it. This is what the book gives: this (re)cognition that had escaped us.

'Oxymoric' writing: perhaps, but it's reality that is oxymoric. When I say take joy in suffering, this is not a trope or a rhetorical effect. This is exactly what waylays us, our chance as human beings. The word suffering has in general a negative connotation, as painful. But it suffices to suffer to know that there is not only pain in the suffering of the soul; that one can suffer without pain. And that for the soul there is sometimes, in suffering, a strange profit. Which is not a joyous profit, but a profit. That suffering cannot do without. Fever, which is unbearable, is a defensive phenomenon. It is a combat. It is the same thing for suffering: in suffering there is a whole manœuvre of the unconscious, of the soul, of the body, that makes us come to bear the unbearable.

Where does the manœuvre lead us? For example to not being expropriated; to not being the victim but rather the subject of the suffering. Of course there are sufferings of which we are the victim, sufferings of the body which nip our mind and from these we die. But human beings try to live through the worst sufferings. To make humanity of them. To distill them, to understand their lesson. This is what the poets did in the concentration camps. And what we do, ourselves, when the pain that strikes us in our personal life makes poets of us.

We can say the same thing of joy. Whoever has not suffered from enjoying, whoever has not suffered from joy, has not known true joy. True joy, when it attains its paroxysm, drives us crazy. Because – luckily, by the way – it goes beyond us, it is bigger than we are. We suffer from our smallness and we make superhuman efforts to be superhuman. To follow joy.

As for what you call, why not, the Pascalian, that is, dwarf giant side, yes, I would more likely say Shakespearean. If Shakespeare has crossed the centuries, it's because he did not make a rupture in the truth of our states. He always made what happens to us in reality appear: that in the most extreme tragedy, in the most extreme pain, we can feel ridiculous and be ridiculous. This is moreover what we dread. Because we are in the multiple register all the time. The monovocal register does not exist. That is what I recount in *Déluge*: when someone is prey to an atrocious despair, he has a handkerchief problem. All of a sudden, no handkerchief and you remember that you are not an actor in a tragedy but a human person. To be in the depths of anguish, ready to die and to say to oneself: and what's more, tomorrow I'm going to have puffy eyes, this is us. It's that we do not stop being in the process of living, even when we are in the process of dying. At the edge of the tomb, we live, we blow our nose, a mirror watches us.

[. . .]

The word human

As for the human theatre which is not a question of humanism. Yes, the word human comes up very often with me. I see no other word to speak of that direction, of that development, of that progress, of that growth, which happens or does not happen in the course of the length of our life. After all, what do we do? We live, but why do we live? I think: to become more human: more capable of reading the world, more capable of playing it in all ways. This does not mean nicer or more humanistic. I would say: more faithful to what we are made from and to what we can create. The question that I have asked myself in the face of History and which crosses all that I write is the question of the choice people make between two major attitudes. Major and opposed. One is an attitude of protection and upkeep; the other is of destruction.

I continue to be surprised by destructive and self-destructive behaviours. Even if I have understood for a long time that destructive and auto-destructive people get something out of it. But what is it that makes human beings find satisfaction in destruction? It is certain that the people who are in destruction are there *because* it is their means of living. In an ultimate way, all human beings choose life. Choose survival, their own survival. At times, to survive, certain people think they must kill the other; at times, to survive, certain people think they must absolutely save the other. It is the origin of all the conflicts. Most often human beings choose to kill the other. And it is a bad calculation.

The heart is the human sex

When I speak of the human, it is perhaps also my way of being always traversed by the mystery of sexual differences. By the sort of double listening that I have. I am always trying to perceive, to receive, excitations, vibrations, signs coming from sexed, marked, different places; and then, in a certain place – barely a point, a full stop or a semicolon – the difference gives way to (but it is rather that the two great currents mix, flow into each other, so as only to be) what awaits us all: the human. This is how I have come to distinguish 'the sex' and 'the heart', saying that what the sexes have in common is the heart. There is a common speech, there is a common discourse, there is a universe of emotion that is totally interchangeable and that goes through the organ of the heart. The heart, the most mysterious organ there is, indeed because it is the same for the two sexes. As if the heart were the sex common to the two sexes. The human sex.

M.C-G.: What you call 'more human' is an attempt to tear the human away from humanism, that is to say away from anthropomorphism and from anthropocentrism. It is the love of all species.

H.C.: We must absolutely not let go of the word 'human'. It is so important.

193

Fortunately I am not always this vacillating and climbing insect, or this fish that descends in spite of himself in spite of myself. These are pains reserved for the author.

In this world where I was born of my mother, born of my dreams of my mother and where I am born again of my mother in her . . . I am a woman.

I have always said

In what way am I a woman?

In this   (wetnurse)

And in that I am not a man. Nothing seems stranger to me than a man. But on the other hand nothing is as close to me as a being that writes, man or woman (because of the interior). They are animals [bêtes]. *All of them, all my brothers and sisters. The* bêtes, *the animals. And we are all* bêtes *(Dreams of animals)*

Saying this I cry. Because

Better (at being) human

When I say 'more human', I mean: progressing. I ought to say: better human. This means, while being human, not depriving oneself of the rest of the universe. It is to be able to echo – a complex but magnificent labour – with what constitutes the universe. I am not saying that one ought to do it as a researcher, as a scholar. But I think that we are not without an environment, one that is human, personalized, personal; and terrestrial, urban, etc. ('political' comes afterwards for me). We are all haunted by the question of our mortality. And thus haunted by the question of what it is to be human, this thing that speaks, that thinks, that loves, that desires and that one day is extinguished. Everyone incessantly goes towards this term which is lived in diverse ways; and which brings us back to a part of the universe that in general we scorn: dust. But dust can be something else entirely: energy, sublime memory, etc. . . . .

To be *better* human is also: not to be closed in one's small duration, in one's small house, in one's small car, in one's small sex, but to know one is part of a whole that is worth the trip, the displacing of all our ideas.

M.C-G.: Is this 'better human' not connected to the vulnerability of love? In one of your latest books you talk about hate; about how we stop hating when we think that the person who is the object of the hate can die. *Déluge*: 'Knowing that, one day, I will die and that he will die one day suffices for me to lose my angers and my illusions. A great human tenderness had reappeared. All of us who, sensing dying approach, throw ourselves on the nearest big chunks of meat, and hasten to eat down the wrong way' (p.223). Vulnerability, that is to say mortality, makes us more human in your eyes: to become conscious that the other, like myself, is liable to be dust is to 'disarm'. To step back, to put human relations in a less cramped perspective?

H.C.: A small commentary on that sentence of *Déluge*. There is the limit of hate. Hate has a limit? How can that be? For example, how could I stop hating Hitler? The person who is going to die exits from this time which, seen from the centuries of centuries – not to say from eternity – will have been an instant, an error, an illusion. The human being who was bad and worthy of hate, exits from the stage where his meanness was active to go onto a stage where all that makes up historical destruction has simply disappeared. There will be a time when those who believed they were powerful people will have joined an extinguished, disappeared humanity, of which we know nothing, and they will take their place among the ordinary, the unsorted. They will be one among the unsorted goers. At death, at the moment of death, this scene is being produced.

This does not mean one should pardon war criminals. There is the unpardonable. I believe that there ought to be the unpardonable in the History of peoples and of states. But in the personal and intimate order, it is good that the fight to death be extinguished. Death extinguishes death, certainly. Love subsists in memory, but hate, which is a formidable defensive movement, falls by itself ... As for that species of vision I often have of our era, seen by someone who could be outside of time, who could travel round it and thus sees its limits: it transforms my evaluation of the world or the relationship I have with others. I

> *Hate = it's the plague. One* catches *hate. Hate hurts the haters. One hates the person who 'gave' us the plague (sickness).*

always see myself as that ant, that little letter wandering through a book whose end one cannot see. And that ant, that little letter does not see the end of the book. But someone who could see the end of the book would have a different life. I imagine that someone ...

M.C-G.: In a way, to seize the present instant, one must go the distance. Which writing attempts to do. Writing sides with life. That is what gives force to your fiction. If not, how would one be conscious of the present which is already past? Or already hypostatized: a distant block.

H.C.: To live, one must live in the present, live the present in the present. At the same time: the sensation of forming one body with all of time, all the living substance of time. Everything conspires so that we do not manage to live in the present: it is Sunday and we of most people prevent them from ever being in the present. Instead, they are in a menacing future, in a projection that destroys everything around them and beneath their feet; or in a rehashing of a baneful past.

M.C-G.: This relation (that you force yourself to have) with temporality allows the writing of death: the life of death. Because in our vocabulary, and our stereotypical way of hearing words, death is finished, past. On the contrary, you never stop recounting the thousand deaths lived in the present.

H.C.: Death is nothing other than that, by the way. What we are able to experience of death is only allusions to death. What we inflict on ourselves, our innumerable suicides and our way of being absolutely beside our own time; ahead of ourselves without having lived what is behind us . . . Admittedly, being able to live in the instant all the time is nearly impossible. But one can live very often in the instant; it is a practice, a necessity. Perhaps the enemy of the present is something one could call ambition.

> *What I have discovered: how the dead suffer during decomposition*
> *Suffer on the one hand . . .*
> *And keep mulling over (Cf. Hamlet)*
> *their powerlessness.*
> *They* cannot *believe it so long as they still have marrow to*
> *not-feel*
> *not-be-able-to.*

One could also call it: will to power, etc. We are like the fisherman's wife who can never live in her house . . .

I will reconstitute. A fisherman catches a very big fish who says to him: listen, if you throw me back into the water, your wishes will be granted. So the fisherman puts him back into the water. He returns to his house, he says to his wife: I threw a fish back into the water; in exchange, to thank me, he gave me this possibility. Since they are in a cabin, the wife immediately asks for a house! Behold: all of a sudden they have a house! And then, once they have their house, she goes around it and she says: all the same, I should have asked for a palace . . . and there is the palace! So then she becomes emperor of the world, until she passes logically into the void. This story had a terrorizing effect on me when I was little. I must have understood the stakes: that woman never lived in her house. What is annoying is that the story is misogynous. So we must change it! Let us say that it is not the wife of the fisherman but the fisherman himself who . . . to be able to use this fable. The secret of our eternities: one must manage to live in one's house, inside one's time . . .

M.C-G.: Inside the time of writing . . .

Returning to (our) time

H.C.: In this sense, yes, the practices of reading and of writing are an extraordinary help. Because there, in this place, we stop, we return to our time, it is here, we live in it, it lives in us.

M.C-G.: We play with it also.

H.C.: Yes, seriously. Because as soon as one is in time, one sees that it is not what goes by but what stays, what opens itself. What deepens itself. All this is not easy. By definition, we do not have a gift for the present. Because from childhood we begin to fear loss, to see nothing but loss, out of fear.

And to return to the story of love: you said that you love the person with whom you can be vulnerable, yes?

M.C-G.: Or who knows that I am vulnerable, or with whom I do not fear their knowing I am vulnerable . . .

H.C.: In the face of love we disarm ourselves, and indeed we keep the vulnerability. It does not disappear, but it is offered to the other. With the person we love, we have a relationship of absolute vulnerability. Why? First of all because we think they will do no harm to us at the same time that we think and we have the experience that they are the only person who can do all the harm in the world to us. Through death: either by dying, or by killing us, that is to say abandoning us. But also, and this is the childlike and magical side of love, we think that the person who can kill us is the person who, because he or she loves us, will not kill us. And at the same time, we (do not) believe it. In love we know we are at the greatest risk and at the least great risk, *at the same time*.

> *It is the word to love that precedes us and slips from our lips . . .*
> *We live, we sleep, we dream and*
> *across // the beds | four-different-leafed love grows*
> *| pierces*

What the person we love gives us is first of all mortality. It is the first 'thing' they give us. With the person we do not love we are much less mortal.

M.C-G.: We are always playing at being immortal. It's a must!

The person we love gives us mortality
immortality

H.C.: Ah but we are immortal too! The person who gives us mortality gives us immortality. Immortality that has been given can be taken back: we feel it; but we do not enjoy the immortality that is only the absence of mortality. It is inert, apathetic, dead immortality. In a trembling and an anguish of joy, at each moment we feel, taste, etc. the immortality that is given.

M.C-G.: It is love's capacity for enchantment: because of the knowledge of the greatest risk, I also live the greatest tension. Enchantment renewed each moment that the other does not abuse my vulnerability.

H.C.: That is where you risk your life. You don't risk your life elsewhere: you risk it only there.

> *It is the fault of this word to love which*
>
> *It is because of its innocence, of my innocence, of my need to name so many emotions that are violently familiar but violent and always as surprising . . .*

M.C-G.: In that sense, it's true that we have the greatest bereavement when the vulnerability is abused by the other.

H.C.: It is irretrievable. Because in love – if not, there is no love – you give yourself, you trust, you entrust yourself to the other. And, contrary to what one might think, this is not at all abstract. It is true that one deposits oneself. *There is a deposit*, and one is deposited in the other person. And if the other goes off with the deposit, one truly cannot recuperate the deposit. What was given can never be taken back. Even if we do not know it at the moment we give; even if we do not imagine that what we have given cannot be taken back – while most things one gives can be taken back. So in reality, virtually, when we love we are already half dead. We have already deposited our life in the hands that hold our death: and this is what is worth the trouble of love. This is when we feel our life, otherwise we do not feel it.

It is an extraordinary round: what you give, that is to say yourself, your life, what you deposit in the other, is returned to you immediately by the other. The other constitutes a source. You are not your own source in this case. And as a result, you receive your life, which you do not receive from yourself.

H.C.: I am saying things that can appear to be harsh, or belittling of love. No, I simply want to express a certain truth: it's easy to love . . . *once you love*! You have to get there first! [*Laughs.*]

M.C-G.: Exactly: first you have to be in the other world. Transported by magic!

Less self

H.C.: To get there, one needs strength, the real strength of abnegation which is renounce-ment: before all the other renouncements that will follow, in particular the renouncement of the affirmation of an identity. One must open oneself, one must make room for the other. Accept an entirely amazing change in economy that is produced: *less self*. A reduced resistance of the ego. It is also to no longer be the first character of one's life, but the second. Even if the second can become the first in the 'tornament' of love. Even so, one needs an immense narcissistic force to begin, and afterward, one is rewarded! [*Laughs.*] Once you have passed the threshold and you find yourself in the world of love, then everything becomes easy. It is the passage that can appear to be difficult.

M.C-G.: In love, this situation that demands renouncement and that gives gratification supports the paradox: at once the desire to assimilate, to annhilate, and the refusal to do so . . .

H.C.: It must also be said, of course, that we are all wolves in love. I am not sure that we are also lambs. I think we are above all wolves. It is known that love is devouring. It is the great drama of love: we want at once to devour the other and not to devour the other. To not want to devour the other is not a mark of love, but a mark of disinterest. So it's the two at the same time: we want at any price to devour the other, and so it is an homage (the desire for the other, in this form, is a sign of love), and at the same time, we know that if we devour them ... there will be no more ... We must perform this double movement all the time. One must desire above all, be ready to kill for it, and at the same time be able to renounce the satisfaction of one's desires *in extremis*. In extremis. Just before destroying. But *even so it's easy*. The difficult passage is easy too: it happens in a flash. In a leap. Without transition. It is the lightning movement of trust. Without reserve and without calculation. We must realize that to love is not of this world, but of another planet. What can be confusing and misleading is that the other planet, which is ruled by the absolute and by faith, is nonetheless located in this world. So that when we love, we are subject to a double regime: that of the ordinary world with its economy and its common laws, and simultaneously that of the singular planet where everything is different. And what is impossible in this world is at the same moment possible in the sphere of love. Words even change meaning when we change levels. The word lamb, the word eat. In the sphere of love, all is grace, free, without price. All is 'easy': nothing is easy: all is given: all is to be given. Because this sphere must be created, at every instant. In reality, the misfortune is that we do not always see the limit. Sometimes we are already in the process of having destroyed without having noticed that the limit was crossed. In any case, to love well, to belove, is relentless work.

> *If someone asked me what do you prefer: to abandon or to be abandoned, concerning a person dear to me, I would not hesitate, I prefer to be abandoned.*
>
> *However nothing frightens me more than abandonment, but at least in abandonment I do not abandon myself.*

M.C-G.: What is fabulous is that it is never definitively settled.

H.C.: That is why love is fragile. Because very often we rest! We stop. And we no longer love.

M.C-G.: The story of the wolf who loves the lamb he doesn't eat could also be a parable of writing in so far as, in writing (as we have been speaking of it), there is the necessity of abandoning oneself, of abandoning a conventional image of oneself, of letting oneself go, of practising a permeability, a vulnerability with which writing nonetheless works?

H.C.: I think that what one abandons in writing is one's resistance. One must at once be afraid, have or keep fear, and cross through fear. In principle, writing leads to enrichment – not of the self but of the self of the person in labour. But in writing, we do not love anyone. Or rather *we love (no) one. On aime personne*. Niemand.

M.C-G.: I do not want to suggest forced coincidences, but in writing the subject must forget itself a bit (him or her) so as to enrich itself from its non-subject, something in itself that it can only encounter by going out. Outside.

H.C.: But in my experience, forgetting oneself is not a sacrifice. It is exalting in a certain way. Besides, it is only making room. Making room for the other part of myself who is the other, who can only exist, of course, if I am there to receive. In other words: becoming a receiver, withdrawing, putting oneself way in the back – this is the condition *sine qua non*. Perhaps this brings us back to love. That is: to love the other more than oneself. But doing that is of course the best way of augmenting oneself, indirectly.

> *(It is only in the act of love that we are present)*

M.C-G.: This comes back to the difficulty of removing resistance and obstacles. For someone who has never written, this must be as difficult as the beginning in love: removing the resistance that prevents our going towards the other-self. The dawn of another self. Where we become inventors: (dis)placed in a scene that gives us the unknown (person).

H.C.: I think we probably love more easily than we write – which does not mean that we love well. But we have more numerous experiences of love than of writing. Because we cannot not love when we live. It is our motivating force. That is what living is: the search for love. And its substitutes. Because we also discover how few possibilities there are to exercise love. The scarceness, incidentally, is related to the scaredness: the fear everyone has of losing. Of losing oneself. I also ought to say, counselled by human prudence: we cannot not be *tempted* to love. Most people flee the temptation. Some do not flee, knowing, as does everyone, that love is dreadful. As dreadful and desirable as God. But no one *chooses*: the two possibilities – to flee, to succumb – carry us off. It is stronger than we are. We are all subjects of the fortune called grace.

13

MONIQUE SCHNEIDER

Monique Schneider is a psychoanalyst and philosopher. She taught at both the Lycée and the University of Grenoble as well as at the University of Paris VII (Denis Diderot). She has been attached to the CNRS since 1970, where she is currently Emeritus Director of Research. She specialises in the study of psychic suffering and in questions of trauma, incest, fraternity and alterity. Her study of the interconnections between affects and representation has led to both her psychoanalytic practice and to her research into the element of repression and denial at the heart of psychoanalysis itself.

Her works include the following:

De l'exorcisme à la psychanalyse. Le féminin expurgé, Paris: Retz, 1979.

La Parole et l'inceste, Paris: Aubier-Montaigne, 1980.

Freud et le plaisir, Paris: Denoël, 1980.

'Pere, ne vois-tu pas . . .?' Le père, le maître, le spectre dans L'Interprétation des rêves, Paris: Denoël, 1985.

Le Trauma et la filiation paradoxale. De Freud à Ferenczi, Paris: Ramsay, 1988.

La Part d'ombre. Approche d'un trauma féminin, Paris: Aubier, 1992.

Don Juan et le procès de la séduction, Paris: Aubier, 1994.

Généalogie du masculin, Paris: Aubier, 2000.

Le Paradigme féminin (forthcoming).

L'Amour comme passion de la causalité (in preparation).

REPUDIATING THE FEMININE

Exiled to the heights

Is it better to look upwards or downwards? This is not just a question about the nature of the masculine, preoccupied by its search for the father, but one which, in a more radical sense, has a bearing on the nature of the human. In *Civilization and Its Discontents*, in a footnote, Freud establishes a link between the theme of the 'civilizing process' and that of the 'raising up' (*Aufrichtung*) which makes every human being an embodiment of *Homo erectus*. This suggests that the meaning of the human as such – whether male or female – is tied to this movement of ascent that is the defining characteristic of the civilizing process. Yet the jubilation that lies beneath this theoretical formulation nevertheless opens out onto an acknowledgement of loss – the loss involved in what Freud terms 'organic repression'. Whereas in the Mosaic strand of Freud's work, the civilizing cut is located in the *Wendung* ('conversion' or 'transition') by which the individual turns from the sensory to the spiritual, this footnote from *Civilization* places that cut elsewhere. Rather than being repudiated *en bloc*, the field of sensory experience is subjected to a process of internal reorganization which modifies its hierarchical structure. While remaining firmly within the domain of the senses, the individual nevertheless comes to abandon a sensory regime founded on smell in favour of another sensory mode, a transcendent dimension accessed by way of 'visual excitations'.

This redistribution of priorities within the realm of the sensory takes place in the context of concerns about temporality and the stability of the family as an institution. How are we to emerge from a temporality of evanescence if all we know are the movements of the instincts towards their immediate satisfaction? Freud answers this question – with its possible ethical implications – by anchoring a principle of fidelity and permanence in the realm of the sensory itself. This establishing of a principle of 'permanence' does indeed demand that a loss be suffered, but far from affecting the entirety of the sensory domain, the resulting 'depreciation' is directed at one region in particular, that of the 'olfactory excitations', the importance of which will be reduced in favour of the visual mode. For vision alone can offer a guarantee of constancy in relations to an object or sexual partner: 'This change seems most likely to be connected with the diminution of the olfactory stimuli by means of which the menstrual process produced an effect on the male psyche [*die männliche Psyche*]. Their role was taken over by visual excitations, which, in contrast with the intermittent olfactory stimuli, were able to maintain a permanent effect.'[1]

Having analysed this particular civilizing turn, one construed in the first instance in terms of a defence against menstrual odour, Freud then considers another way in which the olfactory becomes subject to repression. The excremental takes the place of the menstrual, becoming the new focus of an attempt to impose distance: 'Anal erotism, therefore, succumbs in the first instance to the "organic repression" which paved the way to civilization.'[2] It is telling that this reference to the repression of anal eroticism serves, in the way in which Freud's text is organized, to conceal what was the first reason for moving to an upright posture: essentially, in order to break free from a world governed exclusively by what might be called, in a profane version of the theme from Don Juan, *odor di femmina*.

In later discussions of the relation between upright posture and the repression of the olfactory, the excremental is often promoted to the position of principal target, thereby allowing, once more, the feminine target to be forgotten or repressed. True enough, the repression of the excremental forms part of a developmental process which can be seen to be at work in each individual history, whereas the first of Freud's themes – feminine odour as the target of repression – invites the reader to become reimmersed in a feminine realm sited at the dawn of humanity, though not necessarily present in each individual trajectory. This is a realm which exerts a kind of negative magnetism over the phylogenetic path, for it leads man to flee the ground, to stand erect and build a world safe from the intermittent grip of menstrual odour. On this depends, according to Freud, the stability of the family as an institution. Yet is Freud justified in placing these various mutations within an entirely linear framework, arranging them in accordance with an order governed by succession? Freud employs both a language of chronological succession and one implying the convergence of different factors, each virtually independent of the others:

> The diminution of the olfactory stimuli seems itself to be a consequence of man's raising himself from the ground [*Abwendung des Menschen von der Erde*], of his assumption of an upright gait; this made his genitals, which were previously concealed [*gedeckt*], visible and in need of protection, and so provoked feelings of shame in him. The fateful process of civilization would thus have set in [*stünde*] with man's adoption of an erect posture.[3]

This analysis has a celebratory undertone, for the description of the upright posture is also an example of rhetorical doubling: when the human being managed to stand upright, a monument was thereby erected (*stünde*), in commemoration, at the threshold of the evolutionary process which led to the human. However, in spite of this celebratory air, something frequently hidden from view in Freud's work is here quite apparent: once 'visible', the genital organs become vulnerable. Whereas the piece on 'Medusa's Head' places the exhibition of male genital organs in a context of brave defiance – '"I am not afraid of you. I defy you. I have a penis."' – the footnote from *Civilization* emphasizes the element of danger involved in this sudden absence of protection.[4] The genital organs are presented as 'requiring protection' (*schutzbedürftig*). Yet the term 'protection' (*Schutz*) carries some fairly strong connotations for Freud because it often refers to what the child expects from its parents. Thus this becoming visible is placed in the context of birth, as though the genital organs were subjected to brutal exposure, exposure to sight, to danger, as a result of being drawn out from their primitive bodily hiding-place.

A related question arises: which sex is it that has to endure this position of exposure? Freud is, in theory, analysing a transformation which applies to both sexes, since it is the human being – whether male or female – that reaches the stage of *Homo erectus*. However, in the metamorphosis he describes, the link between visibility and exhibition is clearer in the case of the masuline position and the term designating the specificity of this human that has become *erectus* points to a masculine erotics. At this inaugural moment, the male being becomes the paradigm of the human being.

In addition, Freud's way of referring to this rupture is not easily translated: *Abwendung . . . von der Erde* – literally, 'turning away from the ground'. The expression is formed from the same root as that which denotes the turn analysed in *Moses and Monotheism*: *Wendung*. Yet it is impossible to convey in French, at least with nouns, the proximity between *Wendung* (the act of turning) and *Abwendung* (the act of turning away), a proximity which can be exploited to make apparent the bridge between these two texts.

Dehiscence in the very midst of the Sensible

In the footnote from *Civilization*, the emphasis is firmly on the possibility of changing the direction of the gaze and 'raising up', in an optical no less than a postural sense. Yet this footnote is a long way from implying that the gaze is thereby induced to cut all ties anchoring it in the sensible realm. What is required is simply that certain modes of sensory perception be elevated at the expense of others. Thus it is within the realm of the sensory that this act of liberation takes place, as modes of perception subject to a regime of proximity and evanescence are pushed into the background. In leaving the ground and beginning to focus on the upper realm, the aim is not to renounce the entirety of perceptual experience but rather to induce within it the equivalent of that 'dehiscence' which Merleau-Ponty identified in the tension between the tangible and the visible. This is what gives rise to the phenomena of divergence and overlap which, in Merleau-Ponty's argument in both *The Phenomenology of Perception* and *The Visible and the Invisible*, forbid us to consider the sensory as a single, uninterrupted, field, opposed in its entirety to the intelligible.

Merleau-Ponty overturns the age-old dichotomies that structure the divisions between fields of knowledge – divisions which, to a very large extent, merely transpose and validate the split between oppressor and oppressed, or superior and inferior, which occurs in the social realm. Merleau-Ponty's work argues for the value of organizing the various facets of sensory experience without making their interaction subject to a hierarchical principle – a principle in accordance with which the intelligible would supposedly become responsible for bringing the senses under its control. A brief digression into Merleau-Ponty's work will better allow us to judge what is at stake in the divergence of interpretations between these two versions of Freud's account of the divide which separates two distinct moments in the process of so-called civilization.

In the footnote from *Civilization*, as in Merleau-Ponty's work, the visible has the special task of reorganizing the entirety of the perceptual field by extracting from the profusion of the sensory those poles capable of being apprehended in terms of distance, poles around which other perceptual outlines can then be arranged:

> In visual experience, which pushes objectification further than does tactile experience, we can, at least at first sight, flatter ourselves that we constitute the world, because it presents us with a spectacle spread out before us at a distance, and gives us the illusion of being immediately present everywhere and being situated nowhere. Tactile experience, on the other hand, adheres to the surface of our body: we cannot unfold it before us, and it never quite becomes an object.[5]

By going beyond what can be verified by touch, the power of sight anticipates what may later be grasped and thereby exercises a power of command over the entirety of perceptual experience. In proposing this particular relationship between the visible and the tangible, Merleau-Ponty is offering both an analysis and a warning: he recognizes in visual experience both its movement and, concomitantly, its delusions of grandeur. For it is effectively the cause of an 'illusion' which causes seeing subjects to extract themselves from the visible realm, an illusion which leads us to imagine that 'we stand nowhere'.

Is it not precisely this aspiration to immateriality that is at work in the definition of the masculine framed by Nicole Loraux, who locates it at the peak of Classical Greek voluntarism? Is to be above the sensible realm not to be predisposed to occupy a position of power? The celebration of the visual principle has a bearing on both the nature of the sensible and the construction of the political. For Alain Roger, just such an inflation of the visual principle is at the structural centre of Western judgements of value:

> If idealism is the temptation of the West, this is because the West *looks* to lend authority to other sensory registers, or at least until recently, in spite of many fruitless efforts. We are all, whether we like to think so or not (or rather because we think in visual terms) incurable idealists. When Foucault distinguishes between the ages of resemblance, representation and so forth, he merely identifies the several incarnations of Western idealism. Thus the blind person really is a refutation of idealism [. . .] because blindness makes idealism incomprehensible: without sight, idealism can neither be conceived of nor *theorized*. Moreover, God is 'Pro-vidence' and it would evidently be impious to force Him to labour under the affliction of taste and smell with their stock of base sensations.[6]

This purportedly aesthetic analysis is closely allied to Freud's hierarchical perspective: for as we climb the ladder of sensory perception – the most elevated mode of which is 'Pro-vidence' – we are gradually unburdened. The highest form of being must be pure, entirely free from the taint of smells and tastes. Moreover, the hierarchical position occupied by vision is not the sole preserve of the deity: anyone in a position of political responsibility must be able to fore-see and the Oedipal drama, which leads to a violent loss of sight, is, from beginning to end, a tragedy about power. As a king – or, to be precise, a tyrant – Oedipus ought to have foreseen the events that were to come. Thus gouging out his own eyes is a kind of partial suicide which strikes at the very faculty destined to wield power.

In granting the visual a monopoly of this sort, has the West succeeded in freeing itself – at least in its own self-image – of these parasitical sensory faculties, smell and touch? Has the West tried to follow Heracles's example and tear off its native skin, to slough it off, as though it were a question of leaving behind the mark of a chthonic femininity, a femininity doomed to dwell close to the ground, like the Eve of Autun. Significantly, in one of his novels, *Hermaphrodite*, Alain Roger has developed the hypothesis of a division between sensory fields by attributing the male side of his protagonist with the so-called 'representational' sensations – visual and auditory – and the female side with the so-called affective sensations, those of taste, smell and touch. The portrayal of his novel's main character thus corresponds perfectly to the bipartite division sketched by Freud in the footnote from *Civilization*.

Surely this exclusive emphasis on the value of the visual constitutes an attempt to amputate the feminine component. When he turns to the second account of the target of 'depreciation' – a second stage which, on this occasion, sees him concentrate on the excremental rather than the menstrual – Freud resorts to an adjective formed from the same root as *Verwerfung* ('foreclosure' or 'repudiation') as a way of denoting the status of the devalued object: 'Here upbringing insists with special energy on hastening the course of development which lies ahead, and which should make the excreta worthless, disgusting, abhorrent and abominable [*verwerflich*].'[7]

Although the object destined to be repudiated here is officially the excremental, it would not be illegitimate for us to recall the first phase of his analysis and accordingly suggest that the menstrual too is destined to be foreclosed or repudiated. Moreover, the menstrual and the excremental are conjoined in the zone of juxtaposition that is the cloaca, a zone corresponding to the impurity of the viscera and in which, in women, the place of birth and the site of excretion are fused together. Witness the Church Father's *inter faeces et urinas nascimur*. Thus by standing upright and repudiating the earth, the human being strives to forget the circumstances of its first abode, as though amnesia were linked to a civilizing imperative, namely that of not wanting to know anything about original conditions, those of the gestation of experience. So the visual realm comes to power on the strength of the repudiation it imposes on those complex sensory interconnections which supported it as it came into being. However, Merleau-Ponty's work is very much geared towards rediscovering the path to these zones that have been subjected to repudiation and foreclosure. This involves exposing the ways in which consciousness, in its promotion of the object, resorts to various techniques of burial:

> *What* it does not see is what makes it see, is its tie to Being . . . is the flesh wherein the *object* is born. It is inevitable that the consciousness be mystified, inverted, indirect, in principle it sees the things *through the other end*, in principle it disregards Being and prefers the object to it, that is, a Being with which it has broken, and which it posits beyond this negation, by negating this negation.[8]

We glimpse here the various forms of founding *méconnaissance* involved in the construction of what has the potential to become an object and to be launched into a system of symbolic exchange. This object is necessarily uprooted from the context that has nurtured the development of its various different characteristics. To reverse this process and undertake what might be called a phenomenological regression, Merleau-Ponty attempts to rediscover the traces of the umbilical cord anchoring the visible in the tangible: 'We must habituate ourselves to think that every visible is cut out in the tangible, every tactile being in some manner promised to visibility, and that there is encroachment, infringement, not only between the touched and the touching, but also between the tangible and the visible'.[9]

The phenomenological account rediscovers a story of betrothal – is the tactile not 'promised to visibility'? – and thereby restores a nuptial dimension (even if this ebbs away to the horizon) where the civilizing imperative had issued decrees of repudiation. Moreover, Merleau-Ponty eventually arrives at the figure of chiasmus and thereby manages to avoid fostering the ardent hope that coincidence will be restored at the end of the process. The chiastic model nevertheless allows him to interrupt the perfect linearity of a civilizing process which only recognizes progress in an upward direction. What remains is indeed the lateral presence of that which has, strictly speaking, been surpassed or left behind.

By arranging things such that apparently opposing realms are continually encouraged to separate and touch once again, Merleau-Ponty subverts the clear-cut version of the story of loss. To hypostasize loss suggests that we have been taken in by the illusion involved in the exercise of visual perception, an illusion leading us to assign a position of exteriority to the world, that of the 'object', when, all the while, a continuous movement of reflux lead us to *take the measure* of the tangible, in the heart of which lies a dimension of sightlessness. Yet far from having to be classified as negative, sightlessness marks the limit beyond which sensory experience finds that all distances are overcome, the place where contact is established. Contrary to Heracles's example, the perceiving being is involved in a continuous process in which the various dimensions of the sensory are endlessly split and rejoined and is forever rediscovering the skin that was supposed to have been furtively repudiated. Thus emergence and anchoring are the two moments, or rather the two sites, of the perceptual pulse.

The traumatic context of the 'decision' and nostalgia for the couple

Entering the theoretical universe of *Moses and Monotheism*, we encounter once again the bipolarity identified in the footnote from *Civilization*, yet this time alongside a vigorously centralizing force: sensibility no longer appears to be split in two but becomes, as a whole, the site where the maternal is anchored and which is destined to be surpassed by the inauguration of a 'realm' (*Reich*) focused on both *Geistigkeit* (spirituality/intellectuality) and the father. The transition from one to the other is supposedly a 'progression'. This Freudian thematic is thus structured around a split which hardens the binary oppositions by lending them a somewhat Manichean air.

How should we place *Moses and Monotheism* in Freud's *œuvre*? The force of this work may seem all the greater because of the temptation to see it as effectively the last will and testament of the master. Something is being pushed to the limit, as though thought had been bidden to erect itself over and above the maternal, to rise up to the heights reserved for the spirit and the father. Moreover, the same kind of elevatory movement is adopted and redeployed by Lacan in his theorization of the paternal function.

The theme of ascent encountered in *Moses and Monotheism* is, without doubt, present from the very beginning of Freud's work and it is tempting to see it as the culmination of a lengthy process of development. If it perpetuates a dualistic vision apparent in the earliest of Freud's theoretical formulations, it also draws on the split between the father and the mother in an attempt to unite this with another division, between the sensible and the intelligible – one which does not always appear to be so clear-cut in Freud's work. Could this conceptual strategy be related to the very conditions in which Freud's work was written, namely the context of war and the increased threat of anti-Semitism, as well as the prospect of exile that was beginning to loom on the real horizon of history? The paternal agency, represented by Moses, the architect of exile, would thus have been called upon to accompany a departure from the homeland. Moreover, the state of Britain – the place of refuge – features in the text as a way of suggesting what the representation of God meant to the Jewish people:

> Anyone who believed in this God had some kind of share in his greatness, might feel exalted [*gehoben*] himself. For an unbeliever this is not entirely self-evident; but we may perhaps make it easier to understand if we point to the sense of superiority [*Hochgefühl*] felt by a Briton in a foreign country which has been made insecure owing to an insurrection . . . For the Briton counts on the fact that his *Government* [in English in Freud's original] will send along a warship if a hair of his head is hurt.[10]

So this 'Government' takes on the tutelary role assigned to the God of scripture. This role cannot, moreover, be separated from a privileged spatial position, for it is by virtue of their faith in protection from on high that human beings find themselves 'elevated', filled with *Hochgefühl* (literally, a feeling of height). Thus by contrast with the footnote from *Civilization*, the theme of raising to the heights has changed domain: it is now the relation to God, or to a tutelary political power that is supposed to enable the move to the vertical imputed to the transition from the olfactory to the visual. The connection is maintained between cultural progress and this elevatory movement but the prescription ordering this elevation to the heights is given an entirely different reading. It is no longer a matter of preferring one sensory regime to another but of turning away from the sensory as disclosed by the human sensory apparatus (*Sinnlichkeit*).

Surely then this sensory apparatus becomes the equivalent of the native land from which it has become necessary to break away? Is not the insistence on an element of 'decision' – an insistence emphasized by Vladimir Granoff in *Filiations*[11] – to be ascribed to the sense of traumatic urgency which accompanies the necessary rupture? Freud seems in this text to engage in an act of self-mutilation which bears an analogy with the work of autotomy in traumatic splitting, as characterized by Ferenczi – a splitting between 'the sensory part and another aspect which knows everything but feels nothing'.

The necessity of giving up belief in the sensible almost certainly corresponds to Freud's movement of obedience when confronted by the Mosaic injunction:

> Among the precepts of the Mosaic religion there is one that is of greater importance than appears to begin with. This is the prohibition against making an image of God – the compulsion to worship a God whom one cannot see . . . But if this prohibition were accepted, it must have a profound effect. For it meant that a sensory perception was given second place to what may be called an abstract [*abstrakt*] idea – a triumph of intellect over sensuality or, strictly speaking, an instinctual renunciation, with all its necessary psychological consequences.[12]

In this way, the sensory field is levelled out, for the primacy of the visual – as this emerged in the footnote from *Civilization* – introduces a transcendent dimension into this field which prefigures the power that, in *Moses and Monotheism*, Freud attributes to name-giving.

The fact that there is analogy between these two versions of the transformation that occurs when the masculine is elevated usually hides the chasm which separates their different approaches to the question of the father. In the two versions Freud proposes, the mother's fate is identical: in the *Abwendung von der Erde* (the process of 'turning away from the ground') and in the *Wendung von der Mutter zum Vater* (translating this as the 'transition from the mother to the father' allows us to forget the meaning of *Wendung*: the act of turning). The mother represents the 'ground' to which an individual must bid farewell in order to 'turn' to a higher dimension. Where is this kingdom of the heights to be found? The hypothesis in *Civilization* suggests a reorganization of the sensory field, a process inseparable from the bodily transformation connected with raising oneself up. The version put forward in *Moses and Monotheism* is considerably more radical because it abandons all possibility of an analogy between the visual and the paternal power. The father is not content merely to stand erect in relation to the ground but seems to renounce all ties to the sensory in order to establish himself as a super-sensory being – all of which places the reference to the father within an idealist framework of Platonic inspiration.

In heeding the Mosaic prohibition, as he does, and using it to shore up his definition of the paternal, is Freud remaining faithful to the spirit of his own discoveries? Even as he celebrates the visual heights towards which Moses's injunction encourages us, he discreetly underlines the ambiguous character of the 'progress' which it brings about. This is progress with a heavy price, for it requires an 'instinctual renunciation' – a programme that is not exactly in accord with the ideal of psychoanalysis and which tends to ascribe absolute value to a 'representation' that is rightly qualified as 'abstract'. But does psychoanalytic method not rest upon a systematic suspicion with regard to all that presents itself in the guise of the 'abstract'? To cash out abstraction into the small change of verbal fragments and sensory experiences is indeed what the work of association aims to do. In this way, the abstract finds itself transformed into 'living' elements – the terms *lebhaft* and *lebendig* are employed with great abundance when Freud gets round to specifying what emerges when the primacy of the abstract has been relinquished.

The psychoanalytic transformation cannot, of course, be inscribed in its entirety within this preference for the 'living'. There is another passion animating its scientific work, one which tends towards the ideal of 'dessication'.[13] Yet rather than the pursuit of a bipolar ideal, is Freud's thought not characterized by a taste for pairs – couples – of antagonistic tendencies? Freud is not just a theorist but also a practitioner of conflict, which explains the tension arising between the two poles: one is concerned with the living, in which the central figure is 'the child who remains alive within us' (*weiter-lebend*), although the encounter with this enduring life provokes, according to Freud, a reaction of 'surprise'. This is surprise at the power of survival of a force against which a whole battery of sacrificial procedures is pitted, not least of which being the dessicating scientific passion that loves nothing more than bony remains or a 'crumpled leaf-skeleton'. In an attempt to develop this fundamental bipolarity, Freud turns to a transferential relationship, a couple: the division between Fliess, the guardian of 'life' and Freud, the custodian of the 'soul' or 'spirit', will resurface in the bond with Ferenczi, who is entrusted, as Fliess was, to handle the interface with biology. Analytic work, in Freud's view, is sustained by this divergence, this tension. Yet this tension vanishes in an entropic translation of *Geistigkeit* as 'life of the spirit', as violent an oxymoron in Freud's scheme as talk of water that has all dried up. The threat of sacrifice bearing down on life is actually an integral part of the strategy which moves this 'spirit', this *Geist*, a close relation of the English 'Ghost'.[14]

Another aspect of the *Wendung*: a task that once fell to the masculine, to the extent that it was a model of the *Homo erectus*, is now transferred to the deity: 'The Mosaic prohibition elevated [*gehoben*] God to a higher degree [*eine höhere Stufe*] of intellectuality [*Geistigkeit*].'[15] The allusion to the elevatory movement is superfluous here: bound together as one and the same are the definition of the civilizing process and that of the place allotted to a father who takes on all the hallmarks of the divine. Although this does indeed correspond to one of the lines of force running through Freud's work, is it true that, in *Moses and Monotheism*, we have the culmination of the psychoanalytic enterprise? Not by a long way. The discreet signs of reticence which this work displays can, if we pay them sufficient attention, allow us to hear some of Freud's hushed reservations.

There is a discernible sense of nostalgia. After presenting Jewish spirituality as the highest achievement of civilization, Freud refers in passing to the prospect of loss looming on the horizon: 'Harmony in the cultivation of intellectual and physical activity, such as was achieved by the Greek people, was denied to the Jews. In this dichotomy [*Zwiespalt*] their decision was at least in favour of the worthier alternative [*trafen sie wenigstens die Entscheidung für das Höherwertige*].'[16] The translation given here[17] – 'their decision was at least in favour of the worthier alternative' – although correct, gives no indication that we are confronted here by the return of terms which punctuate this Mosaic text: *Entscheidung* (decision) and a reference to that which occupies a position of height (*das Höherwertige*). In the light of Freud's merciless attack, in *The Ego and The Id*, on all attempts to offer an unconditional defense of the sublimatory processes, can we not discern here – in the way that Freud tries to justify Moses' choice – an admission of regret? Freud was able, by appealing to the Greek ideal and its mythology, to provide psychoanalysis with a point of anchorage which would allow it to avoid having to present itself as the child of Jewish spirituality alone. The discord (*Zwiespalt*) registered here sounds a little like the grudging acceptance of a divorce.

Yet the great significance ascribed to the *Entscheidung* (decision) can only be understood in the context of the *Zwiespalt*, a term constructed from the same root as *Spaltung* and which includes a reference to the 'two'. What we have here is a scenario of agonizing struggle, one which forces Freud to resort to a surgical separation. If there can be no way of maintaining a relationship between these two equally valuable ideals then it becomes necessary to sever links with one of them, to resort to an equivalent of the autotomy which Ferenczi suggested as the model of traumatic defense: this is a defensive move in which a living being caught in a trap severs the limb it cannot free. Freud's attempt to justify such an act of abandonment makes reference to the 'political misfortune' of the Jews that obliges them to decide in haste: 'The Jews retained their inclination to intellectual interests. The nation's political misfortune taught it to value at its true worth the one possession that remained to it – its literature. Immediately after the destruction of the Temple in Jerusalem by Titus, the Rabbi Jochanan ben Zakkai asked permission to open the first Torah school in Jabneh. From that time on, the Holy Writ and intellectual concern with it were what held the scattered people together.'[18]

Seen in this context, the choice of spirituality forms part of a meditation on the diaspora. Thus the idealist division between material and spiritual occurs as a matter of historical necessity – the imperative to flee the homeland, taking only what can be carried in the exile's baggage – and is not therefore the result of some intrinsic feature of the Jewish tradition as such. For surely this idealistically surgical division utterly destroys the idea of the Promised Land as a founding entity. The Promised Land – a striking expression which implies an unbreakable bond between the land and the word. Yet this link only becomes conceivable with the opening out of the future dimension. This expression also undermines the relation to a homeland which, far from constituting the ground in which a people was originally rooted, gets relegated, by the same token, to a mere prospect on the horizon of exile. It is thus this 'political misfortune' that compels the Jews to abandon both a homeland and a theme from Scripture, one which stands diametrically opposed to the Platonic division. Moreover, when Freud reminds us of Moses's injunction, he leaves to one side the promise of a homeland 'where milk and honey will flow in abundance', as though the thought of exile compelled the traveller to leave behind not just the ground of a native land but also an essential theme of Scripture.

Does Freud not hint that the elevatory thrust represents the other side of an extremely fragile situation when he likens the projected structure of *Moses and Monotheism* to 'a bronze statue with feet of clay [*ein ehernes Bild auf tönernen Füssen*]'?[19] Though he remains shackled to his own quest for a staunchly unitary construction, does Freud not come up once more here against his nostalgia for a bipolar structure within which vertical erection is supported by another dimension? When Freud turned to Fliess, deferring to the latter's knowledge of the living as conveyed by biology, asking Fliess to provide a 'pedestal' on which he could set his own spiritual constructions, he was hoping that his scientific collaborator would provide a suitably solid foundation to bear the weight of his edifice.

This allows us to glimpse a hint of nostalgia for the theme of the coupling of life and spirit. It is in the structure of this couple that Max Dorra identifies the originality of

Freud's relation to the scientific field: 'Freud could only afford to marginalize himself in relation to the medical wisdom of the group because he had a "binomial", a friend, a fellow soldier with whom he enjoyed a passionate and exclusive relationship . . . Freud played the couple off against the group.'[20] This 'binomial' not only took the form of a passionate bond; it also allowed Freud to launch a bifocal scientific project, thereby preventing his science of the spirit finding itself in a situation where it would be forced to levitate above a ground which it would try desperately to ignore. Yet the stumbling block for *Moses and Monotheism* lies in this very risk of levitation, a danger closely tied to the temptation, for Freud, to burn the bridges connecting him to the realm of the living, which thereby becomes the sole preserve of the maternal.

Although this bridge-burning version of duality is the dominant one, it does leave room to think in terms of the couple, provided such thinking be done in semi-secret. Thus it is no longer a question of being clear-cut, but rather of building a bridge between two separate domains: one field is thereby brought into relation with another in this collaboration between two men. Instead of opposing the chthonic feminine to the vertical masculine, Freud turns to a theoretical male couple in order to forge a connection between the two planes that are life and spirit, a connection that will offer psychoanalysis the opportunity to anchor itself to the ground. But does the exodus sound the death knell of such a hope?

Can a text claim, on its own behalf, the rigidity of a statue? Although they are portrayed as signs of fragility, surely these 'feet of clay' serve to recall the presence of the ground which lends its support to erections of all kinds? There thus remains the insidious presence of this earthly matter over and above which both the Mosaic statue and the statute of the paternal are to be erected. This text about Moses is far from being a monolith. For it voices, in a fragmentary way, a few of those earthly insinuations emanating from a ground that has had to be abandoned.

The ways to the father are two

In a discreet and rather clandestine manner, a second centre of gravity exerts its influence over the text. For who exactly is it who brings about this change of direction? Freud would like the father to be the agent of change but (and this recalls his disappointment about the outcome of the seduction scenario centred on this figure), 'the old man plays no active part in my case':[21] the role of the paternal in this vast transformational process is that of beneficiary and not principal agent: 'in the case of the victory of patriarchy [*Vaterrecht*] – we cannot point to the authority [*die Autorität nicht auszeigbar*] which lays down the standard which is to be regarded as higher [*höher*]. It cannot in this case be the father, since he is only elevated into being an authority by the advance itself.'[22]

In view of the importance attached to demonstrability and the sequence of causes in the rise of the paternal, how can it be that the emergence of the paternal role is itself shrouded in a textual lacuna? Moreover, Freud admits to the existence of this lacuna with a degree of perplexity: 'Thus we are faced by the phenomenon that in the course of the development of humanity sensuality is gradually (*allmählich*) overpowered by intellectuality and that men feel proud and exalted by every such advance. But we are unable to say why this should be so.'[23]

This admission seems to live and breathe disappointment. Indeed it marks the beginning of a parenthesis which contrasts quite markedly with the dominant hypothesis of *Moses and Monotheism*. Does Moses not represent the one who instigated the transition to the spiritual, at least if the evolution of the Jewish people is considered in isolation? Yet at the very moment when Freud envisages, in general terms, the inauguration of patriarchy, his account ceases to insist on the necessity of appealing to the hypothesis of a charismatic leader who would guide his people to the higher plains of the mind. We have left behind the model of sudden elevation in favour of a development which moves forward little by little (*allmählig*). In assuming this particular mode of evolution, does Freud not depart from one of the overriding tendencies in his account of the coming of the father? Marie Moscovici, in 'Tearing the father to pieces in Freud's work', rightly emphasizes the homology which emerges between the status Freud accords to the hero and the role falling to the father. She writes: 'His heros can often be recognized by his turn of phrase when defining them. The hero is the one of whom he says "he was the first to . . .".'[24] She also quotes the following remark from *Group Psychology and the Analysis of the Ego*: 'It was then, perhaps, that some individual, in the exigency of his longing, may have been moved to free himself from the group and take over the father's part. He who did this was the first epic poet.'[25] Yet in the hypothesis put forward to account for the process of historical development which leads to patriarchy, the father seems to be borne along by, and born of, this movement, without in any way occupying the position of the founder who is able to 'detach himself from the mass'. Whence the perplexed response: 'But we are unable to say why this should be so.' It is no doubt his being thus reduced to silence that paves the way for the reversal of the following sentence: 'It further happens later on that intellectuality itself is overpowered by the very puzzling emotional phenomenon of faith. Here we have the celebrated "credo quia absurdum", and, once more, anyone who has succeeded in this regards it as a supreme achievement.'[26]

How exactly does this reference to a resurgence of faith have a bearing upon the question of the paternal? Is faith to be attributed to a reawakening of the sensitivity which serves as an emblem of the maternal? The answer cannot be unequivocal and it begins to look as though the path of Freud's inquiries will split in two. If we follow the route which ends with the prospect of the figure of the father becoming entwined with that of the hero, it then proves difficult to place this approach by way of faith in the trajectory leading to the paternal. Marie Moscovici emphasises the limits set in advance on her own inquiries when she admits to according special importance to those passages 'Where Freud himself associates the question of the father with the exercise of thought, as opposed to religious belief.'[27] Yet in that the inaugural division is fundamentally bound up with parricide, does the hero correspond to the model of the father or that of the rebel son? Marie Moscovici cites Leonardo da Vinci's challenge to authority as evidence that he is 'one of the figures of the hero' in Freud's eyes.

A comparison between the fate of Leonardo and Moses does, moreover, bring one point of similarity to light. Dominique Geahchan has remarked, during a seminar,[28] that Moses's relationship to the question of filiation changes entirely if you compare 'The Moses of Michaelangelo' with *Moses and Monotheism*. Whereas Freud sees Michaelangelo's statue of Moses as essentially a representation of the father, the first few pages of *Moses and Monotheism* award the great man the status of a son: 'To deprive [*abzusprechen*] a people of the man whom they take pride in as the greatest of their sons is not a thing to be gladly or carelessly undertaken, least of all by someone who is himself one of them.'[29] An opening remark that proves to be of great significance. Note, first of all, that the connotations of this extreme 'greatness' – he is the 'greatest of their sons' – are not necessarily linked to the father. Such 'greatness' can come to characterize the son, a son who is privileged enough to be raised to the superlative. Furthermore, the elevation granted to Moses is perhaps merely the other side of a rather more sinister process: Freud is effectively getting ready to take Moses away (*abzusprechen*) from his people. For the theoretical undertaking heralded from the very first lines of this text is surely akin to infanticide. Although Moses eventually recovers the place reserved for the father in the parricidal hypothesis, an ambiguity is nonetheless discernible from the very beginning of the text. It is remarkable that Freud, in the opening sentence of this work, should both question whether Moses was a Jew and claim, in his own right, to belong to this people.

Can we not discern a note of challenge in the passage where Freud condemns the powerlessness of an intellectualism that is unable to invest the father with his royal role – a father who remains in the domain of the 'indemonstrable' (*nicht aufzeigbar*) – and proceeds to hypothesise that a reversal occurred, one which led to 'belief' (*Glauben*)? Is this, moreover, a real reversal or a return to the origin? In both the short poem addressed to Fliess and the note to *The Ratman*, belief plays a vital role in gaining access to the father. In this context, the *credo quia absurdum* is not entirely unrelated to the theme of the paternal; it is written in the shadow cast by the grandiose figure of Moses. We glimpse here an 'enigmatic' form of the paternal, which reestablishes a connection to the darkness surrounding the dream's evocations of a father whose kinship is with the absurd. In craving hospitality from these themes of belief and the absurd, Freud is returning once again to a theoretical scene still redolent with the memory of his first encounters with the father. The passing reference to the absurd does moreover allow Freud to launch a challenge to the exclusively ethical direction imparted by Moses to the Jewish religion:

> The religion which began with the prohibition against making an image of God develops more and more in the course of centuries into a religion of instinctual renunciations. It is not that it would demand sexual *abstinence*; it is content with a marked restriction of sexual freedom. God, however, becomes entirely removed from sexuality and elevated into the ideal of ethical perfection. But ethics is a limitation of instinct . . . And even the demand to believe in [God] seems to take a second place in comparison with the seriousness of these ethical requirements.[30]

This passage is indeed paradoxical, to the extent that Freud seems to set himself up as the defender of the true faith, which tends in the opposite direction from that signalled by Moses. How are we to interpret the remark about the 'elevation' of a God 'entirely removed from sexuality'? Is it an invitation to turn to the gods of the Greeks or indeed a whole array of pagan deities, clad fullsomely in the signs of sexuality? This interpretation could hardly be more radical, but it is worth recalling a passing remark of Freud's in a letter to Fliess: 'Zeus seems originally to have been a bull. Our old god [*unser alter Gott*], too, is said to have been a bull prior to the sublimation imposed by the Persians. This is cause for all sorts of thoughts too premature to write down.'[31]

The hypotheses put forward in *Moses and Monotheism* tend in a different direction, yet this letter from 1901 allows us to gauge the depth of nostalgia that Freud may have felt. In setting out resolutely on a path which leads to the heights – terms meaning 'raised' (*gehoben* or *erhoben*) are present in great abundance in this chapter – Moses has ordained a process of purification which will eventually force the individual to jettison a burden that could have been valuable to him, one which the analytic work will encourage us to draw upon once again.

Indeed, in the *Three Essays*, Freud only succeeds in his rehabilitation of sexuality by casting doubt on the hierarchical division which specifies that only that which is elevated deserves to be considered human. Yet with Moses, it is this very model which returns with a vengence. In the 'new kingdom of the intellect', 'recollections, representations and reasoning' are promoted at the expense of 'inferior mental functioning'. Thus the noble functions and their less dignified counterparts are held in a relation of 'opposition' (*Gegensatz*). Yet in Freud's theoretical elaboration of loss, does he attribute an 'inferior' status to that which cannot but be an object of such loss? The Mosaic prescription strives specifically to assimilate that which is lost with the inferior, an elision bound up with a fanatical celebration of upward movement. Thus what we see thrust forward is an infinite psychic erection.

Erection occupies a rather peculiar place in *Moses and Monotheism*: there is not one explicit reference that would allow a connection to be made between the seething mass of terms denoting the value placed on height or on movement to the heights and the function of the male body which could serve as the paradigm of this particular passion. It is as though erection had become characteristic of the human in its most elevated form and had thus ceased to take hold of the body. Such a metamorphosis is, moreover, indicative of the process of sublimation, in the course of which the transposition of sexuality to a more noble plain is accompanied by desexualization. In this developmental process, which leads to culture's highest achievement, masculinity is both privileged and concealed. What remains is, in essence, its symbol – a symbol which simultaneously attests to and denies the presence of that upon which it rests. When reduced to its fundamental expression – a yearning for the heights – the paternal both expresses the utmost achievement of the masculine and represses it. It is as though this particular accomplishment – insofar as it is a sensory performance – remained tainted by the materiality which thenceforth falls to the maternal.

The first few lines of the text did indeed prepare the way for a campaign of symbolic reduction. Freud declared at the outset his intention to use words in order to carry out an operation of ablation or removal: *abzusprechen*. Words are thus invested with 'diabolical' power, in the etymological sense in which the diabolical is the opposite of the sym-bolic, with its unificatory effect.

A 'dia-bolical' plan of this kind, announced at the very beginning, is perhaps to be carried out in the process of 'disjuncture' which Marie Moscovici uncovers in the course of her analysis of *Moses and Monotheism*. She notes the importance of dualisms in the hypotheses that Freud develops – '*two peoples* which join to form a nation, *two kingdoms*, born of the fragmentation of that nation, a deity bearing *two names*'[32] – and she highlights the divide that emerges between the monotheistic project and the process of 'detotalization' on which Freud has embarked. She writes: 'Thus, in the course of a work which studies the triumph of monotheism – envisaged in terms of "spiritual advancement" – Freud simultaneously and somewhat covertly proceeds to strip both this god and his prophet of their status as unique.'[33]

The phenomenon of 'demultiplication' gradually recedes to the horizon because underneath the two characters gathered in the name of Moses, Freud evokes a god who existed prior to the Mosaic phenomena of dematerialization and desexualization, one which his letter of 4 July 1901 called 'our former God', one envisaged as preceding the 'sublimation' attributed, in the letter, to the Persians. There is absolutely no question of Freud's espousing a return to the origin: the overriding tendency in the text is to celebrate the decisive 'progress' achieved by monotheism. Yet the intellectual approach is surely informed by that biphasic rhythm of advance and retreat which Freud analysed in his text on *Die Verneinung*. The 'two' would thus be an essential feature of the text's intellectual respiration, forging an intimate relationship between doubt and adherence, between celebration and retroactive acknowledgement which is necessarily doubtful. The entire section that turns on the *credo quia absurdum* unleashes a volley of doubt that curtails the preceding, unconditional, celebration. The 'exploratory incursion' followed by a 'retreat' – a rhythm that characterizes the faculty of judgement, as analysed in *Die Verneinung* – lies open for all to see in this text about Moses. The two phases are not, of course, equal and the movement of criticism and doubt is discernible only in outline – yet it nonetheless forms a decisive reservation, in the sense that it denounces the effect of this radical progress on the fate of sexuality.

In that the suspicious rejoinder fails to overturn the main project and merely exercises a moderating influence, it encourages us to leave in waiting the possibility of opening another path to the father. Freud does briefly establish a connection between the radicalism of the choice in question – in the exodus, only take that which is most precious and consequently most 'elevated' – and the constraints imposed by a situation of 'political misfortune'. This is a departure in the midst of catastrophe: goods and land must be left behind which are fundamentally valuable yet which, in this logic of haste, it is appropriate to look upon with scorn. Leaving to the Greeks 'harmony in the cultivation of intellectual and physical activity', Freud, in *Moses and Monotheism*, allies himself, for the most part, with the choice of the Jewish people: 'that which has the highest value [*das Höherwertige*]'. Far from representing Freud's last will and testament, *Moses and Monotheism* answers his need to prepare a life raft.

Thus the constraints of exile and the passion for ascent are implicitly bound up with one another, as though danger transformed the higher plains into unassailable places of safety, citadels of sorts, high above the reach of the ground. In this yearning for ascent, which rests on the necessity of a 'split' (*Zwiespalt*), the fate of the Jewish people carries that of masculine sexuality in tow. The latter finds itself condemned to value more highly that which it sees, to use Freud's term of preference, as no more than a 'fragment'.

Translated by Oliver Davis

Notes

1 Freud, *Civilization and Its Discontents*, in *The Standard Edition of the Complete Works of Sigmund Freud*, vol. 21, 58–145, p. 99. *Gesammelte Werke*, XIV, pp. 458–9.
2 Ibid., p. 100. *G.W.*, p. 459.
3 Ibid., p. 99.
4 Freud, 'Medusa's Head', *S.E.*, vol. 18, 273–4, p. 274. *G.W.*, XVII, p. 48.
5 Merleau-Ponty, *The Phenomenology of Perception*, tr. by Colin Smith (London: Routledge, 1962), p. 316.
6 Alain Roger, *Nus et paysages. Essai sur la fonction de l'art* (Paris: Aubier, 1978), p. 31.
7 Freud, *Civilization and Its Discontents*, p. 100. *G.W.*, XIV, p. 459.
8 Merleau-Ponty, *The Visible and the Invisible. Followed by Working Notes*, tr. by A. Lingis, ed. by Claude Lefort (Evanston: Northwestern University Press, 1968), p. 248.
9 Ibid., p. 134.
10 Freud, *Moses and Monotheism*, *S.E.*, vol. 23, 1–137, p. 112. *G.W.*, XVI, p. 220.
11 Vladimir Granoff, *Filiations* (Paris: Minuit, 1975).
12 Freud, *Moses and Monotheism*, pp. 112–3. *G.W.*, XVI, pp. 220–1
13 A theme encountered in an earlier text, 'Father, don't you see I'm burning?', *The Interpretation of Dreams*, *S.E.*, vol. 5, pp. 509–11.
14 Cf. R. Gori, *La Preuve par la parole* (Paris: Presses Universitaires de France, 1996).
15 Freud, *Moses and Monotheism*, pp. 114–15. *G.W.*, XVI, p. 222.
16 Ibid., p. 115. *G.W.*, XVI, p. 223.
17 [The author refers here to a translation into French by Cornelius Heim. I have substituted the version proposed in the English *Standard Edition*, to which the same comments apply – *Tr.*]
18 Freud, *Moses and Monotheism*, p. 115. *G.W.*, XVI, pp. 222–3.
19 Ibid., p. 17. *G.W.*, XVI, p. 114.
20 Max Dorra, *Le Masque et le Rêve: histoire de l'inimaginable* (Paris: Flammarion, 1994), p. 27.
21 Letter of 3 October 1897, in *The Complete Letters of Sigmund Freud to Wilhelm Fliess 1887–1904*, tr. and ed. by Jeffrey Masson (Cambridge, Mass.: Harvard University Press, 1985), p. 268; *Briefe*, p. 288.
22 Freud, *Moses and Monotheism*, p. 118. *G.W.*, XVI, p. 226.
23 Ibid., p.118. *G.W.*, XVI, p. 226.
24 Marie Moscovici, 'Mise en pièces du père dans la pensée freudienne', *Cahiers Confrontation*, 1 (Paris: Aubier, Spring 1979), p. 126.
25 Freud, *Group Psychology and the Analysis of the Ego*, S.E., vol. XVIII, 65–143, p. 136.
26 Freud, *Moses and Monotheism*, p. 118. *G.W.* XVI, p. 226.
27 Moscovici, 'Mise en pièces', p. 124.
28 The seminar remains unpublished. I endeavoured to give an account of some of the issues raised in 'Don Juan et le père en question', a preface to Dominique Geahchan, *Temps et désir du psychanalyste* (Paris: Interédition, 1986).
29 Freud, *Moses and Monotheism*, p. 7. *G.W.*, XVI, p. 103.
30 Ibid., pp. 118–19. *G.W.*, XVI, pp. 236–7.
31 Letter of 4 July 1901, in *The Complete Letters of Sigmund Freud to Wilhelm Fliess 1887–1904*, op. cit., p. 445; *Briefe*, p. 490.
32 Moscovici, 'Mise en pièces', p. 142.
33 Ibid., p. 142.

14

JULIA KRISTEVA

Julia Kristeva was born in Sofia, Bulgaria, and came to Paris in 1966 where she soon became one of the most influential young French philosophers and theorists. She has been a practising psychoanalyst since 1979 as well as Professor of Linguistics at the University of Paris VII, and was for many years on the editorial committee of *Tel Quel*. She worked with Tzvetan Todorov, Lucien Goldmann and Roland Barthes among others. Her relationship with her husband Philippe Sollers is well known and recounted in her fictionalised autobiography *Les Samourais* (1990). She has written on questions of subjectivity, marginality, love, sexuality and motherhood in literature, linguistics, politics and psychoanalysis. Her relationship with feminism is complex, and she has dissociated herself from many of its manifestations (in particular French essentialist or 'difference' feminism, but also liberal, reformist feminism) whilst sharing many of its most significant preoccupations.

Her major works include the following:

Séméiotiké. Recherches pour une sémanalyse, Paris: Seuil, 1969.

Le Langage, cet inconnu, Paris: Planète, 1970.

Des Chinoises, Paris: des femmes, 1974.

La Révolution du langage poétique, Paris: Seuil, 1974.

Polylogue, Paris: Seuil, 1977.

Pouvoirs de l'horreur. Essai sur l'abjection, Paris: Seuil, 1980.

Histoires d'amour, Paris: Denoël, 1983.

Au commencement était l'amour: psychanalyse et foi, Paris: Hachette, 1985.

Soleil noir. Dépression et mélancolie, Paris: Gallimard, 1987.

Etrangers à nous-mêmes, Paris: Fayard, 1988.

Les Samourais (novel), Paris: Fayard, 1990.

Les Nouvelles maladies de l'âme, Paris: Fayard, 1993.

Le temps sensible. Proust et l'experience littéraire, Paris: Gallimard, 1994.

Possessions (novel), Paris: Fayard, 1996.

La Révolte intime: discours direct, Paris: Fayard, 1997.

L'Avenir d'une révolte, Paris: Calmann-Lévy, 1998.

Contre la dépression nationale, Paris: Textuel, 1998.

Le Génie féminin, tome I, Hannah Arendt, Paris: Fayard, 1999.

Le Génie féminin, tome II, Melanie Klein, Paris: Fayard, 2000.
Le Génie féminin, tome III, Colette, Paris: Fayard, 2002.

MIGHT NOT UNIVERSALITY
BE . . . OUR OWN FOREIGNNESS?

Beyond the ordeal of the Revolution, the Enlightenment's moral universalism discovered its masterly discourse in Kant's reasoned longing for universal peace. In contrapuntal fashion, the Romantic inversion, the emergence of German nationalism and most particularly Herder's notion of *Volksgeist*, but especially the Hegelian Negativity – which at the same time restored and systematized, unleashed and bound the power of the Other, against and within the consciousness of the Same – might be thought of as stages on the way to the "Copernican revolution" that the discovery of the Freudian unconscious amounted to. My point here will not be to follow that philosophical journey and trace Freud's indebtedness to the course that preceded him. Hence, from the tremendous Hegelian continent that gave the impetus to and completed the *thought* of the Other, I shall retain only what pertains to the intrinsic foreignness in culture, which Hegel brilliantly expanded starting from Diderot.[1] Nevertheless, so as better to point out the political and ethical impact of the Freudian breakthrough, or rather to outline an area where that impact might be thought out by others, by those who are foreign to the present book, inasmuch as the following pages are meant to be prospective, fragmentary, "subjective," more than demonstrative or didactic – I shall draw a tentative line going from Kant to Herder and Freud. With Freud indeed, foreignness, an uncanny one, creeps into the tranquility of reason itself, and, without being restricted to madness, beauty, or faith anymore than to ethnicity or race, irrigates our very speaking-being, estranged by other logics, including the heterogeneity of biology . . . Henceforth, we know that we are foreigners to ourselves, and it is with the help of that sole support that we can attempt to live with others.

Kant the universalist pacifist

While cosmopolitism is exalted or brought down according to the course of revolutionary events, it fell to Immanuel Kant to formulate the internationalist spirit of the Enlightenment in political, legal, and philosophical terms.

Since it is in the "nature of man" to seek the well-being that he himself created through reason, a man – through the philosopher – finds himself confronted with his "unsocial sociability."[2] By means of that phrase, so singularly apt and compact, Kant conjures up at the same time our tendency to create societies and the constant resistance we put up against them by threatening to split away: reasonable man wishes for concord, nature favors discord. The result is that "the greatest problem for the human race, to the solution of which Nature drives man, is the achievement of a universal civic society which administers law among men" (p. 16). To unbridled freedom and distress, men oppose a state of constraint: they impose a discipline on unsociability, which reminds one of the origin of art (p. 17). On the legal and political level, such a universal law could only be achieved "by a lawful external relation among states" (p. 18). And Kant, like the fiery cosmopolitans of the French Revolution, but with the logical precision of a cool argumentation, would in his turn advocate "a league of nations, [in which] even the smallest state could expect security and justice, not from its own power and its own decrees, but only from this great league of nations (*Foedus Amphictyonum*), from a united power acting according to decisions reached under the laws of their united will" (p. 19).

Kant knew that the idea seemed preposterous – "fantastical," he said, thinking of how it was laughed at by the Abbé de Saint-Pierre and by Rousseau. Nevertheless, it seemed imperative to him "as the necessary outcome of destitution" and an exigency henceforth as pressing as that which forced savage men to give up their brutish freedom for the sake of a security based on the constraint of the first laws. Even though that may be a natural trend, it is nonetheless necessary "to find . . . a united power to give it effect. Thus it is forced to institute a cosmopolitan condition to insure the external safety of each state" (p. 23). This does not mean eliminating dangers, without which mankind might slumber, but it would firmly set aside the risk of destruction. Kant is aware of the *time* necessary for citizens to reach maturity in interior matters as for nations to reach concord in exterior ones: this would be a cosmic time, he asserted, in a comparison involving "the path of the sun and its host of satellites." He insisted, just the same, on the ineluctable need for men to prepare the way for a distant international government for which there is no precedent in world history": "This gives hope finally that . . . a universal cosmopolitan condition, which Nature has as her ultimate purpose, will come into being as the womb wherein all the original capacities of the human race can develop" (p. 23).

Echoing Montesquieu and Rousseau, and also resonating with Clootz – who, as we have seen, took up again in his visionary rhetoric the idea of a universal Republic, even providing "constitutional foundations" for the "human species" – Kant's text inscribed, at the outset of a political ethics and a legal reality that are still to be carried out, the cosmopolitan concept of a mankind finding its full accomplishment without foreigners but respecting the right of those that are different. The notion of *separation* combined with *union* was to clarify such a practical cosmopolitanism that nature foresees and men carry out. Having doubtlessly learned from the clashes between nationalisms and cosmopolitanisms during the French Revolution, Kant elaborated upon that doctrine ten years later in *Perpetual Peace* (1795). In what manner? After having distinguished between *jus civitatis* (the civil code of a people) and *jus gentium* (international law), he defined *jus cosmopoliticum* (cosmopolitan law): "Peoples, as states, like individuals, may be judged to influence one another merely by their coexistence in the state of nature." In order to avoid the state of war that particular states are led to establish for the purpose of imposing their own interests, Kant advocated the "idea of federation, which should gradually spread to all states and thus lead to perpetual peace."[3] Such a "State of various nations" (*civitas gentium*), such a universal Republic would include all the peoples of the World. In that spirit, the idea that was outlined by the cosmopolitans of the French

Revolution concerning the integration of foreigners was taken up in similar terms: "Hospitality means the right of a stranger not to be treated as an enemy when he arrives in the land of another." Whence would such generosity follow? Quite simply . . . because the Earth is round: naturally therefore, inevitably.[4]

Far removed from that ideal, however, European states considered newly discovered countries as being "lands without owners," and they have intensified their injustices toward foreigners. In order to proceed out of that dramatic situation toward the state of nations that he proposed, Kant could only call upon "free practical reason," which will accomplish no more than a design inherent in Nature itself.[5]

This is where the acknowledgment of *difference* is inscribed at the very heart of the universal republic. First, the *coexistence* of states will guarantee their vitality and their democracy better than "amalgamation of states under one superior power, which might degenerate into one universal monarchy – a potential source of anarchy. Second, Nature, whom free practical reason respects and fulfills, "employs two means to separate peoples and to prevent them from mixing: differences of language and of religion" (p. 113). Thus *separation* and *union* would guarantee universal peace at the core of this cosmopolitanism, understood as coexistence of the differences that are imposed by the technique of international relations on the one hand and political morality on the other. In short, since politics can only be moral, the fulfillment of man and of the designs of Providence demand that it be "cosmopolitical."

This reasoned hymn to cosmopolitanism, which runs through Kant's thought as a debt to Enlightenment and the French Revolution, appears indeed, today still, like an idealistic utopia, but also as an inescapable necessity in our contemporary universe, which unifies production and trade among nations at the same time as it perpetuates among them a state of war both material and spiritual.

Once more, the ethical decision alone appears able to transcend the narrow needs of national politics. Could cosmopolitanism as moral imperative be the secular form of that bond bringing together families, languages, and states that religion claimed to be? Something beyond religion: the belief that individuals are fulfilled if and only if the entire species achieves the practice of rights for everyone, everywhere?

The patriotic nation between "common sense" and "volksgeist"

It is nevertheless against a background of national conscience and patriotism or nationalism that the contemporary position of foreigners stands out and can be understood. Now, modern nationalism, which also has ancient roots, does not show up before the second half of the eighteenth century, and it is also during the French Revolution that it will be most firmly expressed.[6] Cosmopolitan and rationalistic, the French Enlightenment laid down at the same time the idea of the *nation* that the lengthy work of humanists had prepared since the Renaissance (particularly through the awakening of national languages and literatures) and to which absolute monarchy had given a centralized political structure. One can trace, throughout the seventeenth century, the progressive shift of a political thought advocating royal authority toward one concerned with the sovereignty of the people and of the nation. Even though a "national feeling" did not yet exist, one can detect in the England of that time the formation of public opinion tied to its geographic particularities and ethical values (*Rule Britannia* was composed in 1740), even if the word "patriotism" still retained ironic overtones in those days. Henry St. John, Viscount Bolingbroke introduced into political theory the notion of "particular law," which, while being of universal, divine inspiration, must nevertheless aim at the happiness of the various national communities. His works, *Letters on the Spirit of Patriotisme* (1736) and *The Idea of the Patriot King* (1738) endow the word with a new meaning and are quickly disseminated in France. The emphasis placed by Voltaire or Montesquieu on the specific passions and character of peoples; the distinction made by Turgot between "State" and "nation," the latter being based on a common language; the expansion of the French language through the publication of translations; the more and more confident expression of the "third estate" in a literature of manners rooted in feelings, landscape, and the social individual (from *Manon Lescaut* to *La Nouvelle Heloïse*) – all these can be numbered among the harbingers of the *national idea*. It is Rousseau (1712–1778) who expressed it best, until a cultural, social, and political community displayed itself in the very act of the Revolution: the *sovereign people* beheading the royal sovereignty.

An essential vein of the Enlightenment, along the same lines as and sometimes contradictory with respect to its universalism, this patriotic and nationalistic Rousseauism still underlies contemporary nationalism. It is, however, only one of its components. Nostalgia for the Geneva hearth, which identifies the individual with his geographic and familial origin; the concern for preserving the person even within its closest kinship; the emphasis on free will, which alone must create a national community – such are some of the features of Rousseau's patriotism, which combine sentimentalism and rationalism, passionate withdrawal and demand for justice and freedom, romantic latencies and political lucidity based on the contract of citizens conscious of their equality and their right to happiness. Beyond its sensitive tones, there is a political rationalism that underlies the national idea with Rousseau, allowing patriotic pride to rest on the "common sense" inspired by the Cartesian "free will" and *cogito ergo sum* as foundation of the national contract. Let us first listen to the heart: "Going through Geneva, I went to see no one, but I nearly fainted on the bridges. I have never seen the walls of that happy city, I have never entered it without experiencing a certain weakness of the heart that came from an excess of emotion."[7] Nevertheless, if the self is to merge into the national community,[8] the latter can be tolerable only if it is subservient to the happiness of its members.[9]

Such a contractual concept, wholly political and founded rationally, thus naturally, on everyone's right to freedom, is already appreciably removed from the first signs of national feeling in France, which the presence of the monarchy readily rooted in inheritance and soil. Rousseau's nationalism can be appreciated by contrasting it with Vincent Voiture's very "personalist" version, for instance, concerning Cardinal Richelieu's feats.[10]

National pride, which ignores neither boasting nor spirited jingoism, also discovered during the French Revolution a predominant terrorist feature, about which one may well ask whether it was a violent distortion of Rousseau's nationalism or its intrinsic consequence. The fact remains that patriotism in *Emile* or *The Social Contract* is subordinate to the universality of human rights. Thus, while signing "the Geneva Citizen" to his preface to the *Letter to D'Alembert* (1758), Rousseau noted: "Justice and truth, such are the primary duties of man. Mankind and fatherland, such are his first affections. Every time particular attentions cause him to change that order, he is guilty."[11] This would lead Rousseau, following upon the Abbé de Saint-Pierre's *Projet de paix perpétuelle* (1713), to consider a confederation of peoples in order to prevent war – an idea that Kant would take up again and expand upon.[12]

Another current came to merge with that rational nationalism, which had been legalistic and respectful of the individual, and gave modern nationalism its definitive hue. Even though it grew out of the later German illuministic movements, this second nationalism was nevertheless not rooted in the *legal* and *political* idea of a sovereign nation whose laws guarantee the exercise of freedom and justice but in the more *feudal* and *spiritualistic* idea of physical kinship and linguistic identity.

The melancholy English sentimentalism was not foreign to its appearance – Richardson's *Clarissa* (1748), Edward Young's *The Complaint, or Night Thoughts* (1742–1745), or James Macpherson's *Fragments of Ancient Poetry* (1760), which rationalized the spirit of Gaelic legends, belong to this current. But it was in Germany that the mystical idea of the nation acquired its full scope.

It can be said that in central and eastern Europe the dissolution of Napoleon's Empire did not lead to the formation of a despotic state sufficiently powerful and well-ordered to further the development of a political will. It might also be suggested that Luther's Protestantism inverted into a pragmatic mystique concerned with individual accomplishment what in France produced a common sense of what social stakes were entailed and in England a democratic public opinion eager for political sovereignty. Undoubtedly numerous elements have, through Klopstock, Moser, and especially Herder, ended in the advent of the notion of national community, *Gemeinschaft*: not a political one, but organic, evolutionary, at the same time vital and metaphysical – the expression of a nearly irrational and indiscernible spirit that is summed up by the word *Gemeinsinn*.[13] A supreme value, such a national spirit, *Volksgeist*, is not, with Herder, biological, "scientific," or even political, but essentially moral. It is only after 1806 that this *cultural* concept of "nation" became *political* and became invested in the national-political struggle. As if, as a first step, the French Enlightenment had aroused in the mind of the Protestant Johann Gottfried von Herder (1744–1803) a burst of national feeling anchored in language and mindful of each nation's differential values at the core of universalistic humanism. And as if, as a second step, the repercussion of revolutionary wars had modified that *national religion* into *nationalist* and even more so *reactional politics*, seeking, in opposition to universalist abstraction, a romantic withdrawal into the mystique of the past, into the people's character, or into the individual and national genius – all irreducible, rebel, unthinkable, and restorative. Within this familial and irrational pouch there was room both for national withdrawal (in times of defeat and difficulties, as a structure insuring an archaic integrity, an indispensible guarantee for the family) and national pride (during periods of aggression, as the spearhead of a policy of economic and military expansion).

Henceforth the supreme good no longer was the individual according to Rousseau but the nation was a whole. And even if, with Herder, that nationalist supremacy was checked by a Christian ethics that caused him to be ironical about the feeling of superiority some peoples might have concerning themselves, the path was thus open to irrationalism. The very worship of the national language was heavily weighed down with ambiguities.

Nationalism as intimacy: from Herder to the Romanticists

A translation, that of the Bible, is what founded the modern notion of German culture (*Bildung*). Indeed, when Luther (1483–1546) translated the Holy Writ into spoken German ("The mother in the house and the common man speak thus," is what he said to justify his work), he not only set himself against Roman authority by "unlatinizing" German. More ambitiously yet, he endeavored to found a national culture that, through a twofold motion of *faithfulness* to models and *expansion* of the national register as it was first given in language, persevered up until its Romantic apogee. The Romantic enthusiasm for the national genius (*Volksgeist*) between 1800 and 1830 should not allow one to forget that this cultural nationalism, from the very beginning, rested upon the need to display one's *own* while modifying it through a confrontation with the sacred or classical canon: national features are thus based upon a broadened *translatability*, which merges with the idea of *Bildung*, understood, to begin with, as a process of formation of a national language.[14]

In contradistinction to the rationalist cosmopolitanism of the Enlightenment, already perceived as hollow, one nevertheless finds in Herder the first and most explicit expression of such an anchoring of culture in the genius of the language. While remaining deeply faithful to a Christian universalism (was not Augustine's *City of God* the first cosmopolitan history of mankind?) this Protestant minister was the true founder of the worship of the national spirit so dear to Romanticists.

As early as his *Fragments on the New German Literature* (1767) Herder extolled the originality of the German language, at the same time demanding its improvement through a continuing competition with ancient and modern languages, something he contrasted with mere obedience to classical models. Following *On the Origin of Languages* (1772), *Another Philosophy of History* developed a violent patriotic polemic both against "enlightened" and cosmopolitan despotism and against the "abstract" rationalism of the Enlightenment. Every nation – whose originality, according to Herder, rests in language and literature before affecting mores, government, and religion – is conceived according to the model of the stages of existence, while being integrated into the chain of civilization where it seeks to be the equal of others. In that spirit, his *Voices of Nations in Songs* brought back into favor the medieval past and the prestige of the German people's poetry.

Meanwhile, having linked his history of mankind to biology, Herder finally formulated his famous *Ideas on the Philosophy of History of Mankind* (1784–1791), closer to enlightened humanism than to the Lutheranism of 1774. Here Herder reveals himself to be less concerned with differences in climate or customs, even though he does blame local bad weather for what he considers the shortcomings of the blacks or the Chinese. On the other hand, he pays utmost attention to God's "peoples" (Herder does not accept the idea of "human races"), who remain brothers in their organisms but become radically differentiated on the basis of their languages and civilizations.

While it is true that he built up the cult of a "primeval national language" that owes it

225

to itself to remain "unsullied" by any translation, since it is, as for Klopstock, "a kind of wellspring of the most original concept of people," Herder is only indirectly responsible for its appropriation by nationalist politicians. Recently still, he has been viewed as a regionalist. He was, in spite of all, a translator: he translated Spanish "romances," was interested in English literature and Greek and Roman antiquity, and often maintained a concern for balance between "one's own" and the "foreign": "I observe foreign customs in order to conform my own to the genius of my fatherland, like much ripe fruit under an alien sun"; in a centrifugal motion the translated work must be revealed "as it is," but also as it is "for us."[15] This *Volksgeist*, rooted in a language that is seen as a constant process of alteration and surpassing of itself, nevertheless becomes a conservative, reactional concept when it is extracted from the *Bildung*'s tempo and exalted of its original purity or consigned to the ineffable. Intrinsically, however, such an assimilation of language to *Bildung* and, conversely, this emphasis on national speech as the lowest denominator of identity – all this removed Christian or humanistic cosmopolitanism from its spiritual, natural, or contractual lack of precision; furthermore, it allows us to consider what is "foreign" under the logical, familiar aspect of language and culture.

Starting from there, it would seem essential to effect a taming of foreignness on the basis of a specific logic, which would find its major developments in the philological and literary interest for national languages and literatures. One discovers such an attitude in the Romanticists' particularism, in love as they were with national peculiarities, as well as in Goethe's universalism and his advocacy of a *Weltliteratur*.

The localization of foreignness thus recognized and even positivized in national language and culture will be repeated within the Freudian unconscious, concerning which Freud specified that it followed the logic of each national language. One can even detect in Heidegger's philosophic philologism, which unfolds the concepts of Greek thought from the resonances of its vocabulary, something like an echo of that philology of the national genius inspired by Herder.

On the other hand, the generations following Herder's have extrapolated the literary autarky – which was indeed advocated by the master, who nevertheless subordinated it to the totality of human culture – to make of it an argument extolling the "cosmopolitanism of German literary taste." The latter was then understood as a *superiority* expressing the result of the cultural absolute and thus being placed *above* other peoples, languages, and cultures – justifying the demand for a German cultural *hegemony*. Such a nationalist perversion of the cosmopolitan idea, vitiated and dominated by a national "superiority" that one has taken care to valorize beforehand is, as is well known, at the basis of Nazi ideology.[16]

Rooting the specific in human universality's (the gift of speech) diversified manifestations (national languages) went hand in hand, with Romanticists, with the concept of an *invisible foundation* of universal, visible nature. One imagined that such a *Grund*, specific to nature itself as well as to the human soul, was engaged less in intellectual research than in an emotional, instinctual, and intimate quest – the *Gemüt*. The Romantic leaning toward the supernatural, parapsychology, madness, dreams, the obscure forces of the *fatum*, and even animal psychology is related to the desire to grasp the strange, and by domesticating it, turn it into an integral component of the human. *Einfühlung* – an identifying harmony – with the strange and the different then became essential as the distinctive feature of the worthy, cultivated man: "The perfect man must be capable of living equally in various places and among diverse peoples," Novalis noted.[17]

The strangeness of the Romantic hero thus assumed substance and shape and presented itself as the fertilizing soil out of which a heterogeneous notion of the *unconscious* sprang froth – simultaneously as man's deep link with nature's dark substratum (with Carus and Schubert), as underlying the will to representation (with Schopenhauer), or as intelligent dynamism of Hegelian inspiration operating blindly beneath the surface of the apparent universe (with Hartmann).

One cannot hope to understand Freud's contribution, in the specific field of psychiatry, outside of its humanistic and Romantic filiation. With the Freudian notion of the unconscious the involution of the strange in the psyche loses its pathological aspect and integrates within the assumed unity of human beings an *otherness* that is both biological *and* symbolic and becomes an integral part of the *same*. Henceforth the foreigner is neither a race nor a nation. The foreigner is neither glorified as a secret *Volksgeist* nor banished as disruptive of rationalist urbanity. Uncanny, foreignness is within us: we are our own foreigners, we are divided. Even though it shows a Romanticist filiation, such an intimist restoring of the foreigner's good name undoubtedly bears the biblical tones of a foreign God or of a Foreigner apt to reveal God.[18] Freud's personal life, a Jew wandering from Galicia to Vienna and London, with stopovers in Paris, Rome, and New York (to mention only a few of the key stages of his encounters with political and cultural foreignness). conditions his concern to face the other's discontent as ill-ease in the continuous presence of the "other scene" within us. My discontent in living with the other – my strangeness, his strangeness – rests on the perturbed logic that governs this strange bundle of drive and language, of nature and symbol, constituted by the unconscious, always already shaped by the other. It is through unraveling transference – the major dynamics of otherness, of love/hatred, for the other, of the foreign component of our psyche – that, on the basis of the other, I become reconciled with my own otherness-foreignness, that I play on it and live by it. Psychoanalysis is then experienced as a journey into the strangeness of the other and of oneself, toward an ethics of respect for the irreconcilable. How could one tolerate a foreigner if one did not know one was a stranger to oneself? And to think that it has taken such a long time for that small truth, which transverses or even runs against religious uniformist tendencies, to enlighten the people of our time! Will it allow them to put up with one another as irreducible, because they are desiring, desirable, mortal, and death-bearing?

Freud: "heimlich/unheimlich" – the uncanny strangeness

Explicitly given limited scope, as it was at first connected with esthetic problems and emphasized texts by E. T. A. Hoffmann, Freud's *Das Unheimliche* (1919) surreptitiously goes beyond that framework and the psychological phenomenon of "uncanny strangeness" as well, in order to acknowledge itself as an investigation into *anguish* generally speaking and, in a fashion that is even more universal, into the *dynamics of the unconscious*. Indeed, Freud wanted to demonstrate at the outset, on the basis of a semantic study of the German adjective *heimlich* and its antonym *unheimlich* that a negative meaning close to that of the antonym is already tied to the positive term *heimlich*, "friendly comfortable," which would also signify "concealed, kept from sight," "deceitful and malicious," "behind someone's back." Thus, in the very word *heimlich*, the familiar and intimate are reversed into their opposites, brought together with the contrary meaning of "uncanny strangeness harbored in *unheimlich*. Such an immanence of the strange within the familiar is considered as an etymological proof of the psychoanalytic hypothesis according to which "the uncanny is that class of the frightening which leads back to what is known of old and long familiar,"[19] which, as far as Freud was concerned, was confirmed by Schelling who said that "everything is *unheimlich* that ought to have remained secret and hidden but has come to light" (p. 225).

Consequently therefore, that which *is* strangely uncanny would be that which *was* (the past tense is important) familiar and, under certain conditions (which ones?), emerges. A first step was taken that removed the uncanny strangeness from the outside, where fright had anchored it, to locate it inside, not inside the familiar considered as one's own and proper, but the familiar potentially tainted with strangeness and referred (beyond its imaginative origin) to an improper past. The other is my ("own and proper") unconscious.

What "familiar"? What "past"? In order to answer such questions, Freud's thought played a strange trick on the esthetic and psychological notion of "uncanny strangeness, which had been initially posited, and rediscovered the analytical notions of *anxiety, double, repetition*, and *unconscious*. The uncanny strangeness that is aroused in Nathaniel (in Hoffmann's tale, *The Sandman*) by the paternal figure and its substitutes, as well as references to the eyes, is related to the castration anxiety experienced by the child, which was repressed but surfaced again on the occasion of a state of love.

The other is my (own and proper) unconscious

Furthermore, Freud noted that the archaic, narcissistic self, not yet demarcated by the outside world, projects out of itself what it experiences as dangerous or unpleasant in itself, making of it an alien *double*, uncanny and demoniacal. In this instance the strange appears as a defense put up by a distraught self: it protects itself by substituting for the image of a benevolent double that used to be enough to shelter it the image of a malevolent double into which it expels the share of destruction it cannot contain.

The repetition that often accompanies the feeling of uncanny strangeness relates it to the "compulsion to repeat" that is peculiar to the unconscious and emanating out of "drive impulses" – a compulsion "proceeding from the drive impulses and probably inherent in the very nature of the drives – a compulsion powerful enough to overrule the pleasure principle" (p. 238).

The reader is henceforth ready to accept the feeling of uncanny strangeness as an instance of anxiety in which "the frightening element can be shown to be something repressed which *recurs*" (p. 241). To the extent, however, that psychic situations evidencing an absolute repression are rare, such a return of the repressed in the guise of anxiety, and more specifically of uncanny strangeness, appears as a paroxystic metaphor of the psychic functioning itself. The latter is indeed elaborated by repression and one's necessarily going through it, with the result that the builder of the *other* and, in the final analysis, of the *strange* is indeed repression itself and its perviousness. "We can understand why linguistic usage has extended *das Heimliche* into its opposite, *das Unheimliche*; for this uncanny is in reality nothing new or alien, but something which is familiar and old-established in the mind and which has become alienated from it only through the process of repression" (p. 241).

Let us say that the psychic apparatus represses representative processes and contents that are no longer necessary for pleasure, self-preservation, and the adaptive growth of the speaking subject and the living organism. Under certain conditions, however, the repressed "that ought to have remained secret" shows up again and produces a feeling of uncanny strangeness.

While saying that he would henceforth tackle "one or two more examples of the uncanny," Freud in his text actually continues, by means of a subtle, secret endeavor, to reveal the circumstances that are favorable to going through repression and generating the uncanny strangeness. The confrontation with *death* and its representation is initially imperative, for our unconscious refuses the fatality of death: "Our unconscious has as little use now as it ever had for the idea of its own mortality." The fear of death dictates an ambivalent attitude: we imagine ourselves surviving (religions promise immortality), but death just the same remains the survivor's enemy, and it accompanies him in his new existence. Apparitions and ghosts represent that ambiguity and fill with uncanny strangeness our confrontations with the image of death.

The fantasy of being buried alive induces the feeling of uncanny strangeness, accompanied by "a certain lasciviousness – the phantasy, I mean, of intra-uterine existence" (p. 244). We are confronted with a second source of the strange: "It often happens that neurotic men declare that they feel there is something uncanny about the female genital organs. This *unheimlish* place, however, is the entrance to the former *Heim* of all human beings, to the place where each one of us lived once upon a time and in the beginning." "There is a joking saying that 'Love is homesickness'" (p. 245).

The *death* and the *feminine*, the end and the beginning that engross and compose us only to frighten us when they break through, one must add "the living person [. . .] when we ascribe evil intentions to him [. . .] that are going to be carried out with the help of special powers" (p. 243). Such malevolent *powers* would amount to a weaving together of the symbolic and the organic – perhaps *drive* itself, on the border of the psyche and biology, overriding the breaking imposed by organic homeostasis. A disturbing symptom of this may be found in epilepsy and madness, and their presence in our fellow beings worries us the more as we dimly sense them in ourselves.

A semiology of uncanny strangeness

Are death, the feminine, and drives always a pretext for the uncanny strangeness? After having broadened the scope of his meditation, which might have led to seeing in uncanniness the description of the working of the unconscious, which is itself dependant on repression, Freud marked its required limits by stressing a few particularities of the semiology within which it emerges. Magical practices, animism, or, in more down-to-earth fashion, "intellectual uncertainty" and "disconcerted" logic (according to E. Jentsch) are all propitious to uncanniness. Now, what brings together these symbolic processes, quite different for all that, lies in a weakening of the value of signs as such and of their specific logic. The symbol ceases to be a symbol and "takes over the full functions of the thing it symbolizes" (p. 244). In other words, the sign is not experienced as arbitrary but assumes a real importance. As a consequence, the material reality that the sign was commonly supposed to point to crumbles away to the benefit of imagination, which is no more than "the over-accentuation of psychical reality in comparison with material reality" (p. 244). We are here confronted with "the omnipotence of thought," which, in order to constitute itself invalidates the arbitrariness of signs and the autonomy of reality as well and places them both under the sway of fantasies expressing infantile desires or fears.

Obsessional neuroses, but also and differently psychoses, have the distinctive feature of "reifying" signs – of slipping from the domain of "speaking" to the domain of "doing." Such a particularity *also* evinces the fragility of repression and, without actually explaining it, allows the return of the repressed to be inscribed in the reification under the guise of the uncanny affect. While, in another semiological device, one might think that the return of the repressed would assume the shape of the somatic symptom or of the acting out, here the breakdown of the arbitrary signifier and its tendency to become reified as psychic contents that take the place of material reality would favor the experience of uncanniness. Conversely, our fleeting or more or less threatening encounter with uncanny strangeness would be a clue to our psychotic latencies and the fragility of our repression – at the same time as it is an indication of the weakness of language as a symbolic barrier that, in the final analysis, structures the repressed.

Strange indeed is the encounter with the other – whom we perceive by means of sight, hearing, smell, but do not "frame" within our consciousness. The other leaves us separate, incoherent; even more so, he can make us feel that we are not in touch with our own feelings, that we reject them or, on the contrary, that we refuse to judge them – we feel "stupid," we have "been had."

Also strange is the experience of the abyss separating me from the other who shocks me – I do not even perceive him, perhaps he crushes me because I negate him. Confronting the foreigner whom I reject and with whom at the same time I identify, I lose my boundaries, I no longer have a container, the memory of experiences when I had been abandoned overwhelm me, I lose my composure. I feel "lost," "indistinct," "hazy." The uncanny strangeness allows for many variations: they all repeat the difficulty I have in situating myself with respect to the other and keep going over the course of identification-projection that lies at the foundation of my reaching autonomy.

At this stage of the journey, one understands that Freud took pains to separate the uncanniness provoked by esthetic experience from that which is sustained in reality; he most particularly stressed those works in which the uncanny effect is abolished because of the very fact that the entire world of the narrative is fictitious. Such are fairy tales, in which the generalized artifice spares us any possible comparison between sign, imagination, and material reality. As a consequence, artifice neutralizes uncanniness and makes all returns of the repressed plausible, acceptable, and pleasurable. As if absolute enchantment – absolute sublimation – just as, on the other hand, absolute rationality – absolute repression – were our only defenses against uncanny strangeness . . . Unless, depriving us of the dangers as well as the pleasures of strangeness, they be the instruments of their liquidation.

Subjects, artists, and . . . a king

Linked to anguish, as we have seen, the uncanny strangeness does not, however, merge with it. Initially it is a shock, something unusual, astonishment; and even if anguish comes close, uncanniness maintains that share of unease that leads the self, beyond anguish, toward depersonalization. "The sense of strangeness belongs in the same category as depersonalization," Freud noted, and many analysts have stressed the frequency of the *Unheimliche* affect in phobia, especially when the contours of the self are overtaxed by the clash with something "too good" or "too bad." In short, if anguish revolves around an *object*, uncanniness, on the other hand, is a *destructuration of the self* that may either remain as a psychotic *symptom* or fit in as an *opening* toward the new, as an attempt to tally with the incongruous. While it surely manifests the return of a familiar repressed, the *Unheimliche* requires just the same the impetus of a new encounter with an unexpected outside element: arousing images of death, automatons, doubles, or the female sex (the list is probably not complete, as Freud's text leaves such an impression of a rather distant reserve – because it is passionate), uncanniness occurs when the boundaries between *imagination* and *reality* are erased. This observation reinforces the concept – which arises out of Freud's text – of the *Unheimliche* as a crumbling of conscious defenses, resulting from the conflicts the self experiences with an other – the "strange" – with whom it maintains a conflictual bond, at the same time "a need for identification and a fear of it" (Maurice Bouvet). The clash with the other, the identification of the self with that good or bad other that transgresses the fragile boundaries of the uncertain self, would thus be at the source of an uncanny strangeness whose excessive features, as represented in literature, cannot hide its permanent presence in "normal" psychical dynamics.

A child confides in his analyst that the finest day in his life is that of his birth: "Because that day it was me – I like being me, I don't like being an other." Now he feels other when he has poor grades – when he is bad, alien to the parents' and teachers' desire. Likewise, the unnatural, "foreign" languages, such as writing or mathematics, arouse an uncanny feeling in the child.[20]

This is where we leave the extraordinary realm of literary uncanniness to find its immanence (a necessary hence commonplace one) in psychism as the experience of otherness. It is possible, as Yvon Brès said, that Freud's recourse to esthetic works in order to set up the notion of uncanny strangeness was an admission that psychoanalysis could not possibly deal with it. Man would be facing a kind of "existential apriorism," in the presence of which Freudian thought merges with Heidegger's phenomenology.[21] Without going so far as to assume such a link, let us note, however, that Freud picks up the phrase again in *The Future of an Illusion* (1927): civilization humanizes nature by endowing it with beings that look like us – it is such an animistic process that enables us "to breathe freely [and] feel at home in the uncanny [so that we] can deal by psychical means with our [previously] senseless anxiety."[22] Here uncanny strangeness as no longer an artistic or pathological product but a psychic law allowing us to confront the unknown and work it out in the process of *Kulturarbeit*, the task of civilization. Freud, who "must himself plead guilty to a special obtuseness in the matter" of the uncanny,[23] thus opens up two other prospects when confronting the strange, which is related to anguish. On the one hand, the sense of strangeness is a mainspring for identification with the other, by working out its depersonalizing impact by means of astonishment. On the other hand, analysis can throw light on such an affect but, far from insisting on breaking it down, it should make way for esthetics (some might add philosophy), with which to saturate its phantasmal progression and insure its cathartic eternal return, for instance with readers of disturbing tales.

The violent, catastrophic aspect the encounter with the *foreigner* may assume is to be included in the generalizing consequences that seem to stem out of Freud's observations on the activating of the uncanny. As test of our astonishment, source of depersonalization, we cannot suppress the symptom that the foreigner provokes; but we simply must come back to it, clear it up, give it the resources our own essential depersonalizations provide, and only thus soothe it.

And yet, the uncanny strangeness can also be evacuated: "No, that does not bother me; I laugh or take action – I go away, I shut my eyes, I strike, I command . . ." Such an elimination of the strange could lead to an elimination of the psyche, leaving, at the cost of mental impoverishment, the way open to acting out, including paranoia and murder. From another point of view, there is no uncanny strangeness for the person enjoying an acknowledged power and a resplendent image. Uncanniness, for that person, is changed into management and authorized expenditure: strangeness is for the "subjects," the sovereign ignores it, knowing how to have it administered. An anecdote related by Saint-Simon provides a good illustration of that situation.[24] The Sun-King (French psychoanalysts strangely avoid questioning major political and artistic figures of national history, even though the latter is so weighed down with discourse and psychological enigmas as well) erases the uncanny and his fear in order to display the whole of his being exclusively within the law and the pleasure of Versailles' pomp. Disturbed innerness is the courtiers' lot; they were the compost of the psychic subtlety that the brilliant writer of memoirs has handed down to us, often remarkably anticipating Freud's speculations.

Finally, some might change the weird into irony. One imagines Saint-Simon, a shrewd smile on his lips, as far removed from regal censorship as he was from the courtiers' embarrassment: the humorist goes right through uncanny strangeness and – starting from a self-confidence that is his own or is based on his belonging to an untouchable universe that is not at all threatened by the war between same and others, ghosts and doubles – seeing in it nothing more than smoke, imaginary structures, signs. To worry or to smile, such is the choice when we are assailed by the strange; our decision depends on how familiar we are with our own ghosts.

The strange within us

The uncanny would thus be the royal way (but in the sense of the court, not of the king) by means of which Freud introduced the fascinated rejection of the other at the heart of that "our self," so poised and dense, which precisely no longer exists ever since Freud and shows itself to be a strange land of borders and othernesses ceaselessly constructed and deconstructed. Strangely enough, there is no mention of *foreigners* in the *Unheimliche*.

Actually, a foreigner seldom arouses the terrifying anguish provoked by death, the female sex, or the "baleful" unbridled drive. Are we nevertheless so sure that the "political" feelings of xenophobia do not include, often unconsciously, that agony of frightened joyfulness that has been called *unheimlich*, that in English is *uncanny*, and the Greeks quite simply call *xenos*, "foreign"? In the fascinated rejection that the foreigner arouses in us, there is a share of uncanny strangeness in the sense of the depersonalization that Freud discovered in it, and which takes up again our infantile desires and fears of the other – the other of death, the other of woman, the other of uncontrollable drive. The foreigner is within us. And when we flee from or struggle against the foreigner, we are fighting our unconscious – that "improper" facet of our impossible "own and proper." Delicately, analytically, Freud does not speak of foreigners: he teaches us how to detect foreignness in ourselves. That is perhaps the only way not to hound it outside of us. After Stoic cosmopolitanism, after religious universalist integration, Freud brings us the courage to call ourselves disintegrated in order not to integrate foreigners and even less so to hunt them down, but rather to welcome them to that uncanny strangeness, which is as much theirs as it is ours.

In fact, such a Freudian distraction or discretion concerning the "problem of foreigners" – which appears only as an eclipse or, if one prefers, as a symptom, through the recall of the Greek word *xenoi*[25] – might be interpreted as an invitation (a utopic or very modern one?) not to reify the foreigner, not to petrify him as such, not to petrify *us* as such. But to analyze it by analyzing us. To discover our disturbing otherness, for that indeed is what bursts in to confront that "demon," that threat, that apprehension generated by the projective apparition of the other at the heart of what we persist in maintaining as a proper, solid "us." By recognizing *our* uncanny strangeness we shall neither suffer from it nor enjoy it from the outside. The foreigner is within me, hence we are all foreigners. If I am a foreigner, there are no foreigners. Therefore Freud does not talk about them. The ethics of psycho-analysis implies a politics: it would involve a cosmopolitanism of a new sort that, cutting across governments, economies, and markets, might work for a mankind whose solidarity is founded on the consciousness of its unconscious – desiring, destructive fearful, empty, impossible. Here we are far removed from a call to brotherhood, about which one has already ironically pointed out its debt to paternal and divine authority – "In order to have brothers there must be a father," as Louis-François Veuillot did not fail to say when he sharply addressed humanists. On the basis of an erotic, death-bearing unconscious, the uncanny strangeness – a projection as well as a first working out of death drive – which adumbrates the work of the "second" Freud, the one of *Beyond the Pleasure Principle*, sets the difference within us in its most bewildering shape and presents it as the ultimate condition of our being *with* others.

Notes

1 See above, "The Nephew with Hegel: Culture as Strangeness."
2 Immanuel Kant, "Idea for a Universal History from a Cosmopolitan Point of View," in *On History* (New York: Bobbs Merrill, 1963), p. 15. Page references hereafter given parenthetically in text.
3 Kant, "Perpetual Peace," *On History* p. 100.

4 "It is only a right of temporary sojourn, a right to associate, which all men have. They have it by virtue of their common possession of the surface of the earth, where, as a globe, they cannot infinitely disperse and hence must finally tolerate the presence of each other. Originally, no one had more right than another to a particular part of the earth" (Kant, p. 103).

5 "I do not mean that [nature] imposes a duty on us to do it, for this can be done only by free practical reason; rather I mean that [nature] herself does it, whether we will or not" (Kant, p. 111).

6 Hans Kohn, *The Idea of Nationalism* (New York: Macmillan, 1951).

7 Jean-Jacques Rousseau, *Les Confessions*, "Bibliothèque de la Pléiade" (Paris: Gallimard, 1959), 1:144. [All translations of Rousseau texts by LSR.]

8 Thus: "The civilian is only a fractional unit attached to the denominator and whose value resides in its relation to the whole, which is the social Body [. . .] Good social institutions are best able to change the nature of man – taking away his absolute existence in order to give him a relative one and shifting the *self* to the common unit. As a result, each individual no longer believes himself to be one but a part of the unit and is perceptible only in the whole" (Rousseau, *Emile*, 4:249).

9 "The police is good, but liberty is better" (Rousseau, "Considérations sur le gouvernement de la Pologne," ibid., 3:983). "Public liberty is the most precious good. And every man, in the name of the fatherland, is entitled to tear it away from the hands of the usurper: avenging such a capital crime is the right of each individual. Teach these truths to all men, let them reach down to the lowest order of citizens." Rousseau, *Correspondance générale*, Dufour-Plan, ed. (Paris: A. Colin, 1934), 20:346.

10 "But when, two hundred years from now, those who come after us read our history and see that, as long as he presided over our government, France did not have a single neighbor over whom it did not win fortresses and battles: if they have a few drops of French blood in their veins, some love for the glory of their country, will they be able to read such things without feeling an attachment for him?" Voiture, *Œuvres* (Paris: Charpentier, 1855), 1:272, quoted by Hans Kohn, pp. 202–203.

11 Rousseau, *Lettres à D'Alembert* (Paris: Garnier-Flammarion, 1967), p. 43.

12 Rousseau, *Extrait* (1756–1760) and *Jugement sur le "Projet de paix perpétuelle"* (1782).

13 See Kohn, p. 429.

14 See Antoine Berman, *L'Epreuve de l'étranger. Culture et traduction dans l'Allemagne romantique* (Paris: Gallimard, 1984). One might compare that formation of the national concept through encounters with foreigners with what A. W. Schlegel (quoted by Berman, p. 62) observed in France: "Other nations have adopted in poetry a wholly conventional phraseology and it is consequently purely and simply impossible to translate something poetically into their language, as into French for instance [. . .] It is as if they wanted every foreigner, in their country, to behave and dress according to their customs; it follows that, properly speaking, they never know any foreigner."

15 See Berman, p. 70. Beginning with his translation of the Song of Songs and including his collection of *Volklieder* and his famous biblical exegesis *On the Spirit of Hebraic Poetry*, Herder's impulse is continuously to assimilate the foreign tongue while nevertheless maintaining its particular character in order to make of it a gift to a German language in the process of expansion and reformulation. The peoples of Central Europe have drawn on his thought in order to further the development of Slavic languages and cultures. One might note, however, that this juxtaposition of German *Bildung* with foreign elements – particularly with Hebrew – reaches a critical point with late Romanticism. And it was Herder himself who suddenly hardened his political interpretation, initially a fruitful one, changing the other into an object of assimilation, or even of murderous rejection, to the benefit of German "originality."

16 Herder on his part and through his own contradictions had nevertheless issued this warning: "How the dickens did the Germans, who were ordinarily praised for showing a manly modesty, and who were known for their cool equity in appreciating the merits of foreigners,

come to be so unjustly and crudely scornful of other nations, and precisely of those they have imitated, from which they have borrowed?" Quoted by Max Rouche in his introduction to Herder's *Idées* (Paris: Aubier, 1962), p. 33. And again: "Those who study their own customs and languages must do so when they are distinct; *for everything in Europe tends toward the progressive dying out of national characteristics.* But in doing so, the historian of mankind should be careful not to choose a given people exclusively as a favorite of his, thus diminishing the importance of lineages to which circumstances denied good fortune and fame" (p. 309).

17 As quoted in Henri E. Ellenberger, *A la découverte de l'inconscient* (Paris: Simep-Editions, 1974), p. 170.

18 See above, "The Chosen People and the Choice of Foreignness."

19 Sigmund Freud, *The Uncanny,* in *The Standard Edition of the Complete Psychological Works of Sigmund Freud,* 17:220. Hereafter page numbers given parenthetically in text refer to this volume (17) of the *Standard Edition* (*SE*). [There are, as usual, discrepancies between the French and English translations of Freud. Here it is especially bothersome as *Das Unheimliche* comes out in French as *l'inquiétante étrangeté,* a phrase that matches Kristeva's vocabulary very neatly but is at a linguistic remove from our "uncanny." While following Strachey's translation, thus letting "the uncanny" stand in all the quotations from Freud's text, I have tried to bridge the gap between French and English words by occasionally rendering the French phrase, *inquiétante étrangeté,* in Kristeva's text, as "uncanny strangeness" – LSR].

20 See Paul Denis, "L'Inquiétante Etrangeté chez l'enfant," *Revue de Psychanalyse* (1981). no. 3, p. 503.

21 See Yvon Brès, "Modestie des philosophes: modestie des psychanalystes," *Psychanalyse à l'Université* (October 1986), 11(14):585–586. Beyond the frequency of the word *Unheimliche* in German, which removes a bit of spice from the encounter, Brès notes a certain thematic convergence in its use between Freud and Heidegger. With the latter, anguish, which resides in the being-in-the-world, is uncanniness ("In der Angst ist einem 'unheimlich'" – *Sein und Zeit,* section 40): "But this distressing aspect, this strangeness, signifies at the same time the not-being-at-home." Later, *What Is Metaphysics* (1929) clarifies existential anguish as experienced when facing the impossibility of any determination, and it is again described as *Unheimlichkeit.*

22 Freud, *The Future of an Illusion,* SE, 21:17.

23 Freud, *The Uncanny, SE,* 17:220.

24 "Five or six days later I was at the King's supper [. . .] As sweets were being served, I noticed something or other, rather large, seemingly black, in the air over the table, which I was unable either to make out or point to, so rapidly did this large thing fall at the end of the table [. . . .] The noise it made when falling and the weight of the thing nearly caused it to give way and caused the dishes to jump, but without upsetting any [. . .] The King, after the impact, half turned his head and, without being disturbed in any way, I believe, he said, those are my fringes. It was indeed a bundle, larger than the hat of a priest. . .It had been thrown from far behind me [. . .] and a small bit that had come loose in the air had fallen on top of the King's wig; Livry, who was seated to his left, saw it and removed it. He came near the end of the table and saw that they were indeed fringes twisted into a bundle [. . .] Livry, wanting to remove the bundle, found a note attached to it; he took it and left the bundle [. . .] It contained, in a misshapen, extended writing, like that of a woman, these very words: Take your fringes back, Bontemps; they are more trouble than pleasure. I kiss the King's hands. It was rolled but not sealed. The King again wanted to take it from D'Aquin's hands who stepped back, sniffed it, rubbed it, turned it every which way, and showed it to the King without letting him touch it. The King asked him to read it aloud, even though he himself read it at the same time. That, said the King, is rather insolent! – but in an even, somewhat statesmanlike tone of voice. After that he asked that the bundle be removed [. . .] Afterwards the King no longer mentioned it and no one dared speak about it, not aloud at any rate; and

the remainder of the supper was served as if nothing had happened." Saint-Simon, *Mémoires*, "Bibliothèque de la Pléiade" (Paris: Gallimard, 1983), pp. 632–633. Christian David accompanies this excerpt with a keen commentary in "Irréductible étrangeté," *Revue de Psychanalyse* (1981), no. 3 pp. 463–471.

25 Freud, *The Uncanny*, *SE*, 17:221.

15

SARAH KOFMAN

Sarah Kofman (1934–94) taught for ten years in lycées in Toulouse and Paris, until she went to teach at the Sorbonne (University of Paris I) in 1970 where she became Professor of Philosophy. She is arguably France's best-known contemporary woman philosopher after Simone de Beauvoir. Her work focused on a wide variety of thinkers, from Nietzsche, Freud and Plato to Derrida and Nerval, and on issues ranging from aesthetics and theories of metaphor and laughter to deconstruction, psychoanalysis, and the role of women in philosophy. Kofman published over two dozen books, mainly with Éditions Galilée, where she also directed the 'Philosophie en effet' collection together with Jacques Derrida, Jean-Luc Nancy and Philippe Lacoue-Labarthe.

Kofman's works have been translated into many languages and include the following:

L'Enfance de l'art. Une interprétation de l'esthetique freudienne, Paris: Payot, 1970.

Nietzsche et la métaphore, Paris: Payot, 1972.

Camera obscura. De l'idéologie, Paris: Galilée, 1973.

Quatre romans analytiques, Paris: Galilée, 1974.

Autobiogriffures, Paris: Christian Bourgeois, 1976.

Aberrations. Le devenir-femme d'Auguste Compte, Paris: Aubier-Flammarion, 1978.

Nerval: le charme de la répétition. Lecture de "Sylvie", Lausanne: L'Age d'Homme, 1979.

Nietzsche et la scène philosophique, Paris: UGE, 10/18, 1979.

L'Énigme de la femme: la femme dans les textes de Freud, Paris: Galilée, 1980.

Le Respect des femmes (Kant et Rousseau), Paris: Galilee, 1982.

Comment s'en sortir?, Paris: Galilée, 1983.

Un Métier impossible. Lecture de "Constructions en analyse", Paris: Galilée, 1983.

Lectures de Derrida, Paris: Galilée, 1984.

Pourquoi rit-on? Freud et le mot d'esprit, Galilée, 1986.

Paroles suffoquées, Paris: Galilee, 1987.

Conversions. Le Marchand de Venise sous le signe de Saturne, Paris: Galilée, 1987.

Socrate(s), Paris: Galilée, 1989.

Séductions. De Sartre à Héraclite, Paris: Galilee, 1990.

Don Juan et le refus de la dette, with J-Y Masson, Paris: Galilée, 1991.

Il n'y a que le premier pas qui coûte: Freud et la spéculation, Galilée, 1991.

Explosion I. De "l'Ecce Homo" de Nietzsche, Paris: Galilée, 1992.

Explosion II. Les enfants de Nietzsche, Paris: Galilée, 1993.

Rue Ordener, rue Labat, Paris: Galilée, 1994.

L'Imposture de la beauté, Paris: Galilée, 1995.

FREUD AND PLATO

The mirror and its mirages:
Plato, Freud's forerunner on dreams

In *The Interpretation of Dreams*, Freud quotes Plato on two occasions. In the chapter entitled 'The Moral Sense in Dreams', as he reviews various authors' opinions on the subject, Freud writes: 'Plato . . . thought that the best men are those who only *dream* what other men *do* in their waking life.'[1] On the last page of his book, Freud returns once again to the philosopher, agreeing with him and using him to underwrite the distinction between latent and manifest content which makes any judgement of dreams illegitimate:

> I think, however, that the Roman emperor was in the wrong when he had one of his subjects executed because he had dreamt of murdering the emperor. He should have begun by trying to find out what the dream meant; most probably its meaning was not what it appeared to be. And even if a dream with another content had had this act of *lèse majesté* as its meaning, would it not be right to bear in mind Plato's dictum that the virtuous man is content to *dream* what a wicked man really *does*? I think it best, therefore, to acquit dreams.[2]

This allusion, in almost the same terms on two occasions, to the famous passage from Book IX of the *Republic* (571a ff.), is astonishing, to say the least. For if Plato indeed believes, as Freud does, that dreams are the royal road to the unconscious, or to those desires which 'we probably all contain', that 'can be kept under control (κολαςόμεαι) by convention and by the co-operation of reason and the better desires . . . the ones that wake up while we sleep', he does not, however, distinguish between manifest and latent content; he believes, on the contrary, that our dreams betray our desires and that we can accordingly be judged by them.[3] For Plato, the good man is precisely the one who would not, even in a dream (hence his superiority), do those things which the evil man alone will do in both his waking hours and his sleep alike. If all men, even those who seem entirely self-disciplined, possess a type of 'desires which are terrible, wild, and lawless', desires which become manifest during sleep, some who are well in body and mind experience visions in their sleep which are as far removed from savagery as they could possibly be; some even come into contact with truth better then than at any other time. So it is the dreams of evil men which are the source of our knowledge of the desires which their superiors manage to repress so successfully through reason that they are left in peace, even in their sleep. Or rather, they are the least (ηκιστα) troubled by such desires, for all are born with these disorderly (παρανόμοι) desires.

So Freud seems to have read Plato rather hastily and this would also explain why he fails to cite the philosopher elsewhere, particularly when he discovers that dreams are expressions of incestuous and parricidal desires. For Plato writes: 'I'm sure you're aware of how in these circumstances nothing is too outrageous: a person acts as if he were totally lacking in moral principle and unhampered by intelligence (αἰσχύνης καὶ φρονήσεως). In his dreams, he doesn't stop at trying to have sex with his mother and with anyone or anything else – man, beast, or gods; he's ready to slaughter anything; there's nothing he wouldn't eat. In short, he doesn't hold back from anything, however bizarre or disgusting.' (571d). His silence about Plato is all the more surprising in view of the fact that Freud, who offers in support of his discovery just Sophocles's *Oedipus Rex* and *Hamlet*, complains in a note added to a later edition of the disgust and outrage which greeted his interpretation with its unbearable, shocking, revelation of incestuous and parricidal desires. And in the main body of the text, he writes: 'Like Oedipus, we live in ignorance of these wishes, repugnant to morality, which have been forced upon us by Nature, and after their revelation we may all of us well seek to close our eyes to the scenes of our childhood.'[4]

Was it that *Oedipus Rex* had so powerful an effect on Freud that he forgot the passage from the *Republic*? Or did Freud close his eyes to Plato, in favour of Sophocles, because the philosopher had anticipated his discoveries all too clearly, thereby depriving him of the originality which he so jealously craved?

In any event, his readerly 'slip', repeated twice, his silences and the return of Plato's name on the last page strike me as sufficiently significant to call for closer inspection of the text.

The savage theatre of dreams

It is in the course of his analysis of the transition from democracy to tyranny, or rather from the democratic to the tyrannical person,[5] that Plato appeals to dreams in an attempt to discover what kind of desires predominate in and characterize the tyrannical individual. Having already analysed the aristocratic regime and the corresponding 'soul' or personality-type, governed by the intellect (or *noûs*); the timocratic man and the timocratic regime, in which *thumos* and ambition preside; oligarchy and the oligarchic man, both characterized by the supremacy of desires (*epithumia*) for money, among other things; democracy and the nature of the democratic soul, in which the desire for freedom predominates, Plato comes to the last of all the possible types of soul and regime, namely the tyrannical.[6] Both forms of tyranny arise when the desire for freedom is taken to excess, which necessarily leads to servitude (the trigger occasioning changes of regime[7] being a disturbance in the motive principle produced when this becomes excessive, each type of regime being governed by the desire for what it thinks of as good, without regard for anything else). Plato's aim in this analysis of the different types of regime and person is neither theoretical nor descriptive, but normative. His question, which is that of an idealist, is: Which type of regime and soul are best able to bring the life of greatest happiness?[8] In his scheme, then, the final analysis of the inferior extreme proves to be of the utmost importance, for it is on the basis of this comparison alone – between the most unjust of men, the tyrant, and the most just, the philosopher – that the choice of life and regime is to be determined. What is really at stake here is the need to refute the argument advanced by Thrasymachus in Book I, in favour of the most unjust form of life, that of the tyrannical man, and which, according to him, is the happiest of all:

> This will enable us to see which of them is the least moral; we can then contrast him with the most moral type, and that will complete our enquiry into how absolute morality compares with absolute immorality in respect of the happiness or unhappiness they entail for people who possess them. Then we'll be in a position either to follow Thrasymachus and pursue immorality, or to follow the argument which is developing at the moment and pursue morality.
>
> (545a)

It is some indication of the importance of the discussion that nothing short of the ten books of the *Republic* are needed to counterbalance this argument, with the final myth of Er offering a response to that of Gyges's ring.

The analysis of the tyrannical individual requires one hitherto neglected class of desires to be taken into account, one which had been omitted from the dichotomy of desires established in order to characterize the oligarchic and democratic types (554a – 558d). The former is driven by necessary desires and pleasures, the latter by superfluous ones. Indeed, the democratic man, by making all his desires equals, allows unlimited freedom and complete anarchy to hold sway in his heart – and hence the many colours of disorder and injustice.[9] Prior to this point, there had been no discussion of the class of desires which characterizes the tyrannical individual, because this was not required in order to understand the other 'psychic' and 'political' structures and, above all, because tyrannical desires are harder to uncover than other desires. Indeed, in most they are usually 'repressed by laws and better desires'. This is, moreover, what distinguishes them from the desires of the democratic man, which, although superfluous, are forbidden by neither the laws of society nor those of reason. We might say that theirs is a 'good' superfluity.

'Tyrannical' desires, which are superfluous and bad, are nonetheless still natural and probably innate in all (κινδυνεύουσι ἐγγίνεσθαι παντί). Because they pose a threat to the very existence of the social realm, they are forbidden, either by law and reason (in the case of the aristocratic and the timocratic types), or by better desires (the oligarchic and the democratic types). Repression in tandem with reason can, in a few individuals, bring about their complete eradication; or it can lead to a reduction in their strength and number; or, if repression is unaided by reason, it will fail to some degree and leave these desires to thrive in number and strength alike.

Because these desires are 'repressed', to a greater or lesser extent, it is dreams most of all that testify to their existence. Dreams are the 'royal road' to knowledge of what the law, reason, or better desires, censor in waking hours. During sleep, because reason itself slumbers, forbidden desires stir to varying degrees of wakefulness (in proportion to the strength or weakness of repression in each individual). This mechanism described by Plato, by which the repressed returns, 'anticipates' in every respect the description and the metapsychology advanced by Freud. For during sleep, the censoring agency (which Freud calls the conscious or superego and Plato refers to as the reasonable part of the soul, gentle and born to govern: the intellect) and those sentinels and guardians of reason that are good principles (cf. 560a and 591a) relax their hold and find rest. It is then that the repressed desires can have free rein and satisfy their hunger: 'monsters are spawned in reason's sleep'.

Sleep frees the savage and bestial side of the soul (the unconscious), which is already more or less sated, not on nectar and ambrosia,[10] but on food and drink of a more earthly kind, indeed of too earthly a kind,[11] allowing it to invert the hierarchy in its favour. Yet this assimilation of superfluous, forbidden, desires to a wild animal – which has become a commonplace – should not be taken for granted in Plato's work. For earlier (at 563c) he demonstrates that bestiality is only unleashed in animals when they 'imitate' the lawlessness of men, for example in the democratic regime: 'If you hadn't seen it, you'd never believe how much more freedom pets have in this community compared with any other. The dogs really do start to resemble their mistresses, as the proverb says, but so do horses and donkeys as well, in the way they learn to strut about with absolute freedom, bumping into anyone they meet on the road who doesn't get out of the way. And everything else is just as saturated with freedom.' Dogs, donkeys and horses are animals that have been domesticated by man's reason and, when this is made subordinate to his desires, they inevitably fall back into a feral state. In the city, man alone is responsible for the lawlessness of the 'beast' within and without. It is only the wild beast, free and yet to be tamed, which serves as a metaphor for the savagery of tyrannical desires when these are no longer mastered, *bound* by laws, reason or better desires. In such circumstances, they throw off their chains and are no longer held back by shame and modesty, the two virtues which (according to the *Protagoras*) form the foundations of social existence. On the stage of the dream, this simulacrum, still more so than in the theatre, where the tears and laughter of even the most superior spectators testify to the abdication of reason and to a shameless abandon,[12] like the tyrant who laughs in the face of every written and unwritten law (cf. 563a), when these desires are intoxicated by their new-found freedom, there is no limit to their daring. They will do *anything*, the text says, before spelling out in no uncertain terms, first and foremost, incest with the mother (Μητρὶτε γὰρ ἐπιχειρεῖν), only to then recoil immediately, obsessively, with oedipal horror before its own shamelessness,[13] by generalizing: rape 'of any other, whoever it may be, man, god, animal'. In the same way, the text only hazards allusions to parricide and cannibalism under the cover of the more general form of mad and brazen criminality which results from a universalized injustice and impropriety.

Thus dreams flout all of the three major prohibitions constitutive of the human, just as the tyrant does, whose desires they indeed expose. Even while awake, the tyrant will not hesitate to eat his own children, or kill his father or elder brother, to beat both his father and mother in an attempt to make them satisfy his carnal urges; the tyrant, who is mad beyond redemption, will suffer eternal punishment in Tartarus for these vile crimes, without ever being reincarnated (cf. the myth of Er), except perhaps as a wolf or some other wild beast.[14] For breaking all the laws of humankind, he will be transformed, both while awake and asleep, into a wild beast, a real madman.[15]

Yet the madness of dreams, in contradistinction to that of the tyrant, is purely imaginary. As Freud will later remark, the satisfaction of superfluous and forbidden desires is, in dreams, hallucinatory. We should refer here to the *Timaeus* (71 ff.) which draws on all the resources of an elaborate topological explanation in order to account for the possibility of such hallucinatory satisfaction. According to Plato, the gods created a sort of trough for the nourishment of the body between the diaphragm and the level of the navel and they attached the appetitive soul to it, like a wild beast that must be tied up while feeding, for fear of bringing the race of mortals to an end. It seems that the gods placed it where they did – as far as possible from the faculty charged with deliberation – in order that this would remain undisturbed as it deliberated in the interests of the whole.[16] The appetitive soul does not know how to listen to reason; it merely succumbs *day and night* to the fascination of images and fantoms, simulacra, mere reflections in that other mirror, the liver, that other dark cave, which reflects thoughts from the intellect in the form of images: 'Knowing that [the appetitive soul] would not understand reason or be capable of paying attention to rational argument even if it became aware of it, but would easily fall under the spell of images and phantoms by day and night, [the gods] played upon this weakess and formed the liver, which [they] put into the creature's stall. [They] made it smooth and close in texture, sweet and bitter, so that the influence of the mind could project thoughts upon it which it would receive and reflect in the form of visible images, like a mirror.'[17]

The dream is one of these simulacra, one of these shadows, which the appetitive soul is duped into taking for real. However, and it is here that Freud misunderstood Plato, it is possible to control the delirium of dreams, to avoid being duped and falling prey to images of the bestial; namely, by knowing how to exercise control, during waking life, over one's desires. This requires, first, a healthy body and above all a liver that is in good working order, for nobody chooses to be evil. Rather, 'those of us who are wicked acquire our faults owing to two causes entirely independent of our will. The responsibility lies with the parents rather than the offspring, and with those who educate rather than their pupils' (*Timaeus*, 87d). It follows that those who fail to live a temperate life are not to be blamed on that account: intemperance 'is generally a mental disease caused by a single substance (the marrow) which overflows and floods the body because of the porousness of the bones. And indeed it is generally true that it is unjust to blame over-indulgence in pleasure as if wrongdoing were voluntary' (ibid.).

The second step towards controlling one's dreams, which accordingly depends very much on the first, is temperance. The third is a kind of ritual of exorcism to be carried out before indulging in sleep: strive to keep your soul in a state of wakefulness, nourish it with beautiful thoughts and speculations, direct it towards its better part, towards its higher rather than its lower regions, such that even while it sleeps, instead of forgetting itself, it will still be dominated by the highest principle and all desires will sleep. This sleep of the desires, which leaves the nobler part in peace, is only possible if they too have been calmed by the even hand of temperance, which demands neither fasting nor gluttony.[18] For it is with their extremes of want and satiety that these desires are able to disturb the soul, yoking it to the body, or to its suffering or joy, and preventing it from fulfilling its task. If the best part of the soul also manages to entirely subdue all anger before going to sleep, by pacifying the θῡμος, the heart – an intermediary designed to help master the appetites[19] – then it will paradoxically succeed in accomplishing its task of knowledge even more proficiently than in waking life. We might say that the state of sleep prefigures death, the limit position at which the soul, restored to its primal divinity and freed from the vexations of the body, can finally know the truth.

For the soul which falls to sleep in complete self-mastery, with all its various parts in their proper place in the hierarchy, will not only find that its slumbers are spared visions of illegality, but will also be blessed with powers of divination[20] over the past, present and future, enabling it 'to make contact with the truth better than ever'. Indeed, this is the only way that humans in their mortal weakness can grasp something of the truth, knowledge which is ordinarily the sole preserve of the gods. This is to say that dreams are not, in themselves, deceitful and delusionary: if the 'simulacrum' is 'crafted' by a well-trained soul then it can be a vehicle of truth. There are good and bad dreams and philosophy is a medecine which, by transforming lies into dreams for the good, allows you to sleep in peace. So the good man will not, even in dreams, do as the wicked man does in reality. This dream theatre no more produces a cathartic effect than real theatre (Plato differs here from Aristotle and his scion, Freud). Such concern about the proper way to sleep and dream is driven by the fear that he who gets used, in dreams, to killing his father or sleeping with his mother, far from unburdening himself of these crimes in a hallucinatory fashion, will end up, by force of habit, committing them in real life. In exactly the same way, the spectator who imagines he can identify quite safely with a sorrowful or ridiculous hero, under the pretext that he does not himself appear in the play, who indulges unrestrainedly in lamentation or laughter while at the theatre, will end up behaving as a coward or a fool in everyday life: 'You see, few people have the ability to work out that we ourselves are bound to store the harvest we reap from others: these occasions feed the feeling of sadness until it is too strong for us easily to restrain it when hardship occurs in our own lives . . . And doesn't the same go for humour as well? . . . There's a part of you which wants to make people laugh, but your reason restrains it, because you're afraid of being thought a vulgar clown. Nevertheless, you let it have its way on those other occasions, and you don't realize that the almost inevitable result of giving it energy in this other context [i.e. comic representation] is that you become a comedian in your own life' (*Republic*, X, 606b–c).

So if the well-ordered soul can and should, while asleep, 'give birth' to the good simulacra which alone permit divination and access to the truth – gifts of the gods and generous supplements to mortal human weakness – it is, however, the prerogative of waking reason to interpret these dreams. Plato does not leave even the good dream with the last word, which belongs rather to the noble part of the soul: on its own, the good simulacrum would be unable to speak and tell the truth; it could at most be sufficiently fascinating to allow the appetitive soul to sleep in peace. On waking, reason entirely reasserts its rightful hold:

> The influence of the mind could project thoughts upon [the liver] which it would receive and reflect in the form of visible images, like a mirror. When the mind wants to cause fear, it makes use of the liver's native bitterness and plays a stern and threatening role, quickly infusing the whole organ with bitterness and giving it a bilious colour . . . By contrast, gentle thoughts from the mind produce images of the opposite kind, which will neither produce nor have connection with anything of a contrary nature to their own, and so bring relief from bitterness, using the organ's innate sweetness to render it straight and smooth and free, and making the part of the soul that lives in the region of the liver

cheerful and gentle, and able to spend the night quietly in divination and dreams, as reason and understanding are beyond it. For our makers remembered that their father had ordered them to make mortal creatures as perfect as possible, and so did their best even with this base part of us and gave it the power of prophecy so that it might have some apprehension of truth. And clear enough evidence that god gave this power to man's irrational part is to be found in our incapacity for inspired and true prophecy when in our right minds; we only achieve it when the power of our understanding is inhibited in sleep, or when we are in an abnormal condition owing to disease or divine inspiration. And it is the function of someone in his right mind to construe what is remembered of utterances made in dream or waking by those who have the gift of prophecy and divine inspiration, and to give a rational interpretation of their visions, saying what good or evil they portend and for whom, whether future, past, or present. It is not the business of any man, so long as he is in an abnormal state, to interpret his own visions and utterances.

(Timaeus, 71b ff.)

If none can escape from dreams, which are signs of human weakness and also, ultimately, its remedy, it is not the case that all dreams are alike: Plato, who differs here from Freud, would have agreed with the Roman emperor who had a man executed for dreaming of murdering him, because our dreams judge us; they gauge the violence of our superfluous and forbidden desires and our ability to master them, or lack of it. And far from cleansing us of these desires, our dreams help to strengthen them.

It is characteristic of the tyrannical soul to be unable to transform bad dreams into good ones. The tyrant never sleeps in peace – and his waking life is a nightmare, since without fearing punishment he can unrestrainedly satisfy his most savage desires, those which dreams have succeeded in disclosing.

The tyrant

So how is such a man, at the very limit of the human, possible? Plato's account of the development of the type of personality which characterizes the tyrant follows on from the 'degeneration' of the democratic type. As ever, this is precipitated by a division between the desires, a conflict between father and son. Indeed, the democratic man had emerged out of just such a conflict: on one side were those desires that were necessary and useful (to the oligarchic type), those respected by the father, the educator, who instilled principles in his son that were as parsimonious as him and which served as sentinels and guardians of the law of the father in the soul of the son (as his 'superego'). On the other side were the superfluous desires, those bound up with luxury and *mimesis*, with rivalry unchecked by law and due proportion, those repressed by the father and awakened in the soul of the son by frequenting unsuitable characters whose lives have not been ordered in accordance with need but rather by a luxurious supplementarity (cf. 561a–561c). In the end, the seductive charms of these principles win out, repressing the paternal ones: a model and a *mimesis* are established as substitutes; the authority of the 'second' father replaces that of the 'first', though not without leaving the son with a lingering feeling of guilt in the aftermath of this transformation, a feeling which serves to perpetuate inner conflict. Hence the adoption of rules of behaviour which fall midway between the two others, neither entirely disorderly nor completely parsimonious. It is this final, mediocre, compromise which characterizes the democratic soul.

A democrat becomes a tyrant by repeating an analogous seduction scene: the democratic father instills his mediocre principles in a son who is lured away by the attractions of a way of life which has, as its only principles, those desires forbidden by the law. These source of their seductive power – for nobody chooses to be evil – lies in a whole arsenal of techniques for counterfeiting and falsifying names. This limitless slide into the dissolute is called *freedom*, a pretty name which covers the anarchic equality of every desire and an absence of order and constraint in human behaviour (cf. 564d ff.).

If, however, the young man succeeds in resisting the seductive temptations of 'freedom', one trick that is guaranteed to turn him into a tyrant is to entice his heart to love, the most tyrannical of desires, their chief and master (cf. 574c ff.), which, from an extreme of freedom will lead him into the greatest possible servitude. Chief though it may be, it is not, however, a hierarchical ordering principle for the soul but introduces instead the same kind of disorder as is created in the body by bile or phlegm, for it is only the chief of the superfluous, anarchic, desires. Plato compares these desires, which have no need to work but spend a great deal, to drones of various kinds. Thus at 552c, he writes: 'His home is equivalent to the cell in a honeycomb where a drone is born, and he becomes the bane of his community as a drone becomes the bane of the hive.' Plato distinguishes between winged drones without a sting, who end up as beggars in old age and stinging drones that go on foot, who form the class of criminals. At 554d, he declares: 'When it's a case of them spending someone else's money . . . the drone-like desires most of them contain will be exposed.' At 556a, money-lenders are describes as wingless drones who cause injury with their sting while increasing their capital a hundredfold. At 559d, Plato writes that 'the type of person we've been calling a drone is overflowing with these pleasures and desires, and is ruled by the unnecessary ones'; the democratic individual is likened to a drone, in opposition to the oligarchic, domestic, type, who is governed by necessary desires. 'When a young person, whose upbringing has been as uncultured and mean as we were saying a short while ago, tastes the drones' honey and starts to associate with ferocious, dangerous beasts who are capable of arranging for him pleasures of every conceivable kind, form, and description – that, I suggest, is how the transition begins from an internal oligarchic state to a democratic one.'

Love has all the characteristics of a winged drone. It is the scourge of the hive and only seemingly in control, for it will end up begging, living at the expense of the other superfluous desires which it enslaves as its subordinates but which – just like the tyrant's flatterers – eventually rule as kings. Whereas Eros in the *Symposium* escapes from aporia by having more than one poros to his bow, tyrannical love has by way of *poros* only a profusion of diadems, incense, perfume, and wine; but no sting in the tail. The flatterers take it upon themselves to sharpen the sting of unsatisfied desire. This, indeed, is their strategy for winning power: to literally drive the other, their chief, mad with desire, ridding him of anything that could possibly make him listen to reason (reason and also the wisest desires, the oligarchic and parsimonious desires, which are governed by the reality principle and demand, out of avarice, prudence in the search for pleasure). Just as the tyrant exiles from the city, or exterminates, all who seek to restore him to reason and will not hesitate to kill both his father and mother (cf. 560–7c), tyrannical love, this 'evil love' – which works in the opposite direction to the philosophical catharsis of true Eros – pulls out every paternal principle by the root. Tyrannical love is not seduced, this time, by a principle opposed to that which had hitherto guided it, by a false good that it mistakes for The Good; it no longer even acknowledges that there is any value in Good at all. Herein lies the tyrant's total perversion, his madness, his way of 'becoming bestial'. So love, through intoxication, leads to tyranny. And the tyrant, in his madness and his complete lack of self-mastery, no longer recognizes either human or divine law but aspires to impose his law on all.

By now it is a simple matter to answer the initial question, Does the tyrannical life lead to happiness or its opposite? Is Thrasymachus right, or not? The tyrannical man can only be unhappy – and to the highest degree – since he has been entirely dispossessed of himself and his true lineage; he is afflicted by an incurable madness which knows no bounds; there is no guilt-inducing principle to temper or arrest his megalomania; awake and asleep, he behaves in the most savage and bestial manner and is prey to the most terrible of desires: 'attitudes which had formerly – during the period when there was still a democratic government within him, and he was still subject to the laws and to his father – broken free only at night, while he was asleep. Once he's under the dictatorship of lust, however, his constant waking state is one that was formerly rare and restricted to dreams: there's no form of murder, however vile, that he isn't willing to commit; there's nothing he won't eat, no deed he isn't ready to perform' (574e).

Plato does not specify whether the fully fledged tyrant continues to have bad dreams (but could he, in his madness, tell the difference between dreams and waking life?). At any rate, the dreams born in his democratic past could not have served as a *catharsis* and may even have strengthened his parricidal, incestuous and cannibalistic desires by giving them nourishment.

So if you want to live and sleep in peace, rather than the lunatics described in the myth of Er who rush headlong into the tyrannical life, you would do far better to choose a life which is philosophical and well ordered. For if these terrible desires exist in you, as they do in everyone, you will need a course of psychoanalysis before you can recognize them. In the meantime, trust Plato, sleep in peace and dream good dreams.

Translated by Oliver Davis

Notes

1 Freud, *The Interpretation of Dreams*, translated by James Strachey (London: Penguin, 1991), p. 134.
2 Ibid., p. 782.
3 Plato, *Republic*, tr. by Robin Waterfield (Oxford: Oxford University Press, 1993). This and all subsequent translations from the *Republic* are from Waterfield's edition.
4 Ibid., p. 365.
5 In accordance with the general scheme of Book VIII, Plato always begins by examining the transition in political regimes before turning to the types of person, for if it is true that the type of regime depends upon the way in which the soul arranges a hierarchy between its different parts, then conversely the type of regime serves as the paradigm for knowledge of the type of individual which corresponds to it because it displays, writ large, that which is inscribed in small print in the person (cf. Book I).

6 The deduction of the different types of regime and individual can indeed be carried out *a priori* because it is a function of the different ways in which the soul hierarchizes its various parts.

7 As for the originary change which first afflicted the ideal regime, the harmony of which allowed no room for either alteration or decay, Plato explains this by referring to the universal law of the corruption of all that is born (cf. 546a). The real and occasioning cause of decay is a principle of division within the party which governs. As in the *Iliad*, discord lies at the root of all evil and discord is said to be caused by the ignorance of the guardians, who sometimes failed to reproduce in the correct geometrical proportions, and at the right moment for a given generation, in order to allow for suitable couplings. These ill-assorted unions are responsible for the mix of 'castes' and for schism in the guardian class, between the elders of pure blood and the newcomers, who are half-breeds: 'discrepancy and discordant incongruity will occur, and they always breed hostility and antagonism, wherever they occur' (574a). One consequence of the division is that the two castes of iron and bronze turn themselves towards money, while for the two others (of gold and silver), the only riches worth having are those of the soul and its virtue. The appeal to the myth of the four castes justifies the qualitative structural differences between souls and their destinies.

8 Cf. the beginning of Book VIII, 545a.

9 Note the similarity between the democratic man and the practitioner of mimesis who appears in the city when luxury and superfluity hold sway and whose soul is not guided by a single 'proper' principle.

10 Cf. also *Phaedrus*, 580e and *Republic*, 580c, 588d, 589b.

11 The satisfaction of the appetite for food functions as a metaphor for the satisfaction of desire in general. Similarly, in dreams as described by Freud (cf. the dream referred to as that of the 'Three Fates'), sexual desire appears in disguised form as the desire for food.

12 Cf. *Republic* X, 606a ff. 'Consider this. What a poet satisfies and gratifies on these occasions is an aspect of ourselves which we forcibly restrain when tragedy strikes our own lives – an aspect which hungers after tears and the satisfaction of having cried until one can cry no more, since that is what it is in its nature to want to do. When the part of us which is inherently good has been inadequately trained in habits enjoined by reason, it relaxes its guard over this other part, the part which feels sad. Other people, not ourselves, are feeling these feelings, we tell ourselves, and it's no disgrace for us to sanction such behaviour and feel sorry for someone who, even while claiming to be good, is overindulging in grief; and, we think, we are at least profiting from the pleasure, and there's no point in throwing away the pleasure by spurning the whole poem or play . . . And doesn't the same go for humour as well? If there are amusing things which you'd be ashamed to do yourself, but which give you a great deal of pleasure when you see them in a comic representation or hear about them in private company – when you don't find them loathsome and repulsive – then isn't this exactly the same kind of behaviour as we uncovered when talking about feeling sad? There's a part of you which wants to make people laugh, but your reason restrains it, because you're afraid of being thought a vulgar clown.'

13 Indeed before Freud, Plato and fellow Greeks of his time could not have failed to think here of lines 981–2 of *Oedipus Rex*: 'Many are the mortals who sleep with their mother in dreams'.

14 Cf. *Republic*, 565e, 574a, 615b.

15 Plato is not keen on madmen . . . In *Republic*, in Book III, guardians are forbidden from imitating them (as indeed they are forbidden from imitating women) and the Laws will see to it that they are locked up. Cf. *Laws*, tr. by Trevor Saunders (London: Penguin, 1970), Book XI 934d ff: 'Lunatics must not be allowed to appear in public; their relations must keep them in custody in private houses by whatever means they can improvise . . . If they fail to do so, they must pay a fine . . . There are several kinds of madness, brought on by several causes. The causes we have just mentioned are the result of illness but there are some people with an unfortunate natural irritability made worse by poor discipline, who in any trivial quarrel will shout their heads off in mutual abuse . . . In gratifying his ugly emotion, anger, and in thus disgracefully stoking the fires of his fury, the speaker drives back into primitive savagery a

side of his character that was once civilized by education, and such a splenetic life makes him no better than a wild beast.'

16 Cf. also *Phaedo*.

17 *Timaeus*, tr. by Desmond Lee (London: Penguin, 1965). This and all subsequent translations from the *Timaeus* are from Lee's edition.

18 Plato, once again before Freud, knew very well that the complete sublimation of desire was impossible and that the base part of the soul, like Schilda's horse which Freud describes in the fifth of the *Introductory Lectures*, also has need some small need of nourishment, even if only to allow the better part to live in peace.

19 'The part of the soul which is the seat of courage, passion and ambition they located nearer the head between the midriff and neck; there it would be well-placed to listen to the commands of reason and combine with it in forcibly restraining the appetites when they refused to obey the word of command from the citadel' (*Timaeus*, 70a).

20 In the *Phaedo*, divinatory delirium is one of the forms which good delirium takes.

16

MONIQUE DAVID-MÉNARD

Monique David-Ménard is a philosopher and psychoanalyst, specialising in eighteenth and nineteenth-century German philosophy, and in questions of the body in psychoanalysis and biology. She is Professor and Director of Research at the University of Paris VII (Denis-Diderot), Assistant Director of the Centre d'Études du Vivant, and Secretary of the scientific commission of the Society for Freudian analysis. She is also a doctor of clinical psychopathology. Monique David-Ménard has been in charge of a unit for phenomenological research at the CNRS, and directed a programme at the Collège International de Philosophie; she continues to teach Philosophy at the Lycée Janson-de-Sailly in Paris. She has published widely on Lacan and on Kant, as well as on women and issues of pleasure and sexuality.

Her works include the following:

L'Hystérique entre Freud et Lacan. Corps et langage en psychanalyse, Paris: Éditions universitaires, 1983. (Translated into English as Hysteria from Freud to Lacan. Body and Language in Psychoanalysis, Cornell University Press, 1989.)

La Folie dans la raison pure. Kant lecteur de Swedenbourg, Paris: Vrin, 1990.

Les Constructions de l'universel. Psychanalyse, philosophie, Paris: PUF, 1997.

Tout le plaisir est pour moi, Paris: Hachettes Littératures, 2000.

THE STRUCTURES OF DESIRE
AND THE CONCEPT OF THE
UNIVERSAL

Introduction

The concept of a universal – which structures much of our logic, our political philosophy, our ethics, and indeed our understanding of sexual difference – is not only more complicated than is usually imagined but it is also steeped in confusion. It combines disparate elements, without either recognizing or justifying this process; sometimes it is redefined in a supposedly foundational field, such as logic, without the need being felt for it to be modified in others. Or, as in the case of Lacan's theory of sexual identity, an attempt may be made to modify the concept in order to account for a real paradox – the difference between the sexes – yet it remains, all the while, saddled with the inheritance of confusions to which I have just alluded.

The present work is a critique of the concept of universality from a variety of different perspectives. I do not, however, presume for one moment to offer any systematic replacement. When crisis rocks the foundations of a certain way of thinking, the solution is not to start issuing decrees. Moreover, the incoherence and confusion inherent in the notion of universality should perhaps prompt us to reevaluate the universalist conception of the human being, to appreciate, as we are just beginning to do, both why this particular construction is necessary and what it is about it that means it will sometimes prove illusory. In fact, as Nietzsche said in *Daybreak*, it is a matter of changing our way of feeling: 'We have to change our way of judging if we are finally to be able – perhaps after a very long time – to go one better and change our way of feeling.' By appraising some of the weak points in our use of the concept of universality, I hope to contribute to our being able to feel differently about what this concept is all about.

In the course of this painstaking, often loving, sometimes violent, work on those bastions of thought which have their foundations in the notion of universality, psycho-analysis will be accorded the role it habitually plays in my writings, that of an instrument of criticism which reveals how concepts and fantasies are intertwined in philosophical thinking. Yet it is also part of the problem, for the question of sexual difference is an issue which pushes the notion of univerality into crisis. It may accordingly be asked whether or not I am a feminist. I do indeed draw upon the structure of certain women's dreams in order to show that the substitution of objects of desire does not operate in the same way in these dreams as it does in male sexuality, that the accompanying experience of guilt is different for men and women and that the way in which the concept of universality is constructed by Kant (and also by many other male thinkers) is bound up with a commitment to a certain anthropology of desire and a very particular, somewhat masculine, analysis of the experience of guilt. I do not mean to suggest by this that women have no relation to the universal nor that their thought is destined by nature to particularity. But nor is it entirely by chance that it has been women readers, rather than their male counterparts, who have pinpointed what it is about the very foundations of Kant's thinking on universality that remains nothing more than a poorly justified but supposedly 'self-evident' truth, namely his reliance on a conceptual structure derived from an anthropology declined in the masculine. For the blindspots in any way of thinking will always be clearer to those excluded from it. This does not mean that an anthropology derived from a feminine position would be any more true than the thought of Kant, Lacan or Sade, nor that the ways of gaining access to the concepts which it would allow would be any more rigorous or true. They would merely be different, but it is nonetheless extremely important to bring this difference to light. The basic pairings which undergird conceptual thought are inflected by the question of the sexual identity of thinking subjects, just as they are by myth. It is not at all clear why philosophers should be so reluctant to accept that the way in which concepts are constructed stems from the fantasies involved in a thinker's self-definition as a sexed being, when they purport to accept that philosophy must always concern itself with myths, myths from which concepts may certainly be distinguished, though never in any straightforward fashion. For the question of sexual difference creates myths which are necessary and which are bound up with the fundamental oppositions which form the basis of philosophical problems. Sensible and intelligible, general and particular, are among these basic oppositions which open up a way of interpreting the world that we designate as 'philosophical'. If women, or certain men whose way of being men is unorthodox, have representations of the masculine and the feminine that do not naturally allow themselves to be transformed into the pairs of opposites which have held sway since the birth of philosophical thinking, then philosophical thinking may itself be encouraged to change, without our being able, in advance, to say how, for the pathways between fantasy structures and concepts are fixed in neither their nature nor their essence. Myths change slowly, as do representations of the masculine and the feminine, and so too, therefore, does that which flows from these representations into philosophical thinking. This then is the slant of what might be called my feminism, but which many feminists may not, perhaps, recognize as such. For I am not claiming that the feminine is a higher truth than the masculine. The value of those fantasies involved in elaborating a sexual identity lies entirely in their competence and not in their content. Fantasies and dreams such as those which feature in this book allow us to construct identities which only hold good in relation to those interlocutors – imaginary and real – who are either different from, or the same as, ourselves. One fantasy is never any more true than another, only different. And yet it partakes of thought and it establishes relations to thoughts which are constructed differently from it, in accordance with other rules. These then are the aspects of thought which I hope to bring to the fore in the concept of universality.

The Structures of Desire and the Concept of the Universal

'Any number of times . . .'

The human being with human rights

The moral outlook which Hegel tore to shreds, one which rests on the confrontation between our actions in all their materiality and an unconditional imperative, one which defines the human in terms of a universal relation to the law (a moral, and later a juridical, relation) seems, at the end of the twentieth century, to be unequalled in its capacity to defend against human violence and to serve as an obstacle to conflict on both a national and an international level. We keep coming back to Kantian ethics and the philosophy of human rights in spite, or so it is said, of the philosophical objections which appear to have shown them to be abstract and therefore illusory. Hegel dismantled the logic of this abstraction, which is constantly forced to disguise its ignorance of the real content of human action. Nietzsche has sensitized us to the stench of cruelty that quite openly powers Kant's categorical imperative. More recently, Lacan has drawn a parallel between Sade and Kant by demonstrating that the formalism of the imperative to pleasure can claim authority – just like the moral imperative – from the requirement for universality inherent in the juridico-political concept of the human. In such discussions, Kantian philosophers and those seeking to defend an ethic of human rights are tireless in bringing to the fore the reductive and caricatural sides to the attempt to destroy the moral conception of the human. They also emphasise the dangers involved in attempting to provide a definition of the human being in supposedly concrete terms, as situated within the class-struggle, for this human being is no less abstract, no less unreal, than the universal human being with human rights. But the critics of moral formalism reply that it is high time we abandoned a conception of universal reason which fosters and disguises manifold evils simply because it is ignorant of the violence bound into every strand of its being. This discussion takes the form of a conflictual antinomy: each side believes it is demolishing the other even as the other is demolishing it. The end result, accordingly, is nill all, or deuce, as it were.

Changing objects

Perhaps we need a change of perspective before we can circumscribe the terrain which forms the battleground for advocates and opponents of the universalist conception of the human. Before developing a philosophy of morality, Kant, in 1764, observed that half the human race have no knowledge of their relationship to the law, that women lack that sense of the sublime which is conducive to constancy in the principles of action and that on the occasions when they do behave morally, this is never out of respect for the law. He added that when a woman is moral, this is because she finds morality beautiful, an attitude which the man of morals can only find repellent, even if he allows himself to be seduced by it.

> The virtue of a woman is a *beautiful virtue*. That of the male sex should be a *noble virtue*. Women will avoid the wicked not because it is unright, but because

253

it is ugly; and virtuous actions mean to them such as are morally beautiful. Nothing of duty, nothing of compulsion, nothing of obligation! Woman is intolerant of all commands and all morose constraint. They do something only because it pleases them, and the art consists in making only that please them which is good. I hardly believe that the fair sex is capable of principles . . .[1]

The position here is clear: if moral behaviour is empirically rare in both men and women, this apparent equality should not blind us to a fundamental difference. Men are constituted by the encounter between the maxim of their actions and an unconditional imperative which cuts across and paralyses all the interests of their sensibility. Is this option of foregoing the pathological in favour of a purely formal demand really only thought to be possible in the case of men? If this is meant to be a joke, then it is a joke which articulates a truth that philosophers, Kant included, had previously failed to question. We shall leave Kant with this notion (which is a male fantasy of femi-ninity) that, if women are strangers to moral obligation, this is because they value only beauty. Rather than simply brushing aside the first part of his observation, we shall take it seriously: morality is a male prerogative, an interesting constuction, yes, but one rooted in a structure of masculine desire. In an attempt to elucidate his meaning, we shall be best advised to attend to what Freud called the 'substitutability' of the objects of the sexual instincts and to compare the forms which this substitutability takes in men and women. We shall then be in a position to return to the question of the equivalence of subjects before the law, which forms the basis of the universalist conception of the human.

The psychoanalytic consulting room and the experience of love have both demon-strated that women do not have the same relationship to the Highest Good and to guilt as men, the reason being that the extreme variability which characterizes instinctual objects is inflected differently when these objects are substituted in female sexuality. Women, or those identifying as women, do not change objects of desire in the same way as men, or those identifying as men. Let us be quite clear about this difference: the variability of the instinctual object, which can change, as Freud wrote, 'any number of times', holds good in the case of men and women alike. But this single, generalized, formulation embraces instincts and sublimatory processes which are different for each sex. Moreover, Freud encourages us to consider the great variety of possible functions which an object may perform and thereby the diversity of possible ways in which one object may be substituted for another: 'The object [*Objekt*] of an instinct is the thing in regard to which or through which the instinct is able to achieve its aim. It is what is most variable about an instinct and is not originally connected with it, but becomes assigned to it only in consequence of being peculiarly fitted to make satisfaction possible. The object is not necessarily something [*Gegenstand*] extraneous: it may equally well be a part of the subject's own body. It may be changed any number of times in the course of the vicissitudes which the instinct undergoes during its existence; and highly important parts are played by this displacement of instinct. It may happen that the same object [*Objekt*] serves for the satisfaction of several instincts simultaneously, a phenomenon which Adler has called a "confluence" of instincts [*Triebverschränkung*]. A particularly close attachment of the instinct to its object is distinguished by the term "fixation". This frequently occurs at very early periods of the development of an instinct and puts an end to its mobility through its intense opposition to detachment.'[2]

This passage has been discussed many times. It has also been the occasion of decisive misunderstandings, notably by Lacan, who replaces Freud's idea that the object may change 'any number of times' with the very different view according to which the object as such is altogether devoid of importance.[3] His misreading leads him to develop a perverse model of instinctual satisfaction: 'Kant with Sade'. Or, more precisely, it is the idea that perverse sexuality gets most out of a circuit of instincts by fully exploring an object which is itself indifferent that leads Lacan, while reading Freud, to invent another text. It is clearly not without significance that the moral man of the sublime, the Kantian man who bends the pathological to fit the the principled constancy demanded of action, resembles Sade's libertine in that the variability of the objects of their instincts is interpreted by both as indifference, indifference with respect to the sole requirement to pursue the interests of pleasure, in Sade's case, and indifference in the face of the moral law, which makes all concern for sensibility irrelevant in the face of the imperative, in Kant's. Note that this interpretation of the inherent variability of the object in terms of indifference, or non-differentiation, also recalls Don Juan, who makes each woman indifferent in turn, in order that she not take on too quickly the appearance of an Elvira or a ghost who would call him to account for his pleasures.

Yet according to Freud, the theme of the variability of instinctual objects admits of many other possible interpretations. Consider, in particular, his last sentence, which is formidably subtle: if an instinct becomes fixated on an object too early, he says, then this blocks the mobility of the drives by impeding their *Lösung*. This is a term which denotes both the dissolution of an exclusive tie to too early an object and the satisfaction of an instinct by the experience of pleasure which, for a moment, discharges the pressure of that instinct. To be unable to abandon particular objects and unable to find objects which allow for pleasure because they are all replaceable, prone to substitution, are thus two aspects of the same fixation. Most interestingly in the context of the present discussion is this connection between the possibility of pleasure and the capacity to give up certain objects without this necessarily entailing that objects cease to be differentiated.

Guilt in the feminine: a nightmare

Consider the following example: a woman analysand, just at the moment when she may be forced to give up on the love of a man who is becoming increasingly distant while she waits expectantly, has a dream the night before meeting him. She is standing in a queue with her daughter. The atmosphere is overwhelmingly one of pain, which she describes using the expression "going to the abattoir". She leaves for a moment, to go to the busy part of town on an errand. As she is leaving, in a nice car, she realizes that she is no longer with her daughter and that she should not at any price have left her alone, that by going away she has prevented herself from taking advantage of these last moments of life with her daughter. She wakes up, horrified by this nightmare, with the feeling that she has had exactly the same experience as the Jews during the war when they realized that they were going to die.

Many associations emerge in the course of the analytic session. Her friend said to her recently, "I shall come to see your daughter". And her daughter had recently taken to criticizing her for going out too often in the evenings. Finally, the nice car reminds her of the advances made to her recently by another man, who does indeed have a nice car, unlike the man for whom she is waiting. Moreover, this idea of waiting to die recalls to her an accusation sometimes levelled against the Jews – of having remained passive during the last war – which then brings her to something her friend said: he described himself as passive with women when talking about his relations with a woman other than the patient, another woman for whom, in fact, he might well leave her – the prospect of which was precisely the cause of the present period of anxious anticipation.

Listening to such a dream hardly leaves us with the impression that this woman has no sense of guilt. For this nightmare stages what might be considered a desperate attempt to take on the responsibility for a man's 'misdemeanour'. In fact, guilt is staged in two ways in this nightmare. At the deeper level, this feeling of foreboding about going to a meeting as though to an abattoir leads this woman to an experience of suffering and humiliation (in dreams, the signifying matter for such experiences is often provided by the predicament of the Jews threatened with death). It is entirely impossible for a subject to come into being in such a register: what cannot be represented here is an act by virtue of which a human being would make themselves a source of violence, even if this were to involve feelings of guilt and responsibility, or of solidarity with those other human beings who are raised, by the very repression of this shared violence, to the universal status of subjects before a moral law. This, in fact, is the way in which guilt and the relation between particular acts and the moral law is elaborated in masculine sexuality. This is Freud's argument, in 1913, in *Totem and Taboo*.

But it is not so for this analysand: the ways in which a subject comes into being are different. In relation to the experience of suffering which her present difficulties have awakened, this theme of awaiting death, with its reference to the accusation of passivity levelled against the Jews, amounts to an admission of her being fundamentally ashamed to be alive. This admission can be compared with the sign, to which Lacan drew our attention in the not too distant past, denoting a complete refusal of existence – the sign which constitutes the character of Sygne de Coûfontaine in Claudel's *L'Otage*.[4] But in our analysand's nightmare, there is no sign of a refusal of existence addressed to another, but merely the irrevocable representation of a wish destined not to be fulfilled.

Irrevocable? Not quite, for there is another instance of guilt in this nightmare which is, this time, a subjective construction that serves to contain the raw feelings of un-happiness. In this dream, the patient is telling herself that she is guilty of not having spent enough time with her daughter as death approaches and of having been too preoccupied – for the daughter's liking – with her relationships with men. In this register, not only is the guilt not about her existence as such, but the allusion to her running an errand allows for the expression of a substitution: a man without a car is replaced by one with a nice car. Thus, in the midst of her passive anticipation of a death to be endured but not hastened, there is the sense of a rather more negotiable kind of guilt. The grievances addressed to the mother refer to something other than the inexorable anticipation of a death in which she would not even be with her daughter. A man with a car versus one without: this substitution of one object for another allows for a secondary, eroticized, sense of guilt. Thus, as is invariably the case, the erotic, or instinctual, sits alongside this anxiety about a threatened identity. We also get a fairly clear sense of the way in which the instincts constitute themselves by limiting the death drive, by simultaneously repeating and displacing various aspects of it. Eroticization transforms and sublimates the death drive, without – in the strict sense – repressing it, that is without resorting to the imaginary scene of crime and castration which makes those human beings we call men what they are, by connecting the 'suppression' of an experience of suffering to the universalization of guilt.

Kant was no doubt wrong to say that women have no sense of guilt but he was not wrong in his intuition that their experience of guilt is different from that of men. Women's experience of guilt involves an act of self-dispossession which can only resolve itself into one of the various archetypal situations of expecting the worst. The sense of guilt weighs heavily upon her but remains unconnected to any representation of the desire to commit a murder in which the distinctions between self and other, between love and hate, would be annihilated, as is often the case in men's dreams. This sense of guilt gains no relief from such a construction in which the phallus intrudes to represent what must be lost in order to lessen the gravity of the crime.

The nightmare, in and of itself, gives shape to an anticipated experience of dispossession which will affect the very being of the dreamer; it outlines a fear of breaking up with a lover by making this a deadly prospect. Women have a certain capacity to represent and indeed to live hopeless situations, situations devoid even of the hope that law brings by forbidding something or other; the only way of containing the threat is by producing an exaggerated representation of it. Yet it is against the background of a suffering so intense that it threatens to unravel her very existence that the strands of the erotic scenario are woven together. The smile which enables our dreamer to surface from her nightmare changes the nature of the guilt. The inventive substitution of the man with a nice car for the one who is leaving is a fabrication which allows her to emerge from the dream just as the representation of anxiety reaches its peak. This substitution does not render the objects of desire equivalent, nor does it consign them to the same insignificance in relation to a law binding the subject to ideals which, by virtue of their being unchanging, would ensure that whichever objects were to be given up would become indifferent. Rather, our dreamer devises a substitution which establishes an opposition between two objects by way of the attribute 'car'. This substitution allows a hierarchy to be established between the two levels of anxiety and it makes room for a smile in the nightmare. I called this a sublimation rather than a repression because, when repression occurs, the identification with an ideal suppresses the instinctual objects by incorporating them, arranging them in a series in which they are substitutable and indifferent in relation, precisely, to the law which redefines the subject. There is probably a connection between this way of relegating objects and the mode of a subject's coming into being described by Lacan when he remarked that a subject is that which represents one signifier to another signifier. One object, one signifier, is worth the same as any other since it is by virtue of their position alone that the subject is able to come into being in the eclipse that forms their union. The opposition between the man with the nice car and the one without performs a different function. The nice car makes a mockery of an act of destruction which cannot be construed here as an eclipse of the subject: when destruction occurs, there is no subject and when a subject emerges, this is by laughing in the face of a form of destruction that is not an eclipse. The nice car is not a sign, in Lacan's sense of that which represents something for someone.[5] Nor is it exactly a signifier, for the reason given above. It is more the representation of a possible other presence which suddenly makes the absence bearable. A man with a nice car instead of one who is leaving: this fabrication of the dream does not open the way to an indefinite series of objects, precisely because this symbol is the symbol of a possible presence and of an absence which is thenceforth capable of representation. One other object will suffice: it is not necessary for the substitution to be infinitely open in order for anxiety to be eroticized and the need to move on to another does not entail devaluing the object in general. The dream retains one characteristic of the abandoning object and elaborates – in a ludic, oppositional, fashion – a possible way out in the form of the nice car. It is enough that this procedure allows the dreamer to emerge from the nightmare without forgetting it, for the material which allows her to surface remains related to the missing object. In this sense, the object is neither suppressed by incorporation, nor is the more fundamental form of anxiety subjected to repression. But there is a transformation. Will it be said that women are not subjects? Let us suggest instead that they become subjects differently from men, by way of a certain sort of ludic sublimation of those elements in their desires which cause suffering and guilt.

The logic of guilt in Kant

The foregoing remarks should allow us adopt a different approach to the question of moral understanding, specifically of the categorical imperative and transgression. The difference being that we are now in a position to approach this imperative as an instinctual manifestation – one which undoubtedly exists for a good reason, but which could never be an unconditional standard of truth. For a number of the claims made by Kantian ethics, which are presented as rationally self-evident, in fact turn out to rather more confused as soon as serious consideration is given to the idea there may be other ways in which guilt can manifest itself, aside from morality. Other ways which are real, thus possible – that is, conceivable.

From 1763 onwards – from the *Essay to Introduce the Concept of Negative Magnitude into Philosophy* – and consistently in all the later texts which attempt to define the relationship between our actions and a universal law which stands in judgment over their maxim, the concept of guilt in Kant is two-sided. The experience of guilt is, first of all, one of being overwhelmed by an imperative which lies at the very foundation of our moral consciousness and before which we always feel ourselves to be at fault. The logic of real conflict (*realer Widerstreit*) presupposes an opposition between two forces, both formidable: our awareness of being determined by the law stands opposed to our awareness that the interests of our sensibility resist the unconditional moral imperative. Kant's various different formulations become gradually clearer on this matter as his *œuvre* advances and all point in the same direction. In 1763, Kant is preoccupied by the experience of breaking the law, noting that it presupposes both the recognition of the law and the reality of the force which contravenes it. In the *Groundwork to the Metaphysic of Morals* (1785) and the *Critique of Practical Reason* (1788), he defines both the freedom of the will and respect as negative feelings, that is as products of reason which 'demolish the presumption' of sensibility by casting aside its demands – this casting-aside being the consequence of the paradoxical presence of the unconditional in sensible existence, a mode of being which Kant continues to refer to as pathological. In his late works, such as the *Essay on Radical Evil* (1793), that notorious chapter of *Religion Within the Bounds of Mere Reason*, the very concept of an evil that is radical but not original makes the disposition to evil into a mode of deliberate resistance to our prior inscription within the order of the law. An original will to evil, or a will to destroy the law, is declared to be 'manifestly impossible', which is to say that radical evil must be attributed to a will which runs counter to that which lies at its very foundation. Kant returns to the logic of real conflict as the way of negotiating logically this relation to the law which is always accompanied 'in the men that we are' by an awareness of its being infringed. This then is one side of the guilt which, according to Kant, forms the foundation of the human being as such, including even the criminal behind bars: we are taken by surprise by an unconditional authority which prescribes what we owe and before which we are always at fault.

What is the relation between serial universality and the unconditional?

Yet there is, according to Kant, another side to our relation to the law: the suppresssion of the pathological, of our sensibility and its peculiar effects upon us. This is the anthro-pological condition which makes every intention to act in a certain way into a pretext for the logical exercise that is the universalization of its maxim. Even if our acts are different and specific in concrete terms, the fact that they are capable of being subjected to the test of the universalizability of their maxim, makes them into mere fodder for the formalism of the law – and this is how the moral subject becomes a person, an entity for whom the law has value, irrespective of his particular wishes. One person is worth neither more nor less than another – this is part of the definition of the moral and legal subject – that is, the universality of the person is supposed to be the rational explanation, or commentary, running alongside the experience of being overtaken by an unconditional law, a law which suppresses our pathological side. The law holds good for every human being. This does not mean that the actions of my sensibility are always overtaken by the law but that, whatever the acts I perform, their moral worth is determined only by being confronted with a universal imperative before which they are all equal and before which all those subject to the law are likewise equal. This universalization of the maxim of our actions as a way of testing their moral worth transforms the experience of being found at fault before an unconditional imperative into the relative non-differentiation of the content of our acts with respect to the universal status they may attain for a will. Thus, in the first instance, guilt is the presence of the unconditional in the conditional, while in the second, guilt is the occasion of this redefinition of desire as will – provided that our desires offer no more than opportunities for the definition of a universal. The inclinations of our sensibility are, in this second instance, mere pretexts for definitions of principle, which is quite different from the experience of being at fault before an authority which is both transcendant and foundational. The unconditional is our surprise at finding ourselves before the law; the universal is the formal test which submits our acts to a common standard and by way of which subjects become persons of equal worth, or indeed identical worth, in the eyes of the law: 'Act in such a way that the maxim of your action could always at the same time serve as the law of a possible human world.' Is it not plain to see that the idea of being at fault before a founding imperative is entirely distinct, in rational terms, from this formal process by which acts and subjects acquire equal worth on account of their being universalizable? But when we read Kant, we tend to take these two aspects of his ethics together, as though they were one and the same thing and we ask no further questions. The 'for any man' seems to us to be the natural explanation for the experience of being at fault before the absolute imperative. Yet in logical terms, the fact that the imperative is unconditional has nothing to do with the serial universality of acts and subjects before the law. Each of these ideas is clear and they are distinct one from the other.

What then is responsible for this false sense of sameness, if not the fact that the only point in common between these two aspects of morality is the suppression of sensibility? The unconditional requirement only becomes one with the test of the universalizability of the maxim of our acts if we think of both in terms of methodically casting aside the pathological. The unconditional is the experience of an internal rupture, caused by the upsurge of a commandment which forms the very foundation of our being. The universal is the non-differentiation of cases and subjects produced by the formal test to which we submit our acts. The unconditional and the universal only become the same if they have the same cause – the suppression of the pathological.

The ethics of the universal: truth of a concept or truth of a fantasy?

An unconditional imperative came to light in the analysand's dream with which I began. She had to give up a man she loves, even if this meant 'going to the abattoir', yet no universalizing authority made this one, necessary, renunciation into an example of a trial fit for every human being. The substitution of one object for another was the dream's way of opening up the possibility of a separation when one was called for. It may be objected that the imperative in question is of a different kind from Kant's categorical imperative, that it is still a conditional imperative. Yet in so far as it makes an unconditional demand for something to be given up, it is of the same order. The difference between the need to effect a separation and the moral imperative lies in the fact that the former lacks the backing of a transcendental authority. Rather, the obligation appears simply as a stark necessity, bound up with the departure of a man she loves, a departure she must acknowledge if she is not to go mad and hallucinate that he is there when he is not. Yet this does not correspond to the juridical aspect of the categorical imperative, which defines, in principle, an order of obligation superior to any factual necessity. This juridical aspect supposedly establishes our relation to the law, which forms the basis of our humanity; thus any feelings of suffering engendered by the presence of the law when it casts aside our desires is simply a consequence of what Kant calls our autonomy, that is, our belonging to a juridical order which breaks definitively with the various forms of servitude that characterize the pathological. Yet the analysand's dream expresses disbelief at the possibility of a definitive break of this sort, one accomplished once and for all. In this dream, the fact that she is forced unconditionally to give something up does not lead to an idealization of the principle which demands this of her. This is precisely why, in the process of substitution, one of the qualities of the first object (no car) is retained and transferred to the second (the other man has a nice car). This avoids idealizing the principle which forces her to give up the object. The act of giving up must occur without the reality of her love becoming detached from a principle of an autonomy which would deny that love or relegate it to the realm of the pathological. But by the same token, there is no serialization of objects in this dream: objects are only made equivalent to one another when they are dismissed by a law which creates an opposition between facts and principles. In the nightmare I have analysed, by contrast, the dreamer can move from one object to another because she has established an imaginary bridge – and also that there is a difference – between the two objects. Our dreamer takes her men one by one, to paraphrase Don Juan's motto, yet the arithmetic of her desire is quite different from that of this male hero. It is a question for her of being able to make the transition from one singular object to another while acknowledging her loss, even if the blow is softened somewhat by the wit of substitution. The experience which psychoanalysts call castration – the fact that our desires are not omnipotent and that this strikes us as nightmarish – does not naturally lend itself to an attempt to formalize existence which would enable us to decide in advance what we ought to give up in order for our lives to to be held fast by principles that would save us from nasty surprises.

Thus Kant's observation that women lack a moral sense could be developed as follows: for women, the process of reining in the pretensions of the pathological – our desires – takes place without facts being devalued in favour of principles. In other words, there is no idealization of the principle which calls for something to be given up, even when it is necessary for something to be given up. We might accordingly ask whether the difference between fact and the principles which judge them is not itself a construction – an interesting one, for sure, in that it enables the particular form of giving up known as autonomy, but relative, in its 'truth', to certain structures of desire, to those which conspire to make objects of desire interchangeable in order that one particular object may be given up. Were that the case, we would be dealing with the truth of a fantasy – one inseparable from the particular type of instinctual transformation that it enables – and not the truth of a concept. Clearly, the categorical imperative makes intellectual sense to women no less than men. Yet because, in practice, it is always accompanied by this effect of casting-aside, exercised against our sensible faculty of desiring, the question arises of whether the explanation of its power of obligation in terms of universal applicability does not in fact depend upon that which, in certain organizations of desire, demands both the subjugation of the pathological in favour of a serial, or 'one by one', approach, and simultaneously, a definitive, 'once and for all', separation between these empirical desires and the imperative which allows them to be dismissed *en bloc*.

If there is common ground between Kant and Sade, as Lacan has suggested, does this not lie in the characteristic connection between, on the one hand, the role of a law which only functions unconditionally by dismissing the sensible once and for all, thereby instigating the rule of principle and, on the other hand, the repeated exercise of this particular test of strength, on one object after another, that is universally, the casting aside of one's own desires or those of another?

What is striking about Sade's *La Philosophie dans le boudoir*, Molière's *Don Juan* and Kant's *Critique of Practical Reason* is, in all three cases, the remarkable parallel between the arrangement of objects of desire into an indefinite series and the sacrifice of all these objects in the name of an ideal posited as absolute but which differs in each of the three. In Sade's case, it is the libertine's pleasure, which is validated only by its expression, which justifies sacrificing anything, including the other's charm and the subject's attachments. In the case of Don Juan, as Monique Schneider has emphasised, his revelling in a momentous series of conquests remains subject to a clause which will curtail his pleasure at the moment when a 'pretty face' appears to demand that the entire series be cast aside.[6] 'When a pretty face asks me to, even had I had ten thousand, I would give them all' (Act I, Scene II). Finally, in the case of Kant, we are well acquainted with the idea that the 'deed of reason', by bringing us within the compass of the rational will, relegates our every desire to the domain of pleasure and displeasure. Because pleasure and displeasure cannot be determined *a priori*, our desires and all their particular characteristics pale into insignificance, since it is only their ability to serve as the matter for a non-contradictory law of a possible human world which inscribes them within the moral order.

There is room for further discussion about whether the term sacrifice is wholly appropriate in each case as a way of characterizing the detachment of the unconditional from the serial universality of the terms which it relegates. This point deserves close attention, for on it alone rides the difference between Kantian rigorism, Don Juan's bravado and Sadian impassivity. But it is worth noting that each of these options may be described in terms of the same logic of the universal and the unconditional which governs the determination of the Highest Good. Does this mean that women, or people identifying as women, are capable of acting without referring to this Highest Good of the philosophers, even if, as in Kant's case, it is purely formal?

Conclusion: is thought gendered?

What is gender-specific in thought is the way that fantasies connect with concepts, the process by which particular thoughts, having first been elaborated in a particular, subjective, context, subsequently become detached from that context. This process of detachment, which should be viewed here as a mode of transition, does not follow straightforwardly from the genesis or history of the idea in question. The notion that the thinking subject could be present in the genesis but absent from the result is far from convincing. Rather, we are forced to question this simplistic opposition between history and structure in the course of this very investigation into the connections between fantasies and concepts, connections which are always active when a text is read and interpreted.[7] An awareness of the various ways in which the transition between fantasies and concepts can be effected encourages a tendency to characterize particular ideas not in terms of their universal aspect but rather in terms of how they became detached from the instinctual life of the thinker. Thought is, very probably, universal – but this is perhaps the least interesting way of approaching it, for we remain blind to the way in which particular thoughts become detached from their thinkers. To focus on the universal is to erase the traces of this process of production. Whenever a particular system of thought presents itself as universal, by so doing it tacitly performs this very act of erasure, wiping away the traces of the relation between fantasy and concept, a relation which nonetheless remains active in the finished product. The view that thought comes into being as the product of a constructive process – whether in the case of conceptual thought such as Kant's or Lacan's, visual thought such as Leonardo da Vinci's, or the oneiric thought of dreams – implies we ought to pay attention to those aspects of a particular system of thought which bear the hallmarks of contingency. For deduction alone will get us nowhere in the attempt to establish how a concept displaces the play of instincts in the thinker (their 'sensibility', in Kantian terms) when it builds on this foundation. For example, the Kantian principle according to which 'Nobody can know *a priori* which representation will be accompanied by pleasure and which by pain', bound up as it is with the opposition between pathological and rational determinations of the will, is itself a displacement of the melancholic fantasies which govern Kant's entire anthropology – nothing is constant in the realm of sensibility[8] – for it arranges those objects which might interest our sensibility into a series in which each is equivalent to the other in the eyes of a law which downplays the differences between them. The conceptual structure of the *Critique of Practical Reason* is bound up with the logic of this movement which erases its own contingency by declaring victorious the universality of the Deed of Reason. Conversely, when one stops ignoring the transitions between fantasies and concepts, of which the text is the performance, the self-proclaimed universality of the theoretical edifice known as 'practical reason' emerges as a construction which is called for, in part, by a series of conceptual weaknesses. The same is true, as we have demonstrated, in aesthetics, in the transition between disinterested appreciation and a non-conceptual universal. Even in a mode of thought which claims to be universal – indeed especially in this case – there will be assertions which cannot be justified in terms of the conceptual framework that is being elaborated. And this absence of justification, this incapacity on the part of rational thought to fully justify itself is where it begins to be creative.[9] For its creative, constructed,[10] part emerges out of the fantasies which sustain it, albeit while modifying themselves along the paths of displacement that are grammar, style, logic and the inherent inventiveness of the conceptual mode. These connections between fantasies and concepts, or instincts and concepts, make for a measure of contingency in every thought, which is precisely why thought lies mid-way between an architectonic and a hodge-podge. As Kant and, more recently, Deleuze, have both said, to think rationally is to construct problems. When these problems are worked on conceptually, they gain a common intelligibility because they represent transformations of subjective questions, ones which the thinker may not choose to address, into a conceptual framework which serves as a place of convergence and misrecognition for differing fantasy structures. This transformation and this misrecognition are both at stake in any reading of philosophical texts. Lacan's theory of sexual difference emerges in accordance with a similar logic. The initial choice of a particular anthropology privileges certain features of the way in which objects are substituted in male sexuality. Then comes a reworking of the idea of the unconditional by way of a confrontation between Kant and Sade, and between Kant and Freud's myth of origins in *Totem and Taboo*; then we have the appeal to Frege in an attempt to conceptualize identification and formalize the positions of each sex in terms of this framework. Finally, the universality of the conceptual framework is asserted and the ways in which it came into being are thereby erased.[11]

The question arises of whether the conception of thought which erases the connections between fantasy and theory, by declaring ideas to be universal, is itself masculine; and conversely, whether the conception of thinking which draws attention to these transitions between fantasy and theory can be qualified as feminine. Yet such a move would amount to yet another attempt to naturalize or essentialize sexual difference and would involve a misunderstanding of how the sexual identity of thinking human beings is reflected in the open space of a conceptual field. The elements of sexual identity which do become incorporated into systems of thought are never particular arguments or positions, set in stone forever. The sexual identity of the thinker does determine their choice of the contingencies in their system of thought and indeed the way in which these will be partially covered over by the systematizing force of the constructive process. This contingency is what makes a system of thought both unjustifiable and creative, arising as it does out of the play between masculine and feminine (terms which do not refer to essences) in the postulates of any given system of thought: they seek each other out and stand momentarily transfixed before one another, nowhere more than in those propositions which the system cannot itself recognize as contingent while it is engaged in the task of elaborating a new field of thought.

Yet it is no coincidence that it is been women – or men both perverse and creative – who have pinpointed the weak points, the unjustifiable elements, in given systems of rational thought. Nor is it a coincidence that the present study has read Kant rather differently from the way he has been read in the past, the canonical readings having been by men. The reason is that, for a women who reads Kant (and indeed many other philosophers), even if the intellectual coherence of his thought is clear, this by no means makes it compelling. If the moment of universality in a system of thought marks the site of the most determined attempt to erase the link between fantasies and concepts, it should be apparent why women, rather than taking on trust the supposed universality of reason, will choose instead to bring to light the extent to which the system's presumption of universality rests on a blindness to its own inner workings. It is no coincidence, then, if it tends to be women, or men whose sexual identity resists being placed in the official category 'men', who choose to emphasise these points of transition between fantasies and concepts within systems of rational thought.

It is not possible both to define a system of thought in terms of the universality of its concepts and simultaneously to be attentive to the way in which its concepts become detached from the play of instincts which are transformed in this claim to universality. These two approaches are mutually exclusive and the necessary, but unconscious, choice of one rather than the other is itself invested with fantasy. The reason why some people find it necessary to bring this aspect of systems of thought to the fore – an aspect we shall call detachment from the work – is not always because they consider the claims to universality made by these systems to be bogus but because this universality is only one of their many facets. For these individuals need to reopen a question which the philosophers of the universal have foreclosed, by describing the way in which systems of thought actually function and how this differs from the image which such systems project of themselves. But once decribed, this connection between fantasy and concept is not (any more than the concept of a universal) either masculine or feminine. For the reality of sexual difference is not ontological: it continues to produce effects in registers of thought in which it no longer features as such.[12] Thus it can only ever be in a provisional sense that a philosophical argument or a particular way of formulating a problem seems relevant solely to a specifically masculine or feminine question. But there can be no dispensing with this provisionality. Sexual difference is inscribed in conceptual thought as the necessity of a contingency.

Translated by Oliver Davis

Notes

1 Kant, *Observations on the Feeling of the Beautiful and Sublime*, tr. John T. Goldthwait (Oxford: University of California Press, 1991), p. 81.
2 Freud, 'Instincts and Their Vicissitudes', *Penguin Freud Library*, vol. 11, *On Metapsychology*, 113–38, p. 119.
3 Lacan, *Le Séminaire*, XI, *Les Quatre Concepts fondamentaux de la psychanalyse* (Paris: Seuil, 1973), p. 153. On this point, see Monique David-Ménard, *L'Hystérique entre Freud et Lacan. Corps et langage en psychanalyse* (Paris, 1983), p. 205.
4 Lacan, *Le Séminaire*, VIII, *Le Transfert* (Paris: Seuil, 1991), pp. 325–6.
5 Lacan, *Le Séminaire*, XI, op. cit., p. 144.
6 Monique Schneider, *Don Juan et le procès de la séduction* (Paris: Aubier, 1994), pp. 124–5.
7 This is an issue in the case of the relation between the way in which laws in theoretical physics are written down and the way they are read. Cf. Françoise Balibar, 'Traduire, dit-elle . . . La traduction, une affaire de femmes?', *L'Exercice du savoir et la différence des sexes*, pp. 63–75.
8 The underlying aim of psychoanalysis, by contrast, is precisely to demonstrate that there is a certain constancy in the realm of sensibility, that what characterizes a particular human subject is the law which determines the objects of his or her desire. The fact that the subject may be unaware of this *a priori* act of determination by no means undermines the hypothesis, indeed quite the reverse. Thus Kant and all the other philosophers of desire failed to distinguish between this act of determination and the subject's mastery of what determines him or her.
9 This view should be contrasted with the work of Didier Vaudène on the role of the unknown in the structure of scientific theories. Cf. 'Écriture et formalisation (un effet de finitude ordinaire)', *Césure*, no. 10.
10 Compare the understanding of 'construction' in the above with what Étienne Balibar calls the 'universel fictionnel' [the fictional universal], one of the three aspects of universality which he identifies. See 'Ambiguous Universality' in *Différences: A Journal of Feminist Cultural Studies*, 7:1 (1995); this article appeared in French as 'Universals' in Étienne Balibar, *La Crainte des masses* (Paris: Galilée, 1997), pp. 421–54.
11 This is also the gist of Michel Tort's interpretation of Lacan's remarks on sexual difference in 'Le Différent', *Symboliser. Psychanalystes*, no. 33, *Revue du Collège de psychanalystes*, 1989, pp. 9–16.
12 On the paradoxes of sexual difference in the conceptual field, cf. Geneviève Fraisse, *La Différence des sexes* (Paris: Presses Universitaires de France, 1996), especially chs. 4, 5 and 8.

Part 4

THE RATIONAL AND
SCIENTIFIC SUBJECT

INTRODUCTION

In this section six philosophers give different accounts of one of the questions that lies at the heart of this collection, that of the nature of knowing; five of these consider the relationship between rationality, philosophy and science and the gender of the human subject.

Françoise d'Eaubonne explores directly the history of women's exclusion from the realm of philosophy; she argues that the French (and English) use of 'man' to include both men and women gives a false impression of interchangeability which is revealed as soon as the term 'woman' is used to replace it in certain significant contexts. She takes for her purposes writings about the Nazi death camps, an extreme situation which shows up particularly vividly our reactions to any change of language usage. It is a situation which serves to demonstrate the most fundamental of human needs, that of relations with others, which frequently take precedence over what might initially appear more basic needs such as those for food. This, d'Eaubonne claims, shows that the fight for survival ultimately exalts rather than abolishing the 'relational'. She goes on to argue that the attempt exemplified in the death-camps to reduce men to the status of objects has been going on in other disguised forms 'since time immemorial' in the case of women. This objectification of women represents a form of what she calls 'repressive defence', that is to say, a tactic of masked violence designed to reduce women's potential to threaten male supremacy and dominance. The subordination of women in both theory and practice as the 'Other' sex, always relative to men, has however only recently become a subject of philosophical disquiet. Their exclusion from the realm of philosophy and reason itself is a symbolic representation of their general exclusion and subordination, and is part of the violence entailed in any discourse of Sameness. This discourse may no longer be considered valid, d'Eaubonne argues, but it persists, and can only be overcome by a deconstruction of totalitarian, phallogocentric dualism and the concomitant establishment of the legitimacy of relational need, that is, the primacy of human relations. This will not only free women from violence and oppression but will thereby also free men from the threat of retaliatory denunciation always endemic in dualistic oppression.

Geneviève Fraisse focusses rather on women's exclusion from historical agency. Her essay on the constitution of the subject stresses the fundamental ambiguity of the term 'constitution', hovering between passive and active, as both material composition and act of establishing. Like Françoise Collin, she focuses on the paradoxical implications of women's claims to agency and subjecthood at a moment when philosophy and politics are precisely questioning the pertinence

269

of the subject as a fundamental reference point. She explains the necessity for the promotion of the feminist subject in the light of different types of discrimination against the female subject, be this explicit prohibition, or implicit and unacknowledged exclusion, as in the establishment of so-called 'universal' suffrage in France in 1848. Fraisse delineates and theorises the implications of the feminist individual's attempt to become a subject, and to escape her position as object of exchange for a more collective kind of sorority. Unlike the class struggle however, where a classless Utopia is at least thinkable, there is no possibility of even imagining a sexless society. The feminist subject seeks to neutralise discrimination but she does not exclude the recognition of sexual difference. The feminist struggle ultimately seeks its own dissolution.

Michèle Le Doeuff continues this historical and philosophical line of thought in her reflections on the way in which women's mode of thinking is always downgraded, however it is described. In *Le Sexe du savoir*, she argues that reason and thought are not specifically male domains, and that the institutional domination of philosophical education by men impedes the freedom to know and the critical exercise of thought for both men and women. In this extract she explores the history of the notion of intuition: etymologically derived from *intueor*, to consider, it was originally epistemologically neutral. For Descartes it was 'the conception of a pure and attentive mind', distinct and beyond doubt, as in the intuition of the nature of a triangle. For Rousseau and the German Romantics, it was the form of divine knowledge, immediate and without need of reasoning. But Hegel preferred the 'patient work' of the concept and downgraded intuition to an unselfconscious means of thinking, not productive of knowledge. Since then intuition has come to imply unverifiable and unjustified, and to be applied especially to women. But Le Doeuff is quick to demonstrate what she describes as Geneviève Lloyd's 'error' in attributing the downgrading of intuition to seventeenth-century rationalism and opposing it to Cartesian methods. As she has already shown, Descartes prized intuition, and Lloyd has over-simplified. Le Doeuff refuses the commonplace association of rationality and the masculine, whether women are encouraged to aspire to its rigour or to reject it.

Françoise Balibar and Nathalie Charraud both question the view held by some feminist theorists that contemporary science is masculine. As a scientist herself, Balibar argues firmly against the position, put forward by Luce Irigaray in 'la mécanique des fluides',[1] that we should aim for a feminine science. In her essay, 'Is there a feminine science?' she reflects on the vexed question of the relationship between women and science which, she claims, is an issue of far greater moment for feminists in Britain and the US than in France. Balibar supports the idea that science is not a purely intellectual, disembodied activity, but considers it ultimately dangerous to the women's movement itself to move from this position to one that argues that science is *only* the expression of specific interests with no universal value, which can easily lead to the idea that women should not concern themselves with science at all. Nor does she espouse a simple view of the need to introduce a feminine perspective into science. Both these positions depend on different versions of a belief in the incompatibility of women and science as it is presently constituted which she contests. However, she does maintain that women might be able to free science from the stranglehold of scientism in which she believes it is currently caught, and suggests in a memorable phrase that the women's liberation movement might also be a movement for the liberation of science.

Nathalie Charraud's essay on the 'Apparent subject, real subject' is included as an example of reflections on the question of science and gender from a scientist who is also a psychoanalyst. Like Balibar, Charraud too contests the idea that the subject is excluded from science, and further maintains that the gender of the subject is not biological in origin but is rather related in psychoanalytic terms to narcissistic satisfaction. Charraud defines her own approach as part of an attempt to elaborate a Lacanian epistemology starting from his reflection on science whch develops out of his distinction between the categories of the Real, the Imaginary and the Symbolic. She turns to a selection of scientists including Einstein and Marie Curie to contest the facile identification of masculine with the objective and feminine with the subjective. Indeed, Charraud's position is very different: she interprets the relation that exists between the subject and scientific knowledge in terms not of objectivity but rather of *jouissance*. She explores the writings of the scientists she has chosen and highlights their references to love, wonder, visionary delight, sensuality and beauty. In this way, Charraud opens reflection on the relation between women and science up to a broader reflection on subjectivity and ethics.

In conclusion to this section, Anne Fagot-Largeault considers a different aspect of the relationship between science and the subject: that of bio-ethics and some of the major deontological questions raised by research on living human beings. Her essay provides a timely reminder of the importance of the questions under discussion, and of the indissoluble link between theory and practice, in that these philosophical issues impact so dramatically upon our lives and ultimately, perhaps, our right to life. The survival of the human species itself can, she argues, be an ethical value only if it is deemed that 'man contributed to the perfection of the universe'. Fagot-Largeault points out that even the most apparently self-evident goods, such as health, are only ever hypothetical: science can never prove, for example, that an increase in life-expectancy outweighs the pleasures of smoking. Such an assumption involves an alliance of puritan values and economic calculations. It posits health as a value for humanity, which cannot be proven by science alone. Fagot-Largeault tackles the question of the existence or otherwise of 'human nature', and argues that evolution itself can be responsible for the development of apparently altruistic as well as apparently egotistical behaviour, in so far as both may be useful to the species. In this sense, morality itself may be genetically determined, and rational morality may be an illusion. The danger however of taking evolutionary development as a positive direction is that it risks justifying everything if we feel that nature is somehow 'complicit with our moral ends'. Fagot-Largeault takes a more ambivalent position which recognises that scientific understanding will face us with having to choose which values we want to keep, and that it will provide some 'objective bases' for our choice but no principle of selection. She herself does not believe that knowledge itself suffices as an overarching ethic. However, science cannot be neutral in relation to values, since the choice of scientific research implies an 'ethics of knowledge'and posits truth as a fundamental value, which in turn suggests an ethics of existentialist inspiration, and the recognition that it is we who create our own values. The danger of the promotion of the values of science lies in the risk of scientific imperialism, in the promotion of science over all other values, artistic or poetic, and the refusal of pluralism. Does

271

experimental science have the monopoly on truth, she asks? 'We do not . . . have absolute criteria for science any more than we do for morality.'

Note

1 Luce Irigaray, *Ce sexe qui n'en est pas un,* Paris: Minuit, 1977.

17

FRANÇOISE D'EAUBONNE

Françoise d'Eaubonne is a feminist theorist, historian and novelist, author of over fifty works, and widely translated. She is General Secretary of SOS Sexism. She is also the founder of what in 1974 she called 'eco-feminism', which contends that the oppression of women and of nature are mutually reinforcing, and that women's struggle can contribute to the fight to save and protect the environment. She was a friend of Simone de Beauvoir, Violette Leduc and Nathalie Sarraute.

Her works include the following:

Une Femme témoin de son siècle: Germaine de Staël, Paris: Flammarion, 1966.

Les Écrivains en cage, Paris: A. Balland, 1970.

Le féminisme ou la mort, Paris: P. Horay, 1974.

Les femmes avant le patriacat, Paris: Payot, 1976.

Écologie, féminisme: révolution ou mutation?, Paris: ATP, 1978.

Contre violence ou la résistance a l'État, Paris: Tiercé, 1978.

Une femme nommée Castor: mon amie Simone de Beauvoir, Paris: Encre, 1986.

Féminin et Philosophie (Une allergie historique), Paris: L'Harmattan, 1997.

THE FEMININE AND PHILOSOPHY

> Man discovers himself to be the one who needs nothing other than
> need itself in order – denying that which denies him – to maintain the
> primacy of human relations.
>
> (Maurice Blanchot, *L'Expérience-limite*)

> It is no simple chance that the great civilisation of homosexuality,
> Greece, should have also given rise to the cults of Sameness and, above
> all, of Logos.
>
> (Stephen Zagdanski, *Le Sexe de Proust*)

The epigram from Maurice Blanchot which opens this essay also features on the back
cover of the re-edition of Robert Antelme's book on Nazi death camps, *L'Éspèce
humaine*. The 'man' in question has been reduced to 'stealing vegetable peelings': that
is, dragged down to his absolute human minimum, to a minimum of humanity, and this
by the very thing that denies him and which must be denied.

Differing in this respect from other languages such as German or Russian, the French
word for 'man' describes both the male of the species and the human race in general.
In principal, then, 'le féminin' is subsumed within 'l'homme'. According to a precept
which will be treated in due course, this absorption is part of a wider function critical
to linguistics as a whole; at the same time, the function's abolition of differentiation
obscures its intent. Paradoxically, this universalism eliminates the second term in play:
instead the Earth becomes populated by the same exclusive masculinity found in
Athenian democracy's vision of the origins of mortals.

Read with due regard for its accuracy and sincerity, the Blanchot quotation raises
the following sorts of preliminary questions: 'How can we possibly deny something so
powerful that it reduces man to stealing vegetable peelings?'; or, 'are relations or survival
the primal human need?, and do these two needs come into being simultaneously?'

However, in addition to these initial reflections there also arises another issue. For
example, in the case of Nazi deportees does the figure of the man as a microcosm of all
humans (le déporté) apply equally to the deported female (la déportée)? That is, does it
describe not only the dead man walking of Dachau, but also the dead woman walking of
Ravensbruck?

Linguistic convention dictates that these kinds of questions seem rhetorical. By the same turn, it is easy to imagine the kind of response they might generate: a perplexed shrug of the shoulders, perhaps, and a 'Well, of course'. After all, 'man' refers to both sexes of the human species, and in the face of such questioning an interlocutor would like as not hastily move on to some previous issue. However, it seems to me that this supposedly superfluous distinction is related to the question of the primacy of need mentioned earlier. That is to say that to my mind the need for survival and the need for human relations are perhaps – and nothing more than perhaps – equally manifest but unequally observed, and this in accordance with sexual difference. What's more, it would appear that the only thing stopping us from flagging up this kind of problem is exactly this negation (for it is undoubtedly a negation that we are dealing with here) of one of the two terms in play. In turn, the negation is not just philological but also philosophical, leading as it does into an order in which it is possible to reduce *a human being* to the level of stealing vegetable peelings.

Now, I am not proposing here simply to open the back door to a certain kind of outmoded feminism or pseudo-feminism in which, as at the start of the twentieth century, various feminine characteristics are specified and exalted. In this scheme of things, the singularity of relational need as primary instinct would prevail over the *egotistic* need for survival at any cost, here a masculine characteristic.[1] Rather, we also know that each and every human being exists and subsists in a world in which this animal instinct to survive – an instinct found right down to the lowest rungs of the evolutionary ladder – is exacerbated by an infinite range of threats. What is particular about the human race is that whereas in other species relationships with other members is a simple extension of the survival instinct (as, for example, in the 'rat king'),[2] in humans this relational tropism extends far beyond practical collectivity.

This type of human-specific solidarity would appear to be one the of evolutionary characteristics that leads to civilisation; indeed, it may well account for Patrick Tort's assertion that, according to Darwin, 'natural selection selects civilisations that are in fact opposed to it.' Analogous to the twist of the Moebius loop, the dynamics of this distortive mechanism might in turn serve to explain in materialist – or at least anti-idealist – terms the ethics that structure primitive Communism.[3]

It does not seem to be the case that this relational instinct – which as an object of study has been relatively neglected by the social sciences, tainted as they remain by Freudianism and by the endeavours of what Sartre in his *Questions de méthode* calls those 'lazy Marxists' – manifests itself according to a subject's gender: rather, age appears to be the determining factor. Close in this respect to young monkeys, the human child exhibits an order of need in which affect and physical contact override even food and water. If deprived of those who provide for her, an infant female monkey will let herself waste away and die, even if her need for physical survival continues to be met. A French journalist working in the famine-torn wastes of Bangladesh was left stunned by the experience of offering food to skeletal children: ignoring the food, they instead clambered all over her arms and legs, searching for the caresses which were for them as vital as water to a plant. While this instinct is most visibly evident in the infant, who is still not far from animal symbiosis with the maternal, that is not to say that for an adult reduced 'to stealing vegetable peelings' the primacy of need for relations with other

275

humans constitutes a return to the symbiosis of childhood. Even less is it a distortion of the libido, which is one of the first instincts to perish in the grip of famine (such was the motive behind the inhuman dietary regime followed in monasteries).

In one of his short stories, Jean-Louis Curtis uses documents such as *L'Espèce humaine* to build an imaginary death camp in which – and this is a device original to Curtis – any move by the prisoners to come into physical contact with each other is punished by electric shock.[4] The punishment does not, however, succeed in eliminating these pathetic attempts at contact, which are obviously devoid of any erotic charge. This appetite for proximity with others, for reassurance that one's own singularity is not mere solipsism, will endure any amount of degradation, any level of physical deterioration. Long forgotten if not dead, the primacy of the relational instinct is thus revived: for this is an instinct whose origin is easily camouflaged by a network of familial and erotic affects. In this civilisation which, contrary to Darwinian hypotheses, offers such weak resistance to the natural selection of origins,[5] the instinct is cloaked by the social jungle of daily life.

To my mind, it is not insignificant that of our contemporary writers it should have been a woman who, through the use of Sartre, first attempted to establish the primacy of the relational within the discipline of psychoanalysis. While that is not to say that femininity necessarily enjoys a special engagement with this instinct, in documentary research – and above all in laboratories of Abjection such as prisons, concentration camps, famine fields and so on – it does appear that the human female is more responsive to the expressions of the instinct and its need than her male Other, even if she has no inherent hold over it, or at least only develops one as a result of social forces. In other words, she is not fatally predisposed to exhibit the symptoms of the instinct and to satisfy the need, but is simply able to recognise and refer to them. All of which leads, on a scholarly level, to research such as that carried out by Betty Canon.

Canon stresses that the dynamic of satisfaction/frustration central to traditional theories of the drives is unable to explain the numerous interpersonal phenomena which are also observed. She cites studies made by Spitz (1945–65) that demonstrate the consequences of a childhood break in the maternal bond, and which resonate with the previous remark about young monkeys. Moreover, Spitz's work shows that it is impossible to understand this break by simply using Freudianism (which would see it as the interruption of aggressive libidinal discharge). In the same way, Freudianism cannot explain the infant's vital need for empathic responsibility or for its mirror image.[6] There thus emerges a pressing need to interpret human experience in terms of metaprincipals, 'in order to understand what being human actually means'.[7]

And yet in evoking these theories in the context of the Blanchot quotation we run into a serious potential objection. For example, the extract itself introduces a text whose aim is to present an ultimate claim of belonging to humanity as primordial among the supreme needs, as the last remnant of an otherwise denied and destroyed human specificity. But surely, given the circumstances, this claim of human membership is intimately entwined with the need to survive and persist, and with the negation of that which denies; a negation that the power of surrounding destruction has transformed into 'the only sacred'. Where, it could be argued, is there any allusion in Blanchot's comment to the relational instinct?

> There can be no doubt that it is still a question of egoism, but of an egoism without ego, in which man, desperate to survive . . . bears this need as one which no longer belongs to him, bears it as the need of virtually everybody; thus, life is the beginning and the end of the sacred.
>
> (Maurice Blanchot)

The sacralisation of this 'egoistic' need springs from the fact that the death of but one person makes for the victory of inhumanity, thereby in a sense tolling the death of every human.

> By denying us as men, the SS made us into historical objects which could no longer be the objects of simple of human relations . . . Individuals were so abstracted from the community . . . that, barely had these relations been traced out, they soon extended forth into history, as if they were the very paths – secret and narrow – that the prisoners were forced to follow.
>
> (Robert Antelme, op. cit.)

In this way, the bitter fight for survival – which tends in the short-term to favour self over the Other – does not actually lead to the abolition of the relational at all: on the contrary, the relational is the subject of its final exaltation. That is to say that this 'egoism without ego' is merely the form taken by a battle of the most barren desolation to maintain membership with the rest of the species. It is the link that joins up with all other egos against the reification of humanity, that most destructive and persistent tendency of historical dynamics.

Contrary to the surprised shrug of the shoulders and 'but of course' evoked in the first few pages, I would like the reading of my recent remarks about the quotations from Blanchot and Antelme to stress the shocked indignation that would be caused by replacing the word 'man' with the word 'woman'. I would like us to pause a moment on the perplexing questions that may be generated by this discomfort: for, if 'man' really does represent the human neuter, how, culturally speaking, is the feminine distinguishable from the universal? To the point that in works aiming to treat so fundamental a subject of reflection as *L'Espèce humaine*, there thus emerges an implicit and problematic connotation. While nothing of the kind would be aroused by a text written in the masculine form, it would leave a feeling of incompleteness and surprise if in the same text one were to read that *woman*, reduced to stealing vegetable peelings, becomes a microcosm of humanity where the passion to survive at all costs can be identified with a claim to belong to the human race. The reader would look for some kind of detail to qualify this assertion, some local specificity: is there, for example, a side effect relating to the question of sexuality?; or an allusion to the mediatised event of maternity? In what ways was the SS 'able *to make us into historical objects*' by denying us as *women*? And with whom would simple human relations remain forbidden? In addition to the obvious question of sexual exploitation by rape, was this achieved through the suppression of the menses and of those attributes associated with seduction? These are the sorts of issues raised by this rather different reading, and which, as with every other demonstration of nominalist myopia, contradict with such force the 'Well, of course' of false claims to universalism. This in turn takes us back to a firmly anchored convention that thinks of the feminine in terms of a separate category, so that the refusal to allow it access to the symbolic keeps the feminine outside the realm of the universal.

We thus find ourselves in the following situation: while totalitarian ignominy continues today in equally violent and murderous forms – for example, the current madness of Islamic fundamentalism, in which the category of women suffers the same attempts at reduction and dehumanisation as that of the Jews in Nazi death camps – it cannot be said that such ignominy only seeks to reduce human groups to the state of historical objects, even outside of any exploitative intent or vision. Instead, even in these extreme cases the reification of the Other is unable to completely abolish the most basic human relations. As with the myth of Athenian origins, this is because it is marriage – even when temporary, even when restricted to a brief and sinister farce[8] – and, above all, procreation which make up the final, ultimately indestructible fragments of 'simple human relations'. The purpose of these remarks is to both debunk and denounce the universal tendency of cultures – cultures that were patriarchal yesterday, and 'filiarchal' today[9] – to eliminate one of the equation's two terms while at the same time maintaining a nominalist alibi. It shall be tirelessly repeated that, long before Fascism and Islamic fundamentalism, across a myriad variations of philosophy and ideology (religious or otherwise), and from subgroups to the great civilisations of the past, this tendency has contributed since time immemorial to locking the feminine sex within the same status of historical object aimed for by the SS in the management of sub-men. The strategy of reifying a sex able to *reduce* its other is a defence mechanism; the reduction itself, in symbolic terms, an act of castration.

Repressive defence, a tactic of which the masked passive violence does not always pay dividends, is not the dominant sex's only response to this terror as it leaps from Pandora's box. Rather, it also employs this same, inescapable fact: the presence of the Other. Historical philosophy testifies to this, and the new strategy is clearly determined by Thomas Aquinas. Joining with Aristotle in wonder at how 'plants and animals procreate not by seed but by virtue of their celestial bodies' (itself proof of procreation's peccant element), the theologian proposes this path of salvation for the sinful sex – incriminated as it was by Tertullian[10] and Origen alike – by working from the Aristotelian reduction: 'Woman, a truly defective and accidental being, was created only in order that man be free from contingencies, and that he be allowed to accede to the mind.'[11]

In the same way that Pascal talks of a good usage of illness, the early Christian philosopher wants to clear Creation of its accidents and defectiveness, and he rediscovers in the presence of this Other the legitimacy that had eluded Tertullian. This mode of thinking relates closely to Plato's description of the usefulness of a category which allows man (in the masculine form) to be relieved from daily concerns in order that he may apply himself to his civic duties. Ovid also reasoned in this way, while Creon confined himself to repressive defence. The perspective of Thomas Aquinas, however, can be distinguished by the fact that whilst ancient man was dedicated to serving the State, Christians are devoted to the Creator. Certainly, the 'contingencies' of Aquinas are not those of Sartre: aside, it is true, from the body, for the saint the limits of freedom have nothing to do with this space or historical moment. It is simply a question of the squalid problems of daily life, of the whole miserable network of lived experience, and of which the subject-sex is to be relieved by the defective and accidental sex. It is a fundamental shift in perspective for the age of Faith. For in the myth of Aristophanes' rationalisation of homosexuality, this subject-sex (which was sometimes freed – *horresco referens*! – by carnal exchange with its own kind) was able to turn to matters of the mind. Does Thomas Aquinas count the aforementioned exchange, this time with the Other, with the defective sex, among limitative contingencies? Saint Aquinas implicitly responds to this question through his approval of prostitution, which the moralist sees as a cesspool necessary 'to keep the palace from becoming a place of infection'. In this way, the female sex that is born accidentally or according to the humidity of the southern winds will have its servility justified by making possible man's spiritual freedom. All of which recalls that, in Pauline logic, 'It is better to marry than to burn'. However, Saint Paul nuances this consent with a concern: 'He who takes a wife is worried about pleasing her', he says, when this worry should be directed only to God. Such a reservation does not seem to affect Thomas Aquinas in his theory, so close to that of Aristophanes, of the masculine need to be relieved of contingencies; it never crossed the theologian's mind to please so much as his cleaning lady. The argument for salvation through slavery is in this case pursued to its extreme limits: although for man the Other will always represent the threat of diminution and sin, its role of slave conditions his freedom – which is no longer simply civic but also spiritual – while at the same time offering the sole justification for its own existence. Such was the salvation through subservience ceaselessly preached to abused wives by Saint Monica, the mother of Saint Augustine (his *Confessions*).

'The 'I' finds in the world a place and a home,' says Emmanuel Levinas. Thanks to the women's red-light district, man will keep his home uncontaminated. Through economic developments of which ideology composes but the superstructure, this process will doubtless extend throughout the dynamic of History. However, my argument is concerned with the way in which the original infrastructure – that is, the subordination of one sex by another – appears to arise at the same time as the first foundations of society and technology, thereby bearing just as much responsibility for one of the principal elements of Western philosophy: the allergy to the Other spoken of by Levinas.

Effectively, writes Levinas, this historical mode of thought 'is from its earliest days affected with a horror of the other *who remains other*': therein lies 'an insurmountable allergy'.[12] In turn, philosophy makes itself a 'place of Sameness'. And a place of violence, too, if indeed it is a question of violence when 'one acts as if one were alone in acting'.[13] Husserl never went beyond 'the moment of the supremacy of Sameness': it is perhaps this that explains the mistake made by Hannah Arendt – a disciple of his who is both a woman and a philosopher – with regard to the feminine.[14]

The astonishment generated by this discourse of Sameness – so fervently held by Thomas Aquinas after Aristophanes, and which, unlike other categories, was to undergo philosophical development in the following centuries – is but a very delayed phenomenon, appearing after the collapse of the successive systems on which Western supremacy was founded. The discourse itself has been maintained in a context of anxiety and penury in other territories of millennial patriarchy.

'Through the constant thought of difference in terms of opposition and symmetry which dooms her to oblivion, woman has been excluded from philosophy.'[15]

This is the clearest response to the amazement of someone like Alice Colanis, who collaborated on *Dialogue de femmes*, and who is not afraid of stating the obvious: writes Colanis, 'Throughout history we have not been the philosophical subjects that men have'. However, the same woman that talks of 'those two inseparable sisters, philosophy and History,' does not raise the question of how it is impossible for a human category to be rejected by one of these sisters without also being rejected by the other.

'Excluded from the reasoning of the city, to this day women continue to lead an existence without memory.'[16]

Derrida does not fail to stress that 'today, that which is called philosophy is the site of the greatest disparity between discourses.' This uncertainty – which reflects that of History, the Siamese sister crowned sovereign – is disputed down to the most archaic foundation of its existence: this 'insurmountable allergy to the Other'. This element of security and imperialism structures the discourse of Sameness – this thirsting for the Unique (*Erâd*) – perhaps linking man to his distant origins: it is the thing that most distinguishes his own aggressivity from that of animals, this need to be not simply strongest but also the only one (the survivor).[17]

Again in *Dialogue de femmes*, Catherine Valabrègue writes that, 'There are no women philosophers. Why? This is a statement of truth that must be reflected upon.' But this is a mistake, not a statement of truth, and it is one that the second part of this study proposes to rectify. The correct enquiry would be, '*Why* have there been so few women philosophers?' – to which we could first of all respond as Levinas's work does to Alice Colanis. However, a modification is necessary, and I will be guided from the outset by an observation made by Jean Bernard: namely, that the situation of philosophy has radically changed, and this in the same way as the so-called 'exact' sciences. From the very beginnings of Western thought, two currents have developed symbiotically: that of Archimedes, and that of Aristotle. Today, the acceleration and sophistication of the techniques of the former have largely exceeded the impact of the second, philosophical current. A philosopher may be reproached for being unfamiliar with the latest discoveries in astrophysics or quantum mechanics – but to this statement another must be added: for those sciences at the extreme tip of modern upheaval soon encounter the question of philosophy. Shall we not take our questioning right to the very sovereignty of mathematics? And in the latest endeavours of the supposed exact sciences, in subatomic physics, shall we not equally call into question the unshakeable determinism of the Parmenidian Einstein? In this time of general turbulence philosophy has indeed become a site of the most unexpected and conflicting discourses. The discourse of Sameness is no longer valid – and yet it persists.

It can be noted that dualism, which offered to Western thought two parallel rails, and along which its discourse formerly travelled so smoothly has, in corollary with those of History, come to experience successive derailments. After all, how can we continue to use a discourse based on 'opposition as a mode of symmetrical difference'? (This could equally be formulated as 'difference as a mode of harmonic opposition'.) On the level of sociological scholarship, this impossibility corresponds to an observation made by Marcel Mauss: 'We have written neither the sociology of women nor the sociology of men and women: we have written nothing but the sociology of men.'[18]

One cannot help but evoke the latest research into the nature of matter. Her devastating growth threatening to disrupt their own trajectory, today Philosophy and History have another sister: so-called exact science, spreading its multiform and unitary range from nuclear to astrophysics. Speaking fifty years ago of 'the impossibility of attributing rigorous determinism to a succession of phenomena on the corpuscular scale' (*L'Avenir de la science*, 1944), Louis de Broglie was the precursor of what Mauss expresses above in the field of sociology. The renouncement of determinism within subatomic calculations corresponds, in the study of humans, to the impossibility of establishing laws and rules as precise and thorough as those of an engineer working on the nineteenth-century dream of macrocosmic matter. From the sciences to the study of human society – to sociology and anthropology – the abandonment of old, reassuring formulas proves inevitable. Now at the end of the twentieth century, how can any kind of determinism based on symmetrical opposition really generate decent investigation of a human category, whatever its nature?

Contemporary philosophy can no more ignore the conquests and upheavals of the supposed exact sciences that it can the evolution of society and the political problems that it poses. One of the most striking features of our time, this latter factor has consigned philosophical idealism to oblivion. What Prigogine and Stengers call a 'new alliance' thus becomes necessary.

This is why we discover that totalitarianism, as such and independent from its content (which can range from the fertile economic analysis of socialism to the catastrophic aberrations of fascism), entails in sociology the same negativity as does determinism in the field of quantum calculations. In this way, totalitarianism reveals itself to be the last resort of the *discourse of Sameness*. In the same way that in subatomics the physicist can only go as far as probability, so too the researcher of new political truths cannot move beyond statistics.[19]

Here we are, then, confronted with the excess of the Other, and with the analogy between the human race and the field of the corpuscular. It is a question of breaking with the last resort of dualism, with the phallologos,[20] in order to uncover a perspective where – unlike the mode of opposition which has lead, and which in certain areas continues to lead, to the murderous eradication of the second term – the Other is no longer relative to the Same. Through this and this alone the Other will cease to threaten and denounce the Same that *thinks* it, that represses and obscures it – but which in so doing lays itself open to denunciation, increasing its own peril.

In this way, we will perhaps establish – and not *re*-establish – the legitimacy of relational need: that is, the primacy of human relations.

Translated by Stephen Forcer

Notes

1 For more on this moral specificity, see the entry under 'Woman' in Darwin's dictionary.
2 When rats finds themselves in danger, be it from plague or fire, half a dozen of them will come together and interlink their tails, thereby forming the figure of the 'rat king'. The exact mechanism behind this formation remains unknown.
3 Willi Durant has discussed this social order in which, in times of penury, the collectivity asserts itself so naturally that an individual member would rather die of hunger than not share.
4 Jean-Louis Curtis, *Un Saint au néon* (Julliard, 1956).

5 Written twelve years after *The Origin of Species, The Descent of Man* was completely misunderstood by Spencer and his fellow commentators. The work itself explains how, as soon as it reaches the point at which the weak are to be protected rather than destroyed, human evolution begins to resist the struggle for existence. Before urban development, primitive Communism provided an example of this process. Patrick Tort, an expert on Darwinism, has refuted the spurious interpretations of it.

6 Betty Canon, *Sartre et la psychanalyse* (PUF, 1993).

7 Ibid., p. 34.

8 Temporary marriage has been instituted by the mullahs of Iran as a valve for masculine urges.

9 Antoinette Fouque, "Il y a deux sexes," in *Lire la différence* (Éditions des Femmes).

10 "Woman, it is because of you that the Son of Man is dead . . . You should go about clothed only in rags."

11 Accidental, certainly, since if a woman is born it is simply 'by imperfection of active virtue', or due to an external cause, such as 'the moisture-laden winds of the Midi' (Aristotle, *De Generatione Animalium*, IV, 2).

12 *En découvrant l'existence entre Husserl et Heidegger / Discovering Existence with Husserl and Heidegger* (1967).

13 *Difficile Liberté* (1963). Levinas adds: 'The other *par excellence* is the feminine through which the world is perpetuated by a backstage world' (*De l'existence à l'existant*). These observations were made several years after *Le Deuxième sexe*. It will be noted that there is no distortion of such clear philosophical thought in this study. This 'horror of the other', that is, of the feminine, furthermore relates to the conclusions of Dr Lederer's documentary work, *Gynophobia* (PUF, 1970).

14 On several occasions Arendt paradoxically expressed doubts about the abilities of her sex for philosophical reasoning (see final chapter).

15 Catherine Chalier, *Figures de femmes chez Levinas*.

16 Without memory does not mean without history. In recent years the work of Riane Eisler (*Le Calice et l'épée*) and of Harvard professor Marilyn French (*La fascination du pouvoir*) – to which I would respectfully add my own contribution, *Les femmes avant le patriarcat* – has prepared some of the ground for a sometimes voluntarily forgotten history of women.

17 Dr Juliette Boutonnier, *L'Angoisse* (1956).

18 Quoted by Serge Moscovici in *La Société contre nature*, 10/18.

19 'By suggesting the complementary law between element and system, and by showing us an individual that loses its personality within an organism that incorporates and rediscovers that personality through self-isolation, does not recent physics research present suggestions *from which philosophy and sociology should be able to profit?*' (Louis de Broglie, op. cit.).

20 It was Jacques Derrida who invented the term 'phallogocentrism'.

18

GENEVIÈVE FRAISSE

Geneviève Fraisse is a historian and a philosopher and Director of Research at the CNRS. She is Visiting Professor at Rutgers University, USA. She was an interministerial delegate for Women's Rights (1997–8), and has been a Deputée at the European Parliament since 1999. Her work focuses on the history of the controversy over sexual equality which she explores from an epistemological as well as a political point of view. In Fraisse's view, sexual equality must be worked for on several fronts simultaneously: through an analysis of the works of women philosophers; through a critique of political traditions and their terminology (such as notions of fraternity); through a study of myths of women and the feminine; and through an exploration of notions of female genius and rationality. For Fraisse, such intellectual work is inseparable from more practical feminist issues such as contraception, political parity, professional inequality and domestic service.

Fraisse's works include the following:

Femmes toutes mains: essai sur le service domestique, Paris: Seuil, 1979.

Clemence Royer, philosophe et femme de sciences, Paris: La Découverte, 1985, re-edition 2002.

Muse de la raison: démocratie et exclusion des femmes en France, Aix-en-Provence: Alinéa, 1989; Paris: Gallimard, 1995.

Histoire des femmes en Occident, Vol. IV (XIXème), (eds G. Duby and M. Perrot), Paris: Plon 1991 and 2002.

La raison des femmes, Paris: Plon, 1992.

La différence des sexes, Paris: PUF, 1996.

Les femmes et leur histoire, Paris: Folio Gallimard, 1998.

La controverse des sexes, Paris: PUF, 2001.

Les deux gouvernements: la famille et la cité, Paris: Folio Gallimard, 2001.

INDIVIDUAL, ACTRESS, FEMINIST SUBJECT[1]

For some years, the history of women in general, but above all the history of feminism in all its specificity, has had recourse to the concept of the subject; to an historical subject doubled by a political subject which expresses the idea that it is necessary to know and to recognise woman as an actor, an agent of history.

The feminist subject views itself in terms of a dual collective membership of the unity of all women, a gendered unity, and of a group of feminist individuals, a political group. There has only been a group, that is to say, a feminist movement, since 1789, or, to be more precise, since 1830, or perhaps not even until today. The subject views itself as both individual and collective.

As the appearance of the neologism 'feminism' during the nineteenth century shows, feminism has been, for one hundred and fifty years, not only an historically recurrent social reality, but also an ideological representation. As a contemporary political practice of democracy, and in spite of some practical and theoretical divergences, one can assert its unity as a doctrine since it is characterised by its denunciation of the oppression and exploitation of women and by the assertion of a strategy, the aim of which is to achieve equality of the sexes. It is possible to question this nominalist use of feminism in so far as these real divergences are also ideological contradictions. But it seems to me to be historically important, theoretically useful and politically necessary to under-stand feminism globally. Similarly, although the term equality also has a multiplicity of definitions, they all have the same basic foundation: the denunciation of inequality between the sexes. I readily subscribe to this nominalist approach.

Historical reconstitution

If we are to take the feminist historical subject fully into account, some observations are required. It perhaps seems paradoxical to assert the existence of an individual and collective subject at a moment when philosophical history since the end of the nineteenth century, and political history since the middle of the twentieth, have questioned the pertinence of the subject as a fundamental referent. From the perspective of the positivity displayed by feminism, the theoretician's suspicion with regard to the conscious subject on the one hand, and the political subject, group or class on the other, appears misplaced. For feminism plays on precisely this double register: the collective representation of the contesting of an order and a tradition supports the proclamation of the individual woman as an autonomous being, as founder of her own law.

A single historical consideration can in itself unravel the logic of this paradox. Indeed, it is easy to understand the emergence of this subject, of woman or women, when one appreciates the force with which political discourse (with the philosophical text in the background) places the feminine being in the position of non-subject. This can occur either in an explicit manner, when a professional, civil, political, indeed even intellectual prohibition is applied to women, a prohibition which turns out to be discrimination, that is to say, in the proper sense of the term, a separation of the two sexes; or more implicitly, when a generic discourse fails to make its exclusion of women clear (the best example being the establishment of so called universal suffrage in 1848), an oversight which is not a matter of discrimination, but is rather the negative absorption of one sex by the other.

Let us not be mistaken: the paradox of making use of the notion of the historical feminist subject does not in any way imply that this subject is constructed against the flow of history. Indeed, we must not conclude (even if it can be found episodically and locally) that it is necessary to assert the essence of a specific feminine being or the evidently revolutionary aspect of the feminist movement. As I stated earlier, the representation of the collective feminist subject serves potentially to support the representation of woman or women as historical subjects and as subjects constructing their own history. If the notion of the actor is enough to account for the place of women in the eyes of the historian, the term subject repositions them within the dynamic of a political process. The assertion of the subject does not necessarily imply a claim to specificity; the point here is neither to establish a new conscious subject based on a femininity rich in speculative originality, nor to view the feminist movement as a revolutionary subject, the bringer of an ultimate social utopia. Whatever is at stake for a becoming-subject is balanced between the two extremes of the collective and the individual. And if it appears evident that the collective feminist subject is no more relevant than any other revolutionary subject, such as the proletariat, blacks, or the colonised, it is no less legitimate to view the collectivity of feminist actors as a group of witnesses to the search for an historical identity; witnesses, since these actors are the key figures in a process which goes beyond feminism as such. If feminism is an historical reality, its finality can only be its own disappearance, and if it succeeds in acquiring an historical identity by virtue of the assertion of the feminist subject, it does so in order to reveal a woman-subject ['un sujet femme'] and not a feminine subject.[2] The woman-subject recognises sexual difference, but does not put it to ideological use: discourses on the difference or the resemblance of the sexes are only grafted on to it at different levels as an afterthought. The point is not to avoid a debate on the feminine, but to put it back in its place. What is at stake for the history of contemporary feminism and for democratic society is the inclusion of women in that society.

Whether we say women or woman, their public representation is not immediately self-evident, and they often appear to be socially atomised. For if in the public sphere individuals can mass together, a multitude of private individualities rarely constitutes a unified group, with the exception of those rare housewives who take their protest on to the streets, mothers who protest against war, wives who lend support to a military society, women who demand new laws . . .

The status of feminist that is accorded or granted to an individual emerges in discourse in one of two ways: it is either used to characterise, in a retroactive manner, every person who, before the appearance of the neologism in the nineteenth century, revolted against the oppression of women and called for equality between the sexes, or it has been given, since the beginning of the democratic period, to those who claim to adhere to an ideology or doctrine which favours the emancipation and the liberation of the feminine sex. Thus the adjective 'feminist', even before it was used to describe an individual, was made a necessary part of the French language by the emergence of a social event, of a collective reality and not just of an individual act. Feminists are in a behavioural minority, and a group of individual feminists is always non-representative of the social whole where, by definition, the relationship between individual and multitude is played out. One can well imagine that if feminism is the vehicle of the contestation of an order, an analysis of the feminist individual risks being neither analogous nor even comparable with that of the various representations of the individual that have emerged since the nineteenth century.

We are therefore travelling against the path of history: two kinds of suspicion bear straight away upon the historical reality of feminist individuals. Firstly, there is suspicion regarding numbers, as the feminist movement in the nineteenth and twentieth centuries is only ever considered in a confusing form and described globally as ideology, rather than quantified in terms of the sum of actors that might serve to show its importance. Feminism resembles, therefore, a volatile idea that approaches fantasy, and this encourages an underestimation of its historical function. Secondly, there is suspicion regarding the status of actor, for feminism, as an ideological abstraction, makes it possible to imagine the feminist individual in the form of a caricature: providing neither the image of a good woman nor that of a good militant, the feminist is reduced to a collection of attributes, from intellectual to hysteric, which deprive her of her character as an historical actor. It is always *en passant*, but in precise terms, that it is said that such and such a feminist event only means something to a handful of intellectuals, or else is merely the product of hysteria. Essentially, and this deserves to be studied, feminism cannot escape caricature.

Support for feminism develops not only inside a group, but also at its margins, or even on the outside. And this ambiguity regarding the precise location of support is perhaps more noticeable than it is in the case of other social movements. The second question can be inferred from the distinction between the individual woman and the individual feminist: how are they to be described, and how do we determine their character? This is a problem of definition which swiftly introduces a notion of value.

The history of feminism is part of social history, a history in which individuals, caught up in a network, a political movement or pressure group, act in protest, revolt or revolution. For if these individuals are the bearers of social and political change, how do they represent this change? The question is double-sided: who represents this history, and who wears the badge, be it real or symbolic, of a collective practice? And inversely, how is each individual, or every individual, representative?

Representatives

It took a century after the French Revolution for a social and collective reality to be formulated in terms of the crowd in sociology, the masses in history, and also in terms of social class. The focus of the debate on causality in history is refined thus: when not considering the evolution of structures and the sequence of events, we reflect on the fact that men are and make history. As Henri Berr said at the beginning of the twentieth century: individuals are what is most tangible in history.[3] Berr outlines three levels of historical causality: contingency, necessity, and logic. He identifies the individual at two of these levels. With regard to contingency, the social whole becomes 'the jumbled collection of individualities in the midst of which the true actors of history are to be found'; and the 'insignificant' individual is set against the dignitary, the great man, the ground-breaker, etc. Logical discourse alleviates this antagonism by seeking less to understand the importance of individuals in history than to appreciate the degree of their representativeness: 'The *leader* is thus only distinguished from the crowd by the *degree* rather than by the nature of his activity'.

How, therefore, is the individual separated from the jumble of the multitude? 'Precisely because individuals are social beings and because society is not external to them, but *passes through them* in some way, they can arrogate a socially superior role to themselves: instead of being simple social elements, they can be social *agents*, social *inventors*'. From element to agent, agent to inventor: we see the spectrum of the varying degrees of representativeness.

Social historians immediately encounter the problem of the representational relationship between individual and group. Since the thirties, they have been progressively altering the elements of their analyses. They no longer use two terms, but three: the masses, pioneers and the obscure. Whether these masses are 'workers', as is the case in Lucien Febvre's preface to a text by Édouard Dolléans,[4] or 'popular', as they are for Jean Bruhat,[5] they are set against pioneers, 'small groups of men', 'cells of intelligent workers', and the elite, the aristocracy of the workers. What is particularly interesting for my argument is the category of 'unknown militants' that emerges between the two.

In his *Dictionnaire biographique du mouvement ouvrier*, Jean Maitron rightly aligns himself with this reckoning of the obscure.[6] What are militants if they are not individuals separating themselves from the crowd or the masses in order to belong to a network or to a movement? Even if this movement has official representatives, leaders or inventors, militancy makes each individual the intermediary of a cause, of an idea, in short of an historical reality which is their intimate concern but which goes largely beyond their person.

In the face of that haughty view which judges militants as 'small-time anonymous workers', Jean Maitron highlights the more lowly perspective from which the 'jumble of individualities' appears as an 'abundance of obscure and active men'.

A new idea of representativeness is thus sketched out: to name, to give a name to a social actor, even if this only means devoting one or two lines of a dictionary to them, is to highlight the unknown militant as the unrecognised militant; it is to attribute a role to the individual who intervenes at least once in their life in the social and political scene (by signing a petition, being arrested in a strike) as well as to the individual for whom militant action is an integral part of life. And there is no need for an opposition between the two: 'Militancy is synonymous with continuity. But the episodic preceded the continuous in working life, as it does in this dictionary.' What is important is the spirit in which this process is conducted: to align oneself with obscure lives and individualities is to question that form of representation which is founded on the analysis of the context that frames a movement. The lives, statements or acts of leaders are not sufficient if we are to understand this movement.

Nevertheless, in order for a biographical dictionary of a movement to be objective, it must conform to a vision of collectivity in which hierarchical criteria are necessarily in operation. Jacques Rancière's choices in *La Nuit des prolétaires* change the stakes: speaking of the itinerary of Saint-Simonian workers, he describes them from the outset as 'a few dozen non-representative individuals'.[7] Is this a preference for micro-history? I do not believe so. Its initial aim is to evade the all too weighty problematic of representativeness, and to transform the way in which the individual is perceived. Jacques Rancière uses the terms 'legions' and 'legionaries' to describe the popular masses and to criticise the simplified image of adherence to a collective identity and to the idea of the positivity of the popular subject. His analytical energies appear to be directed elsewhere: how can we expect to see with any clarity the face of a plurality of subjects who are implicated in a collective discourse, but are at the same time removed from any representativeness by their individualist wandering? They are neither representing nor representative, and it is only the question of their becoming subjects that explains our interest in them.

Numbering is naming

The history of recent feminism rightly underlines the collective reality of a women's movement and its importance as a social and political phenomenon. Paradoxically, however, a defensive reaction is discernible: the group is recognised, but the number is denied. Suspicion is cast on the number of participants in the movement, as if, within a process of reductive abstraction, an attempt at annulment was being carried out. Henri Berr speaks of 'tangible' individuals, and it is true that the aim of the project of establishing a biographical dictionary of the feminist movement analogous to that of the worker's movement was, in its counting of feminist individuals, to express a collective reality in concrete terms.[8] Numerical research allows for an evaluation of the significance of a reality beyond the limits of a global representation: discussing the feminist movement often involves the idea of a confusing mass where ideology replaces numerical truth. This means that the historical impact of a feminist moment can be exaggerated, to an almost fantastic extent, while we at the same time refuse to believe that that moment concerns a not inconsiderable quantity of individuals. This is itself an ideological practice, the result of which is a diminishment of the social and political role of feminism.

In addition to a suspicion concerning quantity and numbers, there is generally a suspicion with regard to status and image. Recognition of the validity and legitimacy of feminism can be performed in abstraction and from a distance: one can be convinced of what is at stake theoretically and practically for feminism and still, if possible, dissociate oneself from those individuals who are actors within it. The feminist individual provides neither a good image of a woman nor of a militant: the feminist loses her status as a woman without ever acquiring status as a militant.

Thus the interminable counting of both the principal characters and the more obscure figures of contemporary feminism to infinity closely resembles Jean Maitron's approach to the worker's movement. Nevertheless, if the militant worker can be the object of caricature and imitation, he still participates in history. For the feminist individual, this question remains unresolved. In affording her a social and political role, we alter the way in which women, too, are presented as making, and what is more, as having always made history. There is now something specific at stake.

Numbering individuals allows them to be taken into account, and this involves naming. Numbering tends to prove and to test the reality of a movement, while naming is concerned with the predominantly symbolic representation of this reality. The passage from an individual history of feminism to a collective history at the beginning of the nineteenth century does not simply signify historical 'progress' or a moment when the insufficiencies of individual strategies or exceptional acts will be analysed and exceeded. It announces the composition of the group in a symbolic manner: the group is a designation and an assertion of a membership, one that is historically recognisable and reflected in a 'class'.

By analogy with the notion of 'legal capacity', in an article on the women of the French Revolution, Élisabeth Guibert-Sledziewski proposes that we use the expression 'the historical capacity of women' heuristically.[9] As the object of a legal revolution, with divorce fully installed by virtue of the acts and discourses of men, woman could well have become simply a *subject* of the Revolution. For this to occur, women must identify themselves as such, say and write the feminine 'they' ('elles') or 'women', and finally, use the category 'we/us'. Asserting this collective identity provokes a voluntary and symbolic break within the larger whole, that of the people. A group names itself and a connection is made: women, referring to every woman, say 'we/us'. This question of the self-constitution of a group of women-subjects was first posed in any clear form only after 1830, and it continues to be posed today.

Even if feminist discourse speaks of women as a social category, a 'class' as certain recent texts have it, the collectivity of women will never be transformed into a feminist collective. In contrast with the worker, who is always potentially a union or political militant, not every woman is regarded as a virtual feminist. The working masses were conceived of as the possible prefiguring of an organised proletariat. But this logical representation is unthinkable and inapplicable with regard to the collectivity of women of a given society or nation. Feminists are marked definitively by the avant-garde and by marginality, by a radical conscious realisation, and by a rejection of the norm which is both undergone and demanded.

The assertion of 'we/us' inserts a break and permits the constitution of a group. This is a double break: feminists isolate themselves within the people and separate themselves from the collectivity of women. In appealing to all women, they are well aware that they themselves can only ever be some women. As Christine Planté shows in connection with the Saint-Simonian women, texts introduce the plural 'you' as the addressee, while the feminine 'they' serves as the support of 'we/us', its sometimes faintly voluntaristic representative.[10] In fact, the position of 'we/us' is none too clear: textual analysis shows the ways in which the irruption of 'I' oscillates in its reference between 'we women' and 'we Saint-Simonians'. (In the seventies, a strand of the Women's Liberation Movement referred to themselves as 'we, women on the move'.)

The individual feminist emerges from this perpetual shift between 'I' and 'we/us'. Separating oneself from all other women and acquiring an identity of one's own becomes a necessity. In refusing the traditional model, the feminist woman puts herself on the margins. She makes herself conspicuous. In order to invent a new feminine identity, she must cut herself off from other women. The group, in the wide sense of the class of others or in the narrower sense of the feminist movement, is not sufficient support for this search for a redefinition of self. Collective identity in the avowed form of sorority might be interpreted as an end in itself, but it is also often interpreted as a means of becoming a subject. And finally, with the Saint-Simonians, comes a relatively new reality that subsequently became integral to feminism and which slides across the hesitations of feminist texts when it comes to saying 'I' amidst usages of 'we/us', the collective 'you' and the feminine 'they': they sign articles, brochures and petitions with their forenames.[11] What purpose did the forename serve in 1830 or in 1970, if it did not simultaneously refer to 'I' and to 'we/us', to an interchangeable individual, perhaps, who is nevertheless certainly not anonymous and is conscious of working towards a constitution of the subject?

Where does this will to represent 'we/us' which would permit the assertion of 'I' come from? This political practice in fact mirrors the analysis of the position of women in society. Indeed, I would say that woman is not a subject in the discourse of the subject; and, moreover, she is in an excluded position. The individual feminist therefore denounces her lack of this or that civil right, and underlines her exclusion from the realm of political rights. Now this exclusion, even though it is shared by others who are excluded from civil and political society, is most frequently intensified within the hierarchy of priorities in the struggle: even those who support feminism's denunciation of exclusion are the first to exclude feminism from the struggle, and to seek to annul the differences between the sexes as they are represented politically. The status of exclusion is characterised by a lack of any descriptive particularity: the word to express exclusion is itself lacking in so far as terms from quite different domains are always used to express it: women are slaves or enfranchised, serfs or pariahs, colonised or made proletarian . . . There is no proper name that stands for exclusion, and every excluded person can lend her name to another and each uses alien terms to describe her specific state. Consequently, the problematic developed here concerning the singularity of the feminist subject carries within itself a function of generality which is valid for different categories of excluded people: we must be careful here not to over-determine the analysis.

Using the feminine 'they', 'we/us' and 'I' in order to denounce exclusion is precisely to call for the inclusion of women in the economic, civil and political society that is formed in conjunction with industry and democracy. The plural necessarily passes through the singular: the end of the collective process is a demand for autonomy. Natural law implies that woman is both a civil being and a political citizen; participation in the economic life of an industrial society justifies independence at work and the power to control one's salary, and individualisation suggests the appropriation of one's own body and the governance of one's sexuality. Thus exclusion is not a synonym for absence, nor is inclusion a synonym for presence; rather, we have an historical time-lag: the individualist demands that emerged during the Enlightenment keep intact the familial holism in which woman became the central element, blending her into a totality. Nineteenth-century feminism insists that the woman be permitted to circulate, as a free individual, between domestic society and civil and political society. Free circulation was achieved in the twentieth century. In fact, the issue is no longer one of social life. Today, the articulation between family and 'society' is more subtle: the presence of women is referred to as 'participation', which is itself a sign that the nature of this presence is not always obvious. The end of exclusion has not engendered a new equilibrium.

Describing is identifying

Feminists are the instigators of a discussion about women which calls for a new woman. This new woman situates herself between the image of the old woman and the dream of the new man; and she acquires attributes that are both positive and negative. The negative attributes are those which refer to exclusion only in order to take advantage of it: if exclusion merges the woman into a familial group, it atomises her within the social body, and this atomisation marks her as the object of exchange between men. The object of exchange always incites competition, or perhaps, in language that is more specifically human, rivalry. To stop being an object and to present oneself as a subject requires that sorority supplants rivalry, that the collective movement bursts on to the political and social scene, breaks the circulation of objects of exchange, and leaves a space for the assertion of subjects. That this sorority has also turned out to be historically fallible, and that certain women have chosen a more solitary path in their refusal to be an object of exchange, does not detract from the logic of the argument.

Now these subjects are not abstractions. On the contrary, discourses list the different traditional positions of woman, the girl, the wife and the mother, positions which are criticised in order to be redefined and revalorised. One could add the qualities of female worker and female citizen, whereby we create a mixture of a redefinition of the feminine and an integration of masculine universality, a mixture of specificity and generality.

Isolating the feminist individual raises a two-part question: which qualities and properties are common to every individual, and what kind of 'new woman' does the becoming-subject imply? In spite of the fact that feminist individuals are in a minority compared with the collectivity of women, we know that, in contrast to the worker who can change class, for example, a feminist is affected definitively by her sex, a biological sex as much as a socially constructed gender. Moreover, if we can formulate the utopia of a classless society, there is no possibility of speaking of a sexless one; whence the permanent and occasionally difficult slippage between the position of woman and that of feminist.

If the feminist individual is attempting to become a subject, what is this subject in relation to the problematic of the universal subject which, more often than not, is a masculine subject? In *The Jewish Question*, Marx criticises the abstract man of the Declaration of the Rights of Man precisely because this abstract man does not exist and in fact serves to hide the bourgeois man and the capitalist. In the case of woman, the problem is exactly the reverse: reality, like discourse, shows that woman cannot be thought of in abstraction. She is a being that is relative by virtue of her familial status, possessed rather than possessing, and whose qualities, rather than essence, receive expression. Since this period, in the middle of the nineteenth century, history has been caught up in a double movement in which the identity of the man of the Rights of Man has been precisely defined and in which the search for a woman who is abstracted from her qualities has been refined. It goes without saying that woman's universality as it is evoked by the notion of the eternal feminine, and which is so overwhelmingly present in masculine discourse, is irrelevant here; its imaginary reality precisely masks the dimension of the real and of the symbolic.

To stop appearing as a being relative to others in the familial structure and, consequently, in social life, to cease being subjected to the constraints of feminine sexuality in social life: the possibility of separating sexuality from maternity is an irreversible stage. In so far as procreation is a function of the sexuality of an organism, it is not sufficient to characterise the existence of the individual. What is more, the technical skill of maternity shows it less and less as a function of belonging to a species and more and more as a social function.

In texts, finding oneself as an individual is expressed in a call for the 'new woman'. It would be interesting to compare this new woman with the new man, the generic man, sought by generations of revolutionaries. We can only say here that this new woman, even if she signifies the end of the connection and conquest of the individual, does not disregard the time that is necessary for this invention to occur and does not ignore all or part of the traditionally feminine attributes. In one of her novels, Clémence Royer presents her characters as 'hybrid beings'.[12] A century later, Yvette Roudy entitled her ministerial report *Full Female Citizens*.

From individual to new woman: there is more than one way of becoming a subject, and the woman as becoming-subject goes beyond the feminist becoming-subject. What is more, the numbering of the actors in the history of feminism suggests that a certain number of limits and boundaries have not been respected. Indeed, if every woman is not perceived as virtually feminist, then inversely, the proclamation of her feminism does not exhaust the category of feminist individuals. In other words: access to the position of subject is achieved as much through collective identification as through a solitary journey in which the feminist sign is not necessarily relevant. We could also say that the collective permits or prevents the work of the subject. As such, a new light is thrown upon the position of the exceptional woman, the analysis of whom in the recent feminist tradition remains ambiguous: she represents a transgression in which a desire for assimilation to the masculine world is sometimes played out, but conversely she also serves as a mouthpiece or, often retrospectively, as a symbol within the struggle.

There is no precise intersection between the collectivity of women and that of feminists. As an ideology, doctrine or state of mind, feminism goes beyond the individual feminist. Sometimes, an interest in feminism incites or even implies a rejection of the feminist individual by women themselves: in the seventies and eighties, it was common to hear 'I'm not a feminist, but . . . ' I said earlier that we must number in order to make tangible. Yes, but to number is not to classify; and it seems to be difficult to provide a good definition of representativeness. First, we must analyse how an assertion of 'we/us' suggests a symbolic rupture within the social whole, and, conversely, how a new 'I' may be constructed, an 'I' that is no longer excluded nor an objectified atom prevented from complying with a scale of values, or indeed from creating one. There is never any question of representing only one cause, and the point here is the transformation of self: neither real heroines nor pure, new women, these are the rather 'uncommon' women, those who are often 'unclassifiable' in the eyes of the historian.[13] The refusal to classify individual feminists takes us away from the problem of the degree of representativeness. In writing *La Nuit des prolétaires*, Jacques Rancière charts the wanderings of some non-representative individuals; without being contradictory, I conclude here that every feminist individual is representative.[14]

Thus the feminist search for the woman-subject follows a path that is the reverse of that of western man: the woman-subject seeks to distance herself from her relative and determined being in her quest for universality.

The search for identity is only abstract because it seeks to legitimise a political subject and because this political practice is necessarily inscribed within subjectivity. It does not abandon concrete descriptions, seeking rather to make them irrelevant with respect to an inscription within civil and political society. Essentially, the feminist subject seeks to neutralise discrimination, that is to say, sexual division understood as a place-ment according to sex, but she in no way excludes the recognition of sexual difference. Ideally, we would combine an analysis of social relations between the sexes with that of sexual and loving relations. Unfortunately, the strategies of domination have, historically, fed off this mixture to such an extent that we must initially proceed via a separation of relational levels.

The woman-subject constructed by the history of feminism is both neuter and gendered, and seeks an equilibrium between two movements: first, the movement which puts an end to the dependence of a being that is divided up according to its relative qualities, and second, the movement which is aware that the woman-subject is but one of a number of positions available to a woman as a human being, for this subject does not exhaust the totality of her relation to the world. If feminist thought is working for a constitution of the subject, the operation of legitimisation turns out to be more significant than that of definition. A subjective totality is not therefore required: the emphasis is put on an historical process, the finality of which implies its own dissolution.

Translated by Tom Baldwin

Notes

1 Translator's note: I have translated 'actrice' as 'actress' as the author uses this feminine form once in the title of the essay ('Individue, actrice, sujet féministe'), reverting subsequently to the masculine form 'acteur' throughout the main body of the text.
2 I have deliberately positioned myself outside two problematics: the first makes a distinction between the woman-subject and the feminine subject in order to dispose of the term feminism, which is suspected of signifying the desire to have rather than the desire to be, this separation seeming to me to be ineffectual as far as qualifying a search for identity is concerned (cf.

Antoinette Fouque, 'Féminisme et/ou Mouvement de libération des femmes', ed. Martine de Gaudemar (Aix-en-Provence: CEFUP, 1982), pp. 177–87); the second denounces the usage of the term subject because, in so far as it eventually provides a positive image of oppression, it will be used abusively to describe the condition of women (cf. Nicole-Claude Mathieu, 'Quand céder n'est pas consentir', in *L'Arraisonnement des femmes, Essais en anthropologie des sexes, Cahiers de l'homme*, number XXIV (Paris, 1985), pp. 169–245). The latter criticism is justified, but in my opinion, it is a symptom of those analyses which, in aiming to demonstrate oppression, in fact prevent themselves from articulating their argument through a reflection on the practices of resistance to which the history of feminism, for its part, bears witness.

3 Henri Berr, *La Synthèse en histoire, essai critique et théorique* (Paris: Alcan, 1911).

4 Édouard Dolléans, *Histoire du mouvement ouvrier, 1830–1887* (Paris: A. Colin, 1936).

5 Jean Bruhat, *Histoire du mouvement ouvrier français*, tome I (Paris: Éditions sociales, 1952).

6 Jean Maitron *et al.*, in the foreword to volumes I and II of the *Dictionnaire biographique du mouvement ouvrier français* (Paris: Éditions ouvrières, 1964 and 1973).

7 Jacques Rancière, *La Nuit des prolétaires* (Paris: Fayard, 1981); new edition by Paris: Complexe, 1997.

8 This project was supported by the ATP Femmes du CNRS, under the auspices of Laurence Klejman, Michèle Riot-Sarcey and Florence Rochefort.

9 Élisabeth Guibert-Sledziewski, 'Les Femmes, sujet de la Révolution, in *Révolutions du sujet* (Paris: Méridiens-Klincksieck, 1989).

10 Christine Planté, *Les Saint-Simoniennes ou la quête d'une identité impossible à travers l'écriture à la première personne*, doctoral thesis, University of Paris (III), 1983.

11 Lydia Elhadad, 'Femmes prénommées: les prolétaires saint-simoniennes rédactrices de *La Femme libre*, 1832–1834', in *Les Révoltes logiques*, nos. 415, 1977, pp. 62–88 and pp. 29–60; more recently, two women attached the names of two feminist 'heroines' to their own forenames when signing a book: Anne de Pisan and Anne Tristan, *Histoires du MLF* (Paris: Calmann-Lévy, 1977).

12 Clémence Royer, *Les Jumeaux d'Hellas*, 1864. Let us add that there is nothing more eloquent than the frequent use by late nineteenth-century novelists and essayists of the title 'The New Eve'. Villiers de L'Isle-Adam's *L'Ève future* also belongs to this tradition.

13 Cf. Geneviève Fraisse, 'Singularité féministe: historiographie critique de l'histoire du féminisme en France', in *Une histoire des femmes est-elle possible?* (Paris: Rivages, 1984), pp. 189–204.

14 On the problem of the representation of the group and of the individual, see Jacques Rancière, 'La representation de l'ouvrier ou la classe impossible', in *Le Retrait du politique* (Paris: Galilée, 1983), pp. 88–111.

19

MICHÈLE LE DOEUFF

Michèle Le Doeuff specialises in seventeenth-century British philosophy. She has taught in the École Normale Supérieure de Fontenay and was Professor of Women's Studies in the University of Geneva. She is currently Director of Research in Philosophy at the CNRS and works much of the time in Oxford. She has published widely on seventeenth-century English writers, especially Bacon, whom she has also translated, and Shakespeare's *Venus and Adonis*, a narrative poem which she analyses in terms of questions of freedom, death, sexual difference and identity. In the field of French philosophy, she has worked on women philosophers, including Gabrielle Suchon of the seventeenth century and Simone de Beauvoir, as well as on the philosophical 'imaginary' and a broad spectrum of political and social feminist issues, including the vexed question of parity.

Le Doeuff's major works include the following:

Recherches sur l'imaginaire philosophique, Paris: Payot, 1980. (Translated into English as *The Philosophical Imaginary*, London: Athlone, 1989).

L'Étude et le Rouet. Des femmes, de la philosophie etc., Paris: Seuil, 1989. (Translated into English as *Hipparchia's Choice, an essay concerning women, philosophy, etc.*, Oxford: Blackwell, 1991.)

Le Sexe du savoir, Paris: Aubier, 1998; Paris: Flammarion, 2000. (Translated into English as *The Sex of Knowing*, London and New York: Routledge, 2003).

HOW INTUITION CAME TO WOMEN

Blue stockings: these were blue worsted stockings, knitted in thick warm wool and worn in England by men even where it was not appropriate – hence, the negative connotation of the term since its origin. You may be quite indifferent to all of this, but since I have just learned something about it, allow me to tell you the story of a word. In the seventeenth century, perhaps from one day to the next, these blue stockings, hitherto worn at home for warmth, evolved into a metonymy to refer to the Parliament of 1653. For the members of this *Blue-Stocking Parliament*, Cromwell's chosen few, had little interest in fashionable clothing; velvet and lace had no place in their political program, and they probably thought nothing of appearing in the House dressed in the kind of stockings they wore at home, instead of the black silk stockings deemed essential for such ceremonial occasions, even if they were not so comfortable, especially in winter. So, "Blue-Stockings, Blue-Stockings" grumbled those who certainly had other grudges against this Parliament. The *Oxford English Dictionary*, which I am meticulously plundering, does not specify whether these members of Parliament actually wore blue worsted stockings or were merely judged capable of something so inappropriate. Let us say these parliamentarians thought – or were reputed to be inclined to think – that any one, without standing on courtly ceremony, could offer an opinion on questions put to him. Perhaps no one ever came in blue stockings, but they were capable of doing such a thing – hence, the epithet – and who knows whether in fact they did not earn it? A century later, still in London, some people began to meet informally for literary conversations, at Montagu House, rather than playing cards like everyone else. "Rather than playing cards" figures in the dictionary definition; you can see what kind of subtle sociohistorical knowledge is required to determine the meaning of a word. One of the pillars of this cardless society, Benjamin Stillingfleet, is reported to have been there and really to have worn such stockings. In a private house, and his hosts tolerated it! A certain Admiral Boscawen, noting the consequences of turning up one's nose at whist, nick-named the group "the bluestocking society," underscoring the threat some people pose to the best society.

Since then, a lot of water has flowed under Tower Bridge and several other bridges. No one makes much fuss when a man delivers his lectures at the Sorbonne or at Galloway College sporting his most threadbare clothes; in any case, little fuss is made in the university world, which, after all, has always had its traditions of careless dress or ostentatious indifference to the body. How it might be in high-society salons, I have no idea, but no matter: no one expects a gentleman to play cards to prove his unimpeachable morality. So there was no longer any reason to keep the metaphor alive in the

296

repertoire of insults, rude names, common taunts, and invective. The word has none-theless survived in French and English, thanks to a later meaning, derived from its second metonymic usage: a bluestocking is a woman interested in intellectual pursuits, who, had she frequented Montagu House, might have worn ugly knit stockings beneath her long skirts. For this third use of the word entered both languages at a time when no woman showed her legs: obviously, unprovable charges have the greatest effect and the longest life. Thus, a reproach levelled by gentlemen against austere Puritans has become a term by which even today it is possible to ridicule women who like to read or think, and do not hide the fact. It is a strange story: without a dictionary, no one would know that all of this apparently originated in a clothing choice that may or may not have been made by men who scorned a certain political style. Besides, blue stockings, very blue stockings, could be quite an attractive fashion, now that we show our legs. Alas, the reference to fashion has no effect, and, although its original use has been forgotten, the expression has kept its connotation of austerity, like an unacceptable rejection of all kinds of pleasure in favor of things deemed more essential.

"My grandmother was an odd woman. Her name was Flora Tristan. Proudhon said she was a genius. Since I don't know anything about it, I'll take his word for it . . . She probably didn't know how to cook. A socialist, anarchist blue-stocking," Gauguin wrote about Flora Tristan, whom he had never met.[1] They both had exceptional and terrible destinies. The outcast painter's insensitivity toward the woman who called herself a "pariah" is all the more harsh: his tragedy reduces hers to the level of trivia. Whether or not Flora Tristan knew how to cook (and in any case what does that mean?), her grandson, who knows nothing about it at all, will concoct a hypothesis out of thin air to counterbalance the genius Proudhon attributed to her. "She created a lot of socialist stuff," he said, although acknowledging that he could not untangle fact from fiction in the hearsay which was all he had to go by, and then he adds that "nevertheless" she was "a very pretty and noble lady." *Bas-bleu* does not imply ugliness in this instance, but rather the very antithesis of *cordon-bleu*, which is just as serious. From this sketch, we can conclude that whenever a woman shows some talent for ideas, an automatic reflex is triggered: ipso facto and gratuitously, she is judged somehow deficient, unable to satisfy certain male expectations, whose legitimacy, moreover, is never questioned.

Because the Puritans, who thought they were working for the republic, were committed to sobriety in clothing and demcanor, we can be sure that an intellectual woman has no taste whatsoever when it comes to dressing well or keeping a good table. Of course such a flaw is still reprehensible today, even when the expression "she's dressed to the nines" would provoke guffaws at every level of society, and even when lack of culinary talent is easily forgiven in those who have no other abilities either. We come to the heart of the problem when we realize that those qualities which used to be thought incompatible with intellectual activity have themselves become optional for women. One of these days, no one but *agrégées** de philosophie* will try to be attractive

---

* An *agrégé(e)* is a person who has passed very competitive examinations (concours) to earn the *agrégation* and is therefore qualified to teach in upper two years of the secondary school system or in the lower ranks of the university.

and display their housewifely talents, as if they had to redeem themselves. But from what? And the most irritating thing is that this suspicion never dies out. Recently I invited a good seventeenth-century scholar to a conference, and was showered with compliments by colleagues with whom I usually go for a drink after the seminar:

"Thanks for inviting such a nice woman!"
"Etc., etc.,"
"And besides, she isn't a bluestocking at all!" one woman marvelled.

Hence my recourse to the dictionary, at a time of night when scholars of both sexes are asleep and dreaming, sometimes, but not always, in each other's arms.

How intuition came to women

Are women – are we women – reliquaries or dustbins of history, especially for unflattering language? A word was born of the antagonism between Roundheads and Cavaliers; in the normal course of events, once the antagonism had faded or taken on a different form, the word should have become a linguistic cast-off, but in this case it acquired a new life, and a new referent, just as it was about to lapse into disuse. Of course, that is one more reason for irritation: the insults hurled at us were not even made to measure for us. But let us pose a theoretical question: anthropology (by which I mean any project of knowing human beings as they are supposed to be – as empirical givens) examines the sexual division of labor, functions, responsibilities, characteristics, and so on, in a particular society, frequently with the aim of finding one or two good reasons to show that the division is as it should be, the raw being the domain of one sex, the cooked belonging to the other, or vice versa.* As if, given the identity of one sex and the other, anyone could understand why something is symbolically attributed to one sex and something else to the other – for example, tailored to men, flowing to women, in the order of thought as in the world of fashion. But if we can show that there may be slippage of a symbol from one sexually identified category to another within a given society, then it is superfluous to try to justify the association of ideas, that is, the link between sex and symbolic attribution. Instead, it now becomes possible to speculate that the slippage is regulated by certain principles or laws that should be elucidated. By this I mean it would be pointless to analyze the image of the bluestocking by trying to explain why the color and reference to legs are associated with women, since the term was originally coined with respect to men. But perhaps the transfer from the first application (to male politicians) to its later one (to intellectual women) obeys some sociosymbolic law. You may object that I am offering only one example. Certainly in good logic a single instance suffices to destroy the theory to which it poses a contradiction, but not to establish a new one.

---

* "The raw and the cooked" is the title of Claude Lévi-Strauss's important work in structuralist anthropology. Lévi-Strauss argues that the binary pair (i.e. the raw and the cooked, feminine and masculine) is the basic, universal structure of all human cultures and signification.

This is not a single instance. Take the concept of intuition, which in classical language designates a mode of immediate apprehension, a direct intellectual grasp of something true, which is distinct from, though not necessarily radically opposed to, mediated knowledge achieved through reasoning, discussion, internal debate, dialectic, experimentation, deduction, language, applying or trying to apply some form of proof . . . in short, what is generally called discursive knowledge. For a long time, intuition was considered, first, as an important and valid mode of knowledge; second, as one that can work in cooperation with other modes of thought; and third, as either the best possible form of knowledge and the completion of a process of discovery, or as the form of knowledge without which nothing would take place because it is what sets the process in motion. For example, Descartes says: "By 'intuition' I understand . . . the conception of the pure and attentive mind which is so simple and distinct that we can have no further doubt as to what we understand; . . . thus everyone can intuit in his mind that he exists, that he thinks, that a triangle is bounded by three lines . . . " Descartes thinks the first principles of metaphysics and mathematics are known in this way, yet the extended consequences drawn from these principles can be known only by deduction[2] For Plato, the philosophical itinerary is different: the process begins with debate, failure, working toward a definition, suffering, reasoning; and it has its outcome, if indeed it has an outcome at all, and its reward in a direct, clear grasp of the True. Some of Plato's disciples will even say "in an ineffable and unintelligent contact with Being," which is not necessarily everyone's ideal, but to each her or his own. Plato distinguishes *noêsis* (generally translated by intelligence) from *dianoia* (reasoning or discursive knowledge), but, even though he ranks these modes of knowledge – *noêsis* is superior to *dianoia* – he posits their coexistence in the cognitive activity of anyone, man or woman, who undertakes the long apprenticeship that leads to philosophy.[3]

In the long history of philosophy, discursivity and intuition are not inevitably contradictory or antagonistic, nor is this duality projected onto the duality of the sexes. Moreover, according to philosophers who write in Latin, *intueor* may simply mean "to consider," and *intuitus* an opinion; this vocabulary refers to a looser usage, and the related terms have no particular positive or negative epistemological value. Finally, I can assure you of one thing even though it cannot be verified: if Saint Thomas Aquinas had heard anyone use the term "feminine intuition," he would certainly have recoiled in horror, and more than a few others would have done so too. Hence a question to put to historians of ideas, or should I say pertaining to a history of ideas that are never examined because they are considered too silly, but which carry considerable weight in the debates that sometimes obliquely determine our destinies: how did intuition come to be attributed to girls and women? And beyond this question, should we not be troubled by the fact that thinking about what thought is – about what it is to know – functions in mythical mode, as though there were an epistemic imaginary that is a law unto itself, regulating our perception of what it is to think, to know, to have knowledge, and so on?

This question must be turned into a more complex problem: when the difference between intuitive and discursive modes of thought was accentuated to the point that each of these modes was attributed to one and only one type of being, sexual dualism was not immediately invoked to attribute superior discursive powers to one sex, while assigning only a mediocre or obscure intuition to the other. Jean-Jacques Rousseau draws the distinction along different lines: "God is intelligent; but how? Man is intelligent when he reasons, and the supreme intelligence has no need of reasoning; for it, there are no premises or consequences, there are not even any propositions; it is purely intuitive, etc."[4] Decide as you will whether or not "man" as Rousseau uses it includes women. It will make no difference to intuition, since it is literally divine; or perhaps it is more appropriate to say that divine intelligence is intuitive, which is not exactly the same thing. There is something slippery in the grammar of the adjectives used to qualify a substance; God's intelligence is posited as intuitive, which does not necessarily imply that intuition is part of God's essence nor that only he is intuitive. But the language slips from the attribution ("God's intelligence is intuitive") to the idea of an essential property, one belonging exclusively to God, and thus the quality becomes substantive. It would follow, then, that every intuitive act would become divine; when a human being "intuits' supposing the possibility of such a thing, that act implies some kind of deification.

Though he was perhaps not the first to propose a radical distinction between intuition and reason, Rousseau does not regard it as a sexual difference; for him, this distinction refers to the duality between God and man. However, the problem takes shape in his philosophy, since he posits a stark dichotomy between the two modes of knowing, as though they were no longer complementary, nor did they coexist in the same mind, and from that moment on, it had to be a matter of one or the other. The German Romantics took up this opposition, affirming that the Absolute must be intuited and not conceptualized – probably a recurrence of the neoPlatonic idea of an ineffable and unintelligent contact with Being. This affirmation was in fact a Pyrrhic victory for intuition, because soon afterward, philosophy placed itself at a careful distance from Romanticism, to the point of defining itself in distinction from it. Before long, *The Phenomenology of Spirit* effectively ruled out intuition of the Absolute, which Hegel taxes with being "a view which is in our time as prevalent as it is pretentious."[5] This same Hegel was to replace intuition with the painstaking labor of conceptual analysis as the norm of philosophical thought, and many people endorsed his view that this method should be the only admissible way of doing philosophy. "This intuitive perception which does not recognize itself is taken as a starting-point as if it were absolutely presupposed; it has in itself intuitive perception only as immediate knowledge, and not as self-knowledge: or it knows nothing, and what it perceives it does not really know . . . ": thus runs his radical critique.[6] As far as I know, he did not go so far as to utter the ultimate anathema – "intuition is feminine" – but he came within a hair's breadth of inventing it. For he limits women to "taste," "elegance," and he writes that "women correspond to plants because their development is more placid and the principle that underlies it is the rather vague unity of feeling."[7] Now, according to him, a plant "does not attain to a beingfor-self"[8] and he recognizes that at its best, intuition, *which does not know itself*, "consists of beautiful thoughts, but not knowledge."[9] Thus, moving from botany to the lack of self-knowledge, one may establish a more or less adequate transitivity: intuition does not know itself, a plant never achieves being-for-itself, woman is a plant. Let knowledgeable people of both sexes decide, as they wish, whether the connection is valid, and whether it is therefore possible to attribute to "woman-as-plant" – this anthropological fiction – a discredited way of knowing: intuition, devalued to the point of having lost its status as productive of knowledge. A century later, Anna de Noailles* initiated unanimism, "it is not the meadow, but rather my eye, that is in flower." In the fullest sense of the term, she actualizes the Hegelian figure of the woman of taste and refinement, producer of lovely plantlike thoughts intuitively spreading throughout Nature, thus obligingly leaving philosophy, science, and politics to those who claim them as their rightful domain; she cultivated a form of poetry that the public forthwith labelled minor, but charming.

If intuition came to be synonymous with unprovable allegations or unjustified claims, it no longer had a place in the real philosophy taught in institutions of learning under the name of theory of knowledge. For from the moment rivalry emerged between the intuitive and the discursive, the die was cast, at least in the academic world: since intuition can hardly be taught (unless of course we turn our lectures and seminars into transcendental meditation sessions!), it was a foregone conclusion that discursivity would win out wherever learning is transmitted. In point of fact, one could speak of a "field effect" when a given conflict occurs in an environment structured in a particular way – and universities are places structured in a particular way – it is inevitable that the structure will shape the outcome of the dispute. Today, the word intuition might survive only as a relic of antiquated philosophical discourse, a term that takes us back, as many others do, to notions of which we no longer have any idea: vegetative soul, spermatic Reason, or the Absolute. It is true that Descartes's oeuvre always figures prominently in school curricula, and the passage in the *Regulae* that elaborates the distinction between intuition and deduction and articulates one with the other appears frequently on examinations. How can one make sense of this passage if one believes intuition is mere whimsy, a woman's affair, "woman" being the antithesis of "the learned" about whose sex there can thus be no doubt? It is a mystery; but, as a matter of fact, we manage to make sense of this passage when the curriculum requires it without considering Cartesian views in the light of what we commonly assume in other circumstances.

"What we commonly assume in other circumstances" (the category extends beyond the single issue of supposedly feminine intuition) tends nevertheless to slip into commentaries and translators' choices, inflecting the discourse bit by bit; from one approximation to another, the history of philosophy succeeds in propagating rumors that blatantly contradict the texts themselves; in such situations, "common assumptions" always triumph. Thus, a colleague on the other side of the world explains that the influence of seventeenth-century rationalism is such that the term "intuition" refers to "a thought style that is not sharpened and systematized in the manner of which Cartesian method is the paradigm." And she continues: "Intuition, inevitably, has come to be associated with specifically female thought styles?"[10] With respect to the history of philosophy, this is a mistake. Because intuition cannot be set up in opposition to Cartesian method, which in fact incorporates it as a primordial element and indispensable anchoring point. Anyone who invokes Cartesianism must at least bear in mind that it

---

* Anna de Noailles (1876–1933): French poet and novelist who combined romantic themes with neoclassical forms.

presupposes intuition followed by an articulation of intuition and reasoning. Moreover, from an epistemological point of view, Genevieve Lloyd's simplification is difficult to accept. Cartesian method is neither the only model nor the paradigm for any and every formalization of thought; there are other models competing for the intellectual space opened by the question: "how must one go about thinking and knowing with certainty, or with more certainty than usual?" Here in a nutshell is the effect of the dualism created by projecting the duality of the sexes on to the question of knowledge, for example: create two categories and simplify them both. Basically, all of this contributes to sustaining a reification – certain styles of thought are said to be specifically *women's* [*female*], and although the commentator appears to contest the identification of intuition with these modes of thought, she does not question the notion of "specifically" masculine or feminine thought. Or rather, in this instance, as so frequently happens, "specificity" applies only to the feminine, as if the masculine were the norm and the universal. "Field effect" again: when universities establish women's studies as a separate little world, defined only by specialization in feminine questions (while the rest of the academic world is busy with what?), the field is thus defined by the idea that specificity pertains only to the feminine. In the end, it devotes itself, and thus limits itself, to studying what differentiates us. Another disturbing corollary: in the guise of critique, all of this ends up once more flattering the masculine half of humanity, which takes comfort in the idea that there really is a "man of reason," systematic and methodical, from whom women who really are women differentiate themselves. As long as the equation of a crude notion of rationality with a class of individuals cursorily defined as "masculine" is not exposed as a myth, there is no point in valorizing or rejecting this hollow idea of reason on the basis of this equation. "Reason is masculine, and that's why I'm in favor of it" is as empty a declaration as "Reason is masculine, and that's why I want no part of it." Neither has anything to say about what the issue of rationality might be, and both base a completely fantastical division of the sexes on a set of ill-defined questions.

Considered as nothing more than the direct opposite of reason, intuition could still have been useful as a foil: you can imagine philosophy courses explaining that there are various ways of knowing, some bad and some good, the value of the latter being all the more striking in contrast with the others. And since rumor already had it that women do not reason – a nice idea, suggested by Malebranche in a description of the fibers of the brain, developed by Rousseau, given added muscle by Hegel, driven home by Auguste Comte, lurking sometimes in John Stuart Mill's rhetoric, and still successfully pursued in works published less than twenty years ago – it became only too easy to evoke "feminine" intuition, condescendingly or otherwise. Both erudite language and ordinary language have done this, the latter under the influence of distant debates conducted by the former, whose ultimate significance eludes me somewhat. How is it that, one fine day, toward the end of the eighteenth century, people began to see such sharp contrasts between intellectual capacities, such conflicts between faculties and incompatibilities between ways of knowing, that one and the same being could no longer be said to contain them all? From a feminist perspective, beating the philosophical bushes flushes out a swarm of more and more interesting questions, even if there are no ready answers. And I cannot have an immediate response, since the very concept of "intellectual faculties" seems obscure to me.

Under the influence of Brouwer, a Dutch topologist, some mathematicians, especially in the English-speaking world, go to great lengths to claim that their work incorporates something like intuition, even though it also demands considerable intellectual labor. None of them has concluded that women alone can be truly creative in mathematics, though logically this is what should emerge from the encounter between common views of intuition and the epistemological position of these intuitionists. Must we infer that feminine intuition is not intuition after all? Or that there is no connection between what they say about mathematical objects (which must be intuited) and what is said in the folk epistemology embedded in everyday conversations?[11] Between the garden and the dining room, people take pleasure in detailing the supposed cognitive differences between women and men, without ever establishing even a minimal critical distance: how do we know these differences, and do we *know* them? Since we are discussing mathematics, let us note that the debate has a comic dimension. In Francophone countries where Bourbakian constructivism prevails, intuition of mathematical objects is strictly forbidden: if after manipulating these objects for a long time, you begin to see them, do so on the sly and don't brag about it. In the anglophone world, intuitive or imagist representations of mathematical objects are legitimate; you may confess that you see a convergent series as a collection of small points racing off in a particular direction. From ridicule south of the Channel to relevance on its north shore, how amusing to note that epistemology is divided by an arm of the sea. Yet, on both shores, female mathematicians are equally marginalized.

Notes

1 Paul Gauguin, *Avant et après*. Quoted by Pierre Leprohon, *Paul Gauguin* (Paris: Gründ, 1975), 15.
2 René Descartes, *Rules for the Direction of the Mind*, trans. Laurence J. Lafleur (Indianapolis: Bobbs Merrill, 1961), 10.
3 Book V of the *Republic* (451d, 454e, 546a . . .) indicates that women and men are equally called upon to be Guardians of the polis, and thus to receive an education that culminates in philosophy. This is mentioned again in Book VII, 540c, in which Socrates says: "You mustn't think that in what I have been saying I have had men in mind any more than women – those of them born with the right natural abilities." Plato, *The Republic*, ed. G.R.F. Ferrari, trans. Tom Griffith (Cambridge: Cambridge University Press, 2000), 250. For *noêsis*, see the *Timaeus* 28a, *Republic* VI, 511d; mathematics (and the operations of reason) produce contemplation in the soul, itself the work of a discursivity that relies on hypotheses (VI, 511 c–d); even if this form of contemplation is inferior to the intellectual activity attained in dialectical reasoning, the study of mathematics is a propaedeutic to philosophy, particularly because it "radically cleanses" the organ of the soul which is the power to know. If Platonic philosophy distinguishes between intellection and reasoning, it is nonetheless impossible within the framework it puts in place to isolate intellection by attributing it to people who possess only it, and no reasoning whatsoever.
4 Jean-Jacques Rousseau, *Émile*, trans. Barbara Foxley (London: Dent, 1993), 248.
5 G.W.F. Hegel, *Phenomenology of Spirit*, trans. A.V. Miller (Oxford: Clarendon Press, 1977), 4.
6 G.W.F. Hegel, *Hegel's Lectures on the History of Philosophy*, vol. 3, trans. E.S. Haldane (London: Routledge and Kegan Paul, 1955), 550.
7 G.W.F. Hegel, *The Philosophy of Right*, trans. T.M. Knox (Oxford: Clarendon Press, 1942), 263.

8 Hegel, *Phenomenology*, 149.
9 *Hegel's Lectures*, 550.
10 Genevieve Lloyd, "The Man of Reason," in *Women, Knowledge, and Reality*, ed., Ann Garry and Marilyn Pearsall (Boston: Unwin Hyman, 1989), 124. Author's italics.
11 The term "folk epistemology" appears in an article by Miranda Fricker, "Intuition and Reason," *Philosophical Quarterly* 45, no. 179 (1995): 181.

20

NATHALIE CHARRAUD

Nathalie Charraud is a mathematician and psychoanalyst. She holds doctorates in mathematics and in psychology, as well as diplomas in psychopathology. She is a member of the École de la Cause Freudienne. She has lectured in the history of science at the University of Paris XII and in mathematics at the University of Rennes.

Her major publications include the following:

Infini et inconscient: essai sur Georg Cantor, Paris: Anthropos, 1994.

Lacan et les mathémathiques, Paris: Anthropos, 1997.

APPARENT SUBJECT, REAL SUBJECT

The subject is not as excluded from current science as it is usually said to be. According to the viewpoint discussed below, the question of the sex of the subject is not reducible to biological differentiation, but leads, in particular, to that of narcissistic satisfaction. Thus Albert Einstein, Marie Curie, Barbara McClintock and Georg Cantor attest to a different division of the 'masculine' and 'feminine' positions.

From Aristotle to Galileo, traditional science developed a description of reality that had a specific coherence. This was a science that spoke of a harmonious Nature with affinities that exactly mirrored human emotions, to such an extent that the metaphor of sexual relations often served as an explanation, particularly in the field of alchemy.

With Galileo and Descartes, the status of the reality that is the target of science changed radically. The *cogito* engendered such a powerful break with acquired knowledge that any fantasy of a pre-established harmony was definitively swept aside. In its place are tiny algebraic symbols and mathematical equations that serve to quantify questions regarding space and matter. Experiments based on increasingly sophisticated constructions succeed in procuring ever more precise responses from a material in which it is difficult for us to recognize Mother Nature.

Is the subject as absent from this modern science as we might think? If it is, then it is up to psychoanalysis to ensure that its voice is heard there. But the relationship between psychoanalysis and science is not quite this simple, and cannot be reduced, even though it may seem pertinent to do so in some cases, to one of straightforward complementarity. Psychoanalysis is far from wishing to be situated outside science. On the contrary, it can lead to a conception of science that would take the subject into account. It would do so without falling into that brand of fundamental relativism exemplified by a recent movement in Anglo-Saxon epistemology, in which every field of knowledge, indeed even the smallest fragment of meaningful human activity fits comfortably into the vague and dilute notion of 'science'.

Throughout the work of Lacan, there is a reflection on science which develops out of the distinction between the categories of the Real, the Imaginary and the Symbolic, and which, if drawn out systematically, might lead to a Lacanian epistemology. We can only hope to provide a brief outline of it here. Taking the fundamental Freudian notions of *reality* and *repetition*, we shall lay down markers for defining the object of science, not as a given, but with reference to a subject which is itself always already the subject

of science. Questioning the gender of the subject will allow us to make some observations concerning the 'feminine' position in science.

Real, reality, mathematics

How are we to conceive of a scientific approach to reality given that, according to the
view of the school of psychoanalysis that I am referring to, we can only access reality
along lines of desire and through the double matrix of language and fantasy, and that,
according to Freud, there is only psychic reality? The category of the Real introduced by
Lacan allows us to move outside this solipsism.

In accordance with the pleasure principle that governs the Freudian unconscious, the
young child, at an early stage, hallucinates the object of satisfaction (the breast). It is
the subsequent experience of disappointment that gradually leads it, according to the
reality principle, to distinguish the real object from the hallucinated one, and to detach
itself from it. As the child acquires language, the primordial object of jouissance is lost
forever, while external reality is divided up according to the laws of the signifier. The
renunciation of the primordial object leaves a scar in the form of *fantasy*, which, from
that point onwards, supplies the framework of reality.

A sense of loss is thus inserted into the heart of the subject, a fundamental absence
that is covered over by fantasy which contains, adorns and displays an object that masks
the lack. Fantasmatic scenarios, at the service of the pleasure principle, are part of the
category of the Imaginary. The extent to which reality is coextensive with images
determines the extent to which the Real is perceived as a hole, a dead end for the
Imaginary and the Symbolic.

Lacan underscores the structuring function of this lack which attests, in particular, to
the indestructibility of desire. As Freud made clear, whatever repetition, indeed whatever
compulsion towards repetition there might be in the life of a subject, is repetition of
disappointment. The subject is not free within the network of signifiers. Instead, it circles
continuously around the same void in accordance with a certain automatism. Only an
act can modify the relation of these signifying orbits to the fundamental fantasy that
surrounds this void.

Sublimation, the sole satisfying outlet for drive, according to Freud, introduces,
through artistic or scientific creation, the equivalent of an act which displaces us in
relation to the automatism of repetition. Sublimation provides the means by which we
can grasp hold of the Real from the hole, from within the Symbolic or the Imaginary.

At bottom, repetition is the repetition of failure, and can be transformed, through the
work of sublimation, into a repetition governed by artistic or scientific experimentation.

Lacan has noted that, in language itself, or more specifically among the cardinal
numbers, only the first numbers are significant to the subject. After 4 or 5, the numbers
are no longer signifiers, but have become part of the real. For the subject, numbers, which
are part of language, run naturally alongside the hole of the real.

From a scientific viewpoint, Einstein (among others) marvelled at this concordance:
physical reality obeys mathematical laws. The reality of physics thus comes up against
the reality that is hidden from the subject by language. The mode of scientific sublimation would therefore be the result of the possible encounter between the real of the

subject and that of physics, and science would be that branch of knowledge constituted by the mathematical bridge between the symbolic and the real. 'Mathematical' must be understood in the wider sense. If the heart of the atomic structure and the equations of general relativity require highly elaborate mathematics, the diagrams of molecular biology or the descriptions of genetics, indeed of the 'social sciences', also introduce mathematics into their respective fields, and thus render them 'scientific'.

Psychoanalysts have a long way to go before they can understand all the implications of these Lacanian constructions. They might be of assistance in elucidating the relationship between mathematics, fantasy and jouissance, for example, which, in the end, provide the subject's three approaches to reality. In particular, the link between mathematics and jouissance, which is evoked by the 'accounting of jouissance', is the origin of an inhibition that can be considered as natural vis-à-vis mathematics.

Being or having?

Contrary to what happens in science, where the real always has the final word, from a psychoanalytic viewpoint, the question of being a man or a woman is not reduced to simple biological differentiation of the sexes, but involves the subjective consequence of the difference, which emerges during infancy, between having and not having a penis. Freud attempted to reduce this difference to an opposition between activity and passivity, and subsequently to two positions relating to castration (fear of castration, penis envy). With Lacan, for whom the subject represents itself to itself by a signifier which stands for another signifier, the focus has shifted to phallic significance and the dialectic of *having* and *being* the phallus, the signifier of the desirable in the discourse of the unconscious. From the 'being' viewpoint, the feminine position, through a play of identifications, presents itself phenomenologically as 'masculine' with relative ease. Hence there are three possibilities to consider.

Firstly, the phallus is the most desirable thing there is, and to be the phallus through the medium of science is the height of sophistication. Women of science have frequently found themselves in the position to challenge men's limited knowledge in scientific terms.

Secondly, the question of 'being' is connected to that of identification. It could be the case that a woman, disappointed by a scientific father who does not supply the love she demands, responds by identifying with a father who has a scientific vocation. But the constant striving to be loved by the father will prevent her from entering into true competition with her male colleagues.

Lastly, the same identification with her father can lead a woman to occupy a position of 'having', to behave as if she had a phallus and therefore to become involved in science and to be unequivocally competitive with men. Furthermore, in her love life, she would occupy a homosexual position.

A forced choice

We shall attempt to illustrate these three positions by examining the lives of four scientists: A. Einstein, B. McClintock, M. Curie and G. Cantor.

Einstein and Marie Curie clearly require no introduction. Barbara McClintock is less famous, but her life is discussed elsewhere.[1] Georg Cantor was one the greatest mathematicians of the second half of the nineteenth century. After having identified the different properties of real numbers, which until then had been merged within the idea of a continuum, he invented transfinite numbers.

Marie Curie seems to characterise the second, and even the first position, and B. McClintock very probably the third. G. Cantor is situated in an equally feminine position (for reasons we cannot elaborate on here), while Einstein represents the masculine position in a fairly typical manner.

Like many other actors in science, during adolescence, all four experienced a depression that was sufficiently severe to require a decision that would have a lasting effect on their future. Any attempt to return to the past represented a threat to their balance and well-being.

Thus Einstein, in his autobiography, writes: 'I was still a very young man when I was struck by the vanity of the hopes entertained and the battles fought by most men throughout their lives.' And subsequently: 'This feeling was overwhelming, and out if it was born my distrust of all forms of authority and my sceptical attitude regarding the opinions that hold sway in different social circles.'

Similarly, Barbara McClintock once confided to Evelyn Fox Keller: 'Because of this hypersensitivity, these disproportionate reactions, I was taken out of school on several occasions.'

By the same token, at the age of fifteen, Marie Curie was sent for a year's rest in the country to recover from a nervous breakdown; while Cantor, at boarding school at the same age, received letters from an alarmed father seeking to coax him away from his dark ideas and pleading with him to work less.

In response to the depression that was the expression of their relationship to the external world during adolescence, Einstein and McClintock had something in common, namely, that they were both in the position of 'having'. The lack is on the side of the Other and they will therefore dedicate themselves to completing it, through the advancement of science. Somewhat impervious to their own image, they continuously praised the world of science for its extraordinary logical and mathematical beauty, and did so with a fervour that Einstein referred to as 'cosmic religiousness'.

This 'masculine' position in relation to the phallus means that they are subjected to a far more piercing anxiety of castration. Both attest that they never stopped working, that the object of their research was ever-present in their minds and that anything that distracted them from it frustrated them, even if Einstein, as we know, did not hesitate to become embroiled in the political battles of his time.

While McClintock, like Einstein, reconstructed the world through her discoveries, Marie Curie's aim was to construct herself through science. In contrast to those who were in positions of 'having', Marie Curie, as she emerged from adolescence, made the decision to 'be somebody' by embracing the scientific ideals of her father. Her entire life was to be focused on this ideal and her scientific work yielded to it. However, as primordial as this ideal may have been, she still chose to marry and to raise children who served to complete her narcissistic image.

Cantor, in what is for the most part a typically feminine position, viewed mathematics as a means of increasing his popularity among those close to him. He decided to do mathematics so that his father 'would experience great happiness' by reason of his son's vocation. Later on, he wrote to his sister: 'My work is and will remain the true centre of my life, and I wish for nothing more than to find myself in a position to devote myself without difficulty to this activity and thereby to make myself useful and pleasant in the eyes of a circle of human society.'

Knowledge and truth

Beyond this fundamentally narcissistic position between being and having which determines a subject's choice of a scientific field, a further order of truth slips into the relation that exists between that subject and scientific knowledge: a loving relation, indeed one of jouissance.

Lacan describes feminine jouissance as supplementary and mystical. This means that women are 'not entirely' consumed by the phallic jouissance, which is associated with sexual relations with men. It certainly seems that the kind of satisfaction experienced by the scientist at work, be it a man or woman, is an example of this type of jouissance. However, women in science sometimes have ways of their very own of achieving it.

To the astonishment of her male colleagues, Marie Curie, after the death of her husband, went back to purifying tons of pitchblende by kneading small lumps of it with her hands so as to extract a few grams of radium, and this in spite of the fact that more efficient industrial methods were beginning to be developed. Even in the service of science, a woman can allow this kind of mystical jouissance to seep into her body, while a man must clearly make a detour via abstraction.

Einstein speaks of mathematics in loving terms. It was like a first love, and subsequently, after having fled from it, nostalgia returned him to it. Two of his utterances suffice to reinforce this thesis: 'I started with Euclid at eleven . . . It was one of the most important events in my life, as passionate as my first love. I would never have imagined that there could be anything as wonderful as that in the world.'

The second utterance demonstrates the harshness of the reunion: 'There is at least one thing that is certain, and that is that I have never worked as hard in my entire life, and that I have acquired a great respect for mathematics, the most subtle aspects of which, in my innocence, I considered to be a superfluous luxury. Next to this problem, the first theory of relativity is child's play.'

We have already underlined the fact that the natural relation to mathematics is inhibition, but it is particularly remarkable to encounter it in an Einstein. This is how he explains his avoidance of mathematics: 'I no doubt showed less interest in mathematics than in the other exact sciences, but this is not enough to explain why, to a certain extent, I neglected mathematics. I experienced a curious feeling when I realised that it was divided into a multitude of specialities, and that each one was enough to keep us busy for what little time we have to live . . . ' So if he shrank back in the face of mathematics, it was because of its voracity!

The special theory of relativity is limited in its use of mathematical terms. By contrast, one of the reasons for Einstein's prolonged detours before arriving at the general theory of relativity is of a mathematical nature, and when, much later on, he took on the problem of unified field theory, he wrote to a friend: 'I need more mathematics.'

He spent every day of the final years of his life aligning pages and pages of calculations in the hope of discovering a cosmology that was compatible with the general theory of relativity. Such a man could do nothing else: reconstruct the world on paper, on a cosmic scale. At the end of his life, in spite of his political commitments and two marriages, he wrote: 'I fled from I and WE to the THERE of *there is*' – a concise and lucid formula for designating a preference for knowledge to the detriment of truth!

A special kind of sensual delight

McClintock also speaks of the appearance, in her early infancy, of 'a love affair with the world'. Her aim was not, like Marie Curie's, to make herself loved by the world, but to penetrate deeper into its mysteries.

Having begun to overcome the crisis of adolescence, and having noted that she was 'not like other people' (this certainly seems to be indicative of her homosexuality), she decided to suffer the consequences and embarked on a brilliant career as a biologist.

To achieve the kind of virtuosity that characterises her in her laboratory, she became 'pure regard', to the extent that, when she was behind the lens of a microscope, she lost all sense of herself. In place of Einstein's thought we have McClintock's vision. For these two visionaries, who were both extremely proud of an intuition in which they had absolute confidence, thought and vision are not without connection. 'Suddenly,' says McClintock, 'you see the problem, something happens, and even before you can translate it into words, you feel as if you have the solution. Everything happens in the subconscious. That has happened to me on so many occasions, and I know exactly when to take this type of impression seriously. I just know it. I am absolutely certain of it. I don't speak about it; I don't need to discuss it with anyone. I'm just certain that I've got the solution.'

As important as these dazzling moments of anticipation may be, she eventually had to resort to scientific rigour, and in so doing she received support from her peers. 'It was logic that fuelled my conviction, implacable logic.'

But, unlike Einstein, McClintock is not party to a search for that kind of mastery which is conducted entirely through mathematics. Her connection to the 'not entirely', described above as peculiar to 'feminine' jouissance, is more corporeal. Whatever is neglected by this mastery receives expression within Buddhism. A certain tendency among physicists meant that the likes of Schrödinger, Niels Bohr and Oppenheimer had already been drawn to it. McClintock identifies with Tibetan Buddhist monks' experience in controlling moments of depersonalisation and mystical jouissance. 'What is ecstasy? I don't know what it is, but I know it feels good when it pays me a visit. Ecstasy is rare.'

Similarly, Cantor expresses a special kind of sensual delight in mathematical work: 'In conceiving of the infinite, as I have done here and in my past efforts, I experience a true pleasure (to which I gratefully abandon myself). And if I return to the finite from the infinite, I witness, with equal clarity and beauty, the two concepts (cardinal and ordinal numbers) merging once again into one and converging within the concept of the finite whole number.'

There is no need to appeal to a pre-scientific conception of science to find a subject that has been banished from it. The harmony between subject and world, exalted by traditional science at the level of affects, re-emerges in today's science at the level of mathematics. We must therefore take into consideration the place of mathematics within subjectivity. This involves skirting along the edges of language and being at the same time almost without signification. We need only follow the subject of science when it expresses itself within a scientific context. The more subjectivity is thought to be unacceptable within scientific circles, the more the subject is given the opportunity to express itself, to talk about itself and to construct a vision of the world.

The four scientists cited here attest to the fact that a jouissance in knowledge is accompanied by a knowledge of jouissance. As a result of this possibility of reversal, scientists can be viewed as the subjects of an ethics, and what is at stake for this ethics in the current debate concerns a limitation of their jouissance.

Translated by Tom Baldwin

Note

1   Translator's note: the author writes here that McClintock's 'life is discussed in other articles in this collection'. She is referring to *Le Sexe des sciences. Les Femmes en plus*, ed. Françoise Collin (Paris: Éditions Autrement, 1992).

21

FRANÇOISE BALIBAR

Françoise Balibar is Professor of Physics at the University of Paris VII. She is married to the political philosopher Etienne Balibar. Attached to the CNRS, she directed the Seuil edition of the selected works of Einstein in six volumes.

Her works include the following:

Quantique, Paris: Inter Éditions, 1984.

Galilée, Newton lus par Einstein, Paris: PUF, 1984.

Pourquoi ça vole?, Paris: Hachette, 1987.

Œuvres choisies d'Einstein, 6 vols, Paris: Seuil-CNRS, 1984–92.

La Science du cristal, Paris: Hachette, 1991.

Einstein 1905: de l'éther aux quanta, Paris: PUF, 1992.

Einstein, la joie de la pensée, Paris: Gallimard, 1993.

IS THERE A FEMININE SCIENCE?

The relationship between women and the sciences has been studied extensively in the Anglo-Saxon world. A dominant thesis belonging to the American feminist tradition maintains that science is naturally masculine and that it is the responsibility of women to develop another science that is feminine in nature. In what follows, this sexing of the sciences is called into question.

Contrary to what happens in France, in the United States, the question of science is, and has been for some time, the object of numerous inquiries within the feminist movement. Some American feminists[1] even go so far as to assert that this question, which, until now, has been repressed and hidden behind other questions, is crucial, and that feminist theory (if such an expression makes sense) can only really progress if the bonds that tie the three concepts of *masculinity*, *femininity* and *science* together are unravelled. In more 'European' terms, we might say that for the American feminist movement, the question of the effect of the difference between the sexes within scientific activity is of fundamental political importance. The aim of this article is not only to provide a critical description of the opposing positions, but also to attempt to understand the reasons why American feminists attach such importance to the relatively specific question of science.

If reflection on the question of women and science is more advanced in countries where English is spoken than it is in France, this is almost certainly because, at a very early stage, female scientists, who are nevertheless far fewer in number in those countries than in France, occupied a not inconsiderable position within the feminist movement. While, in France, female scientists 'kept their mouths shut', often giving the impression of satisfaction at having known how to surmount, on an individual level, obstacles placed in front of them in a traditionally masculine world, Anglo-Saxon – above all English – female scientists have not hesitated to denounce the sexist harassment that they have encountered at different stages of their career. There is, therefore, in England, and in spite of the highly elitist nature of studies leading to a scientific career, a tradition of women who demand the right to practice a scientific profession that is without equivalent in France. Furthermore, in their efforts to occupy positions to which they have no birth-right, English women have benefited from a more sustained support than French women of a certain number of eminent (male) scientists, the most illustrious of these being J.D. Bernal, who is famous for his Marxist perspective on science,[2] its history and social practices, and for his reflection on the inequalities – particularly those of a sexist nature – within scientific activity.

The mechanisms of exclusion

These different historical factors mean that in countries where English is spoken, there is a tradition of feminist writings on science that is sorely lacking in France. The first of these feminist studies were distinctly corporatist in character. It is tempting to call them egalitarian; above all, they aimed to dismantle those mechanisms which, historically, had sought to exclude women from the field of science. A case in point is an article by Alice Rossi, adapted from a paper delivered at a seminar organised in 1965 by MIT students on the theme of 'Women in Science' . In this article, which remains popular, A. Rossi asks 'Women in Science. Why so few?', and responds by analysing the 'social and psychological factors that prevent women from pursuing scientific careers'.[3] To speak of 'psychological factors' was to pin the responsibility for the exclusion of women largely on women themselves, and this was an aspect of her argument for which a number of her detractors reproached her tirelessly. Approaching the question from the opposite direction, in an article entitled 'A Feminist Critique of Scientific Objectivity', Elizabeth Fee responded to Alice Rossi by placing the responsibility for the exclusion of women in the hands of the scientific institution, with its rules of work, restrictions and prejudices. She asked if it was possible (and if so, to what extent) to modify scientific institutions in such a way that women would be *naturally* accepted in them.[4] Without equivocation, Donna Haraway responded to this question in the negative, maintaining that it is illusory to expect anything at all from an eventual evolution of the institution.[5] Having noted, with statistics to reinforce her argument, that the recruitment rate of women in scientific domains, after suffering a heavy fall between 1930 and 1960, suddenly increased during the 1960s, Donna Haraway explains – quite convincingly, it must be said – that this increase did not, as we may naively have believed, coincide in any way with the adoption of a more egalitarian legislation. Instead, it coincided with the launch of the Sputniks by the Soviets and the resulting mass recruitment in the United States of anyone with the necessary expertise – a kind of general mobilisation, similar to a 'war effort' – with a view to regaining the technological lead. Thanks are therefore due to a social governance that was better equipped than the feminists and egalitarian lobbies to convince American scientists that women were also capable of making calculations and conducting experiments without making mistakes.[6]

There is no question, however, that these 'egalitarian' studies, as informative and necessary as they may be, provide nothing more than a basic inventory of facts and call for more profound analyses that might explain why so few women are interested in science. It should nevertheless be noted that each of these studies with egalitarian aims is based upon an implicit presupposition that it is also important to discuss, namely that the objective of women is and indeed must be to be 'everywhere and always like men'. Here we should not forget Virginia Woolf's horrific description in *Three Guineas* of a procession of important (and therefore ridiculous) men (lawyers, doctors, professors, etc.) whom the 'daughters of educated men' might wish to imitate. We cannot help but recall Woolf's speculation: 'For we have to ask ourselves, here and now, do we wish to join that procession or don't we?'

A political critique of science

In fact, this question occupies a central position within those more militant debates which, in recent years, have borne upon the question of 'Women and Science'. Should women (that is to say, is it in their interest to) enter upon a scientific career? While for Virginia Woolf it is clearly the status of the professions in general – irrespective of whether they belong to the scientific medical, literary, ecclesiastical, legal or artistic domains – that is at stake, it seems clear that for American feminists, the profession of 'scientist' should be the object of a specific examination. According to the representatives of this line of thought, from a woman's perspective, doing science does not carry the same significance as creating literature or paintings. This for one simple reason: scientific activity is, in itself, uncertain and open to question.

That science should not be understood as what it claims to be in its public presentation of itself, namely a pure and disinterested activity, is not a novel idea. It might even be said that few people today (including scientists) would be prepared to support the idea that science is thoroughly free and disconnected from non-cognitive interests – especially in the United States, where the *political critique of science* has been an essential component of intellectual and political life over the last thirty years. In any case, it should be remembered that in the United States, the feminist movement and the political critique of science have a common origin; from the 1970s onwards, in the tradition of what in France we might be tempted to refer to as 'post-68'[7] and of what Americans call 'radical thought', each movement increased to a previously unknown scale.[8] We should therefore not be surprised that when the American feminist movement came to focus on science, it quite naturally assimilated, even if only to modify them, a certain number of 'political' critiques of science which had been developed by men (since they are in the majority in this domain also).

In the last thirty years, the essential contribution of the critique of science movement has doubtless been its demonstration that science is not a purely intellectual, 'disembodied' activity, but maintains relations constitutionally with different forms of power: state power, financial power, military power, the power of multinational corporations. It is a fact that, for many years, masculine power (or *patriarchal* power, as it is known in English) has been omitted from the list of powers which impose themselves on science. Given the obviousness of masculine power, it is astonishing (or is it?) that it should have taken so many years for the political (read masculine) critique of science and the women's movement to come together on this basis. It is a persistent claim that finally, today, the job has been done and that we have a 'feminist critique of science'.

A feminist critique of science

This critique brings together two kinds of contributors. On the one hand, there are the old combatants – both male and female – in the 'political' critique who have converted to the struggle against masculine power. On the other, there are the original feminists who have become aware of what is at stake for women themselves regarding the question of science. As an example of a representative of the first category, consider Hilary Rose, the author of a work written in collaboration with her husband Steven Rose,[9] who for some years has devoted the bulk of her time to developing a 'feminist episte-mology', and who writes: 'the achievements of those who sought to analyze and critique capitalist science's existing forms and systems of knowledge . . . (which may well have been developed with a conscious opposition to sexism) are theoretically sex blind.'[10] A typical example of those feminists who situate the question of science in the context of the development of the feminist movement itself is Sandra Harding, the author of a work which has experienced a certain notoriety.[11] The first chapter is entitled 'From the Woman Question in Science to the Science Question in Feminism'[12] – the clearest way of saying that the problem is not women, as A. Rossi suggested in 1965, but science itself.

It is interesting to note that both parties claim overtly to be adherents of the work of Thomas Kuhn, and more specifically, of his *The Structure of Scientific Revolutions*.[13] What on the one hand is not particularly surprising (wasn't Kuhn himself of the May 1968 generation?), is nevertheless troubling, since it is not clear how the distinction between 'normal' science and 'non-paradigmatic' science, which is the crux of Kuhn's argument, can help us to think about the question of women and science. In fact, it seems that the feminists – and they are not, as it happens, alone in this[14] – have read something in Kuhn's text that, it seems to me, is not there, namely proof of the fact that science is neither as autonomous nor as absolutely progressive (that is to say offering an increasingly more exact view of 'reality') as scientists and certain epistemologists (with Karl Popper in the lead) would have us believe.

So far so good with this argumentation – even if to get to this stage we have to appeal to Kuhn's text; nobody would support the idea these days that science is a 'pure' activity produced within the walls of an ivory tower. Unfortunately, the critique that uses Kuhn as a starting point, be it feminist or not, does not stop there and often descends the slippery slope that leads to the assertion that 'science *is only* the expression of specific interests' and has no universal value. If this position were only false, it would not provide much cause for concern, but, as I shall now attempt to show, this thesis which views science as an expression of specific interests constitutes, in my opinion, a danger to the women's movement.[15]

'Inhuman' science

A simple, perhaps even simplistic way of connecting the question of women in science to the thesis according to which science has no universal value consists in establishing a certain number of 'natural' oppositions in terms of which women are located on one side and science on the other. The reasoning is perfectly logical. The premises: (1) humanity is divided into men and women; (2) science, which has always been practised by half of humanity (men), can only be an expression of the interests of men. The conclusion: science is not 'human' (this is Londa Schiebinger's expression),[16] since it ignores half of humanity. The corollary argument: the less women, the forgotten part of humanity, have to do with science, the better equipped they are to behave as women should and the less their 'feminine being' is damaged. In short, everything is for the best in the best of all possible worlds: it is a stroke of good fortune that, historically, women have been excluded from science, since to allow them to become involved in it would only be to tarnish them, damage them in their capacity as women.

We need not waste energy criticising this indefensible position. We will note only that to adopt this point of view is to produce precisely the inverse of the desired effect and to abolish radically the subversive potential of the question: why do women not do science? Women have had to endure for years the leitmotif that the effect of science is to destroy femininity and have consequently avoided flying into a violent rage on reading this kind of argument (which is extreme and caricatured, it must be said). To recommend that women become involved in a haughty boycotting of scientific activity, that they retreat on to Mount Aventine, is once again to mistake a renunciation for a victory; it is to militate in favour of women being *denied a pleasure* that they should be free to savour without compunction, without being seen as traitors to their own sex. This is a pleasure that stems from the fact that science is precisely not 'human'. Whatever L. Schiebinger's view on the matter (her article does contain some otherwise useful information), the objective of women is not to 'make science more human',[17] but, on the contrary, to ensure that they are granted the right to take pleasure (in every sense of the term) from an activity that is defined by its non-humanity. In his scientific autobiography, Einstein speaks of the desire to 'flee from the personal' which always drove him to practice physics, and of the immediate pleasure to be found in the world of objective understanding.[18] Of course, Einstein was a man (and not one of the most admirable, given his view and treatment of women), but nobody would dare deny that he knew what he was talking about when it came to science. Nor would anybody dare deny that women are equally as susceptible to the desire to 'flee from the personal' – these are the women who we already have too great a tendency to confine to the lived, the private, the subjective, etc. Isn't the discourse which consists in distancing women from science on the pretext that they will not be true to their own being the most hackneyed and reactionary there is?

As I have already said, this is an extreme and simplistic position. There are, however, more refined versions of the same argument that give further cause for reflection. Basically, the argumentation is built on two hypotheses that are seemingly unquestionable. The first hypothesis is 'naturist' in character: there is an irreducible opposition (in the sense that a fracture is irreducible), and that is the opposition men/women. The second hypothesis is epistemological: it consists in a term for term redoubling of the men/women opposition in the form of a distinction between objective and subjective. A more progressive and critical version of this argumentation consists in taking these oppositions as they are and in showing that the term for term correspondence, the effect of which is to identify the objective with the masculine and the subjective with the feminine, is in fact nothing but the result of a deviant historical process during which objective thought, which, while originally unsullied by either more masculine or more feminine connotations, was misappropriated in favour of men, who used it as a tool in the domination of one sex by the other. Let us cite, as an example of this tendency, Carolyn Merchant's book *The Death of Nature*,[19] in which she develops a thesis according to which the 'scientific revolution' of the seventeenth and eighteenth centuries was motivated by the wish to exclude, indeed to eliminate women from Nature, by reducing the latter to a pure mechanics.[20]

Towards the science/gender system

It was in order to combat this apparently indisputable *a priori* logic that, some years ago now, Evelyn Fox Keller developed an analysis based on psychoanalytic theory (which, unfortunately, is identified with the work of Piaget) and which aimed to unravel the origins of the associations masculine/objective, feminine/subjective.[21]

> The most immediate issue for a feminist perspective on the natural sciences is the deeply rooted popular mythology that casts objectivity, reason, and mind as male, and subjectivity, feeling, and nature as female. In this division of emotional and intellectual labor, women have been the guarantors and protectors of the personal, the emotional, the particular, whereas science – the province par excellence of the impersonal, the rational, and the general – has been the preserve of men . . . In its attempts to identify extrascientific determinants of the growth of scientific knowledge, the social studies of science have for the most part ignored the influence of those forces . . . that are at work in the individual human psyche. Just as science is not the purely cognitive endeavor we once thought it, neither is it as impersonal as we thought: science is a deeply personal as well as a social activity.[22] In other words, despite its rejection of 'scientific neutrality', the social study of science has pursued its critique in terms that tacitly support the divisions between the public and the private, impersonal and personal, and masculine and feminine . . . A feminist perspective on science confronts us with the task of examining the roots, dynamics, and consequences of this interacting network of associations and disjunctions – together constituting what might be called the "science-gender system".

Politically, the system of analysis denounced by E. Fox Keller, which consists in repeating and reinforcing the dichotomies of personal/impersonal, masculine/feminine, etc., leads to one of two diametrically opposed attitudes: on the one hand, an outright withdrawal, which has already been discussed, and on the other, a call in favour of the mass entrance of women into science, with the obvious intention to transform it, to 'modify it from the inside', to 'make a woman's voice heard there'. As soon as one speaks of 'transforming science', the most extreme caution is required, as the spectre of the 'Lyssenko affair' looms large. Are feminists not in the process of repeating the disastrous error of the opposition between bourgeois and proletarian science?[23] In any case, we must think twice before diving headlong into this kind of enterprise.

Can science be otherwise?

Women are of course right to point out that the contraceptive pill could have been developed much earlier had pharmaceutical laboratories not been populated predominantly by men; and they have good reason to suspect that it is due to a lack of interest on the part of researchers (and of those who decide on the programmes of research) that menstrual pains have still not been abolished, etc.[24] But to get from this point to the idea that science in general, without being more precise, could be *otherwise* if women (or men and women on an equal footing) were practising it, involves a step we are not willing to take. This is because to do so would be to be a victim of a well-known positivist illusion, under which modern science has already suffered considerably, an illusion according to which science is reduced to an activity of 'rational prediction' and is not a primarily *speculative* activity. If it is true that we can influence the applications of science politically (by insisting that the decision-makers choose this programme of development rather than another), the fact remains that so-called fundamental science, for its part, obeys an *internal* necessity, which the 'scientific subject', whether it is male, female, black, white, rich or poor, cannot change. It is important to note here that Virginia Woolf's phrase, 'Science, it would seem, is not sexless; she is a man, a father, and infected too', quoted time and time again and unavoidable in Anglo-Saxon literature as soon as there is talk of women and science, is usually, in my opinion, cast against type, if not entirely misinterpreted. Indeed, to quote this phrase without being precise about what Virginia Woolf means by 'infected' is to risk implying that what is being asserted is the intrinsically harmful character of science. 'Infected' refers here to a form of pathological attachment of fathers to their daughters that is analysed at length by Virginia Woolf in the preceding pages and which encourages them to maintain their daughters in a state of dependence for as long as possible. If science is 'infected', this does not occur from within science itself, but as a result of the pathological desire of fathers who stoop to appealing to so-called scientific results to satisfy their fantasy. Moreover, it is not merely coincidental that the phrase quoted above is inserted between a passage in which Virginia Woolf pokes fun at craniologists who believe that they have detected an underdevelopment in women's craniums and another in which she fulminates against doctors who refuse to introduce analgesics into the birthing room. For Virginia Woolf, it is clearly these 'infected' fathers' use of science that is to be proscribed, and not science itself.

In concluding this analysis, the question remains: why are there so few women scientists? And why are women scientists more inclined than their male colleagues to venture along interdisciplinary paths away from the glorious realm of pure and hard science? In any case, one thing is for certain: we will not find an answer without making the analytical effort to understand what science is; women cannot content themselves to assimilate uncritically the scientistic view of science. In fact, the stakes are high for the feminist movement. As soon as it tackles the problem of science (and how could it avoid doing so, since science is of pivotal cultural and political importance in the contemporary world?), the feminist movement must not set itself the wrong goals; it must first find the right tools for the job.

In fact, the feminist movement must at this very moment grasp hold of an historical opportunity: not to 'change' science, but to extricate it from scientistic (and, it should be noted, masculine; but how could they be otherwise?) notions that hinder its development and suffocate it. In this sense, we can hope (dreaming is permissible) that the women's liberation movement would also be a movement for the liberation of science, and would overcome the obstacles placed in its way by one hundred years of scientism and a reification of the so-called 'scientific method'. At least this is the position adopted by Evelyn Fox Keller in her remarkable biography of Barbara McClintock.[25] Faithful in this matter to Virginia Woolf, for whom the ideal of intellectual work was certainly not to be sought in the intensification of 'feminine' qualities, but rather in a certain form of intellectual androgyny (consider the figure of Orlando), Evelyn Fox Keller defends the viewpoint according to which 'the elements of the feminist critique that are opposed most strongly to the generally accepted conception of science are a liberating force for science itself' – and are therefore a factor in *universal* progress. She adds: 'I would go so far as to say that feminist thought could be useful in accomplishing that task which consists in shedding light on and clarifying what the substance of science is, in such a way as to keep hold of the lessons we have learned from it.'

Translated by Tom Baldwin

Notes

1 It is a distinctive feature of the American feminist movement that its representatives are not uniquely female; this, we might add, is not entirely unproblematic – if only because men have an unfortunate tendency to believe that they are more feminist than women.
2 J.D. Bernal, *The Social Function of Science* (London: Routledge and Kegan Paul, 1939).
3 A. Rossi, 'Women in Science. Why so Few?', reproduced in *Science*, 148, 1965.
4 E. Fee, 'A Feminist Critique of Scientific Objectivity', *Science for the People*, 14, no. 4, 1982.
5 D. Haraway, 'Class, Race, Sex, Scientific Objectivity of knowledge', in *Women in the Scientific Engineering Profession*, ed. V. Haas and C. Perruci (Ann Arbor University Press, 1984).
6 The fact remains that women in the United States, while they constitute 45% of the active population, represent less than a quarter of people working in the scientific domain (all disciplines). Cf. 'Women and Minorities [!!] in Science and Engineering', a report published by the National Science Foundation, a governmental organisation analogous to the CNRS in that it finances a significant portion of research on a confederal level, January 1984.
7 This periodisation will make little sense in the United States, where political protest took active forms well before 68.
8 The critique of science movement, sustained for the most part by scientists, began in the United States after the Second World War, as a consequence of the shock at the detonation of the first atomic bombs over Nagasaki and Hiroshima. The use of the atomic bomb, a result of science if ever there was one (thousands of scientists were employed to perfect it in Los Alamos), immediately escaped the control of its inventors, sending shockwaves through the scientific community. But it was only in the 1960s, in reaction to the Vietnam war, that the critique of science movement really took off. It experienced a new lease of life in the 1980s with the development of the ecological critique of industrial society.
9 H. Rose, S. Rose, *Ideology of/in the Natural Sciences* (Cambridge, Mass.: Schenkman, 1976).
10 H. Rose, 'Hand, Brain and Heart: A Feminist Epistemology for the Natural Sciences', *Signs: Journal of Women in Culture and Society*, 9, 1983.
11 S. Harding, *The Science Question in Feminism* (Milton Keynes: Open University Press, 1986). (S. Harding teaches in the United States and is published in England.)
12 See also E. Fee, 'Critiques of Modern Science: The Relationship of Feminism to Other Radical Epistemologies', in *Feminist Approaches to Science*, ed. R. Bleir (New York: Pergamon Press, 1986).
13 T. Kuhn, *The Structure of Scientific Revolutions* (Chicago: University of Chicago Press, 1962). According to Kuhn, science proceeds in long periods of 'normal' science – during which references, problematics and methods are the object of a vast consensus among

members of the scientific community – that are separated by 'non-paradigmatic' periods during which new methods are developed and new questions asked. The paradigm example of the latter is the upheaval in physics that took place at the beginning of this century.

14 See, for example, J. Ravetz, *Scientific Knowledge and Its Social Problems* (New York and Oxford: Oxford University Press, 1971).

15 This attitude is not only dangerous for the women's movement. Generally speaking, the entire modern gloss surrounding the theme of the end of history, the post-Auschwitz, the post-Chernobyl, the end of reason (totalising, totalitarian?) constitutes an over cautious discourse that is objectively disarming and destined to discourage (or has the effect of discouraging) those who may wish to engage in closer inspection.

16 L. Schiebinger, 'The History and Philosophy of Women in Science, A Review Essay', in *Sex and Scientific Inquiry*, ed. S. Harding and J.F. O'Barr (Chicago: University of Chicago Press, 1987).

17 Since when did science have to be 'human'? Do its value and attraction not stem, on the whole, from the fact that it is 'divine'? Consider Leibniz, who made it his aim to reveal the plans of the Creator. As will become clear, the origin of many of the errors in the feminist critique of science is a misunderstanding of what science is.

18 A. Einstein, *Autobiographisches*, in *Einstein, Scientist Philosopher*, ed. A. Schilpp (Evanston, 1947).

19 C. Merchant, *The Death of Nature: Women, Ecology and the Scientific Revolution* (San Francisco: Harper and Row, 1980).

20 Generally speaking, in this type of literature, all of the sins are laid at Descartes' door. See Susan Bordo's article, 'The Cartesian Masculinization of Thought', *Signs*, 11, no.3, 1986, and K. Stern's *The Flight from Woman* (New York: Noonday Press, 1965).

21 E.F. Keller, *Reflections on Gender and Science* (New Haven, Conn.: Yale University Press, 1984). See also E. F. Keller's article 'Gender and Science', *Psychoanalysis and Contemporary Thought*, 1, no. 3, 1978, reprinted in *Discovering Reality: Feminist Perspectives on Epistemology, Metaphysics, Methodology and Philosophy of Science*, ed. S. Harding and M. Hintika (Dordrecht: Reidel, 1983).

22 This in no way contradicts the quotation from Einstein we have just read. What is at stake is the possibility for individuals to escape from the category (personal/impersonal) assigned to them by popular myth for reasons unrelated to the question.

23 It seems that not everybody has learned the lessons of the Lyssenko affair. For example, Marcuse, as late as 1968, in *One-dimensional Man*, supports the idea that it is sufficient to construct 'another scientific project' to prevent the domination of man by man (man in this case is clearly asexual: Mensch). For a further discussion of this subject, see D. Lecourt, *Contre la peur* (Paris: Hachette, 1990).

24 I have deliberately not drawn attention, due to a lack of space and biological expertise, to a debate that is currently raging among American feminists and others concerning new reproductive techniques and, more generally, questions of so-called medical ethics.

25 E.F. Keller, *A Feeling for the Organism: The Life and Work of Barbara McClintock* (New York: Freeman, 1983).

22

ANNE FAGOT-LARGEAULT

Anne Fagot-Largeault is a doctor and a philosopher. She currently holds the chair of 'Philosophie des sciences biologiques et médicales' at the Collège de France, and has taught at many universities including the Universities of Paris I, Paris X and Paris XII. She is also a psychiatric specialist at the Henri Mondor hospital in Créteil. She works on bio-ethics and has been influential in the philosophy of medicine, especially in issues concerning medical experimentation and patient consent. Her ethical stance focuses in particular on the necessity to ensure that medical objectivity is always accompanied by a recognition of the specificity of the human and of human values. She is a member of the Comité National de l'Éthique and many other related commitees and organisations world-wide.

Her works include the following:

Causal vs. teleological explanation of behaviour, Stanford, CA: Stanford University Press, 1971.

Médecine et probabilités (ed.), Paris: Université de Paris XII et Didier-érudition, 1982.

L'Homme bio-éthique: pour une déontologie de la récherche sur le vivant, Paris: Maloine, 1985.

Les Causes de la mort. Histoire naturelle et facteurs de risque, Paris: Vrin, 1989.

L'Éthique environmentale, edited with P. Acot, Chilly-Mazarin: SenS, 2000.

Philosophie des sciences (with D. Andler and B. Saint-Sernin), 2 vols, Paris: Gallimard, Folio, 2002.

SCIENCE AND ETHICS

Problems of foundations

Problems of foundations

> With humanity constituting, fundamentally, but the principal degree of animality, the loftiest notions of sociology, and even of morality, necessarily find in biology their earliest outline, for the truly philosophical spirits who are able to grasp them there.
>
> (Auguste Comte)

4.1 'Can science provide the foundations for ethics?' This small Washington colloquium (ed. Gingerich, 1975) saw Daniel Callahan wish for the return of a 'philosophy of nature', which, putting man back into the universe as a whole, and discerning therein an order, would discover in that order some kind of general principle of ethics. If Darwinian theory is largely correct, the human race is the product of a long process of selection, and is the first species to be able to deliberately influence selection. In what way? Species seem to have always fought to survive: to make *survival* into a value (to continue to procreate, to protect the environment, and so on), it must first be accepted that man contributes to the perfection of the universe. As for taking the direction of evolution into our own hands, 'as long as we have no clear consensus on what is good, it would seem prudent not to intervene,' concludes Bernard Davis.

Today, the medieval ideal of an understanding of the universe that is both scientific and teleological is somewhat harder to achieve. In the absence of a global synthesis, it was hoped to draw from biology some universal principles of a 'scientific ethics'. Arnold Berleant (1977) considers that 'normative facts' emerge from certain regions of knowledge. Biological universals revolve around the maintenance of homeostasis: first, *one must survive* (if not, ethical questions cannot even be asked); next, *one must adapt* ('adaptation is the central moral concept'), and if the style of this adaptation is largely imposed by social life, the primary conditions are those of biological good and bad (the preservation of health, of genetic heritage, and so on). Psychology and anthropology complete the picture, in that they sketch in the conditions of individual development (Fromm, Maslow, Rogers and Skinner) and of insertion within the collectivity (Murdock, Kroeber, Kluckhohn and Harris), between which conditions we naturally observe a 'convergence'.

While finding it contradictory to base moral universals on an evolutionary science, let us state that *health* has without doubt been the most popular norm of a period that has devoted substantial sums to medical research, and which has counted among its urgent imperatives 'jogging' and the intake of natural foods. Certainly, these attitudes are founded on scientific notions: the cost of sickness for the collectivity is calculable, and it has been established that, for example, sedentary living and an overly rich diet are risk factors in cardiovascular illnesses. However, the scientific imperative is hypothetical: *if* you want to reduce your chances of developing bronchopulmonary cancer, *then* refrain from smoking. The biomedical sciences do not prove that the gain of a few years' life expectancy is worth sacrificing the pleasures of smoking or hearty eating. Insofar as they presuppose that any human being would, if enlightened as to the risks of excessive consumption, opt for a long life of sobriety, the biomedical sciences implicitly adopt cultural representations in which puritanism goes more or less hand-in-hand with economic calculations. Here, we find an example of what Englehardt and Callahan (vol. I, 1976) call the 'reciprocal importation' of concepts between science and ethics, with the biomedical sciences absorbing value judgements that are widespread among the collectivity, and collective values being dependent upon factual knowledge that science helps to establish. It is possible that universal values are constructed in this exchange. However, there is the same gap between *total health* ('holistic health' is our modern saintliness; cf. Guttmacher, *Hastings Center Report*, 1979, 2) and the statistical normality defined by biologists, as the gap between Aristotle's man of the 'happy mean' and Quételet's 'average man'. The conference organised by UNICEF and the WHO at Alma Ata in 1978 reaffirmed 'the insistence that *health, which is a state of total physical, mental and social well-being, and which does not simply consist in the absence of illness and infirmity, is a fundamental human right*' (Art. 1). If the objectives laid down by international organisations constitute progressive norms, then health as it is defined here is a value for humanity – that is, precisely not a state of fact that can be scientifically observed or characterised.

It is, however, difficult to dissociate the objective judgement of illness from judgements of value (an illness is an ill), and well-being can only be posited as a value if we are able to explain the objective conditions of realisation. 'Both evaluation and explanation are done by the same reasoning creatures,' says Englehardt, who, in an assessment of four years of interdisciplinary thinking on 'the foundations of ethics and its relationship with science', concludes that the two enterprises – explaining *what is* and outlining *what should be* – must have common roots (Englehardt & Callahan, vol. 4, 1980). That is not simply to say that, as disciplines of reason, science and ethics share the same demand for rational coherence (for instance, non-contradiction and efforts of systematisation). This aspect is stressed by H. Margenau (1978, 1979), who suggests a 'methodological parallelism' between the processes of validation (by confrontation with experience) of scientific axioms and of moral commands. The Hastings group goes further, calling for a dual awareness of how rational ethics are founded on scientific fact, and of how, conversely, numerous scientific concepts already have a normative dimension.

4.2 'There is a human nature,' of which ethics must take account. Issued by E. Wilson (1975, 1978) with a promotional sense of its effect, this proclamation contrasts with those heard throughout the preceding decades. 'There is no such thing as human nature,' affirmed Sartrean existentialism; 'man is the product of situations,' said Marxism; 'man *chooses himself* in the face of situations,' summed up Sartre. Having made the human race into a *cultural* species, radically different from other animal species, here we see in it an animal species like any other where social evolution results from populations' genetic adaptation to ecological constraints, within the limits imposed by the inertia of the genome (1975, ch. 3). 'Sociobiology' has aroused bitter controversies (see, for example, *La recherche*, 1977, 75). Only the question of a 'scientific ethics' will be examined here.

'Human beings are guided by an instinct that is itself founded on genes' (1978, ch. 2). In order to explain the affective reactions which lie at the root of ethical judgements, it is necessary to dismantle the neurological machinery from which these judgements proceed, in the deep structures of the encephalon (the limbic and hypothalamic zones). To understand the finality of the attitudes that are programmed into our central nervous system, we must reconstruct an evolutionary history that illuminates the adaptive significance of selection of those genes responsible for the development of these struc tures of the brain. Once neurophysiology and evolutionary sociobiology have conjointly shown how (that is, by which circuits) and why (to respond to which environmental demands) the human brain functions as it does (for example, triggering, in certain situations, altruistic behaviour), a scientific ethics will exist. In the same stroke, this will banish the phantasms of philosophers of ethics, who seek reasons for the individual to exist without seeing that our species is an evolutionary experiment among many others (1978, ch. 2), or that individual organisms are ephemeral forms of one of the possible genetic configurations of the species – what Schopenhauer might have called 'a superficial phenomenon'. The message of this new 'scientific materialism' is austere, even melancholic (1975, ch. 27): the total knowledge of human nature is, ultimately, *dehumanising* – but it is also inevitable. 'It is man's destiny to know' (1978, ch. 9): this is the price of survival.

We make ourselves unhappy if we attempt to fight our innate dispositions (1978, ch. 4). The knowledge of these dispositions will be liberating, insofar as it opens the way for the only real moral progress: that is, the product of social structures acting upon the selection of our genes, or even the direct modification of certain genes (Wilson is nevertheless silent on the possible manipulation of genes). Today, this knowledge is only taking its first steps, only allowing us to repudiate certain illusions, such as those of personal autonomy and free will.

Like Auguste Comte in the past, E. Wilson avoids all reductionism: he recognises that, in relation to the biological order, the social order presents properties that are *emergent* (1975, ch. 2). However, Wilson lets psychology, as well as any science of individual animal development, be cannibalised on the one side by biology, both cellular and molecular (the biochemistry of neurotransmitters), and on the other by sociology (here understood as the neo-Darwinian study of animal populations). No organism performs acts for their own sake (for pleasure, beauty or interest), and all individual behaviour – whether it be apparently egoist, like homosexuality, or apparently altruistic, like self-sacrifice – is always 'utilitarian'. The calculation of utility is not made up by the individual but by his or her genes, which optimise their chances of reproduction (in this way homosexuals bring an advantage to the selection of their relations' genes – that is to say, indirectly, of their own genes). 'Genes hold culture on a leash . . . Morality has no other demonstrable function than to assure the permanence of human genetic material' (1978, ch. 7).

Another illusion is that of a rational morality. Quoting with timeliness Abba Eban's aphorism that 'men only turn to reason as a last resort' (1967), Wilson insists on the essentially emotional character of our moral motivations (the 'limbic oracle' speaks in terms of fear/aggressivity, love/hate and happy effusiveness/gloomy withdrawal; 1975, ch. 1). The impossibility of bringing a coherent and universal moral code into relief is connected to the innate pluralism of these affects, which are vestiges of the adaptations of different ages to evolutionary situations. In particular, mammals, whose survival has required a high degree of social co-operation, are intimately torn between irreconcilable loyalties (such as narcissism of the self, the family and the tribe – the egoism of the group imposing the reciprocal altruism of its members: true 'mammalian ambivalence'). In L. Kohlberg's description of stages of moral development in the infant human (1971), Wilson seems to see an ontogenetic recapitulation of phylogenetic evolution, where cultural (and educational) systems give rise to a growing level of compromise between egoism and altruism. It is here that a science of the biological foundations of morality would be useful, in that it would facilitate distinction between those values which today retain an adaptive meaning (for example, the mammalian imperative that 'injustice does not pay – it is in your interests to co-operate'), and those that are no longer valid (for example, that certain aggressive reactions might be the archaic remnants of behavioural adaptations to the environment formerly lived in by our hunting ancestors in glacial times). This science would give the human race the means to act upon its own evolution, either by ensuring that certain innate tendencies become obsolete, which would in turn lead to their extinction (our population densities and social systems can be planned to render the majority of aggressive behaviours maladjusted; 1975, ch. 11), or by deliberately selecting those traits to which our societies attribute value (a spirit of co-operation, creativity, and so on; 1975, ch. 27).

In response to that 'great human problem, the subordination of egoism to altruism' (*Catéchisme Positiviste*, 1852, dialogue 4), Auguste Comte proposed a positive solution, in the form of a politico-religious system destined to construct the 'Supreme Being'. Wilson insists that, before utopias are built, it is necessary to ensure that they are biologically practicable, and he believes that science will show us that the number of possible trajectories is really quite small. In fact, in its zeal to rid itself of undesirable phenotypes the 'planned society' would at the same stroke risk killing off other interesting phenotypes, with which the former might be genetically linked (1975, ch. 27). While waiting for a finished bio-medical science that would allow us to make judicious decisions, Wilson meanwhile inclines towards a circumspect conservatism, proposing that 'the preservation of the total batch of human genes' be chosen as the 'primordial value' (1978, ch. 9). As for future generations, for whom is envisaged the Promethean possibility of modifying human nature, these will find in biological knowledge the conditions of a realistic choice. Will they also find therein the norm of an optimal choice? Evolution has *some* goals, but not a *single* goal. Neo-Darwinian theory is perhaps 'the greatest myth we have ever had', but as a source of morality it does not have the emotional attraction of religious myths: it does not say where to go. Our affective brain is programmed to preserve values, not create them: this is the silence of instinct. 'There are no signs in the world,' says Sartre, 'man is condemned to invent man'. Curiously, and having rejected existentialist individualism as illusory, Wilson is driven back to a kind of existentialism of populations, or of the human species: scientific ethics is the choice of a system of values (of a genetic constellation, of a human essence) made on the basis of an objective knowledge of historico-chemical determinisms of which human nature has thus far been composed. While perhaps motivated by the awareness of inconsistencies in this nature that are the result of evolutionary chance, this system does not have a rational or *a priori* conception of what human nature should be.

Some have reproached the author of sociobiology for this abstention from norms. 'Let us be guided by our emotions,' says R. McShea (1978), since they are the only regulating principle and certain indicator of ultimate values. And if our emotions are disparate? Then they are unified by the influence of our cognitions. Already in Freud and several of his contemporaries (Dewey and Baldwin, for example) we find the idea that moral development is organically determined, but that intellect (society) ends up shaping instinct by obliging it to find satisfactions that are more and more complex and deferred. This idea is again taken up by psychologists of the Piagetian school, who see in learning a process of reciprocal regulation 'between the assimilation of things by the mind and the accommodation of the mind to things' (Piaget): in this case, between evaluative moral emotions and the situations that give rise to them. The man who – instead of acting on the impulse of immediate emotion – takes a wider awareness of a situation, and who lets his emotions regroup, acts as we *should* act: that is, in a way that is 'more human', inspired as it is by a more complex feeling, and born out of a more comprehensive view of things (McShea, 1978). From obeying in order to avoid punishment, through to the acceptance of a system of rules that institute common good, the moral maturation of the child is regulated by its cognitive maturation. And what *should* be done is what *is* done by an individual who has reached the stage of development to which society tends to lead the majority of its members (Kohlberg, 1969).

The idea that the moral 'norm' might be found in the 'practice' of the evolved individual, rather than in a theory of good, was moreover already suggested by Aristotle, and recent explorers of mankind's 'moral nature' have consciously rediscovered the inspiration of Aristotelian naturalism (cf. Stent, 1978). Stegmüller (1977) would prefer that the 'subject' of moral theories was not an abstract subject (as in Kant or Rawls), but rather, having submitted its motivations to the test of cognitive therapy, an informed and mature subject.

There is no doubt that ethics has much to gain from an objective study of networks of normality and biophysical development, or of procedures of social harmonisation. Without going so far as to say that, like scientific hypotheses, moral rules are constructed by rational imagination and extrapolation after examining the aspirations of mature and well informed people (Walter, 1974), it is tempting to seek to identify the direction in which evolution is leading us, and to read in it, if not a destiny or prescription, then at least – and as hoped for by Kant (1795) – the sign that nature is complicit in our moral ends. Wilson's personal conviction notwithstanding (he sees human societies as drifting towards the uniformity of an ant-hill), the research mentioned above tends to convey the impression that the evolutionary process creates the conditions for the development of individual potentialities. The danger, if we interpret this as a form of morality, is that it justifies everything: 'I'm okay, you're okay, and anything that is 'fully human' is good'.

The ambivalence of Wilson is preferable to this vague optimism. Wilson, when he is not sheltering in the provocative security of genetic determinism ('we have been programmed . . . '), lurches towards a naked liberty which rejects all excuses ('no guru' can tell us what to do . . .). In his view, nature only provides norms that are outdated (our predispositions are vestiges of archaic adaptations) or negative (certain behaviours are biologically impracticable, such as the failure of systems of slavery, which would suggest that the human genome is resistant to slavery; 1978, ch. 4). Out of this comes the triple 'dilemma' (1978). By measuring the constraints that weigh down on our moral evaluations, science firstly forces us to choose those values that we want to keep. Secondly, science provides 'objective bases' for this choice (that is, indicates those trajectories which are impossible), but does not give any principle of selection for those trajectories that are possible. Finally, science allows us to influence the nature by which we ourselves are influenced.

We have identified in Wilson the mythical (and romantic) idea that moral characteristics are dependent on genes. By contrast, the determining influence of the socio-cultural environment has also been stressed (*Science for the People*, Nov–Dec, 1975; Lewontin, *The Sciences*, Mar–Apr, 1976). The argument is ambiguous. By way of continuing, let us consider a thesis of Karl Popper (1962, I, 5), namely that we can attempt to change a state of affairs (for instance, privileges of race or sex), or we can resist the attempts made to effect this change, or we can decide to let things go and refrain from intervention altogether. However, these decisions only have any meaning if the state of affairs can be modified. Are we accusing Wilson of implying that moral traits cannot be modified, or of being mistaken in his hypothesis on how to modify them? Do we believe that socio-economic causality is easier to manipulate than organic causality? (Despite the fact that we know that it is easier to prescribe antidepressants than to create less stressful living conditions!) With the progress of biology, it might become easier to tinker with genes than with social structures. Indeed, Wilson believes that we can be freed from a particular state of affairs by the exact knowledge of the mechanisms that led to it. If we knew that in order to eliminate a sexual or racial prejudice it was enough to change one gene (or juridical disposition), we could effectively undertake our own liberation. Would we decide to do it? Would we oppose those who would want to do it? Would we abstain? What role would science play in this decision? What seems to me unclear lies at the heart of the aforementioned dilemma: if positive knowledge is, as the author repeatedly says, 'a source of emancipation', then it must also be a source of morality. Not in its contents (once again, the observation of nature does not show what must be done), but in its project (scientific research is not neutral, since Wilson puts it in competition with religions). However, if presented as a militant science, sociobiology hardly provides any elucidation of the role of the scientific adventure in the 'epic of evolution'.

Many scientists would rather remain outside of such developments. 'To problems that articulate the biological and the social, biologists do not, as such, have any response to make. Limiting themselves to the identification of its stages, they can only state the conditions of possibility for evolution' (Gros, Jacob and Royer, 1979, 5). Others have pushed further than Wilson in their questioning of a 'natural philosophy of modern biology'.

'Is science in a position to give man goals in life, having proved that it can take goals away and destroy them?' (Nietzsche).

4.4   Does evolutionary biology confirm 'the absence of any meaningful reason to live'? E. Wilson (1975, ch. 27) quotes the following passage by Camus: 'In a universe suddenly stripped of illusion and light, man feels himself to be a stranger. Since he is deprived of the memories of a lost heritage and the hope of a promised land, this is an exile without exit.' 'Unfortunately, this is true,' concludes Wilson, who consoles himself with the thought that it will be several generations yet before religious mythologies give way to positive phylogeny, which would give us an explanation of ourselves that is both 'total and mechanistic'. Monod also holds that science 'ruins all the ontogenies' on which traditional values rest, and that it implies 'the demand for a total revision of the foundations of ethics': 'at last man knows that he is alone in the indifferent immensity of the universe from which he has emerged by chance. As with his destiny, his duty is nowhere written. It is up to him to choose . . . ' Monod's quasi-stoical response is borrowed (as an epigraph) from the same book by Camus:

> a blind man who wishes to see and who knows that the night has no end, he is always moving onwards . . . He, too, judges that all is well. This universe, henceforth without master, appears to him neither sterile nor futile . . .
>
> (*The Myth of Sisyphus*)

Science puts our values in danger – is this an old quarrel? Even in Galilean cosmology it was believed that science would ruin the moral order . . . Through a reasoning that is analogous to that of Duhem (1905), who 'denies theories of physics any metaphysical import', towards the end of the 1960s 'creationists' (cf. Nelkin, 1976) had no difficulty observing that dogmatism is a stranger to the true scientific mind, or that the system of neo-Darwinian hypotheses was constructed in order to take account of a certain number of facts; no difficulty observing that a construction is not an objective truth, or that there exists at least one other system of hypotheses (creationism) which allows the same elements of experience to be represented (and predicted) just as well, or that the preference for one theory or another must be respected in the name of democratic pluralism and freedom of thought. Monod takes the scientific enterprise less lightly. In his view, the choice between two theories which are, in the main, compatible with the facts is not a question of *taste*, but of *objectivity*. The confrontation with experience selects those ideas that are pertinent, and ends up eliminating those hypotheses that correlate badly with reality. The hypothesis of evolution has supplanted that of creation: this is not a question of intellectual fashion, but rather that, through observing the living world, it was realised that things must have happened this way, and not otherwise. Certainly, the neo-Darwinian explanation is still only approximately true, and as new data are analysed its errors are rectified . . . The point is that, in order for there to be ideas that are less false than others, it must be supposed that there exists an objective reality that can decide between them. The enterprise of knowledge is founded on the 'postulate of objectivity'.

Two conceptions of scientific truth are opposed here, and of these it is possible that at least one is not compatible with any old ethics. To ensure science's metaphysical innocuousness – that is the attitude of conventionalist positivism, which is perhaps the inheritor of polytheism. Either because its observations only treat phenomena (that is, appearances – true reality cannot be experienced), or because its observers do not have at their disposal criteria of choice between different descriptions of the real, scientific discourse has no depth (no ontological import): one may say all one likes, a theory always agrees with the facts, because the observation of the facts is completely impregnated with theory. In the extreme, this tends towards relativism: all ideas are valid, and everyone is right (a position that is unassailable, even perverse, since it makes any criticism pointless). By the same turn, all morals are good – at least, it is not science that will decide between them. Relativism is the natural ally of religion: a science lacking any ontological kick would not be able to criticise any single revelation concerning the nature of beings. And if men are devoid of a sense of truth, perhaps it is better that they undergo the rule of some prophet or Father-God, rather than embroiling themselves in fratricidal combat, which is the price to pay for the tolerance of ideas. In effect, if no one can be convinced of error, some must be persuaded that they are wrong (it is especially enjoyable to put into a minority those who believe in the existence of objective truths). *Science is not neutral*: each researcher works for the victory of his or her point of view, and the hypothesis which, at a certain moment, does triumph is the one whose defenders have been best able to defeat their rivals, or find the best support, be it financial, political or otherwise.

Moral conscience (if indeed such a thing exists) can only take offence at this state of affairs: at the very least, it demands that the democratic rule of decision be applied, rather than that of Mandarinic absolutism. If scientific truth is elaborated in a competition between researchers (on the level of what Popper calls 'world 2'), it is conceivable that we should seek to reform this competition: for example, by guaranteeing all researchers the same funds, the same facilities for publication, and so on (thereby substituting socialist science for capitalist science).

However, is truth better decided upon by a majority of opinion, rather than by submission to a single authority? Monod believes in the selection not of researchers, but of ideas (Popper's 'world 3'): true ideas are those that resist the confrontation of our logic (the outline of experiences acquired by the species) with objective reality (actual experience). What corresponds to the facts is true: only objective (scientific) knowledge can be true; and there is no other source of knowledge. The mythical (Judeo-Christian) and philosophical (Hegelian) ontogenies by which man imagined the history of his own destiny were at one and the same time explanatory and normative (they founded their values on the idea of nature, speaking, for example, of 'natural rights'). These ontogenies were not true (not objective). Science attains objectivity at the price of abstention from any kind of normativity: on this level, '*science is a threat to values*,' in that it demonstrates that a value judgement is never founded on a reality judgement, and that values' only foundation is the human will to promote them (Popper – whom Monod read – would have said that, even if we truly believed that God exists, we would still have to decide whether or not divine commandments are just and acceptable; 1961, §13). So, 'is science neutral'? No. In believing that truth is accessible if we decide to take the trouble to look for it, we define an attitude towards life: that is, an ethics, or even a politics. Science is not neutral in relation to values – not because morality can be founded on science, but because, on the contrary, any party (an individual or a society) that engages in scientific research has made a choice of an ethical order and has, by the same turn, already chosen a morality. The 'ethics of knowledge' is that asceticism of the mind that consists in forcing itself to accept as true only objective knowledge. This ethics implies the moral solitude of man in a universe that is 'deaf to his music, and as indifferent to his hopes as it is to his sufferings and crimes' (1970, ch. 9). In short, a solidly realistic science would call for an ethics of existentialist inspiration: what we *must do* is written nowhere, neither on earth nor in the sky, and our values are created by us.

4.5   Monod's proposition embraces three interlocking arguments: that truth is a value; that, as a value, truth is fundamental (it is the 'measure' for all other values); and that any human group that decides to put its institutions in the service of this value erects a legitimate socialism.

The first of these arguments cannot really be contested, in that the choice to seek truth is an ethical one (the 'postulate of objectivity' sets up a norm of knowledge). As an idea, it is also ancient: Descartes says that we can refuse to acknowledge evidence of the true and/or the good (i.e. refuse God; cf. Descartes' letter to Mesland, 9 Feb. 1645). Monod is right to stress that modern science has not developed by chance in the heart of a Judeo-Christian culture: rather than escaping into fantasy or nirvana, our Western societies have resolved to accept the world as it is, to 'make do with it', and to collaborate with the work of the creator (by saying 'yes', by playing the game: it is the reality principle). This existential engagement, taken in a fashion that is barely conscious, would seem to underlie our techno-scientific civilisation.

Monod's second argument holds that, having destroyed ancient value systems, only the ethics of knowledge is capable of giving man an ideal, and of reconciling man with himself by recognising both his socio-biological nature (as an object of scientific study) and his freedom (the creator of 'transcendence'). Does Monod think that the control of the passions as well as the other virtues all flow from intellectual honesty? The proposition might reek of Spinoza, except that the author of *Ethics* makes it clear that it is knowledge of the sovereignly perfect Being that gives perfection. Should we infer that Monod is transposing *Deus sive natura* . . . ? The idea appears to remain ambiguous: in order to be good, is it enough to be wise?

The third argument generalises the second by extending it to collective life: any society that founds its social and political institutions on the axiom according to which true knowledge must be promoted, and which measures the legitimacy of such institutions by this same axiom, will be just and respectful of the human person. All of which leaves us perplexed. Is the democracy of a human community proportionate to the research and the circulation of information that it undertakes? Does scientific and technical education make better people? Does the presence of scholars prevent concentration camps? Can totalitarianism be avoided simply by recognising that there are no objective laws of universal history? It is not ridiculous to say that a society that restricts the freedom of knowledge is not democratic (a negative criterion). The unease felt in following

Monod to the end of his argument comes, I think, from the implication that science alone holds the criterion of truth, which offers the threat of another kind of absolutism.

4.6 It is pleasing to acknowledge, like Monod, that scientific prudence demands that facts be respected: in addition to a certain humility before the world (facts are what they are, not what we should like them to be, and ultimately our conjectures and extrapolations are subject to the verdict of experience), this idea also expresses a certain mistrust (let us believe only that which can be observed: souls, flying saucers and phenomena that start with 'psych' are not scientific objects). Undoubtedly, to choose to respect the facts is an ethical choice – it might also be utilitarian, in that true ideas have, according to Monod himself, a high 'power of performance' (they succeed). The important thing is to recognise that by anchoring a discourse in objectivity (a guarantee with multiple methodological precautions: techniques of observation, definition of margins of error, review of results, and so on) we make it impossible to posit any old nonsense. In this respect, scientific practice can be understood as a 'moral therapy' (Crombie, 1975), not in the sense where the rectitude demanded of the researcher is a virtue, but where the intolerance of false ideas facilitates tolerance of people. If people make a mistake, their errors are judged by experience (it is useless to use force to impose truth); if they express a value preference, that preference cannot be erroneous, since it is not a matter for experimental criteria.

However, no sooner has a certain scientific realism been deemed healthy than its limits become visible: limited, for example, by positivist blinkers, to the level of facts (as Roland becomes cachectic he is subjected to a battery of blood tests, and he explodes, 'Damn your eyes, can't you see that I'm dying of shame?'; Oliver Sacks, 1973–6); limited by the illusion of objectivity (what facts, and as established by whom?: interference with the object by the observer, the dependence on perception of acquired knowledge, and the formulation of data in terms that are subtly normative: all these necessitate a critique of the 'postulate of objectivity'); or, finally, limited by theoretical difficulties concerning the notion of the 'confirmation' of a hypothesis by the facts (Monod seems to make the position of naïve verification his own). By maintaining a 'transcendence of truth', where the sanction of facts assumes the role of divine judgement, Monod reveals himself to be the inheritor of monotheism (the same could be said of Wilson).

'There can be no set of general criteria for truth': having recalled Tarski's result, Popper (1961) insists on the fact that we approach truth negatively (by identifying our errors). The neo-Darwinian theory of evolution is not true – it is less false than the theories that have preceded it (it corresponds better to reality). Accompanied by Popper, when he changes pitch to say that 'it can be proved that we were wrong, but we can never be sure when we are in the realm of truth,' Monod's axiom that 'we must seek the truth' keeps its ethical impact. In seeking truth, the researcher undertakes to exercise critical vigilance, to doubt. A society that organises itself in such a way that liberates criticism (Popper's 'open society') institutes conditions necessary for democratic pluralism. In order to believe that these conditions are sufficient, we must either more or less suppose that nature has spontaneous wisdom (let the freedom to contest set in, and you will be given the rest – democracy – as well), or presume that the cult of true knowledge as a 'transcendent value' implies an absolute respect for 'man, the creator and guardian of this transcendence' (Monod, 1970, ch. 9). In either case, and to fall back on a situation that conforms to common moral aspirations, a Kantian precept is injected: that is, the categorical imperative, or regulating principal of a natural finality.

But do we want a society dedicated to the progress of science? We can agree with Monod that Western civilisation has in practice opted for objective knowledge, and that it has virtually swept away other civilisations. What is less certain is whether the 'unease of modern societies' is due to the ideological lie by which societies disguise the fact that 'man is the measure of all things': it could just as well have to do with the awareness that there is no absolute measure of values. Meanwhile, it is to be doubted that the 'proud and austere' ethics of knowledge can cure this ill. When one has the choice of one's values, why hold onto the aestheticism of saying *what is* rather than preferring the distance of irony, the imaginary and the 'counter-factual'? It could be replied that the aestheticism of research pays off: it is a factor in development. Herein lies the ambiguity. Enthusiasm for disinterested research is demanded, and it is expected that those who, failing to be moved by curiosity for truth, prefer another, more personal ethics will accept that the collectivity sacrifice everything to scientific progress, because scientific progress is progress full-stop. Is 'the transcendent ideal of truth' being preached here, or rather a technological model of development? The two things do not coincide: the discovery of one more meson or pion is hardly of any import to collective development. If a fundamental value has to be chosen, truth does not impose itself (Plato chooses to see the Good). To see art and poetry as epiphenomena, in the eyes of the 'serious' activity of scientific research, is a scholar's blunder: a dance or a musical phrase can calm existential anxiety better than the exact knowledge of our phylogenetic origins. Monod would doubtless say that he does not scorn poetic discourse at all, on the condition that it does not think of itself as a discourse of truth – but there is a degree of latent imperialism in the refusal of a pluralism of values. Plato threw artists out of the city.

Does experimental science have, moreover, a monopoly on truth? It must be admitted that, for Monod, the import of this proposition is above all negative: it is a question of excluding from the realm of knowledge whatever cannot be scientifically validated. However, the question of the 'criteria of demarcation' between science and non-science remains open: for example, if we admit, like Popper, that the non-scientific is not non-verifiable, but rather unfalsifiable; or if we recognise, with Lakatos (1974), that falsifiability does not suffice to distinguish between scientific hypotheses, since great theories resist the 'anomalies' encountered in the facts (Duhem-Quine argues that a single experiment is never crucial, and that to refute is no more decisive than to confirm. When experience is in disagreement with theory, 'common sense is the judge,' says Duhem). Rather than remaining with the image of a scientific institution that delivers labels of truth, in the same way as the Church formerly administered the sacraments, it is preferable that this question of science and non-science remain open. For all that, the question of demarcation is not a pseudo-problem, and Lakatos (1974) recognises that it has 'serious ethical and political implications': for example, depending on whether we take them as scientific or non-scientific, we react differently to views held on 'race and intelligence'. There exist *some* criteria for the non-scientific: we can criticise the method by which a result has been established (for example, an insufficient sample: the statistics are insignificant); we can contest the manner in which the result is interpreted (for example, a finalist explanation: look for a causal explanation); or we can challenge the concepts upon which the research is founded (for example, 'intelligence': as measured by what test?). We do not, however, have absolute criteria for science any more than we do for morality. As Claude Bernard has said, 'In experimental method, as everywhere, *the only real criterion is reason.*'

5.5 In one of the *Peanuts* albums (quoted in *Hastings Center Report*, 1980, 3), Lucy asks, 'Who are there more of in the world, good people, or bad people?' 'How can we know,' observes Charlie Brown, 'Who would tell the good people from the bad people?' 'Me,' says Lucy.

Beyond a contesting of received norms, perhaps the dominant characteristic of the period 1965–80 was the apprenticeship of decisions about values, carried out through trial and error by a rationality lucid about its limits. Here, the anxiety which accompanied awareness of the arbitrary nature of ultimate human choices in post-war existentialism was tempered by the occasionally rediscovered feeling of an amorous complicity with nature.

Translated by Stephen Forcer

References

The Hastings Center Report (1970–). Institute of Society, Ethics and the Life Sciences, 360 Broadway, Hastings-on-Hudson, NY 10706, USA.

Berleant, A. (1977). Ethics and Science: Some normative facts and a con-conclusion. *The Journal of Value Inquiry* 11: 244–258.

Crombie, A.C. (1975). Scientific objectivity and social choice: The Western experience of scientific objectivity. Volos lecture. Mimeo.

Engelhardt, H.T., Jr. and Callahan, D. (eds) (1976–80). *The foundations of ethics and its relationship to science.* 4 vols. Hastings-on-Hudson: Institute of Society, Ethics and the Life Sciences (Vol. 1: Science, ethics and medicine, 1976; Vol. 2: Knowledge, value and belief, 365 p., 1977; Vol. 3: Morals, science and sociality, 339 p., 1978; Vol. 4: Knowing and valuing: the search for common roots, 286 p., 1980).

Gingerich, O. (1975). Science and the foundation of ethics. In O. Gingerich (Ed.), *The nature of scientific discovery*, pp. 587–95.

Gros, F., Jacob, F. and Royer, P. (1979). *Sciences de la vie et société.* Rapport présenté à M. le Président de la République. Paris: la Documentation Française.

Kohlberg, L. (1969). Stage and sequence: The cognitive-developmental approach to socialization. In D.A. Goslin (ed.), *Handbook of socialization theory and research*, pp. 347–480. Chicago: Rand McNally, xiii + 1182 p.

—— (1971). From is to ought: How to commit the naturalistic fallacy and get away with it in the study of moral development. In T. Mischel (ed.), *Cognitive development and epistemology*. New York: Academic Press.

Lakatos, I. (1974). Science and pseudoscience. *Conceptus: Zeitschrift für Philosophie* 8 (24): 5–9.

Margenau, H. (1979). Science and ethics, their parallelism and some of its consequences. *Epistemologia* 2 (numéro spécial): 167–82.

Monod, J. (1970). *Le hasard et la nécessité: essai sur la philosophie naturelle de la biologie moderne.* Paris: Seuil. 244 p.

335

ANNE FAGOT-LARGEAULT

Nelkin, D. (1976). The science textbook controversies. *Scientific American* 234: 33–9, and 235: 6–9 (lettres).

—— (1961). Facts, standards and truth: A further criticism of relativism, first addendum to Vol. 2 of: *The open society and its enemies*, fifth ed. revised, 1966.

Sacks, O.W. (1973). *Awakenings*, rev. ed. Harmondsworth: Pelican Books, 1976.

McShea, R.J. (1978), Biology and ethics (discussion). *Ethics* 88 (2): 139–49.

Stegmüller, W. (1977). On the interrelation between ethics and other fields of philosophy of science. *Erkenntnis* 11: 55–80.

Stent, G.S. (ed.) (1978). *Morality as a biological phenomenon*. Berlin (West): Abakon Verlagsgesellschaft (*Life Sciences Research Report* 9).

Walter, E. (1974). Reasoning in science and ethics. *The Journal of Value Inquiry* 8: 252–65.

Wilson, E.O. (1975). *Sociobiology: The new synthesis*. Cambridge, Mass.: Harvard University Press. ix + 697 p.

—— (1978). *On human nature*. Cambridge, Mass.: Harvard University Press. xii + 260 p.

Part 5

THE JURIDICAL AND POLITICAL SUBJECT

INTRODUCTION

The final section of this collection brings together six bold explorations of racism, human evil, citizenship, natural law and human rights. Apart from Nicole Loraux's discussion of the exclusion of women from Athenian citizenship, these essays are not concerned primarily with gender, but rather with other fundamental questions affecting human subjects and their interrelationships.

Colette Guillaumin offers a paradigmatic example of the way in which reflection on feminist concerns is inextricably intertwined with other issues central to the question of the human subject. Guillaumin's essay examines the etymological history of the notion of race from its early sense as family group to its current popular, pseudo-biological usage which posits a genetic totality contested by both anthropologists and scientists. The discussion is part of an exploration of the construction of both race and gender, and an attempt to expose their false unities and dichotomies. Guillaumin's work as a social scientist focuses on the practical and theoretical question of the status of categories such as race and gender. She is not easy to place for while rejecting 'essentialism' she cannot simply be described as a 'constructivist'. She considers categories such as gender and race to be neither simply natural/biological nor merely social/cultural. Her position has been described as a form of deconstruction of the belief in 'natural' categories. Guillaumin also situates herself outside the binary oppositions of radical and Marxist feminism, subscribing neither to the view that women's oppression is primary and prior to capitalist oppression nor to the contrary Marxist position which maintains that the end of capitalism would necessarily bring in its wake the end of sexist oppression. Guillaumin considers 'woman' to be a class in the Marxist sense, which means that she can attempt an analysis of women's oppression while still opposing the notion of 'woman' as a natural category. Her work on race runs parallel to her work on gender: she contests the category of race itself in what I would describe as a kind of nominalism, maintaining that race is a product rather than a cause of racism. This bold position is backed up by convincing analyses of biological, historical and linguistic data which show that the idea of race can be traced back to the eighteenth century when the African slave trade coincided with the growth of 'natural' taxonomies. Guillaumin does not deny the existence of sexes or races but she does deny that they are immutable and natural. On the contrary, she argues, they are the product of socio-historical factors such as sexism and racism. This essay constitutes the first chapter of Guillaumin's major work in English on racism and sexism and explores 'the specific characteristics of racist ideology' today which she argues are threefold. First, race has changed from being a legal category to being a geneticist one; second, it concerns different social groups, far wider than the noble families to whom it used to refer; and third, it is now organised spatially rather than temporally. The detail of Guillaumin's textual and definitional analysis make her essay extremely convincing, even though its premises run radically counter to the common-sense view of race with which we are most familiar.

Dominique Schnapper provides a sociological analysis of the phenomenon of racism, and traces its contemporary development away from the perennial xenophobia instigated by fear and incomprehension of the Other, towards a position with scientific pretentions if not scientific credentials. Schnapper believes modern racial hostility to be an unintended by-product of the political move to establish formal equality between races, which brings in its wake a refusal of difference and an ironic sanction for the devalorisation of cultural heterogeneity. In this extract from *La relation à l'autre: au cœur de la pensée sociologique*, Dominique Schnapper gives a chilling account of the necessary relation between modernity and racism. Drawing on sociology (Leon Poliakov, Colette Guillaumin), anthropology (Lévi-Strauss, Louis Dumont) and Marxism (Etienne Balibar, Immanuel Wallerstein), Schnapper argues convincingly that it is precisely the nature of modern, Western, capitalist society that has produced modern racism. Paradoxically, perhaps, the very expansion and globalisation of Western civilisation lies at the origins of modern racism, just as the enshrinement in law of theories of human equality has led cultural and national differences to be redescribed in terms of biological, racial inferiority. The inevitable tension between the world-wide diffusion of Western culture and the need for all cultures to maintain their own specificity has disturbed the essential balance between unification and diversity and produced a demand to reconcile what is clearly unreconcilable. The modern refusal to privilege one culture over another, at least explicitly, has led similarly to the rebaptism of cultural difference in terms of inequality. The proclamation of equality for all citizens runs radically counter to experience and leads perversely to the idea of inferiority as biological rather than legal. The repression of a hierarchical conception of society has driven hierarchy underground and caused it to emerge as biologically grounded racism. Anti-Semitism, for example, has replaced Christian anti-Judaism. In short, racism – like sexism – is a product of modern structures of class and nationalism and is a specific characteristic of modern Western societies.

Myriam Revault-D'Allonnes's essay is taken from *Ce que l'homme fait à l'homme. Essai sur le mal politique*, and proposes a striking interpretation of Kant's understanding of radical evil, which she argues is not psychological or empirical but rather a matter of a fundamental opposition to the moral law. Evil is radical (in Hannah Arendt's term, 'banal') in that it is rooted in the human will, irrespective of whether it is acted on in individual cases: 'it is the evil common to everyone even if not everyone does it'. For Kant, evil does not originate in a perverse or demonic will to disobey the law, which would mean that it was outside the common rule of humanity. On the contrary, and far more disquietingly, it is a universal possibility, and one which depends not on revolt or disobedience but rather on dissembling and self-deception. Evil depends on our making ourselves an exception to the law, and on our willingness to convince ourselves that we are acting within it. Eichmann, the 'bureaucratic criminal', claimed to have 'lived his whole life according to Kant's moral principals', by which he meant, Revault d'Allonnes surmises, that he had taken the laws of his country as the principle of his own actions. But in so far as such evil-doers are not demonic but are rather mediocre, banal and weak creatures like us, we must accept that we too could ourselves be responsible for such atrocities. National Socialism depended not on revolt against the law but rather on a monstrous caricature of it, which involved the perversion of the idea of 'duty' (as in 'Thou shalt kill'), the separation between personal motives and obedience to a pseudo-law, and finally the demand for absolute obedience to the letter of the law. Revault d'Allonnes argues that despite our attempts to understand it, the reason for the existence of evil remains totally unfathomable: absolute evil is perpetrated without reason which makes it all the more radical and disturbing. Retrospective reconstruction may be possible, but no causality or explanation. This does not, however, lessen human responsibility in any way. Even in extreme situations, abstention from (evil) action is always possible; and furthermore, if such radical evil seems to elude our comprehension, this does not mean that we can deny our association, as human beings, with its perpetrators.

Nicole Loraux's work as a philosopher and classicist focuses on the intertwining of myth and politics in fifth-century Athens, in an exploration of what she calls 'the Greek imaginary'. In her first book this was carried out through a study of the political discourse of Athens in an analysis of the funeral orations honouring the Athenian war-dead. Then, in her second book, from which this essay is taken, Loraux explores the significance of the division between the sexes in Athenian notions of citizenship, and in particular the complex and contradictory implications of the exclusion of Athenian women from the status of citizens. The Greek myths of the origins of mankind are discussed by Loraux: in one version, Erichthonios, father of Athenian men, was born directly of the earth, fertilised by the sperm of Hephaistos which dripped to earth from Athena's leg as Hephaistos refused to take no for an answer. In another version all Athenian citizens are born directly from the earth. Athenian women were born separately from Pandora. In no case are women directly implicated in the birth of Athenian men, despite their name's origin in the goddess Athena. The essay included here addresses the ensuing problems for the women of Athens, enshrined linguistically in the lack of a feminine form for 'Athenian': the women of Athens are only 'a race of women', not female citizens. Loraux's work articulates close reading, lexical and rhetorical critique, structuralist analysis of myth, and scholarly scrupulousness within the overall enterprise of uncovering the cultural imaginary of the Athenian *polis*.

Mireille Delmas-Marty and Blandine Kriegel close the collection with two robust explorations of international law, natural law and human rights. In *Trois défis pour un droit mondial* (1998), Delmas-Marty explores the possibility of global law. *Pour un droit commun* (*Towards a Truly Common Law*) of 1994 already considered the current move towards a more global legal community and applied it to concepts such as human rights for European citizens. *Trois défis* offers a counter-attack to current pessimism surrounding human rights issues, and attempts to construct a way forward towards international harmonisation that would avoid the pitfalls of both hegemonic uniformity and of the conflict of national particularities. The three challenges to be answered are first, is the globalisation of law possible in a world where the very notion of human rights is put in question; second, is such globalisation juridically rational in view of the apparently disordered proliferation of norms; and third, is it ethically desirable, given the fact that international institutions cannot guarantee respect for democratic values. Delmas-Marty's aim is to rise to all three challenges in order to open the way for a common law of humanity for the first time in history. She sees various paradoxes as attendant on the project: the possibility of a superimposition of national and international laws risks producing a further proliferation; furthermore, for the first time in history, human rights legislation can now be used against the legislators and even the State itself if its laws run counter to human rights. However, this apparent disorder is envisaged by Delmas-Marty as an opportunity for the creation of a new political, judicial and even epistemological order. She concludes with a discussion of the relationship between ideas of democracy and humanity and the implications of this for the very identity of the human.

In the final extract, drawn from *Les droits de l'homme et le droit naturel*, Kriegel compares the American Declaration of Independence of 1776 and the French Declaration of the Rights of Man of 1789, contrasting the US concept of natural law ('loi'), which depends on a notion of divine creation, and the French conception of national citizenship and rights ('droit') which depend rather on human decision, and presenting a critique of legal positivism. She shows how the US Declaration has always been intimately linked to the Constitution, and reinforced by the bills of rights that head the US States' written constitutions as well as by the Federal Constitution of 1787. Subsequently the Declaration has always had a direct influence on US legislation. The French Declaration, on the other hand, has been variously changed and side-lined and finally re-entered the Preamble of the Constitution only in 1946. Its influence on legislation has therefore been far less pronounced, and indeed the rights of man are not properly part of French law. Kriegel uses the distinction between the individual and the subject to argue that the philosophy of the rights of man should reroot itself within a conception of natural law rather than ally itself to a philosophy of the subject which is not its appropriate source. Her analysis makes fascinating reading for any British or American philosopher interested in understanding the deep-seated differences between French and English ways of thinking about human rights. The collection ends, then, on a question intimately linked to the one with which it started: that of the status, constitution and deconstruction of the subject, and its role in ethical and political philosophy.

23

COLETTE GUILLAUMIN

Colette Guillaumin is known as a materialist feminist. Her doctorate at the University of Paris Sorbonne was in sociology, and she was a researcher at the CNRS (National Center for Scientific Research). She was a founder member of the collective that established the journal *Questions féministes* in 1977 and was also on the editorial board of *Le Genre Humain*.

Her major work includes many articles translated into English, and in particular the collection *Racism, Sexism, Power and Ideology*, Routledge, 1995.

Works in French include the following:

L'Idéologie raciste: genèse et langage actuel, Paris: Mouton, 1972, republié chez Gallimard Folio, 2002.

Sexe, race et pratique du pouvoir: l'idée de nature, Paris: Côté femmes, 1992.

THE SPECIFIC CHARACTERISTICS
OF RACIST IDEOLOGY

Introduction

Racism can be reduced neither to racist theory, nor to racist practice. Theory and practice do not cover the whole field of racism, which extends beyond conscious thought. As an ideology racism is opaque, unconscious of its own meaning.

The aim of this essay is to cast light on the specific characteristics of contemporary racist ideology. After first showing that it cannot be defined simply in terms of aggressivity, stereotyping or 'doctrine', we shall set out to delimit the four characteristics which give it its particular form. These characteristics are defined in relation to those which guided perceptions of race in the past, and can only be understood by comparison with them. They are as follows:

(a) Race today is a 'geneticist' category, whereas in the past it was a legal one.
(b) It is altero-referential in nature rather than auto-referential, as it used to be in the old system. In other words, racist thinking is now centred on 'others', instead of on the 'self'.

  The social groups which bear the mark of race are no longer the same as formerly. In the distant past the term 'race' was applicable only to 'noble families', whereas now it is wider social groups, in a minority or marginal situation in relation to the holders of power, who find themselves so designated.
(c) Finally, the concept of race has become spatial in character, and so radically different from earlier temporal perceptions. We are now faced with a synchronic organization instead of a diachronic one.

The hypothesis that the emergence of racism can be traced to a precise point in history is hotly debated. Even if agreement were to be reached on the possibility of such a dating, the actual date chosen would remain controversial. This is primarily because the phenomenon itself has been inadequately defined. Some see it as a form of practical social behaviour, others as a doctrine, and these different views lead to divergent datings.

If we adhere to the notion of a racist 'practice', then the hypothesis of a possible dating is undermined by arguments so strong as to appear irrefutable: its existence from time immemorial would seem to be proven by well-known and unquestionable historical facts. The constant presence (or frequent re-appearance) of such facts throughout history does indeed tend to suggest that racism is an omnipresent and constant factor. The long history of slavery, the Greek concept of the 'barbarian' peoples, the status of foreigners in ancient societies, the ghettos and the status of Jews in Europe and the Arab world, the widespread tendency to reserve the attribution of human status to one's own group (national, religious or social), are all facts. So is the feeling, from which few cultures seem exempt, that the customs of foreigners are always strange. Finally, and above all, hatred, exclusion, hostility, aggression and genocide are anything but modern phenomena. All of which contributes to a picture which seems to prove that racism has always existed.

Racism and aggressivity

That is indeed correct, as long as racism is defined solely in terms of aggressivity. But while aggressivity is often associated with racism, in our view that only happens at a secondary stage. Moreover, aggressivity is a form of behaviour which is in no way limited to situations of social alienation. Aggressivity often connotes racism, but does not denote it. It is neither a sufficient condition (aggressivity is not always racist), nor a necessary one (racism exists before overt hostility, in a certain type of relation to the other in society). To confuse racism with aggressivity is to leave out of account both the specificity which it introduces into relations between human groups, and the particular form which it gives to the use of force. Racism is a specific symbolic system operating inside the system of power relations of a particular type of society. It is a signifying system whose key characteristic is the irreversibility which it confers on such a society's reading of reality, the crystallization of social actors and their practices into essences.[1] Aggressivity as such does not depend on the essentialization of signs which is the specific mark of racism. In the present situation (the one in which we have been living since the first half of the nineteenth century), aggressivity and racism tend increasingly often to coincide, which no doubt explains the widespread confusion between the two. Yet the link is by no means an obligatory one; racism can be, and sometimes is, benevolent and even laudatory. In the absence of any immediately explosive situation (either because power relations are so overwhelmingly unbalanced that there is no possibility of revolt on the horizon, or on the contrary because they are approximately balanced), racism remains 'pure', restricted to establishing the other as essentially different. Do we need reminding of the political Far Right's fascination with the 'Other', be it Tibet or Nepal. Judaism, the Eternal Feminine, Islam . . .?[2] Fanatics of the esoteric and the 'vital impulse', browsers in the flea market of archetypes and essences, all rivet their blind gaze on such fantasy-emblems. This is a cultural phenomenon, which may or may not be accompanied by physical violence, depending on the circumstances: history may have the power to reveal what is latent, to transform ambivalence into aggressivity, but the signifying system of racism, with its notions of 'essential nature' and 'biological specificity', remains the single necessary ingredient.

Racism and stereotyping

The same is true of stereotyping, which as far as anyone can tell is as old as aggressivity and is often regarded as a specific characteristic of racism. However, we also see it being used both towards those of our own group and within other professional groups, and in general within any activity where over-simplification takes the place of knowledge. Unlike aggressivity, stereotyping is undoubtedly always associated with racism, but not with racism alone, so to that extent it cannot be regarded as an explanation of racism in its specificity.

Racism and racist doctrine

If, in line with the other current approach, racism is regarded as a doctrine and defined as the theory of the inequality of races, then there will be a large measure of agreement about its historical dating. Historians, sociologists, anthropologists and psycho-sociologists concur in situating its origin at a precise moment in the history of the West.[3] That the complete theory of the inequality of races coalesced between the end of the eighteenth century and the opening decades of the nineteenth is a hypothesis as difficult to challenge as that which sees aggressivity as an ancient form of behaviour. Bringing together these two conceptions of racism, it is easy to conclude that it is a tendency which has existed since time immemorial, but was theorized in the West during the nineteenth century; that is certainly the position of the human sciences today.

However, that would be to leave out the ideological character of racism. Taking this into account raises the possibility of a third definition which allows its specific features to be more accurately delimited. It involves taking the analysis into a realm where behaviour patterns have not yet evolved beyond being simple mental schemata, the realm in which, well before any explicit theory (which is only the final stage in the process), the specific organization of perceptions within a given culture comes about. This ideological level covers the complete set of meanings, whether empirical or doctrinal, which direct social behaviour. At this level there is much disagreement among experts. Some set the origin of race ideology back in the twelfth century, at the end of medieval feudalism, while for others it began at the time of the first European journeys to the 'New World', or again in the sixteenth century with the birth of capitalism; finally, a considerable number of scholars locate its origin in the way other peoples were perceived by the ancient inhabitants of the Mediterranean region.[4] To differing degrees these datings still rely on an identification of racism with aggressivity; while such approaches do privilege a certain type of relation to others, they do not distinguish it clearly from aggressivity, which remains a necessary component. Hence the privileging of conflictual periods of active aggression or doctrinal formulation. These divergent interpretations are largely due to the fact that the ideological character of racism has not been clearly defined theoretically.

The search for understanding in which we are now engaged is in fact already heavily mortgaged to the ideology of racism. Research has adopted as one of its basic concepts a notion, that of race, which itself is a specific product of racist ideology, and taken as its field of investigation the very topic in which racist theory situates the problem: aggressivity. In creating and hypostasizing race, racist ideology set up a metaphysics of relations of social heterogeneity which was adopted as it stood by everyone. However, the human sciences have now reached the point where we are starting to realize that if race is indeed real, it is so as a symbolic rather than as a concrete object. It will be granted that this is an important difference, though one which is far from having passed into scientific practice.[5] Yet this difference opens up the possibility of analysing the meaning of the notion of race, and thereby of gaining access to the ideological core of both racist behaviour and race theory. We shall thus concentrate on the notion of race as the medium of racist ideology, attempting to describe its specificity and discover its origin in time.

Historical circumstances of the birth of race ideology

The ideological notion of race was formed in the course of the nineteenth century in Europe. The process by which this came about was part of a wider movement, many aspects of which were then new, and cannot be seen separately from the other mental and social productions of the time; to treat race as a phenomenon closed in on itself, set apart both from other ideological developments and from its own social substrate, would be to reduce it to the status of a 'psychological trait' and so mask its singularity and diminish its importance.

History

These new developments took place in a society undergoing radical political and economic change. The socio-economic organization and practice of power were evolving with a rapidity accentuated by the brutal alternation of monarchic and revolutionary regimes (in France: 1789, 1792, 1798, 1815, 1830, 1848, 1852 . . .). By 1789, the traditional governing class had been dispossessed, practically and symbolically, of political power, in favour of a class vastly more numerous than itself. The nobility, which accounted for only 2–3 per cent of the population, was supplanted by a section of the third estate – the bourgeoisie – who, after acquiring a substantial share, if not the entirety, of the economic power, would now take over political power too. Unlike the group that it replaced, which was highly conscious of being a coherent caste, it did not regard itself as an institutional group. In its own eyes, 'the bourgeoisie [was] so far from being a class that its doors [were] open to anyone wishing either to enter, or to leave';[6] it saw itself not as a class, but as a sum of individuals who made up an 'élite' and had gained power through their own abilities.[7] With the growth of industrialization, the third estate also produced the industrial proletariat. The urban and rural poor became the 'industrial men' whose consciousness of constituting a working class crystallized in the course of the nineteenth century. A large portion of the population moved in this way from a peasant existence into industry, from a subsistence to a wage economy, from a low- to a high-density living environment. Over a hundred-year period these changes affected more than a third of the population, of whom more than half were peasants; at the turn of the nineteenth century 80 per cent of the population was rural, while a century later the figure had fallen to 41 per cent.[8] This gives a measure of the scale of the changes, economic, ecological and in type of work. In addition to these changes affecting the socio-economic conditions of the members of each class, the global economy became transformed by the growth of colonization, which from about 1830 led to the world's being divided up among the western nations, and turned a hitherto indigenous production system into a colonial economy of the type we still have today.[9]

Associated cultural traits

The seizure of political, by way of economic, power by a class which had taken several hundred years to emerge from political non-existence, the birth of the working class, the subjugation of foreign peoples, all bore the hallmarks of individualism, the claim to equality, and nationalism, which formed the background against which the ideology of race made its appearance. These ideological characteristics have remained largely unchanged to the present day. The European nationalisms were born in the revolutionary period and served to cement the desire for popular unity;[10] they embodied a new group consciousness radically different from the organization into 'orders' which preceded them. This period was also marked by the spread of an individualistic morality and sensibility,[11] which led to the definitive fragmentation of the earlier 'societal' identity: the social group lost its referential priority to the individual. Finally, revolutionary aspirations to equality had a profound effect.[12] The striking novelty of this ideological picture is obvious when it is compared to what went before.

These ideological changes were tied term by term to politico-economic developments. The bourgeoisie took over power, and its legitimacy was proclaimed in the doctrine of equality, from the *Encyclopédie* to the society of the first Revolution. At the same time, among the ruins of those theologically based bastions of community organization that were the orders, individualism was breaking out everywhere in support of an intoxicated but unsure bourgeoisie which regarded itself as a collection of individuals. Initially the fruit of economic success, individualism became an alibi for political domination once power had been acquired; from Protestant free will to the free market (liberal) economy, or the success of those best equipped to succeed, it moved from being a means of laying claim to power, to one of asserting the legitimacy of power. 'All political power, all privileges, all prerogatives, the whole of government became enclosed and as if heaped up within the boundaries of that one class', wrote de Tocqueville. Finally, there came into being the 'nation', the name given to itself by the 'people' as it formed itself into the quasi-caste which it had never been in the past. In a world governed by aristocrats and constrained within jealously guarded boundaries,[13] the people, from being nothing, entirely without definition, utterly relative (X's serf, Y's subject, Z's Jew . . .), suddenly started to invent itself, fixing its territory, its language,[14] its constitution, its laws, and affirming its opposition to the hierarchs. (The same phenomenon can be seen today in the opposition of Third World nationalisms to the hierarchs of the West.) Territory, language, laws came in to fill the void left by the people's earlier status, maintained by subjection, as subjects (a word which, by a striking linguistic paradox, actually means the state of being an object).

Finally, the theory of the inequality of races itself crystallized in the middle of the nineteenth century, at the moment of the bourgeoisie's triumph and the birth of class consciousness among workers.[15] Gobineau's *Essai sur l'inégalité des races humaines* was published just as the Second Republic, born in 1848, was collapsing to make way for the Bonapartist socio-political order.[16] A few decades later the theory would enter into social practice and become a systematic part of the country's institutions, a process of application which in no way suggests any causal link between theory and institutionalization.[17]

Race (or racist) ideology

But the theory, a mode of perception rationalized into a doctrine, attracts all the attention at the expense of the ideology that engendered it, and people tend all too readily to confuse two things, one of which feeds on the other but without exhausting its potential. Ideology, more diffuse but also more widespread, is the mode of apprehension of reality shared by a whole culture, to the point where it becomes omnipresent and, for that very reason, goes unrecognized. The ideology of race (racism) is a universe of signs: it is what mediated the specific social practice of western society as it became industrialized, and as political activity was taken over by a class which had formerly been excluded from it. It is a universe of signs far more extensive than simply the 'theory' into which it crystallized in the course of the nineteenth century.

Indeed, the theory stresses human 'differences' and inequalities, and affirms the superiority and inferiority of groups of people in line with criteria more or less explicitly defined, according to author, but that is all. The theory takes race as something irrefutably given, practically as an 'immediate datum of the senses'; as a self-evident truth, rather than a scientific tool or concept. Thus the *Essai sur l'inégalité* gives no definition of race; worse still, it makes no attempt to establish any causal link whatsoever between physical phenomena and mental or social ones. When Gobineau compares the brain weights of Blacks and Whites, the meaning he attributes to the comparison is syncretic: brain weight equates to degree of intelligence. A causal link between mental and physical facts was subsequently deduced a posteriori, in an over-zealous attempt to rationalize the idea, with the result that the assertion of a causal link is now presented as the distinguishing characteristic of racist doctrine.[18] Nothing could be further from the conscious intentions of the theory, whose only explicit postulate is one of hierarchy,[19] but the effect is to hypostasize the existence of races. As for a theory of biophysical causality, there is none; in terms of the biophysical argument, syncretism rules the day.

These two things, the hypostasis of race and biophysical syncretism, are the key characteristics of racist ideology in that they are unconscious, experienced as natural, spontaneous and self-evident.[20] In other words, the theory grows in ground ready prepared to receive it, which it would not dream of trying to define or of questioning. It presupposes that ideology, the inventor of the perceptive term 'race', is there in the background to support it. In treating (and perceiving) race and culture from the start as if they were identical, theoretical racism shows that both its premises and its methodology are motivated by a racist ideology. Even today, anti-racism campaigners only bolster this system when they try to prove propositions such as 'race and culture must be separated', 'culture is not dependent on race', 'race is not properly defined biologically', etc.. negations which all implicitly accept the original syncretic position.[21]

Inequality, superiority, inferiority, differences in ability, are in fact no more than secondary aspects of an overall belief, never expressed because it is obvious and imperative, that human activity is a biophysical phenomenon. And this proposition is a new invention of the industrial era. We have come a long way from aggressivity, and further still from the simple theory of a hierarchy of 'races'.

We shall therefore leave to one side the subject of aggressivity, and racist theory itself, because they not only contain nothing more than the ideology, but do not even contain all of that. If we understand the ideology we will understand its theoretical ration-alization, whereas understanding just the theory would give us only a partial view of the ideology. What we shall therefore attempt to illuminate is the perceptive and signifying system, the ideology, which unlike the theory is shared by all the members of a given culture.[22] If we examine the birth of the ideology of race, we will see that it does indeed turn out to be a historically datable phenomenon.

Juridical and geneticist views

There is a subtle trap laid for us by words whose forms do not alter over time, for we tend to ascribe to them with no hesitation the identity of a fixed meaning. At best, we may note semantic changes as they are presented in the manuals of linguistic history, while still hypostasizing the current sense, and only mentioning the recognized variants around a supposedly stable denotation. This is clearly what happens with the term 'race', of which the human sciences, from anthropology to social psychology, have made such widespread use. It has become the backbone of racist ideology, and we saw a clue to its importance in the fact that it seemed so self-evident that the theory itself did not even bother to define it.

At the end of the last century Freud, looking back over his own life, remarked: 'my origins, or, *as people were beginning to say, my race*',[23] thereby noting a new usage of a term which was far from new. So the meaning of the word could not be taken for granted at the very period when it was coming into widespread use. This meaning is actually quite recent, for as with the all-conquering families of the nineteenth-century bourgeoisie, its pedigree is a modern invention; in the words of one of Lampedusa's characters: 'Yours is an ancient family, or at least, it soon will be'.[24] Like these families, the word 'race' became venerable very quickly. From its attested use in France from the early sixteenth century, but long restricted to a particular social group,[25] the existence of a permanent signified underlying the signifier was extrapolated. This was helped by the fact that the old sense, used in and by a class steeped in the prejudices of 'inheritance' and very touchy on the subject of purity of 'blood', seemed closely related to the sense we give it today. But this is, of course, an illusion, which can blind us to what is specific about the modern use of the term.

In the successive uses of a word we often observe a phenomenon comparable to homonymy, whereby signifieds diverge beneath a common signifier. But the comparison is only valid up to a point, because in the process of historical drift, a term's identity is not wholly reducible to its use in individual utterances; there is a 'remainder', a minimal core sense which stays constant from one period to another. It is this minimal core sense that leads to confusion because it can too easily be regarded as a guarantee of the whole of the meaning, and so of its permanence. That is the case with the notion of race. If the word designates a restricted, well-defined object specific to the period of its use, that object nevertheless has a real relationship with its predecessors, an abstract relation-ship that shrinks down into the skeleton of a meaning. In this way, race comes to have as its permanent semantic core the meaning 'coherent group of people', and nothing else.[26] Each period then adds a certain number of connotations, giving the term a more specific meaning. Each period also tends to charge recurrent old meanings with the new connotations, thus masking the profound changes undergone by people's perception and grasp of social realities. In the current meaning, the core sense of 'coherent group of people' has added to it a biological or somatic content. This other sense is dominant and dictates our whole understanding of the term. The biological idea is the current hypostasis of the notion of race, and it tends to be taken, whether spontaneously or on reflection, as a constant component of the word's usage and meaning, thus unifying over time a notion which closer examination shows in fact to be extremely heterogeneous. For this feeling of permanence is an illusion, the biological colouring is new and was not part of the old term 'race'. Such a shift in meaning is highly significant for our understanding of human groups in industrial societies, for what seems like an age-old reality is actually quite the reverse.

In order to detect shifts in meaning behind the façade of permanence, we have at our disposal that most commonplace of tools, the dictionary. It needs to be consulted in accordance with certain rules.

- The first rule is that we must use dictionaries of different periods, rather than being satisfied with the datings given in a single work. A single dictionary of whatever period will provide only the contemporary sense of a given term, and the date suggested for its origin will apply to the word, rather than the notion, so that the signifier will be dated but not the signified (except where there is a sharp break in meaning). The current signified will be taken as the primary sense, and older signifieds which seem significantly out of tune with the modern sense will often be relegated to the role of minor or specialized senses, without any mention being made of the central role they occupied in the past. Even when (in the best possible case) senses are arranged in chronological order, connotations will become transferred and overflow from the modern meaning to those of earlier periods. At least, that is what happens with the semantic cluster which has built up around the term 'race'.
- The second rule is to compare definitions from different periods. Isolated definitions, however significant may be their 'period' flavour, lose much of their meaning if studied on their own, for they become totalizing and trap us with their appearance of a 'full sense', whereas comparing them with their counterparts from other periods reveals the variations and gaps in meaning characteristic of a particular moment, the novel elements and particularities which trace the evolution and successive content of ideologies.
- The third rule is to compare one with another the elements of the same semantic field, at the same period, in order to check the conclusions drawn from the historical comparison.
- The fourth and most important rule is to treat a definition not as a thing, completely contained in and delimited by the explicit meaning of the term, but as a set of connotations. A definition can actually work on two different levels, one explicit, the other implicit.[27] The first, visible, level is a definition in the usual sense of the term, clear and well-articulated, both logically and syntactically. The other, rendered invisible by its very self-evidence, is created by juxtaposition of terms: logic and syntax are completely evacuated, as is negation, whose status of logical production is well known, whether in a Russellian or a psychoanalytic perspective.[28] The terms

used to lay down the definition all come together to form a connotative portrait of the notion. It is this connotative portrait, rather than the clear exposition which actually conceals it, that creates the meaning, closely following the line of the ideology and pointing up its variations. The type of semantic analysis employed here will therefore deliberately turn its back on anything consciously elaborated, whether in terms of social discourses (ignoring theory in favour of ideology), or articulated definitions (preferring sets of connotations to explicit definitions). However, this decision results in the adoption of a particular attitude, rather than a different field of investigation: the same texts are examined whichever approach is used.

Our analysis will therefore be synchronic in so far as it takes account of the whole semantic field of the notion under investigation: the term 'race' will be examined not in isolation, but in the company of those other words which, according to a common-sense view, would be grouped together with it. It will be diachronic in the comparisons made between successive usages.

The semantic field of the notion of race is that of racist ideology in general, with the word 'race' itself at its epicentre. Around it stand its present-day associates, the designators of racialized groups (Arabs, Israelites, Asiatics, Jews, Negroes, Blacks), as well as certain of its much older corollaries (blood, nobility). The term 'inheritance', for its part, is characteristic of both the older and the modern period; like the word 'race', it is a constant, and can therefore be used as a measure of the changes of meaning which have occurred since the eighteenth century.

The hypothesis advanced above,[29] that racist ideology was born in the revolutionary period and developed through the nineteenth century, will now be tested by reference to two dictionaries of French: the first, the *Wailly*, a popular dictionary published in Year IX of the Revolution (1802), and the second, the *Robert* (first edition), which came out in 1953.

Each definition will be quoted exactly, but the connotative discourse will also be highlighted, so combining denotation and connotation in the same assessment. The eighteenth-century text will always be given first; the quotations are complete, despite their brevity.[30] This method of presentation will bring out the great burden of biology which the modern definitions carry, in comparison with the much 'lighter' older text.

Let us look first at the term 'race', which prior to the Revolution (honour to whom honour is due) was applied solely to noble families.

Race. *18th c.*: *Lignée*: (line of) descent, all those who come from the same family.
[Conversely, under *lignée* we find race]

So the term refers strictly to family continuity. NB: continuity of the family, not genetic continuity, which is not mentioned here, in contrast to later definitions.

20th c. [we are told that the word goes back to the 16th]: 1) Family considered in its successive generations. 2) Subdivision of species, itself divided into sub-races and varieties, constituted by individuals with common hereditary characteristics which represent variations within the species[31] 3) With reference to human groups: subdivision of the human race, equivalent to the division of an animal species into 'races' (breeds).

1749. (Buffon). In the strict sense, each ethnic group which is differentiated from others by a set of hereditary physical characteristics representing variations within the species. *19th c*. (By ext., or improperly). Natural group of people with similar characteristics deriving from a common past . . . This broad meaning, quite close to that of '(line of) descent', is often used and understood as in 2), in disregard of the scientific facts.

These meanings all seem self-evident to us today, and are completely integrated into our perception of the term. The word generation marks a shift, for in becoming the corollary of the 'family' definition, it introduces a biophysical schema ('generation' comes from 'engender') in place of a legal concept, that of 'line of descent'. Thus a biological continuity replaces a juridical continuity.

Hereditary species, animal species, hereditary physical characteristics, species, natural group, scientific facts . . . are among the terms which order the current definition; they take us to the heart of the geneticist assumptions underlying the modern meaning of the term. By the nineteenth century, the whole field had become highly coloured by physiology and nature, evidence of a faith in the physical solidarity of humans and animals. Moreover, this somatic density of race was consecrated by the prestige of science, the new metaphysics; in an age when people believed only in tangible things, skeleton, brain, skull, height, weight, skin-colour were the new realities of the day. They were now felt to be the entire truth behind human phenomena, and seemed to drag along in their wake their anaemic elders, language, religion, law, economics, which were no more than their pale and wavering reflection.

Moreover, we see the use here of the word *hereditary*, whose properly biological meaning dates from the end of the first half of the nineteenth century. It casts its shadow over the earlier usage of notions which have only come to imply it in more recent times: can we now think of 'race' without reference to 'inheritance' in the physical sense? Yet such a reference was unthinkable before the nineteenth century, so much so, as Goblot notes, that:

> A remarkable characteristic of the modern French bourgeoisie is . . . the importance it attaches to the purity of the family. In this, it is infinitely superior to the *ancien régime* aristocracy. It is a matter of some astonishment that a hereditary caste, so obsessed with its ancestors and attributing such importance to blood and race, should have been so little concerned with authenticity of filiation. In this aristocratic society of the 17th and 18th centuries adultery, by both husband and wife, is commonplace, and meets with no reprobation at all. The writings of the period, and in particular the memoirs, leave us in no doubt about that. Natural, physiological filiation is of no importance; all that counts is conventional, legal filiation: *is pater quem nuptiae demonstrant*, the father is, by legal definition, the mother's husband. In fact, it is neither blood nor race that carry value, it is name.[32]

Neither blood nor race carry value? On the contrary. How can we avoid being convinced of their importance when it is ceaselessly proclaimed by the caste that defines itself by reference to them? It is just that blood and race are synonymous with 'name', and 'name' lacks the biophysical content grafted onto the other two terms in the nineteenth century, a content which Goblot assumes in his use of them. This blood and race are not the same as ours, and that is what Goblot fails to recognize at the very moment when he succeeds so well in grasping their deeper meaning. Meaning simply a legal line of descent, race had not yet picked up the genetic overtones we know today; name was what mattered, not genes. It is now scarcely possible for us to identify imaginatively with such a meaning, so strong has been the recurrent contamination by the modern meaning. Let us then look at the changes affecting the terms 'blood' and 'noble', which filled the semantic field of 'race' before the nineteenth century.[33]

> Blood. *18th c.*: Red liquor flowing through the veins and arteries of animals. *Fig.* Race, descendance. *20th c.*: 1) Physiology: red, viscous liquid of insipid flavour, etc. 2) Particularly from 1170: in speaking of blood spilled . . . etc. 3) Blood traditionally considered as the carrier of racial and hereditary characteristics. *See* Inheritance, race . . . *See* Blood, mixed . . . *See* Consanguineous, related. *See* Relationship. *See* Half-blood . . .

The appearance of 'race' in both definitions should not be allowed to mislead us. The first sense, which we know means household or family, has been transformed in the modern version into 'racial and hereditary characteristics', expressing the utterly metaphysical idea of a physical path of transmission.

> Noble. *18th c.*: One who, by birth or royal patent, is superior in rank to the third estate. *20th c.*: Superior to other beings or objects of the same type. 1) In the domain of intellectual or moral qualities, and human values in general. 2) In the domain of behaviour or physical appearance, that which commands respect and admiration by its distinction and natural authority. Specially, 'one who is elevated above the common people by birth, appointment to high office, or royal favour' (Furetière), and therefore belongs to a privileged social class within the State.

The current 'special' definition in fact repeats word for word the old sociological definition given in Furetière's *Dictionary*,[34] which is, as can be seen, virtually identical to that in *Wailly*. Moreover, it shows very well how, in contrast to modern races, an aristocrat could be made (by royal patent or appointment to high office). There is no appeal here to some *sui generis* virtue, whereas nowadays notions like being, species, physical, natural . . . introduce just such a biological colouring. Not, incidentally, without a certain reticence that we shall find in no other definition, reflecting perhaps the daring required to draw such a vulgar association between a prestigious left-over social distinction and today's resolutely proletarian notion of race. To see the concept of nobility and other ideas of the same epoch through modern eyes as aspects of a racist system of thought, to read the religion of 'blood', line of descent and 'race' in this racialist light, is adventurous in the extreme, given the historical absence of any reference to a biophysical basis for human social and mental activity, on which the whole of our current use of such terms is predicated. Without that, there is no point of comparison, and the old aristocracy's touchiness on the subject of its own continuation must be seen as purely legal in origin. Saint-Simon's snobbism and his enthusiasm for the legitimate Bourbons are well known, as is the zeal with which he attacked the social status of the royal bastards. But on the subject of the legitimate filiation of the Condé branch, he writes in tones that will surprise a modern reader:

> Mlle. de Condé died in Paris on 24 October after a long chest illness, which consumed her less than the upset and torment occasioned her by Monsieur le Prince, whose constant whims were the curse of all those at whose expense he exercised them, whims which had rendered this princess inconsolable because two inches in stature had led to her younger sister's being preferred as a bride for M. du Maine, thereby denying her an escape from intolerable servitude. All the children of Monsieur le Prince were near-dwarfs, except the Princesse de Conti, his eldest daughter, though she was still small. Monsieur le Prince and Madame la Princesse were small, though not exceptionally so, and the elder Monsieur le Prince the hero, who was tall, liked to joke that if his race were to go on shrinking in that fashion, it would eventually disappear. The cause was put down to a dwarf whom Madame la Princesse had long had in her household, and it is true that in addition to being short and stocky, Monsieur le Duc and Madame de Vendôme had exactly his face. Mlle. de Condé had a handsome face, and a soul more handsome still, with much wit, common sense, reason, gentleness, and a piety which sustained her throughout a less than happy life. She was therefore sorely missed by all who had known her.[35]

Line of descent, blood, nobility form the whole of the semantic field covered by race up to the nineteenth century. Then the social objects implicated in the field changed, and if we are to assess the shift in meaning between the old social universe and our own, we must look at the group which replaced the aristocracy as the bearers of racial meaning, people for whom race was to be, from then on, their social emblem.

The change in the meaning of the term 'race' from nobility, blood, family, household, to Arab, Asiatic, Jew, Israelite, Negro, Black is one which has passed almost unnoticed. A word which in the old days applied only to the aristocracy is nowadays reserved for 'racialized' peoples, two groups which could not be further apart in terms of both economic and political power. From designating an institutional power-group, it has shifted to cover categories of people without any legal definition, who have nothing to do with the exercise of power.

We shall trace the emergence of the racist meaning of the modern semantic field by comparing the old definitions with those of our own day. For while they may not in the past have belonged to any such highly élitist field of meaning, they did already exist at that time.

> **Arab**. *18th c.*: Which is from Arabia; figuratively, one who demands his due with extreme harshness. – Arab(ic): the language of the Arabs; – arabic

numerals, our ordinary numerals taken from the Arabs. *20th c.*: Which originates from Arabia. The Arab people. An Arab horse (*See* Nedji). An Arab greyhound (*See* Sloughi). *Subst.* The Arabs, Semitic people, and by extension the indigenous islamicized populations of the Maghreb. *See* Barbary, Bedouin (desert Arab), Moor, Saracen. Arabs refer to Christians as 'roumi'. – Of or pertaining to Arabs.

We might begin by noting that the early stereotype, 'one who demands his due with extreme harshness', is no help in the area that concerns us here. We shall come across such stereotypes again in other definitions, and there are a few things which might be said about them, but in general stereotyping is a marginal aspect of racism, and not even specific to it. In this particular case it is enough to point out that the image of the man who is hard with money seems to have disappeared from modern usage.

In the old definition, the references are: (a) geographical (from Arabia); (b) cultural (Arabic language and numerals). There is no mention of biophysical characteristics.

The current definition, on the other hand, takes us into the realm of geneticism ('which originates . . .'), and introduces animal associations (Arab horse, Arab greyhound) alongside a reference to the Arab people. This is the only definition where we find such an association with animals through contiguity, but the underlying drive towards bodily hypostasis finds expression in other ways too, as we shall see. Racial vocabulary then follows, with Semitic; it might be objected with some appearance of plausibility that the linguistic, not the racial term is being used here, but if so, we might have expected 'people of Semitic language', to avoid any ambiguity. The same dictionary also uses 'Semitic' in an explicitly racial sense in other definitions. Moreover, the main meaning of a term at a given time encapsulates all its other meanings, whether we like it or not, and that happens here as much as anywhere else. Finally, 'indigenous' further strengthens the racial colouration.

For a group now considered to be one of the 'fundamental races', we find:

Yellow (-skinned).[36] *18th c.*: Colour of gold, lemons, saffron, eggyolk. *Adj.* of colour yellow. *20th c.*: 1) One of the seven fundamental colours of the spectrum. 2) Yellow-coloured object. 3) Individual of yellow-skinned race. 4) Blackleg, strike-breaker.

There is one straight fact here far more basic than any shift in meaning or connotations: until the twentieth century, 'yellow' did not serve to designate any human group. Those people who, when the West was seized by the craze for somatic designations and Europe discovered the need to order humankind according to the colours of the spectrum, suddenly found the colour yellow thrust upon them apparently had no specific skin colour before that. Now the term 'race' is applied to them too, without anyone thinking of protesting. It is perhaps this term, which has undergone the clearest and most abrupt development, which best illustrates the change that has occurred. What we see here is the overlaying of a totally new meaning on an old word, and its further crystallization into the notion of 'race'.

After this perfect elliptical synthesis of our argument in a single definition, let us move on to look at two terms which seem at first to suggest the opposite. The ancient roots of their usage, and of the social group they designate, appear to support those who see 'race' as an age-old, if not eternal, notion. However, their very age shows up the inconsistency of this belief.

> Jew. *18th c.*: One who professes Judaism. *Fig.* Man who makes usurious loans or sells at too high a price. Rich as a Jew, very rich. Wandering Jew, one who is constantly wandering from place to place. *20th c.*: 1) Noun. Name given to the descendants of Abraham since their Exile (4th century BC). *See* Hebrew, Israelite. Semitic, monotheistic people who lived in Palestine, and whose dispersal lasted from the period of Exile to the 2nd century BC. Name given to the descendants of this people scattered throughout the world, who have generally remained faithful to their religion and attached to Jewish tradition. *Fig.* One who seeks profit above all else, usurer. 2) *Adj.* Jewish: of or pertaining to the community of Jews, ancient or modern.

Here again, and by no means for the last time, we find that the old definition is based on a socio-cultural reference, in this case to religion: 'One who professes Judaism'. We might notice in passing the assumption, long since vanished, that being a Jew is a matter of choice, and not, as people now tend to believe, of biology. This old definition certainly contains stereotypes, but there are no geneticist assumptions, unlike in the modern definition, which reflects our western culture's obsession with such things in words like 'descendants' and 'Semitic'. To this is then added the thoroughly coherent racism of genetic continuity, whereby a religious group is essentialized into a genetic monolith which goes on reproducing itself unchanged through time and space: 'Name given ... since their Exile', 'who lived in Palestine, and whose dispersal lasted from ... to ... descendants ... remained ....' The variations on Israelite readily confirm these observations.

> Israelite *18th c.*: Ancient Hebrew people. A good Israelite, an honest, simple man. *20th c.*: (18th century, from Israel). Descendant of Israel, one who belongs to the Jewish community or religion. *See* Hebrew, Jew.

Here again a modern, geneticist definition ('Descendant') contrasts with an older, historical one ('Ancient ... people').[37]

Prior to the nineteenth century human differences were classified according to 'phenomenological' systems, be they social (appointment to high office, royal favour), religious (one who professes a given faith), or historical (ancient people). Nowadays, geneticist systems are the ones used, as will be confirmed in the case of the term 'Negro'.

> Negro. *18th c.*: Black slave employed in colonial work. Treated like a Negro, very harshly. *20th c.*: Used in common parlance to refer to those of black race, especially Blacks belonging to the so-called melano-African race. *Remark* the word Negro does not correspond to any scientific anthropological classi- fication. In modern-day speech 'Black' is generally preferred to Negro, seen as

pejorative. – Physical type of the Negro: wiry hair, snub, splayed nose, fat lips. – White or albino Negro. Negro dance, customs, music, religion. *Specially*: Black formerly employed as a slave in certain hot countries.

The eighteenth-century definition mentions 'black' as a physical trait, which is particularly interesting as this is the only time that we find such a trait in an old definition. The meaning and function of this detail of pigmentation are important, however. In the eighteenth century definition, 'black' is the qualifier, not the determinant. The determinant is 'slave', a socio-historical designation, which is secondarily qualified by 'black'. In contrast, the word 'black' acts as the determiner in the modern definition because it is the reference: to be a Negro now is no longer to be a slave, it is to be black, and someone who in the eighteenth century was 'a black slave employed . . .' would nowadays be 'a Black employed . . . as a slave'. So the definition has come full circle, with the racial aspect now dominant over the social one. This leaves behind an awkward feeling, however, because why should we worry about the word 'Negro' not corresponding to 'any scientific anthropological classification', unless we have completely lost sight of the fact that it is actually a social, not a scientific, term?

In the current definition there is an abundance of anatomical and biological terminology, but the logic (as opposed to the fantasy value) of such a deluge of physical characteristics remains far from clear, particularly as they are totally absent from the antonyms 'white' and 'yellow (-skinned)'.[38] Finally, the sense presented as special is actually, as we have already observed in other cases, the original meaning (here, the socio-historical one: slavery).

The term 'black' itself undergoes the following evolution:

> Black. *18th c.*: The colour black. – To see the black side (take a gloomy view) of everything. – To leap from black to white, from one extreme to the other. – Think black (gloomy) thoughts, – Negro (by opposition to white). *20th c.*: 1) The colour black . . . 2) Darkness, night . . . 3) Black (paint, etc.) 4) Black as symbol of melancholy, pessimism . . . 5) Black part of a thing . . . 6) (*mus.*) Crochet. 7) *17th c.*. Man or woman of black race. *See* Negro. Specially, black slave, black servant.

In the eighteenth-century definition the colours are seen as a relational system, as indicated in 'by opposition to': black is a comparative quality ('Negro, by opposition to white'), which takes us back to Negro as a social designator, because it is necessary to point out that the word can also mean 'black'. Conversely, the definition of 'white' contains the corresponding observation: 'person whose skin colour is white, by opposition to Negroes'; this has totally disappeared from the present definitions, which deal in all-embracing, self-sufficient, absolute realities ('man or woman of black race' on the one hand, 'man or woman of white race' on the other). Furthermore, the modern definition makes use of the term 'race' which, as always, is absent from the eighteenth-century definition. Thus we have two distinct descriptive schemas:

- the relational, eighteenth-century one: colour X 'by opposition to' colour Y; absence of the term 'race';

- the non-relational, twentieth-century one: race X . . . or . . . race Y; use of the term 'race'.

The current perceptual system is both geneticist and absolute, and is definitely the result of a historical process, since it did not exist at all before the nineteenth century, but is universally present today. It is quite a rare thing to observe such regularity in the expression of an ideology, for the coherent use of terms at a given period, and the sharp divide revealed by comparison between periods, are not just limited to 'race' and 'races'. Line of descent, nature, genealogy, all concepts at the periphery of the 'race' field, yield exactly the same results, but to examine them in the same detail would be overly fastidious, and in any case beyond the scope of the present essay.

However, there is one important term which allows all the foregoing observations to be brought together and checked for validity, a word which lies at the heart of the conflict we are investigating, and is the key to all geneticist thinking: inheritance.

> **Inheritance**. *18th c.*: Right of succession, property a man leaves behind on his death. *20th c.*: 1) Total amount of property a person leaves behind on death. 2) Hereditary character; transmission by line of succession. *Biol. 1842.* (Mozin). Transmission of characteristics of a living being to its descendants. Specific, racial, inheritance: rigorous transmission of specific, racial characteristics by which two individuals (or a single hermaphrodite individual) of a given race or species can only engender individuals of the same race or species. In common parlance, set of characteristics, dispositions, aptitudes, etc. inherited from parents, forebears; hereditary inheritance. Unfortunate inheritance; inheritance of physical and mental defects. *By ext.* Characteristics found from one generation to the next in certain geographical, social etc. milieux, as consistently as if they were hereditary . . . provincial, peasant, foreign inheritance.

'*Living being, descendants, racial, hermaphrodite, engender, race, species, aptitudes, forebears, hereditary inheritance . . .* ': we are here deep in the black-magic territory of bodily nature, a long way from the modest inheritance of the Age of Enlightenment. The 'property a person leaves behind on death' has become swollen with another, more threatening meaning: 'unfortunate inheritance . . . physical and mental defects . . . ' paint a rather curious picture of the term's sinister implications, and it is perfectly clear that it is 'other people' who form a 'race' by virtue of their heredity, for there is nothing particularly narcissistic about such a cheerful catalogue as this!

From one example to another a clear pattern has now emerged. It is hard to deny that the modern senses are indeed based on the old ones, as no new terms have been created. But new meanings have certainly been superimposed on old terms. This has come about largely under the patronage of the natural sciences which, unlike popular, everyday language (which has no objection to lexical creation), prefer to find new meanings for old words, rather than invent new words. That is what has happened here, for the terms we have analysed are the fruit of prolonged scientific efforts to re-describe the world. We know just how successful this vocabulary, new only in terms of meaning, was to be; it quickly took over in the human sciences as well, which became directed

359

towards providing a physical, mechanistic account of human behaviour. These developments are all the more obvious as they involve not a change in the meaning of just a single term, but the drift of a whole semantic field. Without exception, the words in this field are now all markedly different from their older homonyms, showing that the somatic-biological ideology they carry, completely absent from earlier usage, was indeed something quite new.

Auto- and altero-reference

Change of signified group

The internal shift of meaning that we have just analysed is not the only change undergone by the race system. Not only has the descriptive sense of the word, in its religious, historical or social aspects, lurched towards innate meanings and become swathed in an aura of biological inevitability, its field of application has also altered. Thus, in addition to a change in meaning, there has been a change in object. We of course noted in the course of our analysis of the semantic field of the term 'race that it had been extended from the aristocracy to cover the somatic groupings created in the nineteenth century. The aristocracy now having disappeared from the socio-political stage, no single group can be said to have borne the 'race' emblem without interruption.

Change of referential topology

They may not be the same ones, but there are still groups which bear that emblem. In any system which privileges the race symbol by assigning it a referential role, whether it be the old-style phenomenologically-based system or the modern naturalistic one, the two opposing terms are always Self and Other.[39] Which of these social terms is invested with the racial characteristic depends on whether the old or the new system is in operation. Thus, while race remains the referent, that does not mean that it occupies the same position in the system, for it can be either auto- or altero-referential.

The auto-referential system, centred on the Self, was historically the first to be put in place; it coincided with the pre-eminence of the aristocracy, to whom its race symbolism was specific. The system gravitates around the social Self: all social relations between groups are governed by the definition which those who institutionally control power give of themselves. Their eyes remain fixed on their own existence which, both in their own minds and in reality, regulates the course and the symbolism of social activity. It is perhaps legitimate to see in this system a form of ethnocentrism, in the sense that value is derived from those characteristics specific to the dominant group. However, 'aristocratism' is not yet racism because unlike racism, it is not founded on a belief in its own 'naturalness'.

Altero-referential racism is centred on the Other, and seems to arise only in egalitarian societies. A fundamental trait of such a system is the occultation of the Self, of which people have no spontaneous awareness; there is no sense of belonging to a specific group, so the group itself always remains outside the frame of reference, is never referred to as a group. This can be seen clearly in the everyday ways in which groups are designated.

For instance, present-day French society designates Jews as a group but not Christians, Blacks but not Whites, Being White, Christian, etc. 'goes without saying'. This trait is so deeply ingrained in our social universe that it distorts language for its own ends. What conclusion can we draw from the fact that 'Christian' and 'white' are still used mainly adjectivally, whereas Black, Jew ('Juif') and Asiatic ('Jaune') have become nouns, if not that the dominant groups have escaped the process of substantivization which has befallen those whom they dominate?

Furthermore, violence in relations between groups is always explained by reference to the other. We are all familiar with the peculiar logic which produces expressions such as 'the black problem' or 'the Jewish question', but it extends further than is generally realized, because all contact situations (if the use of such a euphemism is permissible) are named by reference to an Other: slave-hatred, anti-Semitism, xenophobia . . . Conversely, none of these words has an antonym: proChristianism, pro-masterism, indigenophilia, etc. obviously do not exist, which confirms the one-sidedness of the relationship. Whatever approach one takes to this question, only the Other seems to be present in people's minds as the explicit referent behind the perceived situation. Our social discourse is no longer directed out from a dominant sense of Self, but towards a dominated Other. Race is no longer associated with power, but with lack of power. Whereas in auto-referential societies difference is the declared property of the dominant group, and used to its advantage, in altero-referential societies it is the Other (in the form of the various dominated groups) who is always different. And underlying this difference is the fact that the Other has now become a regulator, rather than a producer, of social discourse; a regulator deprived of power, and so reduced to the status of an object.

In an auto-referential system the subject group, which controls power, makes the assertion: 'We are different'; by contrast, in an alteroreferential system that group asserts: 'the Others are different'. With the common factor being that race is the signifier of the perceived difference.

The purest form of altero-referential racism is probably what we are seeing in France today, whereas anti-revolutionary aristocratism is the most typical example of the auto-referential type. But the composite forms of modern racism nevertheless retain large residues of auto-referentialism. Such is the case with Nazi Aryanism. American Caucasianism, and the Celticism and Latinism of the French Far Right. However, modern forms of auto-referentialism all appeal to biological criteria, and, above all, are only secondarily auto-referential; they are mainly, and centrally, altero-referential. An obsession with the Other remains their dominant characteristic. The Nazis' anti-Semitism was more of a driving force than their Aryanism; Negrophobia is far more powerful in the United States than Caucasianism.

It is highly likely that the most serious situations are those in which the two systems occur together. In combination they form a structure of explosive rigidity, all the more so as the proportion of the two types of reference becomes more equal. A case in point is that of the Nazi regime, where the law governed both who was an Aryan and who was a Jew, thereby dictating a substantially equal degree of closure of both groups in on themselves.

The form of racism prevalent in France today represents the ultimate expression of altero-reference in that it recognizes only others and not itself. Ultimately, it shows a complete failure to recognize and define any Self group at all. It offers its own completely adequate explanation of lived experience, one that is literally so blindingly obvious that it prevents its proponents from also seeing, specifying and designating themselves as a race at the very time when they are busy designating Others as belonging to one. We have moved as far as it is possible to go from aristocratism, where the Self group alone had the right to such a definition. This type of racism is characterized by blindness about oneself as much as by an obsession with the Other, two traits which it unites into a single system.

Synchronic and diachronic perceptions

We therefore perceive and conceive of race today in a profoundly different way from our predecessors. This difference is not just a result of the introduction of socio-genetic syncretism, a shift in the object designated by the term 'race', or a change in the position of the referent in the social system; it is also marked by a profound modification of temporal perspective. Let us now return to the minimal sense put forward earlier as the semantic core of 'race': a coherent group of people (as defined by whatever criteria, which will obviously vary over time as we have already seen: common legal and administrative status in the early period, common biophysical inheritance nowadays).

The old-style temporal perspective, which for convenience we shall term 'pre-racial', is diachronic. It is organized in terms of line of descent, genealogy, family, as a mechanism for handing down a name. This perception of race therefore follows a line from past to present, in which the individual represents a moment in history. Though essentially a perspective wedded to the passage of time, it can also forge links in space by way of family relationships and alliances, but its main kernel is resolutely temporal. The solidarity between individuals of the same race is that of the passage of time. Moreover, it depends on a legal and institutional system which brings together under one 'family' name a well-defined group of people, 'the Bourbons', 'the Rohans', etc. In this old system, where the term 'race' was only used in the specific context of a family's line of descent, it therefore referred to a set of concrete individuals, limited in number at any given moment, and of ascertainable extension backwards in time. In short, 'race' covered a finite number, graspable by an ordinary person's imagination, of individuals who ensured the continuity of a name through time. A name which was always embodied in the individuals so named, who were generally also known by a personal name distinct from that of the family, and possibly also a number (X, III, V, etc.) or a place in the system of relations (son of . . . , mother of . . . , first cousin of . . .); individuals, in other words, who were listed in various ways and so were easily identifiable. Thus the social reality of race was defined by an extension in time and space that was graspable by everyone's imagination, and the relative individualization of those involved in the system.

In contrast, the present notion of race is characterized by a substantification of time, an enormous extension in space, and the complete disappearance of the individual. Paradoxically, the introduction of geneticism into the picture has broken up the linear temporal perspective specific to the old institution. Biophysical similarity now implies a spatial but atemporal commonality. The perspective has become synchronic and now links together a society composed of contiguous contemporaries, an unlimited number of individuals spread across a huge material space (the whole world). The groups thus formed are vastly bigger than they could ever have been in the past, and a particular physical feature is the only recognizable sign they have in common. The individualized 'filiation' of the old-style races has been replaced by an undifferentiated mass whose obscure origins are lost in the mists of time. The individual does not stand out; he remains unnamed, a mere actualization of the species.

Paradoxically, this takes us into a completely non-concrete domain. Paradoxically, because we would not spontaneously associate the physically dense notion of race, with its litany of somatic and biophysical characteristics, with abstraction. Yet that is indeed the case, for there is nothing more abstract than this undifferentiated mass, floating somewhere outside the passage of time, like an eternal essence from which no single individual stands out in space or time. No name, no number, no family relationship specifies anyone, classes anyone individually, in this mass. A succession of individuals in a family tree has been replaced by a collection of unspecified atoms (Negroes, Jews, Asiatics [.]). The aristocracy were not one race but many (the Xs, the Ys), whereas now we say in the singular 'the black race', 'the Jewish race' . . . We have gone from multiplicity to singularity.

The two perspectives on race thus belong to two profoundly different social topologies. Whatever the characteristics (and consequences) of the old-style view may have been, it did have built into it an evolutionary variable: time. By contrast, the modern system of perceptions has expelled any reference not only to change, but to the very passage of time itself. Time only figures in the form of an immobile archetype, which is eternity. The pre-eminence of succession in time has been broken, to be replaced by juxtaposition in space. Race today is a collection, an agglomeration of contemporaries, brought together under a noun which is no longer the name of a family, but a nominalized adjective. There are no longer any proper nouns, only an undifferentiated and immemorial mass.

Conclusion

The characteristics which we have identified above give, we hope, a somewhat broader picture of race ideology and show more accurately what makes it specific. They at least allow us to differentiate clearly between the ideology and its accompanying racist theory and doctrine, which can be regarded as a secondary edifice. A hierarchy among human groups, a system of biophysical causality underlying social and mental forms, are actually rationalizations of the ideology itself. The ideology implies much more than these doctrinal claims, and possesses specific characteristics which are, as we have seen, quite far removed from the field to which the 'race question' is normally assigned.

Geneticism is, of course, part of this field, but the change in the objects designated by the term 'race', the shift from a temporal to a spatial perspective, and the move from a system referenced around 'Self' to one based on reference to 'the Other', are not generally linked to this question. However, it is precisely these things which are specific to race ideology, i.e. to the perception of race and its sociological meaning. They are not secondary or optional characteristics, but essential and differentiating ones.

The old-style, 'pre-racial' notion of race (in the sense that its ideological field was quite different from that of modern racism) was legal and institutional in nature, applicable to a single, powerful social group, and set in a temporal perspective. It acted as a means for the dominant group in society to designate its own membership, and so can be said to be narcissistic.

The present-day idea of 'race', the cornerstone of racist ideology, refers to social groups which are very different from their aristocratic predecessors. They are the members of minorities, the oppressed, those on the margins of society, who have no power. As a mass biological 'entity', race today brings together a collection of undifferentiated elements widely scattered in space. Finally, it allows members of the dominant group to designate the groups to which 'others' belong.

It is this latter concept of race which forms the foundation of racist theory. A theory which exploits, expresses and rationalizes the reversal of a particular type of belief, itself grafted onto a reversal in the socio-political situation. The theory took shape during the first decades of the nineteenth century and crystallized around 1850, at the moment when the French monarchy was disappearing for good. Thus it came exactly at the point of junction between two different social topologies: auto-referential aristocratism on the one hand, altero-referential racism on the other. Before, a dominant class which literally did not see other people; after, a dominant class which literally did not see itself.

This was the moment in history when the bourgeoisie became the élite and took over power. In so doing, they also took over the élitist views of the dispossessed class, but without the same means of justifying them: no long-standing genealogical practice guaranteed their status, no divine or royal assent legitimized their situation. They thus carried with them into their new position of power the lack of ideological goods and chattels of the common herd from which they had risen, and to which they did not wish to return. Torn between the nobility to which they did not yet belong and the populace which they had left behind, this aristocracy in function but not in name set about laying the foundations of a new élite which is still with us today. In the absence of coats of arms, titles and great houses, they therefore invented ability, aptitude, merit . . .

They also needed to define a common herd of their own, and they found it ready and waiting at the gates. At the gates of the cities, into which the peasants moved to swell the ranks of industrial workers. At the gates of the nation, where conquered peoples came to pay tribute to their victors. At the gates of a strengthened and newly prominent religion. Workers, Negroes, Asiatics, Jews . . . plebeians, primitives, foreigners . . . Others. The guarantors of the legitimacy of the bourgeoisie's conquest of power.

The theoretical discourse of the bourgeoisie thus managed for a brief period (until its efforts were deflected by the unforeseen need for practical social action) to fuse together the auto-referential system and altero-referential racism. In Gobineau's book of the mid-nineteenth century, the nobility on its way out meets up with the people on its way in: gods on the one side, Negroes on the other . . . Thus racist theory, at the moment of the bourgeoisie's triumph, half a century after the fall of the aristocracy, twenty years after the start of modern colonialism, thirty years before the Dreyfus Affair, bound tightly together an ancient, Germanic nobility and an obtuse Gaulish populace, a demi-gods' ethereal paradise lost, and the solid animality of Negroes and half-castes who were busily corrupting a doomed world. But the gods and the aristocracy had already left the political stage, and thus *de facto* the ideological universe . . .[41] A ruler deposed has no further existence. Enter the Others, who will act as a mirror, an inverted image, for this bourgeoisie anxiously seeking its own identity. Since the bourgeoisie did not know what it was, unlike the nobility which had a very clear view of itself, it wanted at least to know what it was not. The era of positive definition was therefore followed by a time of definition by negation,[42] and auto-reference by altero-reference: the bourgeoisie is not black, nor Jewish, nor proletarian.

So this leads to an apparently paradoxical situation. Racism in the modern sense first arose in a 'democratic' society, a mass society whose expressed ideals were fraternal and egalitarian, one in which individualism was becoming accepted, cultural difference was no longer a hindrance to citizenship, and different forms of popular nationalism were attaining almost religious status. At the moment in history when the murder of the king had opened the door to a 'society of equals', when the night of 4 August 1789 had thrown privilege of all types to the winds, when Catholics, Jews and Protestants were no longer anything but citizens, when slavery was about to be abolished, there lurked behind this rosy picture of egalitarianism (which is, of course, also accurate in its own way) the grim shadow of an unbreakable determinism, a closed world: human groups were no longer formed by divine decree or royal pleasure, but by an irreversible diktat of nature. Frontiers which before could be crossed by dispensation from on high had now become fortified walls, defended by the strongest argument available in the young secular and scientifically orientated society of the day: 'such are the laws of Nature, from which no one is exempt . . .'. The gradually accumulating doctrines of the existence of races, their inequality, the survival of the fittest, progress, the protection of the weak by the strong, the forward march of peoples, all came to take their place in the construction of this fortress.

In this way, the combined forces of atheism, determinism, individualism, democracy and egalitarianism in fact served to justify the system of oppression which was being built at the same time. By proposing a scheme of immanent physical causality (by race, colour, sex, nature), that system provides an irrefutable justification for the crushing of resourceless classes and peoples, and the legitimacy of the élite.

First published in 1972

Notes

1 This irreversibility is not a concrete one: power could, at least in theory, change hands. What remains immutable is the underlying symbolism.
2 Notice that we are not using socio-historical designations here because these are, in the eyes of the ideology in question, all Essences.
3 We might look back in this context to observations of R. Benedict, O. Klineberg, C. Lévi-Strauss, G. Myrdal and L. Poliakov, among others.
4 Hypotheses put forward, for example, by M. Duchet and M. Rebérioux in *Racisme et société*; P.-J. Simon in "'L'école de 1492'", *Cahiers internationaux de sociologie*, vol. XLVIII, 1970.
5 What has passed into the literature, in fact, is the association of the two. But this still leaves the 'concrete reality' in place, and accepted as such.
6 *Journal des Débats*, 17 December 1847. Quoted by F. Ponteil in *Les Classes bourgeoises et l'avènement de la démocratie*, Paris, Albin Michel, 1968.

7 See Noëlle Bisseret, Notion d'aptitude et société de classe', *Cahiers internationaux de sociologie*, vol. LI, 1971.

8 Figures taken from Jean Fourastié *Le Grand Espoir du vingtième siècle*, Paris, Gallimard, 1963.

9 See Pierre Jalée, *Le Pillage du Tiers Monde*, Paris, Maspéro, 1967.

10 Marc Bloch underlines the popular nature of these nationalisms in *La Société féodale*, Paris, Albin Michel, 1939.

11 For an analysis of individualism as a class phenomenon, see Félix Ponteil, op. cit., and for its history as a philosophical concept, see Louis Dumont, 'The Modern Conception of the Individual', *Contributions to Indian Sociology*, no. VIII, Mouton, 1965.

12 Diderot made himself the most impassioned spokesman for equality, not only in the *Encyclopédie* (whose role in bringing about these changes is well known), but also in his many political, scientific and literary writings.

13 This attitude is incidentally often wrongly assimilated to modern racism: we shall see below how great a gulf divides aristocratic narcissism of this type from the racist ideology of the industrial world.

14 *L'Histoire de la langue française*, by Ferdinand Brunot, describes in detail the conquest of French as a common language in the revolutionary period, and shows how motivating and emotive a process it was. What more vivid illustration of this could there be than the picture of Bougainville [t.n.: Comte Louis-Antoine de B., navigator, author of *Voyage autour du monde* (1777) and member of Louis XVI's Cabinet] taking the examination to become a primary school teacher?

15 The mid-nineteenth century was marked by the birth of the trades unions and the founding of the First International.

16 It was published in 1852, having taken three years to write.

17 It is being over-generous to Gobineau and his followers to credit them with the paternity of such a major development, or suggest a causal role for them. This view, a survivor from an 'élitist' conception of history, with its preoccupation with tracing the cause of events back to a single important political, military or intellectual figure, fails to take account of the ideology behind all social movements. Key figures only succeed in integrating themselves into such social movements to the extent that they fit in with this underlying ideology. They may perhaps be catalysts of events, they can certainly be the spokespersons of a latent ideology, but it is highly doubtful whether they are ever founders.

18 See Lalande, and the standard dictionaries of French.

19 A postulate which is, in any case, fairly imprecise: see C. Guillaumin, 'Aspects latents du racisme chez Gobineau', *Cahiers internationaux de sociologie*, vol. XLII, 1967.

20 This raises the fascinating problem of the unconscious as a sociological trait. Unlike the individual unconscious, which only reveals its objects by way of symptoms (i.e. trans-positions), the social unconscious shows itself at face value, without concealment. Society holds up its fantasies just as they are, ideologies, like uncensored dreams, literally speak the obsessions and magic imprecations of their culture.

21 This is where the sociological and the individual unconscious link up again. The practice of negation is a conscious superstructure which can never filter down into the unconscious infrastructure, where the logical mode of negation is unknown. Everything that is said, whether in negative or positive form, is an affirmation. Saying 'that is not true' is strictly equivalent to saying 'that is true'. Hence the bitter disappointments of some anti-racism campaigns.

22 Theory is here regarded as an 'opinion'. Whatever objections might be raised against this assertion (and we would certainly subscribe fully to them), it is sociologically accurate: theory operates on a conscious level, and is shared to differing degrees by different social groups and individuals. It falls within the domain of a sociology of attitudes or doctrines, not one of ideologies. Theory provides answers to questions such as: 'Do you think x . . .?', 'Do you believe that y . . .?'; ideology neither thinks nor believes, it assumes.

23 Sigmund Freud, *Ma Vie et la psychanalyse*, Paris, Gallimard, 1950 (our emphasis).

24 In G. Tomasi di Lampedusa, *Le Guépard*, Paris, Le Seuil, 1958.

25 Incidentally, a group very different (the aristocracy) from those who currently find themselves so designated.

26 By 'coherent' we mean 'symbolically coherent'. The modern notion of race involves a belief in the biological cohesion of racial groups which is objectively false, for example. The criterion of this coherence is what society believes.

27 In fact, definitions always work in that way, but with one level remaining inaccessible to conscious scrutiny.

28 See Bertrand Russell, *An Enquiry into Meaning and Truth*, London, Allen and Unwin, 1961, who classifies 'no' as a characteristic of 'hierarchic' language, by opposition to the 'object language'.

29 And based on an earlier work: see Colette Guillaumin, *L'Idéologie raciste. Genèse et langage actuel*, Paris-The Hague, Mouton, 1972.

30 T.n.: As the relevant English semantic fields do not always match the French, it has sometimes been found necessary to adapt a definition, and occasionally to omit one or other section.

31 T.n.: This sense, usually applied to animals (= 'breed'), is commonplace in French but very rare in English.

32 Edmond Goblot, *La Barrière et le niveau*, Paris, Alcan, 1930.

33 The old conception remains [in French] in relation to the animal kingdom, where the term 'race' is applied according to the same hierarchical schema as in human groups: animals 'of race' (i.e. thoroughbreds) are supposed to be the best (the aristocrats), while the rest (mongrels and other half-breeds) are said to be 'without race' (i.e. without breeding). We shall see this dichotomy appearing again later in the present study, but reversed, in the fact that in humans it is the 'others' (the rest) who are said to have a 'race'. We might remark in this connection that the practice of intensive 'racial selection of animals (dogs, and especially horses) goes back precisely to the nineteenth century. The Jockey-Club and other horse-racing societies came into being at a time when 'race' was in fashion. Up to the eighteenth century, memoir writers do not seem to have been particularly interested in this question. As far as we know, Saint-Simon, for instance, says nothing about that passion for thoroughbred animals which is supposed to have been characteristic of the class to which he belonged, and which Balzac, Stendhal and even Proust were careful to attribute to their elegant heroes.

34 This is a clear example of the demotion of a strong (principal or original) sense to a secondary heading ('Specially' or 'By extension'). Thus the senses on which usage is founded end up exiled to the periphery, leading us to think that that was where they had always been. This is particularly striking with the definition of the term 'race', where 'group of people with similar characteristics' is demoted under 'By extension', whereas in fact it forms the basis of the modern meaning. The perception of these groupings underlies the whole synchronic perspective which characterizes modern racism, and in turn the modern usage of the term 'race'. Thus the third estate, the 'Gaulish people' of Thierry, Guizot or Balzac, the 'laborious and rural populations' of Gobineau, the 'Semites' of the linguists and Renan, and 'Negro slaves' (very different from today's Blacks), were the first to bear the race emblem, the first to be given the dubious privilege of being of a particular race. This was not so much on the basis of physical characteristics, as people today think, but rather because of common social characteristics which distinguished them from other groups.

35 This passage forms a single paragraph in Saint-Simon, with his remarks on the paternity of Monsieur le Prince's children occurring as if quite naturally in the middle of a commentary on the character of Mlle de Condé. Saint-Simon, *Mémoires*, Paris, Gallimard (La Pléiade), vol. 1, p. 768.

36 T.n.: The French noun 'un Jaune' means a person of 'yellow' skin; there is obviously no equivalent nominal term in English.

37 Note also the inversion of meanings between the eighteenth century and our own day, first in the stereotype (the honest Israelite has become a schemer), but particularly in the historical

and religious references. In the old days, the term Israelite carried the historical meaning, with Jew being kept for the religious sense, whereas now the situation has been reversed: Israelite [in French] is taking on the religious sense, leaving the historical connotations to the term Jew. With the added difference, of course, that both now carry a racial sense which they did not have in the eighteenth century.

38 We are here adopting modern racial logic, which distinguishes three main races, black, white and yellow (in alphabetical order).

39 Self and Other are obviously being used here to refer to social groups, not individuals.

40 Even if only mythically, by reference to a founding ancestor or a dated origin for the family.

41 They were, of course, still very much a part of the world of conscious images: no class has ever been more fascinated by the aristocracy than the bourgeoisie of the nineteenth century. But it was now merely an object of contemplation; it no longer had a role as a creating subject, or producer of institutions.

42 Something emphasized by Goblot (op. cit.), who shows that the bourgeoisie did not so much define as differentiate itself.

24

DOMINIQUE SCHNAPPER

Dominique Schnapper is a sociologist who also holds a doctorate in literature. She is the daughter of the philosopher and sociologist Raymond Aron. In 2001 she was appointed to the French Conseil Constitutionnel. She has been Director of Research at the École des Hautes Études en Sciences Sociales in Paris since 1980, and member of numerous Governmental commissions, including those investigating nationality reform (1987), drugs (1994) and education (1995–6). She is president of the Société Française de Sociologie. She specialises in the study of minorities, immigrants, Italians, Jews, and the unemployed. She is a Republican and a universalist, but although she does not believe that cultural or linguistic differences should be enshrined in institutions, nor that the Declaration of Human Rights should include 'cultural rights', her dialogue with American Communitarians has led her to maintain that 'democratic citizenship' should make more room for historical and religious particularities than is currently permitted by the French Republic.

Her works include the following:

L'Italie rouge et noire, Paris: Gallimard, 1971.

Juifs et Israëlites, Paris: Gallimard, 1980.

L'Épreuve du chômage, Paris: Gallimard, 1981.

La France de l'intégration, sociologie de la nation en 1990, Paris: Gallimard, 1991.

La Communauté des citoyens, sur l'idée moderne de la nation, Paris: Gallimard, 1994.

La Relation à l'Autre. Au coeur de la pensée sociologique, Paris: Gallimard, 1998.

La Compréhension sociologique, Paris: PUF, 2000.

Qu'est-ce que la citoyenneté?, Paris: Folio, 2000.

Questionner le racisme, Paris: Gallimard, 2000.

La Démocratie providentielle: essai sur l'inégalité contemporaine, Paris: Gallimard, 2002.

RACISM AND THE RADICAL
CONDEMNATION OF MODERNITY

Previously I indicated some essential distinctions between racism as a theory, racist modes of thought, and the racialism and behaviour that result from various ideologies.[1] In so doing I adopted what is, to my mind, one of the crucial products of French thought, and in this discussion the most important stages in the development of this thought will be clarified. The definition of its terms is both the condition and the consequence of sociological research.

Today, sociologists all agree that race is a social construct and that the heart of racist thought lies in the establishment of a deterministic link between the biological and the social. Every sociologist states that we must distinguish between the theory of racism as it is strictly understood (that is, in the biological sense of racial determinism) and wider social phenomena, which can be described as racialising, naturalising or essentialist and which can appear within the social world without recourse to the idea of human races.

With this in mind, most sociologists therefore hold that there is a necessary link between racism and modern society. However, it is in the characterisation of this society that they differ. For Claude Lévi-Strauss, for example, modern racism results from a contradiction between two phenomena: the necessity of cultural exchange and the diffusion of a single civilisation on the one hand, and a necessary 'relative incommunicability' (which is the condition of survival for individual cultures) on the other. Louis Dumont, meanwhile, sees the problem as the inevitable return of the repressed in a society that is, contrary to the deeper nature of the social world, based on the individual. By extending the inspirational work of Léon Poliakov, Colette Guillaumin conceives of modern racism as the result of a new form of the sacred (namely, the biological) in societies that aspire to be rational and scientific and that refuse transcendence. The question has also been dealt with recently by Marxist thinkers such as Etienne Balibar and Immanuel Wallerstein, who see it as a necessary result of the global expansion of capitalism and the rise of nationalism. It can thus be said that sociologists locate the origins of modern racism in, respectively, the existence of a global civilisation, individualism, poorly controlled scientific ambition, and capitalism and nationalism.

'Global civilisation and self-loyalty'

Claude Lévi-Strauss holds that racism is born out of the contradiction between the worldwide diffusion of an individual civilisation and the need, common to any culture, to remain loyal to itself in order to survive. The existence of a global civilisation is probably unique within history, but today all of mankind adheres to the Western lifestyle and recognises its superiority. Certainly, this adherence springs not from the free will of the people: rather it is the product of a dominance asserted the world over by traders, entrepreneurs, missionaries and soldiers from Western nations. However, this is an objective fact that must not be disregarded, since 'it would be useless to want to defend the originality of human cultures from themselves.'[2]

This contact and exchange are conditions of cultural progress. That is to say that isolated cultures die, and that every human advancement lies within the exchanges that take place between diverse cultures. Progress is a function of a 'coalition between cultures', of a pooling of the opportunities that are available to each culture during its development. The more diverse the cultures, the more fertile the coalition. However, a contradiction now emerges, for in the course of these exchanges each culture risks losing the basis of its originality, and their resources become homogenised. Communication leads to homogeneity and homogeneity 'leads to death'. In human societies there are certain forces that tend to reinforce individuality and maintain diversification, and others that move towards unification and the homogenisation of diverse cultures. This diversity must be wide enough to make exchange profitable, since this is the very condition on which cultures exist and develop. However, diversity should not be too wide, as this would make exchange impossible and therefore condemn each culture concerned to decline. As Lévi-Strauss says:

> When we consider their mutual relations we start to wonder if human societies are not defined by a certain optimum of diversity – an optimum beyond which these societies are incapable of moving, but below which it is equally impossible to pass without coming into peril.[3]

Furthermore, this optimum of diversity also exists within single societies. Thus, as the size and homogeneity of a particular society increase the groups which comprise it – variously organised according to ethnicity, class, profession and religion – tend to affirm their differences and individual characteristics.

Unlike individual, concrete cultures, the idea of a global civilisation must not be understood in the sense of an actual reality. It is an abstract notion, and remains weak and schematic. Rather, the reality is one of individual cultures which bring real solutions to the eternal problems of communal human life.

> The true contribution of cultures lies not in the list of their individual inventions but in the amount of 'differential space' that they establish between each other . . . There is not and cannot be a global civilisation in the absolute sense that is often attributed to the term. This is because the idea of civilisation implies a state of coexistence in which cultures offer an optimum level of diversity, whilst

itself being composed of this same coexistence. It is not possible for global civilisation to be anything other than a worldwide coalition of cultures that each preserve their originality.[4]

In order to retain this originality, each culture must remain loyal to itself:

All true creations imply that they are deaf to the calls of other values. This can extend to the outright refusal of other values or even to their negation . . . One cannot, at one and the same time, take part in the pleasures of the Other, identify with it, and remain different.[5]

Lévi-Strauss's 'relative incommunicability' and a certain 'impermeability' constitute the very condition of survival of a given culture. The original development of cultures can only be assured by the communication that takes place between them, but complete fusion would condemn them to lose their originality and their creative potency. We must denounce the way in which racism, 'a theory that is wrong but explicit', is commonly amalgamated with the idea of 'attitudes that are to be expected, even legitimate, and which are in any case unavoidable'[6] (that is, the attachment of people to their own culture, their self-loyalty). We will otherwise fall into a so-called 'global civilisation', which would destroy 'those old individual qualities which have the honour of creating the spiritual and aesthetic values that make life more worthwhile.'[7]

It is clear that what Lévi-Strauss is evoking here is the double 'sacred duty of humanity', which consists in developing the process of unification without compromising cultural individuality. However, Lévi-Strauss's ethnological sensibilities mean that he is professionally alert to the range of solutions that different cultures have developed in order to organise collective living. This leads him to privilege the maintenance of cultural diversity and to fear, above all, the birth of a world where 'monotony and uniformity' reign supreme.

Let us now consider the view that racism is an inevitable product of modern society. Peaceful relations can only be established on the basis of reciprocal indifference, with each culture affirming itself as the only one that is true and ignoring all others. However, this indifference has become impossible in a world where all cultures are in contact with one another, and where we are witnessing the progressive fusion of populations. Lévi-Strauss writes that, 'Reciprocal tolerance presupposes two conditions that modern society is further than ever from actually realising: relative equality on the one hand, sufficient physical distance on the other.'[8] The world in which small groups are permanently separated from each other is no more. Relations between cultures changed forever when the West proclaimed its superiority and brutally imposed its civilisation on the rest of the world. In place of the recognition (be it positive or negative) of cultural diversity has come the affirmation of cultural inequality. Along with the speed of modes of communication and transport, the upheavals of industrial society have built a single world, one founded on global trade, direct competition and inequality between cultures.

However, it cannot de denied that, despite its urgent practical necessity and the fine, high morals that it sets itself, the struggle against all forms of discrimination participates in the very same movement that is leading humanity towards a global civilisation.

Furthermore, the Promethean project to master nature has ended up denying the natural relationships between humanity and its environment: the exclusion of certain peoples only prolongs that of other 'living beings'. From this point of view, there is no foreseeable end to racism.

Consequently, in 1971 Lévi-Strauss stresses the importance of antinomies in the 'pious words' of civil servants of international institutions, who claim to reconcile the irreconcilable and who refuse to acknowledge contradictions. What, for example, does it mean to 'reconcile self-loyalty with openness towards others' while at the same time advocating 'the creative affirmation of each identity and the bringing together of all cultures,'[9] when these two goals are clearly contradictory?

'The return of the repressed in individualistic society'

Louis Dumont joins with Lévi-Strauss in the radical critique of modern society.[10] However, his analysis is based on individualism and the ensuing principle of equality. For Dumont, racism is not a universal phenomenon but a specific feature of modern society. In turn, most societies attribute their superiority to their culture, and not to biological characteristics. By proclaiming a condition of equality modern society eliminates differences in status, and ceases to be able to recognise *de facto* inequalities and reinscribes difference as inequality; in so doing it also necessarily engenders racism, which has become the social disease of modernity. The proclamation of equality for all citizens is abstract and utopian in the sense used by Karl Mannheim,[11] and it contradicts the communal and immediate experience of a people's concrete diversities and inequalities in the social world. Moreover, the universal dimension of this affirmation of equality has the perverse effect of making 'modern' racism worse than that of pre-modern society. Is it not true that slaves in the American Deep South were less unhappy than black citizens of the great industrial cities of the North?

For Louis Dumont, if we observe Western realities from an Indian perspective it is possible to see how localised and artificial the ideals of our societies are, even if we hold these ideals to be morally superior. The idea of hierarchy, for example, which in India is expressed in a pure state, constitutes a fundamental feature of societies that are complex in ways different from our own. A principle of Indian conceptual or symbolic oneness, the 'function' of hierarchy expresses the unity of society. 'To adopt values is to make things hierarchical, and a certain consensus on values – a certain hierarchy of ideas, things and people – is indispensable to the social world.'[12] This principle, crucial to all societies, is expelled by the value systems of Western societies, who 'go so far as to automatically inscribe the principle of equality within their Constitutions.'[13] Modern society makes the individual 'the measure of everything,'[14] and the rationality that it institutes leads to proclamations of an autonomous human order, one founded on the individual and which is alien to natural human aspirations. The principle of egalitarianism is the fruit of such an attitude. Modern society represses hierarchical feelings, which remain unthinkable in our conception of social order. By proclaiming the formal equality of individuals, modern democracy ends up denying 'the more or less essential demands of the social world,' and 'is at odds with the general tendencies of societies'.[15]

However, as in all repression, the hierarchy that the proclaimed principles of the social order repress is always likely to return in the form of a pathology. By making the 'universal necessity' of direct and natural hierarchy illicit, modern egalitarian societies provoke the return of a more monstrous hierarchy. In contradiction of the facts, it is difficult for popular consciousness to think of equality without also evoking an identity. That is to say that human beings do not have the same physical abilities or intellectual gifts; nor do we share the same amounts of wealth or power. In turn, observable differences between individuals and communities are lived in terms of inequalities and can no longer be explained through differences in their legal status. The justification for these differences is a disastrous explanation made in terms of somatic characteristics: that is, racism. This process is illustrated by the history of the United States of America, where racism developed when the abolition of slavery prohibited inequality in legal conditions. It is here that Louis Dumont again sees a link between the slavery of the South and the segregation of the North in that, by denying the reality of differences in social status experienced in the North, America replaced slavery with discrimination based on a 'somatic pretext'.

> The history of the United States shows us that, once abolished, black slavery was succeeded by racist discrimination . . . In place of the former distinction between master and slave there followed discrimination against blacks by whites. But why the development into racism? The question is in part resolved simply by asking it: that is to say that the essence of the master/slave distinction was legal, and that removing it favoured the transformation of its racial aspect into substantive racism. For things to have developed any differently, victory would have had to have been achieved over the distinction itself.[16]

Let us here remember Alexis de Tocqueville, who wrote that:

> I can see that slavery is on the retreat, and the prejudice that it has spawned is immovable . . . Racial prejudice seems to me to be stronger in States that have abolished slavery than in those that have not, and nowhere is prejudice more intolerant than in States where slavery has never been known.[17]

'Biology, or the sacred of modern society'

Several different researchers have developed and universalised the inspirational historical research of Léon Poliakov, which shows how the advent of modern society is also characterised by the emergence of a racial anti-Semitism. Defined in terms that are biological and therefore definitive, this phenomenon has superseded traditional religious anti-Judaism. Subsequently fuelled by the idea of 'the Jewish race', racial anti-Semitism has replaced Christian anti-Judaism, which was founded on the centuries-old hostility of the Catholic Church against a rival religion. We have therefore moved from a world dominated by religious intolerance (the Church protected Jews in order to preserve them as witnesses) to one of modern anti-Semitism which, since it is rooted in the natural and insurmountable fact of race, is based on Jews' radical alterity. In a society which is convinced of the absolute value of scientific research, and which is filled with its spirit, racist attitudes and behaviours are thus legitimated by the name of science. Beyond the case of anti-Semitism, could we not also suggest that modern society is most notably characterised by the sacred position it accords to the biological?

This is a central theme in the work of Colette Guillaumin.[18] For her, racist ideology – that is, an 'essentialist system of perception' – is not 'natural' or eternal, but rather appears at a given moment in history. Guillaumin notes that a different conception of the Other starts to emerge towards the end of the eighteenth century so that, in a radical shift, difference comes to be posited within humanity rather than according to divine dependence. Previously, the Other had been both strange and a stranger, but now Otherness has become more radical. In the fourteenth century there were great discussions about whether women had souls, and in the sixteenth century Indians were subjected to the same question. However, in both cases the objects of discussion belonged to the same universe and, with the help of religious conversion, they could be defined by the divine project and included within true humanity. With modernity, we shift from the religious to the 'racial': this is the moment at which the term 'race' no longer designates a particular line of descendants and comes to describe a wider human group. The word 'Negro', for example, which previously had a social sense in that it described a slave employed in the colonies, has come to assume a racial meaning. There follows a crucial rupture in that it is no longer God and free will that are held to lead the world; rather, the keys of history come to be located within the biological and the deterministic. Alterity cannot be eliminated because it is a human essence, and the radicalisation of difference becomes irreversible and ineffaceable: racist modes of thinking establish a link between alterity and belief in biology, uniting them in a system of power. The idea of the inferiority of the Other has been eclipsed by the denial of his or her human status.

At the end of the eighteenth century, science discovered laws of heredity, origins, filiation and development that became the bases of scientific thought; Darwinism is a privileged example of this. Even the new field of sociology attributes an important place to the passage of time in the life of a given society, and here we are reminded of Auguste Comte when he notes that theological and militaristic society has been succeeded by one of industry and science. Thus, holds Comte, societies move from a theological state, through a metaphysical period and on to an age of positivism. Meanwhile, Joseph de Gobineau is really a racist thinker in that he confuses the biological with the social. Thus, even though he never called for murder on the grounds of race or directly stated that one race holds rights over others, Gobineau's beliefs about racial specificity, the catastrophic nature of interracial relationships and, above all, the causal relationship between race and historical phenomena mean that his thought is essentially racist.[19]

Three factors therefore need to be taken into account in order to explain the appearance of racist ideology in the nineteenth century: (1) the increased awareness of cultural diversity in conjunction with the postulation of the unity of the human species; (2) the development of the sciences and the concentration on biology and internal causality within the passage of time; (3) the colonisation and proletarianization induced by industrial development, and which produced a new type of society. By decreeing that factory workers or colonised peoples are biologically different, racist ideology (that is, postulated radical difference) facilitates the justification of behaviour that contradicts the perceived logical fallacies of egalitarianism. It also resolves the antinomy between declarations of humanitarian values and the concrete development of European economic history.

Like Louis Dumont, Colette Guillaumin stresses that the development of racist ideology parallels the emergence of egalitarian values:

> The growth in racist ideology is in fact very closely linked to egalitarian values, with the former a response to the claim of equality. These two phenomena draw their meaning from the new conception of humanity that arose in the eighteenth century. On the one hand, and with regard to egalitarian ideology, industrial and colonial exploitation are justified on the basis of irreducible and inevitable natural essences. On the other hand we find that, when they are confronted with the ever-fundamental value of humanitarianism, the ideological expressions of these concrete phenomena – such as biological selection, life force and the survival of the fittest – reappear in the form of democratic competition, missions of civilisation, 'progress' and so on.[20]

For Colette Guillaumin the idea of race must be replaced with that of acts of racialisation, and she rejects Michael Banton's behaviour-based distinction between racist theories and racialism and criticises the efforts of classical sociology to understand relations between races. In so doing, Guillaumin posits that racist thought and racist action are united, and that the two express the self-same ideology. Guillaumin therefore offers a radical critique of the sociology of so-called 'race' relations, which for her participates in a general (mis)understanding about race: that is to say that, by thinking about the relationship between races, sociology implies that races exist. As specialists in the field, sociologists have sought to define racism rather than race in that, for them, the latter is an observable fact, a given. Although they did not mean to do so, the social sciences have thus positioned themselves at the very heart of racist ideology. In other words, by selecting the social perception of difference as their object of study, sociologists imply that such perception registers actual physical characteristics. This, however, is not true. There are, for example, certain races that are purely imaginary, and which play the same role in the process of racialisation. The idea of differential physical characteristics is also wrong. We do not, for instance, distinguish Jews from Christians or the working classes from the bourgeoisie on the basis of phenotypes; neither does the term 'blacks' now refer to the same people or civilisations that it did in the fifteenth century. In each and every case, physical traits only serve to designate minority groups who are in a position of dependence or inferiority. A person's appearance is nothing more than a sign, and performs a relatively secondary function.

The idea of race comprises three key elements, namely, 'alterity, a relationship to power and biological type'. The last of these elements goes beyond what is commonly understood by the idea of race, in that it applies to any category that is negatively defined by a biological characteristic, such as sex, age and social class. In the nineteenth century, for example, it was held that factory workers were from a different 'race'. The concept of race has since been pursued by the natural sciences and prehistory, so that we have moved from the observation of 'social or historical differences' to the analysis of 'the physical differences that symbolise them'. Thus, biological usage of the term 'race' also underpins its sociological meaning. As Guillaumin says, '[in the beginning race] was used just as frequently in purely social contexts. Inadequate elucidation of the concept produced a residual indeterminacy at the very heart of the term's generalised somatic implications.'[21] For her, sociology has not escaped 'the biologisation of social thought, which has used this bias in an attempt to posit all difference, whether established or supposed, in absolute terms.' Sociology holds that race is a reality, when it is in fact but a sign. That different groups have been objects of racialisation clearly shows that racism cannot be 'explained' by objective characteristics.

It is impossible to distinguish modes of thought from behaviour. That is to say that, whether we are dealing with words or deeds, both are rooted within the same mental structure that underpins all 'material manifestations of racism'. This 'racist ideology' is 'the place where the phenomenon of racism is to be found "before" the appearance of its material manifestations and the processes that these involve.' Guillaumin writes:

> Although it is a logical break that can be useful on the level of methodology, by separating the doctrine from the facts we also obliterate the perceptual origins of both verbal and physical acts. Such a separation leads these two levels to be viewed as heterogenous. The otherwise negligible risk of all this is thereby transformed, in that the positing of heterogeneity is profoundly complicit with the unconscious desire to reject responsibility for acts considered unacceptable by the value system of our society. This complicity would certainly seem to be the source for the refusal to recognise the solidarity between the racism of Gobineau and Hitler. The dichotomy that is established between the two levels of racism is a defence mechanism that protects against awareness of its deeper reality. If the analysis of racism is to be given the chance of even provisional accuracy, we cannot separate the doctrine from its material facts.[22]

Guillaumin says that in order to understand racism we must go beyond what is described as 'race' in the social world. Racism does not need to use the word 'race'; it should rather be defined as the biologisation or radicalisation of all difference. For Guillaumin, any interpretation that features somatic characteristics must be called racist:

> In fact, the *conscious meaning* of the word 'race' is practically irrelevant in that *it describes, in symbolic form, the radicalisation of all difference* and its institutionalisation within the realm of the immutable. In racism, the causality of race is merely superficial – race is rather the basis of support for perceived difference . . . At one and the same time race is both sign (within the order of perceptual logic), and justification (within the order of behaviour).[23]

Whatever the justification offered for racist ideology, at its heart lie the biologisation and radicalisation of all difference. In this way, racist ideology holds that heterogeneity is definitive and radical in nature, and institutes 'an internal break with humanity'. The use of the term 'ethnic' as an alternative to 'racial' is nothing but euphemism; and sociology – in its wider sense – has failed to find a word that describes cultural categories in such a way as to be absolutely independent from bio-physical phenomena. This failure shows that our unconscious mode of thought continues to link the somatic with the socio-cultural. Whatever the term used to describe it, any way of thinking that 'amalgamates physical causality with mental causality' is racist, expressing as it does the characteristic unconscious psychological structure of our society.

For the racist, a person from a 'minority' is no longer an individual, but rather is exclusively defined as a component of his or her community. The notions of hostility and aggression – as described by Albert Memmi in 1964 – are insufficient to analyse racist feeling, in that racism is not necessarily contemptuous, hateful or violent.[24] However, racism does display certain other characteristics, such as the idea of interracial relationships as both catastrophe and fantasy producing a cultural breakdown involving heterogeneity, exchange and mobility. Indeed, it can be observed that 'racists in power exhibit certain consistent characteristics: they either refuse or specify the nature of education for women and peoples or classes who are poor'; they safeguard or consider as folkloric cultures that oppress minority groups; and they promote 'separation within equality' (in the sense of men and women, different religious groups, social classes and 'races'), 'dependence within interdependence', 'equality in difference', and so on.[25] As Guillaumin says,

> The nature of race . . . is *to evoke the majority through difference and, at the same time, to evoke security through permanence* . . . In racism, race is the sign of permanence . . . racism is defined by its description of heterogeneity, strangeness, foreigners and the Other, as opposed to homogeneity, normality and the self.[26]

Whatever the different forms of racism, the various groups that it targets all share the same 'form of relationship to the majority': that is, a state of 'oppression', dependency and minority. Positioned as specific in relation to the norm, such groups are by definition 'minor'. As for the majority, they are neither different nor specific because they are the central point of reference: the member of the majority is both general and an individual, while the member of a minority is both a peculiarity and a pure expression of the group to which he or she belongs. All minorities are ascribed with the same traits of infantilism. The system of majorities and minorities functions because both sets of groups exist within a communal symbolic network. Hostility is therefore a secondary reaction, in that it is based on characteristics that have already been defined. Racism is 'any separatist behaviour that is cloaked in the sign of permanence.' However, in modern society, which is essentially mobile, this feeling of permanence is provided by biology, which our civilisation holds as sacred.

Christian Delacampagne is another sociologist who holds that the biological is sacred in Western society. Unlike Poliakov, Delacampagne argues that racism does not date from the eighteenth century or even the great voyages of discovery undertaken in the fifteenth century, but that it has been instilled within the deeper structures of the West from the time of Ancient Greece. We are therefore imbued with racism, and it is a particular characteristic of the West to treat those it excludes in the terms of biology and science, thereby reducing them to the status of sub-humans so that 'all conflicts *also* have a racist dimension'.[27] Why has nature come to take the place of the sacred in the West, and why does racism lie at the heart of Western reason? According to Delacampagne, the Arabs invented the slave trade but would also accept blacks as equal if they became Muslim: in this case, prejudice is therefore social and religious, rather than biological. The obsession with the biological is specific to the West and is bound to the idea of the sacred, which is itself central to every society. However, for the West the secularisation of the world is an ancient notion. The European vision is a rational one, and therefore naturalistic and biological. Poliakov, for instance, proposed that the Aryan myth is bimillenial, while Greek differentialism was already founded on natural categories, such as 'women' and 'children'. In the third century BC Manethon, an Egyptian priest, based his condemnation of the Jews on physical characteristics, such as leprosy and body odour, and stated that their presence induced nausea. As we have already seen, in the Middle Ages Jews were attributed extravagant bodily traits. They were depicted, for example, with devil-like horns, and the character of the sanctimonious Jewish hypocrite, who took over from the leper, was also given physiological defects, so that Jews were once again associated with nauseating smells and bizarre diseases. So even though they were in fact indistinguishable from those around them, from start to finish the alterity of the Jew was justified on the basis of hereditary physical characteristics. The ancient weakening of the sacred in the West (which began around the eleventh century) gave rise to anxieties which were in turn dispelled by racist and sexual fantasy. Biology came to assume a magical and religious importance, and the idea of natural differences was imposed at the expense of the universality of the human species. The discovery of North American Indians was made in the context of a world where non-whites were already likened to death and the devil, and where the notion of race was associated with skin colour. These ideas were given a 'scientific' foundation by the anthropological work of the Enlightenment, and were then spread far and wide by colonialism.

For Delacampagne, racism comes from the very heart of Western society in that, from the time of Ancient Greece, it has been mobilised by critical thinking. Thus, having used critical thought to raise such questions in the first place, Western society is the only one to have sought to affirm its existence and its unity through the persecution of others. Delacampagne says that we should distinguish between critical thought's valorisation of disagreement and the logic of persecution. However, in the absence of such a distinction Western (self-)critiques have produced only intolerance, both with regard to itself and to others:

> The West tolerates itself no better than it tolerates the Other. The West cannot bear to be faced with the Other, for it knows that it itself is nothing, that it has lost all specificity and that it is no longer a culture because it has chosen to be universal. As long as this attitude persists, so will racism.[28]

It is clear that the analyses summarised here display undeniable points of contact. The thinking behind them is at least partially cumulative in that, for all their diversity, the analyses establish the necessity of distinguishing between two phenomena. The first of these is racism as a theory, which is today scientifically discredited despite its regular reappearance on the surface of current affairs, made in the name of obvious fact and 'common sense' ('Well, I mean, when it comes down to it there are blacks and there are whites . . . '). The second is racialising thought, which turns all presumed biological difference into alterity. Racism as a theory holds that there exist a number of different races, that these races are immutable and impervious to each other and that the observable differences and inequalities between human groups are rooted in biological characteristics. Racialising modes of thought are characterised by their basis in the idea that, however they are described, human groups never lose their essential differences or their permanent, definitive inequalities. Furthermore, racist modes of thought cannot be broken simply by changing the word 'race' to 'culture'. Replacing 'racism' with 'culturism', 'classism' and 'sexism' makes logical sense, but here again the establishment of an individual's category according to his or her culture, social class or gender is based on substantive alterity. Instead, the notion of racism must be replaced with the process of racialisation, a process in which categories of people are marginalised in the name of supposed differences proposed by biology, and which are therefore essential and permanent. Essentialism, or naturalisation (that is, arguments based on nature), therefore lies at the heart of racialising modes of thought. This is the context in which the formula 'social race' was invented, a term that allowed Quebec French Canadians to analyse their own situation from the standpoint of 'white Negroes'. Similarly, anthropologists have used the idea of the 'invisible race' to describe the Burakumin people of Japan: indistinguishable from other Japanese on the level of their phenotype, religion or culture, the Burakumin have been victims of a brutal and age-old process of racialisation and segregation.

There is a great contrast between the current of French thought described here and the numerous empirical studies that English sociologists carried out until about 1990 on the relationships between races, but without troubling to define what racism actually is (for them it was simply a fact of social reality).[29] We have since seen how researchers such as Robert Miles have come to internalise this debate within their work.

'Marxist sociological criticism'

Marxist critiques are close to anthropological approaches in that both see racism as a phenomenon that is intrinsically and necessarily linked to modern society. The difference is that Marxist commentators define modern society as capitalist.

As can be seen in the classic example of Oliver Cox, orthodox Marxist theory reduces the 'racial' to the 'social'.[30] A further such formulation is given in relation to anti-Semitism by Abraham Léon, who proposes that, 'above all, Jews are seen by history as a social group that has its own fixed economic function. Jews are a class, or rather a people-class.' In this context, anti-Semitism is simply the expression of the class struggle. The suppression of the class struggle and the advent of socialism will therefore lead to the end of Jews as a people-class and, in turn, to the end of anti-Semitism. In this way the 'Jewish question' will come to be answered.[31] We should further remember that in 1972 Robert Blauner introduced the idea that there exists within American society a racial order – in recent years British sociologists have taken on the baton in order to propose analyses that are inspired by Marxism, but which concentrate on the racial aspects of social orders.

Etienne Balibar and Immanuel Wallerstein have recently advanced a new conception of class, nationalism and racism.[32] In their view, modern racism is not simple prejudice or 'the mere delirium of racist subjects,'[33] but rather operates within social relations that are themselves indissociable from the combined structures of the capitalist world. Unless we consider it in the context of class determinations and the contradictions of the nation-state, racism will always escape our understanding. If racism is on the increase, it is because there is an institutional structure behind it, which is itself a product of the structures of class and nationalism.

For Wallerstein, the critique of 'bourgeois' citizenship rests on interpreting the spread of capitalism as the basis of the global economy. He also believes that, in becoming the first economic system to spread across the whole world, capitalism necessarily leads to racism and the ethnicization of certain ethnic or racial groups. By colonising peripheral regions and exploiting their inhabitants, Europe has been able to operate as a capitalist hub and organise global development. The citizens of these capitalist countries have kept the highest salaries and the most prestigious jobs for themselves: they form an international aristocracy of employment, with the acquisition of citizenship guaranteeing their respective privileges. As for the peripheral regions, these produce the basic raw materials and provide cheap manual labour. This international system of economic and political stratification is both rationalised and justified by racism. The exploitation of colonised peoples allows States at the top of this stratification to resolve internal problems with the control of the workforce and with the wider development of capitalism.

The proclamation of the legal equality of citizens and the invocation of universalist principles, which exclude racism, have served to mask true realities about the ethnic and sexist division of labour, the exploitation of States that are peripheral within the global capitalist economy and the internal contradictions of the bourgeois nation-state. The proclaimed universalism of bourgeois society is nothing more than a way of dissim-ulating – and therefore legitimating – difference. In this way, societies with egalitarian ideals and aspirations transform difference into inequality. Humanist discourse and the invocation of citizenship have consecrated the hierarchies and exclusions brought about by the global division of labour and, by legitimating them, have strengthened global structures of oppression and exploitation. Colonisation is inherent to capitalism and racism, and is therefore necessarily linked to capitalist society. Despite the 'universalism of bourgeois ideology',[34] racism continues to spread.

Wallerstein's analysis stresses the importance of strictly economic factors. Thus, in Balibar's words, he

> attacks universalism for having the same form as the stock market (that is, as a process of accumulation), racism for splitting the workforce into centre and periphery and sexism for the opposition between masculine 'work' and feminine

'non-work' within the domestic dynamic of the household, which Wallerstein sees as a fundamental institution of historical capitalism.[35]

Capitalism necessarily engenders racism and sexism because, in both cases, a system of exploitation 'makes it possible to pay whole sections of the workforce very low wages,' and to make such salaries 'far lower than could ever be justified by meritocratic criteria'.[36]

For his part, Balibar underlines the link between racism and nationalism which, for him, is indistinct from the notion of the nation. He writes that, '[in that] they reciprocally imply each other, the specific expression of racism is always supported by nationalism.'[37] Thus, while racism is not manifest within every instance and type of nationalism, 'racism always represents a crucial tendency within its composition'.[38] French nationalism comprises the two classic forms of racism – that is, colonial racism and anti-Semitism – because it assumed its modern form 'in the context of the class struggle and the "social question", which it tended to control and, where possible, supersede.'[39] It is no coincidence that in France universal suffrage was granted to the working class at the time of colonial expansion. The 'social question' was resolved by external colonisation and the racism that came with it. The workers' struggle had brought them relative protection within European capitalist nations, and now they were transformed into the foremen of Imperial domination. In the guise of nationalism, colonialism and racism contributed to the resolution of what at the time was called the 'social question'. Some decades ago Albert Memmi produced a discussion of racism, which is essentially based on his experience of colonial Tunisia, and which demonstrates that 'racism illustrates, summarises and symbolises the colonial dynamic'.[40] Racism is not a perversion of nationalism or colonialism, but rather re-articulates them historically.

Colonialism institutionalises racism within the State. For example, the official attitude towards immigrant workers is simply an extension of colonialism in that, by distinguishing the citizen from the immigrant (who remains a subject without achieving citizenship), the State perpetuates a colonial state of affairs. The nation-state is a legitimate instrument of exclusion, with citizenship consisting in excluding those who are citizens from those who are not. National racism is not 'abnormal' – on the contrary, it is necessarily tied to nationalism. In other words, national racism constitutes

> a 'logic' of interpreting social networks that is rooted in the very way in which the modern nation-state controls and configures alliances and relations with a range of mechanisms, be they legal, educational, social, medical or, in the words of Michel Foucault, 'bio-political'.[41]

Both anthropological and Marxist critiques agree that racism is not a form of xenophobia – which has always been evident in any society – but rather that it is a specific characteristic of modern societies. In turn, such critiques posit a radical break between the xenophobia found in pre-modern societies and contemporary racism. Pre-modern xenophobia is an age-old phenomenon which springs from the incomprehension and hostility spontaneously exhibited by humans when faced with the Other: a being who comes from outside their own society, who has a different way of life and who has values that are alien to their own tenets, which are held to be natural. Until the constitution of modern nations, the Other was external and different – he could arouse curiosity or even sympathy as much as he could hostility, and he could hold prestige. However, two things caused the Other to be subsumed within the realm of the internal: first, the formal proclamation of equality between men; and, second, the idea of (relative) cultural homogeneity engendered by the organising of the political order into nations. The foundation of nations forced ethnically different populations to live together at the same time as it invoked their ethnic homogeneity. As Ernest Gellner has already stressed, it is this contradiction between the rational project of nationalist movements on the one hand, and their ethnic arguments on the other, that has served to give difference its scandalous quality. Definable as a doctrine with scientific pretensions in which biological characteristics are used to devalue certain sections of the population from within one's own society, racism would therefore seem to be a specific characteristic of modern Western societies.

Translated by Stephen Forcer

Notes

1 [Translator's note: in the Introduction to the book as a whole, the author writes that, 'Racism refers to a theory with scientific pretensions which is defined by two key tenets: firstly, the existence of races that are biologically different and which are therefore unequal; and, secondly, the existence of a necessary link between these biological characteristics and social behaviour, such that the biological determines the social. Along with social Darwinism . . . this theory enjoyed its peak between 1830 and 1930, and was most popular among German and English-speaking thinkers. It therefore seems prudent to reserve the term 'racism' for the ideology that grew out of this theory of races, and to distinguish it from behavioural racism (that is, racialism) on the one hand, and racialising ideology on the other, which is not based on a biological theory of races'; Dominique Schnapper, *La relation à l'autre: au cœur de la pensée sociologique* (Paris: NRF-Essais, Gallimard, 1988), p. 22.]
2 Claude Lévi-Strauss, *Anthropologie structurale II* (Paris: Plon, 1973), p. 402.
3 Ibid., p. 381.
4 Claude Lévi-Strauss, *Le Regard éloigné* (Paris: Plon, 1983), p. 417.
5 Ibid., p. 47.
6 Ibid., p. 15.
7 Ibid., p. 47.
8 Ibid., p. 44.
9 Ibid. p. 16.
10 See 'Caste, racisme et 'stratification',' in *Cahiers internationaux de sociologie*, XXIX, 1960, 91–112, reprinted in Louis Dumont, *Homo hierarchicus* (Paris: Gallimard, 1966), Annex 'A'.
11 Translator's note: the author is probably referring to Mannheim's famous work of 1929, *Ideology and Utopia* (London: Routledge, 1997).
12 Louis Dumont, *Homo hierarchicus*, p. 34.
13 Ibid., p. 318.
14 Ibid., p. 319.
15 Ibid., p. 34.
16 Ibid., p. 320.
17 Alexis de Tocqueville, *De la démocracie en Amérique* (Paris: Michel Lévy, 1868), vol.II, p. 306.
18 See *L'Idéologie raciste. Genèse et langage actuel* (Paris: Mouton, 1972).
19 This point was stressed by Lévi-Strauss in 1952, and is one on which all the commentators cited here agree.

20 Colette Guillaumin, *L'Idéologie raciste*, p. 40.

21 Ibid., p. 58.

22 Ibid., p. 47.

23 Ibid., p. 67. The emphasis is Guillaumin's.

24 Memmi writes that, 'Racism is the generalised and definitive valorisation of real or imaginary differences, and is made for the benefit of the individual from whom it issues to the detriment of the victim and in order to justify acts of aggression.'; *Le Racisme* (Paris: Gallimard 'Folio', 1994), pp. 113–14. The strict definition of racism (that is, one that deals in terms of biological races) requires that the adjective 'biological' be added to Memmi's description of 'differences'.

25 Colette Guillaumin, *L'Idéologie raciste*, p. 75.

26 Ibid., p. 77. The emphasis in Guillaumin's.

27 Christian Delacampagne, *L'Invention du racisme. Antiquité, Moyen Âge* (Paris: Fayard, 1983), p. 45. The emphasis is the author's.

28 Ibid., p. 300. Delacampagne's book closes with these words.

29 The first French empirical studies of racism were carried out at the start of the 1990s by a team led by Michel Wieviorka. See, for example, his *L'Espace du racisme* (Paris: Seuil, 1991) and Wieviorka *et al., La France raciste* (Paris: Seuil, 1992), as well as Didier Lapeyronnie's *L'Individu et les minorités. La France et la Grande-Bretagne face à leurs immigrés* (Paris: PUF, 1993).

30 See Oliver Cox, *Caste, Class and Race. A Study in Social Dynamics* (New York: Doubleday, 1948).

31 In 1946 Jean-Paul Sartre also wrote that, 'Anti-Semitism is a primitive and Manichean conception of the world where hatred of the Jew assumes the place of a great explanatory myth [. . .] What else is there to say, other than that socialist revolution is both necessary and sufficient to eradicate anti-Semitism?'; *Réflexions sur la question juive* (Paris: Gallimard, 1954), p. 182.

32 See *Race, nation, classes. Les identités ambiguës* (Paris: La Découverte, 1988).

33 Ibid., p. 59.

34 Etienne Balibar, ibid., p. 18.

35 Balibar, ibid., p. 18.

36 Immanuel Wallerstein, ibid., p. 50.

37 Ibid., p. 86.

38 Balibar, ibid., p. 69.

39 Etienne Balibar, *Les Frontières de la démocratie* (Paris: La Découverte, 1992), p. 104.

40 Albert Memmi, *Le Racisme*, p. 50.

41 Etienne Balibar, *Les Frontières de la démocratie*, p. 160.

25

MYRIAM REVAULT D'ALLONNES

Myriam Revault d'Allonnes was Professor of Philosophy at the University of Rouen until 2002 and is currently at the École Pratique des Hautes Études in Paris. She has also been Director of a programme in the Collège International de Philosophie. A phenomenologist by orientation, she has published widely on the work of Merleau-Ponty, Ricoeur, Claude Lefort, Spinoza and Hannah Arendt, whom she has also translated. A specialist in ethical and political philosophy, she has worked on the paradoxes of Revolutionary terror, on the question of political evil, and on the bedrock of passions which found the links between human beings. She is currently preparing a book on the question of affects, in particular pity and anger.

Her works include the following:

Montesquieu. Lecture de l'esprit des Lois, Paris: Belin, 1987.

D'une mort à l'autre. Précipices de la Revolution, Paris: Seuil, 1989.

La Persévérance des égarés, Paris: Christian Bourgeois, 1992.

Spinoza. Puissance et ontologie, ouvrage collectif, Paris: Kimé, 1994.

Ce que l'homme fait à l'homme. Essai sur le mal politique, Paris: Seuil, 1995 and 1999.

Politique et pensée. Colloque Hannah Arendt, Paris: Payot, 1996.

Le Dépérissement de la politique, Aubier, Paris: 1999 and 2002.

Merleau-Ponty. La chair du politique, Paris: Michalon/Le Bien commun, 2001.

Fragile humanité, Aubier, 2002.

Doit-on moraliser la politique?, Paris: Bayard, 2002.

KANT AND THE IDEA OF
RADICAL EVIL

For Kant, the 'radicalness' of evil has nothing to do with the kind of profundity which Arendt rejects in her response to Scholem, profundity which proves, in the end, to be somewhat superficial. It has nothing to do with psychology, whether individual or collective, nor with the deep roots of ideas or ideologies, nor with the presence of any particular motive. Kant would have described all such determinations as 'empirical'. Evil is *radical* because, in the face of the reason for acting that is the moral law, it sets itself up, antagonistically, as a rival reason. Thus Kant positions himself, from the outset, beyond the dichotomy of traditionally-available responses to this question: either anthropological pessimism linked to the Fall *or* optimistic wishful thinking which would have it that man can, by persistent effort, overcome evil. Yet because evil must be thought of as a *negative magnitude* (and not simply in terms of absence or privation), Kant is not prepared to accept any middle term between a morally good will solely determined by respect for the moral law and a morally bad will that allows other motives to enter into its maxim. Thus propositions of the following kind cannot be accepted: man is good in some respects but bad in others, sometimes good and sometimes bad . . . It is from this viewpoint that what will come to be known as *human nature* must be redefined: this is neither an empirical (sensible) nature, nor a psychological nature, nor in more general terms, a nature that is *given*. This moral (or intelligible) nature of the human being is none other than 'the subjective ground . . . of the exercise of the human being's freedom in general . . . antecedent to every deed that falls within the scope of the senses. But this subjective ground must, in turn, itself always be a deed of freedom . . . Hence the ground of evil cannot lie in any object *determining* the power of choice throught inclination, not in any natural impulses, but only in a rule that the power of choice itself produces for the exercise of its freedom, i.e. in a maxim . . . Whenever we therefore say, "The human being is by nature good", or, "He is by nature evil", this only means that he holds within himself a first ground (to us inscrutable) for the adoption of good or evil (unlawful) maxims, and that he holds this ground *qua* human, universally – in such a way, therefore, that by his maxims he expresses at the same time the character of his species.'[1] Such talk of a 'subjective ground' runs counter to any interpretation in empirical terms. Evil is radical not because it plumbs psychological depths but rather because it manages to get at the ground, to bring corruption to the principle of every maxim. This nature 'before' experience, 'before' observable actions, can only correspond to the intelligible fact of freedom and, as such, cannot be restricted to one individual or another but must instead be allotted to every member of the species. If the *propensity* (*Hang*) for evil takes root in the human heart, this is not as a result of the presence of particular motives of whatever kind (this is Arendt's point when she speaks of Eichmann's lack of profundity as an individual). The propensity takes root by grafting itself onto the very same *predispositions* (*Anlagen*) that make up our humanity, that constitute its possibility, that is its concept. It is true that, of these predispositions, only the first two are susceptible to corruption: the predispositions towards animality and humanity. The third, the predisposition towards personality, an aptitude to life as a moral being swayed only by respect for the moral law, is a predisposition onto which no evil can be grafted. It cannot be perverted, or turned against its own end. The heterogeneity of *propensities* and *predispositions* is, then, crucial in Kant's thinking: the *predispositions*, which may be termed original because they form part of the very possibility of human nature, are predispositions towards the good, which they further. The propensity, because it is contingent – born of freedom – is not objectively, but rather *subjectively*, necessary. As such, it can be understood in two ways: first, as a deed that has actually been carried out, in time, and which by virtue of its content (or 'matter') stands in opposition to the law. But it can also denote an *intelligible* act, one that may be known by reason alone and one that altogether lacks temporal form. And the reality of this act *remains*, even if it turns out that wrong-doing has in fact been avoided in experience and one considers oneself to be justified before the law. This, then, is the meaning of the *radicalness* of evil: the root of the problem, for Kant, lies at the level of the formation of maxims, in an intelligible act prior to any experience and not just in the actual exercise of freedom within the temporal series. Radical evil, which is the evil of the species – a notion that will have crucial consequences – refers back to the originating power of a freedom capable of aligning itself towards either good or evil. This power of choice is in some sense the root or matrix of every sensible action, 'prior to' any particular exercise of freedom in experience (although not in a temporal sense). It will already be apparent why radical evil could be said to be 'banal': it is radical because it is banal. *It is the evil common to everyone, even if not everyone does it.* Thus Kant questions the supposed 'peace of mind' with which those who have 'just luckily slipped by the evil consequences' content themselves. They ought instead to ask whether 'they would not have practiced similar vices themselves, had they not been kept away from them by impotence, temperament, upbringing and tempting circumstances of time and place'.[2] Arendt pursues Kant's line of questioning to its 'political' conclusion when she asks, 'how long it takes an average person to overcome his innate repugnance toward crime'?[3]

The significance of Kant's *rigorism* – misunderstood though it so often is – must accordingly be reassessed. No-one can except themselves from this propensity for evil. Here Kant echoes the words of St. Paul: 'For all have sinned, and come short of the glory of God'.[4] Or again: 'There is no cause for exempting anyone from it, and . . . the character therefore applies to the species'.[5] Even if Kant's rigorism is derived from a profoundly religious experience – and this cannot be denied – it has many wider implications and is not intended simply to serve as an indictment of humanity. Taking the opposite view from classical moralists, Kant denies that the root of evil lies in the irrationality of the passions. Desires, physical propensities and the inclinations of the senses are all morally neutral: they can, at most, offer an occasion for evil-doing. Animality, Kant argues, contains too little and an animal humanity could not be held responsible for the instincts associated with its finitude. However, the discontinuity Kant identifies between evil and the senses does not prompt him to look for the root of evil in a 'depravation' of human reason which would turn the moral agent into a 'demonic' being driven by the intention to do evil for evil's sake.

Why does Kant refuse to let the will to disobey the law be a motive capable of having a decisive impact on the power of choice? The first reason is due, to some extent, to the internal workings of Kantian doctrine: as we noted, the predisposition to personality, which makes man a moral and responsible being, cannot be impinged upon. The moral sense is indestructible and reason as such is incorruptible. But it has all too often escaped notice that the 'demonic' hypothesis is actually rejected by Kant, in the name of *rigorism*, because it contains 'too much' and is therefore no less *detrimental to responsibility* than the idea that evil can be put down to animality. In both cases, the human being is set free – by deficit and then by excess – and placed beyond the reach of the moral law. Beneath good and evil or beyond good and evil; in a sense, it amounts to much the same. Moreover, how could the stipulation that no man may make an exception of himself be entertained concurrently with the hypothesis of a will that is absolutely evil? How to gain assent for the idea that *everyone* is demonic? We know just how reassuring the idea that criminals are driven by the demonic can be, for it implies that the common run of humanity bears no relation to such inhuman creatures. The strength of the Kantian position lies precisely in its capacity to shield us from this false comfort which both Hannah Arendt and Primo Levi will later denounce. By ruling out the demonic drive, Kant arrives at a more radical version of what might be called *responsibility by belonging*. This is not to say that we should (or could) *identify* ourselves with those who, in their uncommon banality, have perpetrated extreme evil. But nor can we absolve ourselves of the responsibility which comes of our belonging to the human kind, which Kant names, precisely, the *species*. Kantian rigorism is what mediates banality, making it an 'operational' concept and bringing it into contact with this mode of responsibility that is neither strictly individual nor strictly collective. For although we have not perpetrated extreme evil and perhaps we would even be unable to do so, for reasons which may be contingent, can this 'innocence', in virtue of which we consider ourselves justified before the letter of the law, be entirely put down our own merit?[6] And Arendt once more transposes Kant into her own terms when she asks 'how long it takes an average person to overcome his innate repugnance toward crime'?[7]

Contrary to common belief, it is not clear that Kantian rigorism (because it is implacable in its denunciations of good conscience) serves merely to heighten a sense of bad conscience. Nor indeed is it intended to elicit a 'long and melancholy litany of accusations against humanity'. Rather, it is the demand for universality which is crucial here and the refusal to make exceptions is bound up with the idea that the quintessence of evil, 'the evil of evils' (as Ricoeur puts it) consists not in disobeying or transgressing the law but in lying and self-deception. The 'evil' man is not the one who *wills* evil (the evil man is not, as I have already argued, a demonic being) but one who has a 'secret tendency to make an exception of himself'. Although neither the will nor practical reason can ever be inherently perverse, the moral order of those motives which man embraces in forming maxims can, however, be perverted. When this occurs, evil can be said to be a *perversion* – though one spawned by freedom – in the sense that it overturns the order governing the relation between inclinations and respect for the moral law. Evil is *perversion* because it subordinates respect for the moral law to self-love, which it sets up as a rule of the will. Thus radical evil is a lie much more than an act of revolt or disobedience, a fraudulent way of behaving in accordance with the law rather than an open transgression of it. This is precisely the sort of 'dishonesty which allows people to be taken in and that stands opposed the establishment within us of a genuinely good will, which develops on the outside into deceitful, untruthful, behaviour towards others. If one is reluctant to view this as malicious, then it should at least be thought base'. It does, moreover, render any attempt to attribute moral qualities, whether internally or externally, entirely 'uncertain'.[8]

The fact that the place of radical evil is along with dissembling, falsification and self-deception is of great import for anyone who wishes to understand its banality. For the 'bureaucratic criminal', of which Eichmann is but the exemplary archetype, is not an enemy of the law. He neither makes out that his will is to revolt, nor that he is doing evil for evil's sake. In *Eichmann in Jerusalem*, Arendt tells of a remarkable incident: Eichmann, who always made out that he had behaved, in everything he did, as a citizen with respect for the law, repeated over and over again that he was doing his duty, not just obeying orders but also obeying the *law*. No doubt he was vaguely aware that some such distinction was required here, but he was never called upon to say more about it. On one occasion, while being cross-examined, he declared that 'he had lived his whole life according to Kant's moral precepts, and especially according to a Kantian definition of duty'.[9] And amid general consternation, he produced the following makeshift definition of the categorical imperative: '"I meant by my remark about Kant that the principle of my will must always be such that it can become the principle of general laws."'[10] In the eyes of a bureaucratic criminal, this meant that one should act as though the principle of one's actions were the same as that of the laws or the law-makers of the country in question. This example of falsification is of more than merely anecdotal value. Over and above the fact that stereotypes, clichés and stock phrases are the most obvious forms of the organized lie and of self-deception, it is worth insisting on the fact that, on no occasion, does this new breed of criminal voice even a hint of hostility to the moral law: he is no enemy of morality. It is never immoralism that guides his actions. These considerations may cast doubt on the relevance of George Steiner's analysis, which starts out by taking seriously Hitler's claim that 'conscience is a Jewish invention' and concludes that the Holocaust testifies to a murderous hatred of the rigorous ideal incarnated in the monotheism of Mount Sinai, in early Christianity and in messianic Socialism. This would mean, in Kantian terms, that a demonic will had established itself as a motive contrary to the law and that the negation of the law and of reason had been promoted as a principle of action.

According to such an hypothesis, the origins of the exterminatory enterprise and of National Socialism in general lay in an anti-moral will (a sort of 'nihilism') which may rightly be described as 'demonic'. Yet it places these 'devils in human form' on the outer reaches of humanity – and it is far easier, as Arendt has emphasised, to be the victim of devils than of mediocre men, of respectable citizens or fathers with children. In the face of radical evil – the evil which belongs to the species and is hence banal – the demonic hypothesis is, it should be insisted, a weak hypothesis. Weak because reassuring and reassuring because selective: the possibility of the inhuman is relegated beyond the reaches of the human, which is thereby relieved of responsibility for it. From the standpoint adopted by Steiner, for example, a distinction could always be made between those who have taken this immoralism as their rule of action and those who, since they have defended moral values, can consider themselves justified and to have no obligation to take others' failings upon themselves. This paradoxical position – to consider onself to be justified before the moral law ('I would never do that') and simultaneously to release oneself from the responsibility for human weakness – is diametrically opposed to Kant's: for Kant, the responsibility of belonging to the human kind is grounded in an undetermined ground. Rather than compare the intelligible and sensible aspects of man, to the detriment of the latter, by demonstrating the self-coincidence of good, Kant makes the enigma of evil dependent upon *freedom* and the exercise of that freedom. Radical evil is accordingly the original form of every act: it is the deed of a freedom which uncovers in itself the powerlessness at the heart of power, the weakness within strength.

But our concern here is not to speculate about the 'metaphysical' aims of National Socialism, but rather – to return to the criminality of ordinary people – to understand the significance of deception, lying and duplicity; the duplicity with which 'the human heart deceives even itself about its benevolent and malevolent intentions' and the 'propensity to deceive even oneself with mendacious interpretations of the moral law, ones which in turn weaken it'.

In *The Destruction of the European Jews*, Raul Hilberg offers an extremely detailed analysis of the way in which the exterminatory enterprise was lent a 'moral' disguise. The 'mobile' killing missions had to be made legitimate: if a planned operation could not be justified (essentially by reference to some fictitious Jewish plot) then it did not take place. Acceptance had to be gained for the notion that the killing of the Jews was 'historically necessary', which in turn meant that personal motives and responsibility had to be ruled out. If a soldier 'killed a Jew spontaneously, voluntarily, or without instruction, merely because he *wanted* to kill, then he committed an abnormal act . . . Herein lay the crucial difference between the man who "overcame" himself to kill and one who wantonly committed atrocities. The former was regarded as a good soldier and a true Nazi; the latter was a person lacking self-control'.[11] Addressing the killers, Himmler declared on one occasion that: 'the *Einsatzgruppen* were called upon to fulfill a repulsive duty. He would not like it if Germans did such a thing gladly . . . They had undoubtedly noticed that he hated this bloody business and that he had been aroused to the depth of his soul. But he too was obeying the highest law by doing his duty and he was acting from a deep understanding of the necessity for this operation.'[12] This understanding of 'duty' implied an injunction to avoid lax behaviour. For not only was there a risk that a dissolute administration might disintegrate, but the occurrence of random atrocities might also discredit the 'ideal' underlying the entire enterprise. This also explains why Himmler exhorted his audience to stamp out pillaging, on the grounds that Jewish property was thenceforth to belong to the Reich: '"We had the moral right vis-à-vis our people to annihilate *this* people which wanted to annihilate us. But we have no right to take a single fur, a single watch, a single Mark, a single cigarette, or anything whatsoever . . . I will not stand by while such an infected spot appears, we will burn it out. But on the whole we can say that we have fulfilled this heavy task with love for our people, and we have not been damaged in the innermost of our being, our soul, our character."'[13] So the killers were obliged to banish all hint of uncontrolled behaviour: an act carried out while under orders was an 'expression of idealism', whereas one carried out under impulse (from an egoistic, sadistic or sexual motive) deserved to be punished. This 'moral' disguise rested on a professionalization of murder and a *separation* between the sphere of personal inclinations (a private life of passions and emotions) and an activity that was judged according to technical and industrial criteria. More so still than blind obedience to orders from above, it was this separation which allowed both a monstrous falsification of the idea of 'duty' to occur and, at the same time, a relaxation of the sense of personal responsibility. And the same is true of those ordinary bureaucratic criminals, implicated to whatever degree in the exterminatory enterprise, and who may very well never have laid eyes on a dead body. For one of the most crucial rationalizations designed for those involved in this enterprise was – in addition to obedience to orders which, once pronounced, were tantamount to absolution – this distinction between impersonal duty and personal sentiment. In this respect, the position of the bureaucrats in charge of the Soviet camps was very similar. In *Into the Whirlwind*, Evgenia Ginzburg describes the man in charge of the Sovkhoz as follows:

> He wasn't a sadist. He got no pleasure from our suffering. He simply did not see us, for in all sincerity he did not consider us as human beings. A 'sudden increase in losses' among the imprisoned workforce was, as far as he was concerned, merely a technical worry like any other – one comparable to a farmer's knife finally wearing out. In both cases, there was only one solution: to replace it with a new one. In the midst of his swinish self-assurance, which was continually bolstered by his sense of the unshakeable firmness of the various propositions and quotations etched into his brain for ever more, he would have been extremely surprised, I think, to hear himself called a slave-trader to his face . . . The firm belief that this world, with its hierarchy and its forms of daily life, was unshakeable, emanated from his every word and from every action of those in charge of us.

This monstrous perversion of morality was, just as much as the politically orchestrated lie, one of the mainstays of the system. In place of morality, what we see emerge is its death-dealing caricature, one far more terrifying than revolt against the law: the exclusion of personal motives (cruelty, cupidity, sadism, etc.) is promoted as the condition of the possibility of mass murder, which is itself established as an 'ideal' and executed in accordance with criteria of productivity. If, for Kant, the 'evil of evils' is the lie, the falsification, the simulacrum, then we could say that National Socialism developed the most terrifying kind of falsification there is. (I am not referring here to particular historical and political conditions, nor am I claiming to offer a 'privileged' response to the question '*Why* evil?') At least three simulacra are put in place in this system of generalized imposture: the perversion of the idea of 'duty' ('thou shalt not kill' is inverted and becomes 'thou shalt kill'), the separation between personal motives and obedience to a 'pseudo-law' (the will of the leader) and, finally, the demand for absolute adherence to the letter of the law, which is evident at every stage of the process.

It is well known that one of the essential features of the totalitarian experience lies in the creation of a *fictitious* world: an ideology that is both rigid and 'fantastically fictitious' (Arendt) creates a world that is both a lie *and* a coherent whole, a world which real experience finds itself powerless to circumvent. But little attention has hitherto been paid to those varieties of *subjectivization* (ways of submitting to the rule of law, of 'elaborating' a relationship to the self) which might accompany the construction of this fictitious world. We would be entitled to think that the spread of evil, like that of a fungus which comes as of nowhere and takes hold everywhere, is bound up with the kingdom of the generalized lie. This kind of lie is not just politically organized but must also have been 'morally' instituted. When Kant finds in falsification, imposture and 'duplicity', the most radical form of radical evil, he is relying implicitly on an ethic of veracity which is the correlative of the natural human vocation to communicate one's thoughts. 'It is a natural calling of humanity to communicate with one another, especially in what concerns people generally.'[14] Thus the demand for universal communicability is not unrelated to the ban, in principle, on lying: the lie establishes for itself 'an end which runs counter to the natural use of the faculty for communicating one's thoughts'. If veracity (which should not be confused with truth) plays a leading role in the institution of the human, what can be said of a system in which the lie is universal, except that it accompanies (though again, I do not claim that it 'causes' but at most that it 'crystallizes') the institution of the inhuman?[15]

This discussion should not be seen as an attempt to offer a privileged viewpoint on evil, still less to 'explain' its origin; for what remains insurmountable is that, to the agents of the exterminatory process, at all levels, there was never a moral problem that proved to be insurmountable. In this descent into the abyss, the reason why evil exists is *unfathomable*: its presence cannot be reassimilated. It is in these terms that Kant blocks the temptation to return to the origin: 'The rational origin, however, of this disharmony in our power of choice . . . i.e. this propensity to evil, remains inexplicable to us . . . there is no conceivable ground for us, therefore, from which moral evil could first have come in us.'[16] There is simply nothing to look for in causal terms: we must learn to do without it. There is no 'why' of radical evil, no more than of the banality of its perpetrators. The absolute evil which ordinary men do is *without reason*. If we contrast this view, once again, with the hypothesis of demonic intent, evil emerges as still more radical. Demonic intent is not unfathomable because it is already a cause. As a cause – perhaps even the cause of causes – the desire to do evil for evil's sake would resolve the enigma of evil's origin. Because demonic intent is, so to speak, 'fixed', its power to unsettle is far less than that of radical evil, which is subject to a principle of uncertainty. Demonic intent is not truly the evil of freedom in all its nakedness. For in the face of the evil of freedom, as Jaspers writes, 'there is no cure for anxiety' and we have no idea where this evil could have come from, even when it is all our own work. When he speaks of 'the limit beyond which we cease to understand', Kant signals that we must abandon our faith in all 'explanatory' schemata: evil, once it happens, will always happen again. That which is 'unprecedented' is 'already present', but what is already present defies scrutinty (is *unerforschbar*).

When faced with the new evil born under totalitarian oppression, all the presuppositions and conditions put forward by economics, history, and mass psychology, may very well be entirely accurate, but even if they are, the fact remains that beyond a certain point there lies a yawning abyss. When it becomes truly the case that 'everything is possible', this event cannot be reduced to any of its antecedent causes, whatever they may be, nor can it be *deduced* from its past: 'It is only when something irreversible has taken place that we can struggle to reconstruct its history retrospectively. The event sheds light on its own past but can never be deduced from it.'[17] In her attempt to develop a methodology which replaces causality with 'elements' that shed some light on, or 'crystallize', their past, Arendt is closer to Kant than she thinks. Not because the philosophical thesis of radical evil can be conflated with the more 'political' approach adopted in *The Origins of Totalitarianism*, but rather because the light cast by these explanations is simply snuffed out on the rock of the inexplicable. There is no reason which could explain the emergence into the present of 'everything is possible'. The devastation which totalitarianism brings is matched only by the failure of all explanation.

But to give up causality for the idea of a ground without a ground by no means implies that the perpetrators of evil should not be held responsible (or should be held to be 'less' responsible) for their actions. The fact that ordinary men are capable of extreme evil does not make evil banal (does not lessen its impact) but rather, makes it radical, because it is the evil of *their* freedom. Its being without reason means that evil leaves us unable to account for its origin: there is no answer to the question 'Where does evil come from?' But the question 'How is it that we come to do evil?' concerns not only our freedom *qua* intelligible fact, but also its *use in experience*. The ordinary man acts, but the inscrutability of origin which renders powerless every explanatory scheme does nothing to lessen the impact of this act. The bureaucratic criminal could, for example, abstain from acting: in extreme situations where the choice of options is very limited and in which the agent altogether lacks political power, the possibility nevertheless remains of 'doing nothing'. Once these ordinary men are no longer either heroes or demons (or indeed saints), 'it is this possibility of "non-participation" that proves decisive in determining how we judge not the system but the individuals, their choices and arguments.'[18]

It is this blind spot of the inexplicable that Primo Levi was thinking of when he wrote: 'Perhaps one cannot, what is more one must not, understand what happened, because to understand is almost to justify. Let me explain: "understanding" a proposal or human behaviour means to "contain" it, contain its author, put oneself in his place, identify with him.'[19]

In this rejection of an idea of comprehension that would be a form of 'identification' – the recognition of like by like – Primo Levi recalls Arendt's trenchant remark in *The Origins of Totalitarianism*, which we have already mentioned, concerning this new breed of criminals who lie 'beyond the reach of human solidarity in crime'. What does it mean to say that, in the face of this new form of criminality, we have exceeded or erred beyond the limits of recognition?

We must return here to the question of *identification*. It will readily be granted, in the first instance, that we identify more willingly with another's suffering and distress than we might with a criminal act; yet, within certain limits – and we must explain where these lie – both are conceivable and to the same degree. Indeed they form the very foundations of social existence. For Aristotle, for example, the process of identifying with the distress of a fellow human being occurs by way of fear as I watch a tragedy being performed. The spectator's fear is born of *analogy*: in the suffering of another, I recognize, virtually, my own suffering. Because an other like me is suffering, I too could suffer. The other's distress is very much that of a fellow human being, one whom I resemble. The role accorded by Aristotle to fear is put down, by Rousseau, to the principle of pity, but the underlying concepts are not dissimilar: the principle of pity, which is pre-rational (though reason will not reject it), can be stated as 'an innate repugnance at the sight of the death or suffering of any creature with sensory organs and principally our fellow human beings'. By describing pity in these terms, Rousseau attributes to it the same properties that Aristotle attributed to fear: the recognition of beings who resemble me and my concern for their distress. 'When by strength of an open spirit I identify with my fellow being and I feel that I am, as it were, inside him, it is because I do not want to suffer that I do not want him to suffer' (*Emile*). And where we can identify with the motives beneath certain human failings (passion, revenge, self-interest, the desire for power, etc.), the same kind of recognition of a fellow being can take place; in such circumstances, our judgement is that of human beings with similar weaknesses. We can pass judgement to the extent that we 'comprehend' what it is that we are punishing and/or pardoning. By punishing we put a stop to evil's machinations; by pardoning we free the criminal and allow them to start afresh.[20] The problem now, however, is that we are faced with crimes which are as unpunishable as they are unpardonable, crimes which no 'motive' can explain and no recognition of the perpetrator as a fellow being can allow us to 'comprehend'. Members of this new breed of criminal therefore lie beyond the limits of any possible 'identification', if indeed it is true that the murderer's acts still occupy a ground that is familiar to us, namely that of life and death. More terrifying still than this observation – although it follows from it – is the idea that the victims, who have been degraded, deprived of their humanity and reduced to an equality-in-indifference that is worse than death, are themselves beyond the limits within which the recognition of fellow human beings can take place. 'That was no world. That was not Humanity. I was no part of that; I didn't belong to that', cried in horror an observer who gained entry to the Warsaw ghetto in 1942.

The advent of radical evil, this product of the ordinary man's freedom, marks the disappearance of human scale and accordingly that of the world. Yet it falls perhaps to a *responsibility by belonging* to take on the burden of that which can no longer be made good by an act of 'identification' that has become too problematic. Radical evil has destroyed the world which both separates and connects one human being to another. Yet this same radical evil implies a form of responsibility that tends towards the recreation of the world. The same radical evil which has implanted the possibility of the inhuman into the human, for ever more, also compels us to take stock of just what humanity is capable of. This appears to know no bounds. For the victims, 'responsibility by belonging' could play a *redemptive* role, restoring them to the humanity that they have been denied. If radical evil in its modern guise has brought with it a loss of world – a loss of the common ground and, as we have seen in the case of the 'crisis' of identification, a loss of the capacity to share the world with another – then the abandonment of a causal framework moves us forward, in the direction of an endless task. The world is a task without end.

If radical evil brings to the fore the aporia in a certain speculative way of thinking, its historical and political 'staging' locates the breaking point beyond which our traditional political categories and criteria of moral judgement are simply redundant. It would be fair to say that the failure of causality is also a crisis of comprehension. When she makes the emergence of radical evil the key to her analysis of the century, Hannah Arendt asks what becomes of *comprehension* – the continuous process of forcing ourselves to live in accord with the world that is our shared abode – in the wake of irreparable loss. If totalitarian phenomena are the key events of the century, how are we to reconcile ourselves (I do not mean in a Hegelian sense) with a world in which such events are even so much as possible? We come up against an obstacle which is doubly insurmountable: on the one hand, it defies understanding and literally 'pulverizes' our categories of thought – as the crisis of explanation testifies – and on the other, its perpetrators are people from whom, it seems, we are separated by nothing save the use they make of their freedom in exprience. It is thus doubly that we are confronted by an experience of absolute non-belonging to the world, a *radical* or *extreme* experience. It is not only the victims, who have already been annihilated before they are put to death, who have been affected by this but also the functionaries of evil, who have been deprived, *by the use of their freedom*, of the ability to differentiate between good and evil, between right and wrong.

Thus the problem of 'evil defying thought' is not only one of the frustrations arising from a fruitless search: evil 'defies thought', Arendt argues, because thought strives to get to the bottom of things, to reach root causes and, in the case of evil (by which we should understand the evil committed by Eichmann), it finds nothing, or rather only the absence of thought. We have seen what becomes of 'depth' and 'radicalness' in the Kantian perspective and we noted that the problem there is not viewed in terms of the way in which motives take root but rather in terms of the ground without a ground that is freedom *qua* intelligible act. If evil defies thought, this is also and above all because it marks the failure of the power of explanation. Absolute evil – after we reject the hypothesis of demonic causes – confronts us with a basic aporia: 'there is no reason we can comprehend that explains from whence moral evil could first have come upon us'. To the enigma of its origin should be added the *scandal* of its *banality*, this *scandal of scandals*, as it might be called, which exposes us, in fear and trembling, to anxiety in the face of irreparable harm. Once we have dispensed with the idea that the perpetrators of evil partake of an alterity that is absolutely other, their *banality obliges* us, in ethical and political terms, to accept *the responsibility of our belonging to the human kind*. The idea of banality protects us not only from a bogus intelligibility but also from all false consolation and fallacious justifications. Evil challenges thought if it is true that the profoundly Kantian question of 'How long does it take before an ordinary person conquers their innate repugnance to crime?' is indeed one of the most unsettling there is.

Yet already implicit in this very challenge to thought is the possibility of a reversal, of a reorientation. If we have lost our grasp on sense and renounced the search for an origin – by recognizing that an aporia haunts this kind of speculation – we thereby release the question of evil from the hold of concepts: as Jaspers has written, reason confronts its limits. But this is the price of its being able to turn back towards the practical domain, the sphere of politics and action. The reinscription of the question of evil within the sphere of the practical follows precisely from the inscrutable character of its reason for being. It is by way of a 'response' to the unintelligibility of evil's origin (there is evil but we do not know why) that we can attempt to reinscribe evil within the realm of the practical. The rejection of theodicy[21] and the critique of rational theology both point towards a reorientation of the question in terms of human activity. How is it that we *do* evil? Are there 'privileged' moments in history and politics for the production of evil?

Radical evil in history and politics

Kant's attempt to problematize the idea of radical evil does not come to an end, as one might expect it to, with this acknowledgement of its unfathomability. Rather, the discussion continues, running alongside the third and fouth parts of the essay on religion. Moral anthropology is concerned not only with the species but also with the *world*: it is both in the world and of the world. Thus the question which follows on from our non-knowledge of the origin of evil, the question which reorientates our approach, is not 'What ought I to do?' but rather, 'What may I hope for?'[22]

If we have succeeded in imagining, albeit with some difficulty, the corruption of an individual who was once good, is the opposite unthinkable? Is it inconceivable to hope, conversely, that 'evil will be raised to good', or in other words to hope that the *predisposition* to good will be 'restored'? This formulation captures the connection between evil, freedom and hope: because the predisposition (*Anlage*) is invincible, human beings who were created for the good but who, as free beings, have been corrupted, can neither view evil as an irreversible course, nor as the effect of an external cause which lies entirely beyond their control. If human beings can never cease to act freely then the *aim* of the good cannot be annihilated by a choice of evil. Because freedom must be protected, in principle, from determination, it would be a mistake to conclude either that evil is necessary or that it is irresistible. Thence springs the hope for a re-establishment of the predisposition to good. As far as practical or institutional politics is concerned, however, we should be careful not to confuse the *aim* with the *accomplishment*. One can certainly hope, but *for what* can one hope? Let us recall that the human being is not morally good but rather has been created *for the good*. Thus it is less a question of realizing what one hoped for and more a question of the good as an *end*. It is precisely at this nodal point that the promise becomes tinged with alienation and the radical evil of the institution emerges as the counterpart to the evil of freedom. By paying close attention, as Ricoeur does, to the fact that the question of radical evil runs alongside the entire argument of Kant's essay on religion, it becomes clear that what Kant is concerned with there is not only the radically non-determined character of evil's origin, which is dealt with explicitly there, but also the process of its totalization. The way in which Kant, even before he moves on to the question of religious institutions, apprehends the figure of Christ is revealing in itself: it is by virtue of being a *mediator* that Christ is an *exemplary* figure and not because he represents the Idea – which would lie beyond the limits of our understanding – of the Principle of the Good. If Kant thereby warns against the deification of Christ, this is because Christ's *validity as an example* depends upon the possibility of a form of *imitation* which remains untarnished by the superstition of false worship and the false Church; imitation is, to a certain extent, the path to the infinite suggested to us by the figure of Christ, but it will never bring about the coincidence with an end which is declared to be unattainable. The same anti-dogmatic tenor holds sway over Kant's discussion of grace: all I can do is hope for grace but without that hope ever becoming knowledge. Hope cannot be relinquished (to do so would be to grant the irreversibility of evil) but just like our non-knowledge of the origin of evil – to which it corresponds, to some degree – hope is also a non-knowledge. It is *as though* the human being were evil by nature and therefore, correlatively, *as though* the human being were unable to give up hope.

But the synthesis of hope cannot be accomplished by the individual alone. Kant's commitment to the principle of universal communicability – which serves as the foundation, as we have already noted, for an ethic of veracity – leads him to situate the individual subject within an organized totality, in other words a Church, or in more general terms, an institution. It is against the background of an original experience of communicability[23] that the synthesis of hope leads us to a world in which human beings relate to one another within an organized totality. They need to be part of an empirical totality but this will always be under threat from false worship, or falsification. So at the threshold of institutionalization, we find what might be thought of as an *analogon* of radical evil: the Church, by reversing the order of relations between the maxim and the motives and thereby subordinating the moral law to urges born of fear and desire, is capable of generating superstition. True evil, the 'evil of evils' thus appears, as Ricoeur once again emphasises, in the very same field from which religion arises. This is a field subject to the requirement of totalization proper to the Dialectic but which is institutionally corrupt, for its institutions are, first and foremost, institutions 'of gathering, recapitulation and totalization'. The argument on radical evil is developed in and concluded by this discussion of the 'pathology of hope' which is a feature of falsified expressions of synthesis:

> Truly human evil concerns premature syntheses, violent syntheses, short circuits in the totality. It culminates in the sublime, with the "presumption" of the theodicies and their numerous successors in modern politics. But this is possible precisely because the aim of the totality is an irreducible aim and because it opens the space of a Dialectic of *total* will which cannot be reduced to the simple Analytic of the *good* will. There are indeed perverse syntheses because there is an authentic question of the synthesis, of the totality, in what Kant calls the total object of the will.[24]

The radicalness of evil points to the imbrication of the desire for totality with its very own pathology. If institutions are in some sense privileged sites for the production of evil, this is because they presume in their *activities* to equate the aim with the accomplishment and to make of the end something that can be fully realized, thereby failing to acknowledge that an irreducible distance separates the work from the task. There is undoubtedly hope and expectation, but they cannot be fulfilled. To make out that the task has been accomplished is to offer a falsifying synthesis, to take a fraudulent final step on the path of totalization. For instance, to seek to rid the human heart of the very desire to do evil, by a politics of moral regeneration, is to deny the unfathomable power of freedom: evil is *freedom's* evil. A politics of virtue – Jacobinism, for example – which aspires to eradicate evil, casting itself as reformation and salvation, will fall prey to the excesses which typify all moralizing politics. For inherent in the ideal of regeneration is a basic ambiguity which implies the possibility of perversion: this ambiguity causes a political will based on the urge to moralize to develop, even in spite of itself, into a kind of demiurgic manipulation, a technology of power. To advocate dispensing with 'despotic' oppression, in favour of an order 'driven by itself in accord with its own design' (Saint-Just), is also to lay down the preconditions of a regime in which power is exercised with complete technical precision, to herald a liberation which contains within itself all the seeds of the greatest conceivable oppression.

Politics as such is certainly not evil. It merely offers an occasion for the realization of evil when it presumes to usurp the kingdom of ends and, by way of a dogma of redemption, to become a way of *realizing* the good. When modern politics, and particularly revolutionary politics, finds itself charged with the task of changing the world and changing people's lives, when politics acquires an aura of saintliness and a kind of messianic faith crystallizes around the desire for 'regeneration', then politics becomes a necessary evil resulting from the will for the good, or, in Kantian terms, from the will's search for a total object. The fraudulent step in this work of totalization is then the raising of politics into a substitute for theodicy. Yet as Brecht remarked, 'strong indeed is the temptation to be good': the positive hyperbole in which politics is identified with the *kingdom of lightness* is thus simply the equal but opposite version of the negative hyperbole, according to which politics is the *kingdom of darkness*.

Kant must take the credit for offering the most trenchant analysis of the reversals to which moralizing politics is prone, as of the excesses of a politics that aspires to be a secular theology. The metaphor of the 'curve' (the human being is *curvus in se*, made of a 'knotted wood', of 'wood with a curved grain') to which Kant has recourse in numerous texts,[25] rules out all 'perfect' or 'complete' solutions – indeed all 'solutions', insofar as this term has only a mathematical and not a political meaning. The task of politics – the institutional organization of rational beings who are driven by 'unsociable sociability' – no more calls for citizens to be *angelic* than it justifies resorting to despotism as the ultimate obstacle to human evil. Thus Kant ranks moral despotism ('But woe to the legislator who would want to bring about through coercion a polity directed to ethical ends! For he would thereby not only achieve the very opposite of ethical ends but also undermine his political ends and render them insecure.')[26] alongside political despotism, the kind of despotism to which anthropological pessimism might lead. Now Kant's decision to reject this option, to deem it inadmissable, stems from his discussion of radical evil. The undecidability of Kant's judgement on the French Revolution (its undeniable significance as a 'historical sign' which discloses the human moral disposition yet which cannot be separated from the inexpiable crime of regicide) is born of a conception of radical evil as a propensity of human nature which cannot be eradicated and an understanding of the unfathomable abyss of an originary power capable of turning itself towards either good *or* evil. The Terror can therefore be understood as the 'historical sign' of the radicalness of evil, which no kind of moral despotism could succeed in eradicating. But conversely, there can be no justifying political despotism which, while being entirely indifferent to ethical criteria, simultaneously pretends to offer resistance to human evil.

In both cases, the target of Kant's criticism is the confusion between the state *qua* juridico-civil (political) entity, governed by the 'laws of public order' and the state *qua* ethico-civil (ethical) entity, governed by the 'laws of virtue'. The very principle of the juridico-political community – the laws of which are concerned only with the 'legality' of actions which 'make a visual, but not a moral (internal) impact' – prohibits, according to Kant, intrusion into the interiority of hearts and minds, just as it does any confusion between the political task (to guarantee the exercise of a republican constitution, even among a nation of 'demons') and the ethical ideal ('to become as good as once we were evil'). The Kantian perspective, which is explicitly structured around the question of radical evil, should not be interpreted in purely restrictive terms, as though all that were at stake for Kant were the limitation of the power of the sovereign and the defence of individual freedom from the power of the state (even if, in certain respects, some of his works lend themselves to such a reading). Kant is not (or not only) on the side of a 'politics of understanding' which would resist the illegitimate aspirations of a 'politics of reason'. But the question raised here – as evinced by his perplexity in the face of the revolutionary event, his admiration for the 'historical sign' and his condemnation of the revolutionary undertaking as such – is infinitely more complex: if something is left 'empty', is it the role of practical politics to fill the void? And if so, how? Should this be its 'work' or its 'task'? Even if the purpose of the religious bond is the regeneration of the will, this is not, however, the purpose of the political bond, which is rather to bring 'impure' wills into accord under a common law.

This distinction between the work (destined for completion) and the task (the very 'principle' of which is to remain incomplete) underpins Kant's famous analysis in the second section of *The Conflict of the Faculties*, in which the distinction between the point of view of the participant undertaking an action and that of the onlookers (*plural*), who are closely connected to one another by 'a sympathy of aspiration which comes very close to enthusiasm', offers a key to his view of the revolutionary event:

> The revolution of a gifted people which we have seen unfolding in our day may succeed or miscarry; it may be filled with misery and atrocities to the point that a right-thinking human being, were he boldly to hope to execute it successfully the second time, would never resolve to make the experiment at such cost – this revolution, I say, nonetheless finds in the hearts of all spectators (who are not engaged in this game themselves) a wishful *participation* that borders closely on enthusiasm the very expression of which is fraught with danger; this sympathy, therefore, can have no other cause than a moral predisposition in the human race.[27]

The question of radical evil is implicated in this essay by way of a meditation on the *tragic partiality of action*. For action, which is, of necessity, both partial and partisan, involves a suspension of the adequate exercise of the intellect. So it is as though the suspension of action, on account of the way it is inevitably drawn into polarizations and also because of the 'end' it implies, were a condition of intelligibility – the intelligibility of the 'historical sign' which bears witness to the human *moral* disposition. Thus Kant's reflections on tragic partiality open out, in the arena of practical action, onto the question of whether there could be a political institution of freedom that would not present itself as a 'work' to be undertaken. Far from having escaped the reach of Kant's analysis, the awareness of a difficult tension between the end and that which is without end brings us back to the question of the synthesis of hope. For human evil also manifests itself in the premature syntheses induced by the fatality of action.

So if radical evil is concerned with freedom 'in the process of its totalization', as much as in its initial non-determination, it may come as something of a surprise that Arendt – who elsewhere is so very attentive to both the irreducibility of finitude and the uncertainties attendant upon acts that can neither be foreseen nor controlled – did not consider at greater length the questions raised by Kant's discussion. Surprising, too, is that her reflections on the evils of totalitarianism were not more deeply rooted in Kant's condemnation of 'short-circuits of the totality', a condemnation which stems from his discussion of the specificity of radical evil.

Yet in *The Origins of Totalitarianism*, Arendt suggests – as though in passing – that if radical evil involves a loss of all our familiar points of reference, then this provides a veiled indication that something has come to pass in modern politics: 'something seems to be involved in modern politics that actually should never be involved in politics as we used to understand it, namely all or nothing – all, and that is an undetermined infinity of forms of human living-together, or nothing, for a victory of the concentration-camp system would mean the same inexorable doom for human beings as the use of the hydrogen bomb would mean the doom of the human race.'[28]

Yet the relevance of this 'all or nothing' is considerably wider than the phenomenon of the concentration camp. Indeed, it may even be said to be of paradigmatic value as far as modern politics is concerned. For the radical evil of politics is precisely this jump into the radical, as exemplified by the dogma of redemption which, after all, is simply one way of saying 'everything is possible'. The ultimate incarnation of the perverse synthesis is this leap into the radicalness of 'everything is possible'. We merely intensify the paradox by noting that the architect of this synthesis – the civil servant of evil – is usually an ordinary man, a 'typically grey specimen' who is 'neither vile nor heroic' (Primo Levi). In the passage we cited above, Arendt refers to what she considers to be the two fundamental experiences of the century: that of totalitarian regimes, which highlights the antinomy of politics and freedom and that of the potential for annihilation inherent in the rational organization of modern states, which offers a glimpse, edging towards apocalypse, of the antinomy of politics and the preservation of life. In both cases, it is the radical character of 'everything is possible' that marks the horizon of the experience. And we do not appear to be all that far from Leo Strauss's position in 'The Three Phases of Modernity', where he writes that, in the the politics of Modernity, knowledge becomes 'a means of action' and that 'man can transform a corrupt material into a material free from corruption'. In other words, to go beyond the incompleteness of freedom by radicalizing the possibilities of human *action* is, at the same time, correlatively, to suggest that there are no longer any obstacles to an almost limitless degradation of human beings, just as there are no longer any obstacles on the path of human progress, or any impediments to the human capacity to be rid of evil. 'Man is, by his very nature, almost infinitely malleable. As the Abbé Raynal put it, the human species is what we want to make it. Man does not have, strictly speaking, a nature that sets limits on what can be brought forth from within it.'[29]

However, the issue of radical evil forbids precisely this kind of malleability, for, paradoxically, it enables us to resist the radicalization of human *action*. 'Liberation' is no more a matter of knowledge than hope. There is no attainable final goal on the path of perfectibility – not because, as Leo Strauss maintains, 'there is not in fact any such thing as a natural human constitution', but because to free onself from evil is to free onself from the evil of freedom and, therefore, from freedom as such. The perverse synthesis of 'everything is possible' cuts two ways: it can be used to justify either the attempt to free human beings from the evil which inhabits them, transforming a corrupt material into one free of corruption, or, alternatively, to justify the attempt to transform the human being into an animal, a denatured being whose only 'freedom' consists in preserving the species. Kant's *methodological* rigorism leads him accordingly to reject these twin possibilities of a radical politics based on the radicalization of *action*; liberation and debasement without limits are the two faces of the same perverse synthesis.

By reimmersing politics in the medium of radical evil, Kant opposes the development of all forms of radical politics. He does not, however, mean to imply that politics is to be identified with evil: he no more allows himself to bewail the manifold evils of politics than he indulges himself in a litany of accusations against humanity. If there is political evil, this is because politics exists in a medium that is freedom, the depths of which are unfathomable, and because totalization always involves a risk of perversion. Radical evil exposes a specific pathology which is not, for all that, a hyperbolic incarnation of evil. Kant rejects the alternative of the kingdom of darkness and the kingdom of lightness, of a politics radicalized negatively (made demonic, in a sense) or a politics which, by speaking the language of theodicy, would presume to be the embodiment of promise and expectation. By so doing, Kant attaches politics to a principle of the discernment of evil while maintaining an irreducible distance between what is and what should be. Radical evil places politics on a path which leads from the enigma of the origin to the relative non-determination of the end. Yet this is a journey to be undertaken rather than a destination that has been reached. So politics is not declared to be 'evil', for its pathology is rooted in an evil more unfathomable than the corruption of power: freedom's evil. The evil of freedom could also be called the evil of living together, the radical evil of politics, more 'original' in its unspeakable banality than the evils of power and oppression. There is no form of rational government that could ever overcome this paradoxical 'truth' of politics – neither political nor moral despotism. So the question of radical evil is not unrelated to a certain 'political style' in Kantian philosophy. If the propensity for evil partakes of the essence of human liberty – thereby preceding any determined act – then every beginning may be said to be 'terrible', terrifying and admirable, unforgettable and incapable of being expunged. The greatness of the act of freedom is terrifying in itself because it points to a beginning that is absolutely enigmatic. When Kant moves on to question the very concept of a project, just as he questioned that of a foundation, he finds that it involves the same non-determination and the same non-coincidence of what is established with that which established it: how could something absolutely straight be made out of wood with a curved grain?

This political style, which is buttressed by the argument on radical evil and reveals a kind of insurpassable 'inbetween', a 'vertiginous' aspect to the political entity that cannot be reabsorbed by any artificial construction, is not without its affinities with one of the inaugural moments in the history of philosophy and political philosophy, with the work of a thinker who viewed politics as no more than an infinite elaboration of living together and who avoided resorting to the authority of the concept in order to provide a 'philosophical' over-justification for this lived reality. A thinker for whom the reasonable institutions of the human 'political animal' could not exclude the threat of tragic excess. For to place these two aspects of Aristotelian thought – that of the *Politics* and that of the *Poetics* – alongside one another is to reveal how the human 'political animal endowed with the *logos*' is rooted in the murky depths of the *deînon* that no kind of rational construction can exhaust. What Aristotle offers up for consideration is the originary pathology of the political, which might be called the *abyss of sociality in the constitution of life together*.

Translated by Oliver Davis

Notes

1 Kant, *Religion Within the Boundaries of Mere Reason*, tr. Allen Wood and George di Giovanni (Cambridge: Cambridge University Press, 1998), pp. 46–7.
2 Ibid., p. 60.
3 Arendt, *Eichmann in Jerusalem. A Report on the Banality of Evil* (London: Faber and Faber, 1963), pp. 87–8.
4 Romans III:23.
5 Kant, *Religion*, p. 50.
6 In *The Question of German Guilt* (tr. by E.B. Ashton, New York, Capricorn, 1961), Jaspers' term for this co-responsibility which binds human beings because they are human is 'metaphysical guilt'. Yet this notion does not involve the ascription of guilt either to an individual *stricto sensu* (for this is the role of criminal or moral guilt) or to a group or collectivity. Responsibility by belonging is not this vague and uncertain notion of collective guilt which always tends to blur the distinctions between crimes of varying degrees of seriousness. Yet according to Jaspers' notion, all humanity is implicated by virtue of the same demand for universality familiar from Kantian rigorism. And responsibility by belonging acknowledges this same demand.
7 Arendt, *Eichmann in Jerusalem*, pp. 87–8.
8 See *Eichmann in Jerusalem*.
9 Ibid., p. 120.
10 Ibid., p. 121.
11 Raul Hilberg, *The Destruction of the European Jews*, (London: Holmes & Meier, 1985), abridged edition, pp. 131–2.
12 Ibid., p. 137.
13 Ibid., p. 275.
14 Kant, 'On the common saying: That may be correct in theory, but it is of no use in practice',

The Cambridge Edition of the Works of Immanuel Kant, Practical Philosophy, tr. & ed. by Mary J. Gregor (Cambridge: Cambridge University Press, 1996), p. 303.

15 Describing the system he calls 'post-totalitarian', Vaclav Havel writes that it is as though it were 'taken in by its own lies' and thereby destined to persist in the falsification of being. The rape of reality by ideology makes the 'post-totalitarian' world a kingdom of the *generalized lie*. Its characteristic practices (of both knowledge and power) are practices of falsification which function such that all without exception become implicated, regardless of their position in the hierarchy. This involvement of each person (in proportion, of course, to their power of action) thus contributes to the formation of the general norm. It is in the name of an ethic of veracity that Havel analyses in these terms what he maintains is a fundamental constituent of *political entropy*. It would be wrong to see in this a confusion between the ethical and the political. Nor is it even an attempt to restore the ethical dimension. Rather, Havel's is an attempt to articulate the effects of ideological ritualization and to describe the modes of subjectivization or elaboration of a relationship with the self. *Politics and Conscience* (Stockholm: Charter 77 Foundation, 1986).

16 Kant, *Religion*, p. 64.

17 Arendt, 'Compréhension et politique', in a special edition of the French journal *Esprit* from 1980 devoted to Hannah Arendt.

18 Arendt, Letter to Scholem.

19 Primo Levi, 'Afterword', *If This Is A Man* (London: Abacus, 1987), tr. by Stuart Woolf.

20 On the power of punishment and pardon to unproot those concerned from an irreversible situation in which they cannot undo what they have done, see Hannah Arendt's impressive analysis in *The Human Condition*.

21 Kant never wrote a theodicy but he did write an essay entitled 'On the miscarriage of all philosophical trials in theodicy' (1791). We shall see later that a certain understanding of 'radical evil' enables us, in line with the critique of speculative theology, to make sense of the distinction between the *a-theistic* and the *a-theological*.

22 I must acknowledge here my indebtedness to Paul Ricoeur's analysis in *The Conflict of Interpretations. Essays in Hermeneutics* (Evanston: Northwestern University Press, 1974). Ricoeur insists on several occasions on the fact that the theme of radical evil concerns not only the *Analytic*, that is 'the regressive demonstration of the formal principle of morality', but also the *Dialectic*, that is 'the agreement and reconciliation between reason and nature'. It is on account of this in particular that the *Essay on Radical Evil* marks a departure from mere formalism. The requirement for totality or totalization (which is a feature of the *Dialectic*) places us in an altogether different realm from that of 'What ought I to do?'. It implies the hope of a 'fulfilment' in which the promise becomes inextricably bound up with alienation.

23 'Common sense' is not only the precondition of all judgments of taste but is also a necessary condition of knowledge and moral action.

24 Ricoeur, 'The Demythization of Accusation', *The Conflict of Interpretations* (tr. by Peter McCormick), op. cit., 335–53, p. 345.

25 In particular in the third part of *Religion*: 'The sublime, never fully attainable idea of an ethical community is greatly scaled down under human hands, namely to an institution which, at best capable of representing with purity only the form of such a community, with respect to the means for establishing a whole of this kind is greatly restricted under the conditions of sensuous human nature. But how could one expect to construct something completely straight from such crooked wood?' (p. 111).

26 Kant, *Religion*, p. 107.

27 *The Conflict of the Faculties* (1798), in *The Cambridge Edition of the Works of Immanuel Kant, Religion and Rational Theology* (Cambridge: Cambridge University Press, 1996), tr. by Mary J. Gregor and Robert Anchor, p. 302. It may be worth noting that Arendt derives support from this text – and from the privilege it accords to spectators who are not involved in the action and are accordingly able to discern a meaning in the course of events which is beyond the partial and partisan perspective of the agent – using it as the basis of her reading of the

faculty of judgment. Her aim in so doing is to establish the *political* significance of judgment, a faculty which, rather than being exercised by a self in isolation, constitutes the public domain which, in turn, determines the meaning of the particular event. Yet it will be apparent that the question of evil is conspicuously absent from this reading, as is the theme of the tragic partiality of action.

28 Arendt, *The Origins of Totalitarianism* (London: Allen & Unwin, Revised Edition 1967), p. 443.

29 *Droit naturel et histoire* (Paris: Flammarion, 1986), p. 235. Strauss's position consists in the attempt to discern in the entirety of modern political philosophy the seeds of a form of historicism that tends towards the abolition of the distinction between what is and what should be, the real and the ideal. Historicism renders bankrupt the idea of a natural law based on a transhistorical standard of the just and the unjust and thereby places once more in question the very possibility of thinking in terms of the just and the unjust. According to Strauss, the first phase of modern political philosophy involves the reduction of the political problem to a technical problem, which paves the way for a philosophy of history centred around the 'ruse of reason' and a reversal of the relation between ethics and politics. As opposed to classical political philosophy, in which the question of the 'best regime' is posed in relation to a normative Nature, modern political philosophy abandons the representation of an order of ends and replaces it with a non-teleological conception of the natural. In such conditions, the initial nature of the human being consists in not having a 'nature'. The human being is 'by nature' a sub-human being capable of becoming either good or evil. From this fundamental state of non-determination comes the 'modern' idea of a kind of freedom that is not justified by reference to something higher than the individual or simply than the human being *qua* human being. My concern here is not with the plausibility of Strauss's wholesale interpretation of German Idealism as reliant upon historicism but rather to demonstrate that the idea of radical evil in its relation to the enigma of freedom runs counter to the reduction of the moral and political problem to a technical one and to show that it forbids any radicalization of action on the basis of a 'natural' human being assumed to be both pre-human and pre-moral.

26

NICOLE LORAUX

Nicole Loraux (1943–2003) was retired Chair of the Department of History and Anthropology of the Greek Polis at the EHESS (École des Hautes Études en Sciences Sociales) in Paris. Previously she taught in the University of Strasbourg, and was later attached to the CNRS as a Scientific Advisor. She was a member and then President of the Commission 'Sciences de l'homme et de la société' of the CNL (Centre National du Livre), as well as Professor at Cornell University. Her work took her into the fields of history, politics, myth, literature, psychology, anthropology and philosophy to an extent that is considerably less common in Anglo-Saxon classical studies.

Her works, almost all of which have been translated into English, include the following:

L'Invention d'Athènes: histoire de l'oraison funèbre dans la cité classique, Paris: Mouton, 1981.

Les Enfants d'Athéna: idées athéniennes sur la citoyenneté et la division des sexes, Paris: Maspéro, 1981.

Façons tragiques de tuer une femme, Paris: Hachette, 1985.

Les Expériences de Tirésias: le féminin et l'homme grec, Paris: Gallimard, 1989.

Les Mères en deuil, Paris: Seuil, 1990.

Né de la terre: mythe et politique à Athènes, Paris: Seuil, 1996.

La Cité divisée: l'oubli dans la mémoire d'Athènes, Paris: Payot, 1997.

La Voix endeuillée: essai sur la tragédie grecque, Paris: Gallimard, 1999.

La Grèce au féminin (ed. N. Loraux), Paris: Les Belles Lettres, 2003.

THE ATHENIAN NAME

Imaginary structures of lineage in Athens

> It is no meager proof of the dignity of Attic history that a single
> feminine figure appears there – a single one, but she dominates it from
> one end to the other: the Virgin of the Acropolis.[1]
>
> Wilamowitz-Moellendorff

To be born Athenian: this requirement is the only condition that defines the citizen of
Athens. There is no route to becoming Athenian other than being Athenian already.[2]
Undoubtedly this version, the Athenian version, is one of many; it is one variant of a
definition that was shared by much of ancient Greece.[3] But no Greek city had formulated
it to such a radical extent as did the democratic *polis*.[4] Because of the city's refusal of all
intermediary categories and degrees of citizenship, the democracy established the same
status for all its members. One point can never be too strongly emphasized: to provide
democracy – a political model but also a luxury – Athens had to keep a strict watch, so
that it could preserve the security of the civic body, tightly closed in on itself. Birth is a
better criterion for exclusion than any other condition, and when the Athenian orators
deduce "the political equality established by law" from "the equality of origin established
by nature,"[5] the historian can hardly resist the temptation just to reverse the order of these
propositions. Reversing the order, however, would bring us only as far as the halfway
mark – and would cover just the easier half. Indeed, if it matters to the historian to
understand how the Athenians could think about citizenship in these terms, it is necessary
to restore the Athenian method of reasoning, to allow the city to speak for itself, even if
in a restricted fashion.

Leave it to the philosophers to define the citizen by the power he wields.[6] In the
polis, only the crucial equivalence between citizenship and birth has the right to define
the city. If we were to give these conclusions their Aristotelian formulation, we would
say that "the citizen is defined by practice as the man who is born from two citizen
parents and not from one, whether father or mother."[7] This "quick and civic" definition,
to use Aristotle's own words, does not function perfectly smoothly, when we realize what
happens when we try to go all the way back to origins. The philosopher notes with irony
that from this perspective there is no response to the question: "And how can an ancestor
three or four times removed still be a citizen?" Indeed, he says, "the definition of the
citizen as one who is born from a male citizen [and] a female citizen could not be applied

to the first inhabitants or founders of a city." Must the language of birth always be lost in the shift backward to the period of origins? Probably. No doubt this subject was always perplexing for the philosophical *logos*. Yet in the interest of the city, there is a language for discussing the subject of origins in which the family is used as a metaphor for the *polis*,[8] and lineage is a way of referring to the fatherland. We have already noted the myth or group of myths by which a community assures itself of its own identity and immediately recognizes itself.

Myths about the origin of Athens – and the imaginary in the Athenian city.

Let us begin with a series of myths: the stories that explain the name the city, which the Athenians simply derived from that of Athena, without any other form of trial.[9] One story claims that the goddess gave her name to the city as the outcome of the conflict with Poseidon over the possession of Attica, a conflict settled by the Athenians themselves – or by Kekrops, the primordial king – in Athena's favor. One version of this story is of particular interest: in this account, it is the women who sway the decision by voting for Athena, while the men choose Poseidon; there is always one more woman than there are men, and this day is no exception. Thus, leading by one feminine vote, Athena wins the title of civic goddess.[10] Yet another account claims that Erichthonios, the autochthon born from the Athenian soil and "raised up" by Athena, named the city after the goddess.[11]

The women on one side, Erichthonios on the other. The women, deprived of all their power in the historic city; and the myth informs us of their former power only to take it away from them again forever, on the very day of their victory. Erichthonios, the autochthonous hero, founding king of the *polis*, thanks to whom the present life of the city inherits an uninterrupted past from time immemorial. Either Erichthonios or a legitimacy already long established; the women vanquished in their victory,[12] and deprived of their names – the ones they formerly transmitted to their children and, above all, their title "Athenian women," although they had in fact helped invent it. ("What is an Athenian woman?" To the great satisfaction of Wilamowitz-Moellendorff and others, the myth responds: "She does not exist.")

Erichthonios, the women: at the heart of this asymmetry, caught between dispossessed citizen-women and the happy inventor of politics, is the name of Athens.

Most importantly, there is Athena, united by close links both to the autochthonous Athenian and to the "race of women" through the intermediary of their ancestor, Pandora. As a civic divinity, Athena protects the royal infant born from Attic soil; as the goddess of *mētis*, or ingenuity, she adjusts the seductive finery of the first woman and initiates her into the craft of weaving.[13] Yet it is not insignificant for us that the first Athenian and the first woman, an apparently asymmetrical couple, occupy the same place on the Acropolis in Athens, at the feet of the goddess and under her protection. Pausanias, describing the chryselephantine statue of Athena Parthenos, observes after just a single glance that there is a snake at her feet, who "would be Erichthonios,"[14] and that "sculpted on the base of the statue is the birth of Pandora . . . the first woman, because before her birth . . . the race of women did not exist."[15] The presence of Erichthonios is hardly surprising on the sacred hill, where the festival of the Panathenaea periodically celebrated his birth. But Pandora's presence seems astonishing at first. Indeed, there appears to be an irreducible distance between the woman, that artifice, that product of artisanal craft, and the autochthon, rooted in the soil that brought him into the world. Moreover, the first woman certainly founds a whole *genos*, but belongs to no city; no other Greek *polis* besides Athens, at any rate, seems to have tried to claim her for its own. To justify Pandora's presence on the Acropolis, scholars have generally looked for some clue that relates her "birth" to that of Erichthonios, and for some factor that might make her naturally Athenian. It is not too difficult to show that one divine couple, Athena and Hephaistos, link these two unusual births, and that by installing Erichthonios and Pandora at the feet of the goddess, Pheidias meant to illustrate the solidarity between the Artisan and the Parthenos, which was a particularly strict bond in Athens.[16] Identifying Pandora as a specifically Athenian figure is a more complicated matter: is she a woman-artifice or a mother-goddess?[17] If she is inserted into the royal genealogy of Athens, which link of the chain is she attached to: Kekrops or Erechtheus?[18] I will not enter into these unresolvable debates, because what is at stake is not Pandora alone (who is brought in, not in a personal capacity but in her role as the ancestor of womankind), but rather *Pandora and Erichthonios* – the couple, whether well or badly matched, that declares the Athenian asymmetry between citizens, *andres Athēnaioi*, and "women".

Athenians, women: the *dēmos Athēnaiōn*, which is the city, and the *genos gynaikōn*, a fantasy that Attic tragedy willingly borrows from Hesiod. Our aim in taking this asymmetry as our object of interest – an asymmetry inscribed in the myths of Origin as it is in the religious space of the city – is to try to dislodge the question that is always asked about "the status of the women of Athens" from the legalistic and sociological quagmire that periodically swallows it.[19] If the opposition between masculine and feminine formed the structure of Athenian society, and if the democratic city really tried to supply a primarily political interpretation to explain the division between the sexes, then it was up to myth to furnish the guarantee of immortality for this unequal arrangement. It is an imaginative operation, and a civic one. But that is not all: the civic imaginary sets up the figure of Athena between a belief in autochthony, that founding myth of the city of men, and the necessary integration of women into the *polis*, and it places her between the celebration of the ancestor Erichthonios and the installation of the first woman on the Acropolis. The eponym for Athens, virgin goddess and motherless daughter of the father of the gods and men – who could be better than she to confer her unity on the mythic complex that is the basis of Athenian orthodoxy in matters of birth and citizenship?

Once again: female Athenians simply do not exist

> Attikos, -e, -on: *"from Athens," a secondary adjective related to* Athenai. *In principle, it applies to things (drachmas, ships): rarely to people, and more to women than to men. The name for a citizen of Athens is* Athenaios. Attikos *is used with an expressive or humorous intent.*[20]
>
> P. Chantraine

Athēnaios: the name of the citizen of Athens reveals the closeness of the tie that derives the name of the city from that of the goddess, as Plato emphasizes in the *Laws* with half-serious, half-ironic force.[21] On the other hand – the facts of language agreeing with mythic discourse in this case – the word for "female Athenian" does not exist.

A "female Athenian" would have to be called an *Athēnaia*, to conform to the system of the Greek language regarding ethnic categories.[22] Yet this word is not said: there are no female Athenians; there are only "women of Athens," *Attikai gynaikes*. Less lucky than the Corinthian or Lacedaemonian woman, who are entitled to be called *Korinthia* or *Lakaina*,[23] the woman of Athens is immediately characterized by the idea that she belongs to something other than herself – to the city, of course but by a kind of relay she also belongs to a citizen, within the framework of legitimate marriage.[24] These women are not just "women of Athens." They are women of *Athenians*. Conscious of this problem, ancient commentators invariably explain it as the crucial need to avoid a scandal – the scandal of applying the same name to married women and to the virgin goddess, who was sometimes called Athenaia.[25] The linguists record this phenomenon, observing that "in general, *-ikos* describes slaves or people who do not have the status of citizens."[26] Readers of myths are no longer surprised that there is no Athenian name for the first woman: if there are no female Athenians, there is certainly no first female Athenian, and Pandora slips naturally into that empty place. As for the historians, they are inclined to locate a social reality lurking behind this linguistic fact: the subordination of women, which they find much more severe in the democratic city than in the Spartan *polis* or in the aristocratic cities of Crete.

To reassure ourselves that this business of words really concerns one of the essential structures of Athenian society, we must wander a little, to make a detour by way of Aristophanes' "plays about women," which seem to take a great interest in the female element of the city. This does not mean that we should look in comedy for direct testimony about social reality in Athens, as people too often believe. Yet since the woman is an effective source of laughter, especially when she dares to stray out of her normal role, the comic stage is a precious reserve of glimpses into the Athenian imagination about the division between the sexes.

There are no "female Athenians" in Aristophanes, a playwright who never contradicts the principles of the Attic language in any way, even when he wants to make his audience laugh.[27] Our first surprise however, is that we find scarcely any mention of *Attikai gynaikes* either.[28] There is one play, the *Thesmophoriazousae*, in which we would expect the women of Athens to be called by this name, at least, because participation in the Thesmophoria is limited to the legitimate wives of citizens, and because the women hold an institutional assembly[29] during this civic festival that undoubtedly qualifies as political.[30] In fact, in Aristophanes' comedy, the women establish themselves as a people (*dēmos*) during the hiatus in masculine political power. Yet they do not establish the "people of female Athenians,"[31] or even the "people of the women of Athens,"[32] as a counterpart to the *dēmos* of Athenian men. Instead, they choose to set up the *people of women*, as if every intrusion of women into the political universe had to be offset by a reminder about their connection to a particular sex – the "other" sex.[33] The asymmetry of Erichthonios and Pandora thus takes a new shape: although the women can certainly appropriate the term *dēmos* for themselves, they still cannot call themselves "Athenians." We will further note that the word *dēmos*, when applied to women, is not a very stable term; it is constantly under threat of competition or even actual substitution by the word *genos*, which effectively takes over during the course of the play. The "race of women" – the female species or sex – supplants the "people of women" in the parabasis of the play.[34] It is distinctly as women that the "female Athenians" participate in politics, and it is as women that they conform to the civic model. In the parabasis of the *Thesmophoriazousae*, as in the *Lysistrata*, they conclude by reminding the audience of their procreative function: "We other women have the right to address just reproaches to the men, and one of these is enormous. It should be that if one of us gives birth to a man who is useful to the city, a naval or military commander, she should be honored."[35] But the point is precisely that the city is asking them to do nothing more than keep to their places as women, bearing children who will carry on their fathers' names. Here, the comic stage opens on a civic space where the mother acquires a legal and political status, but only indirectly, by virtue of her role as the wife and bearer of citizens.[36]

With its Periclean law on citizenship, which dates from Athens does indeed seem to make space for maternal lineage by defining the citizen as one who is "born from two citizens" (ἐξ ἀμφοῖν ἀστοῖν).[37] But in fact there is no such thing as a "female citizen," any more than is a "female Athenian."[38] Thus, the Athenian citizen could just as easily be defined as a man who has nothing but citizen fathers on both sides: his own father, and his mother's father . . . Of course, in periods of distress when it was convenient to present Athens as one large family in order to strengthen the solidarity of the city,[39] the Athenians could return to the ideology of a twofold lineage and try to bring the parental couple back into a kind of equilibrium. For example, take the speech that in 403, after the defeat of the Thirty at the Battle of Mounychia, the spokesman for the democrats addresses to both parties on the subject of *koinōnia*, or community: here is a solemn exhortation "in the name of the gods of our fathers and our mothers" (*theoi patrōioi kai metrōioi*), but it is clear that the orator is simply trying to pile up everything that could help cement the community, since he attaches "the relations of lineage, alliance, and friendship" to his reference to the gods.[40] And we will not stake too much on the momentary and circumstantial equality that is established between father and mother just for an instant of rhetorical eloquence.

Despite this insistence on the implications of the Periclean law, we do not want to assign it too much importance: in fifth-century Athens, there is no "clearly defined matrimonial institution, but rather different types of union, and the democratic city strives to favor one form to the exclusion of the others."[41] Athenian law on matters of filiation is fraught with various tensions and certainly forms nothing like a monolithic corpus. Yet at the heart of the laws about lineage, it certainly looks as if only the Periclean law supplied this system of representations with a model of orthodoxy for thinking about Athenian birth: Periclean law, in which *astē* is merely the name given to the married woman who is the daughter of a citizen.[42] It is a model of orthodoxy that is constantly eclipsed by radical fantasies, which certainly reach beyond the realm of actual law. From these fantasies comes the "dream of a purely paternal descent," a dream that makes itself autonomous and forsakes the field of legal thought to invade the civic imaginary and its ideas about reproduction, but not without calling myth to its rescue. Take, for example, the *Eumenides*: denying the mother the reality of childbearing and the title of *tokeus* (parent), Apollo consolidates both aspects of generation, masculine and feminine, in the father. "The woman you call the mother of the child is not the parent: she is merely the nurse of the seed that was sown inside her. The man who makes her fertile is the parent; she, like a stranger, protects the young shoot."[43] A celebrated text, bearing the mark of extremism – that of Apollo Patroos, and perhaps of tragic discourse as well. But this excess is contradicted by the complexity of Athenian law. Indeed, if the mother is truly of so little importance, and if all that counts is paternal lineage, how can we explain the existence of an Athenian law prohibiting all unions between children born from the same mother, but from different fathers?[44] It is true that the imaginary does not trouble itself with the subtleties that shape reality, in law as in other fields. To put it more precisely: when it becomes necessary to be selective in thinking about identity, the imaginary knows how to make its own choices, even at the heart of contradictory reality.

It would seem that generalized autochthony, which the Athenian *andres* collectively attribute to themselves in the civic tradition,[45] must remain beyond the reach of the patrilineal extremism characteristic of tragedy. If they are born from Attic soil, which, if we are to believe Plato, is "both their earth and their mother," are the *andres* not all "brothers, children of the same mother"?[46] Yet if we read the funeral orations, the official speeches that constantly proclaim the Orthodox representation of collective autochthony, we notice that Plato's version is an isolated if not a polemical one with respect to the dominant tradition. Indeed, the Attic earth is never only a "mother" in the funeral orations, but, through a return in full force of the paternal signifier, it is always both "mother and father" (*mētēr kai patris*: mother and earth of fathers). This juxtaposition alone[47] would be enough to prove that sexual reproduction and the image of the parental couple displace all representations of Mother Earth in civic discourse. But there is more: it does not seem possible to stop halfway in the process of neutralizing the feminine principle. Given the uses certain orators make of autochthony, we glimpse the dream of an Athens where women are totally excluded. To affirm, like Demosthenes, that every Athenian inherits a twofold succession – an individual one from his father, and a collective one from his fatherland – is just to intensify the expression of paternity right in the heart of the parental model. Most of all, this assertion forces the woman's role in the city into question again by denying her all utility, even existence itself: there are no more mothers, and women return to silence.[48] Using different and much more subtle means, Pericles is perhaps following an analogous process in the *epitaphios* he gives in Thucydides. Addressing himself to bereaved families, Pericles separates the close relations of the dead into three groups: parents, sons and brothers, and widows.[49] It might be said that the mothers are part of the first group, and that the exhortation to bear more children is addressed to them.[50] Perhaps that is true. But a closer look at the text makes us much less certain: Pericles justifies this invitation to procreation by mentioning the impossibility of someone "intervening in the deliberations (*bouleuesthai*) on an equal footing and in an equitable fashion, when one has no children to risk in the general danger."[51] Is he really still concerned with the mothers, who, as women, are excluded by definition from taking part "on an equal footing" in all deliberations?[52] We must yield to the evidence: in the passage dedicated to the parental couple, the father takes the upper hand once again.

If we look carefully at the collective representation of autochthony, we will not be surprised when, through a conflation of birth and citizenship, the Athenians are declared "legitimate citizen-sons of the fatherland."[53] If in the civic imaginary the fatherland is self-reproducing, what place remains for women, whose role is negated in just that sphere of fertility to which the city, in practice, confines them?

All the examples of the city's imaginary thus coincide, tendentiously whittling down the place made for women in the *polis*: the language denies them a name, the institutions restrict them to their maternal role, and the official representations seem to try to deprive them of everything, including their status as mothers.

It is true that the significance of the Athenian myth of autochthony often overflows into the secular prose of the funeral oration, and we might sometimes fear that it will become impoverished or altogether consumed in this context. Yet if we settle ourselves into the heart of the myth of Erichthonios – as it is celebrated in the Panathenaea, described by the tragic poets, or illustrated by the vase-painters – we will surely find much more in it than just an insistence on the predominance of the father. Erichthonios certainly has a "father," Hephaistos, but he also has a "mother," the earth, and a "nurse," Athena: a rich parentage, but a complex and unstable one, since, among the roles of the three protagonists in the story, certain permutations begin to appear.[54] It is a parentage, above all, in which the "father" generates the child but then has no part in giving him a name. Indeed, this point is proven by the meager way in which the Athenians decided to appropriate the title "sons of Hephaistos" for themselves. We might in fact expect such a name for the citizens, which would grant Hephaistos his place in the city's quasi-official reserve of appellations, a store the poets dipped into freely. In all of Athenian literature, however it seems that this title arises only once, at the beginning of the *Eumenides*.[55] And such an expression can be explained strictly from the perspective of this tragedy, which is dedicated to celebrating the glory of patrilineal filiation.

We must still face the task of clarifying this strange story – the birth of the first Athenian

Mythic births

She [Athena] *constantly refuses natural maternity.*[56]

J. E. Harrison

The birth of Erichthonios is a strange story, the result of a dynamic contest between sexual reproduction and autochthony. It begins like a mythological love story, with the masculine desire that inflames Hephaistos and the flight of the *parthenos* Athena.[57] What follows could be told, as in Ovid, in the style of a metamorphosis.[58] But Athena is no startled nymph, and although she could certainly bring about a metamorphosis, the goddess prefers to save her *mētis* for other circumstances. With her fierce virginity, the *parthenos* succeeds in escaping violation, and it is the earth, made fertile by the sperm of the god, that brings forth Erichthonios into the light of the Attic sky.

It is a complicated affair, and ancients and moderns alike have generally tried to isolate a primitive nucleus within it – either the engendering of the primordial king by Mother Earth or the ultimately trite adventure of a pair of gods. The inventions of poets or the requirements of national honor are supposed to have masked this earlier portion by inserting it afterward into another context. But we must accept that both the earth and the gods play their role in this story, an account that does not simply consist of concealing an original plot that was abandoned in favor of a degraded version of the myth. The autochthonous birth of Erichthonios is no later addition, meant to save Athena's virginity,[59] or to circumvent the scandal of an incestuous conception.[60] In order to understand the significance of the myth of origins – rather than trying to make it into a thematic addition – we must ask what kind of benefit accrues to a city of men, whose dream is to reproduce themselves, by entrusting the civic earth with the task of avoiding all sexual union, *in extremis*. Athena, whom the entire tradition, without exception, credits with an intimate link to Erichthonios, is not introduced afterward into an "Ouranian legend" in which a god – Hephaistos in this case – inseminates the earth.[61] And Hephaistos does not pursue the goddess with the sole intention of introducing a father into what would otherwise have been a parthenogenetic birth achieved by the earth alone.

On the other hand, it is worth inquiring about the value of having Hephaistos and Athena more or less occupy the place of a parental couple.[62] "Parents" they may be, but they never mate, and were themselves born outside the confines of sexuality either from a solitary Hera without Zeus or from a solitary Zeus without Hera. Are they "parents"? Indeed they are, but without the help of Ge, they could not have been: a virgin who steadfastly refuses Aphrodite, and consecrates herself instead to war and *technē* (craft),[63] and a "phallic" god, as they say, although his role in sexual union is not self-evident,[64] since he is doomed to fail both in his desire for Athena and in his marriage to Aphrodite. We might add, perhaps, that the parents of this child, who springs from the earth to become the inventor of politics, are in fact technicians. There are artisans, then, at the origins of an autochthonous city that prides itself on being rooted in the earth, but mobilizes all the *topoi* of its official discourses precisely in order to repress *technē*.[65]

Is *technē* behind the origin of Athens?[66] Is the myth telling the truth about the democratic city, in which the actual importance of artisanal skill is equaled only by the unprecedented scale of the attempt to disengage a kind of pure politics from all collusion with "work"?[67] One more step, and the Athenian myth of autochthony would become a privileged version of the Greek paradox of the artisan.[68] But should we really take such a step? If the issue simply concerns putting *physis* (nature) over *technē*, the gain is small; that is, if we disregard Ge's truly productive role in this affair, we also reduce the irreducible difference between Erichthonios and Pandora, between the son of the soil and the artifice named woman. Yet nothing entitles us to make this move, neither the official discourses, in which autochthony is primarily a matter of noble birth, nor the figural representations, which clearly know how to distinguish between the fabrication of Pandora and the emergence of Erichthonios.[69] Although they are united in a common *philotechnia* when they create the first woman,[70] Hephaistos and Athena form an impossible couple when it comes to real generation, a couple divided every step of the way, beginning with the sterility of the artisan, who must depend on Gaia or Earth for a borrowed fertility. Thus, we must still ask whether it is in their artisanal roles that

Athena and Hephaistos really intervene in the myth of autochthony.[71] The response to this question is not a simple one, nor is the very Athenian association of the blacksmith-god with the virgin goddess a simple affair, since Athenian religion separates the two gods on the Acropolis and reunites them in the Hephaisteion.[72] But we can be certain of at least one point: Erichthonios is born on the Acropolis, and on the Acropolis one power triumphs over all others – the political power of the Parthenos, protector of the city. This, of course, does not permit us to concoct a kind of radical separation between the two spheres, since there is constant interference between them in Athens, between Athena's political domain and the world of her *mētis*, which she shares with Hephaistos: the skill of the Ergane (the Worker) and the power of the Polias.[73] There is a place for *technē* on the Acropolis, just as there is, conversely, a place for Erichthonios in the Hephaisteion.[74] How could the Athenians have possibly thought about autochthony without referring to such religious facts? But for us the essential principle is that there are orders of precedence among powerful forces, and in this case the place of Athena Polias is incontestable – as prominent on the Acropolis as it is in the myth of autochthony, both in words and in images.[75]

Which brings us back to Athenian birth.

Doubtless it was to be the task of philosophy – and more precisely, the task of a philosopher named Plato – to contest this hierarchy by establishing a strict balance between *physis* and *technē* at the origin of Athens.[76] All that matters here, however, is the daily life of civic Athens; from day to day, in the festivals and celebrations, the birth of the first Athenian speaks the language of "nature" to the city of Athens.

And yet we are not finished with the ambiguities of physis. Indeed, in the birth of the child who would become the first truly human Athenian, where is human *physis*?

Ge, Hephaistos, Athena . . . Right from the start, Earth, by producing the child, dispossesses all the Athenian mothers: this point has already been made, and there is no need to return to it here. As for Hephaistos and Athena – a couple as utterly inseparable as it is disunited – they verify by their own parentage that there was a time when it was possible to be born from one parent and not from two.[77] Does their participation in the birth of Erichthonios, whether direct or involuntary (it matters little), mean that miraculous births necessarily inspire other, similarly miraculous births? It is worth taking some trouble to look more closely at this mythical law, which challenges the human law of generation.

* * *

Although the history of foundation told in the *Eumenides* may be a mythical one, let us leave history aside and return to the myth of Erichthonios, which takes place well before all historical time. The myth of origins has nothing to do with accommodating reality, and the autochthonous birth of Erichthonios founds the civic community on the basis of an immense denial inflicted on the maternity of women. It is the earth that produces the child, and the earth that is eager, as on Athenian vases, to entrust him to the goddess without a mother, so that she can bring him up and make him into a man. Let us then take yet another step: if Athena's parentage is really a useful model for casting light on this unusual birth, as I believe it is, we must admit that it is the law of the father, discreet but still all-powerful, that presides at this founding event.

There is an Athenian vase that quietly says it all. On the London hydria,[78] there is no Hephaistos and no Kekrops to attend the scene. The progenitor is forgotten, the inventor of marriage and his hybrid, man-snake body have vanished; there are no extras on the set in this moment that the painter wanted to solemnize, as confirmed by the presence of Nike (Victory) behind Athena. Here, the goddess is in full warrior regalia, the austere Promachos, or champion, and as such receives the child Ge holds out to her. Facing her is Zeus, a strange presence, with thunderbolt in hand, in a posture that immediately reminds us of Hephaistos's bearing on other vases.[79] The aim of the painter, no doubt, was to transform the emergence of the first Athenian into a "quasi-Olympian event."[80] Unlike Cook, I will not hasten to seize on this example as an unexpected opportunity to claim that Zeus is the necessary protagonist at the scene; on the contrary, it is the exceptional nature of his presence that makes it interesting.[81] Instead, I prefer to see it as a recognition of the intimate link that ties the birth of Erichthonios to the birth of Athena,[82] and puts the child produced by Ge under the unique authority of the Virgin of Zeus. Apparently, then, an Athenian painter had no trouble placing the birth of Erichthonios under the sign of the father.

Erichthonios's birth is a paradoxical one: maternity is redistributed, and the very idea is in danger of simply exploding altogether; neither Ge nor Athena is really a mother for Erichthonios. Perhaps the only purpose for Hephaistos's physiological paternity is to represent symbolic paternity – a paternity whose spokesperson is Athena. Thus, the dominance of the paternal role, hidden as it may be at the intersection of a series of complex relationships, must in fact be the underpinning for the Athenian reading of the birth of Erichthonios.

One difficulty remains: by thinking about themselves as autochthons and by giving themselves their name, Athenians, the citizens of Athens claim they owe everything to Athena – Athena, who, for better or for worse, is a "woman-goddess," capable of arousing Hephaistos's desire, to the great scandal of her more austere devotees.[83] A "woman-goddess": in this respect, the women of Athens, less defeated than they might seem, might have turned the tables on the men by voting for Athena. If this were the case – in, other words, if the Athenians had conceived of the story in this way – there is a good chance they would not have reveled in their eponymy to such an extent.

Wilamowitz-Moellendorff, the honorary Athenian, helps us out here, establishing the link of strict dependence on the goddess – *Zugehörigkeit zu Athena* – only to note that this feminine figure, the sole female to make her mark on the city's history, was a *parthenos: die Jungfrau von der Berg.*[84] The definition Aristophanes gives Athena in the *Birds* will complete the explanation: Athena as the "woman-goddess armed with every weapon."[85] Aristophanes brings to light the paradox of the *parthenos*, her double deviance from the norm: first, with femininity, which is normally realized through marriage, and second, with respect to war, normally reserved for men, devoting herself to personifying masculine values "with the greatest possible intensity."[86]

Carrying Athena's name: a tautological way for the Athenian to declare citizenship.

The tragic name of Athens

The relationship between Athena and Athens is made clear by the frequent tragic synonym for "Athens": Pallados polis (*the city of Pallas*).[87]

C. J. Herington

If we are to believe Aeschylus, the relationship between the Parthenos and those whom she repeatedly calls *astoi emoi* – "my citizens," or perhaps "my fellow citizens"[88] – is one of reciprocal love.[89] We might have been satisfied, at this point, simply to recognize the peculiar nature of Athena's relationships: more than any other god, this divine figure conducts "personal" relationships with those she favors.[90] Yet we must take into account the insistent way in which Attic tragedy likes to emphasize the blurring of the borders between the goddess and the city.

Athens belongs to Athena, just as the goddess belongs to the city.[91] This association is an accepted fact, and perhaps rightly so. But in the *Eumenides* itself, as if Aeschylus were trying to draw up a chart of all the possible configurations of this relationship, mutual adherence turns into identity. For example, the goddess identifies herself with the *polis*, sliding imperceptibly from the "city" to "myself" in her discourse,[92] and the citizens are introduced as those who sit alongside the goddess;[93] finally, in a remarkable shift of the Polias toward the people she protects, the epithet *polissouchos* ("who holds the city"), normally used to describe the goddess, becomes a name for the Athenian citizens themselves.[94]

Does either one really *belong* to the other? Let us instead call the relationship one of "mediated lineage," a lineage in which the citizens "descend" from the goddess. An origin without reproduction, a filiation outside the confines of all sexuality: Athena alone, in her role as *parthenos*, arrested since her birth, and by her birth, in this state of indeterminacy where femininity is always partly masculine.[95] Athena is all this for the Athenians.

There may be a tragic way of making this point.

From Oedipus, the outcast, who addresses a prayer to the city that welcomes him ("You who take your name from the great Pallas [*megistēs Pallados kaloumenai*]") to the characterization of Athens in the *Ion* ("There is a Greek city, a city not without glory, which takes its name [*keklēmenē*] from Pallas of the Golden Spear") or the declaration made to Athena at the end of the same play ("I, Pallas, the eponymous goddess of this soil [*epōnymos . . . chthonos*], have come"),[96] the tragic writers pretend to derive the name of the city from Pallas, the "other name" of the goddess.[97] This is a strange etymology that, if taken literally, would give Athens the name Pallene.[98] Some scholars are eager to affirm that Pallas and Athena were used "indiscriminately" in Athens,[99] and others justify the substitution on metrical grounds. Yet even if we accept a purely metrical explanation, we must still ask why Sophocles and Euripides did not resort to the form *Athana*, which they do not hesitate to use elsewhere.[100] A discussion of synonymous words just conceals the real problem: no word is gratuitous, especially in a tragic text, and to use one word in place of another is, essentially, to use *another* word.

The entire question, then, takes on a new form: why did Sophocles and Euripides so insistently claim that the name of Athens was derived from Pallas? The positive response is that by using Pallas, they could more easily derive the name of the city from the name of the Young Girl.

If we are to believe Strabo, Pallas is, in fact, this young girl. Linguists, like historians of religion, do not seem to have challenged this information.[101] It is more important to assure ourselves that the fifth-century Athenians were also aware of this linguistic fact – those who called Athena the Parthenos in order to mark her virginity. It is true, however, that they they did not use this name as a cult title,[102] or at least, it is little used in the religious context.[103] Here the problem becomes complicated, and we begin to regret the hazards of textual transmission, since this fragment from Hermippos's comic *Birth of Athena* (*Athēnas gonai*) stops just at the wrong moment: "Zeus: I give you, he said, the name of Pallas . . . " We will never know any more about it than that.[104] On the other hand, in Euripides's *Ion* and in Plato's *Cratylus*, Pallas becomes "she who brandishes" (the lance) or "she who dances."[105] Should we admit defeat? It would be somewhat premature to abandon the game now, since we should not forget that Plato, like the tragic poets, had a taste for wordplay, and, more importantly, we should not forget that even when Athena is a warrior or an armed dancer, she is so first of all because she is a *parthenos*.[106]

For those who are not satisfied with what can be drawn from Euripides' and Plato's linguistic speculations, I should point out that there is a rich collection of mythic material that speaks about adolescence, the relationship with her father, and sexual ambivalence, surrounding the name of Pallas.[107] It is also worth noting that Pallas conducts some sort of relationship with the "young" in the religious practice of Greek cities – with ephebes in Athens,[108] and with virgins in Argos.[109] But most of all, we must look for evidence in Attic tragedy and comedy, which have guided us through the entire sequence so far. Consider the chorus in the *Thesmophoriazousae*, for instance, who sing their praises to "Pallas, the friend of choruses . . . the virgin free from all yokes, the guardian of our city, who alone visibly retains power there and is called the holder of the keys."[110] Here, the women take the *kratos* (power) away from the Athenian people,[111] and give it instead to the goddess with the "virginity of a young, untamed girl,"[112] a role they are delighted to honor, at precisely the same time that they give her the name Pallas. We must cite Euripides's *Ion* again, in which a similar relationship seems to be established between the name Athena – which is mentioned late in the tragedy to indicate the Kourotrophos of Erichthonios, the benevolent protector of the city – and the name Pallas, which tends to be reserved for the sovereign of the Acropolis, the fighter in the war with the Giants, the slayer of Gorgons,[113] and the wearer of the aegis. Finally, we should add that Oedipus at Colonus, reaching the end of his wanderings, certainly had some reason for invoking Athena as the young girl, leaving it henceforth to the divine virgin, assisted by the Eumenides those other *parthenoi*, to take over for human virgins – his daughters, and Antigone most of all – who, as the text insistently reminds us, were the only ones to protect the life of the blind man.[114]

Is this collection of facts enough for us to judge that the Athenians meant "the Young Girl" when they called their goddess Pallas? I will wager that we have ample evidence – after all, Wilamowitz-Moellendorff took fewer precautions and drew the same conclusions![115] And since Sophocles and Euripides shift the eponymy of Athens toward

Pallas, I will credit them with the intention of reminding their audiences that the city draws its name and its existence from a virgin.

Our voyage into the Athenian imaginary opened with Aristotle, and Plato will help us close it. From the Philosopher who was the most resolutely deaf to the seductions of the imaginary, to the Philosopher who was the most open to them.

Let us give the final word to the old Cretan man in the *Laws*. In the beginning of the dialogue, he names the Athenian for the first time: "O stranger of Athens (*Athēnaios*) – since I would not want to call you an inhabitant of Attika (*Attikos*), so much do you seem to me to deserve a name that evokes that of the goddess (*tēs theou epōnymia*) – you have brought us clarity by taking the argument back to its starting principle, as one should."[116] No doubt Plato meant to say that the stranger from Athens was an Athenian worthy of his name in two ways: since the Athenian knows how to introduce clarity into an idea by moving back to its principle (*archē*), he is the disciple of the goddess, who is the *archē* of Athens and the friend of *sophia* (wisdom);[117] and since he is the student of Athena, he deserves to be named *Athēnaios* after the eponymous goddess of the city. But Plato also enjoyed inventing the fictional choice between the two names – *Athēnaios* and *Attikos*. And it is entirely fictional, since there is, in fact, no choice: *Athēnaios* normally means the citizen, while *Attikos* is used in the feminine to characterize the women of Athens in their subordinate position.

This Platonic wordplay brings us back to our original problem: *the Athenian name*. To be more precise, it brings us back to the mythic overdetermination of masculine values in the name of the Athenian citizen.[118]

The Athenians constructed a network of myths around their name.

The city carries the name of Athens. That much is fact. From fact stems action. And thus we have a collection of stories.

In one of these stories, it is the women who named the city, no doubt believing that by voting for a "woman-goddess," their law would triumph. Yet, in electing the *parthenos*, the daughter of Zeus, who is completely dedicated to the law of the father, they lost the name they had just invented. The myth explains why there are no female Athenians.

No female Athenians and no female citizens. Only women. On the Acropolis, the Parthenos welcomes Pandora, an indirect way of politicizing the race of women, which cannot be politicized. Or, to be more precise, the race of women, which the Athenians do not integrate, and have no intention of integrating, into the *polis*.

But on the Acropolis, Pandora is a guest twice over. A guest of Athena, and a guest of Erichthonios, the first Athenian, the symbolic child of the goddess. And the dominant Athenian tradition claims that it was Erichthonios who gave the city its title, with the help of the name Athena, his secret patronym.

From all perspectives Athena's victory discounts the maternity of Athenian women.

It matters little here whether social reality is more complex than myth. Or, rather, it does matter that it should be more complex, so that the name of Athens – that simple piece of evidence – can settle as a core of truth. The myths of origin crystallize around this core, an imaginary version of birth in the service of a city of men.

Notes

1 Wilamowitz-Moellendorff (1893) 2:99–100 (the end of a note about Aspasia). Doubtless, Wilamowitz-Moellendorff must have felt entirely at ease "in this culture of men," as maliciously suggested by Goosseris (1962) 85 (from whom I have borrowed this quotation).

2 This stipulation holds true beginning with the generation that follows the Kleisthenian reforms and lasting until 167–166. See Davies (1977–78).

3 This definition of citizenship is a Greek one, as opposed to the Roman definition, which strove to be more open: cf. *Sylloge*³ 523, a letter from Philip V to the inhabitants of Larissa. Nonetheless, it is not clear that the radical opposition between *politeia* and *civitas* is necessarily immediately pertinent: see Gauthier (1974). Briefly, however, we could say that Greece as a whole did not make any claims to territorial definitions of citizenship, nor did each city grant rights to citizens on a large scale. But Athens valued "birth" more than did any other city and even the Kleisthenian definition of citizenship, which was based on the distribution of men in civic space, was transformed into a definition by birth, beginning with the next generation: see Nilsson (1951) 65.

4 Cf. Austin and Vidal-Naquet (1977) 80 and 94–95, as well as Ehrenberg (1960) 50. On the severity of bans against mixed marriage in Athens, as opposed to the much more flexible practice of the aristocratic cities, see Vernant (1980) 45–70. On the openness of Sparta, which was at least theoretical, see Jeanmaire (1975) 489.

5 Pl. *Menex.* 239a 3–4: *isogonia kata physin / isonomia kata nomon.*

6 Arist. *Pol.* 3.2.1276a4–5 (a summary of 1275a24–33).

7 Arist. *Pol.* 1275b22–34.

8 I am paraphrasing Duby ([1975] 115), on the subject of the family as a "metaphor for *seigneurie*" in the eleventh and twelfth centuries.

9 We will not raise the famous (but to us irrelevant) question of "which one, the goddess or the city, gave its name to the other?" There is a recent bibliography on the subject in Fauth (1964) and Burkert (1985). The only point that is still in question concerns the ways in which the Athenians themselves viewed the problem.

10 Varro, cited by St. Augustine (*City of God* 18.9): *et quia una plus est inventa feminarum, Minerva vincit.*

11 On the group of myths and on the myth of autochthony in particular, see above, "Autochthony: An Athenian Topic."

12 *Ita illa civitas . . . a victo laesa ipsam victoriam punire compulsa est,* claims St. Augustine. The "victory" of the women is an ephemeral one, and there is nothing to give modern scholars the authority to claim that these are the chimerical traces of a "mother right" (*Mutterrecht*) lodged in the text, a right that has since vanished forever, as Bachofen suggested ([1861] §23). It is worth adding that Bachofen, moved by an ardent desire to prove the existence of "mother right," does not take the temporal logic of the myth into account. In the myth, Athena's victory, Poseidon's anger, and the exclusion of women are all integrated into the same temporal sequence, as opposed to the previous era, when men and women participated equally in making decisions. Bachofen ignores the first time period in order to set up an opposition between two different periods – the era of the reign of Athena, in which the women were called Athenians and transmitted their names to their children, and the era of the reign of Poseidon, which would then, for Bachofen, constitute the true break. This way, "mother right" acquires a time period and an existence – but that is not what the myth says.

13 Hes. *Th.* 573–78, *WD* 63–64, 72, and 76, as well as *Hom. Hymn Aph. 14–15. See above, "On the Race of Women,"* 80. *Presiding over the adornment of a* parthenos who is a guileful trap, Athena is *Zōsteria* and *Apatouria*; when she watches over women's work, she is *Ergane.*

14 The snake-Erichthonios: see the Basel lekythos BS 404, published by Schmidt (1968).

15 Paus. 1.24.7. Note that Pausanias does not mention Pandora's presence in any other Greek

city, and there is no indication that Pandora was represented outside Athens. See Brommer (1978) 47.

16   E. B. Harrison (1967) 34. Frequently associated as gods of *mētis* – see Detienne and Vernant (1978) 177–275 – in Athens, Hephaistos and Athena are often associated in this way. Cf. Cook (1940) 3.1:218ff., Delcourt (1957) 191–200, and Brommer (1978) 157–59.

17   Pandora as a mother-goddess: on the complex relations among Pandora and Pandrosos, Ge, and Athena in the Panathenaic sacrifice, see Deubner (1956) 26–27 Since Pausanias discusses her birth (*genesis*), scholars have wanted to infer from this that Pandora is in the *anodos* position: cf. Oldfather (1949). She is represented in *anodos* on Oxford krater 525: see plate in this book and also Bérard (1974) 161–64. But Pausanias characterizes Athena's "birth" on the east pediment of the Parthenon as a *genesis* as well, which has nothing like an *anodos* about it – and basically nothing like a birth, either: cf. E. B. Harrison (1967). In addition, the *anodos* of Ge is always incomplete: Bérard (1974) 26. It is therefore useful to distinguish between Ge and the *anodos* of Pandora, who on the Oxford krater actually is shown in the course of *passage*. If we add that the *anodos* is first and foremost a pictorial convention used to indicate passage (ibid., 24), Pandora's *anodos* must be interpreted as the simple representation of her essential passage – the arrival of the woman, and the arrival of marriage, symbolized by Eros flying above the couple, into the world of men. Pandora as the mother-goddess disappears, at least insofar as the Oxford krater is concerned.

18   Pandora can be confused with Pandrosos, the daughter of Kekrops: see Deubner (1956) 26. On the other hand, Phanodemos, the Atthidographer, gives the name of the first woman to one of the daughters of Erechtheus (*FGrH* 325, F 4). On Pandora in Athens, it is still worth consulting Frazer (1897) 2:319–20.

19   See, e.g., Pomeroy (1976) chap. 4 (with bibliography).

20   Chantraine, s.v. "Attikos."

21   Pl. *Laws* 1.626d.

22   Cf. Chantraine (1956) 105: "the tendency of the language is to formulate a system based on the following type: *Abdēra*, *Abdēritēs* (a citizen from Abdera), *Abdēritis* in the feminine, *Abdēritikos* as the adjective (that which belongs to the person from Abdera)."

23   *Korinthia* and *Lakaina* are terms that describe ethnic origin. Herodotus (3.134) juxtaposes *Lakainas* and *Korinthias* with *Attikas* in a single phrase.

24   See Chantraine (1956) 110–11. On the status of women in marriage, see Vernant (1980) 45–70.

25   See the evidence in Chantraine, ibid.

26   Ibid., 112. *Attikos* is the *ktētikon* that corresponds to the ethnic *Athēniaos* (ibid., 103, 108).

27   Commentators, however, point out several comic uses of the nonexistent word *Athēnaia* to designate a woman from Athens; it is a word invented to inspire laughter, but Aristophanes apparently refused to invent a female form for "Athenian."

28   There is a single example in Ar. *Lys.* 56; even here the phrase is meant to provoke laughter by being "suggestive": Chantraine (1956) 112–13. Athenian women really have no name other than "women," whereas, in the opening scene of the *Lysistrata*, the Corinthian, Lacedaemonian, and Theban women are specified by their ethic names.

29   And not thanks to the device of a masculine disguise, as in Ar. *Eccl.*

30   There is a president, a clerk (374–75, 432), and so on. On the Thesmophoria as a civic festival: recall that the women of Athens celebrated this festival on the Pnyx, while the women of Thasos celebrated it in the building devoted to the phratries. See Detienne (1977) 78 and (1989b) 131–32. On the *Thesmophoriazousae* as a parody of a political assembly, see Haldane (1965) and Detienne (1989b) 138–39.

31   Despite the absence of *Athēnaiai*, there are certainly the *hapax* terms: *Olympiai, Pythiai,* and *Dēliai*, placed next to their masculine forms (the only ones in use), *Olympioi, Pythioi,* and *Dēlioi*, in a passage (331ff.) in which the accumulation of feminine forms, forged together from all the bits and pieces, is intended to have a comic effect (but at the same time emphasizing the impossible existence of a separate category for the feminine).

32 The expression that comes closest to this idea is *Athēnōn eugeneis gynaikes* (328–33). With this phrase the women attribute *eugeneia* to themselves collectively, a quality that the *epitaphioi* declare belongs to autochthons. *Athēnai* and *gynaikes* are still both joined and separate.

33 Ar. *Thesm.* 305–7, 335–36. The same comments apply to the *probouleuma* of the "*boulē* of women" (372–79), to the formula as *gynaikes . . . mellousi . . . ekklēsiazein* (77–84; cf. 90, 277, etc.), and to the heckling from the audience (the discourse is punctuated with *ō gynaikes*, just as we find *ō andres Athēnaioi* in the discourse of Athenian orators: see 384, 455, 531, 551, etc.). From the masculine to the feminine version of these formulas, one element is always left out: the Athenian name.

34 The problem of the "race of women" is implicit in the kinsman's speech (466–519), and reflected in the joke of the chorus leader (531–32), which could easily figure in Stobaeus's *Peri gamou*. The "race of women" dominates the parabasis (785ff.), and the *dēmos* of women makes only one more appearance: 1145–46.

35 Ar. *Thesm.* 830–33. cf. *Lys.* 649–51. In the *Ecclesiazousae*, a fiction that effectively gives the women power, the situation is different, and procreation is not pushed to the forefront (but see 233–34) Still, it is the *ekklēsia* that *gives birth* to a decree.

36 This procedure is clearly the case in all Greek cities, not simply in Athens. The language bears witness to this asymmetry: *patra* means paternal lineage, while the opposite term, *mētra*, which the legal vocabulary "does not need," since "the family is based on paternal lineage," is just a technical term meaning womb: Chantraine (1946–47) 236–39. The language carries other traces of this legal nonexistence of the woman: thus *mētrōios*, "maternal" is not derived from *mētēr* "mother," but from *metrōs*, "brother of the mother" and Latin, which possesses the adjective *patrius*, does not have the corresponding *matrius*: Benveniste (1973) 219–2, and 175–76.

37 The formulation of the law is borrowed from Arist. *Ath. Pol.* 26.4, in which the the grammatical duality seems to require the equality of the two parents. This kind of duality is a constant in all references to the law: see the evidence collected in Broadbent (1968) 167.

38 See Austin and Vidal-Naquet (1977) 186–87, commenting on the text of St. Augustine; see also Vidal-Naquet (1986) 216. The word *astai* (female citizens) is used only once in the work of Aristophanes, in a passage from the *Thesmophoriazousae* (541): here, Euripides' kinsman who finds himself in a delicate situation believes that, faced with the women's withdrawal into their own *genos* (539), he must flatter them in the realm of politics.

39 Cf. Pl. *Menex.* 243e–244a.

40 Xen. *Hell.* 2.4.21.

41 See Vernant (1980) 49.

42 It is also important to note that the dual form avoids all effective recourse to the feminine *astē*: these are the resources of the language, which insists on the equality of the joined partners, but at the same time suppresses the female sex and the possibility of the woman ever being a full Athenian!

43 Aes. *Eum.* 658–61: see Vernant (1985) 164; Zeitlin (1978), especially 167–69; Peretti (1956) 241 (on the reading *keklēmenē* in place of *keklēmenou*, which I have adopted against Mazon in 658). On *tiktein* as a feminine function and *tokeus* in the *Oresteia*, see Chantraine (1946–47) 245–46 and commentary by Demont ([1978] 375 n. 32). Note that medical thought successfully avoided the prestigious mirage of a completely paternal lineage: see Lloyd (1983) 86–94.

44 On the contradiction between the text of the *Eumenides* and the law prohibiting marriage between children of the same mother, see A.R.W. Harrison (1968) 22–23 and Pomeroy (1976) 65–66. There is a bibliography on the law in Broadbent (1968) 153. At the level of the Greek language, we see an analogous phenomenon in the rejection of *phratēr*, which is replaced in the sphere of lineage by *adelphos* cf. Benveniste (1973) 173. In order to respond to this question, which was once posed by Hume, we can now read Lévi-Strauss (1983) 127–40.

45 See, for example, Ar. *Wasps* 1076 and *Lys.* 1082 (in which the term "autochthonous men" is a synonym for "Athenians").

46 Pl. *Menex.* 237e4 and 239a1–2.

47 For example, see Lys. *Epitaph.* 17.

48 Dem. *Epitaph.* 4.

49 Th. 2.44–45.

50 Pomeroy (1976) 66, on Th. 2.44.3.

51 On this notion, see Aymard (1955).

52 Cf. Ar. *Lys.* 507–20, which should be compared to 587–90.

53 Dem. *Epitaph.* 4: γνησίους γόνῳ τῆς ποτρίδος πολίτας ("citizens of the fatherland of legitimate birth"). Compare this meaning to the definition of the legitimate son (γνήσιος) as the father's "son by blood" (γόνῳ γεγονώς); cf. Vernant (1980) 51.

54 See above, "Autochthony: An Athenian Topic," 57–65.

55 Aes. *Eum.* 13. The Athenians held a *lampadephoria* in honor of Hephaistos during the Apatouria, according to Istros, *FGrH* 334, frag. 2. Because of this celebration, Simon (1969) 215, followed by Burkert (1985) 168, holds that the Athenians were honoring Hephaistos as the father of their race. But Istros's text indicates clearly that the god was honored as the *giver of fire* and civilizer, and his presence at the festival of "those who have the same father" does not give us license to neglect the specific mode of intervention attributed to Hephaistos, even if we call *Eum.* 13 to our aid. Therefore, along with Deubner ([1956] 233) and Toepffer ([1894] col. 2678), 1 think we should read nothing into Istros aside from what is said there.

56 J. E. Harrison (1908) 300.

57 On the young girl as the favorite object of desire and attempted rape, see Calame (1977) 1:65, 139, 256.

58 See Dupont (1972).

59 This interpretation comes from St. Augustine *City of God* 18.12.

60 See the commentary in Peradotto (1977). Only Plato seems to have seen the problem from this angle, since he makes Athena and Hephaistos children of the same father, and the same issue may have caused his reluctance to mention this episode in *Crit.* 109d.

61 Cf. Delcourt (1957) 145–46, who is inclined to overestimate the role of a phallic Hephaistos, to the detriment of Athena.

62 The Athenian vase-painters, who seem to have explored all the possible readings of the myth of autochthony, sometimes present an image in which chthonic birth (through Kekrops's mediation) counterbalances sexual reproduction (the presence of Hephaistos), as on the cup by the Kodros Painter (Berlin 2537; see plate 5). At other times, the representations focus on the image of the parental couple, Athena and Hephaistos, as on a Munich stamnos (2413, plate 4), in which the two gods encircle Ge, and the two illustrations of Eros are an unmistakable allusion to the erotic intrigue. Thus, there is no solid foundation to the attempts made by Brommer ([1978] 21–23) to replace Hephaistos with Zeus, as the result of a rather unconvincing comparison with London hydria E 182 (see plate 3).

63 Cf. *Hom. Hymn Aph.* 9–15, in which we see a play on the triple meaning of the word *erga* (works of love: 9; works of Ares: 10; works of artisans and women: 11, 15).

64 The phallic Hephaistos: Delcourt (1957), passim. We should also note: (1) The union of Hephaistos with Charis or Aphrodite associates him with "unmarriageable" goddesses, and such a union is anything but a fertile one; cf. Borgeaud (1975) 157. (2) In the myth of autochthony, the seducer fails in his endeavor and only inadvertently makes Ge fertile. (3) The artisan is more famous for his creations (Athena, Pandora) than for his children, who are hardly individuals (like the Kabeiroi, who are just Hephaistos's doubles: cf. Hesych., s.v. "Kabeiroi "Strabo 10.3.21) or whose ancestry is problematical to say the least: see the list of "sons" given by Brommer (1978) 137, which includes Apollo and Kekrops!

65 On the expulsion of *technē* in favor of *aretē* in funeral orations, see Loraux (1986) chap. 4.

66 This was the subject of a famous article by Jeanmaire (1956), which dealt with the names

connected with *mētis* in the mythical royal dynasty of Athens: see Frontisi-Ducroux (1975) 89–94.

67 See Vernant (1985) 274–94, especially 285–89.

68 On the "brutal contrast" existing in Greece "between the social status of artisans and the metaphorical status of artisans as a group," see Vidal-Naquet (1986), especially 227 (quotation) and 232–39.

69 With just one exception: the Oxford krater (525) cited above in note 17.

70 I am borrowing the word *philotechnia* from Plato, which he coins in the *Critias* to discuss Athenian autochthony (109c8), and which is much better suited to the collaboration between Hephaistos and Athena when they produce Pandora.

71 Following Detienne (in Detienne and Vernant (1978) 177–78), I am borrowing from G. Dumézil the idea that a god's mode of action, or particular kind of intervention, helps only to illuminate that god's great variety of spheres of activity.

72 We must also note (without overestimating its importance) that Hephaistos had an altar at the entrance to the Erechtheion: cf. Paus. 1.26.5. Pausanias tells us nothing further about its status. On the Hephaisteion and the double cult statue of Hephaistos and Athena, see Brommer (1978) 75–90.

73 Athena is honored as the Worker in some dedications, but not before the fifth century: Raubitschek (1949) 429. Was there then a space devoted to her, as *Erganē*, on the Acropolis? This question is a controversial one, and it is unclear whether we should take our information from Pausanias 1.24.2: cf. R. Schmidt (1926) and the bibliography in Bérard (1976) 104 n. 25. In the Hephaisteion, where Athena is associated with Hephaistos, she seems no longer to have been honored as *Erganē*, and in any case it is too simplistic to set up an opposition between Athena the protector and warrior of the Acropolis and "the simple *Erganē* of the Plain," as Delcourt does ([1957] 194–95). The interference between the religious field of *technē* and the civic cult of Athena Polias is recorded in the Athenian religious calendar: the festival of the Chalkeia marks the time when the peplos of the Panathenaea is set on the loom. Bérard (1976) believes that we can identify a depiction of the Chalkeia in a vase fragment found in the immediate proximity of the Erechtheion, but his argument is not thoroughly convincing, since it rests on the identification of Sophoclean fragment 844 (Pearson) as a reference to the Chalkeia.

74 That is, if the birth of Erichthonios was really represented on the plinth of the double cult statue of the Hephaisteion, as some scholars think: see the bibliography and discussion in Brommer (1978) 45. Brommer insists on the preeminence of Hephaistos over Athena in the Hephaisteion: (1978) 115. On the other hand, I must emphasize that Hephaistos is just a guest on the Acropolis, and his statue there is not placed beside that of the goddess.

75 Note that in the figural representations of the birth of Erichthonios there is never any actual obligation to represent Hephaistos with the attributes of an artisan. As on the Munich stamnos (see plate 4), he could just as easily have been depicted nude, without a *pilos*, without an *exomis*, without any kind of instrument: see Brommer (1978) 21, 23, 140.

76 The confusion between *physis* and *technē* is a systematic one in Plato: whether it be in the *Republic* (3.414d–e), in which the beautiful lie of autochthony is accommodated to the artisanal production of the citizens, or in the *Critias* (109c–d), in which the link uniting Athena and Hephaistos is a *physis* produced by *philotechnia*. Like Vidal-Naquet ([1986] 233), we should note that the two artisan gods certainly presided over the race of artisans in the *Laws* (9.92od), but they presided as well over the ancient Athens of the *Timaeus* and the *Critias*.

77 See Peradotto (1977) 94, who weaves the myth of Erichthonios into Lévi-Strauss's analysis of the myth of Oedipus.

78 British Museum E 182: *ARV*² 580, 2; see plate 3.

79 As on Munich stamnos 2413 (plate 4) or Berlin cup 2537 (plate 5a). Zeus here is clearly a substitute for Hephaistos and not the reverse, as maintained by Cook (1940) 3.1:182–87, and as Brommer would be inclined to suggest.

80 Kron (1976) 56–57.
81 Conversely, his presence does not entitle Metzger (1976) 298 to interpret it as an "iconographical hodgepodge." I should add that the Munich stamnos also associates Zeus and Nike (more distantly, it is true), who are on side B, with the birth of Erichthonios, on side A.
82 This was pointed out by Kron (1976) 57: "*der Athenageburt angeglichen*" (assimilated into Athena's birth). And is it not true that the birth of Athena was celebrated at the same time as the birth of Erichthonios in the Panathenaea?
83 Cook, for example, who is repelled – "a crude, not to say ugly narrative": (1940) 3.1:218.
84 Wilamowitz-Moellendorff (1893) 2:35, 90.
85 Ar. *Birds* 830–31: θεὸς γυνὴ γεγονυῖα πανοπλίαν / ἕστηκ᾽ ἔχουσα.
86 Vernant (1980) 24.
87 Herington (1955) 55.
88 Aes. *Eum.* 488, 707–8, 858, 862; cf. 1045 (*Pallados astoi*).
89 Aes. *Eum.* 999.
90 See Dodds (1951) 35 and 54 n. 38, as well as Burkert (1985) 141.
91 On Athens as belonging to Athena, besides the citations from the *Eumenides* mentioned in note 125, see Eur. *Held.* 770ff., 922–23 and *Iph. Taur.* 1441, 1452. On Athena's belonging to Athens, see Eur. *Ion* 453–54.
92 Cf. Aes. *Eum.* 475 and 481.
93 Aes. *Eum.* 998–1000.
94 Aes. *Eum.* 775, 882–83, 1010. In the institutional context, Athena is known as *poliouchos* in Camarina (Pi. *Ol.* 5.10), in Chios (Hdt. 1.160). and most of all in Athens, as in the Acropolis dedications: Raubitschek (1949) nos. 3, 53, 233; see also Ar. *Clouds* 602 and *Birds* 827, etc.
95 Cf. Vernant (1980) 23–25. The question here clearly concerns the social status of the sexes, and only that. Facile psychologizing about Athena as a "masculine woman" and as an "androgynous being" is not at all useful, as in, e.g., Pomeroy (1976) 4. The issue is neither Athena's physical appearance – which is clearly "feminine" enough to attract Hephaistos, who is not one for ugly women – nor her *psychē* but rather what she fosters and supports.
96 Soph. *Oed. Col.* 107–8: Eur. *Ion* 8–9 (in which the term *chrysolonchos* is used to describe the goddess) and 1555–56.
97 Pl. *Crat.* 406d.
98 As Owen and Wilamowitz-Moellendorff have pointed out in their commentaries on this passage.
99 Mazon's note to Soph. *Oed. Col.* 107–8.
100 *Athanas* fits perfectly in iambic trimeter. This archaic form, along with *Athēnaia*, is the only one used by the tragic poets: cf. Austin (1967) 53, on line 64.
101 Strabo 17.186: see the material compiled by Fauth (1964) and Vian (1952) 270ff. Cf. also Chantraine, s.v "*pallakē*"
102 At least, such is the conclusion given in Herington (1955) 9 and in Fehrle (1910) 196–98.
103 There are only three instances in the Acropolis dedications: Raubitschek (1949) nos. 40, 79, 121, and p.428, on the problems raised by interpretations of this title. On the other hand, there are numerous references to Pallas (*Pallas Thea, Athēnaia*, or *Tritogenēs*: nos. 28, 35, 66, 67, 72, 125, 133, 148, etc.; nineteen instances) as the daughter of Zeus and armed goddess: Raubitschek (1949) 429. If we believe that the Acropolis was structured around the opposition between a peaceful Polias and an armed Parthenos, as proposed by Herington (1955) – and there are substantial reasons for doubt on this point – then the real name of Athena the warrior in the dedications should be Pallas (cf. 148: *Pallas egrēmacha*). In any case, it would be very surprising if the dedications on the Acropolis were not invariably addressed to Athena Polias, contrary to the conclusions proposed by Raubitschek (1949) 429.
104 Hermipp. frag. 1 Kock. No doubt another intrusion on the part of that "evil spirit" mentioned

by Marrou (1954) 71, who seems to take pleasure in depriving the historian of antiquity of just the information needed.

105 Eur. *Ion* 209–11; Pl. *Crat.* 406d–e. In both texts, Pallas is made to refer to *pallein*.

106 Cf. Pl. *Crat.* 406d–e and *Laws* 7.796b on the armed dance of "the one who, for us, is both a young girl and sovereign" (*korē kai despoina*), a passage that some, oddly enough, have wanted to attach to Persephone, but which seems rather obviously to pertain to Athena. On Athena as the dancer, see Borthwick (1969); she performed the Pyrrhic dance to celebrate the defeat of the Giants: see Vian (1952) 211 and 249–50.

107 See Vian (1952) 270ff. and Kerenyi (1952) 29–31 (who sees the "masculine" side of Athena in Pallas).

108 Cf. J. E. Harrison (1908) 301, on *IG* II² 1006, 11–12 (συνεξήγαγον δὲ καὶ τὴν Παλλάδα): "Her image as Pallas, not as Athena, was carried in procession by the ephebes." On the identification of this festival as the Plynteria, see Pelekidis (1962) 251.

109 In Call. *Lav. Pall.* it is young girls who bathe the Palladion (34, 57, 138): cf. Calame (1977) 1:232–33. Moreover, the goddess is described at length as the virile virgin (5, 13–16, 23–30).

110 Ar. *Thesm.* 1136–42.

111 It is also the only passage in which the women establish a *dēmos* for themselves without taking refuge in the *dēmos* of the Athenian men.

112 That is how I would translate παρθένον ἄζυγα κούρην (1139): Pallas is *philochoros*, which associates her with female adolescence Cf. Calame (1977): 1:70.

113 Athena is named for the first time in 269, in connection with the care she takes with the autochthonous child, whereas Pallas has already appeared more than once as an eponymous figure for Athens and the sovereign of the Acropolis (9, 12, 211, 235). Pallas in the war with the Giants: 211, 991, 996; Pallas and the Gorgons: 1001. See below, "Autochthonous Kreousa," 226–27.

114 For Antigone, and Antigone and Ismene: Soph. *Oed. Col.* 445ff., 745ff., 1365ff.; the Eumenides are named in 106, and Athena is Pallas, the daughter of Zeus, in 1090.

115 Wilamowitz-Moellendorff (1931) 1.236.

116 Pl. *Laws* 1.626d.

117 Pl. *Crit.* 109c.

118 Here we meet Wilamowitz-Moellendorff again, entitling his chapter 7 in volume 2 of his text on Aristotle (1893) "Der athenische Name." It is true that in his own way – that is, his German professorial way – Wilamowitz-Moellendorff was sensitive to these problems . . .

27

MIREILLE DELMAS-MARTY

Mireille Delmas-Marty is Professor of Law at the University of Paris I (Sorbonne) and a member of the Institut Universitaire de France where she is Chair of Criminal Politics and Human Rights. Her research is at the interface of economic penal law, human rights and comparative law. She was involved in co-ordinating the drafting of a legal code to protect the financial interests of the European Union, in the *Corpus Juris* project, 1995–6, and subsequently in the follow-up study carried out by OLAF (Office de Lutte Anti-Fraude) in 1998–9. She is President of the Association for European Penal Research and Vice-President of the International Association for Criminal Law.

Mireille Delmas-Marty is author of dozens of books on criminal law, comparative law and human rights. These include the following:

Le Droit de la famille, Paris: PUF, 1972.

Le Mariage et le divorce, Paris: PUF, 1978.

Droit pénal des affaires, Paris: PUF, 1973.

Les Chemins de la répression: lectures du code pénal, Paris: PUF, 1980.

Modèles et mouvements de politique criminelle, Paris: Economica, 1983.

Le Flou du droit: du code pénal aux droits de l'homme, Paris: PUF, 1986.

Les grands systèmes de politique criminelle, Paris: PUF, 1992.

Punir sans juger: de la répression administrative au droit administratif pénal (with C. Teitgen), Paris: Economica, 1992.

Pour un droit commun, Paris: Seuil, 1994.

Trois défis pour un droit mondial, Paris: Seuil, 1998.

DEMOCRACY AND HUMANITY

Humanity has a bad reputation. For some, it carries the risk of a totalitarianism that, in the name of the progress of humanity, makes man a slave. Others, meanwhile, see it as a profoundly subversive notion, one that leads directly to a fundamentalism of human rights, which is hardly compatible with State sovereignty. And this without forgetting the somewhat ostentatious sentimentalism of the humanitarian generation, whose solidarity would seem to take the form of a 'great cosseting'.[1]

While helping to identify pitfalls, all the '-isms' in the world should not, for all that, cause us to abandon the project to combine democracy and humanity. This is because, beyond pluralism and tolerance, there is the intolerable; and the only response to the intolerable is refusal, made precisely in the name of humanity.

It remains to be seen how this refusal could be democratically constructed, and how it could be organised as a tool of resistance which would, in all, be the end of a slow process of hominisation that started in prehistory, and that doubtless remains unfinished: 'man has yet to be born,' proclaims Maurice Zundel,[2] while a specialist in paleo-anthropology recently made the blunt assertion that the infamous missing link between man and monkeys does not exist, 'quite simply because we are not descended from monkeys, we *are* monkeys.'[3] Less provocatively, Henri de Lumley, the great prehistory specialist, has confirmed that the question of defining man appears to be many-sided.[4] For example, as 'bi-pedalism', or standing upright, is certainly not unique to man, human history could begin with the appearance of tools (2.5 million years ago). Or it could begin with manufactured tools, where the implicit idea of a model offers proof of emergent conceptual thinking (1.5 million years ago). Alternatively, we could start from the point at which fire was mastered, thereby facilitating social interaction (400,000 years ago); or with the appearance of sepulchres containing funeral offerings, which indicates the birth of metaphysical anxiety in Neanderthal Man (100,000 years ago); or we could again wait for the senses of harmony and aestheticism to emerge, which came with Cro-Magnon Man and his practice of wall painting (30,000 years ago).

It is a lesson in humility for those jurists who today claim to be able to define humanity. Let us retain the idea – taken from the scientific approach – that we should doubtless proceed from a body of evidence to be variously combined; a kind of 'fuzzy logic' could perhaps also be applied, but where should we draw the line? Rather than claiming to have found *the* single criterion that defines humanity by marking its entry into the field of law, let us accept the idea that this definition is itself a progressive and, no doubt, as yet unfinished process: outlined by the idea of the rights 'of man' (two centuries ago), humanity has become more clearly defined through the founding prohibition of the crime 'against humanity' (half a century ago). By definition, however, the suppression of the crime arrives too late: the wrong has already been done, and humanity, its victim, is shocked to its foundations. The strength of reprobation and of dissuasion from the crime must be combined with protection affirmed in a positive way, like a promise. Herein lies the usefulness of the notion of 'the common heritage of humanity', an expression coined in 1967 in anticipation of an international conference on sea law, and then extended to other fields concerning law and the environment and, more debatably, to the human genome.

'Humanity as victim and the crime against humanity'

Appearing for the first time in the statutes of the Nuremberg Tribunal, an astonishing sort of interaction between the rule of law, in all its coldness, and the events, in all their horror, has meant that the definition of the crime against humanity has in effect been in continuous evolution. At Nuremberg, crimes against humanity were defined – after crimes against peace and war crimes – as: 'murder, extermination, reduction to slavery, deportation and all other inhuman acts committed against any civilian population, before or during the war, and indeed persecution for political, racial or religious motives' (Art. 6c of the Tribunal Statutes, 1945). In later texts by the UN and the Council of Europe on imprescriptibility (Conventions of 25 January 1948 and 26 November 1968), a reference to genocide was added, as defined in the UN Convention of 1948. Later still, in the UN Convention on imprescriptibility, came the reference to inhuman acts resulting from apartheid politics; the crime of apartheid was itself defined in a Convention of 3 November 1973.

The next step was the creation of International Penal Courts: to begin with, these were so called '*ad hoc*' tribunals, the term delimiting both the space (former Yugoslavia and Rwanda) and the time (the duration of armed conflict) of the competence of these jurisdictions. Prepared by various committees of international experts – in particular by the French committee presided over by Pierre Truche and then, following a first Resolution by the UN Security Council, by a substantial report from the UN Secretary General – the Hague Penal Tribunal was finally put into place by the celebrated Resolution 827 (25 May 1973). The Resolution of 8 November 1994 then created the Arusha Tribunal to deal with Rwanda, and on 3 September 1998 the Tribunal pronounced its first sentence for genocide against the former Prime Minister, who was responsible for the extermination of around 800,000 Tutsis between April and July of 1994.

The two Resolutions expressly target genocide and serious breaches of the Geneva Convention, as well as war crimes and crimes against humanity. Of the latter, the UN Secretary General has specified in a report that, 'in the conflict that broke out in the area of former Yugoslavia, such inhuman acts took the form of the practice called "ethnic cleansing", of generalised and systematic rape, and of other types of sexual violence, including forced prostitution'. Latterly, the International Penal Court Bill adopted in Rome on 17 July 1998 recognises four crimes: genocide, crimes against humanity, war crimes and crimes of aggression. The Bill specifies that the crime against humanity, which implies 'a large-scale or systematic attack directed, in full knowledge of the facts, against a civilian population', may include enslavement, torture, rape and forced pregnancy and sterilisation (when they are committed in the circumstances described above). The text also makes it clear that, 'when there is intention to eliminate, completely or partially, a national, ethnic, racial or religious group', genocide has taken place.

All of which demonstrates the complexity of the crime against humanity, which would thus seem to comprise 'crimes that are specifically named, such as genocide and apartheid, and others that are named only by this generic expression'.[5] To this I would add that the generic expression itself encompasses 'ordinary' crimes – if we dare apply this adjective to murder or rape, to take but two examples – when they are, in the words of the Convention Bill of 1998, 'systematic' or 'large-scale' in nature.

Here we can glimpse what it is that distinguishes crimes against humanity from other crimes, however atrocious the latter may be. It is their collective basis, which is, moreover, stressed in the early decisions of the Hague Penal Tribunal: 'it is the identity of the victim – humanity – that makes a crime against humanity'.[6] It remains the case that this method of always starting again from zero is hardly satisfactory, since it risks weakening the notion of humanity: firstly by dilution, in that it opens the door to all the fears of the moment; and secondly by forgetfulness, in that it neglects to include situations that are as yet unknown, but which bio-technological evolution nevertheless shows are possible. In France, the new Penal Code – passed in 1992 and effective from March 1994 – now bears a title 'Crimes Against Humanity', which symbolically heads the list of violations against individuals; but at the other end of the Code (in Book V, which is devoted to 'Other Crimes and Offences') we find an absurd situation where a section entitled 'Protection of the Human Race' is composed of a single crime, that of eugenics. With humanity at the start of the Code and the human race at the end, things seem a little out of place; unless of course the legislator wanted to make such a distinction between the biological species and symbolic humanity, a distinction which would – through the 'biologisation' of the law – represent a formidable advance on the part of biopower.

And so we find ourselves now pondering the question of whether reproductive human cloning comes under the definition of eugenics, which seems to be the position of the French National Ethics Committee; or whether it should be considered a crime against humanity in that, like slavery, it implies the instrumentalisation of the human being. That is to say that the question of cloning is a measure of the conceptions that underpin the very recent juridical notion of humanity – and a particularly powerful measure at that, since it obliges us to reconsider existing texts in their totality, including the bio-ethical laws of 1994. Provided that we do not repeat the mistake of isolating cloning, as happened with other new bio-medical technologies, the debate on cloning could contribute to the continual – but, perhaps, reversible – process of hominisation. It is with this aim that Roger-Pol Droit has set up an interdisciplinary investigation into such questions (using at one and the same time biology, anthropology, philosophy, history and law).[7]

This interdisciplinary approach is necessary because humanity has taken on an ethical and juridical significance that lies beyond known biological data. Whatever the religious, philosophical or scientific hypotheses imagined to explain the articulation between the universal and the historical,[8] it is a fact that the humanity that under-lies the crime against humanity is made up of more than the things known about the biological species. Perhaps the moment has come to 'harden into words' the living essence of personhood. For Hannah Arendt, this was an impossible task, but she gave us the key to it by insisting on the necessity of a pluralist conception of humanity: the Earth is not inhabited by *man*, but by *men*.

In fact, this is a pluralist conception that runs right through the list – which always starts from zero – of crimes against humanity. If, as we have seen, these prohibitions have a collective basis, then the humanity that underpins these crimes is not a totalitarian humanity. What the prohibition means is that a human being, even when deeply inscribed in its familial, cultural or religious community, must never lose its individuality, must never find itself reduced to a simple interchangeable element of that community and thus rejected as such (as André Frossard has said, to kill someone not for what they have done, but because they have been born: that is the crime against humanity). If human beings need to belong to a group, they cannot be confined and tied to their origins without losing their status at the heart of humanity. In all, what is thus affirmed is the singularity of each being and, at the same time, that being's membership of the human community.[9] All of which amounts to saying that the crime against humanity is not limited to the destruction of other humans, but may encompass deliberate political, juridical, medical and scientific practices that, while ostensibly respectful of human life, call humanity, thus understood, into question. Beyond the survival of the species, what is at stake here is the conception of human dignity. The definition of the crime against humanity should at one and the same time comprise the violation of the principle of singularity (an exclusion which could range right up to the extermination of groups of humans that have been reduced to a racial, ethnic or genetic category, or, in the opposite direction, to the manufacture of so-called identical beings, in particular by cloning), as well as the principle of equal membership of the human community (forbidding discriminatory practices such as apartheid, the creation of 'supermen' by genetic selection, or of 'sub-men' by the crossing of species, with eugenics a simple variant).

In this way, the crime against humanity would form the common limit for all cultures, one which marks – despite pluralism and tolerance, but also in their name – a line that must not be crossed. The definition of this line eludes the uncertainties of biological knowledge. Whether or not they involve the physical destruction of human beings, practices thus described as crimes against humanity have in common what I shall call, for want of anything better, a metaphysical destruction – that is, the negation of the efforts by which man constructs his own humanity. In other words, the crime against humanity is intolerable because it contradicts the effort of hominisation, which would, in the symbolic sense of the phrase, appear to be the true 'common heritage of humanity'. This is because such a heritage is a trans-temporal effort that we inherit from the past – one which passes through the present and which, to borrow from René-Jean Dupuy, inscribes man in a 'humanity promise'.

'The humanity promise and common heritage'

While human rights include the right to ownership, the 'heritage' of the individual expresses something else altogether: at one and the same time container and contents, it signals that the subject and his collected possessions – both physical and non-physical – are indivisible. On a wider level, the heritage of humanity has the trans-temporal quality mentioned earlier: it does not belong exclusively to us, but expresses a global solidarity that exists in time, through the generations to come, as well as space. The humanity promise promises to protect future generations as well.

In 1945, at the top of the preamble of the United Nations Charter, these 'future generations' made their discreet entrance into the field of law, the objective of the Charter being to protect them from 'the scourge of war'. Cultural, archaeological and artistic heritage was also to be preserved for these generations. Following the Convention of 4 November 1946 this heritage was placed under the international protection of UNESCO, an organisation created by the same Convention, and which was charged with ensuring 'the conservation and protection of the universal heritage of books, works of art and other monuments of historical or scientific interest, and to recommend to interested peoples International Conventions to this effect'.

Today, however, it is the environment that most concerns these future generations, as underlined by the Declaration adopted at the Rio Summit of 1992. First introduced at a 1967 conference on sea law, the formula 'common heritage of humanity' has been recognised by a range of documents. For example, the 1970 Declaration on the soil and sub-soil of seas and oceans; or, especially, the 1982 Convention on the Law of the Sea (which came into effect in 1994) and which, beyond the distribution of resources, makes provision for a series of obligations that countries must meet.[10] And – since humanity doubts nothing in its conquest of space – an international treaty of 1979 has also classed the moon and its natural resources as common heritage.[11] This slow realisation has throughout been spurred on by civil society, in the form of organisations that defend the environment. It is a role that will be reinforced still further if the World Observatory proposed by the Independent Worldwide Commission on Oceans is set up, a project which the President of the Commission, Mario Soares, presents as 'a sort of Amnesty International for the sea', charged with 'creating a current of opinion' and 'putting pressure upon world leaders'.[12]

Starting from the Stockholm conference of 1972, the idea of 'sustainable development' – that is, a development that takes account of the planet's ecological limits – has thus progressively set into the heart of the United Nations. This was to be the main theme of the Rio Declaration, which also states the necessity of integrating the environment into the rules of international commerce, so as to avoid the imbalance caused by eco-dumping. In this respect the accord added to Alena, the North American Free Trade Agreement between the United States, Canada and Mexico, illustrates the fact that from now on the international character of the environment is shaped by factors that are economic as well as physical.[13]

Moreover, we might wonder whether the notion of sustainable development should be transposed to all forms of life, including human forms. Such could be the justification behind UNESCO's 'Universal' Declaration on the Human Genome and Human Rights, which was adopted on 3 December 1997. The text, however, – which is written in a solemn tone that gives the impression of a brand new declaration for humanity on human rights – seems to mix social and biological issues so strongly that it leaves one feeling rather perplexed. For example, the first Article immediately affirms that, as an obvious fact, 'the human genome underpins the fundamental unity of all the members of the human family,' and that, 'symbolically, it is the heritage of humanity'. The consequence is that a text intended 'to promote and to develop ethical thinking' is given a foundation that is not only biological, but which is limited even to a single genome. By attaching to the genome gratitude for human dignity and diversity – and at the risk of excluding *a contrario* the dignity of beings born as a result of genetic manipulation – the second part of the sentence about the genome brings yet further confusion. Because it would contravene such a definition of dignity, reproductive human cloning is cited as an example of practices that 'must not be permitted' (Art. 11). Granted, Article 2 checks this genetic dominance a little, affirming that 'each individual is entitled to have his dignity and rights respected whatever his genetic characteristics', and that 'this dignity demands that individuals not be reduced to their genetic characteristics and that the unique character and diversity of each person be respected'. This is, however, but a simple reprise of the Universal Declaration of Human Rights of 1948, the essential difference being that this previous Declaration does not give itself a biological foundation: clearly all men are not born free and equal in nature but, on the level of their dignity and rights, they are 'recognised as such'. If the text's careful handling of 'the free practice of research activities' did not foster such prudent ambiguities, the recourse to the notion of humanity's common heritage could be read as a form of self-defence; ultimately, though, it is the mix of biological, symbolic and philosophical arguments that seems unacceptable.

On the condition that this type of amalgamation be avoided, it remains the case that the notion of a common heritage of humanity can contribute to the quest for a global law beyond the extreme diversity of cultures. Granted, the term 'heritage' is indeed sometimes criticised, but for conflicting reasons. Some authors, such as Bernard Edelman, see in it the triumph of universal economic reason: 'Ultimately, this humanity aims to be the universal subject of a global economic strategy of which nature would, in the end, be the sole object . . . Stripped of his human value, man prepares to become a valuable object.'[14] Conversely, others are concerned that what we are seeing is the announcement of a communitisation that will, through the exhausting of resources that each individual will attempt to appropriate 'in terms of the immediate maximisation of their usefulness to him,'[15] lead directly to the ruin of this heritage. Rather, let us keep in mind the possibilities that the notion of the common heritage of humanity offers us, a notion that appeared as 'as a neguentropic leap, a formidable effort of rationality by a humanity that does not intend to be deprived of its future'.[16] Let us learn to use it as such.

All the work of juridical construction remains to be done, involving in particular research into the practical details of how to represent humanity as the subject of rights, as well as reflection on the criteria of definition, which are doubtless multiple. Barely sketched out, this thinking has been made necessary by the debate on the genome.

For, on the level of global law, the conquest of democracy is in effect achieved as much by pluralist and constructivist methods as by the political voluntarism of refusal, which jurists are going to have to help set to music. Democracy feeds not just on tolerance, but also on resistance to the intolerable: the very idea of humanity is composed of these two, inseparable dimensions.

'The hope of an inhabitable world'

Let it not be said that, given the current state of the world, all of this is simple Utopianism. Rather, let us look at the ground we have covered. In this slow ascent towards consciousness that we call hominisation, time is firstly counted in thousands or even millions of years: in all, law is but a very new idea. We are separated from the Hammurabi Code by less than forty centuries; from the French and American Declarations on the Rights of Man by less than two centuries; and from the Universal Declaration by only fifty years.

'Work in progress' – this is how our history is known. We have to agree to this. And we have to admit that progress is neither continuous nor irreversible, have to debunk this illusion and anticipate coming disasters. Such is our heritage:

> Pure eyes in the woods,
> Seek weeping a head to dwell in.[17]

And so once again – but on a level that has never been reached – resistance rhymes with hope. For to refuse the globalist illusion is not to resign oneself to the disorder of the world – on the contrary, it is a question of also resisting scepticism. *E pur si mouve!* And yet the Earth does move! It moves through groping, hesitations and mistakes. During the first half of the twentieth century the fury of two world wars arose in Europe, but despite Bosnia, Kosovo and Cassandras on all sides, today it gives a more peaceful image of a slow march towards a common law. Representatives from so-called hereditary enemies now sit side by side in two parliamentary assemblies, the Council of Europe and the European Union. Judges who come from long-opposed judicial traditions – common law and the Romano-Germanic system – deliberate together and have, again and again, passed sentence on States, including those from which they themselves originate. Governments adhering to ideologies that have sometimes been judged irreconcilable have, out of successive crises, managed to develop common policies – not only on an economic level (from the 1951 European Steel and Coal Community to the single currency of 1999, via the Agreement on social politics appended to the Maastricht Treaty in 1992, which was finally signed by the United Kingdom and consolidated by the Treaty of Amsterdam) but also in respect of human rights (from the European Convention of 1950 to the revised Social Charter of 1996). However insufficient it may be, today there exists a common European law, and jurisdictions to control its actual application. We are even starting to glimpse the silhouette of the European Citizen, which is inscribed in the Maastricht Treaty.

Of course, not all parts of this example can be transposed onto a global scale. But it remains the case that the experiment of the 'European laboratory' brings a counter to systematic pessimism, and that it can provide useful points of reference for the progressive construction of a global law.

In fact, on this level, too, the task may seem Promethean, but however slow its evolution and however disappointing its repeated failures, we should not pass over its first results, which are now emerging. From the Universal Declaration signed in 1948 to the two Pacts of 1966 that juridically engaged the ever-increasing number of States that have signed it, the advancement of global law has continued. In particular, this advancement has seen the application of pressure by organisations. Themselves making their first steps in learning about globalisation, these organisations may well herald the appearance of future citizens of the world.

As difficult as it may seem, it is in this way that the much-promised reform of the UN has cleared its first set of obstacles. Finally, and despite the wide prognosis of failure and the continued objection of the most powerful State, the agreement obtained for the creation of an International Penal Court will, for the first time in history, allow judges from the five continents to sit in a permanent jurisdiction. Beyond the *ad hoc* tribunals that prefigured it, these judges will together apply principles that have been universally defined.

To resist scepticism is to bring together such disparate fragments in order to take up the three challenges, but without dissociating them.[18] Should one of the answers be missing, then the whole will no longer be possible, reasonable or desirable.

To take up the three challenges at the same time: I believe that this is the condition for opening the way to a common law of humanity which could, by dispelling the dangers, preserve the hope of an inhabitable world.

Translated by Stephen Forcer

Notes

1 Alain Finkielkraut, *L'Humanité perdue* (Paris: Editions du Seuil, 1996), p. 131.
2 Maurice Zundel, *Un autre regard sur l'homme. Paroles choisies par Paul Debains* (Paris: Fayard, 1996), p. 171.
3 Pascal Picq, 'Les origines de l'homme,' in the *Journal du dimanche*, April 1998.
4 Henri de Lumley, 'Préhistoire et hominisation,' in Edgar Morin (ed.), *Journées thématiques. Relier les connaissances* (forthcoming; ministère de l'Education nationale, April 1998).
5 Michel Massé in *Actes*, special edition on law and humanity, September 1973. See also Pierre Truche, 'Le crime contre l'humanité,' in *Droits*, 1993, p. 19 onwards, and René-Jean Dupuy, *L'Humanité dans l'imaginaire des nations* (Paris: Julliard, 1991), especially 'L'humanité victime', p. 195 onwards.
6 The Erdemovic ruling, 29 November 1996, *Les Petites Affiches*, no. 26, 1997, p. 6 onwards.
7 See Roger-Pol Droit (ed.), *Réflexions sur le clonage humain* (Paris: Éditions du Seuil, 1999), especially Mireille Delmas-Marty, 'Faut-il interdire le clonage humain?'
8 See *La Nature et la Règle, dialogue entre Jean-Pierre Changeux et Paul Ricœur* (Paris: Odile Jacob, 1998).
9 See Mireille Delmas-Marty, 'L'humanité saisie par le droit,' in *Humanité humanitaire*, op. cit., p. 27 onwards.
10 See Martine Rémond-Gouilloud, 'Le patrimoine commun,' in *Du choix de détruire. Essai sur le choix de l'environment* (Paris: PUF, 1989), p. 149 onwards.
11 See Alexandre C. Kiss, *La Notion de patrimoine commun de l'humanité*, Académie de droit international de La Haye, Recueil des cours, t.175, 1982.
12 Mario Soares, texts collected by Pierre Le Hir, *Le Monde*, 2 September 1998, p. 19.
13 See Michel Prieur, *Droit de l'environnement*, 3rd edition (Paris: Dalloz, 1996), p. 39 onwards.
14 Bernard Edelman, *L'Homme, la Nature et le Droit* (Paris: La Découverte, 1988), p. 140–1.

15 G. Hardin, quoted by François Ost in *La Nature hors la loi* (Paris: La Découverte, 1995), p. 330.

16 François Ost, ibid., p. 337.

17 René Char, 'Fine Building and Forebodings' in Mary Ann Caws and Jonathan Griffin (trans., ed.), *Poems of René Char* (Princeton: Princeton University Press, 1976), p. 4. The poem was published in 1934, a time when, in the very words of the poet, 'the allegory of horror was starting to materialise' behind the fallacious façade of fine buildings; *Le Marteau sans maître* (Paris: Gallimard, collection 'Bibl. de la Pléiade', 1983), p. 11.

18 [Translator's note: these 'three challenges' are the 'Trois défis' of the title, namely: is the globalisation of law possible in practice?; is it juridically reasonable?; and is it ethically desirable?]

28

BLANDINE KRIEGEL

Blandine (Barrett) Kriegel is a political philosopher who has been 'chargée de recherche' at the CNRS and Professor at the Université Jean-Moulin in Lyon and is now Professor at the University of Paris X (Nanterre). She worked closely with Foucault in the Collège de France in the 1970s, and has published widely over the last twenty years in areas such as theories of history, Republicanism, democracy, monarchy, slavery and the Rights of Man. Her aim is 'to construct a reasoned history of the fundamental concepts of rights (*droit*) and human freedom', and she has worked on several national commissions for juridical modernisation and reform. She is founder-editor of the 'Questions' collection and editor of the journal *Philosophie Politique*. In 1999 she intervened in the scandal concerning the use of contaminated blood given to haemophiliacs, and argued that the 'code pénal' was not the appropriate way to examine the questions of the responsibility and guilt of the French ministers and officials involved (Laurent Fabius, Georgina Dufoix and Edmond Hervé). She supported the Parity movement.

Her major works include the following:

L'État et les esclaves: réflexions pour l'histoire des états, Paris: Calmann-Levy, 1979.

Les Chemins de l'état, Paris: Calmann-Levy, 1986.

Les Académies de l'histoire, Paris: PUF, 1988.

Les Historiens et la monarchie, Paris: PUF, 1988.

La République incertaine, Paris: PUF, 1988.

Les droits de l'homme et le droit naturel, Paris: PUF, 1989.

La Politique de la raison, Paris: Payot, 1994.

Propos sur la démocratie: essai sur un idéal politique, Paris: Descartes, 1994.

Cours de philosophie politique, Paris: Librairie générale française, 1996.

L'Histoire à l'âge classique, Paris: PUF, 1996.

Philosophie de la République, Paris: Plon, 1998.

La Cité républicaine: essai pour une philosophie politique, Paris: Galilée, 1998.

Le sang, la justice, la politique, Paris: Plon, 1999.

Réflexions sur la justice, Paris: Plon, 2001.

État de droit ou empire?, Paris: Bayard, 2002.

THE EIGHTEENTH-CENTURY
DECLARATIONS OF RIGHTS AND
THEIR DESTINIES

The American Success of the 1776 Declaration of Independence; Resistance in Europe to the 1789 Declaration of the Rights of Man.[1]

By proclaiming the rights of man and of the citizen, rights found at the heart of modern democracies, the two legal declarations of the eighteenth century are considered to have marked a crucial turning point in the evolution of political law. However, the destinies of the two declarations have not been the same. The Declaration of Independence has never been dissociated from the Preamble of the American Constitution, into which it was inserted at an early stage. Rather, the sprit of the Declaration was reinforced by the Bills of Rights that headed all constitutions written by British colonies that became independent States, and which were drawn up during that same period. Such a spirit was further strengthened by the first 10 amendments of the Federal Constitution of 1787. In turn, the Declaration had a direct and continuous influence on positive American law in that, preceding even the possible intervention of the Supreme Court, the control of diffuse and decentralised constitutionality was entrusted to every court in the land.[2] The 1789 Declaration, on the other hand, was uprooted from its bedding within our French constitutions very early on. Either new texts were substituted in its place, as was the case in 1793, 1795 and 1848, or its insertion was omitted, as happened in imperial and monarchical constitutions. This was even the case under the Third Republic, as much in the constitutional laws of 1875 as in the revisions introduced on 21 June 1879, 14 August 1884 and 10 August 1926. The Declaration only reappeared in the Preamble to our Constitution belatedly, in 1946 – consequently, its influence on positive law has been but very indirect. As Jean Rivero has stressed, today the Declaration of the Rights of Man has no strict legal status.[3] French law has ended up endowing a large number of these rights with a positive quality, but it has done so on the basis of different qualifications which have in turn led to distinct legal consequences. For example, where the case law of the Council of State has 'General Principles of Public Law', the Constitutional Council has 'Principles of Constitutional Value'. Says Rivero,

> The insertion of human rights into positive law is being achieved through the intermediary of categories – categories in which, moreover, the rights of man may come into proximity with principles that are distinct from them, such as the continuity of public service.[4]

Furthermore, from the 'Law of Suspects' that started The Terror, passing through the nineteenth-century 'villainous laws' outlawing propaganda to recent special tribunals, our country's political law has provided multiple opportunities to breach the principles of 1789. Where does the disparity between the destiny of the two texts come from, and how can we understand the misfortune that has befallen our own Declaration?

Let us perhaps begin with the fate that has prematurely marginalised the French Declaration, a fate decided by extremely strong doctrinal oppositions. Widely distributed among different sections of public opinion, these oppositions have durably perpetuated their stand against the Declaration. Of these objections, two are very well known: those of the conservatives, and those of the communists. For the conservatives, the opening of hostilities was signalled by Edmund Burke's stirring *Reflections on the Revolution in France*, published in 1790. This was, in the words of Novalis, 'a revolutionary book against the Revolution'. Its author, a liberal who had nevertheless supported the rights of the American colonies, became a bitter enemy of the French revolutionary experiment. Denying that it was inspired by the 'glorious Revolution of 1688', Burke directly attacked the doctrine of the Rights of Man. Taking advantage of historicist arguments developed previously by Sir Edward Coke and Viscount Henry Bolingbroke, he opposed the abstract principles of the French with the 'rights of the English', which were founded on tradition and heritage. Burke says that,

> it has been the uniform policy of our constitution to claim and assert our liberties, as an *entailed inheritance* derived to us from our forefathers, and to be transmitted to our posterity; as an estate specially belonging to the people of this kingdom, without any reference whatever to any other more general or prior right.[5]

Reacting against the desire of French representatives to found civil rights on the nature of man, Burke also insisted on the insurmountable difference that separates such rights from natural law. For him, the rights of man that had been introduced into communal life were

> like rays of light which pierce into a dense medium, [and which] are, by the laws of nature, reflected from their straight line. Indeed in the gross and complicated mass of human passions and concerns, the primitive rights of men undergo such a variety of refractions and reflections, that it becomes absurd to talk of them as if they continued in the simplicity of their original direction.[6]

This historicist objection was firstly echoed in France by the Restoration tradition of ultra-Royalist thinkers, such as Joseph de Maistre, Louis de Bonald and, later, Pierre Simon Ballanche.[7] It then made its name in Germany in doctrinal works of political romanticism by Haller, Muller, Görres, Baader and the Schlegel brothers.[8]

The rejection of the Declaration of the Rights of Man was affirmed by an especially powerful blow from Fichte and his *Addresses to the German Nation*.[9] Calling for 'the liberty of the individual to be enclosed within limits that are as strict as possible,' and for 'all of the individual's vague desires to be submitted to a uniform rule and constantly watched over,' Fichte also held that the defence of private property was 'a minor objective'. Much like his 'practical' initiative with Brentano and Achim von Arnim to found the first club from which Jews and women were barred, Fichte's theoretical reflection that the rights of Germany were preferable to the rights of man would later inspire the Nazis. In this climate, hostility to the French Declaration sprang from a refusal of equality and from a loathing of democracy. This led its enemies to turn back, before seventeenth-century political theory, to an organicist and seigneurial conception of society and, beyond that, towards doctrines of nature that revalue the idea of conquest, that exalt the difference between peoples and that sometimes magnify distinction between races.

The second identified opposition to the doctrine of the Rights of Man is that of Karl Marx. In his early works, such as *The Jewish Question, The Holy Family* and *The Critique of Hegel's Philosophy of Right,*[10] Marx denies the Rights of Man the slightest value. Holding that the right to security is nothing but 'the concept of the *police,*'[11] he deplores the division of natural rights and civil rights. In this, Marx sees only the alienation that separates private and selfish man from communal man. This kind of difference must be eradicated:

> Only when real, individual man resumes the abstract citizen into himself and as individual man has become a *species-being* in his empirical life, his individual work and his individual relationships, only when man has recognized and organized his *forces-propres* as *social forces* so that political force is no longer separated from him in the form of *political force*, only then will human emancipation be completed.[12]

To the extent that civil liberties are a luxury reserved for those who own property, it is useless to fight to obtain such liberties. Rather, we should put a stop to economic exploitation and social oppression. There is no such thing as the legal liberation of man, only the social emancipation of the collectivity. For Marx, the disparagement of the Rights of Man is part of a wider rejection of all autonomy in political law – 'the spirit of laws is property,' with politics 'a cloudy sky'. By reinstating the question of power in the relationship with property and undoing the work done by modern jurists – themselves concerned with separating power from property and with distinguishing the economic from the political – Marx, too, goes against the course of history. In the case of the Declaration of the Rights of Man, his inspiration was romantic.[13]

Despite the work undertaken by Elie Halévy,[14] the third source of opposition is much less widely known: indeed, the hostility of liberals towards the Declaration of the Rights of Man has passed virtually unnoticed. However, following on from Dumont de Genève – who was nearly one of the writers of the Declaration – Jeremy Bentham poached on Burke's preserves by exposing his own hostility to the Rights of Man.[15] It is true that the development of Bentham's argument was perceptibly different, but while he does not pick up Burke's theory of prejudice and prescription that founds acquired rights, Bentham does hold that man is a being of need and not of law. He also believes that society is not based on the social contract, but on the principle of exchange, and of the natural identity of interests, which is itself one of the forms of the principle of utility. It was this hostility or lack of interest in the Rights of Man that was to influence the whole trend of utilitarianism, and which explains the indifference to the question of man that Solzhenitsyn believed he had identified in contemporary liberalism. For all that, though, the liberals' relationship with the Rights of Man remains complex and tainted with ambivalence. In practice, for example, in England the most fervent supporters of equality – and, especially, of the equality of civil rights – were liberals. It is also the case that in Southern and Eastern Europe the name of 'liberals' was very often given to hard-line supporters of natural and civil rights. It is striking, however, that the distinction subsequently made by Benjamin Constant between the political liberty of the Ancients and the civil liberty of the Moderns[16] does not exactly match the separation between the Rights of Man and those of the Citizen. Essentially, the civil rights that Constant talks about are singular rights of the private individual, rather than the rights of man as a person. Moreover, from 1840 a number of important French liberals, notably including Alexis de Tocqueville and Gustave Beaumont, were won over to security-oriented penal philosophy.[17] Hostile towards philanthropy, and preferring the security of society to the safety of the individual, this philosophy holds that the criminal must be removed from humanity in order to ensure the protection of honest people. This rallying lastingly diverted such liberals from the defence of the Rights of Man, which was itself being brandished against them – precisely on the level of penal and social misery – by heads of political Catholicism such as Montalembert and Falloux,[18] as well as the leaders of the Republican Party.[19]

While it has had its proselytes, the Declaration of 1789 can thus be said to have aroused a tremendous amount of resistance. For it is no small matter to have been simultaneously opposed by conservatives, liberals and Marxists. Today, this hostility has of course very much abated: not one of these former adversaries continues to declare itself openly hostile to the Declaration, and any persistent enmity remains latent. A *de facto* modernisation of the Rights of Man has recently come into effect in two stages. The first stage took place in the 1950s, and was born out of horror at the catastrophe wrought on Europe and the world by the Nazis and their allies, who had openly chosen the rights of man as a target. It was after their defeat that our French Preamble was adopted, and which explicitly evokes this fact:

> On the morrow of the victory achieved by free peoples over the regimes that have attempted to enslave and degrade the human person and that have bathed the whole world in blood, the French People remain loyal to the principle of 1789, the Charter of our freedom . . .

This was quickly followed by the Universal Declaration on Human Rights made at the General Assembly of the United Nations on 10 December 1948, and then, on 4 November 1950, by the European Convention on Human Rights, which was signed by the ministers of 15 European countries. Meanwhile, Article 3 of the Statute of the Council of Europe stipulated that: 'Every member of the Council of Europe must accept the principles of the rule of law and of the enjoyment by all persons within its jurisdiction of human rights and fundamental freedoms . . .'

Coming in the 1970s, the second stage of this modernisation accompanied the unexpected revelations – orchestrated by the genius of Solzhenitsyn – about the Gulag

Archipelago that had been set up within Soviet-style regimes. This provoked democracies to restore the ideology and politics of the Rights of Man as the order of the day.
However, it should be recognised that this *de facto aggiornamento* is not yet *de jure*. If
three traditions as different and powerful as conservatism, liberalism and Marxism came
together for a while in order to block the doctrine of the Rights of Man, and ended up
uniting in an agreement on social law, it is perhaps the case that their hostility reveals a
fundamental trend of European political development that remains to be investigated.[20]
It is still little known that, under the surface of the political theories of the old continent,
the French Declaration was at the centre of an agonising struggle: a struggle that led
certain currents to regress to positions clearly prior to the choices and orientations
of modern philosophy, which is characterised by a general criticism of imperial and
seigneurial models, and others to move in the opposite direction towards the promotion
of the social and the exaltation of the nation. It is a problem that brings a degree of
specificity to comparative observations of political development between America and
Europe. That the political evolution of the two continents has been different is rarely
contested, but this difference is more commonly alluded to than analysed in its own right.
One of the reasons for this may spring precisely from the position that positive law
accords to individual rights: here in France the place of such rights has long been
contested, whilst in America they were planned and guaranteed from the outset. This
belated shift in the destiny of the 1789 Declaration can in turn serve to stimulate research
into the reasons behind it in the powerful pairing of the doctrines of conservation and
European revolution that I have sketched out here, and which deserve to be developed.
It can also be asked whether the delayed implosion of the French Declaration into our
positive law – the sequence of which has been particularly drawn out when compared to
that of its American cousin – is not rooted in the very writing of our text. Let us therefore
continue by comparing the two Declarations.

'A comparison of the texts of the American and French Declarations'

Each of the Declarations is presented as an address, with an author, an addressee and an
object. In the American Declaration of 4 July 1776, the author is defined in a very general
way: it is a question of 'We, the People', although we soon learn that this is the people
that resides in the English colonies of America. The author of the French Declaration of
26 August 1789 is far more specific, both nationally, in that we are reminded that the
Declaration is French, and politically, so that the Declaration is stated to emanate not
from the nation in its entirety, but from the 'Representatives of the French People' alone.
Whilst the Declaration of 1776 is addressed to 'the opinions of mankind', the subject of
the 1789 text is less easy to determine: simple and personalised in the American text, the
French addressee is complex and anonymous. In the latter Declaration, only the
objectives have an addressee, which comes in the form of 'the members of the body
politic'. However, marked with a certain intransitivity, this evocation lies embedded
within the enumeration of the Declaration's aims. The object of the two texts is rather
more difficult to appreciate, and here we must distinguish between purpose and content.
   The aim of the American Declaration (which, as its name suggests, is a Declaration of
Independence) is strikingly univocal:

> When in the course of human events, it becomes necessary for one people to dissolve the political bands which have connected them with another . . . a decent respect to the opinions of mankind requires that they should declare the causes which impel them to the separation.

It is worth remembering that the rights of this Declaration are international or, at the very least, supranational. The purpose of the French Declaration, meanwhile, is strikingly ambiguous. At one and the same time, the stated aims are to establish inalienable and sacred rights, to institute the rights and duties of the members of the body politic, to install the balance of legislative and executive power as well as the maintenance of the Constitution, and to contribute to the happiness of all. It has been repeatedly stressed that the Declaration of 1789 intended to set up a platform for any legitimate political body.

It can thus be said that even a very superficial reproduction of the two texts prevents us from jumping – as sometimes happens – to contrast the universality of the French Declaration with the specificity of the American Declaration. Rather, the two texts have a tendency to intersect. In terms of its author and its addressee, the American Declaration is much more universal than that of 1789. Its object, however, is less so, in that this is constituted by the liberation of the English colonies and by the formation of the United States of America. In the French Declaration the author is very specific. However, since it deals with the institution of a society rather than with the liberation of a nation, this is not true of the Declaration's object or its addressee. In the first case, a people speaks to the opinion of mankind about its right to emancipation; the author and addressee are general, but their object is specific. In the second case, the representatives of the French people set out the inalienable and sacred rights of man and of the citizen; now the author is specific, but it is the object and addressee that are general.

As regards the content of the rights invoked by the two texts, the asymmetrical manner in which they were drawn up precludes a term-by-term comparison. In order to find trans-Atlantic equivalents to the continental terms, it would firstly be necessary to draw on a number of different documents, such as the Declaration of Independence, the first ten amendments to the Constitution of 1787, the Bill of Rights of the Union States, and so on. By the same turn, to discover the mechanisms by which the French Declaration was put into practice and guaranteed would involve reading the Constitution and examining the provisions of the Civil and Penal Codes, without ever being certain of making an exhaustive comparison. Not to mention the fact that we should devote greater attention to respective distances than to coincidence.

The first of which distances has to do with the relationship to rights. A declaration of independence, the Declaration made by the colonies does not newly declare rights but rather, above all, reminds us that rights pre-exist. 'Independence,' it says, 'is a right' – according to whom, exactly? According to 'the laws of nature and of nature's God'. The influence of John Locke can be read here, when he says that 'the rules that [legislators] make for other men's actions must, as well as their own and other men's actions, be conformable to the law of Nature – i.e., to the will of God, of which that is a declaration'.[21]

Also present is the influence of Spinoza, in the questions of God and natural law, or *Deus sive natura*. After this first, almost immediate reference to God, the American

Declaration quickly makes another in the second paragraph, in which the rights themselves are set out: 'We hold that . . . all men are created equal, that they are endowed by their Creator with certain unalienable rights.' *Natural rights therefore depend upon natural law*. In the French Declaration the evocation of pre-existing rights is not made in the same way, in that we are only reminded of them by their negation. This comes in the suggestion that when the natural, inalienable and sacred rights of man are lacking, political corruption and civil pathology inevitably set in. Natural rights thus come to be privileged by a kind of default. As for natural law, this is simply not mentioned. The subject of rights is not God but the will of the Representatives; and the legislator is not nature but a personal act, the singular creation of the nation's delegates and an expression of the 'general will' in Rousseau's sense. This is not to say that God is completely forgotten by the French Declaration, which is written 'in the presence and under the auspices of the Supreme Being.' The text attests the place of God as a witness, who is useful but also neutral and distant – where the American Declaration has God the creator, the French text has God the observer. In response to the question of who the rights are declared by, we can thus posit not the law of nature but the French people. Natural rights do not depend on natural law but on the act of declaration in which they are recorded. Here, natural law no longer exists. *The Declaration of 1789 conforms to natural rights but does not submit to natural law*.

The question of distance between the two texts secondly relates to the quality and order of rights. In the American Declaration, equality is the first right to be evoked: 'All men are created equal.' In the French Declaration, liberty and equality are placed on the same level, with a slight preference for liberty. With equality coming first in the American Declaration, and the French Declaration giving priority to liberty, here, too, we must guard against haste when comparing the American and French Revolutions in terms of the antinomy of liberty and equality. The preeminence accorded to equality by the American text is no longer surprising once we understand that its immediate use-value is to found the right to legitimate independence across all peoples. The Declaration of Independence is not a classical text founded on arguments for sovereign rights and just wars; also, in the absence of a monarch, royal prerogative provides not a single principle of independence for the English settlers. Unlike the days of the Romano-German Empire, when French and English princes used such arguments in order to resist the domineering ambitions of the Holy Emperor, neither do the settlers argue that their leader is 'Emperor in his kingdom'. Rather, they seek their right to independence in natural equity, or *jus genitum*. A modern text that comes from the school of natural law and of the law of nations, the American Declaration is inspired by the idea that the rights of political society should be similar to those of the individual, and that the relationships between individuals and peoples should be governed by the same law. This law cannot be dependent upon States: rather, since the relationship of States to each other is the same as that of individuals within the natural order (that is, equal and without master), the law must be respected by States. Henceforth, States can be linked only by conventions that they must respect. This is why the American Declaration works so relentlessly to demonstrate that the English unilaterally broke the contracts that bound them to the colonies, who from now on are able to speak for themselves. The Declaration of Independence is the first text of modern international law to substitute, for the single sovereignty of the State, the equality of peoples, a natural law that must be continue to be adhered to and pacts that must be respected.

Neither do the two texts set out the rights of man in the same order. After equality, the American Declaration upholds 'life', 'liberty', 'the pursuit of happiness' and, further on, 'resistance to oppression.' The French text upholds 'liberty', 'equality', 'property' and 'the resistance to oppression'. In the American Declaration, civil rights depend upon natural law: governments, the text reminds us, are established in order to guarantee such natural rights, and must attend to the security and happiness of all in respect of this law. The opposite is true of the French Declaration, which leaves us in no doubt that the Rights of Man are those declared by the text itself. Straight away, 'the natural, inalienable and sacred rights of man' are announced, and a few lines later it is added that, 'the National Assembly recognises and declares . . . the following rights of man and of the citizen.' Natural rights, however, occupy minor positions, forming half of Articles 1 and 2, and part of Articles 4, 7, 9, 10 and 11. Meanwhile, Articles 3–17 are almost entirely devoted to political law and to civil rights, comprising definitions of sovereignty, civil liberty, law, the army, taxation and freedom of religion, opinion and expression. Moreover, natural rights are poorly distinguished from civil rights, so that the distinction between what concerns humanity, on the one hand, and citizenship, on the other, is not always made clear. Any attempt to define this distinction in precise terms must involve very close examination of the texts. The First Article, for example, becomes a real headache when we consider it from the standpoint of natural law and civil law. 'Men are born and remain free and equal in rights,' it reads, 'Social distinctions can be founded only upon the common good.' Between the moments of birth (natural state) and life (civil state), let us freely admit that there is no obvious break in continuity. Furthermore, in the French Declaration natural rights are the means and not the end, with the text promising to use them as a remedy for the pathology of the body politic (that is, governmental corruption and public disruption), and to institute the 'constitution' and 'happiness of all.' Natural rights are not simply done away with in favour of civil rights, but they are given the more minor role. The invocation of the Rights of Man drives the institution of a political citizenship. *Where the American Declaration seeks the rights of man within a respect for natural law, the French Declaration builds the rights of the citizen within the foundation of civil society.* In comparison with the American text of 1776, the 1789 Declaration expels both the politico-theological relationship of man to God and the order of natural law, and blunts the sharp edge of natural rights.

Conclusion: 'Philosophy of the subject is not the source of human rights'

'Back to the present'

Let us change eras, return to the present and come back to the recent flourishing of the Rights of Man that has sprung from the establishment within positive law of what we now call 'fundamental rights'. A certain number of public freedoms – previously defined by doctrinarians of modern jusnaturalism as human rights – have now found legal guarantees. This is originally thanks to the intervention made by the French Council of

State in the name of the general principles of rights. More recently, such developments are due to decisions made by the French Constitutional Council relating to the laws of the Republic and to principles of constitutional significance. Does this shift undeniably demonstrate that the insertion of the Rights of Man into law has progressed? And does it make for a definitive clarification of the theoretical bases of the doctrine of human rights? Jean Rivero does not think so. For him,

> The concept remains hazy. We speak of fundamental rights, but in what ways are these different from rights that are not fundamental? What relationships do fundamental rights have with the Rights of Man, or with fundamental freedoms? Even the notion of fundamental rights itself is cloaked in a kind of haze. Granted, on the level of their content there is enough internal agreement to accept the existence of what we could call a core of fundamental rights. Essentially, this is a question of classical liberty, of freedoms that are inherent to the very dignity of a person – what is called the heritage of European common values. But whilst this core is solid it is shrouded in a halo.[22]

Within this halo – this comet trail that is the Rights of Man, and that Mireille Delmas-Marty has elegantly called a 'legal mist' – lie dusty particles that must be expelled. Perhaps the first step must be made by challenging representations that are approximate, and by refusing inadequate genealogy. All too often we applaud a questionable version of history, believing that the appearance of the Rights of Man is linked to legal sub-jectivism and that this same appearance demands the existence of a decentred subject, a subject who has been expelled from nature, and whose singular conscience has turned in on itself in order to present, through metamorphosis, a new programme of action and legislation. We imagine all too easily that the banner of the Rights of Man is necessarily the metaphysical discovery of the subject, and that they defend both the idea of rights as an attribute of personhood and legitimacy as an act of subjective judgement. In short, we are too readily convinced that the notion of the Rights of Man depends upon the subjectivisation of the law. For if all this was true, we would have to explain why those European societies that adopted the idea of subjective idealism have been so reticent with regard to human rights, and so slow to incorporate them into their own constitutional documents. We would also have to fashion a response to the objection formulated by Hannah Arendt when she stresses that nineteenth-century European nation-states could not defend themselves and were unable to guarantee human rights for individuals who did not directly belong to their country. In this way, it was more or less only citizens who had their human rights respected.[23] It would also be necessary to understand the way in which it was peoples rather than individuals who were thought of in the image of man, and to explain the reasons that kept French society from a notion of *habeas corpus*.

'The Rights of Man and of the subject'

Perhaps the picture we have of how the Rights of Man connect up to the theory of the subject, to the will of the individual, is not completely accurate. Perhaps the doctrine of the Rights of Man is not linked first and foremost to the subject and to the theory thereof, but rather is associated with the idea of *species*, so that the doctrine is primarily concerned with man as a member of a given species, and intended for him in a generic sense. 'Man' means the member of a biological genus, a component of humanity, and is not immediately linked to individual, singular subjects. This has been noted by Hannah Arendt and Michel Villey, both of whom remind us that in Rome 'homo' designated men with no rights (slave, as opposed to citizen). Arendt and Villey also note that Roman citizens were in no way deprived of individual rights, having as they did the personal right to vote, to census, to conscription and so on. However, it was precisely secularisers of natural law such as Johannes Althusius, Christian Wolff and Samuel von Pufendorf who rejected the idea according to which natural law is the right of the human species, which Locke and Spinoza had taken up from its central position within the Salamanca School. Through its Biblical references, the Salamancan conception of rights was intended for the human race. For the Scriptures do not foreground society or the individual but rather deal with the human race, so that they begin with Adam – the father of all men – and end with the redemption of the entire species. In the same way, the founding of natural law must be inscribed not so much within society or the subject as within humanity. In order to observe natural law, society must conform to the aims of the species. Certainly, the first human right to find a legal foundation in the thought of the Moderns is itself linked to a process of individuation. This is the right to life which, within civil structures, becomes the right to security. Each individual must take control of his or her life, with sovereign power having no right over whether a person lives or dies. However, this process of individuation is not necessarily one of subjectivisation. Indeed, I would say that, in the juridical terms of the individual's right to security, the subject blocks the individual: far from guaranteeing the right to security, legal voluntarism prevents it from being established within positive law. In fact, one of the principal consequences of legal voluntarism is that the relationship between humans and nature – or indeed between rights and things – comes about only through reason and *recta ratio*. This is what is meant by Hugo Grotius when he says that even if God no longer existed, He would remain the prescription of strict human reason. Thus, this strict reason has come to be substituted for natural law: functioning as an intermediary, reason is the only point of relationship between the human subject and nature. The human subject is but pure thought. Loyal to Cartesian convictions, I am above all a thing that thinks. Straight away, and faced with things and with beings, a human being cannot be said to be arranged as a body among bodies, as a being that is natural within the natural, but rather as a mechanic/manufacturer who is able to think things and to produce them. Such a conception singularly weakens the idea of the body. If, according to Locke, my first natural right is the power of appropriation of my body, the freedom to maintain this control and the right to security, it is because the English philosopher imagines life itself as a gift that has been bestowed upon me by something other or more powerful than myself, a gift that I share with my fellow humans and which no-one must seek to attack, either by destruction or domination. The right to security is a protection of life in so far as it is a gift from nature. As a being of nature who bows to natural law I am a living entity, and it is precisely this living body that I must protect from any despotic domination. Outside of nature, on the other hand, the protection of bodily safety can be less fundamental than the exaltation of the powers of will. Thus, recognition of an individual's natural dimension – that he/she is living, that he/she has a body, that he/she is a nature among natures – weakens and withdraws in favour of a rising exaltation of the individual's mental dimension, of the soul and of *ego cogito*. The idea of liberty is also modified, so that it is no longer a question of delivering life from destruction and domination in order that it be allowed to survive, but rather of enlarging the free self-determination of the subject. The outcome of all this is evident, from the Cartesian conception of man to the absence of *habeas corpus* which characterises French law. In fact, it can be noted that the right to security is only inscribed within the tradition of French political law by default, and this in the limited legal sphere of our public law. The default inscription arises because royal legislators Jean Bodin and Charles Loyseau defined sovereignty at a very early stage by the non-attribution of *jus vitae necisque* – that is, the power of life and death over one's subjects, which was the jewel in the crown of authority in Antiquity. For us French, however, on the penal level this definition was not to receive the extension it enjoyed in English law, and which saw the *habeas corpus* adopted in 1679. In Locke's analysis, the *habeas corpus* provides the pre-eminence of the right to life and security with a triple foundation, one that is simultaneously public, civil and penal. Based on the idea that no-one may be detained or placed in custody without a lawful judicial procedure having previously been set in motion, the *habeas corpus* means that no-one's physical body may be put into illegal detention or custody, and that ownership of one's own body is the principal human liberty. Here, then, the right to security is a continuous human right: it is a civil right (being a question of possession), a penal right (it is inscribed within penal procedure) and a public right (the right must be protected by the sovereign). What the right to security is not is private – in other words, it is an individual right that is not a right of the subject. It is also expressed differently, constituting the very definition of the subject of rights: 'you own your own body,' it says, 'you have the right to security. Your life belongs to you, and you are a human being.' Anyone who has become a citizen may benefit from the *habeas corpus*, but not someone who is simply a civilised subject. We French subjects still do not benefit from the *habeas corpus*, and our right to security remains uncertain and limited. Indeed, perhaps this is why we worry so much about security. It could also be added that, on the level of their links with the human race, the Rights of Man unavoidably deal with man as a member of humanity. In the past, the founder of 'Médecins sans frontières', Bernard Kouchner, has wrongly been mocked for what was seen as the benevolent pretension of wanting to lead a politics of human rights that operated over the heads of States. However, whilst it is obvious that human rights can only be declared and guaranteed by and within lawful States, their scope could never be limited to a purely national level. History bears witness to this since, from the Declarations of 1776 and 1789 up until the United Nations' Universal Declaration of 1948 and the European Convention on Human Rights, the development of human rights has been accomplished through active proceedings (assemblies, treaties and tribunals) that are both inter- and supranational.

From this fairly rapid examination, I would like to draw a lesson that affects the very development of the Rights of Man. If the Rights of Man have no origin in subjective idealism or legal voluntarism but rather, as I have tried to show, draw from modern texts of rights which maintain their reference to natural law then, for those who believe in their future and application, natural law is also where the philosophy of rights must be re-rooted.

By way of precluding any frantic flight outside the sphere of law – where arguments would take place in an intellectual atmosphere dominated by sociologism and anti-juridicism – all this is not to deny the vital contribution made by juridical positivism, which reminds us that the law also has its own substance, institution and morphology. However, the mechanics of juridical positivism are not so well suited today to our quest to understand European political development. Make no mistake: we have to return to the question of natural law, and re-open the portal that it has already established in our nations' founding texts. In future, the legal destiny of human rights will be shaped by a philosophy of natural law – and today, as in the past, that destiny is assured by critique of the philosophy of the subject.

Translated by Stephen Forcer

Notes

1 [Translator's note. Whether talking about the actual texts and traditions of the Declarations or the general notion of human rights, the author refers to 'les droits de l'homme' throughout her article. On the one hand, the English term 'the Rights of Man' indicates a specific historical context and replicates the language of the time; the author herself also prefers 'les droits de l'homme' to 'les droits humains', which is used by many modern French human rights groups. Readers are therefore asked to accept that the following translation is largely obliged to render 'les droits de l'homme' as 'the Rights of Man'. However, in recognition of the fact that such a rendering is untenably problematic in a contemporary setting, 'les droits de l'homme' will be translated as 'human rights' on those occasions where suggestions of the French Declaration, its history and associated traditions are subordinate or absent, or where a modern context is inferred.]

2 Cf. Mario Capelletti, *Judicial Review in the Contemporary World* (Indianapolis: Bobbs-Merrill, 1971).

3 Jean Rivero, *Les libertés publiques* (Paris: PUF, 1974).

4 Ibid., 2nd edition (1984), vol. I, p. 24.

5 Edmund Burke, *Reflections on the French Revolution and Other Essays* (London: J.M. Dents & Sons Ltd., 1950), p. 31. The emphasis is Burke's.

6 Ibid., p. 59.

7 Cf. J. de Maistre, *Considérations sur la France*, 1796 (Brussels: Éditions Complexe, 1988), and *Essai sur le principe générateur des constitutions politiques*, 1810 (Lyon & Paris: J.B. Pélagaud, 1867); Louis de Bonald, *La législation primitive considérée dans les derniers temps par les seules lumières de la raison*, 1802 (Paris: A. Le Clere, 1847).

8 Cf. Jacques Droz, *Le romantisme politique en Allemagne* (Paris: A. Colin, 1963), and Roger Ayrault, *La genèse du romantisme allemand* (Paris: Aubier, 1969–76), 4 vols.

9 Johann Gottlieb Fichte, *Addresses to the German Nation* (trans. R.F. Jones and G.H. Turnbull; Chicago & London: The Open Court Publishing Company, 1923).

10 *On The Jewish Question* and *The Critique of Hegel's Philosophy of Right. Introduction* are to be found in Karl Marx, *Early Writings* (intro. Lucio Colletti; trans. Rodney Livingstone and Gregor Benton; Harmondsworth & London, Penguin Books, in association with *New Left Review*, 1977), pp. 211–41 and 243–57 respectively. See also Karl Marx and Frederick Engels, *The Holy Family, or Critique of Critical Critique*, 2nd revised edition (trans. Richard Dixon and Clemens Dutt; London: Lawrence & Wishart, 1980).

11 *On The Jewish Question*, in *Early Writings*, p. 230. The italics are Marx's.

12 Ibid., p. 234. The italics are Marx's. This criticism does not negate 'the absolute idealism of

law within the absolute distress of reality'. Cf. Bernard Bourgeois, 'Marx et les droits de l'homme,' in Guy Planty-Bonjour (ed.), *Droit et liberté selon Marx* (Paris: PUF, 1990).

13 Cf. 'Marx Romantique,' in Blandine Barret-Kriegel, *L'État et les esclaves* (Paris: Payot, 1988).

14 *La formation du radicalisme philosophique* (Paris: PUF, 1995), 3 vols., especially chapter 1, 'Le principe de l'utilité contre la Déclaration des droits de l'homme,' in vol. II.

15 'Anarchical Fallacies: Being an Examination of the Declaration of Rights issued during the French Revolution,' in *The Works of Jeremy Bentham* (ed. John Bowring; Edinburgh: William Tait, 1843), vol. II, pp. 489–534.

16 Benjamin Constant, *De la liberté chez les Modernes* (ed. Marcel Gauchet; Paris: Le livre de Poche, 1980), pp. 434 and 495.

17 Alexis de Tocqueville, *Ecrits sur le système pénitentiaire en France et à l'étranger* in *Œuvres complètes*, vols. IV and V (ed. Michelle Perrot; Paris: Gallimard, 1984).

18 Michel Prélot, with Françoise Gallouedec-Genuys, *Le libéralisme catholique* (Paris: A. Colin, 1969).

19 Cf. Claude Nicolet, *L'idée républicaine en France* (Paris: Gallimard, 1982).

20 Cf. Luc Ferry and Alain Renaut, *Philosophie politique* (Paris: PUF, 1985), vol. III.

21 From chapter XI, 'Of the extent of the legislative power,' in John Locke, *Of Civil Government, Two Treatises* (intro. W.F. Carpenter; London: J.M. Dent & Sons Ltd., 1949), p. 185. See also chapter XIX, 'Of the dissolution of government': 'Who shall be judge? . . . every man is judge himself, as in all other cases so this, whether another hath put himself into a state of war with him, and whether he should appeal to the supreme Judge, as Jephtha did'; ibid., p. 241.

22 Jean Rivero in Louis Favoreu (ed.), *Cours constitutionnelles européennes et droits fondamentaux* (Aix-en-Provence: Presses universitaires d'Aix-Marseille, 1982), pp. 521 and 524.

23 Hannah Arendt, *L'impérialisme* (trad. Martine Censi; Paris: Fayard, 1982), p. 275.

INDEX